POLITICS IN
INDEPENDENT POLAND
1921-1939

POLITICS IN
INDEPENDENT POLAND
1921–1939

THE CRISIS OF CONSTITUTIONAL
GOVERNMENT

ANTONY POLONSKY

OXFORD
AT THE CLARENDON PRESS
1972

Oxford University Press, Ely House, London W. 1

GLASGOW NEW YORK TORONTO MELBOURNE WELLINGTON
CAPE TOWN IBADAN NAIROBI DAR ES SALAAM LUSAKA ADDIS ABABA
DELHI BOMBAY CALCUTTA MADRAS KARACHI LAHORE DACCA
KUALA LUMPUR SINGAPORE HONG KONG TOKYO

PRINTED IN GREAT BRITAIN
AT THE UNIVERSITY PRESS, OXFORD
BY VIVIAN RIDLER
PRINTER TO THE UNIVERSITY

FOR MY WIFE

PREFACE

In this book I have attempted to describe the political life of the newly independent Polish state from March 1921 (when the Treaty of Riga was finally ratified and the democratic constitution came into force) to September 1939. I have not dealt in detail with the period from the re-establishment of independence in November 1918 to the end of the Polish-Soviet war, because during these years the need to establish the country's frontiers, and the series of military campaigns which this brought about, imposed an artificial and temporary restraint on party differences and thus postponed the tackling of the internal problems inherent in independence.

My main concern has been to investigate the political development of the largest and most populous of the states which emerged in East-Central Europe after World War I. As was true of most of them, the constitution of Poland was highly democratic. I have thus attempted to show the dilemmas of a newly independent state, faced with pressing social, economic, and political problems, in operating a political system evolved over a long period of time in the much more highly developed and socially homogeneous countries of Western Europe. The final breakdown of the 1921 constitution which brought Piłsudski back to power in May 1926 did not, however, result in a decisive break with liberal democracy, for Piłsudski's regime attempted to operate a sort of semi-constitutional 'guided democracy'. The major part of this book is devoted to describing the disintegration of his 'system' and the development of his regime in an increasingly autocratic direction. This development became more pronounced after Piłsudski's death in May 1935; nevertheless his successors had not yet imposed a totalitarian system by the outbreak of World War II.

This book is based principally on the minutes of the Sejm and Senate, on government documents in the Archiwum Akt Nowych and papers in the Archiwum Zakładu Historii Partii, both in Warsaw, on personal accounts deposited in the Józef Piłsudski Institute Archive in London, on published and unpublished memoirs, and on newspapers.

Considerable attention has been devoted to the social and economic background, since Polish history is too often treated as if it took place in a social vacuum, and since there is no readily accessible treatment of these matters available elsewhere. The importance has also been stressed of the political problems which arose from the fact that one-third of Poland's population was composed of people whose language or religion was distinct from that of the majority.

The rendering of Polish place-names in English creates many difficulties. The system followed here is not wholly consistent, but seems to raise the fewest objections. For towns such as Warsaw, Cracow, or Lodz, which have a commonly employed English form, this form is used. For others, such as Poznań, Toruń, and, slightly questionably, Wilno, the Polish form is used. The form Brześć is used throughout, except in referring to the peace treaty of Brest-Litovsk, where to do so might have appeared pedantic. For some provinces (*województwa*) the familiar anglicized form is adopted, as Poznania, Pomerania, Polesia, and Silesia. For the rest, however, such forms do not exist; in such cases Cracow province, Warsaw province, Wilno province, etc., are employed. The names of Russian, White Russian, and Ukrainian politicians and political organizations, and the titles of books in these languages and in Yiddish have been transliterated according to a commonly used English system. An exception has been made in the case of the Uniate Metropolitan Archbishop Sheptytski, which I render as Szeptycki, since the rendering of his name in a form different from that of his brother, General Stanisław Szeptycki, seemed to occasion unnecessary confusion.

It is always a pleasant task to thank those who have helped one in one's work, though considerations of space make it impossible for the list to be comprehensive. First of all, I should like to thank Mr. H. T. Willetts for his much valued aid and advice, and Drs. A. Walicki, J. Milewski, J. Gołębiowski, and F. Parsons, and Mr. A. Ciołkosz for reading and criticizing the manuscript. I should also like to thank Professor (now Minister) H. Jabłoński and Dr. A. Garlicki of the University of Warsaw for their invaluable assistance during the year I spent in Warsaw and on my subsequent visit, as well as Mrs. B. Skrzeszewska and Dr. H. Knoll of the Archiwum Akt Nowych, Dr. F. Tych of the Archiwum Zakładu Historii Partii, Drs. J. Molenda, J. Lewandowski, and A. Ajnenkiel of Warsaw, and General Krok-Paszkowski, Colonel T. Schaetzel, and Mr. W. Stankiewicz of the Piłsudski Institute in London. I also owe a debt to Mr. Michael Kaser of St. Antony's College, Oxford, for teaching me how to use a calculating machine.

Finally, I should like to record here my gratitude to the late Mrs. Regina Szenbaum, who taught me the Polish language and so much else about Poland.

ANTONY POLONSKY

CONTENTS

LIST OF MAPS

LIST OF TABLES

ABBREVIATIONS

A.A.N.	Archiwum Akt Nowych
A.S.S.	Akta Sprawy Świtalskiego
A.Z.H.P.	Archiwum Zakładu Historii Partii
B.B.W.R.	Bezpartyjny Blok Współpracy z Rządem
B.P.P.P.	*Bulletin Périodique de la Presse Polonaise*
C.A.M.S.W.	Centralne Archiwum Ministerstwa Spraw Wewnętrznych
C.A.W.	Centralne Archiwum Wojskowe
D.G.F.P.	*Documents on German Foreign Policy*
D.P.O.	*Dziesięciolecie Polski Odrodzonej*
Dz.U.R.P.	*Dziennik Urzędowy Rzeczypospolitej Polskiej*
G.U.S.	Główny Urząd Statystyczny
J.C.E.A.	*Journal of Central European Affairs*
K.H.	*Kwartalnik Historyczny*
K.P.P.	Komunistyczna Partia Polski
M.R.S.	*Mały Rocznik Statystyczny*
N.D.	*Nowe Drogi*
N.D.P.	*Najnowsze Dzieje Polski*
N.K.N.	Naczelny Komitet Narodowy
N.P.R.	Narodowa Partia Robotnicza
O.E.H.P.	*Osteuropa Handbuch: Polen*
O.N.R.	Obóz Narodowo-Radykalny
O.W.P.	Obóz Wielkiej Polski
OZON	Obóz Zjednoczenia Narodowego
P.A.N.	Polska Akademia Nauk
P.H.	*Przegląd Historyczny*
P.O.W.	Polska Organizacja Wojskowa
P.P.R.M.	Protokóły Posiedzeń Rady Ministrów
P.P.S.	Polska Partia Socjalistyczna
P.P.S.D.	Polska Partia Socjaldemokratyczna
P.R.M.	Prezydium Rady Ministrów
P.Zach.	*Przegląd Zachodni*
P.Z.	J. Piłsudski. *Pisma zbiorowe*
P.Z.P.K. I	Protokóły zebrań periodycznych kierowników władz i urzędów Iej instancji
P.Z.P.K. II	Protokóły zebrań periodycznych kierowników władz i urzędów IIej instancji

R.D.R.L.	*Roczniki Dziejów Ruchu Ludowego*
R.S.R.P.	*Roczniki Statystyki Rzeczypospolitej Polskiej*
S.D.K.P. i L.	Socjal-Demokracja Królestwa Polskiego i Litwy
S.G.P. i S.	Szkoła Główna Planowania i Statystyki
S.P.	*Statystyka Polski*
S.S.S.R.	*Sprawozdania Stenograficzne Sejmu Rzeczypospolitej*
S.S.Se.R.	*Sprawozdania Stenograficzne Senatu Rzeczypospolitej*
U.N.D.O.	Ukrainskie Natsionalno-Demokratychne Objednienie
W.P.H.	*Wojskowy Przegląd Historyczny*
Z.P.W.	*Z Pola Walki*
Z.W.P.O.	*Żydzi w Polsce Odrodzonej*
Z.Z.Z.	Związek Związków Zawodowych

INDEPENDENT POLAND:
THE SOCIAL AND ECONOMIC
BACKGROUND

POLAND in the eighteenth century was a vast country which comprised not only the eastern and central parts of the present-day state, but also much of Lithuania, Latvia, White Russia, and the Ukraine. Its political life was dominated by the landed gentry, or *szlachta*, who elected the king and the parliament. Although in theory all members of the *szlachta* were equal, in practice politics were the preserve of the great aristocratic families who were almost sovereign on their vast estates.

This political system exposed Poland to strong pressure from its neighbours. Although the more conservative gentry still maintained that 'in anarchy lies Poland's strength',[1] the first partition of the country by Russia, Prussia, and Austria in 1772 showed the dangers inherent in this attitude. Attempts to reform the constitution did not prevent the extinction of Poland as a state in 1795, when its remaining territories were divided among the same three Powers. Although at the Congress of Vienna in 1815 a part of Russian Poland (the so-called Congress Kingdom) was granted considerable autonomy, the country remained under foreign rule.

Some of the great aristocrats favoured co-operation with the partitioning Powers, but the loss of independence was bitterly resented by the mass of the gentry, and led to a series of uprisings between 1830 and 1863 which gave Poles the reputation of perpetual revolutionaries all over Europe. All were ruthlessly crushed, and indeed the savage measures which followed the revolt of 1863 effectively suppressed the struggle to regain the independence of Poland by armed insurrection.

On the eve of World War I, the partition of Poland seemed permanently established. All but the most visionary of Polish

---

[1] 'Polska nierządem stoi', literally 'Poland owes her existence to her lack of a central government.'

B

politicians had renounced independence except as the most long-
term of aims. Yet Poland re-emerged in 1918, somewhat unexpectedly, from the military collapse of the Powers which had

MAP 1. The Territories making up the New Polish State

effected her partition at the end of the eighteenth century. The
recreation of the Polish state and the absorption of its disparate
parts, particularly in the difficult years after World War I, was
an enormous task. For more than 130 years, the different areas

which comprised the newly independent country had been ruled by different administrations and had formed integral parts of Austria-Hungary, Germany, and Russia. In the various areas, wide

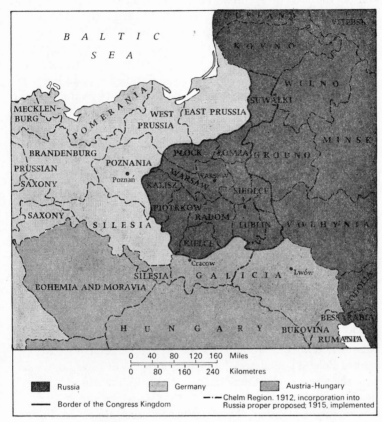

MAP 2. The Polish Lands on the Eve of World War I, showing the administrative divisions of the partitional powers

divergencies of law and custom, of temperament, and even of language, hindered the smooth functioning of the state.

The former Russian territories made up the largest part of the state, covering 67 per cent of the total area.[1] They were divided into two parts, the Congress Kingdom, in central Poland, and the *Kresy*, or eastern borderlands.

[1] Based on *R.S.R.P.* iii (1925), 7–11, Table III.

The Congress Kingdom, which, after the crushing of the revolt of 1863, retained scarcely any vestiges of the autonomy it had been granted at the Congress of Vienna in 1815, comprised 30 per cent of the area of the new state.[1] Its population of 10·5 million in 1912 was largely Polish, although there was a substantial Jewish minority in the towns. Still largely agricultural, it had experienced rapid industrial development from the last quarter of the nineteenth century, supplying principally Russian and Far Eastern markets.[2] By 1913 317,000 workers were employed in mining and industry. The main industrial centres were Lodz, for textile production, the Dąbrowa basin, where a metallurgical industry had grown up alongside the coal-mines, and Warsaw, with its metal-working factories and food-processing plants of which the most important were sugar refineries.

The abolition of the *corvée* in the Congress Kingdom had been administered in such a way as to diminish the power of the Polish gentry, who were feared by the Russian government as the originators of the nationalist risings of 1830 and 1863. As a result, although large landed estates were important in the Congress Kingdom, medium-sized peasant holdings played a stronger part than elsewhere in Poland. As often happens when land reverts on a large scale to a self-sufficient peasantry, the Congress Kingdom could not provide for its own food requirements, and imported grain from the Russian Empire.

The Eastern Kresy, which had formed an integral part of Russia, had in 1921 a population of 4·8 million and covered 37 per cent of Poland's total area.[3] This was a region of mixed nationalities: the peasantry in the north was mainly White Russian, though there were also some Poles and Lithuanians, and in the south it was mainly Ukrainian. The landowners were almost exclusively

---

[1] Based on *R.S.R.P.* iii (1925), 7–11, Table III. These figures are somewhat difficult to calculate because pre-war and post-war administrative boundaries did not coincide exactly. The above percentage was arrived at by assigning the provinces of Warsaw, Lodz, Kielce, and Lublin, and the districts (*powiaty*) of Augustów, Suwałki, Łomża, and Kolno in the Białystok province to the Congress Kingdom, and the provinces of Wilno, Nowogródek, Polesia, and Volynia, and the other districts of the Białystok province to the Eastern Kresy.

[2] For this development see: R. Luxemburg, *Die industrielle Entwicklung Polens* (Leipzig, 1898); S. Koszutski, *Rozwój ekonomiczny Królestwa Polskiego w ostatnim trzydziestoleciu* (Warsaw, 1905); and J. Jedlicki, *Nieudana próba kapitalistycznej industrializacji* (Warsaw, 1964).

[3] Based on *R.S.R.P.* iii (1925), 7–11, Table III.

Polish, while the urban population was Polish and Jewish. Over-whelmingly agricultural, it was a backward region with poor transport and little contact with the outside world. The peasants of the Polesian marshes, for example, still traded almost exclusively by barter. Such industry as existed was concentrated in Wilno, and was concerned with food and timber processing.

The territories formerly under German rule also fell into two distinct parts, Poznania and Pomerania, and Polish Upper Silesia. Poznania and Pomerania in the west, with a population in 1921 of 2·9 million and 11 per cent of the country's total area,[1] were predominantly agricultural. One of the principal suppliers of food for the rapidly increasing urban population of Germany, this area had been among the most efficient and highly capitalized wheat- and rye-growing regions in Europe. Its agricultural structure differed markedly from that of the rest of Poland; it was characterized by the existence of many large landowners and prosperous peasants (*Grossbauer* or *gburzy*), as well as a vast pool of peasants with dwarf holdings and landless agricultural workers who provided the labour force for the first two groups. The only significant industries were food processing and the repair of agricultural machinery. Economically, the area was almost totally dependent on Germany. Between 1911 and 1913 the exports of Prussian Poland have been calculated as reaching 3,000 million marks annually. Of this two-thirds went to the German Reich, and less than one-tenth to the other areas which would later make up Poland.[2] Although strenuous efforts had been made, through colonization and Germanization of the schools, to assimilate forcibly the Polish population, they had proved largely unsuccessful. Only in the towns and among the large landowners did the Germans form a sizeable element.[3]

Polish Upper Silesia, in the south-west, comprised that part of Upper Silesia which was assigned to Poland after the plebiscite of March 1921. It had at the time of independence a population of 980,000 and covered 0·8 per cent of the country.[1]

Before the war, Upper Silesia had been, after the Ruhr and Saxony, the third most highly industrialized area of Germany.

---

[1] Ibid.
[2] A. Rose, *Bilans handlowy ziem b. dzielnicy pruskiej* (Warsaw, 1920), pp. 664–5.
[3] See R. W. Tims, *Germanising Prussian Poland* (New York, 1941).

Alongside its coal-mines, most of which fell to Poland, and which in 1913 had produced 44 million tons of coal, there had grown up vast iron and zinc foundries, as well as an important chemical industry. In 1914 450,000 workers were employed in mining and manufacturing in this region.[1] The agricultural system was characterized by the highest percentage of large estates in all of Poland, and by the many small plots held on lease. These small-holdings reflected the desire of agricultural labourers on the large estates for an independent, additional source of income, as well as the long-standing tradition among Silesian industrial workers of maintaining some link with the land.[2]

Though the industrialists, landowners, and officials had been almost entirely German before 1914, the overwhelming majority of the population was Polish-speaking and Catholic. The whole of Silesia had passed from Polish rule in the fourteenth century, first to the Czechs, then to the Habsburgs, and finally, in the eighteenth century, to Prussia. As a result, nationalist feeling was weaker here than elsewhere in Poland, and it was not until 1903 that a Polish nationalist was returned to the Reichstag.[3] In the plebiscite only 44 per cent of the total population of Upper Silesia voted to join Poland.[4]

The lands formerly under Austrian rule were two areas very different in size and importance, Galicia and Austrian Silesia, both in the south. Galicia, with a population of 7·6 million in 1921 and covering 20 per cent of Poland's total area,[5] was predominantly agricultural. The way in which serfdom had been abolished, and the rapid rise in population throughout the nineteenth century, had caused the greatest fragmentation of holdings in Poland. In 1921 four-fifths of all holdings were of less than 5 hectares.[6] Little industry had developed here until the discovery of oil in East

[1] On the industrial development of Upper Silesia see K. Popiołek, 'Rozwój kapitalistycznego przemysłu na Śląsku, 1850–1910', Konferencja Śląska: Instytut Historyczny P.A.N. (Wrocław, 1954), i. 191–265.

[2] M. Mieszczankowski, Struktura agrarna Polski międzywojennej (Warsaw, 1960), chapter viii.

[3] For the political background see M. Orzechowski, Narodowa Demokracja na Górnym Śląsku (do 1918 roku) (Wrocław–Warsaw–Cracow, 1965), and E. Sontag, Adalbert (Wojciech) Korfanty, ein Beitrag zur Geschichte der polnischen Ansprüche auf Ostoberschlesien (Kitzingen/Main, 1954).

[4] W. J. Rose, The Drama of Upper Silesia (London, 1936), pp. 180–1.

[5] Based on R.S.R.P. iii (1925), 7–11, Table III.

[6] Ibid. 34, Table I.

Galicia at the beginning of the twentieth century. By 1909 the refineries centred around Borysław, which employed about 6,000 workers, had an annual output of almost 2 million tons, nearly 4 per cent of the total world production.[1] At Wieliczka and Kałusz salt was mined and paraffin wax produced, of which Galicia had a world monopoly until 1907. In the west the population was largely Polish, while in the east the peasantry was mainly Ukrainian, the majority of the landowners and of the urban population was Polish, and the Jews formed an important minority in the towns.

That part of Austrian Silesia which fell to Poland had in 1921 a population of 145,000 and 0·3 per cent of the total area.[2] Also largely agricultural, it had in addition a well-developed textile industry in Bielsko-Biała. The population was predominantly Polish, with a sizeable German minority.

The creation of a single economic unit from these disparate areas, differing widely in social and economic development, was a slow and difficult process. It was only in early 1920 that a single currency, the Polish mark, was instituted for the whole of Poland. Until then as many as six currencies had circulated in the different parts. In addition to German marks, Austrian crowns, and Russian roubles, there were Polish marks, 'occupation marks' issued by the German High Command in the area east of the Congress Kingdom, and some of the different varieties of Soviet roubles.[3] As late as 1920 a tariff barrier was maintained between the former Prussian partition and the rest of Poland, and one needed a passport to travel from Warsaw to Poznań.[4]

Poland lacked a unified transport system. The Vistula, which passed through all the partitions, had not been made suitable for navigation along much of its course. Other river communications, excepting those in former Prussian Poland, were of poor quality. The rail networks, fairly dense in Prussian Poland and rather less than adequate in Austrian and particularly Russian Poland, had been constructed bearing in mind the interests of the partitioning powers. More than fifty Austrian and German railway lines led to

[1] S. Bartoszewicz, 'Przemysł naftowy', *Dziesięciolecie Polski Odrodzonej* (Cracow–Warsaw, 1928), p. 1031.
[2] Based on *R.S.R.P.* iii (1925), 7–11, Table III.
[3] Z. Landau and J. Tomaszewski, *Zarys historii gospodarczej Polski* (Warsaw, 1962), p. 39.
[4] A. Ajnenkiel, *Od 'rządów ludowych' do przewrotu majowego* (Warsaw, 1964), p. 44.

the Russian frontier; only ten continued on the other side. There was no direct rail link between Warsaw and Poznań, Kielce and Cracow, or between the centre of the country and the sea. The railway systems in the different areas had different equipment and different methods of administration. There were three systems of signalling and safety devices, three group-braking systems which meant that rolling stock from the different areas could not be run together, and 160 types of engine. Furthermore, Russian rolling stock was of a different width from the rest, and even when converted to the normal gauge could only run in the Congress Kingdom and the Eastern Kresy.[1]

Four legal systems obtained in the new Poland. In the Congress Kingdom, civil law followed the Napoleonic Code, supplemented by a number of laws dating from the period of autonomy before 1863. Criminal law and legal procedure followed the practice of the Russian Empire, as they did in the Kresy, where Russian civil law also prevailed. In Prussian Poland German law obtained, while in Galicia Austrian law was the rule, modified by the legislation of the provincial parliament. The unification of the legal systems caused great difficulties in the first years of independence, and was still not complete by 1939. The legal systems differed considerably, and it was often the case that what was legal in one area was illegal in another. The forming of a joint-stock company, for example, required government authorization in Russian Poland, while in Prussian Poland it was necessary to register the company only after it had been formed.[2]

The economies of the different partitions had been closely linked with those of the partitioning Powers. The creation of a unified Polish economy posed serious problems for the more developed industries which had grown up behind the protective walls of the high Russian and relatively high German tariffs. Of the products exported by partitioned Poland, 83·3 per cent had gone to the respective partitioning Powers, and 85 per cent of imports had come from them.[3] After 1918 the Russian market was virtually closed, while the high tariffs of Poland and the Habsburg successor states hindered trade. Some industries, such as sugar refining, were

---

[1] J. Ginzbert, *Drogi żelazne Rzeczypospolitej* (Warsaw, 1937), quoted in Landau and Tomaszewski, op. cit., p. 51.

[2] Ibid., p. 52.

[3] F. Zweig, *Poland between two Wars* (London, 1944), p. 13.

duplicated in the different partitions, but others, such as machine building and armament manufacture, were almost totally lacking.

The systems of taxation varied greatly. In Russia, the bulk of the state's revenue had come from indirect taxation, nearly half in 1913 from purchase tax. Direct taxation in that year accounted for only 7·9 per cent of the national revenue. Austria had depended on both direct and indirect taxation, while in Germany direct taxation was most important. The tax levels also differed. Between 1911 and 1913 the tax burden per head in the Congress Kingdom was 41 crowns, while in Galicia it was 29 crowns.[1]

The extent and quality of education differed markedly from region to region. Universal education had existed only in Germany, but since the schools were seen as a medium for Germanization, there had been no Polish-language primary schools, to say nothing of secondary schools or universities. In Galicia, where the educational system had been under Polish control, a network of secondary schools, two universities, in Cracow and Lwów, and a technical college in Lwów had been established. Primary education was not, however, as extensive as in Germany. The educational system had been most primitive, and illiteracy most widespread, in Russia. It was only after the German occupation that a state-sponsored network of Polish-language primary schools was established. A Russian-language university and technical college had existed in Warsaw.

The economic problems of the new Polish state were intensified by the devastation of the war. The front in the east, unlike that in the west, was not static, and tremendous damage was done in the Russian offensive of 1914, the German offensive of 1914–15, and the desperate Brusilov offensive. Because of the Polish-Soviet War, armed combat ceased in Poland only in 1920. By then 90 per cent of the country had been directly touched by the war, and, of this, one-fifth had been the scene of heavy fighting. Only the Prussian partition was not seriously affected. By 1920 55 per cent of the bridges, 63 per cent of the railway stations, 48 per cent of the locomotives, and 18 per cent of the buildings in the country had been destroyed.[2] The heaviest losses had been suffered by the Congress Kingdom, particularly around Kalisz and Żyrardów.

Wartime requisitions seriously affected Polish industry. When

[1] Landau and Tomaszewski, op. cit., p. 53.
[2] Ajnenkiel, op. cit., p. 18.

the Russians evacuated the Congress Kingdom they took with them whatever industrial equipment they could. The German authorities, in turn, sent large quantities of machinery back to Germany. The metallurgical industry ceased production entirely as its furnaces were dismantled and removed by the Germans. It was only in 1919 that the first new furnace started operating, and of the eleven functioning in 1914 only seven were still in use in 1922. The textile industry of Lodz also suffered severely from requisitions: miles of transmission belts were sent back to Germany, as well as large quantities of electric motors and copper parts, of which there was a shortage in the Reich. The Polish delegation at the Peace Conference estimated total Polish losses at 73,000 million French francs.[1]

In addition, no new investment was made in Polish industry during the war, apart from German investment in Upper Silesia. It thus fell behind the rest of the world technically. The devastating impact of the war was painfully felt in the next few years, and the level of production of 1913 was never again attained during the 1920s.

The Poles had long dreamed of independence and had attributed their undeniable social and economic backwardness to foreign rule. They believed that the re-creation of a Polish state would solve their problems. Yet, understandable as these feelings were, they could not long disguise the fact that independence had created almost as many problems as it had solved.

AGRICULTURE

In 1921 Poland had 27·2 million inhabitants.[2] Their number had more than tripled since 1800, for in that year the population of the

---

[1] According to a secret memorandum by Władysław Grabski, 'Wyjaśnienia dotyczące ratyfikacji traktatu pokojowego z Niemcami i umowy wielkich mocarstw z Polską przez delegata pełnomocnego Polski na Kongresie Pokojowym', manuscript marked in Polish 'strictly confidential, Paris 1919'; quoted in Landau and Tomaszewski, op. cit., pp. 17–18.

For war damage generally, see *Polska w czasie wielkiej wojny 1914–18*, ed. M. Handelsmann (Warsaw, 1936), vol. iii, and *Zniszczenia wojenne i odbudowa Polski* (Warsaw, 1929). Some statistics on the extent of the destruction caused are provided in Appendix C, pp. 519–20.

[2] *R.S.R.P.* iv (1925–6), 5, Table II. For the territories not covered by the 1921 census, the figures given are, for the Wilno region, those of the preliminary census of 1919, and for Upper Silesia, those of the last German census of 1910.

former Polish Republic, an area somewhat larger than the re-created Polish state, had been barely 9 million.[1] With an annual natural increase of 15·3 per 1,000 inhabitants, Poland had one of the highest rates of population growth in Europe, exceeded substantially only by Yugoslavia, Romania, and the U.S.S.R.[2] This rapidly rising population greatly intensified the already existing social and economic problems of the new state.

Of the inhabitants of independent Poland, a quarter lived in the towns, and three-quarters in the countryside.[3] The largest of the towns was Warsaw, with a population in 1921 of nearly a million; substantially smaller were Lodz, Lwów, Wilno, Cracow, and Poznań.[4] Table I describes the occupational divisions in Poland.

TABLE I. *Occupational Distribution of the Population of Poland in 1921*[*]

	Total	Agriculture, forestry	Mining and industry	Commerce, insurance	Communications, transport	Other
Workers and dependents	100·0	63·8	15·4	6·2	3·3	11·3
Active population	100·0	72·3	10·3	3·7	1·8	11·9

[*] *M.R.S.* (1931), p. 10. Table XIX. This table is based on the census of 1921, but extended to the areas not covered. See p. 16, n. 1.

The overwhelming preponderance of agriculture in the Polish economy emerges clearly. According to the League of Nations figures for the years around 1930 (which do not differ materially from the earlier period), only Albania, Yugoslavia, Bulgaria, Lithuania, and the Soviet Union exceeded Poland in the percentage of the population deriving its livelihood from the soil. As against the Polish figure of 63·8 per cent, the Czech figure was 33 per cent, the French 29 per cent, and that for England and Wales 5 per cent.[5]

A fundamental characteristic of Polish agriculture was the

[1] 'Vie économique', *La Pologne, 1919–39*, ii (Neuchâtel, 1946), 99.
[2] *M.R.S.* (1931), p. 11, Table II.
[3] Ibid., p. 4, Table VI.
[4] Their populations in 1921 were: Warsaw, 937,000; Lodz, 452,000; Lwów, 219,000; Wilno, 208,000; Cracow, 181,000; and Poznań, 169,000. From *M.R.S.* (1931), p. 6, Table XI.
[5] F. W. Moore, *Economic Demography of Eastern and Southern Europe* (Geneva, 1945), p. 26, Table II.

far-reaching fragmentation of peasant holdings. According to the census of 1921,[1] a third of all holdings, or 3·5 per cent of the arable land was held in plots of less than 2 hectares, while almost two-thirds, or 14·8 per cent, of the arable land was in plots of less than 5 hectares.[2] Many of these plots were not self-sufficient, and their owners were forced to supplement their earnings by working on larger farms.

Before 1914 the pressure of population growth had been some-what relieved by emigration, and by absorption into the rapidly developing industries. Between 1895 and 1913, over 2½ million people emigrated from Poland. By 1913, 250,000 were emigrating annually,[3] and 800,000 agricultural labourers were finding seasonal employment abroad.[4] But after the war, as emigration became more difficult, and industry in Poland failed to expand, the problem of the surplus agricultural population became increasingly serious, and was much discussed. In 1934 for every 100 hectares of cultivated land there were 81 people in Poland, 49 in Germany, 64 in Czechoslovakia, and 36 in Denmark.[5] The surplus population was thought to be as high as 8 million, but the most reliable estimate, that of the Instytut Gospodarstwa Społecznego in 1935, showed that with no change whatever in agricultural technique, 2·4 million people could leave the villages.[6] If the number of people only semi-employed is added, the surplus rural population was probably as high as 4·5 million.

Large landowning was a significant feature of Polish agriculture. According to the census of 1921 0·9 per cent of all holdings, but *47·3 per cent of the arable land*, was in farms of more than 50 hectares. Of this, 1·6 per cent was church land, 23·6 per cent government land, and 73·9 per cent in private hands.[7] The average large estate was of considerable size. Of the 10½ million hectares of land held by large private landowners, well over half was in estates of more than 1,000 hectares.[8] Some were truly gigantic: the Zamoyski estate covered 191,000 hectares, the Radziwiłł estate

---

[1] For a discussion of the reliability of this census, see Appendix C, pp. 520–1.

[2] *M.R.S.* (1931), p. 15, Table 1.

[3] 'Vie économique', *La Pologne, 1919–39*, ii. 26.

[4] W. Thomas and F. Znaniecki, *The Polish Peasant in Europe and America* (Boston, Mass., 1918), iv. 73.

[5] A. Żabko-Protopowicz, *Rolnictwo w Polsce* (Warsaw, 1938), p. 34.

[6] L. Landau, J. Pański, and E. Strzelecki, *Bezrobocie wśród chłopów* (Warsaw, 1939), p. 146.

[7] 'Wielka własność rolna', *S.P.* (1925), v, p. viii.   [8] Ibid., p. 1.

177,000 hectares, the comparatively modest Potocki estate 19,000 hectares.[1] In fact, the amount of land held in large estates had diminished somewhat in the fifty years before 1914; this was due principally to the sale of land by large landholders who wished to obtain capital for modernization.

In 1921 the large estates held a strong position. From them came nearly half the harvests of rye, wheat, barley, and oats, as well as most of Poland's grain exports. Their productivity, too, was much higher than that of other agricultural producers. Whereas the average harvest of wheat per hectare on the large estates was 15·3 quintals, on the smaller plots it was only 11·8.[2]

Large peasant holdings of 20–50 hectares were rather rare in Poland, and played a significant part only in Poznania and Pomerania, the former German territories, where they comprised 14·9 per cent of the land in 1921.[3] But medium peasant holdings of 5–20 hectares were common everywhere, comprising 30·8 per cent of the land, and nearly a third of all holdings.[3] The division of larger holdings through inheritance, the sale of land by large landowners in the period of inflated land prices before 1914, and the large-scale emigration, which prevented some fragmentation and brought more capital in the form of remittances, had all contributed to the growth of this group in the fifty years before 1914.

The leasing of land was rather unusual in Poland, outside Upper Silesia. Only a tenth of all holdings, or 6·2 per cent of the land, was wholly or partially leased.[4] This was a result of the high price of land before 1914, which made outright sale more profitable, and of the traditional hostility to the leasing of land on the part of the gentry, who thought it low and tradesmanlike.

Archaic survivals persisted in Polish agriculture. The most important were common lands and servitudes:[5] the former were found everywhere in Poland except Poznania and Pomerania, while the latter occurred only in former Russian Poland. In 1921 common lands comprised 1·5 million hectares, or nearly a tenth

[1] Mieszczankowski, op. cit., p. 21.
[2] For more examples of the higher productivity of the large estates, see Appendix C, p. 528.
[3] Based on *R.S.R.P.* iv (1925–6), 106–9.
[4] Ibid., p. 121, Table IV.
[5] Legally, servitudes were 'easements and services mortgaged on one property for the benefit of another' (Zweig, op. cit., p. 130). In practice, servitudes conferred on the peasants the same rights (to graze cattle, to collect timber, etc.) on certain parts of the large estates as they enjoyed on common lands.

of the area of lesser landholdings.[1] Over a half was common grazing land, particularly important for the small peasants, who were thus able to keep a cow. This was most significant in impoverished Galicia, where 70 per cent of holdings benefited from common lands, as opposed to 46·2 per cent in the Congress Kingdom and 35·5 per cent in the Kresy.[1] Servitudes, an old source of contention between village and manor, were inadequately estimated in the census of 1921. They were almost entirely done away with in the land reform. However, the number of holdings for which servitudes were liquidated between 1921 and 1938 was 278,800, which gives some indication of their former extent.[2]

The medieval strip system, whereby a peasant did not possess a consolidated holding, but strips of land scattered around the village, was also widely prevalent. In the villages investigated by the Instytut Gospodarstwa Społecznego in 1935, only a third of the holdings were consolidated; 39·1 per cent were in four or more strips.[3]

Outside the western areas and a few well-run estates elsewhere, agriculture was undercapitalized and inefficient. The yield of wheat per hectare was 40–5 per cent, that of potatoes 20–30 per cent, below the German average.[4] These deficiencies became even more pronounced after 1918; the use of fertilizer diminished,[5] and very little mechanization was introduced. As late as 1939 only 2,000 tractors were in use, or 1 tractor for 8,400 hectares. This compared very unfavourably with the figures for France: 30,000 tractors (1 for every 700 hectares) and for Hungary: 7,000 tractors (1 for every 829 hectares).[6]

Agricultural production was concentrated in cereals. The largest crop was rye, cultivated mainly in Poznania and Pomerania, and in the Warsaw and Lodz provinces, of which Poland was, after Germany and the U.S.S.R., the world's third largest producer. Wheat, oats, and barley were also extensively grown.[7]

[1] *S.P.* (Warsaw, 1927), xii. 25 (issue II).
[2] *M.R.S.* (1939), p. 70.
[3] K. Czerniewski, 'Zagadnienia struktury agrarnej' in Instytut Gospodarstwa Społecznego, *Struktura agrarna wsi polskiej* (Warsaw, 1937), p. 87.
[4] C. Poralla, 'Die Wirtschaft zwischen den beiden Kriegen', *Osteuropa Handbuch Polen* (Köln, 1959), p. 79.
[5] Mieszczankowski, op. cit., p. 321.
[6] I. Svennilson, *Growth and Stagnation in the European Economy* (Geneva, 1954), p. 250, Table AXIX.
[7] *M.R.S.* (1931), p. 20, Table IV; p. 21, Table VI.

Two other important crops were sugar-beet and potatoes, and one of the more worrying results of the growing impoverishment of the Polish village was the increased cultivation of potatoes at the expense of sugar-beet: the average potato yield increased from 247·9 million quintals between 1909 and 1913 to 276·9 million quintals between 1926 and 1930.[1]

The raising of livestock, especially pigs, was also a significant aspects of agricultural production. From this source came four-fifths of the money income of farmers.[2] However, its development was hampered by the low quality of peasant stock.

In 1930 over a fifth of the land area of Poland was forest, and, as one would expect, forestry was everywhere a major industry, except in some of the more intensively farmed western regions. It benefited primarily the large landowners: most of the forest land (54·9 per cent) formed part of their estates, with 33 per cent in public hands, 8·7 per cent in small-holdings, and 2·7 per cent in common lands.[3]

Agricultural products, particularly sugar, timber, wheat, and livestock made up a considerable proportion of Polish exports, between 1928 and 1930 nearly 60 per cent.[4] The country was thus extremely vulnerable to the catastrophic fall in agricultural prices which began in the late 1920s.

Polish agriculture faced many difficulties after independence. The basically favourable situation which rapidly expanding industry had created before 1914 ceased, and the towns showed little absorptive capacity either for the surplus population of the villages, or for agricultural production on a large scale. The dwindling of the numbers of emigrants reduced the efficacy of another safety valve. Between 1920 and 1929 nearly 1¼ million people left Poland, but with the Depression emigration stopped almost completely, and after 1926 870,000 of the emigrants returned, mainly from France.[5] The Land Reform Bills of 1920 and 1925, which provided for the annual parcellation of 200,000 hectares, could not, in these unfavourable conditions, do more than keep pace with the rapidly rising population.

Small producers, the overwhelming majority of the peasants,

[1] Ibid., p. 20, Table IV.   [2] Poralla, op. cit., p. 81.
[3] M.R.S. (1931), p. 24, Tables VIII and IX.
[4] Based on M.R.S. (1931), p. 59, Table II; p. 62, Tables IV and V. For more detail on Polish agricultural exports, see Appendix C, p. 522.
[5] Zweig, op. cit., p. 20.

met additional problems. State policies of favouring heavy industry and large landowners hurt them. They lacked the capital to modernize their backward holdings, while credit became more expensive, and taxes rose above the pre-war level. The extensive cartelization of Polish industry aggravated the disparity between agricultural and industrial prices, the highly developed system of intermediaries in produce marketing meant that the peasant lost much of his profit to the various marketers, while monopolies in the retail trade kept the prices of the goods he bought high. The Depression intensified these difficulties, and led to the increasing impoverishment of the village. Agricultural problems were among the most complex the new state was to attempt to solve.

INDUSTRY

Despite the preponderance of agriculture in the economy, Poland had experienced rapid industrial development, particularly in Upper Silesia and the Congress Kingdom, in the fifty years before 1914. By 1927 849,500 people worked in the mines and in factories employing more than five persons.[1] Such industry as had developed was closely linked with the economies of the partitioning powers, and its adaptation to the new framework created by independence proved difficult indeed.

Poland possessed some of the raw materials necessary for industrial growth. In the coal deposits of Silesia and the Dąbrowa basin, she commanded, after the U.S.A., Canada, China, and the U.K., the fifth-largest estimated coal reserves in the world.[2] Though the known reserves in the East Galician oil fields were being exhausted, they still provided for domestic needs. Vast reserves of hydro-electric power were also available, but because of both scarcity of capital and the fear of further increasing the difficulties of the coal industry, only 0·1 per cent of the estimated 3·7 million h.p. was exploited in 1926.[3] More serious, the available iron ore reserves were inadequate for Poland's needs, and extensive government searching failed to uncover any new deposits while much of the ore in Poland required enrichment before it could be smelted. In

---

[1] *M.R.S.* (1931), p. 37, Table XXI. In this chapter 'factory' denotes a workshop employing more than five people.

[2] Ibid., p. 32, Table II.

[3] Ibid., Table IV.

addition, Poland possessed no supplies of such important minerals as manganese, tin, and nickel.

In 1929 the coal-mines employed 134,000 people,[1] and extracted 462 million tons, ranking fifth in the world in coal production.[2] Three-quarters of the coal was mined in Upper Silesia, a fifth in the Dąbrowa basin, and the rest in the Cracow basin.[3] However, most of this coal was unsuitable for coking, and coking coal had thus to be imported from Czechoslovakia. On the other hand, coal was an important Polish export. The ending of the three-year period of free export to Germany provided by the Geneva Convention, and the German-Polish tariff war, created some difficulties, but the opportune occurrence of the General Strike in Britain enabled Polish coal to find new markets, particularly in Scandinavia. In 1929 coal made up 13·6 per cent of the total value of Polish exports.[4] Some attempt was made to encourage the use of coal as a domestic fuel in Poland, but it failed because of the cheapness of wood.

A high degree of concentration existed in the coal-mines. There were altogether thirty-three mining firms, eleven of them mixed mining and foundry enterprises; of these firms five controlled almost half of the production of the Silesian basin in 1927 (34·5 per cent of total Polish production), and employed half of all Silesian coal-miners (33·5 per cent of all those in Poland).[5] Coal marketing was also highly concentrated, five companies marketing two-thirds of the coal mined in 1929.[6]

Poland's oil deposits were concentrated in the Carpathians, in the south-east of the country. Although some modernization took place after the war, the average production of 735,000 tons between 1925 and 1930 was little more than half the average annual production in pre-war years.[7] Adequate though this was for Polish domestic requirements, it left no surplus for export. The known deposits, estimated at 60 million tons in 1932,[8] were being gradually exhausted, and the proliferation of small wells hindered

[1] *M.R.S.* (1939), pp. 128–9.
[2] *M.R.S.* (1931), p. 34, Table X.
[3] Based on *M.R.S.* (1931), p. 34, Table IX.
[4] Based on *M.R.S.* (1931), p. 59, Table II.
[5] R. Gradowski, *Niektóre problemy kapitalizmu monopolistycznego* (Warsaw, 1959), pp. 16–18.
[6] Ibid., pp. 19–20.
[7] *M.R.S.* (1931), p. 34, Table XI.
[8] Poralla, op. cit., p. 89.

rationalization. Natural gas production grew, however, particularly from the late 1920s.

There were only two large manufacturing industries in Poland, metallurgy and textiles. Metallurgical and electro-technical plants (including foundries) had the higher output in value, and in 1927 employed 163,000 people (15·2 per cent of the labour force in factories).[1] The foundries were located almost exclusively in Upper Silesia and around Kielce; metal, machine, and electro-technical plants were also found here, as well as in Warsaw and Lodz, and to a lesser extent in Poznań and Cracow. Founding was marked by a high degree of concentration: in 1927 the average number of men employed in a foundry was 1,404.[1] The industry was dominated by five large firms, which were responsible in 1928 for 88·9 per cent of the production of the great ovens, and 84·7 per cent of that of the rolling mills. When two of these firms amalgamated in 1930, they controlled over half the raw steel production.[2]

The metallurgical industry was remarkable for the unequal development of its different branches, a heritage of partition. Machine-tool and textile machinery factories were few in number; ball-bearing, turbine, and armaments factories were totally lacking, making necessary large-scale imports; however, the locomotive and agricultural machinery plants of Upper Silesia were far too large for the Polish market, and relied on export for survival. The low absorption capacity of the Polish market limited the profitability of metallurgical enterprises generally, and hampered modernization. The plants, already outmoded because of the failure to renew machinery during the war, fell further behind world standards.

With 182,100 workers in 1927 (over a fifth of all factory workers), the textile industry was the larger employer of labour.[3] Its centre was Lodz, the 'Polish Manchester', which had grown from a small village in the mid-nineteenth century to a town of half a million. Textile manufacture was also developed in Bielsko-Biała, in Austrian Silesia, in Białystok, Warsaw, and, to a lesser extent, Cracow. Before the war the industry had produced mainly for Russian and Far Eastern markets, but independence saw a fairly successful refashioning to meet local needs. The industry included a large

---

[1] Based on M.R.S. (1931), p. 37, Table XXI.
[2] Gradowski, op. cit., pp. 12–14. The firms were the Upper Silesia United Foundries and the Katowice Mining and Foundry Co.
[3] M.R.S. (1931), p. 37, Table XXI.

number of artisan workshops and cottage workers, but in factory production large and middle factories predominated. In 1925 eight factories with more than 3,000 workers each employed 39·2 per cent of all textile workers.[1] The average number employed in a spinning mill was 209.[2]

After 1918, cotton textiles were produced almost exclusively for the home market: about 5 per cent of woollen cloth was exported. Both these branches were dependent on raw material imports, for government attempts to improve the quality of Polish wool had little success. The hope of saving foreign exchange led the Government to encourage the development of linen production, for flax could be grown locally and would provide a useful supplement to peasant earnings. As a result, linen production grew, particularly in the 1930s. Some attempts were also made to foster the development of artificial fibres, but lack of experience and the conservatism of the Polish consumer hindered the production of synthetic textiles. None of Poland's other industries were very highly developed.

As was the case with textiles and metallurgy, Polish industry generally was characterized by far-reaching concentration. In 1928 100 factories (excluding mines and foundries) employed over a third of all factory workers.[3] But small-scale workshops were also a marked feature of the Polish scene. In 1928 there were 319,400 of these, employing 886,200 people.[4] The most important crafts were blacksmithing, cabinet-making, shoemaking, tailoring, and baking, but many rather more specialized crafts existed, such as gaiter-making, comb-making, and wig-making.

Cartels played a large part in Polish industry. They had grown from 9 in 1919 to 100 in 1929, when they controlled 40 per cent of industrial production.[5] The Great Depression, which led to a breakdown of the internal price structure, saw a further growth in their number. All basic industries were affected by cartels; coal, iron-founding, zinc, cotton, sugar, timber, and petroleum were all highly cartelized. Although this is a feature more frequently found

[1] Gradowski, op. cit., p. 22.
[2] M.R.S. (1931), p. 37, Table XXI.
[3] Gradowski, op. cit., p. 10.
[4] H. Mianowski, 'O rzemiośle', Dziesięciolecie Polski Odrodzonej, pp. 1083–6. For more detail on the different types of artisan trade in Poland, see Appendix C, p. 523.
[5] Zweig, op. cit., pp. 102–3; see also M. Kalecki, 'Udział karteli w działalności przemysłowej na rynku polskim', Prace Instytutu Badania Konjunktur Gospodarczych i Cen (Warsaw, 1933), iii, no. 2, pp. 3–7.

in highly advanced economies, special factors explain its occurrence in underdeveloped Poland. Industry was already very concentrated; high tariffs excluded foreign competition, and the scarcity of capital made it easy to control firms outside the cartel. The difference in costs in different areas of Poland meant that without agreements of this type some industries would be bankrupted. This was true, for example, of the sugar refineries of central Poland, the Cracow coal-mines, and the Kielce steel industry. Moreover the Government, whose export policy depended upon selling abroad at lower than domestic prices, saw in the cartels a convenient economic tool. It was only in 1933, at the height of the Depression, that some action was finally taken against them.

An important aspect of the Polish economy at this time was the large part played by the state. Étatism had been a characteristic of the policies of the partitioning powers. The railways before 1914 had been almost entirely state owned. In addition, the Austrian Government had run state salt and tobacco monopolies, and had owned oil refineries and coal-mines, while in Prussia the Government had owned coal-mines and chemical factories. Étatism had been less developed in Russian Poland; apart from the liquor monopoly the state had owned one coal-mine and one metal factory.[1] The war had everywhere seen a great increase in the role of government within the economy. The inadequate capital resources of Poland, coupled with the need to integrate the economy and to create industries such as munitions and armaments necessary for defence, also led to far-reaching state action.

The state exercised extensive control over the credit system. Though the Bank of Poland, established in 1924, was nominally independent, in practice its freedom of action was limited: the President of the state had the right to appoint its president, it was to hold some free treasury funds, it was watched over by a government commission, and the state held 75 million zloties worth of its shares.[2] Polish private banks were all too often weak and speculative. In 1926 only 43·2 per cent of bank deposits were held in private banks, and by 1930 the amount had fallen to 36·7 per cent.[3]

[1] T. Lulek, 'Przedsiębiorstwa państwowe', *D.P.O.*, p. 930; see also *Etatyzm w Polsce* (Cracow, 1932), and T. Bernadzikiewicz, *Przerosty etatyzmu* (Warsaw, 1936). [2] M. Szawleski, 'Bank Polski', *D.P.O.*, p. 1114. [3] Gradowski, op. cit., p. 125. See also J. Schön, *Die polnische Bankwesen* (Katowice, 1928).

State credit institutions occupied an important position in the economy. The most important of these were the P.K.O. (Post Office Savings Bank), the Bank Rolny (Agricultural Bank), and the Bank Gospodarstwa Krajowego (Bank of the National Economy), of which the last had capital deposits of 150 million zloties in 1927, as against 200 million in all the private banks.[1] This bank also held shares in many industrial enterprises: in 1928 it owned 33 per cent of the stock of the Polish Iron Ore Mines, nearly all the stock of the Potash Exploiting Joint-Stock Co., 89·6 per cent of Ursus, the first motor-car factory in Poland, and owned the Starachowice Iron Ore Mines outright.[2]

The Polish Government extended the individual state monopolies of the partitioning powers to cover the whole country. By 1925 there were five such monopolies: tobacco, spirits, salt, matches, and a state lottery. With the exception of the matches monopoly, which was leased to a consortium controlled by Ivar Kreuger, the Swedish 'match king', and two potash mines, they were all directly run by the state, and accounted for an average of 31 per cent of the national revenue between 1926–7 and 1929–30.[3]

The Government also ran other industrial enterprises. Apart from the state forests, railways, airlines, and commercial fleet, it ran the Brzeszcze Coal-Mines, which it inherited from the Austrian Government, the State Nitrate Factories in Chorzów and Tarnów, and 'Polmin', the State Factory of Mineral Oils in Galicia, which possessed one of the largest refineries in Europe. In addition, the Government participated in joint enterprises with private industry. For example, the state owned half the shares in Polish Treasury Mines, it leased its lead and silver mines at Strynica in Silesia to a company in which it held half the shares, and its coal-mines in the Dąbrowa basin to a joint Polish-French enterprise.[4]

The Ministry of War ran some factories on its own. These included the State Armament Manufactures, with headquarters in Warsaw, which made firearms in Radom and ammunition in Skarżysko; an explosives factory in Zagożdzone; and an aircraft factory, an engineering works, and a uniform factory in Warsaw.[5]

[1] Gradowski, op. cit., p. 141.
[2] Lulek, op. cit., pp. 931 ff.
[3] J. Michalski, 'Monopole skarbowe', *D.P.O.*, p. 925. See also Bernadzikiewicz, *Koncern Państwowy w Polsce* (Warsaw, 1938).
[4] Lulek, loc. cit.
[5] Ibid., p. 933.

Although it is difficult to calculate the exact share of the state in Polish industry, Table II may serve as a rough guide.

TABLE II. *State Ownership in Poland**

	Percentage under government control in 1929
Railways	93
Commercial aviation	100
Merchant marine	95
Post, telegraph, and telephone	95
Iron production	16
Armaments	100
Coal-mines	20
Salt-mines	99
Chemicals	60
Oil refineries	20
Metal industry	30

* The estimate was made by taking the percentages of state ownership in 1938 from Buell, *Poland, Key to Europe* (London, 1939), p. 158, and adjusting them in the light of the nationalizations which occurred between 1929 and 1938. The most important of these were the taking over of the Żyrardów Textile Mills, and of the United Upper Silesia Foundries and Katowice Mining and Founding Joint-Stock Co. (the last two had amalgamated in 1930).

Much of Polish industrial growth before 1914 had been the result of foreign investment, and because the Government and its subsidiary credit organizations absorbed most of the domestic capital after the war, private industry was encouraged to seek capital abroad. It is rather difficult to estimate the amount of foreign capital investment in Polish industry; foreign capital was often disguised as domestic, for the usual reasons, although the inducements which the Government offered to foreign investors caused the reverse to occur as well. In 1929, according to official figures, foreign capital participated in 363 (of 1,552) joint-stock companies in Poland, with a capital investment of 1,831 million zloties (a third of the total of 5,497 million).[1] In addition 67 companies, with a total capital in Poland of 236·6 million zloties, operated in Poland with head offices elsewhere.[2] The proportion of foreign investment was particularly high in certain industries: 51·9 per cent in foundries, 65·4 per cent in the machine and electro-

[1] *M.R.S.* (1931), p. 29, Table IV.
[2] Ibid., Table V.

technical industries, 40·6 per cent in chemicals, and 75·6 per cent in gas, water, and electricity supply.[1]

The most important source of capital was France, from which came a quarter of total foreign investment in 1931. French capital tended to grow in the period, particularly as a result of joint Franco-Polish ventures such as Skarboferm, a mining and founding company in Silesia, and the Silesia–Gdynia railway. It was significant in coal-mining and petroleum, and in the textile and electrical industries. German capital, also a quarter of the total in 1931, was almost entirely pre-war in origin and tended to decline, largely through nationalization. It was particularly important in Silesia, in mining and founding, but also played a part in the chemical, metal, and electro-technical industries.[2] American investment (21·3 per cent) was important in petroleum and zinc, less so in the textile and metal industries;[3] Belgian capital (9·4 per cent) was active in iron and steel, electricity, and chemicals, while British capital (4·8 per cent), almost entirely post-war, was concentrated in banking, electrification, insurance, transport, chemicals, and sugar. Other investors were Switzerland (2·8 per cent), Austria (3·9 per cent), and Sweden (2·0 per cent).[4]

Polish industry failed to expand as rapidly after 1918 as it had before the war. Though most of the war damage had been made good, and some progress in integration had been achieved, the 1928 index of manufacturing production, the highest before the Depression, was only 116·4; in 1913 it had been 135·1.[5] Poland was the only European country whose production figures in 1929 were still below the pre-war level.[5] There were many reasons for this decline. Time was needed to overcome the economic difficulties presented by the integration of territories formerly closely linked with the economies of the different partitioning powers. War damage had been very extensive, and manufacturing production had fallen to 47·4 in 1920.[5] Polish economic development was closely connected with world trade, which did not recover significantly from the war until 1925, and the lack of modernization resulting from under-investment since 1914 hampered competition in the world market. The need to import raw materials and many machine tools created

[1] Ibid., Table IV.
[2] L. Wellisz, *Foreign Capital in Poland* (London, 1938), pp. 151–2.
[3] Ibid., pp. 152–3.   [4] Ibid., p. 153.
[5] Svennilson, op. cit., p. 305, Table ALXVI (100 = average annual production 1925–9).

a balance of payments problem, which was intensified by the repatriation of the profits of foreign capital invested in Poland, and the tariff war between Poland and Germany, her largest export market, also hindered recovery.

In addition, the poverty of the peasantry kept the domestic market for industrial products small. There was a relative lack of Polish entrepreneurs, and many state enterprises were uneconomically managed. Domestic capital was very scarce, and much foreign capital, particularly French and German, was cautious and slow to innovate, while excessive cartelization and concentration led to rigidity. The Great Depression was cruelly to expose these shortcomings of Polish industry.

SOCIAL CLASSES

In Poland before the partitions all members of the *szlachta*, or landed aristocracy, had been equal before the law. In fact, however, both in the eighteenth century and more particularly in the nineteenth and twentieth centuries, a distinction was made between the great magnates, like the Zamoyski's and Radziwiłł's, and the large mass of the gentry. By 1921, both magnates and gentry had lost some of the social and economic pre-eminence they had enjoyed in the eighteenth and nineteenth centuries. The abolition of serfdom, the confiscations of land following the 1863 rising, the agricultural depression of the 1880s, and the importing of large quantities of wheat from the fertile Ukraine, had all somewhat undermined their position. However, as we have seen, both medium and large landowners who, together with their dependents, numbered 178,800 in 1927,[1] still held a conspicuous place in agriculture.

The patriarchal way of life of the Polish country gentleman on his manor still enjoyed great prestige. Industrialists, bankers, and lawyers might have more influence, but the status of a gentleman nevertheless eluded them. Almost all the prominent Polish industrialists bought landed estates. There was, remarked Andrzej Wierzbicki, head of Lewiatan, the organization of Polish industrialists, 'an almost irresistible urge for land' among his associates: for 'To create, according to one's best will and understanding, on one's

---

[1] According to the estimate of L. Landau, 'Skład zawodowy ludności Polski jako podstawy badania struktury gospodarczej', *Wybór pism* (Warsaw, 1957), p. 187, Table V.

own piece of land, in accordance with one's own plan, that was true work! I felt as if I had been born a landowner, and not an industrialist.'[1] Roman Dmowski's supporters, stung by hostile allusions to his artisan background (his father was a roofer), were extremely sensitive about their leader's ancestry. 'Studnicki's remarks [concerning Dmowski's background]', wrote Jędrzej Giertych, 'are so unjust they should be called libels . . . Dmowski's family is a family of lesser gentry from Podlasia.'[2]

A fair number of prominent figures in the inter-war period in Poland came from landed families. In politics, they included Piłsudski himself, who came from a noble family in Lithuania; the two Grabski brothers, Władysław, Prime Minister in 1923–5, and Stanisław, Minister of Education and Religious Cults in 1925; Gabriel Narutowicz, the assassinated first President of the republic, and Władysław Raczkiewicz, Minister of the Interior in 1925 and President from 27 September 1939. Among the writers, perhaps the most important were Jarosław Iwaszkiewicz and Maria Dąbrowska.

Peasants, who with their dependants numbered 15,550,400 in 1927,[3] were the largest social class. Though class stratification had, as we have shown, gone far in the countryside, consciousness of a common peasant identity was much stronger. The peasant differed from the townsman in language, dress, and social customs, and the rate of population growth in the villages was twice that of the towns.[4] The central feature of peasant life was the existence of an extended family group, which comprised all the blood and law relations up to a certain variable limit, usually the fourth degree of consanguinity. Smaller nuclei emerged within this extended group, as a married couple reached a respectable age; it was around these nuclei that social life was organized, and the two family functions of mutual assistance to members, and control over their actions, were exercised.

It is in the light of the existence of the extended family that the peasant's attitude to land must be understood. Land was essentially

---

[1] A. Wierzbicki, *Wspomnienia i dokumenty* (Warsaw, 1957), p. 188.

[2] J. Giertych, 'O rodzicach Dmowskiego', *Słowo Narodowe* 14 January 1939, quoted in I. Wolikowska, *Roman Dmowski: Człowiek, Polak, Przyjaciel* (Chicago, 1961), pp. 227–8.

[3] Landau, op. cit., p. 187, Table V.

[4] A. Zauberman, *Industrial Development in Poland, Czechoslovakia and East Germany* (London, 1964), pp. 70–1.

familial. It could be managed by the father, the older son, the younger son, or the son-in-law. They were temporary managers; what was important was that it was well run. On marriage, a new homestead was generally created, carved out of the parental holding, but those unmarried children who remained with the parents had an obligation to work on the land, and a right to be maintained by it. Their responsibility to contribute to the homestead did not cease if they left the village to work elsewhere, and it was the acceptance of this responsibility which prompted unmarried Polish immigrants in America to send money back to their parents in Poland. 'The familial character of the farm', explain Thomas and Znaniecki,

should not be interpreted as if the family were an association holding a common property. The members of the family [apart from the parents] have essentially no economic share in the farm. They share only the social character of the members of the group, and from this results their social right to be supported by the group, and their social obligation to contribute to the existence of the group. The farm is the material basis of this social relation, the expression of the unity of the group in the economic world.[1]

But because the creation of new holdings for married sons, or for the heirs of the head of the family upon his death, was an established custom, peasants had great difficulty in accepting the idea that land was like any other material possession, and did not necessarily have to be subdivided.

The peasant's sense of the nation was very vague. He was far more conscious of his village and its surroundings. The Government too was something distant and almost incomprehensible. 'The attitude towards government', comment Thomas and Znaniecki,

can perhaps be compared with the attitude towards the material order on the one hand, and towards the divine order on the other; it is intermediate between the two. The political order appears to a certain extent as an impersonal and amoral power, absolutely mysterious, whose manifestations can possibly be foreseen, but whose nature and laws cannot be changed by human interference. But this order has also another side, more comprehensible, but more unforeseen, with some moral character, that is capable of being just or unjust and of being influenced; in this respect it is the exact parallel of the divine world.[2]

Suspicion of strangers was increased by the absence of charitable

---

[1] Thomas and Znaniecki, op. cit. i. 159.   [2] Ibid., p. 141.

traditions outside the family and the Church. Peasants had, therefore, great difficulty in understanding the motives of those who came to help them.

The peasants were deeply religious and superstitious. Religious processions were frequent, and on Sundays the countryside was filled with colour as the villagers, in regional dress, walked to church, holding their shoes in their hands to prevent unnecessary wear. The widespread belief in magic, with the consequent weakening of the notion of cause and effect, was a great obstacle to the introduction of rational farming practices.

One of the more curious features of the Polish peasantry, the result of the wide range of the *szlachta* before the partitions, was the existence of peasant nobles. In spite of their noble surnames and coats of arms, their villages differed in no respect from the rest of the villages in the countryside, and they themselves were distinguished only by a stronger feeling of the humiliating character of personal service.

By 1921 emigration and industrialization, with the new horizons they created, had done something to break down the closed world of the peasantry; but the extended family unit still had great strength, and change came very slowly in the villages. Since the amount of land possessed was held in the village to be an indication of a man's worth, it was to be expected that agricultural labourers should have a very low status. They, together with their families, numbered 3,217,000 in 1927.[1] In 1931 43 per cent lived in their own homes, and were for the most part seasonal workers, while 54·7 per cent lived on the large estates, or with the more prosperous peasants.[2] Most of the permanent workers received a considerable proportion of their wages in kind. Some of those on large estates, who had special skills, such as smiths, cartwrights, gardeners, and hop-growers, lived fairly well, but the majority were among the poorest people in Poland.

Entrepreneurs, who together with their families numbered 119,100 in 1927,[3] did not play a large part in Polish social life. For one thing, industry was not much developed in Poland: Upper Silesia was, in fact, the only highly industrialized area. For another, the old genteel prejudices against trade and manufacturing still

[1] Landau, op. cit., p. 188, Table V.
[2] Based on *M.R.S.* (1939), p. 259, Table II.
[3] Landau, op. cit., p. 187, Table V.

persisted, and had been intensified by the fact that Polish entrepreneurs had been relatively unimportant in the early industrialization of Poland. The industrialists in Upper Silesia were almost
entirely German. Even in the Congress Kingdom, foreign skills
and foreign capital had been very significant. As late as the 1880s,
ethnically Polish firms still kept their books in German, because
of its prestige as the language of trade, and lawyers dealing with
industrial matters often conducted their correspondence in German.[1] The development of Lodz had been achieved largely by
German, and to a lesser extent Jewish, factory owners. In 1914
many of the richest industrialists in Congress Poland were German,
such as the Geyer brothers,[2] the Grohmann brothers, Kindler,
Biedermann, and Scheibler. Andrzej Wierzbicki was very conscious of the accusation that Polish industry was unpatriotic.
He went out of his way to refute the

primitive view, based on *a priori* assumptions, and not on a real knowledge of Polish conditions, that foreign capital affected Government
policy in a manner detrimental to Polish national interests. Capital had
neither the need nor the opportunity to act in this way. It did not have
the need, because its fate was closely bound up with the economic
development of the Congress Kingdom, not with its backwardness.
It did not have the opportunity because Polish institutions represented
our economic interests.[3]

Though the social influence of the industrialists was not great,
they were nevertheless able to exercise strong pressure on the
Government, through the Central Union of Polish Industry,
Mining, Trade, and Finance; originally confined to the former
Russian partition, it came, by 1932, to include the whole of Poland.

In the absence of a strong bourgeoisie, the dominant urban class
was the intelligentsia, which embraced a far wider group than it
would have done in the West. *Świat pojęć*, a popular pre-war
encyclopaedia, defined 'intelligentsia' in this way:

The intelligentsia, in the sociological sense of the term, is a social
stratum made up of those possessing academic higher education,
Typical representatives of the intelligentsia . . . are professors, doctors,

[1] J. Chałasiński, *Przeszłość i przyszłość inteligencji polskiej* (Warsaw, 1958),
p. 171.
[2] Richard Geyer, although a German, was shot by the Nazis in 1939.
[3] Wierzbicki, op. cit., p. 229.

literary figures, etc. The social situation of the intelligentsia does not mean that its members have a rigidly defined social or ideological position. Members of the intelligentsia can identify with the most varied social and political trends. In fact they occupy the leading role in all political groupings.[1]

However, membership of the intelligentsia was not to be identified strictly with the possession of a secondary school diploma. It was more important that one's manners and language should be those of the educated classes, and that one should evince some familiarity with the humanities. This is amusingly brought out in the duelling code of one Boziewicz, who included among those capable of affording satisfaction apart from the gentry, 'all those who have completed secondary education' as well as the self-taught 'who have reached, if not surpassed, the level of secondary education, for example, painters and writers'.[2]

The intelligentsia can tentatively be divided into several groups. The first group comprised the free professions, including doctors and dentists, lawyers, judges and legal personnel, secondary school and university teachers, writers and artists. A second group was made up of senior administrative and technical personnel. It included higher government officials, the directors of government economic enterprises, senior people in the social services, members of the religious hierarchy, engineers, architects, builders, and industrial chemists. Finally, a third group of lower ranking people included primary school teachers, lesser government officials, parish priests, junior technical personnel, and some clerical workers and shop assistants.[3]

In spite of the very marked differences in income within the group in the late 1920s (a prominent doctor or lawyer earned 700–1,200 zloties monthly,[4] the average *inteligent* only 260),[5] the intelligentsia possessed a strong feeling of collective solidarity and responsibility. The press was continually flooded with articles

---

[1] *Świat pojęć* (Warsaw, 1939), pp. 117–18.
[2] W. Boziewicz, *Polski kodeks honorowy* (Warsaw–Cracow, 1936), 6th ed. Quoted in J. Żarnowski, *Struktura społeczna inteligencji w Polsce w latach 1918–39* (Warsaw, 1964), p. 55.
[3] For different methods of classification, see Żarnowski, op. cit., pp. 306–50; and S. Szczepański, 'Struktura inteligencji w Polsce', *Kultura i Społeczeństwo* (1960), pp. 19–48.
[4] Żarnowski, op. cit., p. 263. In 1927 £1 = 44·55 zloties.
[5] Ibid., pp. 189–91.

discussing the role of the intelligentsia, and whether its functions were being adequately performed.[1]

The occurrence in Polish censuses and labour legislation of the category 'intellectual worker' makes it fairly easy to estimate the size of the intelligentsia. It is true that not all intellectual workers could be considered members of the intelligentsia (this applies particularly to minor shop assistants), but the difference involved is negligible. Thus, adding together the census figures for members of the free professions and for intellectual workers, there were in the census area in 1921 488,000 members of the intelligentsia (522,000 in all of Poland), or 1,134,000 with dependants: they formed 3·5 per cent of the economically active population.[2] In independent Poland the intelligentsia grew very rapidly: in 1931 it numbered 716,000 (4·7 per cent of the economically active population), or 1,497,000 with dependants. By 1939, according to Żarnowski, it had reached 862,000 (5·2 per cent of the economically active),[2] but it was still relatively small.

The intelligentsia adopted many of the attitudes of the *szlachta*. A sizeable proportion of its members were of noble origin, and had come to the towns following the ruin of their estates in the difficult years of the 1870s and 1880s. In the towns they hoped to continue a way of life which had become impossible for them in the country. Maria Dąbrowska, in *Noce i dni*, provides a fictionalized account of the process: Hipolit Niechcic, unable to prevent the collapse of his estate, moves to town. 'He fled to the town as if to a foreign environment, where he would be importuned by nothing, and where he could live quietly with what remained to him.'[3] But even those members of the intelligentsia who were not of noble origin took up many of its mannerisms and ideas.

Of these, perhaps the most important was the belief that the intelligentsia was the embodiment of the Polish nation, its conscience and directing force. This feeling became particularly

---

[1] See e.g.: N. Czarnocki, 'Grzechy i omyłki inteligencji pracującej', *Droga* (1924), no. 8, 32–7; B. Heidenkhorn, 'Proletaryzacja inteligencji zawodowej', *Droga* (1930), no. 1, 67–74; A. Hertz, 'Spór o inteligencję', *Droga* (1929), no. 10, 846–55; 'Inteligencja wobec bolszewizmu', *Droga* (1931, no. 3, 193–207; 'Sprawa klerków', *Droga* (1933), no. 1, 229–40; J. Wittlin, 'Inwentarz kultury narodowej', *Skamander*, i (1925), no. 38, 76–93. The list could be extended indefinitely.

[2] Żarnowski, op. cit., p. 135, Table V. For the limits of the 1921 census see Appendix C, pp. 520–1.

[3] M. Dąbrowska, *Noce i dni* (Cracow, 1934), ii. 26–7.

strong when, in the face of Germanization and Russianization from the 1880s, writers bore the main responsibility for the preservation of the Polish language. 'The intelligentsia', wrote Leon Wasilewski, 'was the guard which kindled the national spirit from a spark among ashes and carried its flame to Poland, reborn as a state.'[1] The consciousness of a special responsibility persisted in independent Poland. The professors of the Jagiellonian University, protesting against the maltreatment of prisoners in Brześć, declared, 'In particular, we, as educators, as the intellectual elite, as those who have taken an oath of faithful service and of care for the whole republic, cannot indifferently pass over the Brześć affair.'[2]

From the *szlachta* the intelligentsia inherited a certain disdain for trade and manufacturing. A member of the intelligentsia could not earn his living through small trading or manufacturing on a small scale, though exceptions were made for really large manufacturers, or for endeavours of an artistic character, such as dealing in *objets d'art* or publishing. This attitude applied even more strongly to manual labour. It explains the penchant of industrialists for buying land, and the relative absence of industrial dynasties in Poland. A very common pattern, particularly among Jews, was for a father to build up an industrial fortune; his son would, while maintaining the business, become a dilettante and patron of the arts; his grandson might become a full-time writer, or literary critic.

The hostility to industrial pursuits was strongly criticized by Dmowski. 'The new forms of national production', he wrote, 'were initiated by foreign elements, free of the traditions of Polish passivity, particularly Jews and Germans, and the declassed *petit-noble* intelligentsia made use of them only to obtain ready-made jobs.'[3] Prus gave literary expression to the feeling of social inferiority among industrialists in his novel *Lalka*: Wokulski, a ruined landowner, moves to town, where he makes a fortune in industry; he dies worn out by unrequited love for the Countess Łęcka, to him the personification of aristocratic values.[4] It is significant that in Poznania, which was part of a highly

---

[1] Z. Wasilewski, 'Na widowni', *Myśl Narodowa*, no. 16, 15 April 1934.
[2] 'List otwarty profesorów Universytetu Jagiellońskiego do J. W. Pana Adama Krzyżanowskiego, posła na Sejm R.P.', *Robotnik*, 18 December 1930.
[3] R. Dmowski, *Myśli nowoczesnego Polaka* (Lwów, 1904), p. 88.
[4] B. Prus, *Lalka* (Warsaw, 1934).

industrialized state, these attitudes did not prevail, and that an intelligentsia of the type found in the rest of Poland hardly existed.

The wide cultural interests of the intelligentsia was also part of the *szlachta* heritage. However, this respect for knowledge was essentially that of the amateur and the dilettante, not that of the specialist. In the 1930s there was one university student for every 700 people in Poland, an extraordinarily high proportion for a relatively backward country. (The corresponding proportion in England was 1:1,013.)[1] But the two largest faculties were law and philosophy, hardly the most necessary for a developing state.[2] This overproduction of 'literary intellectuals' had much to do with the fascism prevalent at the universities.

Finally, service to the state, through the civil service, enjoyed great prestige. A feeling also existed that the state had an obligation to maintain gentry forced off the land. Galicia obtained autonomy in the 1870s, and a rapid growth of the bureaucracy was soon evident. The same was true of the rest of Poland, particularly after independence. According to Kajetan Garbiński, head of the Warsaw Polytechnic, writing in 1910,

The desire to be an official has increased to such an extent among Poles, that all youth, whether urban or rural, as if ashamed of the most useful endeavours of their families, have besieged the Governmental Commission and its subsidiary departments like ants. From this results the enormous number of useless, half-baked officials, claiming the right to do anything in the Government, ready to grasp [at anything] . . . rather than work with their own hands for their upkeep.[3]

Poland had a fairly highly developed network of small traders. In 1921 518,000 people, or 3·7 per cent of the working population, were occupied in trade and insurance.[4] By 1927, traders and their dependants numbered 1,372,300 people.[5] There was much talk in Poland of the excess of traders, but in fact the percentage of the population maintained by trade and communications (excluding the post office and the railways) was 6·4 per cent, as against 11·4 per cent in Germany.[6] The figures for the urban population alone,

[1] Chałasiński, op. cit., p. 150.
[2] The Philosophy Faculty embraced all the Humanities.
[3] K. Garbiński, a report, as described by S. Askenazy, 'Pierwsza politechnika polska', *Nowe Czasy* (1910); quoted by Chałasiński, op. cit., pp. 167-8.
[4] *R.S.R.P.* iv (1925-6), 47-51, Table XII.
[5] Landau, op. cit., p. 187, Table V.
[6] Ibid., p. 190.

however, do show a slightly, though not significantly, greater concentration in Poland (17·9 per cent as against 14·9 per cent).[1]

Polish small trade was rather primitive. The typical trader was an individual with his own shop (71·4 per cent of all those in trade, as compared with 36·1 per cent in Germany).[2] His profit margins were small, and when he gave credit, it was often at a usurious rate. But the system was adapted to the level of economic development. The Government's attempts to replace private traders by peasant co-operatives had more negative than positive results. Trade was concentrated in Jewish hands. In 1921 62·9 per cent of those employed in trade and insurance were Jews,[3] and of that number 88·9 per cent were engaged in the retail goods trade.[4] This concentration in the hands of a group who formed almost a separate caste was one of the reasons for the contempt with which trade was viewed in Poland, and for the failure of a Polish bourgeoisie to develop.

According to Landau, in 1927 industrial workers and their families numbered 5,290,000.[5] The Inspectors of Labour estimated the number of actual workers in 1929 at 1,110,248,[6] which is somewhat lower than Landau's figure would suggest,[7] but the difference almost certainly results from the absence of artisans and cottage workers, whose places of work were not inspected.

The working class was divided into two distinct sections. Artisans, as we have seen, owned 319,400 workshops in 1928, in which 886,200 people were employed.[8] Most artisans worked in small workshops, helped only by members of their families, but the smallness of the average workshop is exaggerated in the statistics. To avoid tax, the number of journeymen and apprentices was often falsely lowered in census returns. Arnekker estimates that in 1931 280,000 journeymen worked in artisan workshops.[9] The number of apprentices must have been somewhat less than this.

---

[1] Ibid., p. 191.   [2] Ibid., p. 192.

[3] A. Tartakower, 'Zawodowa i społeczna struktura Żydów w Polsce odrodzonej', Z.W.P.O. ii. 557.

[4] Ibid. ii. 371.   [5] Landau, op. cit., p. 187, Table V.

[6] Based on figures quoted in M. Drozdowski, 'Położenie i struktura klasy robotniczej Polski lat 1918–39 w literaturze naukowej dwudziestolecia', Z Pola Walki, iv (1961), no. 1, p. 36.

[7] In 1921, according to the census, of all those dependent upon mining and industry for their livelihood, 47·5 per cent were economically active.

[8] See above, p. 19.

[9] E. Arnekker, Przejawy kryzysu w rzemiośle i chałupnictwie (Warsaw, 1934),

Artisans were a colourful feature of the Polish scene, a remnant from pre-industrial times, which industrial development had not yet made obsolete. With few exceptions, their standard of living was low, and they worked extremely long hours. A large proportion (39·7 per cent in 1921)[1] were Jews, who were especially numerous in the clothing crafts, in hides and skins, baking, and bookbinding.[2]

There were 849,500 workers employed in large and medium industry in 1927.[3] Great differences in standard of living existed among the industrial workers. Best-off were workers in government monopolies, who were not only highly paid, but enjoyed relative security, and skilled workers. Unskilled workers, often of peasant origin, generally earned the same wage as those on government relief projects, or slightly less.[4] Particularly badly off were the cottage workers; they were most common in the textile industry around Lodz and Bielsko-Biała. According to Arnekker they numbered 200,000 in 1931, and this increased as the Depression continued.[5] Because they were miserably paid, they were forced to work extremely long hours to make ends meet. The unemployed, who had increased from 126,400 in 1926 to 299,800 in 1930,[6] also underwent great hardship as the Depression dragged on.

As often happens in economically underdeveloped countries, the industrial working class was relatively well off, particularly in relation to the peasantry. In December 1929 a skilled metalworker in Warsaw earned 85·92 zloties weekly, a fairly high wage; a spinner in Lodz earned 39·64 zloties, a coal-miner in Upper Silesia 48·35 zloties weekly.[7] However, these figures tend to give rather too optimistic an impression. The estimates made by the Instytut Gospodarstwa Społecznego, on the other hand, show that in 1933, admittedly one of the worst years of the Depression, over half of all workers earned less than 20 zloties weekly.[8] But in addition to wages, the fairly highly developed system of social security must be taken into account. Indeed, one of the real difficulties hampering

p. 14. See also C. Niewadzi, 'Przemysł drobny i rzemiosło w Polsce burżuazyjno-obszarniczej', *Zeszyty Naukowe S.G.P. i S.* ii (1955), 171.

[1] A. Hafftka, 'Żydowski stan rzemieślniczy w Polsce odrodzonej', *Z.W.P.O.* ii. 557.

[2] Ibid. 550–1.

[3] *M.R.S.* (1931), p. 37, Table XXI.

[4] F. Gross, *The Polish Worker* (New York, 1945), p. 35.

[5] Arnekker, op. cit., p. 55.

[6] *M.R.S.* (1931), pp. 99, Table VIII.

[7] Ibid., p. 102, Table XI.

[8] Gross, op. cit., p. 46.

any political co-operation between workers and peasants was the peasant belief that industrial workers were unnecessarily privileged.

The vast majority of industrial workers were Poles. In Lodz and in Upper Silesia, however, many skilled workers were German. Jews generally avoided heavy industry, but were important in the smaller clothing and food-processing factories.

NATIONAL MINORITIES

Independent Poland was a multi-national state. In 1921 only 69·2 per cent of the population gave their nationality as Polish,[1] while in 1931 only 68·9 per cent gave Polish as their mother tongue.[2] Pressure to obtain politically satisfactory results was universal in nationality censuses in Eastern Europe, and these figures are almost certainly too high. The national minorities in Poland were of two types: territorial minorities, which constituted a majority of the population in certain areas, and dispersed minorities, which were found scattered in most parts of the country, but nowhere formed a significant majority.

Ukrainians formed the largest of the territorial minorities. They lived in the provinces of Lwów, Stanisławów, Tarnopol, and Volynia, and to a lesser extent in the provinces of Lublin and Polesia. In 1921 3,898,000 people stated that their nationality was Ruthenian (14·3 per cent of the population),[1] while in 1931 3,220,000 stated that Ukrainian was their mother tongue, and 1,220,000 Ruthenian.[3] These figures do not reflect the true position. Estimates of the number of Ukrainians vary from about 5 million by Polish scholars, to 7 or even 8 million by Ukrainian nationalists.

Religion divided the Ukrainians. In East Galicia they were overwhelmingly Uniate, or Greek Catholic. The Uniate Church was created at the Synod of Brześć in 1596 by the union with Rome of the Orthodox living in the eastern parts of the Polish republic; it preserved many features of Eastern Orthodoxy, such as the Old Slavonic ritual and a married priesthood, but came to approximate

---

[1] *R.S.R.P.* iv. 26, Table V.

[2] *S.P.*, ser. C, xciv a (1938), Table X. In the census of 1931 people were asked their mother tongue and religion, not their nationality.

[3] *M.R.S.* (1937), pp. 20–1. The artificial differentiation between Ukrainian and Ruthenian (Little Russian), reflecting the division between the nationalist and Russophile orientations among Ukrainians, was fostered to some extent by the Polish authorities, but tended to decline in importance in this period.

more and more to Catholic practice. The *filioque* was introduced into the creed, the Roman teaching on transubstantiation was

MAP 3. Nationalities in Poland according to the census of 1921

adopted, and the rulings of the Council of Trent were accepted, the Pope was named in the liturgy as the head of the Church, the

Orthodox were referred to as schismatics and dissidents, and Orthodox clerical dress was abandoned.[1] Many Poles hoped that this process would lead to the national assimilation of the Ukrainians in East Galicia. In fact, the Uniate Church, under Archbishop Szeptycki of Lwów, became closely connected with Ukrainian nationalism, and throughout the inter-war period was one of its main supports.

Until the forcible reunion with the Moscow patriarchate in 1839, the Ukrainians of Volynia had also been Uniate, but in the course of the century they again became deeply attached to Orthodoxy. When toleration was established in 1905, very few of them returned to the Uniate Church or embraced Catholicism, like the White Russians in the provinces of Nowogródek and Wilno among whom this phenomenon was fairly frequent.

The overwhelming majority of Ukrainians were peasants. In the areas in which they lived, only 10·3 per cent of the population in 1931 depended on industry for its livelihood, compared with 19·4 per cent for the country as a whole.[2] In East Galicia fragmentation of holdings had led to a serious deterioration of the agricultural system, but in Volynia the peasants were somewhat better off. There were almost no Ukrainians among the landowners, who were so important in the agrarian structure, and who were virtually all Poles or Polonized. Some of the Polonized gentry were still members of the Uniate Church, but few of them followed the example of Archbishop Szeptycki in identifying with Ukrainian nationalism.

The towns in East Galicia and Volynia had a majority of Poles and Jews. Ukrainians made up only 30·8 per cent of the urban working class, and generally held the lesser-paid positions.[3] Government enterprises such as the railways, and some oil-wells and refineries, usually preferred to employ Poles. There were almost no Ukrainian industrialists. From the late nineteenth century, however, a small intelligentsia had grown up, composed chiefly of priests, teachers, and the managers of the extensive system of Ukrainian co-operatives.

[1] H. Koch, 'Die Unierte Kirche in Polen', *O.E.H.P.*, pp. 109–10. See also J. S. (pseud.), *W kościele i w cerkwi — praktyczny wykład obrządków rzymskiego i greckiego* (Cracow, 1926).

[2] *M.R.S.* (1937), based on pp. 29–31, Table XX.

[3] L. Hass, 'M. Kravets: *Napisy Robitnichogo Ruchu Zachidni Ukrainy v 1921–39* (Kiev, 1959)', a review, *Z Pola Walki*, iv (1961), No. 2, pp. 218–22.

White Russians were the other important territorial minority, and formed the bulk of the population in the provinces of Polesia and Nowogródek, as well as a large minority in the Wilno province, and a somewhat smaller minority in the Białystok province. In 1921 1,060,000 people gave their nationality as White Russian (3·9 per cent of the total population), while 49,000 (0·2 per cent of the total population) stated that they were '*tutejsi*', or 'locals', and were almost certainly White Russians.[1] In 1931 990,000 people (3·1 per cent of the population) gave White Russian as their mother tongue, and 707,000 (2·2 per cent of the population) said that they spoke the local language.[2] These figures are probably rather low, for national consciousness was not strongly developed among the White Russians, and a large number of White-Russian-speaking Catholics were probably persuaded by census officers to state that they were Poles.

The majority of the White Russians were Orthodox (91·3 per cent of the White-Russian-speakers, 98·5 per cent of the 'locals');[2] however, there was a sizeable Catholic minority, composed principally of those who had left the Orthodox Church following the Toleration Edict of 1905. The figure of 7·9 per cent for the proportion of White-Russian-speaking Catholics in the population does not give a true impression of their number, and almost certainly many of them appear in the census as Poles.

The areas in which the White Russians lived were the least developed economically in Poland. Only 8·5 per cent of the inhabitants of the provinces of Polesia, Nowogródek, and Wilno derived their living from industry in 1931.[3] The overwhelming majority of White Russians were peasants and agricultural labourers. As in East Galicia and Volynia, the landowners were either Poles or Polonized. The population of the towns was largely Polish and Jewish. However, a small White Russian intelligentsia did exist, particularly in Wilno.

The Germans must be regarded as a dispersed minority. Only one town, Bielsko-Biała (German Bielitz), in Austrian Silesia, had a German majority.[2] In no single district did Germans constitute a majority of the population, although there were a fair number of predominantly German villages. According to the pre-war census

[1] *R.S.R.P.* iv (1925–6), 26, Table V.
[2] *S.P.*, ser. C, xciv a, Table X.
[3] *M.R.S.* (1937), based on pp. 29–31, Table XX.

figures, which are probably somewhat exaggerated, Germans in the territories which later comprised independent Poland were approximately 1,720,000 in number: of these 1,100,000 lived in Poznania and Pomerania, 150,000 in Polish Upper Silesia, 450,000 in the Congress Kingdom, 100,000 in Volynia, and 70,000 in Austrian Poland.[1] The passing of Poznania and Pomerania to Poland led to a large-scale emigration of German officials, army personnel, and others who did not wish to live under Polish rule. According to the census of 1921 (this time probably too low), 1,059,000 or 3·9 per cent of the population gave German as their nationality.[2] By 1931, the number of people who gave German as their mother tongue had fallen, in the official statistics, to 741,000 (2·3 per cent of the population).[3]

Most of the Germans in Poland were Protestant. In 1931 there were 599,000 German-speaking Protestants and 118,000 German-speaking Catholics.[4] Most of the German settlement had taken place from Protestant areas; Catholic settlers, moreover, both in the medieval and modern periods, tended to be more rapidly assimilated.

Even after the emigration which followed independence, Germans continued to form an important element in Poznania and Pomerania. Many of the large landowners were Germans; according to Radwan, Germans owned 36·2 per cent of the holdings of more than 50 hectares in Poznania and 43·7 per cent in Pomerania,[5] and there were many Germans among the larger peasants. The agricultural labourers, however, who played such a significant part in the agrarian system of this region, were mostly Poles. In the towns, a certain number of officials were still German, and many agricultural processing plants were in German hands.

Upper Silesia was an area in which national and class divisions overlapped to a considerable extent. The indigenous Polish-speaking population, which had ceased to be ruled by Poland in the fourteenth century, had been diluted by the entrepreneurs and

---

[1] Cited in W. Kühn, 'Das Deutschtum in Polen', *O.E.H.P.*, pp. 138 ff.

[2] *R.S.R.P.* iv (1925–6), 26, Table V.

[3] *S.P.*, ser. C, xciv a, Table X.

[4] Ibid. Of the Protestants, 49 per cent were Lutherans, 2·8 per cent Calvinists, 38·6 per cent members of the Protestant United Church, and 11·5 per cent members of other churches.

[5] J. Radwan, 'Agricultural Reconstruction in Poland', *Poland*, ed. B. Schmitt (Berkeley and Los Angeles, 1945), p. 225.

traders from Germany, who came in the wake of industrialization. Almost all the large landowners were German (90 per cent according to Radwan),[1] as were the industrialists. The majority of the peasants and industrial workers were Poles. National consciousness increased among the Poles when they left the large, semi-feudal estates to work in the mines. This emerged clearly in the plebiscite of 1921: the industrial east voted to join Poland, the agricultural west chose to remain with Germany.

The Germans in the Congress Kingdom fell into two groups. In Lodz and Białystok there were 140,000 Germans before World War I, most of whom were connected with the textile industry.[2] By 1914 many of the plants were owned by Poles or Jews, but many German industrialists remained. Among the skilled workers, Germans were also numerous. The remainder of the Germans in the Congress Kingdom were almost entirely peasant settlers, living in German villages along the Vistula, east of Toruń, in the Kalisz and Lodz areas, in the north-west, and around Chełm. The 100,000 Germans of Volynia were also overwhelmingly peasant (94 per cent in 1921).[3]

In Galicia, the Germans formed three distinct groups: 34,000 were peasant colonists, settled principally in the Ukrainian-speaking areas by Joseph II; 6,000 were Sudeten German forestry workers; and 30,000 were textile workers in the largely German town of Bielsko-Biała.[4]

The Jews were the largest of the dispersed minorities. According to the census of 1921, 2,110,000 people, or 7·8 per cent of the population, gave their nationality as Jewish, which meant that 25 per cent of those of 'Mosaic persuasion' gave their nationality as Polish.[5] This could be taken as an index of the amount of assimilation, but is more likely the reflection of a desire to please the census takers. The census of 1931 gives a more satisfactory indication of the extent of assimilation. Of the 3,114,000 people of 'Mosaic persuasion', 2,488,000 (79·9 per cent) gave Yiddish as their mother tongue, 244,000 (7·8 per cent) Hebrew, and 372,000 (11·9 per cent) Polish.[6] The middle figure is almost certainly composed

[1] J. Radwan, 'Agricultural Reconstruction in Poland', *Poland*, ed. B. Schmitt (Berkeley and Los Angeles, 1945), p. 225.   [2] Kühn, op. cit., p. 140.
[3] Ibid., p. 142.
[4] Ibid. See also W. Kühn, *Die jungen deutschen Sprachinseln in Galizien* (Münster, 1930).
[5] *R.S.R.P.* iv. 26, Table V.   [6] *S.P.*, ser. C, xciv a, Table X.

of Zionists who, though they may have wished to, in all likelihood did not use Hebrew in their daily lives, and should probably be divided between the first and third groups.

The majority of Jews were still extremely devout, observing to the letter the 613 Commandments of Orthodox Judaism. The men continued to wear the long caftans and beaver hats, relics of the costume of Polish nobles in the seventeenth century, which had become identified with religious orthodoxy, and let their sidecurls grow long. The women still cut off their hair on marriage, wore wigs, and went once a month for purification to the ritual baths. Chassidism, an eighteenth-century reaction to the unemotional and formalistic character of rabbinic Judaism, was strong, particularly in the regions around Chełm and Lublin, and in Galicia. In many areas it had degenerated into a cult centred round the court of a Chassidic rabbi, and miracle-working rabbis, such as the one at Góra Kalwarja, enjoyed wide renown. But under the influence of urbanization and industrialization, medieval Judaism was breaking up. More and more able men and women left the stifling atmosphere of the small towns to seek freedom in the big cities. This process has often been described in fiction, as in *Głosy w ciemności* by Stryjkowski, and *Three Cities* by Sholem Asch.[1]

The situation of the Jews differed considerably in the various partitions. In Prussian Poland, where in 1921 there were 20,600 Jews (0·67 per cent of the population),[2] emancipation had come early in the nineteenth century. The vast majority of the Jews of that area had emigrated to the centre of Germany, especially to Berlin. In Galicia, where in 1921 there lived 607,000 Jews (10 per cent of the population),[2] emancipation had come in the 1870s. Many Jews had enjoyed educational opportunities, and the percentage of Jews in the learned professions was high. Many Jewish members of the intelligentsia were Polonized, and Jews like Szymon Askenazy and Józef Feldmann were important in the Polish national movement. However, the economic backwardness of Galicia kept the structure of the Jewish community relatively static. In 1921 74·1 per cent of all those occupied in trade and insurance in Galicia were Jews.[3]

---

[1] J. Stryjkowski, *Głosy w ciemności* (Warsaw, 1963); S. Asch, *Three Cities* (London, 1933).

[2] J. Parkes, *The Emergence of the Jewish Problem* (Oxford, 1946), p. 131.

[3] Tartakower, op. cit., *Z.W.P.O.* ii. 367.

In the Russian partition, where in 1921 there were 2,217,000 Jews (12 per cent of the population),[1] full civil rights were achieved only after independence. This was particularly true of the Eastern Kresy, but even in the Congress Kingdom Jews did not have the right to own agricultural holdings, or to be mayors of small towns. With the intensification of persecution in Russia, many Jews moved to the Congress Kingdom, where conditions were somewhat better; the percentage of Jews in the Congress Kingdom rose from 11·1 in 1842 to 14·5 in 1897. Large-scale emigration prevented a further increase, but in 1921 Jews still formed a substantial 14·25 per cent of the population.[2] This influx of Russianized Jews provoked fears that they would be used to Russianize the Congress Kingdom, and led to intensified anti-Semitism. The industrial development of the Congress Kingdom had, however, created new economic opportunities for Jews. The old medieval concentration of Jews in trade diminished, and Jews became important both in the artisanate and in the industrial working class.

The Jews were largely urban. In 1931 over three-quarters lived in towns: 43·3 per cent of the Jews were in towns of more than 20,000 inhabitants, where they formed 26·4 per cent of the population; 29·8 per cent lived in towns of less than 20,000 (28·8 per cent of the population); while 23·1 per cent lived in villages and in the country (3·2 per cent of the population).[3] As one would expect, therefore, Jews were found mainly in urban occupations. In Galicia, however, where the granting of civil rights had enabled Jews to buy land, a class of Jewish landowners developed. In 1912, 4·3 per cent of the land held in large estates was owned by Jews.[4] It was from such a landowning family that Sir Lewis Namier came.

There existed also a certain number of Jewish peasants. In 1921 9·5 per cent of Jews actively employed earned their living from farming, forestry, gardening, and fishing.[5] It is true that the majority were market gardeners, but some were peasants, the result both of earlier attempts to solve the Jewish problem by agricultural

[1] Parkes, op. cit., p. 131.
[2] B. Wasiutyński, *Ludność żydowska w Polsce w wiekach XIX i XX* (Warsaw, 1930), pp. 8–9.
[3] F. Beranek, 'Das Judentum in Polen', *O.E.H.P.*, p. 120.
[4] S. Bronsztejn, *Ludność żydowska w Polsce* (Wrocław–Warsaw–Cracow, 1963), p. 54.
[5] Tartakower, op. cit., *Z.W.P.O.* ii. 366.

settlement, and of the buying of land by small Jewish farmers in the immediate post-war years.

Jews formed a significant part of the Polish intelligentsia. They were particularly numerous in law and in medicine, for in 1931, according to Mahler, they comprised 49–50 per cent of all lawyers[1] and 46 per cent of all doctors.[2] They were also important in Polish literary life: among Polish writers of Jewish origin were Julian Tuwim, Antoni Słonimski, Józef Wittlin, and Bolesław Leśmian, to name only a few.

There were some Jews among the larger capitalists: in banking, Kronenberg, Wawelberg, and Bloch; in sugar refining, Toeplitz and Epstein; and in textiles, Poznański. But the typical Jewish 'capitalist' was either the owner of a small factory or a master-artisan with a large workshop. According to the estimates made by the American Joint Committee (admittedly in the somewhat abnormal year of 1921) 60·6 per cent of all Jewish factories employed less than five people, compared with 7·1 per cent of non-Jewish factories.[3]

The largest occupational group among Jews in 1921 comprised those in trade and insurance: 34·6 per cent of all economically active Jews were engaged in this branch (62·6 per cent of all those in trade and insurance in Poland).[4] Of these, 88·9 per cent were employed in the retail goods trade.[5] The Jewish trader faced great difficulties, both because of nationalist boycotts and because of the general suspicion in Poland of all trade as somehow unproductive and parasitic. As Kwiatkowski, the Minister of Trade and Industry after the May coup, noted

When the period of inflation [1922–6] created as an inevitable consequence a number of unhealthy and highly undesirable phenomena in the field of trade, there spread in the popular mind a certain hostility to trade as such. This hostility even took practical forms, expressing itself in the denial of the need for any aid (such as credit) for trade not directly linked with production.[6]

In 1921 31·7 per cent of the economically active Jewish population worked in mining and industry.[7] This group may be divided

[1] R. Mahler, 'Jews in Public Service and the Liberal Professions in Poland, 1918–39', *Jewish Social Studies*, vi (4), 313–14.   [2] Ibid., p. 325.
[3] Tartakower, op. cit., *Z.W.P.O.* ii. 388.
[4] Ibid., pp. 366–7.   [5] Ibid., p. 371.
[6] E. Kwiatkowski, *Postęp gospodarczy Polski* (Warsaw, 1927), p. 30.
[7] Tartakower, op. cit., *Z.W.P.O.* ii. 366.

into two not entirely distinct parts. Jewish artisans comprised 39·7 per cent of all those in Poland.[1] In the more backward parts of the country, the percentage was even higher. In Polesia, for example, 81·1 per cent of all artisans were Jews, in the Nowogródek province, 77·1 per cent.[2] The Jewish industrial working class was concentrated in the smaller factories, particularly in the food and clothing industries. (46·7 per cent of Jews in mining and industry worked in clothing factories, 15·4 per cent in food-processing plants.)[3] Jewish workers tended to avoid heavy industry, partly because they found it distasteful, partly because of discrimination and the difficulties created for the Orthodox by Saturday work. Many Jews were cottage workers in the textile industry. In general, Jewish workers were rather poorly paid.

Perhaps the most pressing problem facing Jews in Poland was their extensive pauperization. Jewish poverty had been widespread in Eastern Europe before World War I, but emigration and industrialization had done something to alleviate the situation. After the war, however, industrial production did not expand rapidly, and emigration dropped to half its pre-war level. Jews were concentrated in the less-modernized industries, and were adversely affected by rationalization, to say nothing of deliberately anti-Semitic policies. This problem was to grow much worse as time passed.[4]

Of the other minorities, the most important were the 69,000 Lithuanians (0·3 per cent of the population), concentrated in an area separated from the Lithuanian border by a strip of Polish settlement, the 56,000 Russians (0·2 per cent), living all over the Kresy, and the 31,000 Czechs (0·1 per cent) settled in Volynia.[5] In addition, there were some interesting historical survivals, such as the Tartars, Polish-speaking Moslem descendants of Tartar and Turkish prisoners of war, and the Karaites, a people of Turkic origin who had adopted a heretical form of Judaism.

[1] See above, pp. 469–70. See also I. Bornstein, *Rzemiosło żydowskie w Polsce* (Warsaw, 1936).
[2] Hafftka, op. cit., p. 357.
[3] Tartakower, op. cit., *Z.W.P.O.* ii. 369.
[4] On this, see J. Borenstein, 'Zagadnienie pauperyzacji ludności żydowskiej w Polsce', *Z.W.P.O.* ii. 395–407.
[5] *R.S.R.P.* iv (1925–6), p. 26, Table V.

II

POLITICAL LIFE IN THE NEW STATE

Poland, from one cause or another is always unquiet. The
new constitution only serves to supply that restless people
with new means, at least new modes, of cherishing their
turbulent disposition.

Burke, *Thoughts on French Affairs*

THE CONSTITUTION

THE Polish Constitution of March 1921 was modelled on that of
the Third French Republic.[1] It established a democratic republic
with universal suffrage and a bicameral legislature made up of a
Sejm, or lower house, and a Senate. Of these, the Sejm was vastly
more powerful. Elected for five years by a system of proportional
representation, it could be dissolved before this period had
elapsed only by a vote of two-thirds of its own members, or three-
fifths of the members of the Senate acting with the approval of
the President. It had the right to initiate legislation, and to inspect
annually the accounts of the state. The annual adoption of the
budget, the imposition of taxes, and the determining of the size
of the army all required legislative approval. It had, in addition,
the right to question ministers, who were all responsible to it, and
who could be forced, either individually or as a Cabinet, to resign
following a simple majority vote in the Sejm.[2]

The constitution stated that elections were to be 'universal,
secret, direct, equal, and proportional'.[3] All citizens over twenty-
one years of age were entitled to vote in elections to the Sejm,
and a modification of the d'Hondt system of proportional representation was adopted in an attempt to prevent excessive fragmentation of political groups. This modification intensified the
d'Hondt system's bias in favour of larger parties by establishing
a number of indirectly contested seats (72 of the Sejm's 444),
for which only those parties which had put up candidates in more

[1] *Konstytucja 17 Marca 1921 r.* (Warsaw, 1921).
[2] Articles 5, 6, 10, 11, 26, 33, 56.   [3] Article 11.

than 6 of the 64 constituencies were eligible. The seats on this list were distributed in proportion to the number of seats a party won in the constituency lists.[1] In addition, the requirement that no elector should reside more than 6 km. from a polling station favoured the rural parties, as it made constituencies in the country rather smaller than those in the towns.

The Senate was also elected according to the d'Hondt system by all citizens over thirty years of age, and each of the thirteen provinces formed a Senate constituency. The Senate was purely a review body. It could, within thirty days of the passing of a law, suggest amendments which the Sejm could then adopt by a simple majority vote. To reject these amendments, a majority of eleven-twentieths was required.[2]

The Sejm and the Senate, sitting together, constituted the National Assembly. This body elected the President by an absolute majority, and was responsible for the revision of the constitution called for every twenty-five years. Amendments were adopted by a simple majority vote.[3]

Many of the bitterest disputes concerning the terms of the constitution had arisen over defining the nature of the executive. The National Democrats, fearing that their *bête noire*, Piłsudski, might be elected President, succeeded in drastically limiting the powers of that office. According to the constitution, the President was not responsible to the Sejm, but his power was exercised through his ministers, who were. Elected for seven years, he opened, closed, and adjourned the Sejm, but had no veto over legislation. Along with the Cabinet, he had the power to issue decrees in accordance with laws, but his acts were not valid without the countersignatures of the Prime Minister and the minister whose sphere of responsibility was involved. He was the highest-ranking military officer, but in time of war could not be Supreme Commander.[4] He could, however, appoint a Supreme Commander on the advice of the Council of Ministers.[5]

The real executive power was thus exercised by the Cabinet

---

[1] Law of 28 July 1922, *Dz.U.R.P.*, 1922, no. 66, pp. 590 ff. For a description of the d'Hondt system, see E. Lakeman and S. Lambert, *Voting in Democracies* (London, 1955), pp. 87–90.

[2] Articles 35, 36.   [3] Articles, 39, 125.

[4] Piłsudski had held the offices of Head of State and of Supreme Commander between November 1918 and November 1922.

[5] Articles 2, 3, 25, 39, 46.

under the chairmanship of the Prime Minister. Ministers had the right to take part in the sessions of the Sejm, and the Cabinet as a whole, as well as each individual minister, was responsible to the Sejm, and could be forced by it to resign.[1]

MAP 4. Poland, showing Provincial Divisions in 1931

In addition, ministers were constitutionally responsible to the Sejm for criminal acts committed while in office. On the passing of a resolution by a three-fifths majority of the Sejm, a minister could be impeached by a Tribunal of State, composed of the president of the highest court and twelve other members holding no state office. The tribunal was elected for the entire duration of the

[1] Articles 55, 56, 59, 60.

parliament; eight members were chosen by the Sejm and four by the Senate. A minister could not resign to evade trial, and while on trial he was suspended from office.[1]

In local government, despite a constitutional provision that 'the principle of decentralization will be introduced', a centralized system on the French pattern was established. The country was divided into seventeen provinces (*województwa*), each of which was administered by a governor (*wojewoda*). The provinces were, in turn, divided into districts (*powiaty*) under the control of sub-prefects (*starostowie*). Although the constitution claimed that this system was based on 'the principle of broad territorial local self-government', the ideal remained largely a dead letter. However, some attempt was made to promote economic self-government through chambers of commerce, industry, and agriculture, and organizations of artisans and industrial workers.[2]

The constitutional position of the army had provoked great contention in the constituent Sejm, and continued to do so until the May Coup. Nominally, the President was head of the army, but its parliamentary dealings were conducted by the Minister of War, who was to be an army officer, and who was responsible to the Sejm for all acts of military officials, both in time of peace and in time of war. He served as a shield for the Supreme Commander, who was not directly responsible to parliament, and who was nominated by the President on the recommendation of the Cabinet, advised by the Minister of War.[3]

A compromise was reached on the question of Church–State relations which all but established Roman Catholicism as the state religion. 'The Roman Catholic faith', proclaimed the constitution,

being the religion of the overwhelming majority of the nation, occupies in the state a leading position among religious endowed with equal rights (*równouprawnionych*).

The Roman Catholic Church governs itself by its own laws. The relationship of the state to the church will be laid down on the basis of an agreement with the Holy See, which will require ratification by the Sejm.[4]

The traditional liberal safeguards were included in the constitution. The judiciary was to be independent, and judges could be

---

[1] Article 59.   [2] Articles 3, 66, 68.
[3] Article 46.   [4] Article 114.

dismissed only by a judicial decision; members of parliament enjoyed legal immunity for their actions in parliament; persons under arrest were to be brought to trial within forty-eight hours; citizens had the rights of freedom of speech, conscience, and belief, and freedom of petition; the press was free, and freedom of assembly and the inviolability of the mails and of personal dwellings could be waived only under certain circumstances laid down by law.[1] All these rights could, however, be set aside during a state of emergency.

The constitution set forth, in addition, some general principles. According to Article 99,

The Polish Republic recognizes all property, whether owned privately by individuals or collectively by groups, institutions, local government bodies or, finally, by the state itself, as one of the most important bases of social and legal order. It guarantees every inhabitant, institution or group the protection of its property. It will allow expropriation or limitation of ownership only in cases provided for by law, because of the greater need of the state, and compensation will be paid.

'Labour', declared article 102, 'as the main wealth of the Republic is under the particular protection of the state . . . . Each man has the right to state-supervised working conditions and, in case of unemployment, sickness or accident, to welfare benefits.'

Every twenty-five years the National Assembly could revise the constitution, adopting amendments by a simple majority. In the interim, constitutional revision required a two-thirds majority, both in the Sejm and in the Senate. However, the second Sejm elected under the new constitution could effect revision by a three-fifths vote.[2]

Although the constitution was that of a national state (its preamble began 'We, the Polish Nation'), it guaranteed within its borders 'complete protection of life, liberty and property to all, without distinction of origin, nationality, language or religion'. Every citizen had the right 'to maintain his national identity and to preserve his language and national customs'. Minorities were to enjoy the 'full and free development of their national character through autonomous groups, of a public and legal nature, composed of their representatives'. They had the right to found private schools and religious and social organizations, though nothing

[1] Articles 21, 77, 78, 98, 100, 104, 105, 106, 107, 112.
[2] Article 125.

was said of minority rights within the state school system. The practice of any religion not disruptive to public order was permitted.[1]

The rights of the minorities were more closely defined in the Treaty of 28 June 1919 between the Allied and Associated Powers and Poland. This formed part of the fundamental law of Poland,[2] and could not be changed without the agreement of the majority of the Council of the League of Nations.[3] In addition to the rights already guaranteed by the constitution, the treaty provided that the Polish Government could not limit the use of any minority language:

Notwithstanding any establishment by the Polish government of an official language, adequate facilities shall be given to Polish nationals of non-Polish speech for the use of their language, either orally or in writing, before the courts.[4]

It further ruled that Poland must

provide in the public educational system in towns and districts in which a considerable proportion of Polish nationals of other than Polish speech are residents, adequate facilities for ensuring that in the primary schools the instruction shall be given the children of such Polish nationals through the medium of their language.[5]

Finally, Jews could not be forced to violate their Sabbath, and no election could take place on a Saturday.[6]

Upper Silesia enjoyed a special autonomous position within the state. Before the plebiscite in German Upper Silesia, the Sejm passed on 15 July 1920 a law conferring wide self-government on those parts of Austrian and German Upper Silesia which would fall to Poland.[7] The law established as Silesia's legislature a provincial Sejm, elected by universal suffrage, and as executive a governor, appointed from Warsaw, with a council of seven. Two members of the council were appointed by the governor and

---

[1] Articles 95, 109, 111, 112.

[2] Treaty between the Allied and Associated Powers and Poland, signed at Versailles on 28 June 1919, reprinted in J. Robinson, O. Karbach, M. Laserson, N. Robinson, and M. Vichniak, *Were the Minorities Treaties a Failure?* (New York, 1943), pp. 314 ff., Article 1.

[3] Ibid., Article 12, pp. 316–17.   [4] Ibid., Article 7, p. 315.

[5] Ibid., Article 9, p. 316.   [6] Ibid., Article 11, p. 316.

[7] 'Ustawa Konstytucyjna z dnia 15 lipca 1920r., zawierająca statut organiczny województwa śląskiego', *Dz.U.R.P.*, 1920, no. 73, pp. 1298–305.

five elected by the Sejm. The Silesian Government was empowered to deal with questions concerning the use of two languages in Silesia, matters of local government and public health, and the organization of a police force. It exercised control over primary education and all vocational training, and legislated in clerical matters, with the exception of those to be dealt with in the Concordat. Provision for the poor, agricultural legislation, local communications and electricity, the floating of provincial loans and the imposition of provincial taxes all fell within the competence of the provincial administration.

Silesian autonomy was further strengthened by the Geneva Convention of 15 May 1922 between Germany and Poland.[1] Its purpose, as determined by the Council of the League of Nations when it was decided to partition Silesia, was

to preserve for a certain time, for the industries of the territory separated from Germany, their former markets, and to ensure the supplies of raw material and manufactured products which are indispensable to these industries; to avoid the economic disturbance which would be caused by the immediate substitution of the Polish mark for the German mark as the sole legal currency in the area assigned to Poland; to prevent the working of the railways serving Upper Silesia from being affected by the shifting of the political frontier; to regulate the supplies of water and electricity; to maintain freedom of movement for individuals across the new frontier; to guarantee, as far as possible, to the workers that they shall not lose, in the portion of territory assigned to Poland, the advantages which were secured to them by German social legislation and by their Trades Union organization; and finally, to ensure the protection of minorities upon the basis of an equitable reciprocity.[2]

A League of Nations Tribunal of Arbitration was set up in Silesia to deal with any disputes over the interpretation of the Convention. Appeals against its decisions could be made to the League itself.[3]

Before East Galicia was definitely assigned to Poland, a law was passed by the Sejm on 26 September 1922 conferring wide

---

[1] 'Convention germano-polonaise relative à la Haute Silésie faite à Genève, le 15 mai 1922.' Reprinted in G. Kaeckenbeeck, *The International Experiment of Upper Silesia* (London, 1942), pp. 567–822.

[2] Quoted in Kaeckenbeeck, op. cit., pp. 9–10.

[3] 'Convention germano-polonaise, Sixième Partie: Commission Mixte et Tribunal Arbitral de Haute Silésie', Kaeckenbeeck, op. cit., pp. 801–16.

autonomy upon the provinces of Lwów, Tarnopol, and Stanisławów.[1] This was intended to influence the Council of the League
to accept the incorporation of East Galicia into Poland, and once
the question was favourably decided in May 1923, the provisions
of the law were largely disregarded.

THE PARTIES

This sophisticated and highly advanced constitution did not
function well in Poland. Perhaps the principal reason for this was
the extreme fragmentation of Polish political life. In 1925, for
example, there were ninety-two registered political parties in
Poland, including the parties of the national minorities.

In the Sejm thirty-two parties were represented, organized into
eighteen parliamentary clubs.[2] The far-reaching differences which
had developed during 130 years of foreign rule in the former
partitions were partly responsible for this multiplicity. In Galicia,
for example, people had become accustomed to thinking of themselves as Austrians as well as Poles. Stanisław Łańcucki, a socialist
leader, describes the prevailing mood of Galician railway workers
in 1914–15:

Everyone trembled at the mere thought that Austria might undergo
a catastrophe, and no one thought that she could possibly disintegrate.
'And who will recognize my years of service? Who will pay my pension
if Austria falls? No, it is impossible. Austria must win.' These were the
questions and desires of the railwaymen, both Socialist and National
Democrat. This, however, was how almost everyone in Galicia understood the situation.[3]

The contrasting traditions of political tactics in constitutional
Austria and Germany and in autocratic Russia also hindered co-
operation. In no sphere more than in politics, claimed the peasant
leader Stanisław Thugutt, was it so important

whether one became active under the Russians or under the Austrians,
with the tradition of armed uprisings and mole-like conspirational work
in the blood, or with the habit of small struggles for the achievement of
very limited aims. The general aim might be the same, but how greatly

---

[1] 'Ustawa z dnia 26 września 1922 r.', *Dz.U.R.P.*, 1922, no. 90, Article 829,
pp. 1553–5.
[2] A. Bełcikowska, *Stronnictwa i związki polityczne w Polsce* (Warsaw, 1925),
p. 9.
[3] S. Łańcucki, *Wspomnienia* (Warsaw, 1957), p. 152.

these psychological differences influenced tactics, a matter of such importance in politics, that it divided deeply and fundamentally people otherwise extremely close to each other.[1]

Although the electoral system was intended to prevent the excessive proliferation of small parties, the principle of proportional representation which it embodied brought about fragmentation. In addition, the 'self-confidence and exuberant individualism'[2] of the Polish intelligentsia, which played a leading role in all the parties, hindered the formation of more broadly based political groupings.

The unfortunate effects of this atomization were intensified by a lack of political experience. Before 1914 the Polish parties in the Reichstag, the Reichsrat, and the Duma had always been among the Opposition, demanding the redress of grievances. This habit was difficult to overcome. 'In Poland', wrote Thugutt, 'everyone wants to be in opposition; on no account will anyone accept responsibility.'[3]

Widespread poverty and ignorance increased the temptation to indulge in demagogy. As late as 1931, after twelve years of compulsory education, only 69·8 per cent of the population could read and write. In the countryside the proportion of literates was only 64·4 per cent.[4] The Eastern Kresy was the most backward region in this respect: in the Białystok province the proportion was 63·5 per cent,[5] and in Polesia 48·5 per cent.[6]

Polish political life in the 1920s was still to a great extent overshadowed by the increasingly anachronistic conflict between the National Democrats and the followers of Piłsudski, a conflict over tactics and orientation which had arisen before 1914 and had dominated the course of Polish politics during World War I. In his account of Poland between the two world wars, Mackiewicz claimed, 'The history I am writing could be called "Dmowski and Piłsudski". The history of my generation is the struggle of these two men.'[7]

[1] S. Thugutt, *Wybór pism i autobiografia* (Glasgow, 1943), p. 109.
[2] A. Micewski, *Z geografii politycznej drugiej Rzeczypospolitej* (Warsaw, 1964), p. 377.
[3] S. Thugutt, Letter to Juliusz Poniatowski, *Wyzwolenie*, 27 July 1924.
[4] Based on *S.P.*, ser. C, xciv a (1938), Table XVI, pp. 60–73.
[5] Based on *S.P.*, ser. C, lxxxiii (1938), Table XVI, pp. 58–9.
[6] Based on *S.P.*, ser. C, lxxxvi (1938), Table XVI, p. 52.
[7] S. Mackiewicz, *Historia Polski od 11 listopada 1918r. do 17 września 1939r* (London, 1941), p. 34.

THE NATIONAL DEMOCRATS

Roman Dmowski, with Jan Popławski and Zygmunt Balicki, a founder of the National Democratic party,[1] and its principal ideological spokesman, formulated his views in the late 1890s in reaction against Positivism, the belief that nationalist aspirations should be subordinated to social reform, and the general acquiescence in foreign rule, both of which had dominated politics in Poland after the disastrous crushing of the insurrection of 1863. He felt that his position offered the possibility of a new solution for the old problem, a third way:

> Where formerly it was held that the nation had only two alternatives, either armed uprising or complete abdication and acquiescence in the most miserable conditions of existence . . . the Polish nation has now found a new way, excluding both of these. It has realized the necessity of taking as its point of departure in politics the real political situation, the incorporation into three states, but it has understood that within each of these three states it can and must struggle for its national existence, for its separateness, for conditions of general advance, indeed, for its civil rights . . .[2]

As a result of a visit to Japan, he came to see national feeling as a combination of instincts 'independent of the will of the individual'.[3] He hoped to make use of this involuntary national feeling to create among the Poles of all the partitions a sense of national community which would be strong enough to withstand the pressures of assimilation. His movement stressed national solidarity and opposed class parties, which he accused of political immaturity. Although he admitted that one group of Polish socialists had accepted the need for national independence, this 'does not prevent them from being socialists', he wrote:

> they cannot recognize cultural, economic and political antagonisms between nations, they cannot talk of the spiritual distinctiveness (odrębność) of a nation, of the unity of the desires of a nation in a given field, for what would then become of the doctrine of the international proletariat, or of the predominance of class antagonisms over all others?[4]

[1] Narodowa Demokracja, also known as Endecja.
[2] R. Dmowski, 'Niemcy, Rosja i kwestja polska', *Pisma* (Częstochowa, 1938), ii. 227. This is the reprint of a work first published in 1908.
[3] Idem, *Dopełnienie: Myśli nowoczesnego Polaka* (London, 1953), pp. 98–9.
[4] Idem, *Myśli nowoczesnego Polaka* (Lwów, 1904), pp. 169–70.

He placed great emphasis on developing the national sentiment of the peasantry, who did not share the passivity with which he reproached the *szlachta*, and who, following emancipation, were showing 'activity, enterprise, and flexibility of thought'.[1]

But though the National Democrats worked extensively among the peasantry, founding schools and co-operatives, they were not hostile to large landowners. Apologizing for his attack on the policy of the conservatives in Galicia, Dmowski stressed that it was their politics and not their social position he was assailing: 'It is our great advantage, compared with other nations who have lost their existence as states, that we possess historic classes, inheritors of the political culture of the past, a factor of first-rate value in the contemporary evolution of our nation.'[2]

Although he called himself a democrat, Dmowski was opposed to liberal democracy as it was practised in the West, both because he believed it was dominated by 'Jewish-Masonic influences' and because it conflicted with his idea of a coherent national community with a common will. He saw as a feature of Western parliamentary development the polarization of political life between liberals and conservatives:

In general, conservative parties support strong internal policies, vote for greater state impositions, etc., while on the other hand, progressive and democratic elements advance liberal slogans, defend the individual against the state, attempt to reduce the aspirations of the state, and the burdens it lays upon its citizens.[3]

He felt that the uncritical acceptance in Poland of the principles of Western liberalism had placed Polish democracy on 'a false road'.[4] 'Even today', he found in 1904, 'many people are deeply convinced that true democracy cannot be concerned with such matters as the national interest, that it should only struggle for freedom and liberty, opposing broad national and state aspirations.'[5]

Dmowski regarded Germany as Poland's principal enemy. Prussia had played the most conspicuous part in the partitions of Poland, and, unlike Austria and Russia, had gained territories

[1] Ibid., p. 91.
[2] R. Dmowski, 'Upadek myśli konserwatywnej w Polsce', *Pisma*, iv, pp. vii–ix, the reprint of a work first published in 1914.
[3] Idem, *Myśli nowoczesnego Polaka*, pp. 180–1.
[4] Ibid., p. 186.   [5] Ibid., pp. 185–6.

which she held to be indispensable to her national existence. 'To Prussia', he wrote, 'the lands she took from Poland were necessary for the territorial linking of her possessions.'[1] Without them the German desire for dominance in East-Central Europe would be rendered almost unattainable. Prussia was bound to oppose the re-establishment of a Polish state because it would call into question her hold on her Polish lands. Dmowski held that 'Prussia grew up from the fall of Poland; the revival of Poland . . . would be a brake on German eastward expansion and would undermine the leading role which Prussia plays in the German Reich. Thus Prussian politicians understand that they can make no compromise with the Poles.'[2] He believed that German ambitions in Eastern Europe would lead to a clash with Russia, and he hoped to win the trust of the Russian government by his anti-German policies and his general political responsibility so that Russia might reach some agreement with the Poles. Moreover, he believed that the internal difficulties of the Russian state would lead to a liberalization of policy in relation to the non-Russian minorities.

Anti-Semitism formed a fundamental element of National Democratic ideology. To Dmowski, the Jews in Poland were a coherent national group which could never be assimilated, and which was being used by the partitioning powers to reinforce their rule. He saw the Jewish predominance in Polish trade as the principal cause for the failure of a Polish bourgeoisie to develop, and for the political weakness of Poland which had led to the partitions.

The National Democrats first became important in Polish political life during the revolution of 1905, when they vigorously opposed the attempts of the Polish Socialist Party under Piłsudski to begin a national uprising. Dmowski even went to Japan to counteract the effect of Piłsudski's mission to the Japanese High Command. By 1914 the National Democrats had become the strongest political force both in the Congress Kingdom and in Prussian Poland. In Galicia, because of their pro-Russian orientation and the dominance in politics of the large landowners, they had less success; however, their strength grew here, particularly after the introduction of universal suffrage in 1907.[3]

---

[1] Dmowski, *Niemcy, Rosja i kwestja Polska*, p. 30.
[2] Ibid., p. 151.
[3] For a fuller account of the National Democrats before 1914 see: R. Dmowski

Already in 1912, a secret all-Polish conference of the National Democrats in Cracow had decided that in the event of war the party would support the Entente. Thus in August 1914 the party accepted the Manifesto to the Poles issued by Grand Duke Nicholas, and in the autumn of that year formed a pro-Entente Polish National Committee[1] to counteract the influence of the pro-Austrian General National Committee.[2] The Polish National Committee bitterly opposed Piłsudski's legions, and formed Polish units, the so-called Gorczyński legions, to fight alongside the Russian forces. In August 1917, as Russia became a less significant part of the Allied coalition, the committee reformed itself in Lausanne. It adopted Paris as its headquarters, where it was headed by Dmowski himself, and established branches in America, London, and Rome. The National Committee was recognized by the French in November 1918 as the future Polish Government, and its delegation, with some additions to appease the Piłsudski-ites, represented Poland at the peace conference at Versailles.[3]

In independent Poland, the National Democrats entered politics as the Popular National Union,[4] formed in 1919 by the amalgamation of National Democratic and allied groups from the different parts of Poland. These included the Galician National Democrats,[5] the Galician Christian Peasant Party,[6] the National Democrats of the Prussian partition, and the parties which had made up the National Electoral Committee of Democratic Parties[7] in Russian Poland.

Pisma, i–iv; E. von Puttkammer, *Die polnische National-Demokratie* (Cracow, 1943); S. Kozicki *Historia Ligi Narodowej* (London, 1964); W. Feldman, *Geschichte der politischen Ideen in Polen* (Munich, 1917).

[1] Komitet Narodowy Polski.

[2] Naczelny Komitet Narodowy.

[3] For the National Democrats during World War I see: T. Komarnicki, *The Rebirth of the Polish Republic* (London, 1957); R. Dmowski, 'Polityka polska i odbudowanie Państwa', *Pisma*, iv–v; M. Leczyk, *Komitet Narodowy Polski a Ententa i Stany Zjednoczone, 1917–19* (Warsaw, 1966).

[4] Związek Ludowo-Narodowy, also known as the Z.L.N.

[5] Stronnictwo Narodowej Demokracji.

[6] Stronnictwo Chrześcijańsko-Ludowe.

[7] Narodowy Komitet Wyborczy Stronnictw Demokratycznych: formed by the Inter-party Circle (Koło Międzypartyjne), the main pro-Entente grouping here, it had included the National Democrats, the Polish Progressive Party (Polska Partia Postępowa), the Party of Constructive Politics (Stronnictwo Polityki Realnej), the National Union (Zjednoczenie Narodowe), the Christian Democrats (Chrześcijańska Demokracja), and the Union of Economic Independence (Związek Niezależności Gospodarczej). See Bełcikowska, op. cit., pp. 68–9.

The second congress of the Z.L.N., held in Warsaw on 26–7 October 1919, formulated the new party programme. Its links with the pre-independence policies of the National Democrats were explicitly stated:

The principles which gave the nation the strength of spirit necessary to achieve independence, the paths of national politics which led to liberty have not ceased to be appropriate because subjection has ended. They are the most valuable ideological heritage which we take with us into a new life in the independent Polish state.[1]

The party claimed to be democratic. 'Poland', stipulated Article 18, 'if she is to occupy her appropriate place among civilized nations, must be a modern democracy.'[2] At the same time, according to Article 14, 'The Popular National Union demands a strong government which will ensure the maintenance and execution of the law, as well as respect for authority.'[3] The principle of voluntary national activity was maintained, and étatism was criticized. The paragraph in the programme dealing with 'The Relation of the State to the Nation' had the subheading 'As little state compulsion as necessary, as much effort by the citizens as possible'.[4] The need for social justice was stressed: 'National unity in the state is illusory unless there is social equilibrium in the nation.'[5]

The Catholic Church was to be given a leading position in the new state: 'Basing the moral education of the Nation on religion, and recognizing the Church as the director of its moral life, the Z.L.N. demands for the Church complete independence and an appropriate position in the State.'[6]

Rapid industrialization was called for, in order to prevent large-scale emigration, to end the dependence of Poland on foreign capital, and to create a strong middle class.[7] The Z.L.N. also proposed negotiated wages and 'broad social insurance'.[8] Land reform was considered necessary in order to create 'numerous prosperous peasant holdings', but the parcellation was to involve

[1] 'Program Związku Ludowo-Narodowego' (Introduction), reprinted in Bełcikowska, op. cit., pp. 81–2.
[2] Ibid., p. 91.   [3] Ibid., p. 84.
[4] Ibid., p. 85.   [5] Ibid., Article 10, p. 87.
[6] Ibid., Article 14, p. 90.
[7] 'Program Z.L.N.,' Bełcikowska, op. cit., Article 7, pp. 85–6.
[8] Ibid., Article 12, pp. 88–9.

principally state holdings, mortmain lands and 'excessively large' estates.[1]

The traditional policy towards Jews was accepted. The Z.L.N., stated Article 8, 'calls for the securing of the Polish character of the towns, of industry and trade as one of the most pressing needs of national policy'.[2] In relation to the other national minorities, federalism was explicitly rejected. 'The Republic must aspire to the greatest possible unity of state and nation (*jednolitość narodowo-państwowa*).'[3] The eastern parts of Poland were seen as an important source of land for colonization.[4]

Finally, the Z.L.N. adhered to the National Democratic anti-German and pro-Entente orientation in foreign policy. 'It remains true', stated the preamble to the programme, 'that the most dangerous enemy of Poland is Germany.'[5]

Dmowski, exhausted by his efforts at the peace conference, did not play a large part in the life of the party in the first years after independence. The leadership of the party in parliament fell to the veteran Galician parliamentarian, Stanisław Głąbiński, while that of the national party was assumed by another Galician, Stanisław Grabski, who was succeeded in 1923 by Stanisław Kozicki. The party had an extensive press, with *Gazeta Warszawska* as its main organ. It also issued a morning paper in Warsaw, *Gazeta Poranna*, which amalgamated with *Gazeta Warszawska* in October 1925. Among its provincial papers, the most important were *Goniec Krakowski* in Cracow, *Słowo Narodowe* in Lwów, *Kurjer Poznański* in Poznań and *Dziennik Wileński* in Wilno.

It is rather difficult to assess the strength of the Z.L.N., for in order to take advantage of the electoral system, it formed a bloc in the elections of November 1922 with the Christian Democrats, the Christian National Party,[6] and the Christian National Agricultural Party of Poznania.[7] In this bloc, the Christian Alliance of National Unity,[8] the Z.L.N. was by far the most important. The bloc won 29·1 per cent of the votes cast, and 169 seats (38 per cent of the total); 98 of those seats were assigned to the Z.L.N.[9]

---

[1] Ibid., Article 11, pp. 87–8. [2] Ibid., p. 86.
[3] Ibid., Article 9, p. 86. [4] Ibid., Article 11, p. 88.
[5] Ibid., p. 82. [6] Stronnictwo Chrześcijańsko-Narodowe.
[7] Chrześcijańsko-Narodowe Stronnictwo Rolnicze.
[8] Chrześcijański Związek Jedności Narodowej (nicknamed 'Chjena').
[9] A. Próchnik, *Pierwsze piętnastolecie Polski odrodzonej* (Warsaw, 1957), pp. 133–5.

An account of the bloc's successes does give some idea of the areas of National Democratic strength. In the towns, the bloc did particularly well, winning 37·4 per cent of the votes, while in the countryside it won 25·6 per cent.[1] It was especially strong in

TABLE III. *Elections to the Sejm, November 1922**

	Votes in 1000s	Percentage
Right	2,637	30·1
Christian Alliance of National Unity (National Democrats, Christian Democrats, Christian National Party)	2,551	29·1
National—State Union	38	0·4
State Alliance of the Kresy	48	0·6
Centre	1,914	21·9
Piast	1,153	13·2
Polish Centre (Catholic Peasant Party and counterpart in former Congress Kingdom)	259	3·0
Bourgeois Centre	29	0·3
N.P.R.	473	5·4
Left	2,221	25·2
Liberation	963	11·0
P.P.S.	906	10·3
Peoples' Councils	46	0·5
Peasant Party—Left Wing	59	0·7
Radical Peasant Party (Fr. Okon)	115	1·3
Communist lists	132	1·4
National Minorities	1,889	21·6
National Minority Bloc	1,398	16·0
East Galician Zionists	175	2·0
West Galician Zionists	81	0·9
Jewish Populists (Folkists)	53	0·6
Chliborobi (pro-Polish Ukrainians)	87	1·0
Bund	81	0·9
Zionist Workers' Party (Poalei Sion)	14	0·2

* Based on Próchnik, op. cit., p. 133; 'Statistique des élections à la Diète et au Sénat effectuées le 5 et le 12 novembre', *S.P.* viii (1926).

Warsaw, where it won 42·0 per cent of the votes,[2] and in Poznań, where it won 75·9 per cent.[3] Regionally, it was strongest in the

[1] 'Statistique des élections à la Diète et au Sénat effectuées le 5 et le 12 novembre 1922', *S.P.* viii (1926), p. ix.

[2] 'Statistique des élections', 1922, *S.P.* viii (1926); based on Table XII, p. 15.   [3] Ibid., based on Table XII, p. 48.

former German areas. It won 48·9 per cent of the votes in Poznania, 55·7 per cent in Pomerania, and 36·5 per cent in Silesia.[1] In the central provinces (roughly corresponding to the Congress Kingdom), it won 33·2 per cent of the votes,[1] while in the eastern provinces (roughly equivalent to the Kresy), inhabited largely by non-Poles, it won only 5·4 per cent.[1] In Galicia, where its pro-Russian orientation had always been a handicap, it won 18·5 per cent.[1] It did somewhat better in Galicia's eastern provinces, because the struggle with the Ukrainians had made the Poles more nationalistic, and it was helped by the widespread boycott of the election by Ukrainians. In the Tarnopol province, for example, it won 25·5 per cent of the votes.[1]

PIŁSUDSKI AND HIS FOLLOWERS

Piłsudski, the 'noble socialist', as the National Democratic leader derisively called him, was almost the diametrical opposite of Dmowski. Born on a large estate near Wilno, he was in many ways the direct descendent of the romantic Polish revolutionaries of the nineteenth century. To him, the uprising of 1863 was not the criminal folly it seemed to Dmowski.

'Historical currents', he wrote in 1924,[2]

derived from and faithful to the style of our generation, wanted to force us to accept the view that a score of hotheads, of madmen, of idiots, symptomatic of Polish lightheadedness, of Polish stupidity, prevented Polish caution, understanding, seriousness from endowing Poland with I know not what benefits. . . . This was a war, a war, gentlemen, which great Russia had to wage for a whole year in order to win!

Piłsudski first became active in politics in Narodnaya Volya, the Russian terrorist organization. Sentenced in 1887 to five years in Siberia for taking part in a conspiracy against the life of Alexander III (the same conspiracy for which Lenin's brother was executed), he quickly came to the conclusion that Tsarist Russia 'that Asiatic monster covered with European veneer',[3] was Poland's principal enemy, and that he had over-estimated the strength of

[1] Ibid., p. ix.
[2] J. Piłsudski, 'Wpływ Wschodu i Zachodu na Polskę w epoce 1863r.', *P.Z.* viii. 85–6.
[3] Idem, 'Jak stałem się socjalistą', *Promień*, nos. 8–9 (1903). Reprinted in *P.Z.* ii. 52.

the Russian revolutionary movement. On his return to Poland, he soon assumed a leading role in the Polish Socialist Party.[1] It seemed to him that now that both the landowners and the bourgeoisie had decided on collaboration with the Russians, only the industrial working class was interested in national liberation. During the Russo-Japanese War, he tried unsuccessfully to persuade the Japanese to sponsor a rising in Poland, and in the 1905 revolution he took control of the Fighting Organization[2] of the P.P.S. which he led on a series of terrorist attacks on Russian government outposts. His devotion to terrorism and his belief in the precedence of national liberation over social revolution finally split the P.P.S. in November 1906, and culminated in an attack on the railway station at Bezdany, north of Wilno, in September 1908.[3]

Piłsudski was now convinced of the need for military organization and training, so that in the coming war Polish military force could have some influence on the outcome. 'My latest idea', he wrote to Feliks Perl in September 1908, 'is the necessity in our conditions of creating in every party, and most particularly in our party, organizations of physical force'.[4] He moved to Galicia, where the situation was least restrictive, and where the Austrian Government was not unsympathetic to his anti-Russian aims. Already in June 1908 he had formed the Union of Active Struggle[5] to direct the organization and training of military units. Piłsudski's pre-war military activity reached its high point in November 1912, with the formation of the Provisional Committee of Confederated Parties Demanding Independence,[6] which united in support of the legionary movement almost all the Galician parties, except the Conservatives and the National Democrats.[7]

By 1914, Piłsudski's disputes with the Committee, and the

[1] Polska Partia Socjalistyczna, commonly known as the P.P.S.
[2] Organizacja Bojowa.
[3] See: J. Piłsudski, P.Z. i–ii; W. Pobóg-Malinowski, Józef Piłsudski, 1867–1914 (London, 1964); A. Żarnowska, Geneza rozłamu w Polskiej Partii Socjalistycznej, 1904–6 (Warsaw, 1965).
[4] J. Piłsudski, 'List do Feliksa Perla', P.Z. ii. 299.
[5] Związek Walki Czynnej.
[6] Komisja Tymczasowa Skonfederowanych Stronnictw Niepodległościowych.
[7] For Piłsudski's activities in the years immediately preceding World War I see: J. Piłsudski, P.Z. iii; A. Garlicki, Geneza Legionów (Warsaw, 1964), ed. S. Arski; J. Chudek, Galicyjska działalność wojskowa Piłsudskiego, 1906–1914 (Warsaw, 1967).

conflicts within it, had somewhat diminished its strength. On the outbreak of war, Piłsudski had attempted to foment a national uprising in Warsaw by proclaiming a National Government and announcing his intention to support it with his troops. However, the complete failure of the Poles in the Congress Kingdom to respond, and the formation by the pro-Austrian conservatives of the General National Committee (N.K.N.), placed before Piłsudski the alternatives of co-operation with the N.K.N. or the break-up of his legions. He decided on co-operation, and he was almost certainly sincere when he wrote to Władysław Jaworski, the Galician conservative, in August 1915:

the political aim of the war, which I have placed before myself from the start, was and is the incorporation of Galicia and the Congress Kingdom into the framework of the Austrian-Hungarian monarchy. I did not, and do not, believe that it is possible to obtain better conditions for Poland in this war.[1]

Piłsudski remained true to the Austrian orientation until mid-1916, when the increasing weakness of Austria and the hostility of the Hungarians, the Germans, and the Austrian army to the Austrian-Polish solution had become evident. He became convinced that a satisfactory resolution of the Polish question depended on an agreement with Germany. When the Germans established a rump Polish state on 5 November 1916, Piłsudski supported their action. He demanded, however, the creation of a civilian government before he would help in the formation of an army. When this condition was met in January 1917 by the formation of the Council of State,[2] he went ahead. 'You are right', he told Baranowski after 5 November, 'that Austria is finished. From now on we are going to talk only in Warsaw, on a new basis, and with the Germans. . . . I am again going to make a compromise, this time with the Germans.'[3]

Piłsudski realized very quickly that the Germans were interested only in a puppet state, and refused to take the oath of allegiance to the Reich which they demanded of the army, counselling his supporters to follow his example. In July 1917 he was arrested

---

[1] Letter, cited by J. Hupka in *Z czasów wielkiej wojny* (Niwiska, 1936), p. 116. For Piłsudski during World War I see also: J. Piłsudski, *P.Z.* iv–v; S. Migdał, *Piłsudczyzna w latach pierwszej wojny światowej* (Katowice, 1961); S. Arski, *My Pierwsza Brygada* (Warsaw, 1963). [2] Rada Stanu. [3] W. Baranowski, *Rozmowy z Piłsudskim, 1916–31* (Warsaw, 1938), pp. 40–4.

and interned in Magdeburg for the duration of the war. He was thus able to return to Poland in November 1918, following the collapse of the Central Powers, with the aura of a martyr and the reputation of an indomitable fighter for independence. He quickly assumed the role of leader in the new country, holding the positions of Head of State and Supreme Commander of the army. But his plan to exploit the weakness of Russia following the Civil War in order to dislodge White Russia and the Ukraine from the Soviet Union, and thus to ensure Polish security, failed and almost led to political catastrophe in Poland.[1] Internally, the National Democrats, his lifelong enemies, emerged as the strongest force in politics, and were able, in the new constitution, to circumscribe severely the powers of the President. They hoped in this way to prevent Piłsudski from exercising again the personal control he had held before 1922. Piłsudski had determined not to stand for President even before the elections of November 1922, which further strengthened the National Democrats. His position in the army was also being undermined.

No single political group supported Piłsudski, but in the Polish Military Organization[2] which he had set up during the war, he possessed a body of utterly devoted adherents. The P.O.W. had established two organizations, Konwent A, to place sympathetic men in prominent positions in Left-Wing groups, and Konwent B, which was to do the same in Right-Wing groups. Konwent B was rather unsuccessful, but in the Left-Wing parties Piłsudski had many supporters. His influence was naturally greatest in the P.P.S., of which he had been a member until the early years of the war, when he allowed his membership to lapse on account of his other interests. But he had not yet openly clashed with the socialists, and the authenticity of a remark which Mackiewicz attributes to him in 1918 is doubtful: 'For a long time', he is supposed to have said, 'we have travelled together in the socialist tram. I have got out at the stop marked "Independence".'[3] Among

---

[1] On Piłsudski's federal schemes see: T. Komarnicki, op. cit.; J. Lewandowski, *Federalizm. Litwa i Białoruś w polityce obozu belwederskiego* (Warsaw, 1962); M. Dziewanowski, 'Piłsudski's Federal Policy, 1919–21', *J.C.E.A.* x (1950), no. 2, 113–28; no. 3, 271–87.

[2] Polska Organizacja Wojskowa (P.O.W.).

[3] S. Mackiewicz, op. cit., p. 183. On the question of the authenticity of the statement, see W. Pobóg-Malinowski, 'Skoro nie szablą, to piórem', *Kultura* (Paris), 1960, no. 5/151, pp. 99–134.

the P.P.S. leaders, Tadeusz Hołówko, Jędrzej Moraczewski, Leon Wasilewski, Bronisław Ziemięcki, and Rajmund Jaworowski were his direct supporters, and he enjoyed much goodwill among the rank and file and the other leaders.

In the peasant movement, Piłsudski's influence was strongest in the Liberation Party,[1] based mainly in Russian Poland, but he hoped to widen this influence to cover the peasant movement as a whole. He warned his supporters against splitting the United Peasant Party in December 1922, advising them to 'gather [Witos] to themselves, and not force him into the orbit of the National Democrats by opposing him'.[2] When Witos nevertheless decided to make an alliance with the National Democrats in May 1923, his party split. P.O.W. members were prominent among those who engineered the break-up.[3]

In the elections of 1922, Piłsudski, in an attempt to attract adherents on the Right, directly supported two rather small conservative groupings linked with large landowners, the National-State Union in Galicia[4] and the State Alliance of the Kresy in Eastern Poland.[5] Neither won any seats, the former group receiving 38,000 votes and the latter 48,000.[6]

But in spite of his political setbacks, Piłsudski had a wide, charismatic appeal in Poland as a whole, as the dashing and romantic legionary, who was at the same time indomitable and incorruptible.

PARTIES OF THE LARGE LANDOWNERS

Political groups representing the large landowners had been important in Poland before 1914, particularly in Galicia, where the lack of economic development, the relatively small proportion of lesser gentry, and the poverty of the peasantry all contributed to their power. The most important party here was known as the

[1] Polskie Stronnictwo Ludowe—Wyzwolenie.
[2] A. Bogusławski, *Pamiętnik*, quoted in Lato, op. cit., p. 81. Wincenty Witos was perhaps the most important peasant politician in Poland immediately after World War I. See below, pp. 120–2.
[3] The most important were Bogusław Miedziński, Karol Polakiewicz, and Antoni Anusz. See Lato, op. cit., pp. 81–2.
[4] Unia Narodowo-Państwowa. On this, see J. Lewandowski, *Unia Narodowo-Państwowa czyli kryzys liberalizmu polskiego* (Warsaw, 1964).
[5] Państwowe Zjednoczenie Kresowe.
[6] Próchnik, op. cit., p. 133.

Stańczycy, from a work by one of its founders, Józef Szujski's *Teka Stańczyka*.[1] The Stańczycy had paved the way for the achievement of self-government in the 1860s, and controlled the new provincial parliament. They formulated the concept of '*trójlojalizm*' (tri-loyalism), the idea that independence should be renounced, and that co-operation with the ruling powers might at least achieve tolerable conditions. In addition, they founded a historical school, the Cracow School, which argued that the internal defects of the Polish Republic had been responsible for its downfall, and attempted to deal fairly with both Jews and Ukrainians.

As late as 1911, renamed the Party of the National Right,[2] the Stańczycy were the most important force in the parliamentary bloc of Governor Bobrzyński of Galicia, who was one of their principal adherents. But already their power was waning. Universal suffrage had given new political power to the peasants, who had no reason to feel grateful to their landlords; the bitter struggle over the modification of the franchise in East Galicia increased the strength of the National Democrats, who had opposed Bobrzyński's liberal policy towards the Ukrainians; and the growth of a new nationalism made *trójlojalizm* appear tarnished and degrading. During the war the Stańczycy were the most powerful element in the N.K.N., but the bankruptcy of the Austrian solution, reflected in the military weakness of the Habsburgs, the division of Galicia into Polish and Ukrainian halves, and the granting of the Chełm region to the Ukrainians under the Treaty of Brest-Litovsk, robbed the Party of the National Right of most of its former support.

None of the other landowners' groups before 1914 had such importance. In Galicia, they included a number of landlords in the east who objected to Bobrzyński's liberalism towards the Ukrainians, and the group around Stanisław Stroński in Cracow, who were closer to the National Democrats. In the Congress Kingdom, the National Democrats had succeeded in winning over a large number of the landowners; Maurycy Zamoyski, the largest

[1] Stańczyk was a jester at the court of Aleksander Jagiellończyk and Zygmunt the Elder. Through his wit he made the king aware of political realities. For the Stańczycy see: J. Buszko, *Sejmowa reforma wyborcza w Galicji, 1905–14* (Warsaw, 1956); M. Bobrzyński, *Wskrzeszenie państwa polskiego*, vol. i (Cracow, 1920); S. Mackiewicz, op. cit., chap. i.

[2] Stronnictwo Prawicy Narodowej.

property-holder here, was one of their most important supporters. The Party of Political Realism[1] to some extent followed the lines of the Cracow School, and similar groups existed in the Kresy. In Prussian Poland, the Polish landowners were almost entirely National Democratic.[2]

In independent Poland, the landowners' parties were faced with the dilemma that their social base was too small to ensure them many votes, while their hostility to land reform alienated those peasants who might otherwise have supported them. What political tactics to adopt in this situation was a problem best resolved by those groups close to the National Democrats, from whom they differed principally in a stronger opposition to land reform. They were two in number, the Christian National Agricultural Party and the Christian-National Party, which together formed the Christian-National Club[3] in parliament. They fought the 1922 elections together with the Popular National Alliance and received twenty-seven seats in the Sejm.[4]

The patrician Party of the National Right was one of the casualties of independence. Refusing to make any concession to the new situation, it held that the 1921 constitution was too democratic, and called for a weighted franchise. It opposed the 1920 land reform, and called instead for reforms which would 'raise the level of agricultural production'.[5] But it held fast as well to the more creditable aspects of its heritage: it opposed exclusive nationalism, emphasizing its danger to the state, and advocated fair treatment for the minorities. It also proposed a sophisticated set of constitutional controls over the administration.[6] But although the pronouncements of its leaders were listened to with attention, and its daily newspaper, *Czas*, was one of the most important in Poland, its political strength was minimal. In the first Sejm it was fairly influential through the sixteen-member Club of Constitutional Work.[7] Its deputies had entered parliament as former members of the Austrian Reichsrat, since elections were impossible in East Galicia on account of the continued

[1] Stronnictwo Polityki Realnej.
[2] On these groups see Micewski, op. cit., chap. iii.
[3] Klub Chrześcijańsko-Narodowy.
[4] A. Próchnik, op. cit., p. 135.
[5] 'Program Stronnictwa Prawicy Narodowej', Article 13; reprinted in Bełcikowska, op. cit., p. 753.
[6] Ibid., pp. 745–55.   [7] Klub Pracy Konstytucyjnej.

fighting between Poles and Ukrainians. However, in the election of 1922 the Party of the National Right failed to win a single seat.

The small monarchist Conservative Party[1] lacked the intellectual eminence of the Party of the National Right, but shared its political insignificance.

WORKERS' PARTIES

i. *The Polish Socialist Party*

The Polish Socialist Party, the largest of the workers' parties, was formed in April 1919 by the union of the Polish Socialist Party of the former Russian partition and the Galician Polish Social Democratic Party.[2] The Polish Socialist Party in the former German areas, a rather weak group with a limited influence in Silesia, joined them some months later.

The Polish Socialist Party in Russian Poland was created in November 1892 by the amalgamation of four smaller Polish socialist groups active in Russia. After the secession, in March and July 1893, of those elements which believed that social revolution should be the party's main concern, the party came to concentrate its attention on national liberation. As we have already seen, Piłsudski's control of the party and his insistence on terrorist activity against the Russian Government led to a split in November 1906, following which the domination of the party by those elements which wished to stress the struggle for independence was secured. The achievement of a correct balance between social and national goals nevertheless continued to plague the party, and led to a further split late in 1911 between Piłsudski, Walery Sławek, and Leon Wasilewski on the one hand, and Feliks Perl on the other. Perl left the party and formed the Polish Socialist Party—Opposition.[3] The two parties remained close in ideology, however, both believing that social revolution was not imminent, that a Polish military force should be built up in anticipation of a coming conflict between the partitioning powers,

[1] Stronnictwo Zachowawcze.

[2] Polska Partia Socjal-Demokratyczna (P.P.S.D.).

[3] Polska Partia Socjalistyczna-Opozycja. For the P.P.S. in this period see J. Krzesławski, 'Dzieje P.P.S. od 1904 roku do wybuchu wojny światowej w 1914', *Księga jubileuszowa Polskiej Partii Socjalistycznej* (Warsaw, 1933), pp. 62–103; J. Holzer, 'Nurt opozycyjny w P.P.S. frakcji rewolucyjnej i P.P.S. opozycja (1909–14)', *P.H.* lxvi (1959), no. 3, 545–68.

and that in such a war support for Austria, or at least for the Central Powers, was most likely to help the Polish national cause. As a result, they reunited following the outbreak of war in August 1914.

The party remained close to Piłsudski throughout the war. In December 1914 it joined him in acknowledging the leading role of the General National Committee, and it was one of the principal sponsors of the pro-Piłsudski-ite General Committee of United Parties Demanding Independence.[1] The P.P.S. applauded the establishment of a Polish buffer state by the Germans on 5 November 1916, and its representatives sat for a time on the Provisional State Council,[2] the civilian authority set up by that state. In addition, the party supported Piłsudski in the legionary crisis of July 1917.[3] But it was at the same time increasingly establishing its independence from Comrade Ziuk. Piłsudski and his closest lieutenant, Walery Sławek, withdrew from party activity in 1914, and new men such as Norbert Barlicki, Mieczysław Niedział-kowski, and Adam Landy, less subservient to him, became pro-minent in the leadership. The bankruptcy of Activism, as support for the Central Powers was known, grew increasingly evident. The military weakness of Austria was manifest, while Germany was obviously interested in nothing more than a satellite Poland, and preferred to deal with socially conservative groups. The harsh-ness of German requisitions also caused much bitterness. Finally, the attempts of Piłsudski's followers in the P.P.S. to induce the party to co-operate with the National Democrats were resented. But Piłsudski-ite influences were still very strong in the party at the end of the war.

The Galician Polish Social Democratic Party (P.P.S.D.) had grown up in entirely different conditions in a constitutional state, and was based on a wide network of constituency parties, trade unions, and co-operatives. From 1908, under its leader, Ignacy Daszyński, a man of remarkable oratorical talents though not really politically acute, it had been one of the principal supporters

---

[1] Komitet Naczelny Zjednoczonych Stronnictw Niepodległościowych.

[2] Tymczasowa Rada Stanu.

[3] For the P.P.S. during the war see: J. Holzer, *Polska Partia Socjalistyczna w latach 1917–19* (Warsaw, 1962), and 'Polska Partia Socjalistyczna w latach 1914–19', *Ruch robotniczy i ludowy w Polsce w latach 1914–23* (Warsaw, 1961), pp. 319–54; H. Jabłoński, *Polityka Polskiej Partii Socjalistycznej w czasie wojny 1914–18* (Warsaw, 1958).

of independence and of the legionary idea in Galicia. Because of Galicia's general backwardness, it saw as its main goal in internal politics the democratization of Galician society. Socialism was very much a long-term aim.[1]

On the outbreak of war, it declared its support for Austria, proclaiming a 'class truce'. It remained in the General National Committee until November 1917, and broke with its long-standing policy by entering the Polish Club[2] in the Austrian Reichsrat, dominated as it was by the Stańczycy, in 1916. As late as May 1917 Daszyński declared that 'Poland, free and contented, will be a buttress of the Austrian throne'.[3] This policy differed from that of the Polish Socialist Party in Russia, which inclined increasingly towards a German solution. It also led to opposition from the Piłsudski-ites within the Galician party, such as Jędrzej Moraczewski, Zygmunt Klemensiewicz, and Emil Bobrowski. But it was only the increasing unreality of the Austrian solution which led to the party by the middle of 1917 to call for an independent united Poland, and even then sympathy for Austria was expressed.

When the Austrian occupying authority in the southern part of the Congress Kingdom collapsed, both parties played a significant part in the creation of the Popular Government[4] in Lublin, headed by Daszyński. However, the return of Piłsudski, now tremendously popular, on his release by the Germans created difficulties. The Polish Council of State established by the Germans in Warsaw, and now dominated by groups similar in character to the Cracow conservatives, had, somewhat surprisingly, acknowledged him as their legal successor, and he had the overwhelming support of the armed forces maintaining the Lublin Government. Piłsudski, who believed that the primary task was not social revolution, but national consolidation in order to present a united front to the Allies, was unhappy about the radical character of the People's Government. He was even at this time seeking a compromise with the National Democrats. He

[1] For the Galician Social Democrats see: I. Daszyński, *Pamiętniki* (Warsaw, 1957), 2 vols.; J. Holzer, 'Polityka kierownictwa Polskiej Partii Socjalno-Demokratycznej w przeddzień powstania niepodległego państwa polskiego (luty-październik 1918r.)', *Z.P.W.* iii (1960), no. i, 35–57, and *Polska Partia Socjalistyczna w latach 1917–19*.

[2] Koło Polskie.

[3] Speech to the Polish Club, 28 May 1917, quoted in Holzer, *Polska Partia Socjalistyczna w latach 1917–19*, p. 65.

[4] Rząd ludowy.

successfully put pressure on Daszyński to resign, and to acquiesce in the formation of a new Popular Government with Moraczewski as Prime Minister but controlled by Piłsudski himself, who assumed the position of the Head of State and Supreme Commander.[1]

The elections of January 1919 were a serious disappointment for the two socialist parties, which together won 9·4 per cent of the votes and held 35 seats out of 394. This, together with the waning of the workers' council movement, in which the Communists were also important, saw the end of the period in which the socialists had much influence on the course of government action.

The united party adopted a Social Democratic position. It opposed the concept of the dictatorship of the proletariat, which Niedziałkowski defined as 'merely changing places with the bourgeoisie'.[2] Instead, it claimed, 'The P.P.S. wants to build a democratic and republican Poland for the Polish working masses.'[3] The eighteenth party congress in August 1921 decided that the party should participate only in a 'worker-peasant government',[4] but this was amended at the nineteenth party congress (30–1 December 1923): it was resolved that

in situations in which the achievement of a popular government is not possible, the P.P.S. cannot remain indifferent to the formation of a government, and on strictly laid down conditions, can tolerate and eventually support an anti-Right Wing cabinet whose activities will not be hostile to the interest of the working class.[5]

At the seventeenth congress it had been decided to join the Vienna International, the so-called Second and a half International. When the request for membership was refused on the grounds of revisionism, the P.P.S. joined the Second International in May 1923.[6] The party remained very hostile both to Communism and to Russia. It had supported Piłsudski's federal aims for White Russia and the Ukraine; *Robotnik*, the party paper, affirmed on 7 June 1919:

The Russian state must be limited to the solely Russian areas.

[1] See A. Ajnenkiel, 'Z dziejów Tymczasowego Rządu Ludowego w Lublinie', *K.H.* lxv (1958), no. 4, 1057–90.

[2] Quoted in Holzer, *Polska Partia Socjalistyczna w latach 1917–19*, p. 403.

[3] Pre-electoral appeal for the elections of November 1922, Bełcikowska, op. cit., p. 356.

[4] Ibid., p. 354.   [5] Ibid., p. 367.   [6] Ibid., pp. 353–8.

This ethnic Russia must be ringed on the east, west and south by the independent states of liberated nations, strengthened by mutual alliances and enjoying the support of the powers leading in culture (*mocarstw przodujących kulturze*).

During the Polish-Soviet War, Daszyński, the party leader, had joined the Government. The party formed a Workers' Committee for the Defence of Independence, and established a workers' regiment for the defence of Warsaw.[1] Attacking the Communists in Poland, the party declared in July 1924:

Those Polish workers, attracted by fine words about revolution and a better life, make themselves unconscious, passive tools of a foreign staff of military adventurers like Trotsky who, while issuing slogans of liberation, are selling the bloody labour of their own proletariat to the capitalists of the West.[2]

In internal politics, the P.P.S. called for the abolition of the Senate, a proportional system of representation and extensive local government.[3] It demanded the separation of church and state and universal compulsory lay education.[3] In economic matters it called for the maintenance of the eight-hour day and forty-six-hour week, for a minimum wage and for social insurance.[4] The clause on nationalization in the party programme was conveniently vague. It demanded 'the nationalization of those branches of industry ripe for this, in particular mines of all types, foundries, and the means of communication'.[3] In agriculture the nationalization of forests and waterways was proposed. Large landholdings were to be expropriated, 'part remaining in government and communal estates, the remainder to be leased to groups of people with little or no land, and to workers' co-operatives'.[4] For the minorities, the party advocated the recognition of their language rights, and the granting of territorial self-government in areas in which they formed a majority.[5] The P.P.S. tried with some success to work with the socialist parties of the minorities.

[1] A. Leinwand, *Polska Partia Socjalistyczna wobec wojny polsko-radzieckiej, 1919–20* (Warsaw, 1964).

[2] Appeal of the Central Executive Committee of the P.P.S., 23 July 1924, reprinted in Bełcikowska, op. cit., p. 360.

[3] 'Program Polskiej Partii Socjalistycznej (Seventeeth Congress, 1919): "W zakresie wewnętrznych stosunków politycznych" ', reprinted in Bełcikowska, op. cit., p. 362.

[4] 'Program P.P.S., "W zakresie stosunków gospodarczych"', Bełcikowska, op. cit., p. 363.

[5] Ibid., p. 362.

As we have seen, Piłsudski-ite influences were strong in the party, although men like Perl who had reservations about the Marshal were also important. The party possessed a series of newspapers, of which the most influential were *Robotnik* in Warsaw and *Naprzód* in Cracow. It enjoyed considerable support in the Central Alliance of Trade Unions,[1] the largest of the trade union organizations in Poland. The Agricultural Workers' Trade Union formed by Jan Stapiński was also largely sympathetic to the socialists.

In the elections of November 1922 the P.P.S. won 10·3 per cent of the vote, obtaining 41 seats in the Sejm.[2] It won 12·6 per cent of the urban vote and 9·4 per cent of the rural vote,[3] which showed that its campaign among agricultural workers had had some success. In Warsaw itself it won 15·5 per cent[4] and it also did well in the industrial area around Cracow, where it gained 26·9 per cent.[5] In Galicia as a whole, the P.P.S. won 11·3 per cent of the votes, compared with 12·4 per cent in the central provinces of Poland.[6] It did surprisingly well in Polesia, with much support around Pińsk, and received 31·3 per cent of the vote here.[6] In Silesia it won 16·1 per cent, but in the rest of Prussian Poland it did extremely badly, with 1·6 per cent in Poznania and 1·0 per cent in Pomerania.[6]

ii. *The Communist Party of Poland*

The Communist Workers' Party of Poland,[7] renamed in March 1925 the Communist Party of Poland,[8] was formed by the union of the Social Democratic Party of the Kingdom of Poland and Lithuania[9] and the Polish Socialist Party—Left Wing[10] in December 1918. Its ranks were swelled by the adherence in late 1920 of a Polish Socialist Party—Opposition,[11] led by Stanisław Łańcucki and Jerzy Sochacki-Czeszeyko, and in 1921 by Left-Wing secessions

---

[1] Centralny Związek Stowarzyszeń Zawodowych.
[2] A. Próchnik, op. cit., pp. 133, 135.
[3] 'Statistique des élections à la Diète et au Sénat', *S.P.* viii (1926), ix.
[4] Ibid., based on Table XII, p. 15.
[5] Ibid., p. 57.
[6] Ibid., p. ix.
[7] Komunistyczna Partia Robotnicza Polski.
[8] Komunistyczna Partia Polski, known as the K.P.P.
[9] Socjal-Demokracja Królestwa Polskiego i Litwy, or the S.D.K.P. i L.
[10] Polska Partia Socjalistyczna—Lewica.
[11] Polska Partia Socjalistyczna—Opozycja.

from the various Jewish socialist parties, the Bund, the Zionist Workers' Party,[1] and the Fereinigte.[2]

The Social Democratic Party was formed as a result of the withdrawal from the Polish Socialist Party in March and July 1893 of those groups, led by Rosa Luxemburg and Julian Marchlewski, which believed that the Socialist Party's stress on the national question was harmful to socialism.[3] The new party at first took the provocative name of the Social Democracy of the Kingdom of Poland (i.e. the Congress Kingdom), by which it was intended to show that the party renounced independence and limited its activity to Russian Poland. This implication was not abandoned when it amalgamated in 1899 with the ideologically kindred Union of Workers in Lithuania, led by Feliks Dzierżyński.

The Social Democracy never gained widespread support; it remained a small and predominantly Jewish group of impressive but relentless intellectuals. Even one of its admirers describes it as 'more of a pressure group in international Socialism than a political party'.[4] Stress on social rather than national goals was an old tradition in Polish socialism. Ludwik Waryński, the doyen of Polish socialists, had said, 'There is a nation more unfortunate than the Polish nation: it is the nation of proletarians.'[5] With the growth of revolutionary sentiment in Russia and the increased economic dependence of Russian Poland on the Tsarist Empire, this policy had even more justification. But what was new was the almost irrational fury with which Rosa Luxemburg and her followers attacked the P.P.S. for its nationalist deviations. 'Not even the most fertile fantasy of a café politician', she declared on several occasions, 'could envisage the reconstitution of Poland . . .'[6] This extremism made almost impossible co-operation with the Left Wing of the socialists, which had finally emerged as a separate group in November 1906.

It also complicated relations with the Russian Social Democrats, for the Social Democracy refused to join the Russian party unless

[1] Poalej Sion.
[2] See M. Dziewanowski, *The Communist Party of Poland* (Cambridge, Mass., 1959), p. 98.
[3] See above, p. 68.
[4] P. Nettl, *Rosa Luxemburg* (London, 1966), i. 261.
[5] Quoted in Dziewanowski, op. cit., p. 15.
[6] See e.g. the article in the Cracow *Przegląd Socjaldemokratyczny* of 1902, quoted in W. Pobóg-Malinowski, *Najnowsza Historia Polityczna Polski* (London, 1963), i. 268–9.

the independence of Poland was specifically rejected. This, along with Rosa Luxemburg's hostility to what she regarded as the over-centralized ideas of party organization held by Lenin, and disputes over the peasant question, on which the Social Democracy was intransigently Left-Wing, delayed until 1906 its entry into the Russian party. However, internal ideological disputes continued, which together with the resentment by the groups in Poland of domination by emigrés, led to a split in the party late in 1911.[1]

The Polish Socialist Party—Left-Wing, led by Feliks Kon, Tadeusz Rechniewski, and Max Horwitz-Walecki, had emerged as the majority faction in the P.P.S. during 1905. An attempt was made at the eighth party conference in February 1906 to smooth over differences within the party, but this proved impossible. The two groups finally split at the ninth party conference in November 1906. Impressed by the strength which the Russian revolutionary movement had shown in 1905, the P.P.S.—Left Wing believed that Piłsudski's stress on terrorism could have no beneficial results, and held that a constituent assembly in Warsaw would satisfy Polish national demands. However, even this mild proposal was enough to make the Social Democracy refuse to work with them.

Both the P.P.S.—Left Wing and the two factions of the Social Democracy opposed the war in 1914, and a joint committee to co-ordinate action was established in Warsaw. It broke down, however, in March 1915, when the Social Democracy proved intransigently hostile to the self-government finally proposed for the Congress Kingdom by the Russians. Both parties took part in the Zimmerwald and Kienthal conferences, where the two groups of the Social Democracy approached very closely Lenin's views on the war as a revolutionary catalyst. Their links became closer in November 1916, when they passed a joint resolution that only the end of capitalism and the establishment of socialism could end wars.

Both parties hailed the Bolshevik revolution, though with some reservations. The Social Democracy still hoped to prevent the Russian party from supporting Polish self-determination, and on the breakdown of German authority in Poland, called on the workers to assume power. For the P.P.S.—Lewica, the Bolshevik

---

[1] For the S.D.K.P. i L. see: P. Nettl, op. cit.; M. Dziewanowski, op. cit.; J. Reguła, *Historia Komunistycznej Partii Polski* (Warsaw, 1934); *S.D.K.P i L. Materiały i dokumenty, 1893–1903* (Warsaw, 1962), 2 vols.

Revolution seemed fully to justify the Social Democratic position, and calls for a union of the two parties became stronger. Nevertheless when union was achieved in December 1918, the Left-Wing Socialists were faced with the secession of their organizations in Lodz and Poznań, and the breaking of their previously close ties with the Bund, the main Jewish socialist party.[1]

The programme of the new party, adopted at the union conference, was almost entirely Luxemburgist. After stressing that the aftermath of the war would create a revolutionary situation, it reaffirmed the position of the Zimmerwald Left, that a new International was necessary because of the treachery of the revisionists. In Poland, it called for the establishment of the dictatorship of the proletariat through the workers' council movement. It opposed a land reform which would give land to the peasants, calling instead for the establishment of large co-operatives, and appealing almost exclusively to agricultural workers. It again specifically rejected Polish independence.[2]

For the next two years, the party believed that a revolution was imminent. It attempted to gain control of the workers' councils, and in January 1919 refused to register as a political party; it was thus forced underground. During the Polish-Soviet war, it encouraged the Bolsheviks to invade ethnic Poland, and to establish for Poland a Provisional Revolutionary Committee. But the Treaty of Riga in March 1921, and the waning of revolutionary sentiment in Poland, made a reassessment of party policy necessary. In accordance with the tactics of the third congress of Comintern, which stressed the importance of co-operation with Social Democrats, a new line was formulated.[3] It was introduced at the third party conference in April 1922, when the new leadership of Adolf Warski, Max Horwitz-Walecki, and Maria Kostrzewa was established, and it was confirmed at the second party congress in Moscow in August 1923, where Warski explicitly

---

[1] For the war years see: J. Reguła, op. cit.; F. Tych, *P.P.S.—Lewica w wojnie 1914–18* (Warsaw, 1960); J. Kancewicz, 'S.D.K.P. i L. wobec zagadnień wojny, rewolucji i niepodległości Polski w latach 1914–18', *Ruch Robotniczy i Ludowy w Polsce*, pp. 103–88.

[2] 'Platforma polityczna', *Komunistyczna Partia Polski: uchwały i rezolucje* (Warsaw, 1954), i. 36–45.

[3] For these developments see: J. Reguła, op. cit.; M. Dziewanowski, op. cit. For the present-day Communist interpretation of the immediate post-war years see J. Kowalski, 'Z zagadnień rozwoju ideologicznego K.P.R.P. w latach 1918–23', *Ruch Robotniczy i Ludowy w Polsce*, pp. 261–318.

rejected the Luxemburgist 'errors' on self-determination. 'Our mistake', he had written to Dzierżyński in November 1921, 'was in repudiating Poland's independence, for which Lenin always rebuked us.'[1] The party now held that 'only the victory of revolution can give the Polish nation lasting independence in a state (*niepodległość państwowa*)'.[2] It called for a 'democratic' army, and urged the formation of a broad worker–peasant alliance to overthrow the existing Right-Wing government in Poland.[3] Its agrarian programme was modified as well: while some of the estates would be maintained as model co-operatives, most of the expropriated land would be handed over to the poor peasantry and agricultural workers; the slogan 'land for the peasants' was adopted.[4] The party now also demanded 'the national unification of the Ukrainian and the White Russian people',[5] presumably with the Soviet Ukrainian and Byelorussian Republics.

In the 1922 elections, the Communist Party put forward a list under the title of 'The Union of the Proletariat of Town and Country'. It won two seats, and 1·5 per cent of the votes.[6] One of the seats it won in Warsaw, where it received 6·7 per cent of the votes;[7] the other was in the constituency of Będzin in the Dąbrowa basin, where it received 20·8 per cent.[8] Elsewhere it was quite weak. In the town of Lodz it won 6·3 per cent of the votes,[9] while in the province of Silesia its percentage was only 0·1.[10]

The party was fairly influential in the Central Alliance of Trade Unions, and was particularly strong among railway workers, miners, and agricultural labourers. It had a significant underground press, of which the most important papers were *Czerwony Sztandar*, *Głos Komunistyczny*, *Kolejarz-Komunista* for railway workers, *Żołnierz-Robotnik* for soldiers, and the theoretical journal *Nowy Przegląd*, which appeared approximately once every two months.

[1] Quoted in Dziewanowski, op. cit., p. 103.
[2] *Komunistyczna Partia Polski, uchwały i rezolucje*, p. 198.
[3] Ibid., 'Manifest II Zjazdu Komunistycznej Partii Robotniczej Polski do całego ludu pracującego', p. 251.
[4] Ibid., 'Uchwała w sprawie sojuszu robotniczo-chłopskiego', p. 209; 'Sytuacja polityczna i taktyka partii', p. 204.
[5] Ibid., 'Za naszą i waszą wolność', p. 228.
[6] A. Próchnik, op. cit., pp. 133, 135.
[7] 'Statistique des élections, *S.P.* viii (1926), based on Table XII, p. 15.
[8] Ibid., based on Table XII, p. 33.
[9] Ibid., p. 26.   [10] Ibid., p. ix.

iii. *The National Workers' Party*

The National Workers' Party[1] was formed in May 1920 by the union of the already closely linked National Workers' Union in the Congress Kingdom and the National Workers' Party of Prussian Poland. The National Workers' Union had been set up in June 1905 by the National Democrats, in order to counteract socialist influences among the workers.[2] In September 1908, it broke with the National Democrats, accusing them of an excessive propensity to compromise and of neglecting the goal of national independence. The Union joined the Provisional Committee of Confederated Parties Demanding Independence, supported the legionary movement, and advocated an Activist solution of the Polish problem until the Treaty of Brest showed that Germany was interested in nothing more than a puppet Polish state.

In independent Poland, the N.P.R. occupied a position which combined nationalism and social radicalism. Its programme, adopted at the second party congress in Cracow in September 1921, underlined the party's opposition to the dictatorship of the proletariat, and its support for parliamentary democracy.[3] The programme stated that the National Workers' Party 'takes as its most important goal the social and political liberation of the working class',[4] but at the same time it emphasized the party's awareness of a common national interest, in which the working class participated: 'Recognizing that the class struggle is an undoubted fact and an instrument of social development, the party pursues this struggle within the limits of general state interests, and does not push it to extremes.'[5]

In the economic sphere, the party called for a planned economy, with the right to work and a minimum wage, and demanded the gradual extension of nationalization. Some private enterprise would, however, always remain.[6] In addition, it supported the

[1] Narodowa Partia Robotnicza (N.P.R.).

[2] For its history see: A. Micewski, op. cit., chap. iii; T. Monasterska 'Narodowy Związek Robotniczy w latach 1905–14', *Z.P.W.* vii (1964), no. 1, 3–31.

[3] 'Program Narodowej Partii Robotniczej uchwalony na II Kongresie N.P.R. w Krakowie w dn. 4, 5 i 6 września 1921 roku'; reprinted in Bełcikowska, op. cit., Section I, Article 3, pp. 310–11.

[4] Ibid., Article 1; Bełcikowska, p. 309.

[5] Ibid., Article 4; Bełcikowska, p. 311.

[6] Ibid., Articles 5, 6, and 7; pp. 312–13.

1920 land reform.[1] Claiming that it based its activity on Christian ethics, the N.P.R. demanded a predominant position for the Catholic Church, although other religions would enjoy ostensibly equal rights.[2]

In relation to the national minorities, it stressed that Poland was a national state, but advocated for the minorities rights of national cultural autonomy.[3] On the other hand, the N.P.R. held 'that the predominance of Jews in certain branches of trade and production is harmful, and supports the Polish and Christian element in these'.[4]

In the election of 1922, the party won 5·4 per cent of the votes, and eighteen seats.[5] It did particularly well in Lodz, where national antagonisms were strong, winning 19·0 per cent of the votes,[6] in Poznania with 28·2 per cent and in Pomerania with 24·2 per cent.[7] The N.P.R. was led by Karol Popiel, and had its own trade union organization, the Polish Trade Union,[8] especially strong in Prussian Poland. Of its newspapers, the most important were *Głos Robotnika* in Poznań and *Praca* in Lodz

PEASANT PARTIES

One of the features of Polish political life, as indeed of the politics of most of Eastern Europe, was the existence of peasant parties, supporting the peasants' interests and claiming for them, as the majority of the population, a commanding position in the state. These parties all shared a commitment to parliamentary democracy, but particularly emphasized the peasants' dominant role in the nation. Wincenty Witos, the self-educated peasant leader from Galicia, who emphasized his peasant origins by wearing peasant dress and speaking with peasant expressions, articulated this feeling:

Poland fell as a state of the nobility . . . Poland rises again as a state of the peasantry (*państwo ludowe*), and as such can and must survive . . .

[1] Ibid., Section II, Article 3; p. 318.
[2] Ibid., Section I, Article 9; p. 315.
[3] Ibid., Section II, Article 2; p. 318.
[4] Ibid., p. 319.
[5] A. Próchnik, op. cit., pp. 133, 135.
[6] 'Statistique des élections', *S.P.*, viii, based on Table XII, p. 26.
[7] Ibid., p. ix.
[8] Zjednoczenie Zawodowe Polskie.

The peasant masses (*rzesze ludowe*) must assume responsibility for the future of the state, and if they are to bear this heavy burden, they must acquire political influence, the possibility of ruling the state.[1]

Many attempts were made to unite the different peasant parties, and in the first Sejm their representatives formed the Parliamentary Union of Peasant Deputies.[2] But the different levels of economic development and the different political traditions of the three partitions hindered co-operation. So did political inexperience, for the peasant parties were all of relatively recent origin, and the leaders of the smaller groups feared that they would be swamped by the more powerful Piast Peasant Party. Political disputes over whether the peasants should ally with the Right or Left, and over the proper role of the Church, further intensified division.

i. *The Piast*

Five peasant parties put forward lists of candidates in the 1922 elections. The largest of these groups was the Piast,[3] led by Wincenty Witos. It had emerged in Galicia in 1913 from a split in the Polish Peasant Club in the Austrian Reichsrat, and had supported Activist policies during the early stages of the war. It broke with the Central Powers in 1917, however, rather earlier than many other parties, and pursued quite a moderate social line, preferring in many ways to work with the National Democrats rather than the socialists. Its influence was extended at the end of 1918 by the accession of a splinter group from the Peasant Union[4] in the Congress Kingdom, and in November 1920 by the absorption of the Union of Peasants,[5] newly formed in Poznania, where before the war an independent peasant movement had not existed. In October 1919 the Piast had united with the Liberation Peasant Party,[6] the strongest peasant group in the Congress Kingdom. The more radical members of the Liberation Party left the Piast in December 1919, but of its fifty-seven members of parliament, thirty-four remained with Witos.[7]

---

[1] Quoted in Bełcikowska, op. cit., pp. 167–8. For the peasant movement generally see: W. Witos, *Moje wspomnienia* (Paris, 1964), 3 vols; M. Rataj, *Pamiętniki, 1918–27* (Warsaw, 1965); S. Thugutt, *Wybór pism i autobiografia* (Glasgow, 1943). [2] Sejmowy Związek Posłów Ludowych.
[3] Polskie Stronnictwo Ludowe 'Piast'.
[4] Zjednoczenie Ludowe.   [5] Zjednoczenie Włościan.
[6] Polskie Stronnictwo Ludowe — Wyzwolenie.
[7] For these developments see S. Lato. op. cit.

Witos strongly impressed his stamp on the Piast. His attitude towards the other political groups in Poland is clearly outlined in his autobiography:

National Democracy

Contrary to widespread belief, I did not feel a great devotion to, or weakness for, this party . . . I disliked in the National Democrats not only their reactionary social standpoint, but their loudness, and their claim to a monopoly of patriotism . . . I could not deny their virtues, however: a clear and distinct standpoint in national matters, the ability to make compromises, and loyalty in maintaining them.

Socialists

I held the majority of socialists to be unstable and noisy agitators, irresponsible people who knew no limits in building up appetites, and although they knew that these could not be satisfied, did not know how to tell their people this at the appropriate time . . .

Liberation Peasant Party

'Liberation', in my opinion, comprised the rural branch of the socialists, sometimes competing with them in demagogy. Dominated by semi-intellectuals and socialist school-teachers, directed, moreover, by an unseen hand [Piłsudski], it pursued a policy remote from the interests and desires of the peasantry, while appearing to have great concern for them.[1]

The Piast party programme, adopted at the all-Polish congress of November 1921, called for the full implementation of the land reform of July 1920.[2] It maintained that Poland was a predominantly agricultural state, and that the government should foster particularly the development of industries which were linked with agriculture.[3] The programme affirmed that the Polish people were 'deeply religious', and claimed that 'the party stands on the position of observing Christian principles in private and social life, and in the state'.[4] The national minorities were to be granted equality, but the Polish character of the Kresy was to be strengthened.[5]

[1] W. Witos, op. cit. i. 46. It is true that Witos wrote this in the bitterness of exile in Czechoslovakia in 1938, but his position in the 1920s was not markedly different.

[2] 'Program Polskiego Stronnictwa Ludowego "Piast" ', Belcikowska, op. cit., Part II, Article 17, p. 187.   [3] Ibid., Part II, Article 26, p. 189.

[4] Ibid., Part I, Article 4, p. 179.   [5] Ibid., Part II, Articles 4 and 6, p. 184.

In the elections of 1922, the Piast won seventy seats, and 13·2 per cent of the votes.[1] It did particularly well in Galicia, where it won 32·6 per cent of the votes, as against 10·1 per cent in the central provinces and 5·1 per cent in the west.[2]

ii. *The Liberation*

The Liberation Peasant Party, second largest of the peasant groups, was the result of a merger in December 1915 of the three main peasant parties in the Congress Kingdom: the National Peasant Union,[3] which had broken with the National Democrats because it considered them too yielding on the question of national independence, the Peasant Union,[4] close to the socialists, and the peasant politicians grouped around the journal *Zaranie*. It differed from the Piast in that its leaders, Stanisław Thugutt, Tadeusz Nocznicki, and Kazimierz Bagiński, were members of the radical urban intelligentsia and not of peasant origin. The party had belonged to the Activist General Committee of United Parties Demanding Independence, but broke with the Central Powers at the same time as the socialists, and was important in the formation of the Lublin Government. In October 1919, as we have seen, it joined the Piast. However, the opposition of the more radical ex-Liberation Deputies towards the Piast's approaches to Dubanowicz of the Christian National Party, in order to achieve a compromise on land reform, led to the secession of twenty-four members in December 1919, and to the reconstitution of the Liberation Party.[5]

The Liberation Party was much more sympathetic to the socialists than was the Piast. 'We demand', stated the party weekly on 6 March 1921, 'a worker–peasant government which, above all, will have the courage to base itself on the broadest masses of the people . . .'[6] The party also called for the implementation of the 1920 land reform, and for the nationalization of basic industries. 'Neither the state nor political parties', its programme declared,

[1] A. Próchnik, op. cit., pp. 133, 135.
[2] 'Statistique des élections', *S.P.* viii, p. ix.
[3] Narodowy Związek Chłopski.
[4] Związek Chłopski.
[5] See above, p. 138. For a description of the peasant movement, in Russian Poland during World War I see: H. Jabłoński, op. cit., chaps. i and ii; J. Molenda 'Masy chłopskie i ruch ludowy w czasie wojny 1914–1918', *Ruch robotniczy i ludowy w Polsce, 1914–1923*, pp. 355–408.
[6] *Wyzwolenie*, 6 March 1921.

'should interfere in religious affairs, for these are matters for the individual conscience of every citizen.'[1] The national minorities were to be assured full civil rights, and to be granted territorial autonomy in areas in which they constituted a majority.[1]

In the election of 1922, the Liberation Party won forty-nine seats and 11 per cent of the vote.[2] It won 16·0 per cent in the central provinces and 19·3 per cent in the east. Its support in the south, with 2·9 per cent, and in the west, with 0·1 per cent, was minimal.[3]

The other peasant parties were smaller and less significant than the Piast and the Liberation. They included the Right-Wing Catholic Peasant Party, with five seats in the Sejm, and two smaller radical groupings, the Radical Peasant Party with four seats, and the Peasant Party—Left Wing with two.

CHRISTIAN DEMOCRACY

Although Poland was an overwhelmingly Catholic country, Western European-style Christian Democracy was not a major political force. The Christian Democratic Party, until 1925 called the Christian National Party of Labour,[4] was formed in September 1919 by the union of Christian Democratic groups in Galicia and the Congress Kingdom. It was later joined by the National Workers' Party[5] of Poznania, and the strong Christian Democratic group in Upper Silesia led by Wojciech Korfanty. Although Christian Democratic trade unions had been important in all the partitions, and particularly in Prussia, before 1914, the Catholic social movement in politics was of recent origin in Poland. In the 1920s it was still only gradually emancipating itself from its dependence on the National Democrats, with whom it had formed a joint list in the elections of 1919 and 1922. Its growth was further hampered because it did not enjoy the full support of the Church hierarchy, many of whose members were National Democrats. Edmund Dalbor, the first primate of independent Poland, was an enthusiastic supporter of the Endecja.[6]

---

[1] Lato, op. cit., p. 67.
[2] A. Próchnik, op. cit., pp. 133, 135.
[3] 'Statistique des élections', *S.P.* viii, p. ix.
[4] Chrześcijańsko-Narodowe Stronnictwo Pracy.
[5] Narodowe Stronnictwo Robotnicze.
[6] For Christian Democracy in Poland, see: A. Micewski, op. cit., chap. iii;

Led by Ludomil Czerniewski and Józef Chaciński, the party adopted a characteristic Christian Democratic programme. 'The aim of the Christian National Party of Labour', stated the regulations of the parliamentary club, 'is the organization of the Polish state on Christian principles, and the defence of the labouring class from moral, economic and socio-political standpoints.'[1] The party programme called for a democratic state in which the principles of religion would be honoured,[2] and proposed extensive social insurance. It saw the solution of the worker question in the part-ownership of the means of production by the industrial working class,[3] and it called for the implementation of the 1920 land reform.[4]

The party had its own trade union organization, the Christian Trade Union Alliance of Poland[5] in Warsaw, the Polish Christian Trade Union Alliance[6] in Cracow, and allied groups in Pomerania and Upper Silesia. It fought the 1922 elections on a common list with the National Democrats; its total of forty-three seats is therefore not a satisfactory reflection of its own support. In the 1928 elections, the first it contested alone, it won eighteen seats. It was strong in Warsaw, particularly among the artisans, and in Upper Silesia, where Korfanty's popularity as the leader of the Upper Silesian revolts ensured it mass support.

PARTIES OF THE MINORITIES

i. *The Ukrainians*

The political life of the national minorities was almost as fragmented as that of the Poles. Among the Ukrainians, the political differences between those who had lived under Russian rule and those who had lived under Austrian rule were still great. Almost all the Ukrainian parties in former Russian territory (Volynia, Polesia, Podlasia, and the Chełm region), where Ukrainian

---

W. Bitner, 'O prawdziwe oblicze "Partii Katolickiej" w dwudziestoleciu', *Więź*, no. 6, lxii (1963), 110–12.

[1] Regulamin Kół Chrześcijańsko-Narodowego Stronnictwa Pracy, reprinted in Bełcikowska, op. cit., p. 133.

[2] 'Program Chrześcijańsko-Narodowego Stronnictwa Pracy, "Sprawa religijna"', reprinted in Bełcikowska, op. cit., p. 124.

[3] Ibid., 'Sprawa społeczna i robotnicza', Bełcikowska, op. cit., p. 127.

[4] Ibid., p. 129.

[5] Chrześcijańskie Zjednoczenie Zawodowe Rzeczypospolitej Polskiej.

[6] Polskie Zjednoczenie Chrześcijańskich Związków Zawodowych.

nationalism was a fairly recent phenomenon, joined the Bloc of National Minorities,[1] a loose grouping formed for the election of November 1922 to overcome the prejudice of the voting system against the smaller parties. The twenty members from these regions elected on the bloc's list formed the Ukrainian Club in the Sejm, and issued a joint declaration, rather moderate in tone, shortly after the opening of the new parliament:

The aim of the Ukrainian people is the rebirth of an independent Ukrainian state. Recognizing the true situation, however, we express our willingness to co-operate with the Polish nation, and with all the nations in the Polish Republic, on the following conditions: the Polish Republic, not nationally uniform, must be re-formed to allow every nation within it . . . the right of self-determination.[2]

Apart from a group of independent members, the Ukrainian Club was made up of the representatives of three parties. The largest of these, with seven seats, was the Peasant Alliance.[3] It proposed independence for the Ukraine, but stressed much more strongly the agrarian demands of its overwhelmingly peasant supporters. It claimed to be 'the political class union of the Ukrainian peasantry',[4] and called for 'the end of the exploitation of poorer peasants'.[4]

The Ukrainian Social Democratic Party[5] had support both in East Galicia, where it boycotted the 1922 election, and in Volynia and Polesia, where five of its members were elected. Originally closely linked with the Polish Socialist Party, it had broken away before 1914, and after the war it became increasingly sympathetic towards Communism. Eventually, in February 1924, it left the Ukrainian Club, and with the two Communist deputies formed the Communist parliamentary group.[6]

The third party represented in the Ukrainian Club was that of

---

[1] Blok Mniejszości Narodowych (also called Bloc No. 16). For the Ukrainians generally see: M. Hrushevsky, *A History of Ukraine* (New Haven, 1941); J. Reshetar, *The Ukrainian Revolution* (Princeton, 1952); M. Feliński, *Ukraińcy w Polsce* (Warsaw, 1931); and B. Paneyko, 'Galicia and the Polish-Ukrainian Problem', *Slavonic Review*, ix (1931), 567–87.

[2] Speech of Deputy Podhorski, *S.S.S.R.* 23 January 1923, col. 66.

[3] Selansky Soyuz.

[4] 'Program Ukraińskiego Socjalistycznego Zjednoczenia "Selansky Sojuz"', 'Zasady programowe', reprinted in Bełcikowska, op. cit., p. 544.

[5] Ukrainska Sotsial-Demokratychna Partia.

[6] M. Feliński, op. cit., p. 59.

the autonomist-federalists, which had one deputy. This was a pro-Polish group, which called for federal status for the Ukrainian areas within Poland.[1] A similar group, without parliamentary representation, was the Ukrainian National Party,[2] the rump supporters of Semion Petlura, whose alliance with Piłsudski had culminated in the Kiev campaign. They called for the re-establishment of an independent Ukraine, allied with Poland.[3] Neither of these parties had much support.

In East Galicia the Ukrainian national movement was older and better established. Almost all the Ukrainian parties here boycotted the elections of November 1922, believing that participation would confirm the Polish claim to the region, at that time still unsettled in international law. The only Ukrainian party which contested the election in East Galicia was the pro-Polish Ukrainian Peasant Party;[4] it won 87,000 votes and five seats.[5] Its position on the national question was clearly described by its leader, Father Ilkov:

> The Ukrainian people does not have enough strength or enough educated men to form its own state. We have only one alternative: to depend on Poland, thanks to whom we can preserve our national spirit, and in the course of time, united with Poland . . . to unite the whole Ukrainian nation.[6]

Socially, it demanded the full implementation of the 1920 land reform.[7]

The largest Ukrainian party in East Galicia was the Ukrainian National Party of Labour.[8] Before World War I it had been the basis of the Ukrainian national movement, founding co-operatives, and issuing the only Ukrainian daily paper, *Dilo*, in Lwów. It had played an important part in the West Ukrainian Government established after the collapse of Austria; this was crushed by Polish military action, and the party came increasingly into conflict with the Ukrainian Government-in-exile, led by Evgeny Petrushevich.

[1] A. Bełcikowska, op. cit., pp. 452–60.
[2] Ukrainska Narodna Partia.
[3] Bełcikowska, op. cit., pp. 915–22.
[4] Known as the 'Khliborobi'; see Bełcikowska, op. cit., pp. 551–6.
[5] Próchnik, op. cit., pp. 133, 135.
[6] Quoted in Bełcikowska, op. cit., p. 556.
[7] 'Program Ukraińskiego Włościańskiego Stronnictwa', Bełcikowska, op. cit., p. 552.
[8] Ukrainska Narodna Trudowa Partia.

The party still called for an independent West Ukraine as the precursor of an independent Ukraine, but it objected to Petrushevich's political intransigence, and was restive over the electoral boycott of 1922. This conflict led to the victory of the moderates in the party, led by Volodimir Bachinsky, and a declaration was issued in May 1923 stating that an initial step, only autonomy should be demanded for the West Ukraine. The radicals, however, led by Vyacheslav Budzhinkovsky, refused to accept this, and fought to regain control of the party.[1]

The Ukrainian Radical Party[2] was socially more progressive, but also much weaker. It had participated in the 1918 Government, and demanded national independence. In its programme it called itself the 'party of the working masses of Ukrainian nationality',[3] and proposed a far-reaching land reform. Because of its strong anti-clericalism, it provoked the hostility of the Greek Catholic Church.

Though much weaker than it had been, the Russophile orientation, which held that the Ukrainians were really Russian, still had some influence in East Galicia. The movement split in 1921 between the conservative Russian National Organization[4] and the more radical National Will,[5] which based its programme on that of the Russian social revolutionaries.

From 1921, the Ukrainian Military Organization,[6] an underground terrorist group, led from Vienna by Evgeny Konovalets, had been active.[7] In September 1921, it organized an attempt on Piłsudski's life, and in the summer of 1922, embarked on a campaign of burning Polish farms. During the election of 1922, it had enforced the electoral boycott through terror, attacking, even murdering, pro-Polish Ukrainians.

ii. *The White Russians*

National consciousness was both more recent and less developed among the White Russians. They responded favourably, in many cases, to Russianization before 1914, and to the Polonization which

[1] For these developments see Bełcikowska, op. cit., pp. 901–5.
[2] Ukrainska Radykalna Partia.
[3] 'Program Ukraińskiej Radykalnej Partii', Bełcikowska, op. cit., p. 910.
[4] Russko-Narodna Organizatsya.
[5] Narodna Volia.
[6] Ukrainska Voyskova Organizatsya (U.V.O.).
[7] See Pobóg-Malinowski, op. cit., pp. 437–9.

followed the war. The area they inhabited was very poor, and Polish radical parties had considerable strength there. Of the 35 seats in the constituencies which were largely White Russian, the Liberation Peasant Party won 15, the Socialists 5, and the White Russian parties 6.[1] All the large White Russian parties contested the 1922 elections on the list of the Bloc of Minorities, winning 11 seats (9 in the constituencies and 2 on the general list). Their deputies formed the White Russian Club in the Sejm, which in January 1923 called for 'territorial autonomy with a local sejm'[2] for the White Russian areas, and they all sent representatives to the White Russian National Committee[3] in Wilno.

The largest of the White Russian parties, with seven members in the Parliamentary Club, was the White Russian Social Democracy.[4] Founded in 1903, it had functioned before the war as the White Russian Socialist Hromada, with a generally socialist programme; however, it demanded the granting of land to small peasants, and the preservation of individual farming. After 1918, it stressed its allegiance to parliamentary democracy, declaring that socialism could only be achieved as a long-term aim, following industrialization and much preparation. This reformism and emphasis on peasant demands caused great discontent in the Left Wing of the party, and culminated in the secession in January 1924 of four members of the Parliamentary Club, led by Bazyli Rogula. They formed the White Russian Independent Socialist Party, which allied itself with the Communists.[5]

The White Russian Socialist Revolutionary Party,[6] with two deputies in parliament, was also socially radical, and had left the Hromada in 1917. It moved increasingly towards Communism, and in July 1924 expressed its willingness to work with the Communists.

The White Russian Christian Democratic Union,[7] led by Father Stankievich, had one seat in the Sejm. Supported largely by

[1] 'Statistique des élections', *S.P.* viii, Table XIV, p. 118.
[2] Speech of Deputy Tarashkievich, *S.S.S.R.*, 23 January 1923, col. 39. For White Russia generally see: N. Vakar, *Belorussia, The Making of a Nation* (Cambridge, Mass., 1956); V. Poluian, J. Poluian, *Revoliutsonnoe i natsionalno-osvoboditelnoe dvizhenie z Zapadnoi Bielarusi v 1920–1939* (Minsk, 1960).
[3] Natsyonaly Bielarusky Komitet.
[4] Bielaruska Sotsyalno-Demokratychna Partia.
[5] Bełcikowska, op. cit., pp. 620–6.
[6] Partia Bielaruskich Socjalistuv Revolutsyonistuv.
[7] Khrestijansko-Demokratychny Sauz Bielarusinuv.

Catholic White Russians, in particular the priesthood, it was strong in the area around Wilno. Though it had no links with the Polish Christian Democrats, it was based on the same Christian principles, and while it made clear its support for self-determination for White Russia, its programme was primarily concerned with religious questions. It demanded that the state be organized on Catholic principles, and that the freedom of the Church be ensured. The party saw the solution of the industrial question in the extension of ownership and in profit-sharing.[1] Its influence among the large majority of White Russians, who were Orthodox, was minimal.

From the autumn of 1920 Vyacheslav Lastovsky, one of the leading White Russian nationalists, had been living in Kaunas in Lithuania. The White Russian emigration here was greatly strengthened by the deportation by the Polish authorities in the following year of twenty White Russian activists.[2] Lastovsky formed a government-in-exile, and established links with the Ukrainian Petrushevich, now in Prague. The 'government' demanded the annulment of the Treaty of Riga and the establishment of a White Russian state within its ethnographic boundaries. It rejected any co-operation with Poland, and from 1921 organized terrorist attacks on Polish outposts, to which the Lithuanian authorities turned a blind eye.[3]

From 1921, terrorist tactics had also been adopted by the pro-Soviet White Russian Revolutionary Organization, which demanded the union of the whole of White Russia in the White Russian Soviet Republic.[4]

By 1924, the Polish authorities were considerably worried by the domination of White Russian politics by pro-Communist and anti-Polish parties. For this reason they fostered the establishment in May 1924 of the pro-Polish White Russian Democratic Council,[5] led by Dr. A. Pavlukievich. The Council, later renamed the White Russian National Council,[6] did not acquire any significant support.

---

[1] 'Program Chrestijańsko-Demokratyczny Związek Białorusinów', reprinted in Bełcikowska, op. cit., pp. 610–18.

[2] Pobóg-Malinowski, op. cit. ii. 442–3.

[3] Ibid., p. 443.

[4] Bielaruska Organizatsya Revolutsyna. See Ajnenkiel, op. cit., pp. 259–60.

[5] Bielaruska Demokratychna Rada.

[6] Bielaruska Natsionalnaya Rada.

iii. *The Germans*

Among the national minorities, the Germans possessed the greatest political unity, although differences remained between those who had lived in the German Reich and those of the other partitions. Almost all the German parties stressed the importance of the defence of their minority rights over ideological differences. German politicians, particularly Senator Erwin Hassbach, played a conspicuous part in the formation of the Bloc of National Minorities, and all seventeen German members of the Sejm were elected on this list. They formed the Parliamentary Club of German Union, which emphasized the loyalty of the German minority to the new state. Joseph Spickermann, the chairman of the Club, declared in the Sejm on 23 January 1923:

> Our Polish state will not need to be ashamed of the citizens of German nationality for whom it cares . . . We are the best guarantee for lasting and friendly relations with the neighbouring German state . . . [From our behaviour] our opponents will be convinced that one should not regard the German minority in Poland as an undesirable element, but should value it as an important and necessary factor in the state organism.[1]

This, and many similar statements, were made partly, and possibly wholly, in good faith. But the German minority, to some extent against the will of several of its leaders, was forced into a false position by the almost universal support in Germany for the revision of the 1918 frontiers, and by the active efforts of the various German governments to achieve this.

The largest party in the German Club was the German Alliance for the Defence of the Rights of National Minorities in Poland,[2] formed by the amalgamation of all the German political parties in Poznania and Pomerania, from the conservative German National People's Party[3] to the Social Democrats.[4] It had five seats in the Sejm, and called for the union of all Germans in order to establish their minority rights as granted by the constitution

---

[1] *S.S.S.R.*, 23 January 1923, col. 12. For the Germans generally see: S. Paprocki, *Minority Affairs and Poland* (Warsaw, 1935); O. Heike, *Das Deutschtum in Polen, 1918–39* (Bonn, 1955); M. Cygański, *Mniejszość niemiecka w Polsce centralnej w latach 1918–39* (Lodz, 1961); S. Stoliński, *Les Allemands en Pologne* (Warsaw, 1927).

[2] Deutschtumsbund zur Wahrung der Minderheitsrechte in Polen.

[3] Deutschnationale Volkspartei.

[4] Sozialdemokratische Partei.

and the Versailles treaty. It stressed, however, that 'The German Alliance has no anti-Polish tendencies, and endeavours to create peaceful co-existence between Polish and German citizens of the state, upon whom the necessity of fate has imposed co-existence.'[1]

In Upper Silesia, a non-party organization similar to the German Alliance, the German Peoples Alliance for Polish Upper Silesia,[2] was created in 1921. It proved less successful than its counterpart in Poznania and Pomerania in achieving political unity, winning over the nationalist[3] and Catholic[4] parties but not the socialists. It had five representatives in parliament.

In the Congress Kingdom, no over-all political body was created, though the two largest groupings here, the German Labour Party,[5] which represented industrial workers, and the German peasant organizations, both stood on list 16.

The Labour Party, whose strength was in the textile town of Lodz, with two seats in parliament, emphasized the importance of minority rights. Its programme, however, was a fairly orthodox social democratic one, and the party attempted to co-operate with the other principal socialist groups in Lodz, the P.P.S. and the Jewish Bund.[6]

The German peasantry in the Congress Kingdom had elected two members of parliament in 1922, who formed the German People's Party in 1924.[7] It called for the observance of the rights of the German minority, but also stressed the importance of government aid for agriculture.[8]

The only German group which did not stand on list 16 was the German Social Democratic Party in Upper Silesia. Formed by the union in 1921 of the majority Social Democrats and the Independent Socialists, it belonged to the Second International, and based its programme on the 1888 programme of the Austrian Social Democracy. In 1922, it called on its supporters to vote for the P.P.S. The Social Democratic Party in Poznania and

---

[1] 'Deklaracja Niemieckiego Związku dla obrony praw mniejszości narodowych w Polsce', reprinted in Bełcikowska, op. cit., p. 572.
[2] Deutsche Volksbund für polnisch Schlesien.
[3] Deutsche Partei.
[4] Katolische Volkspartei.
[5] Deutsche Arbeitspartei in Polen.
[6] M. Cygański, op. cit., chap. i, pp. 17–48.
[7] Deutscher Volksbund.
[8] 'Program Niemieckiego Związku Ludowego w Polsce', reprinted in Bełcikowska, op. cit., pp. 580–4.

Pomerania, which had won one seat as part of the German Alliance, united with the Upper Silesian party in April 1924.[1]

iv. *The Jews*

Jewish politics were highly complex, a result both of the seriousness of the problems facing the Jews, and of the rapid changes in the structure of the community brought about by industrialization and urbanization.[2] Jewish parliamentary activity was dominated by the Zionists, but the main division between those of the Congress Kingdom and Kresy, organized in the Jewish National Council and led by Isaac Grünbaum, and those of Galicia, led by Dr. Leon Reich, was not connected with Zionism itself. It rather reflected the different position of Jews in former Russian Poland from that of Jews in Galicia, and the resulting differences in political attitudes between them. Grünbaum demanded for the Jews full cultural autonomy, with the right to run their own independent network of Jewish schools, established and financed by the state, and called for the transformation of Poland from a national state to a state of nationalities. He was the principal force in the creation of the Bloc of National Minorities before the election of 1922, and he induced a fair number of non-Zionist Jewish parties, mostly in the Congress Kingdom and the Kresy, to stand on this platform, in particular the orthodox Agudas Israel and the non-political Union of Merchants. Altogether seventeen deputies were elected from the Jewish parties on this list.[3]

The Galician Zionists demanded only the securing of full civil rights for Jews in Poland. They believed in a direct approach to the Polish government, and opposed the creation of the Bloc of National Minorities, both because it would excessively antagonize the Poles, and because the Jews had no real common interests with the other national minorities. The Ukrainians and White Russians wanted national independence or territorial autonomy,

---

[1] Bełcikowska, op. cit., pp. 592–6.

[2] For Jewish politics generally see: S. Segal, *The New Poland and the Jews* (New York, 1938); A. Hafftka, 'Żydowskie stronnictwa polityczne w Polsce odrodzonej', *Z.W.P.O.*, ii. 249–85, and 'Życie parlamentarne Żydów w Polsce odrodzonej', *Z.W.P.O.*, ii. 286–311; M. Eisenstein, *Jewish Schools in Poland* (New York, 1950); L. Halpern, *Polityka żydowska w Sejmie i Senacie Rzeczpospolitej Polskiej, 1919–1933* (Warsaw, 1933).

[3] A. Hafftka, 'Życie parlamentarne Żydów w Polsce odrodzonej', *Z.W.P.O.* ii. 293. For Grünbaum's views, see also I. Grünbaum, *Milchamot ha Yehudim be Polaniya* (Jerusalem, 1946).

while the Germans wanted a revision of the Versailles Treaty. Jews, on the other hand, could accept the existing boundaries of Poland, and their need was for the implementation of the rights granted them by the constitution. The Galician Zionists had seventeen deputies elected in 1922, but this exaggerates their influence, since they won fifteen seats in East Galicia, where the Ukrainians had boycotted the election.[1]

The two Zionist groups agreed, however, on the need for a Jewish state in Palestine, established on a secular basis. They had a large daily and weekly press, including *Nasz Przegląd* (Warsaw) and *Chwila* (Lwów) in Polish, *Lodzer Tageblat* (Lodz) and *Najer Hajnt* (Warsaw) in Yiddish. A network of secondary schools, the Tarbut, had also been established.

Two smaller Zionist groups which stood on the list of the Bloc of National Minorities were the Mizrachi, the party of the religious Zionists which won five seats, and the Zionist Labour Party, Hitachduth, which won three.

The strongest Jewish political group was the Orthodox Agudas Israel. Founded in 1916, during the German occupation and under the influence of German Orthodoxy, its attitude to the Polish state was friendly. It held to the Talmudic principle, 'Dinoh de Malchisoh Dinoh' (the law of the state is law), and believed that a direct approach to the rulers was more likely to alleviate the position of the Jews than political agitation. Its principal strength was in the Congress Kingdom, where the support of the famous rabbi of Góra Kalwaria brought it the allegiance of his many followers. Though not much concerned with parliamentary politics, its political branch, Peace to the Faithful of Israel,[2] had six deputies elected in 1922. Schooling was one of its particular interests, and it possessed the largest network of Jewish private schools in Poland. The Agudas was very hostile to Jewish radicalism, and fought the Jewish socialist parties, in particular the Bund, placing an interdict on the Bund daily, *Naye Folkszeitung*, and founding an Orthodox workers' organization. It favoured Jewish settlement in Palestine, but opposed the revival of Hebrew as a language of daily use.

The Jewish People's Party[3] advocated a programme of national cultural autonomy. Though not opposed to settlement in Palestine,

---

[1] A. Próchnik, op. cit., pp. 133, 135.
[2] Shloyme Emune Israel.   [3] Yidishe Volkspartei.

it held that the Jewish problem in the diaspora would be solved by the granting of autonomy to Jewish communities: they should have the right to tax themselves, establish their own welfare organizations, and run a network of Jewish schools financed by the government. The party was not hostile to the Hebrew revival, but argued that Yiddish was the national language of the Polish Jews. It was strong among the Jewish petite-bourgeoisie and artisanate in Warsaw, Lodz, Lublin, and Wilno, although its support had declined somewhat from a peak reached in the two years following the war. It opposed the Bloc of Minorities, and had one member elected to the Sejm in 1922.[1]

The General Jewish Workers' Alliance, nicknamed the Bund,[2] with which the Jewish Social Democratic Party in Galicia had merged in April 1920, was the largest of the Jewish socialist parties. Founded in Russian Poland in 1897, it had joined the Russian Social Democratic Party in 1898, splitting off from it in 1902, but rejoining it in 1906, and had co-operated with it rather uneasily until the war. Its social programme was very radical. In May 1920, the first congress of the party in independent Poland decided to accede to the Third International, but the party refused to accept the twenty-one points laid down by Comintern for all Communist parties. This led to the secession in August 1921 of the Communist elements in the party (the so-called Kom-Bund). Since the Bund still refused to join the Hamburg International, which it accused of revisionism, it remained for the time being independent of any international affiliation. It strongly criticized the Communists for their destructive tactics within the movement.

The Bund had been on bad terms with the P.P.S. before 1914. The Polish Socialists criticized it as the creation of Russianized Jews and as an instrument for the Russianization of the Jewish working class. The parties differed on the national question, the Bund rejecting Polish independence and calling instead for

---

[1] See A. Hafftka, 'Żydowskie stronnictwa polityczne w Polsce odrodzonej', Z.W.P.O. ii. 268–9.

[2] Algemeine Yidisher Arbeiterbund. For the Bund see: H. Shukman, 'The Relations between the Jewish Bund and the R.S.D.R.P., 1897–1903' (Oxford D.Phil., 1961); Doires Bundisten, ed. J. Hertz (New York, 1956); Finfuntzwantsik Yor Zamlbuch (Warsaw, 1922); B. K. Johnpoll, The Politics of Futility. The General Jewish Workers Bund of Poland, 1917–43 (Ithaca, N.Y., 1967). The atmosphere of the movement is well captured in the photographs of Der Bund in Bilder, 1897–1957, ed. J. Hertz (New York, 1958).

autonomy for the Congress Kingdom. After 1918, many of the Bund leaders were suspicious of the P.P.S.; they found it excessively reformist and prone to compromise with the National Democrats. Co-operation between the two movements was at best sporadic.

On the Jewish national question, the Bund attacked all other Jewish parties, but especially the Zionists and the Orthodox. Nevertheless it demanded national cultural autonomy for the Jews, with a state-sponsored school system based on Yiddish. It had already built up its own private network of Yiddish schools.

In the election of 1922, the Bund, led by Maurycy Orzech and Henryk Ehrlich, put up its own list of candidates. It won 81,000 votes, mainly in the larger towns in Russian Poland, but did not win any seats.[1] It had a strong influence in the Jewish trade union movement, and issued a daily newspaper, *Naye Folkszeitung*.

The Zionist Workers' Party[2] was based on the ideology of Ber Borochov, who held that the Jewish problem could only be solved by the creation in Palestine of a Jewish state in which 'normal class relations' would prevail, and workers and peasants form the majority. The party split in 1920 between a Right and a Left Wing. The Right Wing joined the Second International, while the Left Wing, after applying to join Comintern, rejected the twenty-one conditions, and saw its Communist faction secede. Both groups called for Jewish cultural autonomy in Poland, and formed a common list in the 1922 election; jointly they won 14,000 votes, and no seats.[1]

The assimilationists, who had been important in Galicia after 1863, lost much of their pre-war significance. Their chief organization was the Alliance of Poles of the Mosaic Faith from the Whole of Poland.[3] They opposed Zionism and demands for cultural autonomy, and stressed that the Jewish question was a Polish internal matter. They demanded full civil rights for Jews. At its conference in May 1919 the Alliance declared, 'Poles of the Mosaic faith, filled with a sincere love for Poland, will unshakeably serve their Mother Country as dedicated sons, without regard to the difficult conditions in which they live.'[4]

[1] 'Statistique des élections', *S.P.* viii, Table XIV, p. 118.
[2] Poalej Sion. See A. Hafftka, 'Żydowskie stronnictwa polityczne w Polsce odrodzonej', *Z.W.P.O.*, pp. 270–3, 280, 284.
[3] Zjednoczenie Polaków Wyznania Mojżeszowego Wszystkich Ziem Polskich.
[4] Quoted in Bełcikowska, op. cit., p. 864.

This multiplicity of parties, reflecting not only political differences, but also national, regional, and religious allegiances, dissipated energies and hindered a rational approach to Poland's many problems. It is hardly surprising that the creation of a government based on a parliamentary majority proved exceedingly difficult to achieve, once the enthusiasm engendered by the attainment of independence and the ephemeral solidarity brought about by the Polish-Soviet War had dissolved.

III

THE BREAKDOWN OF THE
PARLIAMENTARY SYSTEM

The economic and financial crisis is the axis of our present-
day politics. On it, above all, is concentrated the attention
of the Government and of society. All those who have any
understanding, however superficial, are aware that our
whole future depends on the way in which we deal with
this crisis.

Roman Dmowski, 1925

THE political stability of the new state was fragile from the very
beginning. This was to a considerable extent the result of the
persistent and longstanding feud between Piłsudski and the
National Democrats. In the immediate aftermath of independence,
the need to achieve secure and settled frontiers had imposed
a certain political unity on the different Polish groupings. It was
because of his realization that internal conflict could only weaken
the Polish cause that Piłsudski, on his return to Poland in November 1918, had hesitated to place himself at the head of the 'People's
Government' which had been established in Lublin. The Moraczewski Government,[1] formed under his aegis and in which he held
the position of Head of State and Supreme Commander, was
explicitly prohibited by him from embarking on a policy of radical
reform. He aimed above all at reaching some sort of temporary
compromise with the National Democrats; he even wrote to
Dmowski, then leading the Polish National Committee in Paris,
on 21 December 1918 as 'My Dear Roman' and expressed the
hope that they would both be able to rise above the 'interests of
parties, cliques, and groups'.[2]

However, the National Democrats were rather less interested
in co-operation, feeling themselves in a strong position because
of their international recognition. But following their abortive

[1] Polish prime ministers and their terms of office from November 1918 to
September 1939 are listed in Appendix B, p. 518.
[2] *P.Z.* v. 21–2.

H

attempt to overthrow Piłsudski in a coup on 4 January 1919 they became more conciliatory and acquiesced in the formation on 16 January of a compromise Centre Government under Ignacy Paderewski.

This compromise masked deep differences over the form the new state was to take and it was not destined to prove long lasting. Dmowski, true to his belief that Germany was Poland's main enemy, aimed at extending the country as far as possible to the West, in order to make it a 'buttress against the German *Drang nach Osten*'. In the memorandum he presented to President Wilson in October 1918 on behalf of the Polish National Committee he made large claims in the West—Poznania, Pomerania, Upper Silesia, and parts of East Prussia. He did not limit his demands in the East to those areas where there was a Polish majority, but included almost the whole of the former Grand Duchy of Lithuania, parts of Volynia and Podolia and the whole of Galicia. These were areas in which he believed Polish cultural influence to be dominant, and the non-Polish groups, with the exception of the Jews, were thus to be assimilated to the Polish nation in a unitary and centralized state.

Piłsudski, on the other hand, continued to regard Russia as the main threat to Polish independence, and he opposed too far-reaching claims in the West on the grounds that they would make impossible a satisfactory relationship with Germany. He saw in the weakness of the Soviet Union following the Civil War the opportunity to ensure Poland's security in the East by fostering the creation of national Lithuanian, White Russian, and Ukrainian States, which would be federally linked with Poland. Though Poland was to be the dominant power in this federation, Piłsudski was probably sincere in his claims that he respected the national aspirations of the Lithuanians, White Russians, and Ukrainians. The same could hardly be said for the Polish landowners in these areas, who saw in federal schemes a means for safeguarding their estates. It is doubtful too, whether Poland possessed the resources to embark on such a grandiose policy. But it accorded well with Piłsudski's dictum, 'Poland will be a great power, or she will not exist.'

The establishment of Poland's frontiers dominated political life until mid-1921. These frontiers in their final form approximated much more closely to Dmowski's views than to those of Piłsudski, and the Marshal's federal schemes were shown to have little sub-stance. The national sentiments of the White Russians and the Ukrainians outside East Galicia were not firmly enough based to make possible the creation of strong national states, while Lithu-anian nationalism proved in the first instance to be hostile to Poland both because of the dispute over Wilno and because of the belief that it was only by weakening Polish cultural links that the Lithuanian national revival could prosper. Piłsudski did succeed, in spite of the bitterness engendered by the conflict over East Galicia, which was finally conquered by the Poles in July 1919, in signing an agreement with the Ukrainian national leader Semion Petlura in December of that year. This was converted to an offensive alliance in April 1920 and was followed by the outbreak of war with the Soviet Union and a successful march on Kiev. Support for the Ukrainian People's Republic proved small, how-ever, and the Soviet counter-offensive drove the Polish forces deep into Poland. It was only the Polish victory in the Battle of Warsaw in August 1920 which prevented the incorporation of Poland into the Soviet Union. The Peace Treaty of Riga signed in March 1921 marked the final abandonment of federal plans. The eastern Polish frontier was, indeed, set somewhat to the west of the line claimed by Dmowski.

The near disaster caused by Piłsudski's schemes brought to the surface again the latent hostility between the Marshal and the National Democrats, who felt his attempt had been in the worst tradition of nineteenth-century political romanticism. Piłsudski, in his turn, bitterly resented their attempts to belittle his role in the victory over the Russians, their claims that the battle on the Vistula had been won by General Weygand, perhaps with divine intervention. (For such was the implication of the phrase 'the miracle on the Vistula'.)

Other factors also contributed to Poland's political difficulties. The multiplicity of parties and interests made it extremely difficult to form a Government based on a stable majority, and the coalition formed to fight the war with the Soviet Union did not long survive the end of the external threat. The constitution of March 1921, sophisticated and complicated as it was, was not well suited to the problems of the new state, and the primacy it gave to the lower house contributed further to the weakness of the executive. It had, moreover, been framed by the National

Democrats to curb the power of Piłsudski, and as a result the political framework it established was never accepted by the Marshal and his followers as legitimate.

The political crisis was exacerbated by the extremely serious problems which the new state had to face. It proved a difficult task to overcome the effects of wartime destruction and to weld the disparate parts of the country into an economic unit. As a result Poland was plagued, as were a number of other successor states, by an increasingly uncontrollable inflation. The dispute between Piłsudski and his National Democratic opponents spilled over into the army and thus further undermined political stability, while the threats to Poland's independence from Germany and the Soviet Union intensified the atmosphere of crisis. The political inexperience of the Poles, and the conditions in which they had lived before 1914, when Polish national survival had been the preeminent consideration, made it difficult to deal fairly with the national minorities, who made up a third of the population of the new state, and who became increasingly alienated by its policies. Finally, the parliamentary system was considerably discredited by the widespread corruption of the deputies, many of whom seized the opportunities provided by the inflation for profiteering. In these circumstances, it is easy to see why the highly democratic constitution of March 1921 functioned so badly. Some action against it seems in retrospect to have been almost inevitable.

THE POLITICAL AND ECONOMIC CRISIS

One of the main reasons for the intractable nature of the political crisis was the continued inability of successive governments to deal effectively with Poland's economic problems. These economic problems were, in turn, intensified by the rapidity with which governments rose and fell. The two crises must thus be seen as closely connected, and mutually interacting.

The weaknesses of the parliamentary system had already become obvious with the collapse, in September 1921, of the coalition government of Wincenty Witos created in July 1920 to deal with the critical situation arising from the Polish defeats in the war with Russia. After Witos's fall it had proved impossible to form a Government based on a secure parliamentary majority. The two Governments of Antoni Ponikowski, rector of the Warsaw

Polytechnic (19 September 1921 to 1 March 1922; 10 March 1922 to 6 June 1922), the short-lived Government of Artur Śliwiński, the Piłsudski-ite historian (28 June to 7 July 1922), and that of the Cracow conservative Julian Nowak (31 July to 14 December 1922) had all been extra-parliamentary Governments, in which the majority of Cabinet positions were held by experts without party affiliation. They depended, for parliamentary approval, on the support of shifting and uncertain majorities, since no single political group felt strong enough to assume the responsibilities of government. The one attempt, in July 1922, by the parties of the Right to form a Government based on a parliamentary majority and headed by Wojciech Korfanty, had led to a violent clash with Piłsudski, the Head of State, and ended in a fiasco. The seriousness of the crisis was obvious after the elections of November 1922, in which no single political group won a clear majority. The Right, composed of the Popular National Union and the Christian National Club, held 125 seats in the Sejm, significantly more than in the previous parliament, but still not a majority. The Centre, comprising the Christian Democrats, the National Workers' Party, and the Piast Peasant Party, had altogether 132 seats. The Left, principally the socialists and the radical peasant parties, had 98 seats, and the national minorities had 89.

'Today', wrote the National Democratic *Gazeta Warszawska*, almost despairingly, on 28 November,

the new Sejm begins its work . . . There is no one who does not affirm that the most pressing problem is the improvement of our financial position and that this can only be accomplished by a parliamentary government based on a firm majority . . . The difficulty is that the elections have not led to a coherent majority.[1]

Only three parliamentary Governments were possible under these conditions. An all-party coalition of the type formed during the Polish-Soviet War was one possibility, but it was extremely unlikely, except in a grave national crisis, because of the hostility of the Left to any co-operation with the National Democrats. According to Witos, Thugutt, the leader of the Liberation Peasant Party, told him that he would join such a coalition only in the case of another Bolshevik invasion.[2]

A Centre–Left coalition was also very difficult to arrange.

[1] *Gazeta Warszawska*, 28 November 1922.
[2] Witos, op. cit. i. 48.

Because the Right–Centre Christian Democrats would refuse to take part, a Government formed in this way would have only a very narrow parliamentary majority. Its survival would thus be dependent on the support of the national minorities. This would render it vulnerable to strong attack from the National Democrats, and some of the party leaders feared such a connection with the minorities as an electoral liability.

However, the principal difficulty in forming such a Government lay in the unwillingness of the two large peasant parties to collaborate. The political gap between them has often been attributed to differences in social support. The Piast, it has been held, was the party of the large peasants, prosperous and conservative, while the Liberation Party was supported mainly by the more radical small and middle peasants.[1] In fact, both parties represented the better-off and more independent peasants, for the poorest were generally most susceptible to clerical influence in favour of the *Endecja*. The differences between them were more the result of the contrasting political conditions in which the movements had evolved. The Piast had a fairly long experience of political activity in semi-constitutional Austria, and the majority of its leaders were of peasant origin. The Liberation Party, though it enjoyed peasant support and had some peasant leaders, was led largely by urban intellectuals, like Stanisław Thugutt, for whose Western radical views the party seemed the best vehicle.[2]

Witos was prepared to form a broad Centre–Left parliamentary coalition, and in this he was supported by Piłsudski. However, Thugutt was opposed, and a meeting arranged between the two peasant leaders by Fryze, the editor of the radical *Kurjer Poranny*, shortly after the election, proved abortive. Thugutt wanted instead to form a Centre–Left Government without a definite parliamentary majority, which would depend on occasional alliances. He felt that 'After such bitter pre-electoral struggles, it was too early to achieve such a far-reaching understanding; it would seem like a division of the spoils.'[3]

As a result, the most likely parliamentary grouping was a

[1] See, for example, Ajnenkiel, *Od 'rządów ludowych'*, pp. 56–7.

[2] The difference in atmosphere between the two movements is clearly reflected in the memoirs of their respective leaders. See Witos, op. cit., Thugutt, op. cit.

[3] Ibid., p. 98. For Witos's attitude towards co-operation with the Liberation, see Witos, op. cit. i. 29, 48, 50.

Centre–Right coalition. The Right had emerged strengthened from the elections of 1922, and had recovered its self-confidence, which had been somewhat eroded in the early days of independence. On 25 February 1920 Dmowski had written to Zygmunt

TABLE IV. *The Sejm in December 1922**

	Seats	
	No.	Percentage
Right	125	28·0
Popular National Union	98	22·0
Christian National Club	27	6·0
Centre	132	29·9
Christian Democracy	44	10·0
National Workers' Party	18	4·1
Piast Peasant Party	70	15·8
Left	98	22·1
Liberation Peasant Party	48	10·9
Left-Wing Peasant Party	2	0·4
Radical Peasant Party	4	0·9
Polish Socialist Party	41	9·3
Communists	2	0·4
Non-party	1	0·2
National minorities	89	20·0
Ukrainians	20	4·6
White Russians	11	2·4
Ukrainian Peasant Party	5	1·1
Russians	1	0·2
Germans	17	3·8
Jewish Club	34	7·7
Jewish People's Party	1	0·2
	444	100·0

* Próchnik, op. cit., p. 135.

Wasilewski, 'It is certain that if we formed a Government—let us assume with me at its head—we should well and truly cut the throat of Poland.'[1] But during the next two years others had tried, and failed, and since the governmental crisis of July 1922, the National Democrats had been determined to create a Centre–Right majority.

[1] Biblioteka Jagiellońska. Papiery St. Kozickiego. Letter of Dmowski to Z. Wasilewski, dated 25 February 1920, from Algeria.

Some difficulties still stood in the way of an understanding with the Piast. Witos, proudly sensitive about his origins, resented the way the National Democratic press mocked his peasant dress.[1] Moreover, the bitterness of the pre-election campaign, scarred by the breaking-up of Piast meetings in Poznania by National Democratic hooligans, had not been forgotten.[2]

The question of the proposed land reform was also still unresolved. This problem had hovered over the first Sejm and had even brought about the fall of the Skulski Government on 9 June 1920. A resolution outlining the principles of the proposed reform had been passed, only after strong opposition, by one vote, on 10 July 1919.[3] The advance of the Red Army, however, considerably increased the willingness of the Right to accept a land reform, and a fairly radical bill was passed on 15 July 1920.[4] It provided for the parcellation of Government land, and of all land in excess of 180 hectares, including forests, in large estates, with a higher limit in the east and a lower limit in industrial areas. Church land was also subject to division.[5] Excess land in private hands was subject to compulsory purchase through a government agency, the Central Land Office.[6] Compensation at 50 per cent of the market price, estimated to make up about 30 per cent of the actual value of the land, was provided.[7] Land acquired in this way was to be sold to peasants with little land, or agricultural labourers, in order to create 'strong and intensively productive peasant holdings, based on private ownership'.[8] Long-term credit was to be granted to those who acquired holdings by a State Agricultural Bank, whose creation was proposed.[9]

The National Democrats had by 1922 accepted the need for

[1] See Witos, op. cit. i. 29 and 60.

[2] Ibid. iii. 11–13.

[3] For this, see C. Madajczyk, *Burżuazyjno-obszarnicza reforma rolna w Polsce, 1918–39* (Warsaw, 1956), pp. 137–44.

[4] 'Ustawa z dnia 15 lipca 1920 roku o wykonaniu reformy rolnej', *Dz.U.R.P.*, 1920, no. 120, 1229–37. For a Stalinist discussion of the issue of land reform, see Madajczyk, op. cit.

[5] 'Ustawa z dnia 15 lipca 1920 r. o wykonaniu reformy rolnej', Articles 1–2, *Dz.U.R.P.*, 1920, no. 120, 1229–31.

[6] Główny Urząd Ziemski.

[7] 'Ustawa z dnia 15 lipca 1920 r. o wykonaniu reformy rolnej', Articles 6–13, *Dz.U.R.P.*, 1920, no. 120, 1231–5. (The estimate of 30 per cent is given in Ajnenkiel, op. cit., p. 114.)

[8] Ibid., Articles 27 and 29, p. 1235.

[9] Ibid., Article 32, p. 1236.

a land reform, although this had led to a split in the party and to the departure of most of the large landowners within its ranks. However, they called for the modification of certain aspects of the 1920 law, in particular the provisions on compensation, which were held to be contrary to the Article in the constitution safeguarding private property (Article 99), and the limit imposed on private landholding, which they felt was too low. The Piast, on the other hand, called for the full implementation of the law.

The parties were further divided by their differing attitudes towards Piłsudski. Although the Piast had broken early with Activism, it was not unsympathetic to Piłsudski, and did not share the extreme hostility which the National Democrats felt for him. In the crisis caused by Piłsudski's refusal to accept a Government headed by Wojciech Korfanty, the Piast had voted against the motion of no confidence in the Head of State proposed by the Endecja.

Finally, the Left Wing of the Piast, led by the redoubtable and popular Jan Dąbski, was hostile to any co-operation with the Right, and threatened to split the party if such an agreement were reached.

The economic problems of Poland in the immediate post-war years, as of many other European countries, took the form of uncontrolled inflation. This had begun during the war itself, and accelerated considerably after 1918. If 100 is taken as the index of food prices in Warsaw in January 1921, the level had risen, by December 1922, to 1298·2.

There were many reasons for this runaway inflation.[1] In part it developed because the supply of goods was insufficient to meet the demands of the available money income. The war in the east between 1918 and 1921 imposed a continuous strain on the supply of manufactures, as did the extensive needs of reconstruction after the devastation of World War I.

Furthermore, the Government proved incapable of balancing the budget. There had been a deficit of 7,503 million Polish marks in 1919, and it rose to 445,000 million in 1922.[2] This was caused,

---

[1] On the Polish inflation see: Landau and Tomaszewski, op. cit.; E. Taylor, *Inflacja polska* (Poznań, 1926), and *Finanz und Steuersystem der Republik Polens* (Jena, 1928); L. Oberlender, K. Stein, S. Ritterman, B. Friediger, A. Zauberman, and O. Lange: *Przewroty walutowe i gospodarcze po wielkiej wojnie* (Cracow, 1928).

[2] Landau and Tomaszewski, op. cit., p. 63.

to some extent, by the inadequacy of the tax system. Many of the taxes inherited from the partitioning powers were no longer levied after independence, and the inexperience of the new Polish financial officials facilitated evasion of those still in operation. Moreover, the Government was forced to meet heavy expenses. During the Polish-Soviet War, the Ministry of War absorbed 50 per cent of the state budget, and even after the Treaty of Riga, its share still accounted for 30–40 per cent.[1] The deficit on the state railways,

TABLE V. *Index of Food Prices in Warsaw, 1921–1922*[*]

Month	1921	1922
1	100	274·2
2	126·7	279·2
3	130·1	300·9
4	125·2	339·6
5	128·6	372·2
6	139·3	395·2
7	180·7	483·8
8	208·4	557·5
9	231·5	612·7
10	284·9	655·4
11	285·0	830·5
12	279·3	1298·2

[*] *R.S.R.P.*, 1920–2, Part ii, p. 215, Table VI.

which swallowed up 20 per cent of the budget, was also a constant drain.

The Government bridged the gap between income and expenditure by printing paper money, thus accelerating the inflation. The amount of money in circulation rose from 1,024 million Polish marks in 1918 to 793,437 million in 1922.[2] Once started, inflation had a momentum of its own. Factory owners held back on the repayment of loans and taxes, aware that by so doing they would considerably decrease the amount they had to pay. In fact, the inflation in its early stages aided the reconstruction of the economy by increasing the profits of industry.

A psychology of inflation had been created by the rise in prices since 1914, and workers and salaried people continually called for rises in wages to meet the spiralling cost of living. At the same

[1] Landau and Tomaszewski, op. cit., p. 63.　　　　[2] Ibid., pp. 63–4.

time, the Polish parliamentary system made the maintenance of any control over wages and prices difficult. The socialists were unwilling to impose any sacrifice on the urban workers, while the peasant parties refused to freeze agricultural prices.

Finally, the adverse balance of payments led to the depreciation of the foreign exchange rate for the Polish mark, and further increased inflationary pressures. A dollar bought 9·8 Polish marks in 1918; by December 1922, it bought 17,808.

TABLE VI. *The Dollar Exchange Rate in Poland**
(*in Polish marks, on 31 December*)

1918	9·8
1919	110·7
1920	579·3
1921	2950·0
1922	17808·3

* Based on *R.S.R.P.*, 1920–2, Part ii, p. 248, Table XXV.

In its initial stages, this fall in the exchange rate also aided industrialists, and facilitated industrialization. Since the fall in the value of the mark was faster than the rise in domestic prices, it constituted a continuous devaluation, an export premium which made Polish goods increasingly competitive in the world market. But as the inflation began to get completely out of control, the fall in the value of the mark ceased to be faster than the rise in local prices, and those engaged in foreign trade to a great extent stopped dealing in marks, preferring to reckon in dollars, pounds, or French francs.

In spite of the help it afforded in the beginning, the results of the inflation were largely harmful. It wiped out the savings of the intelligentsia, and contributed greatly to the growth of political extremism among its members. In his autobiography, Adam Pragier, one of the leaders of the P.P.S. and the son of a wealthy Cracow doctor, describes what happened to his father's estate:

After his death, shortly after the war, his 'estate', which was worth about 150,000 gold crowns, sufficed, when I inherited it, for a three-week holiday in France. My mother placed her savings of 15,000 gold roubles in a mortgage on the house of a relative in Warsaw. After her death, soon after the war, that relative settled the mortgage . . . When he had received it, it had amounted to one-eighth of the value of his house on Marszałkowska [a smart street in the centre of Warsaw].

When I cashed it in a bank at the corner of that street, I could buy myself a pair of brown shoes ... on Chmielna [a poorer shopping area].[1]

The inflation also hurt the industrial working class. Wages failed, after 1918, to reach their pre-war level. By the end of 1921, the average real wage in industry in Warsaw was only 52 per cent of the pre-1914 figure.[2] Moreover, wages did not keep pace with prices. Labour unrest increased, as workers found their pay more and more inadequate. In 1921 there had been 720 strikes, involving 479,000 workers. In 1922 there were 800, involving 607,000 workers.[3]

Finally, speculators were quick to take advantage of the opportunities afforded by the inflation, and since deputies were often involved in their schemes, there was a growing disillusionment with parliament. A striking case in point was the Dojlidy affair. Dojlidy was an estate in Prussian Poland which was bought in August 1921 from the Government Land Office by the Polish-American Peasant Bank, an organization in which several prominent members of the Piast, including Władysław Kiernik and Jan Bryl, were involved. The bank paid 14,400 Polish marks per morgen.[4] Two months later plots were offered to peasants at 120,000 marks per morgen. The land was finally sold to the Lubomirskis, a large landowning family, for several times the purchase price.[5]

The first serious attempt to control the inflation was made by Jerzy Michalski, Minister of Finance in the non-party Ponikowski Government from 21 September 1921. He attempted to balance the state budget by drastic cuts in expenditure. The number of army officers and state officials was reduced, and three ministries were abolished. He introduced a special capital levy, to be imposed once only, which was intended to bring in 80,000 to 100,000

---

[1] A. Pragier, *Czas przeszły dokonany* (London, 1966), p. 220.
[2] W. Fabierkiewicz, *Polska w liczbach* (Warsaw, 1924), p. 73.
[3] *Revue trimestrielle de statistique* (Warsaw, 1924), nos. 2–3, p. 260, Table I.
[4] A morgen is 55 ares, or just over half a hectare (100 ares).
[5] For the affair, see Madajczyk, op. cit., pp. 166–7. W. Bazylowski 'Sprawa Dojlid jako przyczynek do przeprowadzenia reformy rolnej na początku II Rzeczypospolitej', *N.D.P.* (1st series), viii (1964), 19–50. The exchange rate for the dollar, in marks, during this period was:

31 July	2,035	31 August	2,800
31 September	6,300	31 October	3,890·5

(*R.S.R.P.* 1920, p. 248.)

million marks, and a new tax on war profits. He tried to improve the running of state enterprises, and established a lucrative state tobacco monopoly. He hoped also to stimulate the economy by the voluntary abrogation of the eight-hour working day. No new currency was yet to be established, but for the time being the coining of marks was to be halted.[1] This programme had some successes; the rate for the Polish mark fell from 4,550 to the dollar in December 1921 to 3,957 by the beginning of June 1922.[2] But the hesitations of the Sejm led to a dilatory application of the levy, which brought in much less than intended. Government income in 1922 reached only 51·4 per cent of expenditure.[3]

Moreover, the deflationary aspects of the programme, and in particular the attempt to revalue the mark, caused much difficulty. The granting of credit to industry was restricted, production slowed down, and unemployment grew, reaching 200,000 in mid-1922. The attempts by employers to lower wages because of the recession caused a wave of strikes, and the Government felt itself too weak to carry out its programme. After the Government fell on 7 June 1922, as a result of the National Democrats' attempt to secure the support of a parliamentary majority,[4] the finance policy was abandoned, and the inflation grew rapidly worse. Between July and December, the rate for the mark rose from 3,957 to 18,075 to the dollar.[2]

The political crisis re-emerged in an intensified form in the new parliament. The parties of the Right and the Piast reached a compromise over the election of marshals (speakers) for the two houses of parliament: Maciej Rataj of the Piast was elected Marshal of the Sejm, and Wojciech Trąmpczyński of the National Democrats became Marshal of the Senate. However, the election of the state President was not so easily arranged. Piłsudski, who would have had the support of all parliamentary groups except the Right, refused to stand, claiming that the prerogatives of that office had been diminished in the new constitution with him specifically in mind. At a meeting on 4 December of Left and Centre deputies who had asked him to stand, he criticized the limited powers which the President possessed in relation to the Council of

[1] For this programme, see Ajnenkiel, *Od 'rządów ludowych'*, pp. 192–3, and Zweig, op. cit., pp. 35–6.
[2] Ibid., p. 35.
[3] Ajnenkiel, *Od 'rządów ludowych'*, p. 193.
[4] See above, pp. 101, 105.

Ministers and the army. 'I do not believe', he concluded, 'that I possess those characteristics which are indispensable for the type of work laid down by the constitution.'[1]

He proposed instead a broad Centre–Left alliance which would elect Witos President. When Witos decided not to stand, Piłsudski supported the Piast candidate, Stanisław Wojciechowski, one of the leaders of the peasant co-operative movement, and a former socialist.[2] But his plan for a single Centre–Left candidate failed because of the hostility of the Liberation Party, and especially of Thugutt. This party nominated Gabriel Narutowicz, who had worked for many years as a chemist in Zürich, and had been Foreign Minister in the Nowak Government.[3] The Right hoped to take advantage of this situation, confident that Wojciechowski would be eliminated in the voting, and that the Piast would, in the last resort, vote for their candidate rather than that of the Left. They made a great miscalculation, however, in nominating the Polish Ambassador in Paris, Maurycy Zamoyski, who was the largest landowner in Poland, and whose candidacy was bound to be repugnant to all the peasant parties. In addition, both the socialists and the national minorities nominated candidates, but only as a matter of principle.

The President had to be elected by an absolute majority of the National Assembly. If no such majority was attained on the first ballot, the lowest candidate was eliminated, and another ballot was taken. This procedure was repeated until an absolute majority was reached.[4] On the first ballot, Zamoyski received 222 votes, Wojciechowski 105, Baudouin de Courtenay (the candidate of the national minorities) 103, Narutowicz 62, and Daszyński, the socialist candidate, 49. On the final ballot, however, the majority of the Piast voted for Narutowicz rather than Zamoyski; thus the former was elected by 289 votes to 227.

The political situation at once became exceedingly tense and violent. The Right, which had emerged strengthened from the elections, felt that it had been cheated of its electoral victory by a conspiracy of the national minorities, particularly the Jews. The parties of the Christian Alliance of National Unity published

---

[1] Piłsudski, *P.Z.* v. 295. For the whole speech, see pp. 286–96.

[2] For Piłsudski's account of the situation, see 'Wspomnienia o Gabrielu Narutowiczu', *P.Z.* vi. 101.

[3] See above, p. 101.

[4] See above, Chapter II, p. 46.

a statement on 10 December, the day after the election of the President, declaring that they could not, 'in this exceedingly unhealthy state of affairs, take any responsibility for the course of events', and they refused to give any support to 'Governments created by a President imposed by foreign nationalities: Jews, Germans and Ukrainians'.[1]

Press attacks on the new President knew no bounds. The main National Democratic daily, *Gazeta Warszawska*, stated that Narutowicz was 'protected by Jewish world finance' and claimed he could not even speak Polish properly (which was quite false).[2] 'How could the Jews dare to impose their President on us?' asked the National Democratic deputy, Father Kazimierz Lutosławski, in *Gazeta Poranna*.[3] Deputies were molested by nationalist mobs outside parliament, and stones were thrown at the President on his way to the Sejm to be sworn in. It was hardly surprising that Narutowicz was assassinated on 16 December, while talking to the British Ambassador at an art exhibition, by Eligiusz Niewiadomski, a nationalist fanatic.

The assassination brought about a rapid popular reaction against the Right, and all the leading Right-Wing parties denounced the crime. Piłsudski hoped to take advantage of this situation in order to make a final reckoning with the National Democrats. Already on 11 December he had told Rataj:

I cannot give up power at a time when a band of gangsters is disturbing the peace, insulting the President, and the Government does nothing. Give me power, and I will quiet the streets. If not, I will do it alone—I cannot give way in these conditions.[4]

After the assassination, a group of prominent members of the P.O.W., including Adam Koc, Ignacy Boerner, and Ignacy Matuszewski, met Rajmund Jaworowski and other leaders of the Warsaw organization of the P.P.S., in which Piłsudski-ite influences were strong. It was decided to use the occasion of the funeral of one of the workers killed in the political disturbances after the election of the President to start anti-Right-Wing demonstrations. Piłsudski was to allow this 'spontaneous outburst of popular wrath'

---

[1] *Gazeta Poranna*, 10 December 1922.
[2] *Gazeta Warszawska*, 10 December 1922.
[3] *Gazeta Poranna*, 11 December 1922.
[4] M. Rataj, *Pamiętniki* (Warsaw, 1965), p. 126.

to take its course for a day, and then step in as the re-establisher of order.[1] However, the plan was never carried out, largely because Daszyński, informed about the scheme by Jaworowski, went to Koc's house and, 'in a pathetic speech',[2] held out against violent action. He threatened the strongest measures of party discipline against those members of the P.P.S. who took part in the proposed venture.

The situation was also somewhat eased when Rataj, the acting President, nominated a 'Cabinet of pacification', headed by General Władysław Sikorski, on the day of the assassination. Sikorski, one of the ablest men in Poland, had worked as a junior Austrian staff officer with Piłsudski in the Union of Active Struggle before 1914. During the war, they had disagreed strongly on several occasions, since Sikorski's support for the Austrian solution clashed with Piłsudski's belief that Poland should play a more independent role, but after the war their relations again improved for a time, and Piłsudski agreed to serve as Chief of Staff under the new Cabinet.

On 20 December 1922 the National Assembly met again to elect a new President. Agreement was reached between Witos and Thugutt, and only one candidate was proposed by the Centre and Left.[3] This candidate, Stanisław Wojciechowski, was elected on the first ballot, with 298 votes, defeating the Right-Wing nominee, Kazimierz Morawski, President of the Cracow Academy of Sciences, who had 221.

Sikorski acted swiftly to restore order. He proclaimed a state of emergency in Warsaw, and brought new army detachments into the capital. At his first meeting with the leaders of the political clubs in the Sejm, he threatened the Right that if the situation did not become quiet, he would use the army, 'not distinguishing between guilty and innocent'.[4] By the New Year, the country was relatively calm.

The new Cabinet did not have firm parliamentary support, but, for the time being, the widening of the breach between the National Democrats and the Piast meant that its survival was assured. The National Democrats reproached Witos for his hesita-

[1] The incident is described in Pobóg-Malinowski, *Najnowsza historia*, ii. 421–2.
[2] Ibid., p. 422.
[3] See Thugutt, op. cit., pp. 102–3; Witos, op. cit., pp. 32–4.
[4] Quoted in Pobóg-Malinowski, *Najnowsza historia*, ii. 423.

tion about forming a Government based on 'a Polish majority', and held him responsible for the election of Narutowicz. *Gazeta Warszawska* wrote on 15 December, the day before the President's murder, that because of his victory 'A barrier has been thrust between the Right and the Piast.' Witos was disquieted by the involvement of the Right in the assassination and stated, 'I will not associate with people with bloodied hands.'[1] Moreover, as leader of what would be the smaller partner in a coalition, he realized that the longer he resisted, the better the terms he could demand.

In his first speech to the Sejm, on 19 January, Sikorski frankly recognized the non-parliamentary character of his Government, but continued, 'I cannot see a majority in parliament which could create a long-lasting Government. From this difficult situation, I draw the moral right to make clear my readiness still to hold the position of Prime Minister.'[2] On 23 January he received a vote of confidence of 320 to 110, the Left, the Piast, the National Workers' Party and the Slav minorities supporting him.

The financial situation remained pressing, and the exchange rate deteriorated rapidly. A dollar, which had bought 3,957 marks in June, bought 13,435 in October and 17,808 by December.[3] Sikorski called a conference of all former Finance Ministers on 9 January 1923. On 13 January he persuaded the highly gifted and independent Władysław Grabski to become Minister of Finance, and to carry out the reforms suggested by the conference. It was hoped that the budget could be balanced within three years. This was to be achieved by government economy and by the increased commercialization of state enterprises. The system of taxation was to be reformed, and taxes were to be based on an index which would keep pace with inflation. Loans would also be sought to make up the deficit.[4]

For a time this plan succeeded in halting the rise in prices, but its success was cut short by the somewhat unexpected fall of the Government on 23 May 1923. Sikorski had tried to split the Right by dislodging the large landowners and having them form a separate party, but this scheme had little success, and

---

[1] Pobóg-Malinowski, *Najnowsza historia*, ii. 420.
[2] *S.S.S.R.*, 19 January 1923, cols. 22–3.
[3] *R.S.R.P.*, 1920–2, Part II, p. 248, Table XXV.
[4] For this programme, see Zweig, op. cit., p. 36 and Próchnik, op. cit., p. 163.

his Government lacked firm parliamentary support.[1] When the National Democrats and the Piast finally reached agreement, he had no alternative but to resign.

From February, informal discussions had taken place between the Piast and the National Democrats. Witos had become convinced that a Government with a parliamentary majority was essential in order to resolve the serious political problems, and that such a Government could only be formed in alliance with the Right, with whom he would anyway prefer to co-operate.[2] On 4 March the Piast leaders decided to approach the Right, and their decision was approved, though by no means unanimously, by the executive committee of the party on 17 and 18 March. A Centre–Left Government was ruled out, and the executive committee further resolved that

attempts to form a parliamentary Government based on what is called a relative majority cannot be taken seriously, for such a Government will be based, in fact, on a minority. Moreover, it is impossible and unacceptable that a parliamentary Government dependent on the national minorities should be formed.[3]

The National Democrats had by this time somewhat regained their confidence, and were increasingly prepared to compromise on land reform. After prolonged negotiations, agreement was finally reached in Warsaw on 17 May. This agreement, known as the Lanckorona Pact, from the estate where it was believed, incorrectly, to have been signed, held that 'the Polish national character must be maintained in the constitution of the state and in local government'.[4] In the Kresy, the local inhabitants must be convinced 'that they are permanently linked to Poland',[5] and Polish colonization was to be fostered. A *numerus clausus* was implicitly proposed: 'Polish youths will be ensured, in universities, institutions of higher education and trade schools, of the possibility of

---

[1] The attempt is described by Rataj, op. cit., pp. 145, 147, and 156.
[2] Witos, op. cit. i. 47–8.   [3] *Czas*, 21 March 1923.
[4] 'Układ z dnia 17 maja 1923', Article 1, quoted in Witos, op. cit. iii. 36. The text of the agreement is also discussed in detail in W. Stankiewicz, 'Pakt lanckoroński (Metodologiczne omówienie źródeł)', *R.D.R.L.* i (1959), pp. 196–218. For the negotiations see B. Dymek, 'Z polityki Polskiego Stronnictwa Ludowego "Piast" (Pakt lanckoroński z 17.V.1923)', *Zeszyty Historyczne Uniwersytetu Warszawskiego* (1961), ii. 143–60.
[5] 'Układ z dnia 17 maja 1923 r.', Article 5, in Witos, op. cit., p. 37.

study in accordance with the just relationship between nationalities in the state (*słuszny stosunek narodowościowy*).'[1]

In foreign policy, the Versailles Treaty was to be regarded as the basis of Poland's security. Germany was seen as her principal enemy, and the improvement of relations with Czechoslovakia and increased trade with Russia were proposed.[2] The electoral system was to be modified to ensure that it would produce a parliamentary majority.[3] In addition, 'the exclusion of all politics from the army' was demanded, which meant, in effect, the rooting out of Piłsudski-ite influence.[4]

The core of the agreement was the section on land reform. It provided for the compulsory annual redistribution of 200,000 hectares for ten years. The land was to come, in the first case, from state holdings and mortmain lands, concerning which an agreement with the Church would be reached. As for privately owned land, redistribution was to begin with the largest estates. The upper limit on holdings was raised in the Kresy to 400 hectares, and even higher limits were proposed for estates with industrial plants such as sugar refineries or breweries. Full compensation was to be provided. In the case of voluntary surrender, 25 per cent of the market value of the land was to be paid in ready cash; in the case of compulsory purchase, 10 per cent. The rest would be in gilt-edged securities, payable over thirty years.[5]

The pact was signed by the Popular National Union, the Christian Democrats, the Piast and the Catholic Peasant Party. The Christian National Party refused to sign because they disagreed with the land reform provisions, but promised to support the new Government. However, even in the parties which signed, the agreement was not universally accepted. Seventeen of the Piast members of Parliament (fourteen deputies and three senators), led by Jan Dąbski, left the party in protest, forming the 'Peasant Unity'[6] grouping, sympathetic to the Liberation party. Some of the National Democratic landowners, led by Jan Stecki, president of the landowners' league, also seceded.

Nevertheless, a parliamentary majority still remained. On 26 May 1923 Sikorski resigned after losing a vote of confidence by 117 to 279, and a new Government was soon formed. Of the

---

[1] Ibid., Article 1, p. 37.   [2] Ibid., Article 2, p. 37.
[3] Ibid., Article 3, p. 37.   [4] Ibid., Article 7, p. 38.
[5] Ibid., Article 9, p. 39.   [6] Jedność chłopska.

ministers, three were from the Piast, four from the Popular National Union, and one from the Christian Democrats. Six were non-party specialists.[1] Witos took Sikorski's place, and in a speech announcing his programme, claimed that his Government was 'the realization of the democratic principles of parliamentarianism', and that 'the negative feature of extra-parliamentary Governments, for which no-one has a clear responsibility, will be ended'.[2] For the time being, the political future of the Government was secure, and it won a vote of confidence by 226 votes to 171.

Army matters were not so easily settled, for the Piłsudski-ite Minister of War under Sikorski, Kazimierz Sosnkowski, refused to serve the new Government. So did Piłsudski, resigning as Chief of Staff on 29 May. A month later, on 2 July, he resigned his only remaining position in the army, the Presidency of the Inner War Council, claiming that he would not serve under the people he held morally responsible for the assassination of Narutowicz.[3] His position as Chief of Staff was taken over by Stanisław Haller, and General Stanisław Szeptycki, a former Austrian officer, who had been Governor-General in the Austrian-administered part of the Congress Kingdom during the war, ultimately became Minister of War. Other Piłsudski-ites who held high positions in the army, notably General Krzemieński, head of the Military Supreme Court, Colonel Ignacy Matuszewski, Colonel Adam Koc, and Colonel Kazimierz Stamirowski, were also forced to resign.[4]

The economic situation, however, proved too much for the new Government. After its accession to power, the inflation accelerated, both because of the unsettled political situation and because of the effects of the German inflation, which was then reaching its peak. Władysław Grabski had continued as Minister of Finance in the new Cabinet, but resigned on 30 June on account of his general disagreement with the Cabinet's political line and the opposition within the Government to his proposed property tax.[5] He was succeeded by Hubert Linde, head of the Post Office

---

[1] H. Roos, 'Die polnische Regierungen, 1916–39', *O.E.H.*, p. 676.
[2] *S.S.S.R.*, 1 June 1923, col. 5.
[3] For his speech giving the reasons for his resignation, delivered at the Hotel Bristol on 3 July, see *P.Z.* vi. 24–35.
[4] J. Krzemieński, 'Rozmowa Komendanta ze mną', *Niepodległość*, n.s. v (1955), p. 216.
[5] For Grabski's letter setting out the reasons for his resignation, see *Czas*, 2 July 1923.

Savings Bank. The inflation had now reached fantastic proportions. On the creation of the new Government the mark rate for the dollar had been 52,500; by 9 June it had reached 71,300, and by 1 August 231,260.[1]

Shocked by this deterioration and by Grabski's resignation, the Government passed a law on 11 August implementing the property tax. This was to be paid between 1924 and 1926, and was to raise altogether 1,000 million gold francs. However, it was not to be applied in 1923, so that its effect in stemming the inflation was minimal.[2] When Linde resigned on 31 August, his successor, Władysław Kucharski, imposed further drastic cuts in expenditure and tried in vain to obtain a foreign loan to stabilize the financial situation. In addition he proposed the valorization of all taxes and state credits on the basis of a zloty account unit, but the law providing for this was not passed until 6 December.[2] The inflation continued. On 1 September the dollar bought 249,000 marks, on 1 October 380,000.[3] By 20 November, one dollar was worth 2,300,000 marks.[4]

Since the effects of the inflation were only slowly passed on in wage increases, working-class discontent grew. A wave of strikes spread across the country in July, and succeeded for a time in alleviating the situation by forcing the adjustment of wages. In October real wages again began to fall. The Government, anticipating trouble, made Cabinet changes. At the end of October, Korfanty and Dmowski became Ministers, and their entry into the Cabinet was widely taken to indicate the adoption of a policy of strong resistance to working-class demands. Strikes broke out again, first in the coal-mines of Katowice and the Dąbrowa basin, then on the railways, in the Lodz textile mills, and in the Post Office. The Government responded by conscripting the strikers, threatening those who failed to appear with trial for desertion in summary courts. On 5 November the P.P.S. called a general strike. The call was fairly widely obeyed in the country as a whole, and had 100 per cent success in Cracow. Here the Government's prohibition on public meetings led to an open clash between the army and the workers. Fourteen soldiers and eighteen workers

[1] Ajnenkiel, Od 'rządów ludowych', p. 227
[2] Zweig, op. cit., pp. 36–7.
[3] Ajnenkiel, Od 'rządów ludowych', p. 234.
[4] B.P.P.P. 133, p. 5.

were killed, and the workers took over the town. Piłsudski-ite influence was important in the clash: many former legionaries, from Cracow and elsewhere, took part in the fighting.[1]

Already before the strike, the P.P.S. had been negotiating with the Government. By 11 November agreement was reached: the militarization of the railways and the summary courts were ended, in return for the calling off of the strike.[2] Nevertheless the political atmosphere remained tense. *Kurjer Warszawski*, a leading Right-Wing paper, referred nervously to the danger of 'Kerensky-ism',[3] and the Government contemplated restrictions on freedom of speech and assembly to restore order. Several semi-fascist organizations, such as the National Guard[4] and the Polish Patriots' Alert,[5] promised to support the Government. Civil war threatened again.

The events in Cracow had considerably undermined the strength of the Witos Government. Opposition had arisen within the Piast over the waiving of the parliamentary immunity of two socialist deputies who had been involved in the Cracow violence.[6] However, it was the old question of land reform which finally brought the Government down. The agricultural committee of the Sejm had been working on a Land Reform Bill since July. When it was completed, it embodied, to a great extent, the provisions of the Lanckorona Pact. But the seizure of mortmain lands was made conditional on Church approval, and this was criticized by the Left Wing of the Piast as a betrayal by the Right. Fourteen deputies, led by Jan Bryl and Jakub Pawłowski, left the party.[7] Witos no longer had a parliamentary majority, and his Government resigned on 14 December.

Thugutt now attempted to form a broad Centre–Left Government, but failed because of the refusal of the Christian Democrats to participate.[8] As a result, a non-parliamentary Government was

---

[1] For these events see: Ajnenkiel, *Od 'rządów ludowych'*, pp. 234–41; Rataj, op. cit., pp. 169–73; F. Kalicka, *Powstanie krakowskie* (Warsaw, 1963); M. Porczak, *Walka robotników z reakcją w 1923r.* (Cracow, 1926). For Piłsudski-ite involvement, see B. Drobner, *Moje cztery procesy* (Warsaw, 1962), pp. 80–119; *Sprawa brzeska* (London, 1941), pp. 50, 61, 122, 148, 153.

[2] Rataj, op. cit., pp. 171–3.

[3] *Kurjer Warszawski*, 11 November 1923.

[4] Straż Narodowa.   [5] Pogotowie Patriotów Polskich.

[6] Witos, op. cit. iii. 52.

[7] See Lato, op. cit., pp. 81–3; *B.P.P.P.* 139, pp. 5–6.

[8] Thugutt, op. cit., pp. 108–14.

formed by Władysław Grabski on 19 December. It was regarded by both the Right and the Left as a provisional stopgap, but in fact it lasted two years, longer than any other Government before the May Coup. Grabski, though not politically connected with the Right, had many contacts in the Popular National Union through his brother, Stanisław, who was a prominent member. His relations with the Left and the Piłsudski-ites were also satisfactory. In his first Cabinet, the Minister of War, Kazimierz Sosnkowski, was close to Piłsudski, and Ludwik Darowski, his Minister of Labour and Public Works, was generally held to be a man of the Left. Grabski showed great skill in conciliating the political parties, constantly reshuffling his Cabinet. As Feliks Perl summed up in *Robotnik* on 25 May 1925, 'No party is particularly sympathetic to the Government of Mr. Grabski, but no party has any particular desire to overthrow it because of the lack of a majority in the Sejm and the general chaos of relations between the parties.'

Grabski further ensured support for his Government by granting favours, and even bribes, to individual deputies. Marian Dąbrowski, who had strongly criticized the Government, was asked why he did not vote against it. 'Why should we overthrow Grabski', he replied, 'when we have all received money from him?'[1]

When Grabski took office, the economic situation was truly desperate. By 8 January 1925 the rate for the mark had fallen to 10,125,000 to the dollar.[2] Grabski demanded special powers from parliament to enable him to issue decrees on economic and financial matters, and these privileges were granted him for six months. He decided to reject international control over the Polish economy, on the Austrian model, and hoped by vigorous action to revive domestic confidence. The first aim of his reform was to balance the budget. The receipts from the property tax increased government income, expenditure was drastically cut, and railway tariffs raised. A domestic loan was floated. Throughout January and February the mark held steady, and in February no new marks were printed. Grabski now embarked on the second stage of his reform. A new central bank, the Bank Polski, was founded

---

[1] M. Lempicki, 'Dziennik' (unpublished diary deposited in the Ossolineum Library, Wrocław); quoted in J. Tomaszewski, *Stabilizacja waluty w Polsce, 1924–5* (Warsaw, 1961), p. 96.

[2] Zweig, op. cit., p. 39.

in April 1924 with a capital of 100 million zloties. It was to be responsible for the new currency, the zloty, established at a rate of 5·18 to the dollar, and resting on a gold exchange standard. The old currency was called in at a rate of 1,800,000 marks to the zloty. In addition, the Government succeeded in obtaining some foreign loans, including an Italian loan on the security of the state tobacco monopoly, and one from the American firm Dillon, Read and Co. Confidence grew, and the reform seemed to be accomplishing its objectives.[1]

The Government also managed to resolve some pressing political questions. On 17 July 1925 the Sejm adopted a Land Reform Bill which was modified in the Senate, and was finally passed on 28 December. It was a compromise between the 1920 law and the Lanckorona Pact proposals, providing for the voluntary subdivision, under government supervision, of 200,000 hectares annually.[2] The upper limit of landholding was fixed at 180 hectares, and 300 hectares in the east. Forest land was excluded, and exceptions were to be made for highly efficient estates, or those with industrial plants.[3] Full compensation was to be provided, generally half in cash and half in bonds.[4] Land was to be distributed first to agricultural labourers and those with little land, on easy terms.[5] The act left a great deal to the discretion of the authorities, and its character depended, to a considerable extent, on the way in which it was implemented.

The Government also succeeded in signing a Concordat with Rome on 2 February 1925, which was ratified by the Sejm in March. It provided for the appointment of bishops and archbishops by the Pope, subject to the approval of the President. It also gave the consent of the Church to the implementation of the land reform law on Church lands, and stipulated that religion was to be taught in all state schools by teachers appointed by the

---

[1] On Grabski's reforms see: W. Grabski, *Dwa lata pracy u podstaw państwowości naszej (1924–5)* (Warsaw, 1927); J. Tomaszewski, op. cit.; Z. Landau, 'Polityczne aspekty działalności angielskiej misji doradców finansowych E. Hiltona Younga w Polsce (1923–24)', *Zeszyty Naukowe S.G.P. i S.* (1958), no. 9, pp. 71–112; 'Pożyczka tytoniowa', *Zeszyty Naukowe S.G.P. i S.* (1956), no. 3, pp. 61–82; 'Pożyczka Dillonowska', *K.H.* lxiv (1957), no. 3, pp. 79–85.

[2] 'Ustawa z dnia 28 grudnia 1925 r. o wykonaniu reformy rolnej', *Dz.U.R.P.* (1926), no. I, Article 11, p. 4.

[3] Ibid., Article 2, p. 2; Article 4, p. 3; Article 5, p. 3.

[4] Ibid., Articles 27–31, pp. 8–9.

[5] Ibid., Articles 72–6, p. 16.

Church. In addition, the Government was to provide for part of the maintenance of priests.[1]

Grabski failed, however, to secure the return of Piłsudski to the army. After the collapse of negotiations, Sosnkowski had resigned as Minister of War on 17 February 1924. He was succeeded by Władysław Sikorski, whose project for army organization was violently attacked by Piłsudski.[2]

Nevertheless it was not politics which was to bring down the Government, but the recurrence of the economic crisis. By early 1925 it was clear that the Grabski reforms were in serious difficulty. The budget had not been balanced in 1924, and the deficit now reached 190 million zloties, largely because of the disappointing returns of the property tax. Further foreign loans had proved exceedingly difficult to obtain. The harvest in 1924 had been very poor, and the situation was not much improved by the good harvest of 1925, for international prices for sugar, wheat, and wood, the principal Polish exports, fell drastically. The balance of payments remained heavily passive, and control over wages and prices was not maintained. The reform was finally dealt its *coup de grâce* by the German-Polish tariff war which began in June 1925.[3]

In January 1925 the period ended in which all signatories of the Versailles Treaty (including Poland) had Most Favoured Nation privileges in Germany. In June of that year the provisions of the Upper Silesia Convention, obliging Germany to import without tariff 6 million tons of Silesian coal annually, also lapsed. Germany proposed that in return for Most Favoured Nation privileges in Poland, she would continue to accept without tariff one-fifth of this quantity of coal. This very disproportionate offer was intended to strengthen the already powerful hold of Germany on the Polish economy. When these terms were refused, the importation of many Polish products was prohibited: this affected 56·6 per cent of all Polish exports to Germany, and 26·75 per cent of Polish exports generally.[4]

---

[1] For the Concordat, see *Dz. U.R.P.* (1925), no. 72, pp. 1082–94.

[2] See below, pp. 131–4.

[3] See: C. Kruszewski, 'The German-Polish Tariff War and its Aftermath', *J.C.E.A.* (1943), pp. 294–315; J. Krasuski, *Stosunki polsko-niemieckie, 1919–25* (Poznań, 1962), chap. v, pp. 474–510; B. Rzepecki, *Zatarg gospodarczy polsko-niemiecki* (Warsaw, 1930); B. Ratyńska, 'Geneza wojny celnej polsko-niemiekiej', *N.D.P.* (1st series), vi (1963), pp. 77–103.

[4] Rzepecki, op. cit., pp. 7–8.

A run on the banks started, and the outflow of foreign currency threatened to force the amount of cover for the zloty below the legal limit. In August 1925, the Bank of Poland succeeded in stabilizing the zloty at 5·98 to the dollar. However, Grabski's proposals for new savings and for the reduction of industrial taxes and other aids to industry were only grudgingly accepted by the Sejm. When foreign currency again began to flow out, the director of the Bank of Poland stated that he could not maintain the existing exchange rate. Grabski refused to accept his judgement, and in spite of President Wojciechowski's intervention, resigned on 13 November 1925.[1]

After some difficulty, a new Government was formed on 20 November under Alexander Skrzyński, who had been Foreign Minister during the greater part of the Grabski Government. Although he was generally held to be sympathetic to the Left, Skrzyński, a former Austrian diplomat, was also acceptable to the Right. President Wojciechowski originally intended him to form a non-parliamentary Cabinet, but he insisted on obtaining parliamentary support for the Government. 'I could not head such a Government now', he declared, 'when it is essential, nay crucial (*niezbędny*), that a Government be formed in which the parties share responsibility . . .'[2] He succeeded in creating a broad coalition, including the National Democrats, the Christian Democrats, the Piast, the National Workers' Party, and the P.P.S.

The participation of the P.P.S. in this undeniably bourgeois Government followed logically from the decision taken at the nineteenth party conference in December 1923 that the party would support Cabinets 'whose activities will not be hostile to the interests of the working class'.[3] The P.P.S. had throughout, though more or less unwillingly, supported the Grabski Government. Moreover, this conciliatory policy, advocated by the party centre, in particular by Feliks Perl and Mieczysław Niedziałkowski, was approved at the twentieth party conference held in Warsaw from 31 December 1925 to 3 January 1926. It did, however, arouse much opposition in the party. The Piłsudski-ites such as Moraczewski, Hołówko, and Ziemięcki were uneasy about it, particularly as the Marshal became increasingly hostile to the

[1] See Tomaszewski, op. cit., chap. v, pp. 181–223.
[2] *Robotnik*, 20 November 1925.
[3] See above, Chapter II, p. 71.

Government. The Left, in particular Adam Kuryłowicz and, to a lesser extent, Zygmunt Zaremba, also criticized it, seeing in Piłsudski's opposition the means to precipitate the revolution.[1]

The Minister of War in the new Cabinet was Lucjan Żeligowski. Although he was a former Russian officer, and not a legionary, he was close to Piłsudski, with whom he had co-operated in the seizure of Wilno in October 1920, and his appointment was the result of Piłsudski's successful pressure on the President. After Grabski resigned, Piłsudski delivered a letter to Wojciechowski on 14 November warning him against 'neglecting the moral interests of the Polish Army in the discussions concerning the resolution of the present crisis'.[2] On 15 November, the seventh anniversary of Piłsudski's return from imprisonment in Magdeburg, more than four hundred army officers, including twenty generals, gathered in a demonstration at Piłsudski's house in Sulejówek.[3] Their spokesman, General Orlicz-Dreszer, begged the Commander 'not to be absent in this crisis'.[4] Bronisław Miedziński, a prominent member of the P.O.W. and a Liberation deputy, warned Rataj on the following day of the danger of unrest in the army, and of the possibility of civil war if Sikorski were appointed Minister of War.[5]

The economic situation which the new Government faced was critical. By 31 December the number of registered unemployed had risen to 284,000,[6] and the zloty rate for the dollar was 9·10.[7] The new Minister of Finance, Jerzy Zdziechowski, criticized the over-optimism of Grabski, and attempted, in his own programme, to combine proposals of the Right with those of the socialists. Rigid economy was to be practised. The salaries of officials were to be cut for three months, and army expenditure was to be

[1] For the internal situation in the P.P.S. see: A. Pragier, op. cit., pp. 315–16; L. Hass, 'Kształtowanie się lewicowego nurtu w Polskiej Partii Socjalistycznej na tle sytuacji wewnętrzno-partyjnej (listopad 1923 — maj 1926)', K.H. (1961), pp. 69–102, and P.P.S. Lewica, 1926–31, Materiały zródłowe (Warsaw, 1960).
[2] Piłsudski, P.Z. viii. 247.
[3] According to the Gazeta Poranna Warszawska of 18 November 1925, there were 415 officers present. The unlikely figure of 2,000 is given in K. Wrzos, Piłsudski i Piłsudczycy (Warsaw, 1930), p. 67.
[4] For the text of his speech, and Piłsudski's reply, see Piłsudski, P.Z. viii. 248–51.
[5] Rataj, op. cit., p. 316.
[6] Statystyka Pracy (1926), no. 2, p. 43. The figures are for those registered in the state labour exchanges.
[7] Ajnenkiel, Od 'rządów ludowych', p. 285.

limited by reducing the term of service. Action was to be taken against speculation, and industry was to be encouraged by tax reliefs.[1]

These measures did not seem at first to have any real effect. The zloty rate improved somewhat, but unemployment continued to rise, reaching 301,000 registered by the end of January.[2] Differences in economic policy began to split the Cabinet. Zdziechowski called for more deflationary measures and cuts in expenditure. The P.P.S., however, wanted the burden to be shared by all classes, and advocated an increase in the property tax together with public works for the unemployed. These differences were eventually papered over at the end of March. The reduction of the salaries of officials was extended for one month, and 2 million zloties were provided for public works.[3]

The economy now began to revive. The *de facto* devaluation helped exports, and the British coal strike opened up a new market for Polish coal. The inflation constituted in practice a salary cut for state officials, and the Government managed by April to balance the budget.[4] Unemployment fell slightly to 272,000 registered by the end of April,[5] though it was still high. Nonetheless the uncertainty of the political situation and the general atmosphere of crisis accelerated the fall of the zloty, which reached 9·70 to the dollar on 30 April.[6]

Zdziechowski decided on further deflationary steps. He advocated the raising of existing indirect taxes, and the creation of new ones. The wages of state officials were to be lowered until the end of the year, and pensions for retired people and invalids were to be cut. In addition, 18,000 railway workers were to be dismissed. This was too much for the P.P.S. 'This is a budget of rich people', Daszyński told Rataj. 'You want to base improvement on an injury to the poor, you want to throw 18,000 railwaymen out of work.'[7] On 20 April the two P.P.S. ministers resigned. Skrzyński himself wanted to resign, but was persuaded to stay on until the provisional budget for the next two months was passed. He waited until this

---

[1] For the details of this programme, see Landau and Tomaszewski, op. cit., pp. 104–8; Zweig, op. cit., pp. 41–3.

[2] *Statystyka Pracy* (1927), no. 1, p. 32, Table I.

[3] The conflicts in the Cabinet are described in Rataj, op. cit., pp. 353–4.

[4] Landau and Tomaszewski, op. cit., pp. 105–8.

[5] *Statystyka Pracy* (1927), p. 32, Table I.

[6] Rataj, op. cit., p. 360.   [7] Ibid., p. 357.

was accomplished, and a new law on the organization of the army, believed to be acceptable to Piłsudski, had been adopted.[1] Then, somewhat unexpectedly, he resigned on 5 May.

Already before his resignation, the parties of the Centre and Right had been negotiating. They now called on the President to assign to Witos the task of forming a Government. Wojciechowski would have preferred a less provocative personality, such as Jan Dębski of the Piast or Józef Chaciński of the Christian Democrats. However, after both of them refused, he assigned the task to Witos on 6 May 1926.[2] Witos could not succeed in forming a Government, principally because of the intransigence of the National Democrats, who insisted on Sikorski as Minister of War and Stanisław Grabski as Minister of the Interior. This would have meant an open clash with Piłsudski. Wojciechowski again turned to Chaciński, but his attempts to form a Cabinet were frustrated by the hostility of Korfanty, who feared that his own position in the Christian Democratic Party would be weakened. Witos began a second attempt to form a Government on 7 May. This time he succeeded in persuading Skrzyński to take the post of Minister of Foreign Affairs, in order to give the Cabinet a more liberal appearance, but after a long discussion with Niedziałkowski, Skrzyński withdrew, and Witos informed the President that he could not form a Government.

Wojciechowski now called on the Socialists Marek and Niedziałkowski who, in accordance with the resolution of the executive committee of the P.P.S.,[3] tried to form a left-wing Government, with the support of the national minorities, in which Piłsudski would be Prime Minister. However, Piłsudski refused this offer, claiming that he limited his sphere of activities to the army. As a result, Marek fell back on the proposal of a Centre–Left Government, but because of the opposition of Witos and Chaciński the idea had to be abandoned. Finally, Marek's suggestion of a left-wing Government with national minority support was rejected by the President, because it would lack a parliamentary majority.

Desperate by this time, Wojciechowski called on Władysław Grabski to form a non-parliamentary Government. Grabski

[1] For this, see below, pp. 134–5.
[2] For the events of the crisis see: Rataj, op. cit., pp. 360–7; Ajnenkiel, *Od 'rządów ludowych*, pp. 289–96; Pobóg-Malinowski, *Najnowsza historia*, ii. 473–80; Witos, op. cit. ii. 79–91, as well as the contemporary press.
[3] See above, pp. 122–3.

managed to persuade a number of prominent figures, including Skrzyński, to serve under him, but the announcement of his proposed Premiership raised a storm among the parties of the Right and Centre. Witos attacked it particularly strongly. Grabski also failed to obtain the support of Piłsudski. On 9 May he was forced to abandon his attempt. At 11 o'clock that night Stanisław Głąbinski appeared unexpectedly at the Belvedere Palace, the President's official residence, to announce that the National Democrats, Christian Democrats, Piast, and National Workers' Party were prepared to form a Government under Witos. This may have forestalled the reconstitution of the Skrzyński Cabinet, in which Wojciechowski had managed to persuade Piłsudski to accept the post of Minister of War on condition that three of his close supporters, Jędrzej Moraczewski, Bronisław Ziemięcki, and Kazimierz Bartel be given Cabinet posts.[1] Against his better judgement, Wojciechowski accepted the new proposal.

The new Witos Government was formed the following day. In the Cabinet the Piast had three posts and the Christian Democrats, National Democrats, and National Workers' Party two each.[2] The Minister of War was General Julian Małczewski, a relatively unknown figure commanding troops in the Warsaw region. His chief recommendation was his assurance to Witos that he had the situation in Warsaw under control. The formation of this Cabinet was a political mistake of the highest order. Rataj, Wojciechowski, Pragier, the socialist leader, and several others had warned Witos against taking such a provocative step.[3] It was bound to antagonize the left-wing parties. Already on 6 May the P.P.S., the Liberation Party, the Peasant Party,[4] and the Party of Labour[5] issued a joint declaration:

The representatives of the Socialist Club, the Liberation Club, the

---

[1] See: W. Grzybowski, 'Spotkania i rozmowy z Józefem Piłsudskim', *Niepodległość* (1948), no. 1, p. 93, and 'Premier Kazimierz Bartel', *Kultura* (1948), no. 13, p. 104; also see J. Walewski, 'Omyłka Wincentego Witosa', *Kultura* (1964), no. 3/197, p. 116.

[2] H. Roos, 'Die polnische Regierungen 1916–30', *O.E.H.*, p. 677.

[3] For Rataj's warning, see Rataj, op. cit., pp. 362–3; for Pragier's, see Pragier, op. cit., p. 314.

[4] Stronnictwo Chłopskie, a radical grouping with thirty seats in the Sejm, made up largely of those who had left the Piast over land reform, had joined the Liberation, and then seceded.

[5] Partia Pracy, a six-man group, composed of those who had left the Liberation Party when it adopted a resolution on uncompensated land reform.

Peasant Party and the Party of Labour hold it their duty to declare with the utmost vehemence that the formation of a Government representing the social, political and economic views of reaction constitutes an open provocation to the whole of working Poland, and ought to come up against the resolute and unremitting resistance of organized democracy.[1]

When the new Cabinet was formed the same groups 'declared . . . war without mercy and the most absolute opposition against the Witos Government'.[2]

As well as a provocation to the Left, the formation of this Government was an even more open attack on the Piłsudski-ites. It meant the end of the new law for army organization. Moreover, in an interview with *Nowy Kurjer Polski* on 9 May, Witos went out of his way to provoke the supporters of Piłsudski: 'Let Marshal Piłsudski finally come out of his retreat,' he said in reply to a question, 'let him form a Government, let him invite the co-operation of all creative forces which are interested in the good of the state. If he does not do this, it will clearly be because he is not concerned to put the affairs of the state in order.'[3] Supremely over-confident, Witos was convinced that Piłsudski had lost his nerve, that he was a spent political force. In a section of the interview which some members of the Piast had managed to keep out of the press, he had stated, 'They say that Piłsudski has the army behind him; if that is so, let him take power by force . . . I would not hesitate to do it. If Piłsudski does not do this, then it seems he does not have these forces behind him.'[4] The National Democrats believed the same, and no doubt encouraged Witos to go ahead. After the formation of the new Government, the main Endecja paper, *Gazeta Warszawska Poranna* wrote:

The parties of the Left have proved, in the course of the crisis, that they were incapable of any creative or positive work. And this not only because of their numerical weakness. Our Left is totally disorganized, impotent, and is only capable of opposition. The socialists have failed, Deputy Marek has failed. In vain have they awaited 'miracles' from Sulejówek, for from nothing, nothing can be made, and one cannot count on miracles in politics.[5]

[1] *Nowy Kurjer Polski*, 7 May 1926.
[2] Ibid., 10 May 1926.
[3] Ibid., 9 May 1926.
[4] The incident is described in Rataj, op. cit., p. 365.
[5] *Gazeta Warszawska Poranna*, 11 May 1926.

CONFLICTS IN THE ARMY

Piłsudski was provoked to act by the rather unexpected formation of the Witos Government. That he was able to do so was the result of the support which he enjoyed within the army, support which he had carefully fostered, and which had increased because of the way in which army problems had been dealt with before 1926.[1]

The officer corps in the new Polish army had come from a number of different sources. Some officers were former members of Piłsudski's legions or members of the P.O.W. They were, for the most part, without formal military training, but because of their past, as the first Polish army, thought of themselves as an élite group, entitled to special consideration. Unlike those 'who through passive waiting had hoped to make possible victory over the Central Powers', they had acknowledged the need for 'active struggle against Russia'.[2] 'The legions', wrote Wojciech Stpiczyński, a prominent Piłsudski-ite journalist, 'through the genius of their creator and leader were not only the inheritors of the national chivalric spirit, but also the inheritors of the great historic mission of Poland—the Jagiellonian tradition based on modern methods of realization'.[3]

Not all former legionaries were supporters of Piłsudski, however. In the Second Brigade, supporters of the Austrian-Polish solution had been fairly numerous, and many of these men continued to look on the Marshal with reserve after independence.

The legionary officers continually clashed with the officers from the Austrian Imperial Army, a tightly knit group of which the most important members were Generals Stanisław Haller, Stanisław Szeptycki, and Tadeusz Rozwadowski. The legionaries reproached them for their long servility to the Austrians, and for their hostility to the Polish national cause during World War I. 'The Polish army', wrote Adam Uziembło in November 1924, 'will be a

---

[1] For the question of the army in politics see: J. Rothschild's pioneering and thorough, though strongly pro-Piłsudski-ite article, 'The Military Background of Piłsudski's Coup d'État', *Slavic Review*, xxi (1962), no. 2, pp. 241–60. In a slightly altered form, it appears as chap. ii of his *Piłsudski's Coup d'État* (Irvington, N.Y., 1966); Piłsudski, op. cit. vi and viii; B. Podoski, 'Organizacja naczelnych władz obrony państwa. Szkic historyczny', *Niepodległość*, N.S., vii (1962), 181–99; F. Sławoj-Składkowski, 'Wspomnienie z okresu majowego', in *Nie ostatnie słowo oskarżonego* (London, 1964), pp. 50–118.

[2] A. Uziembło, 'Przegrupowanie', *Głos Prawdy*, 6 September 1924.

[3] W. Stpiczyński, 'Po dziesięciu latach', ibid., 9 August 1924.

national army only when there does not remain in it one officer who formerly served in a foreign army.'[1]

The officers grouped around Władysław Sikorski were distinct from the rest of the former Austrian officers. Sikorski had, as we have seen, collaborated closely with Piłsudski in the legionary movement before 1914. However, as head of the military department of the General National Committee he had clashed with the Marshal, who opposed his support for the Austro-Polish solution. The officers sympathetic to Sikorski were linked in a secret pseudo-masonic organization, The Guard,[2] also known from its motto as 'Honour and Fatherland'.[3] It had been created in 1921, and had increased in importance during Sikorski's premiership, when it was joined by more officers who wished to form a coherent resistance to the Right in the tense period after the assassination of Narutowicz. They felt that Piłsudski had acted too weakly in the crisis.[4]

The officers from the former Tsarist army were generally not politically committed. A number of those in the higher ranks, however, were sympathetic towards Piłsudski, with whom they shared a Kresy background. Among these were General Lucjan Żeligowski, Minister of War in the Skrzyński Cabinet, and General Daniel Konarzewski, the deputy Minister of War after the Coup.

Only a small number of Polish officers had previously served in the German army, and these tended to be hostile to Piłsudski and friendly to the National Democrats.

A final group of officers comprised those who had been members of the Polish Corps organized under General Józef Haller in France in 1918. Haller, the commander of the Second Brigade of legionaries, had deserted from the Austrian army at the Russian Front at Rarańcza, early in 1918, in protest against the Treaty of Brest-Litovsk. He was a strong opponent of Piłsudski.

As we have seen, according to the constitution, the President was nominally head of the army, but its parliamentary dealings were conducted by the Minister of War, always an army officer, who was responsible before the Sejm for all acts of military

---

[1] A. Uziembło, 'Siła narodu', ibid., 29 November 1924.
[2] Strażnica.   [3] Honor i Ojczyzna.
[4] On the Guard group, see Pragier (who was a member of the Sejm commission set up to investigate secret organizations in 1924), op. cit., pp. 287–9; M. Lisiewicz, 'Związek wojskowy "Honor i Ojczyzna" ', *Bellona*, xxxvi (1954), no. 3, 47–53.

        K

officials in time of peace and in time of war. He was the shield for the Supreme Commander, who was not responsible to parliament, and who was nominated by the President acting on the advice of the Minister of War.[1] Piłsudski was opposed to this degree of civilian control, which he believed would make the army the tool of politics. He held himself to be morally responsible for the army, and believed that he was entitled to speak on its behalf. In the letter which he delivered to President Wojciechowski immediately after the fall of the Grabski Cabinet on 14 November 1925 he concluded, 'I was obliged to take this step, because I created the army, I fought with it in the most critical circumstances, and because I hold the highest rank in this army.'[2]

While still Head of State, he attempted to forestall the constitutional provisions for the army by issuing, on 7 January 1921, a decree on military organization which established for the army the independence he desired.[3] The decree provided for the management of army affairs by two bodies, the Full War Council and the Inner War Council. The Full War Council comprised the President, the Minister of War, the Deputy Minister of War, the general who was to be Commander-in-Chief, the Chief of the General Staff and two deputies, the generals designed to be field commanders of corps in wartime, and three other generals nominated annually by the Minister of War.[4] Its functions were purely advisory. It could discuss and give advice on questions of military training, armaments, mobilization, communications, technology, fortifications, or any other questions which the President or the Minister of War might suggest.[5]

The real power over the army was exercised by the Inner War Council. It was presided over by the general designated to be Commander-in-Chief in wartime, and on it sat the generals who were to be wartime field commanders of corps. The Minister of War could attend meetings 'according to need and to his judgement'.[6] He had no control over the appointment of the designate Commander-in-Chief or the designate Generals. The Council, in co-operation with the General Staff, prepared operational war plans which the Minister of War was forced to accept, and it

---

[1] See above, Chapter II, p. 48.   [2] Piłsudski, *P.Z.* viii. 248.
[3] 'Dekret Wodza naczelnego o organizacji naczelnych władz wojskowych z dnia 7 stycznia 1921 r.', Piłsudski, *P.Z.* viii, Appendix I, pp. iii–v.
[4] Ibid., Section A: Pełna Rada Wojenna, p. iii.
[5] Ibid., pp. iii–iv.   [6] Ibid., p. iv.

decided on the qualifications of all unit commanders above the rank of major.[1]

The essence of this decree was that it left the Minister of War, who was responsible to the Sejm, with no power to affect the military operations of the army, and thus rendered nugatory the provisions of the constitution. As long as Piłsudski remained Supreme Commander and Chief of Staff, his influence prevented the introduction of a bill to give effect to these provisions, but when he resigned his positions in the army on the formation of the Chjeno–Piast Government, the new Minister of War, General Szeptycki, brought forward a bill on 27 June 1923 to enact the provisions which the Marshal detested.[2] Under its terms, the powers of the Minister of War were to be greatly increased, the Inner War Council to be abolished, and the Full War Council to be transformed into an advisory body to the Minister, who was to sit on it as chairman. The President could no longer sit on the Council, and its membership would comprise the Chief of General Staff, the Chief of Army administration, the designate Commander-in-Chief, and the designate field commanders.[3]

The bill was strongly attacked by Piłsudski, and its adoption by the Sejm was forestalled by the fall of the Witos Cabinet on 14 December 1923. From this time on, the problem of the army had a double character: firstly, how should the constitutional position of the army be regulated, and secondly, under what conditions could Piłsudski be induced to return to active service. Thugutt, in the course of his abortive attempt to form a Cabinet in December 1923, had persuaded Piłsudski to take the post of Minister of War; in return, Piłsudski demanded that the decree of January 1921 be maintained, and that the army be kept independent of parliamentary interference.[4]

Grabski too attempted to facilitate the return of Piłsudski, and appointed as Minister of War Kazimierz Sosnkowski, Piłsudski's Chief of Staff in the Legions. As Grabski wrote in his memoirs, Sosnkowski 'was the person who could best maintain good relations with the camp of the followers of Marshal Piłsudski and with

---

[1] Ibid., pp. iv–v.

[2] The proposed bill is printed in Piłsudski, *P.Z.* viii, Appendix I, pp. vi–viii as 'Projekt ustawy o organizacji naczelnych władz wojskowych z dn. 27. VI. 1923 r.'

[3] Ibid., Articles 8 and 9, pp. vi–viii.

[4] Thugutt, op. cit., pp. 112–14.

Piłsudski himself'.[1] However, Piłsudski demanded that if he return to the army, he be given the posts of Chairman of the Inner War Council and Chief of Staff. Grabski, supported by Wojciechowski, refused, believing that this would excessively antagonize the Right.[2]

Sosnkowski now attempted to secure the Marshal's return by offering him the post of General Inspector of the Army (designate Commander-in-Chief) and by offering to make this post one of Cabinet rank. However, Piłsudski's opposition to the scheme and its doubtful constitutionality led to its collapse. On 17 February 1924, having failed to reintegrate the Marshal, and opposed to Grabski's cuts in the military budget, Sosnkowski resigned.[2]

His successor, General Sikorski, also wanted to secure Piłsudski's return to the army, but only on certain conditions. He told Rataj on 21 February that the most important matter to settle was the definition of the constitutional position of the army:

> He did not want to arrange this *ad personam* for Piłsudski and his whim, but only as good sense should dictate. He would never agree to the independence of the Commander-in-Chief from the Minister of War. He could not co-operate with Piłsudski as Chief of Staff, but after the organization of the higher military authorities according to his own conception, he believed he could 'put up with it' with Piłsudski as Commander-in-Chief with limited functions—the theoretical, abstract preparation of war plans. Of course he [Piłsudski] might prove unwilling.[3]

Sikorski's plan for military organization was endorsed by the Cabinet on 10 March 1924, and came before the Sejm on 14 March.[4] It provided for two bodies to deal with military matters. The Council for the Defence of the State was to comprise the President of the Republic (as president), the Prime Minister, the Ministers of Foreign Affairs, of the Treasury, of Commerce and Industry, and of the Railways, the Chief of General Staff, and the General Inspector of the Army.[5] Its functions were to discuss the co-ordinate questions concerning national defence.[6] The planning of military operations was entrusted to the Council of War,[7] which sat under

[1] Grabski, op. cit., p. 33.
[2] Pobóg-Malinowski, *Najnowsza historia*, ii. 457–8.
[3] Rataj, op. cit., p. 187.
[4] It is reprinted in Piłsudski, *P.Z.* viii, Appendix I, pp. ix–xiii, as 'Projekt ustawy o organizacji naczelnych władz wojskowych z dn. 14. III. 1924 r.'
[5] Ibid., chap. ii, Article 3, p. x.
[6] Ibid., Article 2, p. x.
[7] Ibid., chap. iv, Article 8, p. xi.

the chairmanship of the Minister of War, and included the General Inspector of the Army, the Chief of Army Administration, the designate Commanders of Field Corps, the Chief of General Staff, and two generals nominated by the Minister of War.[1] In the preparation of military plans, the General Inspector of the Army and the Chief of General Staff were subordinate to the Minister of War.[2]

Piłsudski strongly opposed this arrangement. He claimed that it was a copy of French models, and not suitable for Polish conditions. It failed clearly to define the functions of the Minister of War, the Chief of General Staff and the General Inspector of the Army, whose powers were anyway too limited. In addition, it made the army vulnerable to political influence.[3] In an attempt to conciliate him, the Cabinet adopted on 5 December 1924 certain modifications in the proposed law.[4] The General Inspector of the Army was explicitly designated as Commander-in-Chief in wartime, and was given greater authority over the Chief of General Staff, although he was still not empowered to appoint this officer.[5] A meeting was arranged on 11 December between Sikorski, Rataj, Thugutt, Piłsudski, and Stefan Dąbrowski. Piłsudski rejected the proposed compromise with extreme violence and in unmeasured language. According to Rataj, he said, 'The project is either a fiction, or I must assume that the General Inspector is an ass, the Minister of War a villain, and the Chief of Staff a louse on the collar of the General Inspector.'[6] The apparent impossibility of reaching any compromise with him led Grabski to affirm 'There can no longer be any talk either of further discussion with the Marshal or of his return to the army.'[7] Thugutt walked out during the meeting.[8]

The conflict had, by now, become exceedingly bitter. Piłsudski, feeling himself unjustly excluded from the affairs of state, began

---

[1] Ibid., Article 9, p. xi.

[2] Ibid., chap. iii, Articles 6, 7, pp. x, xi.

[3] For Piłsudski's criticisms, see 'List do gen. Sikorskiego (29.II.24)', *P.Z.* vi. 209–11.

[4] This is reprinted in Piłsudski, *P.Z.* viii, Appendix I, pp. xiii–xviii as 'Projekt ustawy o organizacji nacz. wł. wojsk. uwzględniający poprawki przyjęte przez Radę Ministrów w dn. 5.XII.24.'

[5] Ibid., Articles 12, 13, 14, 16.

[6] Rataj, op. cit., pp. 259–60.

[7] Pobóg-Malinowski, *Najnowsza historia*, ii. 462.

[8] Rataj, op. cit., p. 260.

to show increasing signs of a loss of emotional balance. At the Fourth Conference of Legionaries, on 8–9 August 1925, he claimed, for example, that documents in the archive of the Historical Commission of the Army had been destroyed in order to diminish his achievements in 1920.[1] A commission was set up to examine the allegations; it concluded, 'The Commission, in investigating these complaints, must first of all stress the deplorable reasons [the attacks on Piłsudski] which have provoked them, but is compelled to conclude that, for the most part, they are without foundation, or inexact.'[2]

On the fall of the Grabski Government, it will be remembered, Piłsudski was able to put pressure on President Wojciechowski to prevent the reappointment of Sikorski as Minister of War. The new Minister of War, Żeligowski, was a close associate of Piłsudski's, as was Jędrzej Moraczewski, one of the socialist ministers in the new Cabinet. On 9 January 1926 Moraczewski raised the question of Piłsudski's return to the army, but succeeded only in obtaining a Cabinet communiqué on 12 January calling on parliament to speed up its work on the bill on army organization before it.[3] Piłsudski, in an open letter, attacked the communiqué,[4] and on 7 February Moraczewski resigned. Piłsudski met with Wojciechowski, and demanded that the appointment of the General Inspector of the Army be made by simple decree of the President. On 10 February Żeligowski, who had remained in the Cabinet, moved to withdraw the army bill before the Sejm, but his motion was adjourned until the next meeting a week later.

When the Cabinet met on 19 February, it issued a communiqué stating that a reply was being prepared for the President who, interested in the possibility of regulating army matters by decree, had asked to be informed of his constitutional rights. It further stated that the Cabinet had decided to intervene in order to secure the adjournment of discussions of the Sejm Army Commission on the Army Organization Bill, but would wait for the President's

---

[1] For his speech, see Piłsudski, *P.Z.* viii. 195–208. He elaborated his accusations in a series of articles in *Kurjer Poranny* in October and November 1925 These articles are reprinted in Piłsudski, *P.Z.* viii. 217–44.

[2] 'Orzeczenie komisji dla zbadania stanu aktów operacyjnych z 1920 r.', reprinted in Piłsudski, *P.Z.* viii, Appendix II, p. xxx. For the whole report, see ibid., pp. xxix–xxxviii.

[3] *Robotnik*, 10 January 1926, 12 January 1926.

[4] The letter is reprinted in Piłsudski, *P.Z.* viii. 251–3.

reply before deciding on the abandonment of the bill itself. On 28 April the Cabinet finally withdrew the modified Sikorski Bill, and on 4 May it accepted a new proposed law suggested by a special commission composed of the Prime Minister, the Minister of War, and the Minister of Justice.[1] The new proposal increased the power of the President, who was to be Chairman of the Council for the Defence of the State.[2] The General Inspector of the Army was again explicitly designated wartime Commander-in-Chief, and the Chief of Staff was made responsible to him.[3] Finally, the powers of the Minister of War were diminished.

This new arrangement accorded, approximately, with Piłsudski's views, although he did not give it his explicit approval. Żeligowski, when asked by the *Nowy Kurjer Polski* whether Piłsudski would now return to the army, replied, 'The previous plan prevented this return. Now it is a question of only a very short period before the Marshal can finally take up in the army the position which is rightfully his.'[4] However, the adoption of the new bill was forestalled by the fall of the Skrzyński Government. In any case it would probably not have obtained legislative approval, for the Right, firmly opposed to Piłsudski's return to the army, mounted a campaign against him in parliament. General Szeptycki's resignation from active service was made the focal issue: he had resigned on 29 March, incensed by Piłsudski's continual attacks on him, which he felt Żeligowski condoned. Upon his resignation, the Senators of the Popular National Union, the Christian National Party, the Piast, and the Christian Democrats had put a question to the Minister about his action in the matter.[5] Żeligowski's reply was referred to a combined session of the Senate Foreign Affairs and Army Commissions, which decided, on 5 May, to refuse to accept the reply.[6] In the course of the discussion Wojciech Trąmpczyński, the National Democratic Marshal (Speaker) of the Senate, declared:

I do not want to discuss the scandalous situation in the army, in which generals who have been deeply insulted cannot obtain satisfaction from Mr. Piłsudski because he regards himself as standing above the law.

---

[1] For the development of the situation see Rataj, op. cit., pp. 349–61. The new proposal is reprinted in Piłsudski, *P.Z.* viii, Appendix I, pp. xxv–xxvii, as 'Projekt ustawy o naczelnych władzach obrony państwa z dn. 4 maja 1926 r.'

[2] Ibid., Articles 1–4, pp. xxv–xxvi. [3] Ibid., Articles 2, 7.

[4] *Nowy Kurjer Polski*, 5 May 1926.

[5] *S.S.Se.R.*, 31 March 1926, col. 40. [6] *Robotnik*, 6 April 1926.

What I would rather point out is that, according to Minister Żeligowski's letter, the idea of appointing Mr. Piłsudski Commander-in-Chief in wartime still lingers on in his ministry. I see in that the danger of a catastrophe for the country, because I believe that Mr. Piłsudski has not the military education which such functions demand. I, like many others, have had that conviction since 1920.[1]

This declaration caused great anger in Piłsudski-ite circles, particularly in the army. A thousand officers went to the President to say that they wished to defend the honour of the army of which he was head, and that of Marshal Piłsudski. On 10 May, General Rydz-Śmigły wrote to the President to say that 'the views which Mr. Trąmpczyński has felt obliged to air undermine and destroy the indispensable and basic moral values of the army, its faith in its Chief, and its noble pride in the victories it has won under his leadership'.[2] In a clash with Piłsudski, the Government could not depend on the army for support.

FOREIGN POLICY

Faith in the parliamentary system was further undermined by the series of defeats Poland sustained in her foreign policy. Her relations with almost all her neighbours remained unsatisfactory, and only on the small borders with Rumania and Latvia did she enjoy real security.[3] In Germany all the leading politicians continued to demand the revision of the Polish western frontier either peacefully, by international arrangement with the co-operation of the Western Powers, as advocated by Stresemann, or by collaboration with Russia in the event of a Polish-Soviet war. Relations were further embittered by disputes over the treatment of the German minority in Poland, who were being used by the Reich as an argument for a revisionist policy. Moreover, as we have seen, a tariff war between Germany and Poland broke out in June 1925 which greatly increased Polish economic difficulties. Stresemann, Prime Minister and Foreign Minister from August 1923, hoped to

[1] Quoted in J. Malicki, *Marszałek Piłsudski i Sejm* (Warsaw, 1936), p. 276).
[2] Quoted in *Nowy Kurjer Polski*, 11 April 1926.
[3] For Polish foreign policy in this period see: P. Wandycz, *France and her Eastern Allies* (Minneapolis, Minn., 1962); J. Korbel, *Poland between East and West* (Princeton, N.J., 1963); J. Krasuski, *Stosunki polsko-niemieckie, 1919-25* (Poznań, 1962); and Z. Gąsiorowski, 'Stresemann and Poland before Locarno', *J.C.E.A.* (1958), pp. 25-47; 'Stresemann and Poland after Locarno', *J.C.E.A.* (1958), pp. 292-317.

use these economic difficulties to force concessions from the Poles. From mid-1925 German diplomats in the West had done all they could to prevent Poland's floating any new international loans. In April 1926 Stresemann stated that a peaceful settlement of the border question could be achieved after Polish economic collapse; Germany must delay Poland's economic recovery 'until that country becomes ripe for the settlement of the frontier question in accordance with our wishes . . .'.[1] Stresemann had already won British support for his aim of modifying the frontier. In March 1925 Austen Chamberlain told the Cabinet, 'The German-Polish border in its present form, particularly in connection with the corridor and Upper Silesia, [cannot] remain as it is.'[2]

Relations with the Soviet Union, Poland's other large neighbour, were also unsatisfactory. Soon after the signing of the Riga Treaty, the Russians began denouncing the Polish eastern border on the grounds that it did not accord with the principle of self-determination.[3] Russia feared that these territories could be used to foster nationalist separatism in the Soviet Union, and she sponsored revolutionary terrorist movements in them. The Soviet Government was also obsessed by the possibility that Poland could be used as a jumping-off point for an imperialist attack on the Soviet Union, and resented the activities of Russian *émigrés* in Poland.

Polish-Soviet relations improved somewhat in the second half of 1925. However, this was mainly the result of the Russian desire to use the Polish card to prevent Stresemann from abandoning Germany's close links with Russia in favour of her links with the West. After Locarno these Russian approaches to the Poles continued, but remained fruitless. The Soviets resented Poland's relations with the Baltic states and the renewal, on 26 March 1926, of the Polish-Rumanian Alliance. The Poles, for their part, remained sceptical of Russian good faith: at the Third Congress of Comintern in March 1925 Dmitri Manuilsky had stated:

The true function of Poland is to form a barrier preventing the spreading of the Communist idea westward. For that reason the

---

[1] Gąsiorowski, 'Stresemann and Poland after Locarno', p. 299; quoting A.A. 2339/4569, 168665-71.
[2] J. Korbel, op. cit., p. 168; quoting A.A. 1425/2945, 571579, 23 March 1925.
[3] Ibid., p. 105.

international proletariat must consider as its task the smashing of capitalist Poland, turning it into a Soviet Republic.[1]

Relations with Czechoslovakia remained cool, but correct. The Poles still resented the Czech refusal to allow the transit of military equipment in 1920, and were bitter about what they regarded as the unjust frontier settlement between the two countries. Polish-Czech relations improved somewhat in 1924 and 1925, but became chilly again following the ready Czech response to Stresemann's approaches in October 1925.

Lithuania, unreconciled to the loss of Wilno, refused even to open diplomatic relations with Poland.

Polish foreign policy between 1921 and 1926 was based on the strict observance of the Versailles Treaty, and on Poland's alliance with France, concluded on 19 February 1921. The alliance provided for French help in the event of an unprovoked German or Russian attack, and was brought into operation by a secret military convention. The basis of Polish security was thus severely undermined by the Locarno Agreements of 16 October 1925, which seemed to consider the Polish western border a matter for negotiation. The nature of the political defeat which Poland suffered as a result of Locarno was camouflaged by the Franco-Polish Guarantee of 16 October, and the Warsaw press, apart from the traditionally anti-German National Democratic papers, reacted favourably to the Agreements.[2] However, by mid-December the country's new and perilous position had become evident.

The atmosphere of crisis was intensified by the Russo-German Neutrality Pact of 24 April 1926. It revived the 'Rapallo spirit', and seemed explicitly directed against Poland. In fact, the Germans had demanded from Chicherin, the Soviet Foreign Minister, an assurance that Russia would not in any way recognize Poland's boundaries.[3] In this situation, calls for a strong hand to deal with foreign policy fell on friendly ears. On 29 April the radical *Kurjer Poranny* wrote:

The critical and menacing circumstances in which we find ourselves demand that the Government of the Republic command great respect, and it will not have this until it is clothed with the authority of the man

---

[1] Quoted in R. Umiastowski, *Russia and the Polish Republic, 1918–41* (London, 1945), p. 101.

[2] *Robotnik*, for instance, described Locarno on 12 November as an 'important achievement in European politics'. *Robotnik*, 12 November 1925.

[3] Korbel, op. cit., p. 196.

around whom is concentrated the healthy part of the nation, the man who is the symbol of the struggles for Polish independence, and whose name is still capable of moving the worker and peasant masses.[1]

Piłsudski himself was greatly aroused by what he regarded as the misguided and excessively yielding foreign policy of Poland between 1923 and 1926. Never greatly interested in the complexities of domestic politics, his principal concern, after the army, was foreign affairs. According to January Grzędziński, Locarno provoked him to use his most soldierly curses, and led him to call Skrzyński, among other things, 'the little bitch of Locarno'.[2] He was even more upset by the Soviet-German non-aggression pact. 'Our army', he said, 'is very badly armed and poorly clad. We have lost time because of the [political] crisis, and the Germans since Locarno have made their second approach to the Russians since Rapallo. . . . Already the pincers are beginning to squeeze . . .'[2]

THE NATIONAL MINORITIES

The critical state of Poland's relations with her national minorities was also a cause for concern. Ukrainians, White Russians, Germans, and Jews made up one-third of the population of Poland, and had been guaranteed the use of their languages and the preservation of their national identity both in the constitution and in the treaty between Poland and the Allied and Associated Powers of January 1919.[3] The Governments in the early years of independence had, by and large, intended to deal fairly with the minorities, but had been hampered by the pressing nature of other political problems which prevented the formulation and implementation of a long-term policy in this matter. The unimpressive quality of the lesser bureaucrats meant that the liberal intentions of ministers were often frustrated by the chauvinism and incapacity of local officials, and the accession to power of the Chjeno–Piast Government, whose policy in relation to the minorities was strongly chauvinistic, greatly exacerbated the situation.

The problem was most acute in relation to the territorially

---

[1] *Kurjer Poranny*, 29 April 1926.

[2] J. Grzędziński, *Maj 1926* (Paris, 1965), p. 68.

[3] On the minorities see: Ajnenkiel, *Od 'rządów ludowych'*, pp. 161–72, 256–62; Pobóg-Malinowski, *Najnowsza historia*, ii. 436–46; Krasuski, op. cit.; Z.W.P.O., op. cit. ii; Heike, op. cit.; L. Sorochtej, 'Sprawa ukraińska w Polsce a rząd Władysława Grabskiego' (unpublished Doctoral dissertation, University of Warsaw, 1962).

compact White Russian and Ukrainian groups in eastern Poland. The Polish-Soviet War and the Polish-Ukrainian conflict had left a strong residue of bitterness here. In addition, collectivization and the purging of nationalists had not yet revealed the negative aspects of Soviet nationality policy; as a result, the White Russian and Ukrainian Soviet Republics proved extremely attractive to radical nationalists.

In East Galicia, the failure to implement the far-reaching provisions of the law of 26 September 1922[1] caused much resentment. Territorial self-government was not granted, nor was a Ukrainian university established. Moreover, the Polish Government had shown itself extremely maladroit in its dealings with the Greek Catholic Metropolitan, Archbishop Szeptycki. He had been assured, while abroad, by the Sikorski Government that he could go back to his diocese. However, on his return to Poland in August 1923, the new Witos Government, which hoped to have him replaced as Metropolitan by the more pliable Bishop Khomshyn of Stanisławów, went back on this promise, and insisted that he remain in Poznań.[2]

In Volynia and the White Russian areas the grievances were somewhat different. The Polish officials here were often very incompetent, and a peasant had to spend a great deal of time and effort in arranging routine matters, such as the sale of land, which had been very simple before the war. The area had been devastated by six years of war, and suffered as a result of slow reconstruction and the Government's deflationary economic policies, particularly under Grabski in 1924 and 1925. The slow implementation of land reform was resented by the land-hungry peasants, who were also highly aroused by attempts to foster Polish colonization, both civilian and military, in the region.[3] It is true that this colonization did not reach large proportions, for in 1923, when military colonization was stopped, only 8,732 holdings had been created, and most were not occupied by the owners. But the policy was seen by the Ukrainian and White Russian peasants as symbolic of the Government's lack of interest in their problems. The re-conversion of Catholic churches seized in the nineteenth century by the

[1] See above, Chapter II, pp. 51–2.
[2] See *Gazeta Warszawska*, 12 June 1923, 22 July 1923, 25 August 1923, 11 September 1923. In fact, he was finally allowed to return to Lwów in November, after appealing to the President.
[3] See Madajczyk, op. cit., pp. 172–6.

Orthodox Church, and the establishment, in 1925, of an auto-cephalous Orthodox Church independent of the Moscow patriarch-ate, all created friction. So, too, did the liquidation of the system of White Russian primary schools established by the Germans. The number of these schools had dropped from about 300 in 1917–18 to 23 in 1924–5.[1]

In East Galicia, nationalist influences remained dominant. The anti-Polish wing of the Ukrainian National Party of Labour gained the upper hand in 1925, and this led to the formation of a new and strongly anti-Polish nationalist group, the Ukrainian National Democratic Organization (U.N.D.O.) in July 1925.[2] The Ukrainian Military Organization had recovered by 1924 from the mass arrests of 1922, and began a new campaign of sabotage, burning Polish farms and homesteads. On 5 September 1924 one of its members made an unsuccessful attempt on the life of President Wojciechowski in Lwów.

Communist influence among the Ukrainians, with the demand for the incorporation of the West Ukraine in the Ukrainian Soviet Republic, also increased. At its second congress (August–September 1923), the Polish Communist Party set up the Communist Party of the Western Ukraine,[3] and in February 1924 the Ukrainian Social Democratic Party announced its sympathy towards Communism.[4]

Communism, which took the form of a combination of pro-Russian feeling and a desire for land reform, was even more widespread among the White Russians. By 1924 both the White Russian Independent Socialist Party and the White Russian Socialist Revolutionary Party had made clear their pro-Communist position.[5] The Communist Party of Western White Russia had also been set up at the second congress of the Polish Communist Party,[6] and the Independent Peasant Party, a pro-Communist group created in November 1924, had much strength here.[7] In the

---

[1] J. Korus-Kabacińska, 'Położenie ludności białoruskiej w Rzeczypospolitej Polskiej w latach 1924–26', *Zeszyty Historyczne Uniwersytetu Warszawskiego*, ii (1961), 199–201.

[2] Ukrainskie Natsyonalno-Demokratychne Objednienie.

[3] See M. Szczyrba, 'Komunistyczna Partia Zachodniej Ukrainy', *N.D.* (1959), i. 79–86. [4] See above, Chapter II, p. 85.

[5] See above, Chapter II, p. 88.

[6] See S. Bergman, F. Karwacki, and W. Stankiewicz, 'Komunistyczna Partia Zachodniej Białorusi', *N.D.* (1959), i. 86–93.

[7] For this see S. Jarecka, *Niezależna Partia Chłopska* (Warsaw, 1961).

White Russian Hromada, founded in July 1925 and soon enjoying mass support, Communist influences were also predominant, though some nationalist elements demanding full independence for White Russia were found in its leadership.[1]

Terrorism from bases in Lithuania and, in particular, from Soviet White Russia, continued. It culminated in an attack by 100 armed men, led by a Soviet officer, on the district capital of Stołpce, in the Nowogródek province, on the night of 3–4 August 1924. The band took possession of the whole town, pillaged shops and houses, and destroyed the police and railway stations.[2] The Government's immediate response was to set up a Border Protection Corps. General Olszewski was made Governor of Volynia, and General Januszajtis Governor of Polesia. General Rydz-Śmigły, head of the Wilno Military Region, was given full powers to deal with the situation. As a result, terrorism diminished somewhat, but it was clear that military force could not solve the political problems, and that far-reaching changes were needed in the Polish administration.

Already in April 1924 Grabski had set up a four-man commission, which included his brother Stanisław Grabski and Stanisław Thugutt, to investigate methods of improving the administrative, judicial, and educational systems. In July, laws were introduced to allow Ukrainians, White Russians, and Lithuanians to use their languages in the courts and in dealings with the administration in eastern Poland.[3] A new school law was introduced which provided that in areas in which 25 per cent of the population was not Polish, schools with instruction in Ukrainian, White Russian or Lithuanian should be established at the request of forty parents. However, these schools were to be bilingual, and as a result the new law failed to satisfy the minorities, who saw in it a means of Polonization.[4]

---

[1] A. Bergman, 'Białoruska włościańsko-robotnicza Hromada (1925–7)', *Z Pola Walki* (1962), pp. 73–99.

[2] For a contemporary Communist account of this terrorism, see T. Dąbal, 'Ruch partyzancki w Polsce', *Nowy Przegląd* (January 1925), i: new edition, Warsaw, 1959, pp. 291–302.

[3] 'Ustawa z dnia 31 lipca 1924 o języku państwowym i języku urzędowania władz administracyjnych', *Dz.U.R.P.* (1924), no. 73, pp. 1094–5; 'Ustawa z dnia 31 lipca 1924 o języku urzędowania sądów, urzędów prokuratorskich i notarjatu', *Dz.U.R.P.* (1924), no. 78, pp. 1206–7.

[4] 'Ustawa z dnia 31 lipca 1924 zawierająca niektóre postanowienia o organizacji szkolnictwa', *Dz.U.R.P.* (1924), no. 79, pp. 1212–13.

In August Skrzyński, the Foreign Minister, announced that a Ukrainian university was to be established as well, but because of Polish nationalist agitation, it was to be set up in Cracow, and not in a Ukrainian area. It thus proved impossible to gain the support of Ukrainian academics, and the project lapsed.

The new laws were inadequate to deal with the situation. On 17 November 1924, Thugutt entered the Cabinet as Minister without Portfolio, but with special responsibility for minority affairs. He succeeded in obtaining the formation of a 'minorities section' attached to the Political Committee of the Cabinet, but he failed to achieve any real improvement in the treatment of the Slav minorities. He resigned from the Cabinet on 28 May 1925, giving his reasons in a statement to the press: 'I demanded only that one should take one's word seriously, that one should observe the laws and the Constitution. Alas! Reality has not satisfied the most modest of my demands.'[1] After Thugutt left the Cabinet, the situation in the eastern provinces again became extremely tense.

Relations with the German minority were also very unsatisfactory. In a sense this was inevitable, since the Germans in Poland were being used by the German Government as a pretext for demanding the revision of the Polish western frontier. Conflict was also provoked by the Polish determination to undo the effects of the policies of Germanization which had been pursued in Prussian Poland. Further friction arose over the rights of Germans in Poland who had, in accordance with Article 91 of the Versailles Treaty, opted for German citizenship, and over their property. The rights of German colonists brought in to increase the German element in Prussian Poland caused dispute as well. Moreover, the Germans opposed the implementation of land reform in Poznania, Pomerania, and Upper Silesia, where German landholding was particularly affected. The amount of land in large estates in German hands diminished from 1,535,000 hectares in 1918 to 1 million hectares in 1926.[2] The Government's attempts to lessen the dependence on Berlin of the United Protestant Church in former Prussian Poland were resented, and complaints were continually raised about the number of German schools. The bitterness of these conflicts was intensified by the heavy-handedness of many

[1] *Robotnik*, 29 May 1925.
[2] R. Staniewicz, 'Mniejszość niemiecka w Polsce — V kolumna Hitlera?', *Przegląd Zachodni* (1959), i. 400.

Polish officials. Irritating though the activities of the *Deutschtumbund* were, there was little justification for its being banned by administrative order in August 1923.

The Government did, however, manage to reach agreement with the Jewish Club in the Sejm. The dispute between Reich and Grünbaum over the correct tactics to use in parliament had, by early 1925, given way to an increasing acceptance of Reich's moderate position. When Lucien Wolf, Director of the Joint Foreign Department of the British Board of Deputies, visited Poland in June, he was able to initiate negotiations between Reich and Skrzyński.[1] On 4 July the agreement was signed. Two days before, the Jewish Club issued a declaration setting out its position:

> The Jewish club in the Sejm, firmly upholding the principle of the integrity of Poland, and its interests as a Great Power, and recognizing the necessity for internal consolidation, states that it will pursue a policy in the Sejm in accordance with these principles both in general matters and in those concerning the defence of the interests of the Jewish population.[2]

In return, the Government promised to introduce certain measures to alleviate the position of the Jews. Primary schools with Yiddish as the language of instruction were to be established, Jews in schools and in the army would not be placed in a position which would compel them to violate their religious beliefs, Yiddish and Hebrew could be employed at public meetings, and the Jewish Communal Organization (the Kahal) was to be extended and democratized.[3] In addition, Skrzyński wrote a letter to Naum Sokolov of the World Zionist Congress on 1 July in which he stated:

> I have the pleasure to declare that the Polish Government follows with lively interest the development of the efforts of the Zionist Organization to revive Jewish national individuality and Jewish culture in the land which is its historic cradle.[4]

The agreement aroused much opposition in the Jewish Club, but

[1] Wolf's account of his mission is to be found in the archives of the British Board of Deputies.
[2] *Nasz Przegląd*, 1 July 1925.
[3] For the terms of the agreement, as published by the Government, see *Robotnik*, 12 July 1925.
[4] *Nasz Przegląd*, 2 July 1925.

it was finally accepted. However, when it was published by the Government on 12 July, it included only twelve points, as against the forty-two previously agreed on. This was held by many members of the Club to constitute a breach of faith. Although some of the provisions were implemented, the concrete results of the agreement were small. Still it did somewhat ease the position of the Jews, and when the Skrzyński Government was formed in November, Reich, on behalf of his Club, greeted it favourably.[1]

Piłsudski had, before 1914, favoured a federal solution of Russia's nationality problems, and had attempted to foster White Russian and Ukrainian independence after 1918. Now that the Sejm had manifestly failed to reconcile the Slav minorities to the state, Piłsudski seemed to many the man who could achieve this difficult task. He had always opposed extreme National Democratic chauvinism and the demand that Poland should be a national state, absorbing the Slav minorities and expelling Jews and Germans.[2]

Finally, the extensive corruption of deputies, ever ready to accept bribes, had led to widespread disillusionment with Parliamentary institutions. We have already mentioned, in passing, the Dojlidy scandal[3] and the way in which Grabski's man of affairs, Kauzik, used bribery to maintain his Government in office.[4] There were many other examples, such as the Żyrardów scandal, in which an enormous, largely French-owned, textile firm had succeeded in evading tax for a number of years, and in which Władysław Kucharski, the Finance Minister, was involved.[5] In addition, the involvement of General Zagórski in the proceedings of the Franco-Polish armaments firm, Frankopol, and the alleged complicity of the Deputy Chief of Army Administration, Michał Żymierski, in malpractices in the supply of gas masks were widely criticized. Piłsudski, scrupulously honest himself—he had donated his pension, after his withdrawal from political life, to the Stefan Batory University in Wilno—particularly resented this corruption.

---

[1] See his speech in the Sejm on 26 November 1925, *S.S.S.R.*, 26 November 1925, cols. 5–6.
[2] On Piłsudski-ite plans for resolving the problem of the minorities in Eastern Poland, see J. Lewandowski, *Imperializm słabości* (Warsaw, 1967).
[3] See above, p. 108.
[4] See above, p. 119.
[5] For the Żyrardów affair, see S. Nagórski, *Ludzie mego czasu* (Paris, 1964), pp. 140–2.

By 1926 in economic and political life, in the army, in foreign policy and in relation to the minorities, parliamentary government, with its attendant ineffectiveness and corruption, seemed to have brought Poland to the edge of a precipice. The renewal of the Chjeno–Piast Government seemed to promise the intensification of all that was worst in Polish parliamentarianism; the final crisis of the Polish constitution could not long be delayed.

IV

PIŁSUDSKI TAKES POWER

Two nations speaking Polish are in conflict for power,
struggle over every office, contest influence in the army,
and go so far as to involve in their quarrels the symbol of
the majority in the country, the President of the Republic.

Gazeta Warszawska, 25 March 1924

If there are in Poland strong forces which could dream of a
dictatorship of 'honest men', if there are strong hearts and
strong fists ready to destroy the 'order' of today, one should
not look for them in the ranks of reaction . . . The moral
leader of these people who long for honesty in the
state, who understand that the misdeeds of the Sejm and
Government can destroy Poland, is Józef Piłsudski.

Ignacy Daszyński, *Sejm, rząd, król, dyktator*, 1926

By 1926 it was clear that parliamentary government had not been
able to solve the pressing social and political problems of Poland.
Criticism of this system, and in particular of the 1921 constitution,
was widespread. Ignacy Daszyński, the socialist leader, published
a pamphlet early in 1926 in which he stressed that a democratic
republic was the best system of government for Poland and that
most of the faults of the Sejm were the result of Polish social and
political backwardness. Nevertheless these faults could not be
denied. Parliamentary government had led to corruption, to excessive party spirit, and to the exercising of influence (*protekcja*) upon
the Government and the civil service by deputies on behalf of their
clients. It had failed to provide a strong and effective administration or consistent policies. Daszyński believed that increasing
political experience would improve the situation, but also advocated immediate constitutional changes: he called for more frequent elections and for the strengthening of the power of the
President.[1]

Piłsudski, against whom the May constitution had been expressly
directed, was another strong critic of its functioning. It had led,

[1] See I. Daszyński, *Sejm, rząd, król, dyktator* (Warsaw, 1926), *passim*.

he felt, to the excessive influence of party politics in the administration of the Army and in foreign policy. No clear distinction had been drawn between executive and legislative functions; in his opinion

The basis of parliaments, when they served mankind healthily, resided in this, that there existed an executive power which was judged by elected bodies called Parliaments or Sejms. When the sickness began, that is, the disappearance of the division between the executive power and the power which judged the executive, the sense of justice had to disappear, for it cannot exist where no one is responsible for his evil actions.[1]

Criticism of the constitution was not the monopoly of the Left. In January 1925 Witos began a campaign for the revision of the constitution. In a speech at Łuck, in eastern Poland, he maintained that 'Our constitution has gone too far in its liberalism, farther than any other European state.'[2] Already in January of the previous year the Piast Parliamentary Club had adopted a programme of constitutional revision which called for strengthening of the power of the executive and granting to the President the right to dissolve or prorogue parliament. In addition it called for a reduction in the number of deputies, and for a reform of the electoral system in order to introduce single member constituencies which, it was felt, would link deputies more closely to the electorate.[3] In his pamphlet *Czasy i ludzie*, published in February 1926, Witos extended and elaborated these views. He again called for an increase in the power of the President and proposed an electoral reform. This was to favour larger parties and increase the responsibility of the deputies. Disputed results were to be settled by the administration, and not by parliament. In addition, either the power of the Senate was to be strengthened or the Senate was to be abolished, and the grounds for impeaching government officials for fraud and negligence were to be widened.[4] 'In the event of the Sejm's failing to carry out this programme', Witos wrote ominously, 'it will destroy itself, and Poland, not wanting to collapse, will be compelled to seek another way out, in order to be able to carry on her work, which may modify present conditions, but may also have unhappy results.'[4]

[1] Piłsudski, 'Wywiad w *Nowym Kurierze Polskim* z dnia 29 kwietnia 1926 r.', *P.Z.* viii. 330.
[2] *Robotnik*, 11 January 1925. [3] *Piast*, 27 January 1924.
[4] W. Witos, *Czasy i ludzie* (Tarnów, 1926), p. 15.

Revision of the constitution was also demanded by the National Democrats. In 1925 the Parliamentary Club of the Popular National Union had called for various constitutional changes. These included modifications in the electoral law to end proportional representation and to raise the voting age by five years, a reduction in the number of Deputies, and the equalizing of the powers of the Sejm and Senate.[1]

Disillusionment with parliamentary government as such was also widespread on the Right. Dmowski saw a direct link between the political and the economic crises. The weakness of parliamentary governments meant that large concessions had to be made to obtain support, 'And what is the shortest and easiest way to attain this? Prodigality with government money.'[2] For the time being, he felt, writing in December 1925, the formation of the all-party Skrzyński coalition had shown that democracy could provide a stable and lasting government. However, he wrote, 'the idea of dictatorship is not at all revolting to me. . . . If we had a man who had even half the worth of Mussolini, if we could create even half an organization like the Fascists . . . I would willingly agree to a dictatorship in Poland.'[3] The trial of the Fascist Polish Patriots' Alert[4] which began on 4 May 1926 exposed the many links existing between this organization and right-wing politicians. Those who had had contact with the Patriotic Alert included Stanisław Głąbiński, national chairman of the Popular National Union, Stanisław Kozicki, Minister Plenipotentiary in Rome and a prominent National Democratic politician, Władysław Kiernik, the former Piast Minister of the Interior, and General Szeptycki.[5] 'The trial of the Polish Patriotic Alert', wrote *Robotnik* on 10 May, 'cannot be considered an episode of the past. It is full of contemporary relevance . . .'[6]

Finally, the extensive system of welfare legislation and the eight-hour day were coming under strong criticism. 'Our social legislation', Witos held, 'has not been able to find its proper limit. In Poland everyone works as little as possible.'[7] The attack sometimes

---

[1] Pobóg-Malinowski, op. cit., p. 451.
[2] Dmowski, 'Sny a rzeczywistość', *Pisma*, x. 28.
[3] Ibid., p. 34. [4] See above, Chapter III, p. 118.
[5] See *Nowy Kurjer Polski*, 5–12 May 1926. After the coup, two of the group's leaders were sentenced to four months' imprisonment, one to two months' and one to one month. Two were acquitted. *Nowy Kurjer Polski*, 20 May 1926.
[6] *Robotnik*, 10 May 1926. [7] Ibid., 11 January 1925.

assumed grotesque forms: Dmowski regarded the eight-hour day as an attempt by skilled workers to exploit the unskilled: 'The mass of workers is done an injury in this, that the laws do not allow workers to work as much as they should, as they can, and even as they want to, and in this way earn more.[1] Our social legislation', he continued, 'has not grown up from the needs of the country and of its people. It is the abortive fruit of thoughtless imitation, and must undergo fundamental revision.'[2]

The formation of the Witos Government on 10 May 1926 was interpreted by the Left and the Piłsudski-ites as an open provocation, the beginning of a right-wing coup against the constitution. Witos was aware of this and tried, somewhat belatedly, after his initial bellicose statements, to calm the situation. He did convince Skrzyński that he was acting in good faith; after their conversation, Skrzyński told Kajetan Morawski, the Under-Secretary of State in the Ministry of Foreign Affairs, 'He does not want a showdown with Piłsudski, he only wants order.'[3] The statement which Witos issued on 10 May was also intended to relieve domestic tension:

The Government which I have formed was the result of necessity, and not of the desire for power, which at present in Poland is neither pleasant nor attractive, and which often almost slips from one's hands into the street. This has been seen in the last crisis.

Attempts have been made to represent my Cabinet as a Government of provocation and struggle. Nothing could be more false.

The Government was created for the whole country, and not for political parties. I sincerely intend to take steps to broaden the basis of the Government and to engage the co-operation of all those who can overcome pettiness and stand together for the good of the country.[4]

But the Piłsudski-ites could not forget Witos's earlier fire-eating words, his interview with *Nowy Kurjer Polski*, his repeated calls for 'a Government of strong men, and a big programme',[5] and his proposals for constitutional and electoral reforms. January Grzędziński, Piłsudski's adjutant, wrote in his diary on 19 April:

The view that is dominant is that the Cabinet crisis will be exceptionally difficult, and that Witos will decide on a strong-arm Government

---

[1] R. Dmowski, 'Kwestia robotnicza wczoraj i dziś', *Pisma*, ix. 223.

[2] Ibid., p. 225.

[3] K. Morawski, 'Przewrót Majowy', *Wiadomości*, xii, no. 566 (3 February 1957), 1.

[4] Rataj, op. cit., p. 367. Rataj claims to have drafted this statement for Witos.

[5] Ibid., p. 358.

together with the *Endecja*. General Sikorski or perhaps Szeptycki or Stanisław Haller will take over the Army. The Sejm will be dissolved, the electoral law will ultimately be changed, and sub-prefects will conduct Galician elections and find a majority for Government of reaction and corruption. As for us—'order' will be established.[1]

Piłsudski had long planned some sort of action against parliament and the 1921 constitution. General Sikorski had felt that a coup was imminent in November 1925, and the following April he warned the politicians of the Centre and Right against the danger of violent action by Piłsudski if a Centre–Right Government were formed and no prior arrangement made with the Marshal.[2] Unrest was expected on May Day and on 3 May, the Polish national holiday. Witos too believe that some kind of anti-parliamentary *putsch* was in the offing during the second half of April.[3]

Fairly elaborate preparations had gone into the planning of a coup. We have already seen that members of the P.O.W. held prominent positions in many of the Left and Centre parties. In September 1925 Piłsudski had told Kazimierz Bartel, leader of the six-man Club of Labour in the Sejm, to prepare himself for the post of Prime Minister. Bartel had several meetings with Piłsudski at which political problems were discussed in some detail.[4] Also present at these meetings were some members of the underground circle of Roman Knoll, a senior official in the Polish Foreign Office. Non-party radicals, they feared a coup by the Right after the creation of a Right–Centre Government, a development which they held would be disastrous in a multi-national state such as Poland. In their search for a military figure to support them in forestalling the Right, they had originally settled on Sikorski; however, by the end of 1925 they had decided that Piłsudski was more likely to fall in with their schemes.[5] There existed as well other left-wing underground organizations. According to Moraczewski, the P.P.S. and the Liberation, fearing a coup by the Endecja, had created already in 1925 a secret organization modelled

---

[1] J. Grzędziński, *Maj 1926* (Paris, 1965), p. 16.
[2] See the memorandum in the Stanisław Kauzik Collection in the A.A.N., 'Jak doszło do wojny domowej'. It was written by someone close to Sikorski, though not by the General himself, and has been published in the *Kwartalnik Historyczny*, lxvi (1959), no. 1, pp. 126–38, with an introduction by M. Pietrzak.
[3] Witos, *Moje wspomnienia*, iii. 75–9.
[4] W. Grzybowski, 'Premier Kazimierz Bartel', *Kultura*, no. 13 (1948), 99–101.
[5] See Morawski, op. cit., p. 2.

on the People's Militia of the Popular Governments of 1918–19. This body had made contact with another secret group led by Colonel Karaszewicz-Tokarzewski which, it was believed, took orders from Piłsudski. However, attempts by Barlicki and Thugutt to use Moraczewski as an intermediary to unite the two groups failed.[1]

This failure probably occurred because Piłsudski, who believed that the socialists had not shown any real desire to co-operate with him either following the assassination of Narutowicz or in the Cracow riots, was seeking new allies. As far back as the 1922 elections he had co-operated with the conservative large land-owners and supported two of their lists.[2] From 1925 on he was making approaches to them through Mackiewicz, editor of *Słowo*, a Wilno newspaper which represented the views of the Kresy con-servatives.[3] He also attempted to contact Prince Zdzisław Lubo-mirski, who refused to meet him. Piłsudski's efforts are described by the president of the large landowners' Agricultural Credit Association, Władysław Glinka:

From January 1926 on, I learned from some of my friends that Piłsudski was thinking of taking power with the support of the Army, but that he intended to do so completely legally, from a formal point of view, because he was certain that Wojciechowski would do everything he demanded without the need to resort to arms. So would the Government and the Sejm. Preparing to act, and not wanting to be a slave of the Left, Piłsudski was seeking support on the Right. Not from the Right-Wing parties in the Sejm, but from people with conservative convictions and of irreproachable reputation.[4]

The military preparations were even more elaborate. Following the appointment of Żeligowski as Minister of War, the punish-ments imposed by Sikorski for participation in the November demonstration at Sulejówek were rescinded. General Orlicz-Dreszer, who had gone on leave rather than accept his demotion to a post in Poznań, became Cavalry Inspector for the Warsaw Military District and Head of the War Ministry Cavalry Depart-ment. Together with Colonel Bolesław Wieniawa-Długoszowski,

---

[1] J. Moraczewski, 'Pamiętnik' (unpublished, in A.Z.H.P.), quoted in Ajnenkiel, op. cit., p. 294.
[2] See above, Chapter II, p. 65.
[3] Mackiewicz, op. cit., p. 183.
[4] 'W rocznicę przewrotu majowego. Dokumenty', *Polityka*, xi (1957), p. 6.

he supervised the military side of the preparations for the coup. On these preparations General Żeligowski either turned a blind eye or, more probably, was quietly sympathetic.[1]

Prominent opponents of Piłsudski in the armed forces were weeded out. As we have seen, General Stanisław Haller resigned as Chief of Staff in December 1925, and General Szeptycki left active service in March 1926. General Zagórski, head of the Air Force, hounded for his part in the Frankopol scandal, resigned in April and was replaced by a Piłsudski-ite, General Rayski. Within the General Staff itself, the head of the Army Administration Department, General Stefan Majewski, and his deputy, General Michał Żymierski, were replaced by General Daniel Konarzewski and General Norwid-Neugebauer, both supporters of Piłsudski. The same phenomenon occurred in the Second Army Department (Intelligence) where Colonel Michał Bajer was replaced by Colonel Ścieżyński, and in the Third Army Department (Training and Organization) where General Stanisław Burhardt-Bukacki and Colonel Józef Beck took charge. Attention was also devoted to the regional commands. The dominance of Piłsudski-ite officers was secured in the military divisions of Warsaw, Lublin, Grodno, Lodz, Brześć, Toruń, and Wilno. General Sosnkowski, Piłsudski's closest associate in the legions, was Commander in Poznań, the National Democratic stronghold.

These preparations did not go unnoticed. Captain Henryk Picheta, battalion commander of the 22nd Infantry Regiment stationed in Siedlce, writes in his memoirs

Around 20 April, I do not remember the date exactly, but I know it was a Sunday, I was summoned by the commander of the regiment (Col. Krok-Paszkowski) to report to him in the officers' mess. He there informed us that a 'coup d'état' was being prepared by Marshal Piłsudski and asked if he could count on us.[2]

Krok-Paszkowski had himself been informed of the preparations by General Mieczysław Trojanowski, commander of the 9th

---

[1] For the preparations for the coup see: M. Romeyko, 'Przed i po maju 1926 r. Ze wspomnień oficera sztabu generalnego', *W.P.H.* vii (1962), no., 1, pp. 274–316; no. 2, pp. 203–38; no. 3, pp. 262–301; no. 4, pp. 259–94; W. Karbowski, 'Wypadki majowe w 1926 r.', *W.P.H.* iv (1959), no. 2, pp. 328–78; H. Piątkowski, 'Wspomnienia z "wypadków majowych" z 1926 r.', *Bellona*, iii, iv (1961), pp. 182–213; J. Rothschild, *Piłsudski's Coup d'État* (New York 1966), pp. 75–82.
[2] H. Picheta, 'Przełom majowy', *Tydzień Polski*, 9 May 1953, p. 3.

Infantry Division and a former legionary.[1] Adam Pragier has described how in the autumn of 1925, Marian Malinowski, a pro-Piłsudski-ite P.P.S. deputy, put him in touch with an army officer who, under a false name (Pragier by chance knew his real identity), claimed to be helping in preparations to resist a right-wing coup. Pragier, who represented Pruszków, a constituency outside Warsaw in which there was an important railway junction, was to arrange with his party members to paralyse Government troop movements in the event of an armed clash.[2] In April, Colonel Wieniawa-Długoszowski sounded out the officers at the Cadet School about a proposed coup, and found the response unfavourable.[3]

The most bizarre incident which occurred during preparations for the coup concerns a pro-Government general, Tadeusz Kutrzeba. Early in March 1926, having just completed a book on the 1920 war, he arranged to visit Piłsudski so that the Marshal could check the manuscript. When he arrived at Sulejówek, he found himself ushered into a study, along with General Orlicz-Dreszer, by Piłsudski himself. Apparently unaware who Kutrzeba was, Piłsudski proceeded to describe in great detail his preparations for a coup. Kutrzeba afterwards gave Dreszer his word that he would repeat nothing he had heard, and although he fought on the Government side in May, he did not reveal what he had discovered.[4]

Yet, although the preparations for the coup were elaborate, it is still not clear at what point Piłsudski finally decided to act. Unlike his supporters, he had shown great hesitation in resorting to illegal intervention against the Government. He had not, in the end, taken any serious action in the crisis following Narutowicz's assassination, during the Cracow riots or in the crisis following Grabski's resignation, when Dreszer had all but asked him to make a coup.[5] His passivity in 1922 and 1923 had led the radical officers in the army to look to Sikorski instead as a champion against the Right. Piłsudski's behaviour during 1925 and 1926 had convinced many politicians that he was a spent force, and this calculation had

[1] Archive of the Józef Piłsudski Historical Institute (London), 'Relacja generała Krok-Paszkowskiego' (1957).
[2] Pragier, op. cit., pp. 317–18.
[3] J. Rzepecki, *Wspomnienia i przyczynki historyczne* (Warsaw, 1956), pp. 13–14.
[4] Romeyko, op. cit., Part IV, pp. 261–4.
[5] See above, Chapter III, p. 123.

weighed heavily both with Witos and with the National Democrats in their decision to revive the Chjeno–Piast coalition. Neither Skrzyński nor Wojciechowski believed that Piłsudski was planning any action against the Government in May. When Witos told Wojciechowski during the May governmental crisis that he thought Piłsudski was plotting something, Wojciechowski

replied very strongly that this was untrue. He could guarantee that Piłsudski could not be capable of such a crime. Moreover he [Piłsudski] had visited him personally a few days before and had given him his word of honour that he was not thinking of any coup. He did not have the slightest reason not to believe his assurances because he knew that Piłsudski always kept his word.[1]

In addition, there is much evidence that the final eruption of the governmental crisis in May, with the breakdown of the Skrzyński coalition, was neither expected nor welcomed by the Piłsudski-ites. Both Rataj and Pragier, who was particularly sensitive to Piłsudski-ite intrigues in the P.P.S., agree that the resignation of the socialist ministers which precipitated the crisis was the result of the party's unwillingness to support the strongly deflationary aspects of Zdziechowski's financial policies. Piłsudski played no part in this.[2] Grzędziński's diary too shows that many Piłsudski-ites believed that nothing would be done to prevent the Right's dealing with the constitutional crisis as it wished.[3]

Finally, Piłsudski's moderate position in the deteriorating situation after Skrzyński's resignation suggests that he was either playing a very elaborate double game, or, more likely, that he took his decision to move outside the constitutional framework very late. It is true that Piłsudski refused to participate in Marek's proposed Government, giving the rather lame excuse that he confined his attention to Army matters. However, the explanation he privately gave to Stefan Benedykt—that the Government lacked a parliamentary majority and could not last—is convincing.[4] At the beginning of the crisis (perhaps on 6 May) he sent Niedziałkowski to Kajetan Morawski to persuade him to accept the post of Foreign Minister.[5] The evidence concerning Piłsudski's willingness to take

---

[1] Witos, op. cit. iii. 83. For Skrzyński's views see ibid., p. 85.

[2] Pragier, op. cit., pp. 312–13; Rataj, op. cit., pp. 356–7.

[3] See above, pp. 150–1.

[4] S. Benedykt, 'O przełomie majowym', *Wiadomości*, xiv, no. 667, p. 1 (11 January 1959).

[5] Morawski, op. cit., p. 1.

part, as Minister of War, in a revived Skrzyński Cabinet is unclear, but on balance it suggests that he made his offer in good faith.[1]

On the other hand, members of the P.O.W. and other supporters of Piłsudski did much to create the political crisis. Almost from the time the Skrzyński coalition was formed, *Glos Prawdy* had agitated against it, and against the participation in it of the P.P.S. On 19 December 1925 Wacław Grzybowski, secretary of the Club of Labour, wrote:

The leaders of the P.P.S. are suffering from a malignant delusion which could be called 'the parliamentary delusion'. They do not realize that one cannot, from the elevated position of the parliamentary parties, look to the interests of the many-million-strong camp of labour. They do not realize that all the parties in Poland today are only names written on paper.[2]

In the final crisis, compromise at first appeared possible. Marek and Niedziałkowski told Erdman of the Piast that the P.P.S. did not feel itself strongly linked with the bloc of left-wing parties: 'They were prepared, for the time being, to make wry faces, but later would even join the coalition if the Cabinet were not too provocative (Byrka instead of Zdziechowski, and Sikorski not a member) and if Witos decided to solve the Piłsudski question.'[3] However, when Miedziński and Poniatowski, P.O.W. members of the Liberation, heard about this, they created a great uproar, and forced the P.P.S. leaders to withdraw their statements.

On 18 April, when the crisis was just beginning, Żeligowski had, as a precautionary measure, ordered the concentration of a number of pro-Piłsudski-ite regiments for manœuvres at the military camp at Rembertów, near Sulejówek.[4] The manœuvres were to begin on 10 May. Sometime between 8 and 10 May, most probably on the morning of the 10th, when the formation of a new Centre–Right coalition under Witos was certain,[5] Piłsudski decided to act.

On that day the Marshal gave an interview to the radical *Kurjer Poranny* which was printed on 11 May. It was also carried by

[1] See above, Chapter III, p. 126.
[2] W. Grzybowski, 'Ataki na P.P.S.', *Glos Prawdy*, 19 December 1925.
[3] Rataj, op. cit., p. 363.
[4] Archive of the Józef Piłsudski Institute (London), 'Relacja generała Skwarczyńskiego' (n.d.).
[5] Witos had been charged at 1 a.m. by the President to form a Government. At 2.30 p.m. the President signed the decrees nominating the members of the new Cabinet.

Republika in Lodz, *Dziennik Wileński* in Wilno, *Ilustrowany Kurjer Codzienny* in Cracow, and the main Yiddish papers. Asked about his views on the developments of the previous few days, he replied, somewhat ominously, 'I do not regard this process as ended, for on a number of occasions the attempts of Mr. Witos have not succeeded because of the inability or unwillingness of this gentleman to take into account the moral interests of the state.'[1] He strongly attacked the formation of the Witos Government and claimed that the Army and foreign policy, which should be above politics, would now fall prey to party interests. The Government was a revival of the Chjeno–Piast coalition, which he had refused to support: 'I knew in advance that with such a Government there would be internal corruption and the misuse of governmental authority in every direction for party and private advantage.'[2] This Government had, moreover, taken strong action against him personally. 'I was surrounded by paid spies, everyone who betrayed me—the former Supreme Commander—was given advancement, I might even say attempts were made on my life.'[2] 'I doubt', he remarked threateningly, 'whether anyone in the Army would be prepared to die for a Government of this type.'[3]

Even before the Government had been fully sworn in on the evening of 11 May, Witos ordered the confiscation of the papers which had printed the interview. However, some issues escaped and were circulated clandestinely. Demonstrations against the Government began, both spontaneous and organized (largely by Colonel Wieniawa-Długoszowski). Groups of students and officers went from café to café shouting 'We will not allow the bartering of the army', 'We will not let them steal Poland', 'Down with the Chjeno–Piast'. Incidents took place in several of the cafés, including the famous Blikle's on Nowy Świat, when patrons refused to cheer Piłsudski.[4]

Rumours circulated that the Government was about to arrest Piłsudski or certain of his associates, particularly Dreszer. *Rzecz-pospolita* brought out a special issue on the 11th claiming that legal

[1] J. Piłsudski, 'Wywiad w *Kurierze Porannym* z dnia 11 maja 1926 r.', *P.Z.* viii. 333.
[2] Ibid., p. 334.   [3] Ibid., p. 335.
[4] The events of the coup have given rise to a vast literature. Among the more important works, one might mention: J. Grzędziński, op. cit.; S. Haller, *Wypadki warszawskie od 12 do 15 maja 1926 r.* (Cracow, 1926); Karbowski, op. cit.; Piątkowski, op. cit.; Rzepecki, op. cit., Rothschild, op. cit.

action would shortly be taken against the Marshal.[1] In addition, *Kurjer Poranny* alleged that on the night of 11–12 May, an unidenti-field band had attacked Piłsudski's house in Sulejówek, and had fired shots.[2] The paper admitted some years later that this incident had been staged by Piłsudski-ites, but at the time the news broke it raised the emotional temperature in Warsaw still higher.

On the same morning Piłsudski drove from Sulejówek to Rembertów. Żeligowski, in his last order before resigning, had handed over command of the troops here to the Marshal, and with the exception of one battalion from the Officer Cadet School, all the troops acknowledged his command. At about 11 a.m. they moved on Warsaw. By 2.30 p.m. they had reached Praga, on the right bank of the Vistula. They encountered no resistance here, and took control of the entrances to the three bridges (two road and one rail) which crossed the river to the centre of Warsaw.

Piłsudski afterwards claimed that he intended only an armed demonstration, and that he believed the Government would capitulate before his show of strength. The Press Bureau of the City Administration which Piłsudski set up during the fighting issued a statement on the night of the 13th:

Marshal Piłsudski, when he left Rembertów at the head of the military units under his command, intended to protest against the Government which had been formed by Mr. Witos, which the Marshal regarded as a Government of dishonesty.[3]

This clearly reflects Piłsudski's desire not to be held responsible for unleashing civil war, but is it true? There is much evidence to support it. Many contemporary observers accepted Piłsudski's explanation of his intentions: General Sikorski, who was not par-ticularly sympathetic towards his aims, believed that the Marshal intended only an armed demonstration;[4] so did the author of the memorandum 'Jak doszło do wojny domowej'.[5] An armed demon-stration of much smaller dimensions had succeeded in November 1925 in preventing the nomination of Sikorski as Minister of War. Moreover, Piłsudski believed that Wojciechowski shared his own negative assessment of the Witos Cabinet, and would not resist him.

[1] *Rzeczpospolita*, 11 May 1926, Dodatek nocny.
[2] *Kurjer Poranny*, 13 May 1926; *Robotnik*, 13 May 1926.
[3] *Dokumenty chwili*, i (Warsaw, 1926), p. 17.
[4] W. Sikorski, 'Kartki z dziennika', *Żołnierz Polski*, xiii (July 1957), p. 4.
[5] 'Jak doszło do wojny domowej', op. cit., p. 138.

He also believed that his military strength would ensure speedy capitulation. From Rembertów Piłsudski had brought the 7th Regiment of Uhlans, led by Colonel Kazimierz Stamirowski, the 22nd Infantry Regiment, led by Colonel Henryk Krok-Paszkowski, one regiment of mounted riflemen, led by Colonel Stefan Hańka-Kulesza, the Rembertów manœuvre battalion under Major Aleksander Rutkowski, and the exercise division of the 28th Regiment of Light Artillery, led by Major Mieczysław Koraziewicz. In addition, some units in Warsaw had declared for Piłsudski. These included the 1st Regiment of Light Infantry and the 36th Regiment of the Academic Legion. Piłsudski-ite supporters were found in many other Warsaw units as well, and in all departments of the Ministry of War. General Rayski, a Piłsudski-ite, commanded the Air Force in Warsaw.[1]

The 11th Regiment of Uhlans and the 13th Infantry Regiment, both of which supported Piłsudski, were only a few hours from the capital. Moreover, as we have seen, Piłsudski possessed considerable strength in the various provincial garrisons. General Małachowski in Lodz declared himself at once on the side of the coup, and General Rydz-Śmigły in Wilno sent the 1st Legionary Division to Warsaw. Piłsudski expected that General Skierski in Toruń and General Sosnkowski in Poznań would be able to prevent the transferring of Government reinforcements from these National Democratic strongholds. His control of the commands in Skierniewice and Częstochowa would enable him to cut off the pro-Government troops in Cracow and perhaps in Lwów, where General Sikorski had been sent after he had ceased to be Minister of War.

The forces at the immediate disposal of the Government were much weaker. It could count on the Cadet School, commanded by Colonel Gustaw Paszkiewicz, whose one battalion at Rembertów had returned to Warsaw and placed itself under the command of the Government, on the Officers' Infantry School under Major Marian Porwit and, with less certainty, on the 30th Rifleman's Regiment, under Colonel Izydor Modelski, and the 21st Infantry Regiment. In addition, the Government possessed one platoon of the 1st Mounted Artillery Division and an armoured-car platoon.[2]

The disposition of Piłsudski's troops also lends support to the

---

[1] For the military situation see: Karbowski, op. cit., pp. 328–32; Piątkowski, op. cit., pp. 183–5.

[2] Karbowski, op. cit., pp. 333–5, p. 340.

claim that he planned an armed demonstration only. If he had hoped to take Warsaw by fighting, he would not have advanced in such a way as to be compelled to attack over the river. Furthermore, he lacked the heavy infantry which would have been necessary to force the bridges.

The Government realized that it was faced with a crisis when, on the night of the 11th, the 7th Regiment of Uhlans, marching from Mińsk Mazowiecki to Rembertów, disobeyed the orders of the new Minister of War, General Malczewski, to return to base.[1] Early on the 12th the Cabinet began discussing what action it should take. It has been argued that Witos was willing to give way, but that he was prevented from doing so by pressure from the National Democratic Cabinet Ministers and especially from the Government's military advisers.[2] The evidence is inconclusive, however. Witos's memoirs, as one would expect, do not mention any willingness on his part to make concessions. During the last few days of the crisis, one of his main preoccupations had been the fear that he might be thought a coward.[3] This suggests that he too may have favoured a hard line. So does the fact that he failed to inform Wojciechowski, who was believed to be sympathetic to Piłsudski, of the Cabinet meeting on the 12th.[4]

In this Witos misjudged the President. Wojciechowski, who had returned by 3 p.m. from his summer residence at Spała, argued more strongly than anyone else against compromise. His position caused some surprise, and is usually attributed to his chagrin at being deceived by Piłsudski, who had given him his word that he was not planning a coup. Yet even earlier he had shown some resentment at Piłsudski's high-handedness with him. On 5 May he told Rataj that he wanted a Government with a parliamentary majority, since he wished to avoid a clash with the Sejm. 'With Piłsudski', he added, 'I am not going to talk, he treats me in a disrespectful way.'[5]

By 2 p.m. on the 12th the Government had determined on a military showdown, and a communiqué was issued:

The criminal agitation spread for a long time by plotters and over-throwers of order in the Army has had sad results.

---

[1] Grzędziński, op. cit., p. 19.
[2] Pobóg-Malinowski, *Najnowsza historia*, ii. 477–8.
[3] See, for example, Rataj, op. cit., p. 363.
[4] Morawski, op. cit., p. 1.
[5] Rataj, op. cit., p. 361.

A number of units of the Army from various regions, collected at Rembertów, incited by false rumours and deceived by false orders have allowed themselves to break discipline and renounce obedience to the Government of the Republic.

The Government of the Republic, standing guard over the constitution and maintaining law and order, has protected the capital from invasion by the rebellious leaders and the units deceived by them.

The President, as the highest military authority, orders the rebels to come to their senses and submit to the Government.

The Government calls on all citizens to remain completely calm, and to obey the legal authorities of the Republic.[1]

In addition, the President issued a separate appeal to the Army. A state of emergency was proclaimed in the Warsaw province and in the Siedlce and Pułtusk districts of the Lublin province. Supreme command of the troops was assumed by General Malczewski, the Minister of War. General Tadeusz Rozwadowski was placed in command of the defence of Warsaw, and Colonel Władysław Anders was named his chief of staff. General Stanisław Haller became Chief of Staff. There was a conspicuous predominance of former Austrian officers among those leading the Government's troops.

After all the preparations for resistance had been made, Wojciechowski went down to the Poniatowski Bridge, where Piłsudski had established himself on the Praga side. Through an adjutant he arranged a meeting with the Marshal at the centre of the bridge.[2] Wojciechowski refused Piłsudski's proferred hand, and stated at once, 'I uphold the honour of the Polish Army.'

Piłsudski, somewhat surprised, replied, 'Well, well, but not in this way.'

'I represent Poland here', Wojciechowski continued, 'I demand you make your protest legally, that you give a direct answer to the Government's appeal.'

---

[1] *Dokumenty chwili*, i. 5.
[2] The course of their conversation is well documented. Wojciechowski recorded his version, which was published by S. Arski, op. cit., p. 418. See also the account by the President's son-in-law: W. J. Grabski, 'Ostatnie rozmowy Piłsudskiego z Wojciechowskim', *Kierunki*, v. 19 (15 May 1960), p. 11. For Piłsudski's account, see his *P.Z.* ix. 15. In addition, a number of cadets from the Cadet School overheard part of the conversation; see Rzepecki, op. cit., pp. 22–5; Piątkowski, op. cit.; *Bellona* (1961), pp. 186–8; the account of Józef Kuropieska, another cadet is printed in Karbowski, op. cit.; *W.P.H.* iv. 335.

'For me', countered Piłsudski, 'the legal road is closed.'[1] After further vain attempts to persuade Wojciechowski that he intended no action against the President, but only against the Witos Government, and that he should be allowed to pass into the city, Piłsudski turned to the Government troops. When they too failed to respond to his appeals, he returned to his side of the bridge. Civil war was imminent.

Piłsudski was completely cast down by the realization that he had either to submit or to use force. He returned to the headquarters of the 36th Regiment of the Academic Legion. 'The Marshal', writes Stefan Benedykt, an eye-witness,

lay on a couch. He looked bad, was pale, exhausted, and depressed.

For a long time he said nothing. Then he said 'I have come to you. The Poniatowski Bridge is lost. Do you understand, lost . . . lost . . . lost.'

When he was told that a battalion from the 36th Infantry Regiment had taken possession of the Kierbiedź Bridge, he replied 'You are wrong, boys, that is not so, there is no entry to Warsaw.'[2]

In fact, the military situation was not quite as gloomy as it seemed. Following the interview on the bridge, Wojciechowski had returned to the Cabinet meeting, where he again argued against any compromise, and after the meeting ended he promised Witos that he would not allow 'such an indignity to take place as to give in to rebels'.[3] The military advisers to the Government at first resolved to withdraw to safely loyal Poznań and to crush the revolt from there. However, the disastrous political consequences of such a plan led to its abandonment. Instead, the Government entrenched itself firmly behind the three bridges across the Vistula. They reinforced their position heavily, placing one company of the 21st Infantry Regiment, one squadron of light infantry, and the regiment from the Officers' Infantry School on the Poniatowski Bridge, and a police division with another company of the 21st Infantry Regiment on the Kierbiedź Bridge. Nevertheless, when one company of the 36th Regiment of the Academic

---

[1] Arski, op. cit., p. 418.
[2] S. Benedykt, op. cit., *Wiadomości* (1959), p. 1.
[3] According to the report of *Nowy Kur ey Polski*, 13 May 1926.

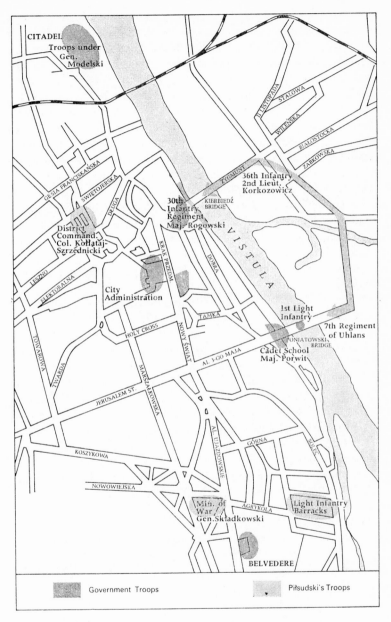

CITADEL
Troops under
Gen.
Modelski

II LISTOPADA
STALOWA
WILEŃSKA
BIAŁOSTOCKA
ŻABKOWSKA

36th Infantry
2nd Lieut.
Korkozowicz

ZYGMUNT

30th
Infantry
Regiment
Maj. Rogowski

KIERBIEDŹ
BRIDGE

GĘSIA FRANCISKAŃSKA
ŚWIĘTOJERSKA
DŁUGA

District
Command
Col. Kołłątaj-
Szrzednicki

VISTULA

LESZNO
ELEKTORALNA

City
Administration

KRAK PRZEDM

DOBRA

1st Light
Infantry

7th Regiment
of Uhlans

TAMKA

TOWAROWA
TWARDA

HOLY CROSS

NOWY ŚWIAT

AL 3-GO MAJA

PONIATOWSKI
BRIDGE

Cadet School
Maj. Porwit

JERUSALEM ST.

MARSZAŁKOWSKA

KOSZYKOWA

GÓRNA
SOLEC

AL. UJAZDOWSKIE

NOWOWIEJSKA

Min. of
War
Gen. Składkowski

AGRYKOLA

Light Infantry
Barracks

BELVEDERE

Government Troops   Piłsudski's Troops

MAP 5. Military situation in Warsaw on 12 May 1926

Legion, which had declared for Piłsudski, crossed from Praga, the 21st Regiment allowed them to take possession of the exit from the Kierbiedź Bridge.[1] The Piłsudski-ites now had access to Warsaw, though they would still have to fight their way up the escarpment.[2]

Piłsudski, thrown into confusion and despair by the unexpected resistance of Wojciechowski and the Government forces, still hesitated to take action. It was left to General Orlicz-Dreszer to assume command of the rebel troops. An attack was mounted at 6.30 p.m., and after about half an hour's fighting Piłsudski's units had scaled the escarpment and taken possession of Zamkowy Square. From here they forced their opponents down Krakowskie Przedmieście, thus compelling the Government, which was deliberating in the Radziwiłł Palace on this street, to withdraw to the Belvedere, the Presidential palace. They then took the complex of military buildings and the headquarters of the city administration on Saxon Square (today Victory Square). By 8.30 p.m. they had reached Jerusalem Street.

Once having taken over the city administrative headquarters, the Piłsudski-ites created an improvised staff. General Orlicz-Dreszer was named head of the military units known as the 'Warsaw Group'. His chief of staff was Lieutenant-Colonel Józef Beck. General Felicjan Sławoj-Składkowski was made Governor of Warsaw, Roman Knoll was placed in charge of the Ministry of Foreign Affairs, and Kazimierz Bartel and Colonel January Grzędziński were made responsible for transport. The necessity of forming a General Staff at this late stage is another indication that Piłsudski had not anticipated any large-scale military action.

Piłsudski's forces were now in a strong position. They controlled the telephone exchange, the Railway Ministry and the District

---

[1] The incident is differently described in Rothschild, op. cit., pp. 63–4, where it is stated that this company of the 36th Regiment was sent by the Government to reinforce the bridge, and there went over to the rebels, thus opening Warsaw to Piłsudski. This account is contradicted by Grzędziński, by Karbowski, who is generally very reliable, and by Colonel Sawicki, who commanded the 36th Infantry. See Grzędziński, op. cit., p. 22, Karbowski, op. cit., *W.P.H.* (1959), pp. 336–8, and Archive of the Józef Piłsudski Historical Institute (London), 'K. Sawicki, 36 p.p. w przełomie majowym', (1957).

[2] Warsaw is built on two levels; the main part of the city is situated on a bluff, with the river below.

Headquarters of the Railways, so that the only reliable link the Government had with the rest of Poland was by air. (The Government had succeeded in replacing General Rayski, the Piłsudski-ite head of the Air Force, by General Zagórski.) They also held the main railway station and the offices of the General Staff. Further-

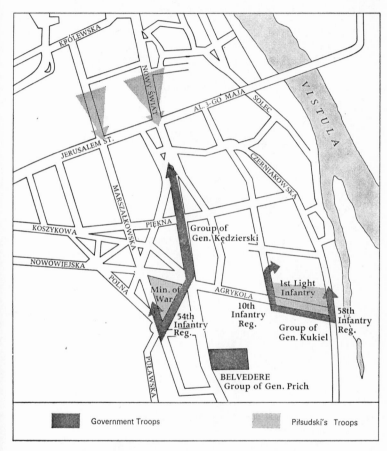

MAP 6. Military situation in Warsaw on 13 May 1926

more, Piłsudski's troops were numerically superior to those of the Government.

Nevertheless, Piłsudski decided to try to settle the conflict by negotiation. Wojciechowski had already refused to see a joint delegation of the Left parties, and he now refused to see Piłsudski's

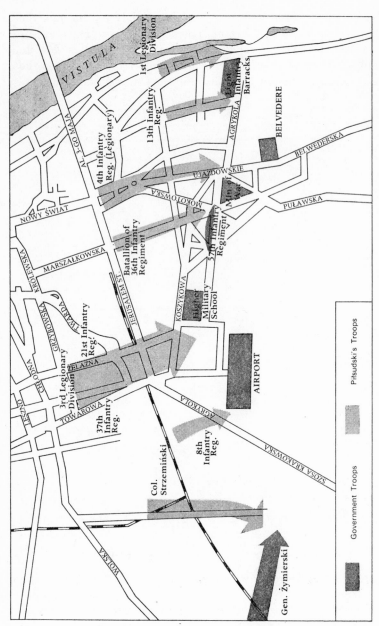

MAP 7. Military situation in Warsaw on 14 May 1926

emissaries, first Rataj and then Żeligowski. Piłsudski also tried, through Stanisław Mackiewicz, to set up a conciliation committee, composed of large landowners such as Prince Lubomirski and Alexander Meysztowicz, on the 13th.[1] However, all these attempts failed because of the absolute intransigence of Wojchiechowski. 'This suppurating abscess must finally be cut out', he told General Haller.[2] He had taken personal charge of military operations, as Head of the Armed Forces, and of the Cabinet he allowed only Witos to deal directly with the generals.[3]

He was affected too by the optimism of his military entourage, who believed that reinforcements could soon be brought in to crush Piłsudski. Already on the 12th two ministers, Stefan Piechocki and Stanisław Osiecki, had been sent to Poznań and their reports about the popular mood there were encouraging.[3] On the 13th the Government expected the arrival of the 10th Infantry Regiment from Łomża, the 57th and 58th Regiments from Poznań, the 71st Regiment from Ostrów Łomżyński, and the 26th Regiment from Lwów; the 6th Regiment from Cracow and the 3rd Regiment from Tarnowskie Góry were scheduled to arrive somewhat later. In addition the Government had ordered General Rybak, Divisional Commander in Brześć, to stop any Piłsudski-ite troops coming from Wilno.[4]

In fact the reaction in the provincial garrisons was not quite what either side expected. Piłsudski, believing that a show of force would achieve his ends, had not devoted much time to preparation outside Warsaw. The District Command in Poznań declared for the Government after General Sosnkowski, who had attempted suicide, perhaps because of the conflict of loyalties with which he found himself confronted, had been replaced.[5] So did that in Toruń, where the Piłsudski-ite commander, General Skierski, was arrested by his lower-ranking officers. Cracow came out for the Government, and General Sikorski in Lwów did as well, though somewhat ambiguously. He refused to send more than a token

---

[1] See W. Glinka, op. cit., *Polityka*, xi (1957), 6.
[2] S. Haller, op. cit., p. 23.
[3] Witos, op. cit., p. 105.
[4] Haller, op. cit., pp. 20–1, p. 29.
[5] The Sosnkowski affair remains somewhat mysterious, and has given rise to a large literature: see, for example, Pobóg-Malinowski, op. cit., pp. 483–4; Romeyko, op. cit. vii, no. 4, pp. 279–83; K. Morawski, *Tamten brzeg* (Paris, 1962), pp. 145–6.

contingent of troops to Warsaw, claiming that the rest were needed where they were because of a threatened Ukrainian uprising.[1]

The garrisons at Modlin and Puławy, near Warsaw, supported Piłsudski. So did the Lodz command and the Częstochowa command, which controlled an important rail link. In Wilno General Rydz-Śmigły won over the civilian authorities and sent a divisional corps to reinforce Piłsudski.

The Marshal spent most of the 13th in attempts to negotiate a settlement. He limited his military operations to defending the position he already held. However, in the afternoon, reinforced by the 10th Infantry from Łowicz which had arrived during the night, and the two Poznań regiments which had reached Warsaw at 3 p.m., the Government forces counter-attacked.[2] They had some initial successes. After taking the headquarters of the Ministry of War on Nowowiejska Street, they moved up Ujazdowskie Avenue and Marszalkowska Street to the Main Station. Their patrols even reached Królewska Street and the Saxon Garden. Some Piłsudski-ite units went back across the river as the situation deteriorated, and so did Piłsudski and his staff, who established themselves in the Eastern Station.

Rozwadowski intended to encircle the Piłsudski-ites who remained in the centre of the city with the help of the troops in the Citadel, behind the rebel lines. But unknown to the Government, these troops had gone over to the Marshal. General Modelski was arrested, and the two regiments there placed themselves at the disposal of General Burhardt-Bukacki, a supporter of Piłsudski. Then, reinforced by the arrival of troops from Kutno, the insurgents were able to force the Government troops back along Marszałkowska to Union Square.

A considerable factor in the frustration of the Government's attack was the success of the Piłsudski-ites in preventing the arrival of Government reinforcements. The 55th Infantry was persuaded to take no part in the conflict. The 71st Infantry from Ostrów was internally divided, and eventually went over to the insurgents.[3] Through their control of the telephone and telegraph systems, the Piłsudski-ites could confuse local commanders. Control of the rail-

[1] For Sikorski's conduct see: Sikorski, op. cit.; Haller, op. cit., pp. 27–8, 44–6.
[2] See: Karbowski, op. cit., pp. 356–60; Haller, op. cit., pp. 31–9.
[3] Karbowski, op. cit., p. 354.

way network was also important.[1] Already, on the eve of the coup, unknown to the central committee of the P.P.S., Adam Kuryło-wicz, head of the Railway Workers' Union, had been discussing ways of controlling the situation with Moraczewski and Ziemięcki, two prominent supporters of Piłsudski within the party.[2] During the fighting his union members sabotaged trains bringing Government troops to Warsaw, but allowed Piłsudski-ite forces to pass. On the 13th he called a railway workers' strike without previously consulting the P.P.S.

This strike had much to do with forcing the hand of the central committee of the party, which had been discussing the situation since the coup began. Those of its members who, like Perl and Lieberman, had reservations about the Marshal, would have liked to impose some conditions before committing themselves to support him. However, the news of the railway strike committee left the P.P.S. virtually no alternative but to call a general strike for the 14th.[3]

It has often been argued that the general strike was decisive in ensuring Piłsudski's success.[4] This is incorrect. If any strike was decisive it was the rail strike, and even had the P.P.S. not called a general strike, the members of the socialist Railway Workers' Union, who had good reason for bitterness on account of the Government's economic policy and the previous Witos Government's conscription of railway workers, would have continued to obey Kuryłowicz's orders.[5] Yet although the rail strike did help the insurgents, it was not universally supported. The railway workers in western Poland, where the influence of the National Workers' Party was predominant, did not strike. Indeed, more important than the strike was the sabotage organized by Kuryłowicz, for example at Kutno and Częstochowa, which

---

[1] For the situation on the railways, see Grzędziński, op. cit., pp. 30–54. Grzędziński was deputed by Piłsudski to take charge of the Railway Ministry during the fighting.

[2] Pragier, op. cit., p. 319.

[3] Pragier, op. cit., pp. 319–22. See also Barlicki's statement during the Brześć trial in *Proces brzeski* (London, 1941), pp. 39–40, and H. Lieberman 'Wspomnienia' (unpublished, in the possession of Mr. A. Ciołkosz, London), pp. 286–8.

[4] See, for example, Rothschild, op. cit., p. 129; H. Roos, *A History of Modern Poland* (London, 1966), p. 112.

[5] See above, Chapter III, p. 124. For Kuryłowicz's contacts with the Piłsudski-ites during the coup, see Grzędiński, op. cit., pp. 26–8, 32.

certainly did much to delay the arrival of Government reinforcements.[1]

The position of the Government on the night of the 13th was
bad. The Citadel had been lost, the airport was cut off, and
reinforcements were not arriving. Piłsudski, on the other hand,
expected substantial reinforcements, the Legionary Division from
Wilno, the 3rd Division from Zamość, Chełm, and Lublin, and the
2nd from Kielce. He made a final attempt, through Żeligowski, to
negotiate a settlement. This failed, and when the reinforcements
he was expecting arrived at 2.30 a.m. he decided to mount a major
attack on the 14th in order to settle the issue.

At 5 a.m. on the morning of the 14th, Piłsudski began his attack,
covered by machine-guns, artillery, and tanks.[2] By mid-morning
his troops had surrounded the airport and were threatening the
Belvedere. The Government's reinforcements from Cracow and
Poznań were still delayed by transport difficulties. By early afternoon the insurgents had taken the airport and had regained
possession of the headquarters of the Ministry of War. At about
5 p.m. they took the Belvedere.

The Government had already withdrawn to Wilanów, about
five miles south. Here a fierce debate was raging.[3] The military
were in favour of withdrawing to Poznań to continue the struggle,
and were supported by Zdziechowski. Witos and Wojciechowski
wanted to submit, arguing that a prolonged civil war would expose
the country to serious internal and external dangers. At 7 p.m. the
Government and the President both decided to resign. A message
was sent to Rataj, the Marshal of the Sejm, who came to receive
Wojciechowski's resignation at midnight. Legally, Rataj was now
Acting President and could call on any one he chose to form a
Government. However, the contrast between the legal and the
actual position emerged clearly in the communiqué issued by
General Burhardt-Bukacki, Chief of Piłsudski's General Staff,
early on 15 May:

The President of the Republic has abdicated his power in favour of
Marshal Piłsudski, and has recognized him as the only person worthy
and fit to govern Poland ... Marshal Piłsudski is working together with

[1] Grzędziński, op. cit., pp. 35, 41, 46.
[2] See: Karbowski, op. cit., pp. 358–66; Haller, op. cit., pp. 31–47.
[3] Witos, op. cit. iii. 110–12; Haller, op. cit., pp. 47–54.

Marshal Rataj to create a new Government of honest men who will be worthy of office.[1]

To the surprise of some members of his staff, Piłsudski decided against taking direct power, and allowed Rataj to hold the position of Acting President. The politicians of the Right hoped that Rataj would make use of the Government reinforcements which had arrived on the morning of the 15th from Poznań under General Łados to strengthen his hand against Piłsudski. The arrival of these troops had even led some of the more fire-eating generals, such as Haller and Rozwadowski, to contemplate a renewal of hostilities.[2] Rataj originally intended to create a 'Cabinet of national reconciliation' headed by the moderate Piast Deputy Jan Dębski, but after a three-hour discussion with Piłsudski on the morning of the 15th, Rataj agreed to name Bartel as provisional Premier. He was to remain in office until a new President had been elected.

Rataj, as Acting Head of State,[3] issued a proclamation demanding the end of all military activity and prohibiting the revival of conflict without his permission. Piłsudski, as Minister of War, was to supervise 'the winding up of this state of affairs'.[4] The members of the Witos Cabinet, who had been interned, were released. However, four generals, Haller, Zagórski, Malczewski, and Rozwadowski, remained in custody. The three days of fighting had cost some 500 killed and 1,000 wounded.[5]

Piłsudski had been deliberately vague, both before and during the coup, about his aims. In his last interview before the conflict, as we have seen, he attacked corruption in the state and the subjection of the Army and of foreign policy to party considerations.[6] During the fighting, perhaps in a bid for left-wing support, he stated, 'There cannot be too much injustice in a state towards those who labour for others, there cannot be too much dishonesty in a state—if it does not want to destroy itself.'[7] Yet he was not eager for active military support from the Left as long as there was no serious deterioration in the situation. This was in part the result of his disillusionment with the P.P.S.'s spinelessness, as he saw it,

---

[1] *Dokumenty chwili*, i. 26.   [2] Arski, op. cit., pp. 430–1.
[3] Ibid., p. 431.   [4] Rataj, op. cit., p. 369.
[5] The official municipal estimate was 371 killed and 918 wounded: *Kronika Warszawy*, 11, no. 5 (May 1926), pp. 88–90. W. Górnicki, 'Ostatni rokosz w Warszawie', *Świat*, 13 May 1956, p. 8, estimates the number of killed at 840–60 and the wounded at 1,500.
[6] See above, pp. 156–7.   [7] Piłsudski, *P.Z.* ix. 9.

after Narutowicz's assassination and the Cracow riots, as well as his fear of fomenting a revolution. Although he had encouraged the formation of workers' militia units, he had been very unwilling to make use of them during the fighting, giving them outdated or non-functioning weapons, or even no weapons at all.[1] 'The Army', he stated, 'will stop shooting at my command. I do not know if civilians will stop.'[2]

The series of press interviews he gave after the coup did not greatly clarify his intentions.[3] He declared himself against dictatorship. In Poland, he claimed, people were too ready to load all responsibility upon one individual. Moreover, Poles could not be ruled 'with a whip'.[4] He prided himself on the return to legality: 'I have accomplished something unique in history . . . I have made a sort of revolution without any revolutionary consequences.'[5] However, although constitutional form was re-established, the return to the 1921 Constitution was not complete. Piłsudski called on parliament to reform itself, threatening that if it did not do so, 'I will not hesitate to fulfil my obligation.'[6]

As regards positive political aims, he declared grandly, 'My programme is the diminution of robbery and the pursuit of the path of honesty.'[7] When asked why he had moved against the Government, he replied that he had been particularly revolted by 'the absolute impunity with which all financial irregularities were committed in the state' and by the state's ever increasing subjection to nouveaux-riches.[8] He linked the widely prevalent corruption with the legal immunity of deputies.

The views he expressed on politics were also vague. A strong government was needed in Poland to unite, after 130 years, the different partitions. Neither the Government nor the President was sufficiently powerful. The Sejm and Senate had too many rights. Their continual intervention hampered the smooth functioning

---

[1] See Pragier, op. cit., pp. 322–4; Pobóg-Malinowski, op. cit., p. 482.
[2] Ibid.
[3] For these interviews, see Piłsudski, *P.Z.* ix. 11–29.
[4] Piłsudski, 'Wywiad z korespondentem "Le Matin" (25.V.26)', *P.Z.* ix. 22.
[5] Piłsudski, 'Wywiad ogłoszony w "Kurierze Porannym" z dnia 25 maja 1926 r.', *P.Z.* ix. 18.
[6] Piłsudski, 'Wywiad korespondenta "Le Matin" u Piłsudskiego w Sulejówku (23.V.26)', *P.Z.* ix. 13.
[7] Piłsudski, 'Przemówienie do przedstawicieli stronnictw sejmowych (29.V.26)', *P.Z.* ix. 33.
[8] Piłsudski, 'Wywiad ogłoszony w "Kurierze Porannym" . . .', *P.Z.* ix. 14.

of the Government. He also attacked excessive party spirit and the multiplicity of parties. Stressing again his independence of the Left-Wing parties, he stated 'Personally, I have not wanted to be a member of the Polish Right or the Polish Left.'[1] If 'Left' and 'Right' referred to social positions, Poland, according to Piłsudski, was too poor at present to embark upon social experiments. Politically speaking, the Right in Poland, unlike the Right elsewhere, was, he claimed, an opponent of a strong executive and had displayed anarchic tendencies, for example in the agitation which had led to the assassination of President Narutowicz.

The new Cabinet created by Bartel had no clear political tendency either. Piłsudski took the position of Minister of War. Of the other ministers one, Młodzianowski, the Minister of the Interior, was a former legionary officer and Governor of Polesia. Four were non-party specialists and five were senior civil servants.[2] 'The Government which has been created . . . and the revolution which has been accomplished have nothing in common', charged *Robotnik* on 16 May.

For the moment, however, the parties of the non-Communist Left were prepared to stifle their misgivings about Piłsudski's statements. They were all intensely relieved by the overthrow of the Witos Government, which they had regarded as a direct threat to themselves, and refused to believe that the Marshal was not basically in agreement with their views. They continued to hope that the coup would mean the initiation of new and radical social and economic policies. On 20 May, therefore, the Left bloc (the P.P.S., the Liberation, the Peasant Party, and the Party of Labour) issued a declaration calling for the election of Piłsudski as President and for the dissolution of parliament 'as an indispensable condition for the reform of public life in Poland'.[3]

The individual parties of the bloc also stressed their belief that the coup would lead to a turn to the Left. Meeting on 15 May, the central committee of the P.P.S., in spite of its irritation at not having been consulted before the coup, welcomed Piłsudski's return to power and called for the dissolution of parliament and the Marshal's election as President. It called for the formation of

---

[1] Piłsudski, 'Wywiad ogłoszony w "Kurierze Porannym" z dnia 27 Maja 1926 r.', *P.Z.* ix. 24.
[2] Roos, 'Die polnischen Regierungen, 1916–39', *O.E.H.P.*, p. 677.
[3] *Kurjer Poranny*, 21 May 1926.

a worker–peasant government, without the participation of those groups which had made up the Witos Cabinet. It also advocated a new policy towards the minorities and the punishment of corruption among politicians.[1] The party continued throughout May to campaign vigorously for Piłsudski's election as President, although many leaders of the party were becoming increasingly unhappy about Piłsudski's calls for strengthening the executive and uneasy about the actions of the Government. 'The statements and first actions of our new rulers', wrote *Robotnik* plaintively on 30 May, 'lead one to fear that they do not see, or do not want to see, the consequences which the coup should bring.'

Demands for the adoption of radical policies were also urged by the Liberation and the Peasant Party.[1] Of the parties of the Left bloc, only the Club of Labour, most strongly under Piłsudski-ite influence, failed to formulate definite demands. The illusion that Piłsudski was about to initiate a social revolution was even shared by the Communist Party, which supported the coup, because it regarded the formation of the Centre–Right Government as the first stage of a Fascist takeover. Piłsudski, it was argued, was the representative of the Polish petit-bourgeoisie, in revolt against the main spokesman for the Polish ruling classes, the Endecja. A new Leftist leadership of Julian Leński, Leon Purman, and Henryk Stein had replaced Warski and Kostrzewa, who had been accused by Stalin at the Fifth Comintern Conference in 1924 of excessively favouring Trotsky. However, this new leadership also fell into disfavour with Moscow for initiatives in the international field, and Warski again took over in mid-1925. Extreme Leftism and terrorism were abandoned.[2] Though some members of the party were apprehensive of the danger of a Piłsudski-ite dictatorship, the party feared much more a possible Fascist coup by the Right. It thus supported Piłsudski in the armed clash, and even offered to form a militia. By the end of May, after Piłsudski's unequivocal refusal to accept any Communist aid, and under strong criticism from Stalin for its position, the party moved into somewhat reluctant opposition. Nevertheless, complete rejection of the 'May error' did not come until later in 1926.[3]

---

[1] *Dokumenty chwili*, i. 30.

[2] For these developments, see Dziewanowski, op. cit., pp. 105–19; Reguła, op. cit., pp. 89–169. For the modern Communist view, see Kowalski, *Zarys historii polskiego ruchu robotniczego*, chap. ii, pp. 250–339.

[3] The consequences of the 'May error' hung heavily over the life of the party

If Piłsudski's interviews did not expose the illusory nature of hopes for radical reform after the coup, the demands put forward by the radical Piłsudski-ites made clear the unlikelihood of the Government's initiating Leftist policies. On 15 May, a group of twelve organizations including the Riflemen's Union and the Union of Polish Youth appealed to the Marshal to 'dissolve parliament immediately, take supreme power yourself and establish new constitutional principles which will separate the executive and legislature and increase the powers of the head of state'.[1] The Piłsudski-ites placed great stress upon the campaign against corruption and founded an occasional paper, *Nakazy Chwili*, edited by Adam Skwarczyński, devoted to advancing the cause. The first issue of 22 May contained a list of senior officials accused of theft, corruption, or incompetence. It included the most prominent members of the Witos Cabinet as well as Stanisław Karpiński, the President of the Bank of Poland, Jan Żarnowski, head of the Main Auditing Office, and Jan Kanty-Steczkowski, President of the Bank of National Economy.[2]

The national minorities were, for the most part, sympathetic to the coup, regarding Piłsudski as a lesser evil than the National Democrats. But at the same time, with a caution bred of previous disappointments, they adopted an attitude of reserve. The White Russian, Ukrainian, and German Clubs decided only at the last minute to vote for Piłsudski if he stood for President. The Jews, relieved at the overthrow of a nationalist and potentially anti-Semitic Cabinet, were more open in their support. Already on 27 May, the Jewish Club, after a day of deliberations, voted to support Piłsudski's candidacy.[3]

The attitude of the parties of the Centre and Right to the coup was not as hostile as might have been expected. They shared the almost universal relief that the civil war had not lasted long enough to tempt either Russia or Germany to intervene. They realized too that they had underestimated Piłsudski, that they had gambled and lost, and that for the moment there was no possibility of

---

in the years following. See Dziewanowski, op. cit., pp. 121–54; Reguła, op. cit., pp. 169–288.

[1] Quoted in *Głos Prawdy*, 20 May 1926.

[2] *Nakazy Chwili*, 22 May 1926. The former were placed on a blacklist, while the latter who were regarded as slightly less culpable, were named in a 'grey list'.

[3] *Nasz Przegląd*, 28 May 1926.

overthrowing the new Government. There were even many, particularly in the Centre parties, who, partly out of opportunism and
partly in the belief that he could provide a better alternative than
the existing parliamentary system, hoped to come to terms with
Piłsudski. Most seriously divided was the Piast. Many members of
the party had opposed formation of a Cabinet by Witos, and at a
meeting of thirty-two Piast senators and deputies in Cracow on
18 May, there was serious disagreement over what course of action
should be adopted; the resolutions passed avoided any clear statement about the new Government.[1] The party split three ways.
The pro-Piłsudski-ites were led by Jan Dębski, while the anti-
Piłsudski-ites included Władysław Kiernik and Alfons Erdman.
In addition, there was a large group of neutrals. In its discussions
over the election of the new President, the party failed to reach a
decision, but the communiqué issued on 31 May stated that 'the
Club of the Piast party, placing the interest of the state above that
of parties, has decided not to oppose the candidacy of Marshal
Piłsudski'.[2] In fact Witos himself did not oppose Piłsudski's
candidacy, regarding it as the logical consequence of the coup.

The National Workers' Party (N.P.R.) was also seriously divided.
In Warsaw and former Prussian Poland its organizations strongly
condemned the coup. However, elsewhere, particularly in Lodz,
there was much support for Piłsudski among its members. The
anti-Piłsudski line of the party was harshly criticized by Ludwik
Waszkiewicz, a former president of the Parliamentary Club, and
Antoni Ciszak, who founded a new weekly, *Nowa Sprawa Robotnicza*,
to advance their views.[3]

On the Right there was also considerable support for Piłsudski.
He had, after all, shown himself victorious, and too strong an
opposition might have unpleasant consequences. People were still
being arrested (though most were soon released), and newspaper
censorship was in full operation. Moreover, to many on the Right,
Piłsudski seemed a more attractive alternative than Communism,
whose strength was believed to have increased greatly as a result
of the coup. In an article headed 'Red Prelude', *Kurjer Warszawski*

---

[1] *Czas*, 20 and 21 May 1926. See also *Głos Prawdy*, 20, 23, and 27 May
1926.
[2] *Kurjer Poranny*, 31 May 1926.
[3] *Głos Prawdy*, 20, 23, and 27 May 1926; *Nowa Sprawa Robotnicza* proved
somewhat ephemeral, however, and ceased publication at the end of August.

affirmed 'One cannot say of the Communists in Poland that they have let pass this suitable opportunity for increasing their agitation. On the contrary, they have exploited it in every direction and let loose a mass of pamphlets on the country . . .'[1] These sentiments were strongest among the conservatives. Already on 17 May Mackiewicz, writing in *Słowo* in Wilno, had called on Piłsudski to be the 'Polish Bonaparte',[2] and by the end of the month, *Czas* was also calling for Piłsudski's election. The Piłsudski-ites took considerable pains to reassure conservative opinion.[3] An article in *Nowy Kurjer Polski* on 26 May stressed the Government's opposition to 'revolutionary agrarian slogans'.[4] A well-known Piłsudski-ite lawyer, Franciszek Paschalski, wrote in *Kurjer Poranny* on the 26th that Piłsudski had made his coup 'not in the name of a social programme, but in the name of public morality'.[5]

The strongest opposition to the coup came from the parties of the Christian Alliance for National Unity. Outside former Prussian Poland, however, this opposition was largely verbal. The executive of the Popular National Union resolved on the 15th that it would take no part in the formation of a provisional government, and it campaigned for holding outside Warsaw the meeting of the National Assembly at which the President was to be elected.[6] Nevertheless, only with difficulty did it manage to hold its allies in line. Both the Christian Democrats and the Christian National party condemned the coup, but both, particularly the Christian Nationals, were determined not to adopt a position of intransigent opposition. It was only after long-drawn-out discussion and bitter conflict that the three parties agreed on the night of 30–1 May to nominate Adolf Bniński, Governor of Poznania, as their presidential candidate.[7]

In western Poland the situation was different.[8] It was to this

---

[1] *Kurjer Warszawski*, 29 May 1926. [2] *Słowo*, 17 May 1926.
[3] See, for example, the articles in *Kurjer Poranny* on 27, 29, and 31 May 1926.
[4] *Nowy Kurjer Polski*, 28 May 1926.
[5] *Kurjer Poranny*, 26 May 1926. [6] *Dokumenty chwili*, i. 31.
[7] *Kurjer Poranny*, 31 May 1926.
[8] For the situation here see: A. Czubiński, 'Wielkopolska i Pomorze wobec zamachu stanu w maju 1926 r.', *Studia i materiały do dziejów Wielkopolski i Pomorza*, vi, no. 1 (1960), pp. 153–207; R. Wapiński, *Działalność Narodowej Partii Robotniczej na terenie województwa pomorskiego w latach 1920–30* (Gdańsk, 1962), and 'Działalność Narodowej Demokracji na Pomorzu Gdańskim w latach 1920–26', *Zapiski Historyczne*, xxix, no. 1 (1964), pp. 7–37.

strongly nationalist and National-Democratic region that those members of the Government who wanted to continue the struggle had intended to retreat. The area was the richest in Poland, and considered itself far superior to the rest of the country whose development, it believed, had suffered harmful effects from Austrian and Russian rule. Hostility to the coup was extremely strong here. On 15 May *Kurjer Poznański* wrote:

All of Western Poland persists and will persist inflexibly in the belief that there has been a rebellion against the legal authorities. He who has provoked this is and will remain a rebel, with whom the country will never have anything in common. For us he has ceased to be a Pole.[1]

The reaction was most violent in Poznania. Here the Governor, Bniński, proclaimed a state of siege on the 15th, and the students of the university formed a Legion of Volunteers to march on the capital. On the 16th a group of forty deputies, mainly from Poznania, met at the house of the National Democratic deputy Leon Pluciński. They issued a declaration demanding that the election of the President be held outside Warsaw, and declaring that the rest of the country was under no obligation to obey orders from the capital.[2] While the extremists called for the resumption of military action, the moderates demanded some form of autonomy for Poznania.

In Pomerania, a state of siege was also announced, and the provincial authorities refused to re-establish telephone and telegraph links with Warsaw. In Silesia the reaction was rather weaker, both because of the autonomy which the province enjoyed and because Piłsudski-ite and socialist organizations were stronger. However, on 17 May a group of fourteen deputies, led by Korfanty, issued a declaration threatening action if all political prisoners were not released.[3]

The Government was understandably worried by the situation. On 16 May Bartel conferred with Trąmpczyński, the Senate Marshal, who was a National Democrat from Poznania. Trąmpczyński agreed to go to the western areas in order to restore calm. He also hoped to use the strong support the Right enjoyed there as a bargaining point with the Government. At first his efforts at pacification had no real success. On 20 May an 'Organization for the Defence of the State' was created in Poznania which held that

---

[1] *Kurjer Poznański*, 15 May 1926.
[2] Ibid., 17 May 1926.   [3] *Dokumenty chwili*, ii. 20.

western Poland should be the base from which social revolution would be crushed. Similar organizations were set up in Pomerania and Upper Silesia. Nevertheless, the proclamation which Trąmp-czyński issued on the 20th did have some effect.[1] He strongly deprecated violent action and called on Poznania to submit to the provincial (though not the national) authorities. Although the situation still remained tense, too many rash threats had been made, and people were tired of words without action. In spite of their statements, all the deputies from the western regions took part in the National Assembly.

The first stage in the further entrenchment of Piłsudski's hold on power was the election of a new President which was to take place on 31 May. Rataj failed to respond to right-wing demands, and agreed to convene the National Assembly in Warsaw, holding that this 'would testify to the outside world and to the country that the situation had returned to normal'.[2] Piłsudski intended to stand for President so that by his election the coup could be given the final stamp of legality, but he had no intention of assuming the office, which he regarded as far too limited in power. All his statements on the subject were deliberately vague, so as not to arouse suspicion. He devoted much time to seeking a suitable candidate actually to serve as President. First he approached two conservatives, Zdzisław Lubomirski and Marian Zdziechowski, both of whom refused.[3] So did Artur Śliwiński, a dedicated follower of the Marshal who had been Prime Minister for a short time in 1922. When, just after Piłsudski's election, Bartel suggested Ignacy Mościcki, an eminent chemist who had been an obscure member of the P.P.S. before 1914, the Marshal agreed, confident (correctly, as it proved) that Mościcki would remain completely subservient to him.

Two days before the election, Piłsudski spoke to a group of Left and Centre deputies. The election was free, he assured them, but no party agreements should be made. His speech was full of implied threats. 'Things have so turned out', he said, 'that I need not have let you into the National Assembly, and could have mocked you all. But I want to see if one can still rule Poland without the whip.'[4]

[1] The text is quoted in *Kurjer Poranny*, 21 May 1926.
[2] *Robotnik*, 22 May 1926.
[3] Morawski, *Tamten brzeg*, p. 159.
[4] Piłsudski, 'Przemówienie do przedstawicieli stronnictw sejmowych (29.V. 1926)', *P.Z.* ix. 32.

He was elected on the first ballot by 292 votes to 193 for Bniński, the candidate of the Right, and 61 blank votes. The Left, most of the Piast, some Christian Democrats, the Jews, and the Germans voted for the Marshal. The Slav minorities abstained. Immediately after the election Piłsudski wrote to Rataj declining to take office. He claimed that his personality was not suited to it, and charged that there were still many in parliament responsible for Narutowicz's death.[1]

The new election took place on 1 June. The P.P.S., angered by Piłsudski's duplicity, nominated their own candidate, Marek, and the 56 votes he won made a second ballot necessary. This time Mościcki was elected by 281 votes to 200 for Bniński and 63 abstentions.

Piłsudski decided for the moment against the dissolution of parliament, a step which had been urged by the Left and even by Bartel himself.[2] He believed that the present Sejm would prove sufficiently accommodating for the needs of the Government. An election would delay the return of calm to the country and would in all probability result in a strongly left-wing parliament, filled with a consciousness of its own rights and demanding radical change. When Baranowski asked Piłsudski in June whether there would be new elections, he replied: 'What I have before me I know, and I know what I can depend on. It is not clear what tomorrow will bring, so I will not hurry . . . Moreover, at present they vote as I like, resolve as I command, because they are afraid.'[3]

After Mościcki's election Bartel resigned, as had been agreed. He was asked by the President, after discussions with Piłsudski, again to form a Government, and after three days' reflection he consented. Although the new Cabinet, finally constituted in the second half of June, included six new ministers, the composition differed little from that of its predecessor. Piłsudski again held the portfolio of Minister of War and Młodzianowski that of the Interior. The rest of the posts were held in almost equal numbers by senior civil servants and non-party specialists.[4] Bartel tried in vain to placate the Left by inviting Juliusz Poniatowski of the

[1] Piłsudski, 'Pismo do Marszałka Sejmu o nieprzyjęciu wyboru do prezydenta Rzeczypospolitej 31.V.26.', *P.Z.* ix. 33–4.

[2] See, for example, the report of his press conference of 24 May 1926 in *Nowy Kurjer Polski*, 25 May 1926.

[3] W. Baranowski, *Rozmowy z Piłsudskim* (Warsaw, 1938), p. 198.

[4] Roos, 'Die polnischen Regierungen 1916–39', *O.E.H.P.*, p. 677.

Liberation and Moraczewski of the P.P.S. to take office; both refused. His approaches to the Right, in particular his offer of the Foreign Ministry to the former Activist, Prince Janusz Radziwiłł, were also unsuccessful. He did succeed in inducing the Christian Democrat Paweł Romocki to take the Railway Ministry, but in order to accept, Romocki was forced to leave the party.

Having elected a President and created a suitable Government, Piłsudski now determined on a number of constitutional changes in order to remedy what he regarded as the worst defects of the 1921 Constitution. These were discussed by the Cabinet on 9 June,[1] and on the 16th a draft bill was placed before the Sejm. It limited the period during which parliament had to be in session to four months. If the budget were not voted during that period the Government's proposed budget would be adopted automatically. The President was given the right to dissolve parliament if the Council of Ministers so resolved. New elections had to be held in 120 days (instead of 90). The President was given a thirty-day suspensive veto over legislation. He was also granted the power to issue proclamations with the force of law when parliament was not sitting and, until the end of 1927, also when parliament was sitting.[2] As a justification for these proposals, Wacław Makowski, the Minister of Justice, informed the Cabinet: 'The . . . law has as its goal the satisfaction of the most pressing needs, the necessity of which has become evident in the years since the adoption of the Constitution of 17 March 1921.'[3]

The Centre and Right for the most part responded favourably. They had frequently demanded such changes and now felt that 'If a coup had been made in May and blood spilt, at least Poland should gain from it, and obtain a good constitution.'[4] They were also prepared for the moment to see what the Government could do. At the same time they took advantage of the opportunity to put forward a number of constitutional proposals of their own which differed from the Government's mainly in demanding a modification of the electoral system.[5] The Left was divided. Both the

---

[1] A.A.N., Zespół Prezydium Rady Ministrów, Protokóły posiedzeń Rady Ministrów, 9 June 1926, item 3. (These minutes are cited below as P.P.R.M.)

[2] The Government's proposal is appended to P.P.R.M., 16 June 1926, as 'Załącznik 20 do nr. 23'.

[3] P.P.R.M., 3 July 1926, Załącznik 1.

[4] Rataj's paraphrase of their views, Rataj, op. cit., p. 376.

[5] These are appended to P.P.R.M., 3 July 1926.

Peasant Party and the Liberation were, with some reservations, favourable to the Government's initiative. The P.P.S. was not. In two strongly worded articles in *Robotnik*, 'Towards Omnipotence for the Government' and 'The Argument of the Whip',[1] Daszyński criticized the proposed changes. In the parliamentary debate he declared, 'Instead of one evil, omnipotence for parliament, we do not want to introduce another, omnipotence for the Government.'[2]

On its third reading on 22 July the bill, somewhat modified by the Sejm Constitutional Committee, was finally approved by 246 votes to 95, thus achieving the two-thirds majority required. The Popular National Union, Christian Nationalists, Christian Democrats, Piast, N.P.R., Club of Labour, and the Peasant Party voted for the Government. The P.P.S., the Communists, and the Slav minorities voted against. The rest abstained. After the Senate's modifications had been rejected, the changes to the constitution were finally adopted on 2 August.

As adopted, the proposals were in two parts. The first, which was not a constitutional amendment, was the law conferring on the President the power to issue decrees with the force of law until the dissolution of the parliament then sitting.[3] The Government thus gained greater freedom of action, since decrees could be used to bring laws into harmony with the constitution and to implement its provisions, to reorganize and modify the administration of the state, to regulate the exercising of justice, and to deal with social and economic matters.[4] Specifically excluded were those matters which, according to the constitution, required legislation, such as the voting of the budget, the size of the Army, the parliamentary control of state debts, the declaration of war, and the constitutional responsibility of ministers. In addition, decrees could not be used to impose new taxes, create new monopolies, materially increase tariffs, or to modify the electoral system, provincial boundaries, provincial autonomy, school and language laws, or the marriage laws.[5]

The constitutional modifications differed little from the Cabinet proposals.[6] The period for which parliament had to sit was

---

[1] *Robotnik*, 18 and 19 June 1926.   [2] *S.S.S.R.*, 5 July 1926, col. 34.

[3] 'Ustawa z dnia 2 sierpnia 1926r. o upoważnieniu Prezydenta Rzeczypospolitej do wydawania rozporządzeń z mocą ustaw', *Dz.U.R.P.* (1926), no. 78, p. 880.   [4] Ibid., Article 1, p. 880.   [5] Ibid., Article 2, p. 880.

[6] 'Ustawa z dnia 2 sierpnia 1926 r. zmieniająca i uzupełniająca Konstytucję Rzeczypospolitej z dnia 17 marca 1921 r.', *Dz.U.R.P.* (1926), no. 78, pp. 877–9.

extended to five months. If the Sejm did not vote a budget in this period, the Senate proposal would be adopted. If neither house voted a budget, the Government's proposal was to have the force of law. However, this provision was not to be applied if parliament had already rejected the Government's proposal as a whole. No alternative provision was made should such a situation arise, except that the budget of the previous year could be applied if parliament was dissolved.[1] The President could dissolve parliament, but he had to give cause, and parliament could not be dissolved twice for the same reason. The period between a dissolution and new elections was again laid down as ninety days.[2] In revising the Senate's modifications, the Sejm discarded the existing constitutional provision which enabled the Lower House to dissolve itself by a two-thirds vote. The suspensive veto of the President was abandoned. He had, however, the right to issue decrees with the force of law when parliament was not in session. These had to be presented to the Sejm within fifteen days of its reassembling.[3] Finally, provision was made for depriving a deputy of his seat if he misused his position for financial gain.[4] While these changes strengthened the power of the executive, they did not, formally at least, amount to an abandonment of the liberal democratic character of the constitution.

At the same time, the Government strengthened its control over the civil service and the Army. On 16 May the Cabinet minutes record:

> The question of changes and displacements in personnel was discussed. The Government is opposed to tendencies to make a party reckoning. The necessity of removing people who do not possess the required ethical or technical qualifications was recognized.[5]

In fact, the changes made were not as radical as might have been expected, although the most irreconcilable opponents of Sanacja, as the Government styled itself,[6] did lose their positions, as did some who had been blatantly guilty of improper practices. On 19 May the Prime Minister sent a circular to all ministerial departments demanding a list of administrative civil servants who sat on

[1] Ibid., Articles 1, 3, pp. 877–8.   [2] Ibid., Article 4, p. 878.
[3] Ibid., Article 5, p. 879.   [4] Ibid., Article 2, p. 877.
[5] *P.P.R.M.*, 16 May 1926, item 4.
[6] 'Sanacja' is rather difficult to translate—it means something between 'purification' and 'reform', and was chosen in order to indicate the Government's desire to clear away the negative features of the pre-1926 political system.

the governing bodies of financial organizations so as to facilitate the investigation of financial abuses.[1] On the 27th Korfanty was suspended as President of the Bank of Silesia, and a government communiqué claimed that he had misappropriated the bank's funds for his personal use.[2] The President of the Polish Mutual Assurance Company was also suspended and the entire supervisory council of the Agricultural Bank dismissed. The senior civil service was reorganized as well. The personnel of the Presidential Chancery was changed. The staff of the Prime Minister's Office was modified and the Under-Secretary, Władysław Studziński, was replaced. In the Foreign Service, Stanisław Kozicki, the Ambassador to Italy, who was alleged to have asked Mussolini to intervene on Witos's behalf, was withdrawn, as was Franciszek Sokal, the Polish Delegate to the League of Nations. Kajetan Morawski, the Under-Secretary of Foreign Affairs, resigned.

There were many changes in other departments too. The most important were the suspensions of Klemens Olpiński, the Under-Secretary of the Ministry of the Interior, Mieczysław Rybczyński, Under-Secretary and Head of the Department of Public Works, and Stanisław Kauzik of the Ministry of Finance.

The provincial governorships were also reviewed and new appointments made. Władysław Raczkiewicz took over as Governor of the Wilno province, and the Governors of the Lublin province and Polesia were suspended. In August, the radical Piłsudski-ite Michał Grażyński was placed in charge of Silesia, while in October, General Młodzianowski became Governor of Pomerania.

On 19 May, Piłsudski had set up a 'Committee of Liquidation' for the Army, headed by General Żeligowski, to 'assign all appointments, bearing in mind the latest changes caused by recent events'.[3] The officers who had been arrested after the coup were soon released, with the exception of Rozwadowski, Zagórski, Jaźwiński, and Żymierski. But the strongest opponents of the Marshal were quickly weeded out of the army. The rank of General Inspector was abolished, affecting four generals, Rozwadowski, Józef Haller, Osiński, and Majewski. General Gruber was replaced as head of the Department of Military Justice at the Ministry of War by

[1] *Nowy Kurjer Polski*, 19 May 1926.

[2] *Robotnik*, 28 May 1926. The other changes in the civil service have been taken from the contemporary press, in particular *Czas*, *Robotnik*, and *Nowy Kurjer Polski*.

[3] Ibid., 20 May 1926.

General Józef Daniec. General Kukiel, head of the Historical Department, and his adjutant received indefinite leave. General Burhardt-Bukacki became Chief of the General Staff, which was thoroughly reorganized. General Rozen replaced Colonel Wieroński as head of the Police, Colonel Dreszer took over the command of the Central Cavalry School from Colonel Przeździecki, while command of the Cadet Corps at Modlin was conferred on Lieutenant-Colonel Trzebuń in place of Colonel Wiśnicki. General Mieczysław Kuliński, Commander of the 5th Corps in Cracow, was replaced by General Stanisław Wróblewski, who had proved invaluable to the Piłsudski-ites at Częstochowa. General Józef Haller and General Szeptycki both resigned, while General Pik, President of the Military Supreme Court was suspended. Colonel Rayski again took command of the Air Force. Sikorski was for the moment left in command of the Lwów military region, although he was forced to accept a Piłsudski-ite, Adam Koc, as his Chief of Staff.

Piłsudski was thus in a very strong position. He was in secure control of the Army and the civil service. He had obtained far-reaching powers for his Government. Moreover the Right, though hostile, did not feel strong enough to challenge him. It could no longer count on its alliance with the Centre. Even in western Poland the Government felt sufficiently secure to end the state of emergency there on 16 June.[1] The Left was still basically favourable to the Marshal. Even the P.P.S., for all its opposition to the constitutional changes, was not prepared to challenge Piłsudski. The new Cabinet could now attempt to deal with those problems which had proved too much for the Governments before the coup. 'The Government', wrote Bronisław Miedziński in *Głos Prawdy* on 4 August,

has before it a month and a half of free time during which it will not need to co-operate with the Sejm or enter into communication with it. The special powers, limited it is true, but corresponding as a whole to what the Government vigorously demanded, have been granted. The country, which has till now focussed its attention on the process of the struggle of the Government with the Sejm to obtain freedom of manœuvre, now shifts its gaze, full of expectation, to the Presidential Palace and the Palace of the Cabinet.[2]

[1] P.P.R.M., 16.VI.26, item 14.
[2] *Głos Prawdy* became a daily newspaper after the May coup.

V

'A GOVERNMENT OF LABOUR'

And now what! What does Mr. Piłsudski want to do? . . .
With what idea has he come? What is his programme?
Kurjer Poznański, 18 May 1926

The Government understands that it is not enough today
to maintain legal order provisionally. It is further necessary
to raise public life to a level of morality which will be the
measure of the internal regeneration and recovery of the
Republic. This moral regeneration, this development of
the Republic, through respect for law and social justice
and by the elimination of all party and individual egoism,
the Government considers, not only its future function, but
also its present task.
Kazimierz Bartel, 16 May 1926

WITH the election of Mościcki as President, the enactment of the
modifications to the constitution and the purges of the Army and
civil service, Piłsudski had securely entrenched himself in power.
His regime differed from many of the other authoritarian regimes
established in Europe in the inter-war period in that he had taken
office with no definite political programme and had no organized
party to support him. Moreover, he had no clear views on how
the internal affairs of the state should be managed, apart from
a strong dislike of the 1921 constitution and of the way in which
it had functioned under the control of the political parties.
Furthermore, although he had come to power as a result of the
support he enjoyed in the Army, he was most concerned after
1926 to keep the military out of politics and in this, at least in
the first years of his regime, he largely succeeded. He did not
envisage, in the aftermath of his taking power, any radical departures in either domestic or foreign policy. The first few years of
the new Government were characterized by an attempt to work
within the framework of the modified constitution and, at the
same time, to create a body of support for the regime. Both these
aims were to prove increasingly difficult to pursue as opposition

built up in parliament but for the moment, by dealing effectively with a number of thorny problems in the economic sphere, in relation to the national minorities and in foreign policy, the Government seemed to enjoy considerable success.

THE NEW GOVERNMENT

The style of the new Government in its first two years in office was set by Kazimierz Bartel, a self-educated locksmith who had become Professor of Mathematics at the Lwów Polytechnic. Bartel had not been a member either of the Legions or of the P.O.W. and had not, indeed, been closely linked with the Piłsudski-ites at all. He enlisted in the Polish Army in 1918, rose to the rank of colonel, and held the post of Minister of Railways in several governments in 1919 and 1920. A member of the Liberation, he was elected to the Sejm in 1922, but broke with the party when, in March 1925, it decided in favour of the uncompensated expropriation of large estates. He then created the radical six-man Party of Labour, one of whose members was Thugutt, at odds with the Liberation since 1924 because of his decision to join the Grabski Government. In addition, Bartel was reputed to be a member of an anti-Endecja masonic organization, which also included Thugutt, Śmiarowski, Raczkiewicz, and Patek, all of whom had been to some degree sympathetic to Piłsudski during World War I.[1] He held the premiership until he was replaced by Piłsudski at the beginning of October 1926, and from then until June 1928 was Deputy Premier. After this he became Prime Minister again, and held the office until April 1929. Piłsudski reserved for himself control over the Army and questions of foreign policy, but during this period most of the day-to-day running of the Government was left to Bartel. The Marshal had already gathered around him his inner group of advisers, which was to become more important as the political situation deteriorated. It included such men as Józef Beck, Bogusław Miedziński, Walery Sławek, Kazimierz Świtalski, Adam Koc, Aleksander Prystor, and Janusz and Wacław Jędrzejewicz. Many of them were already attached to Ministries as 'advisers', or held specific positions in them.[2]

[1] Ajnenkiel, Od 'rządów ludowych', p. 220.
[2] See Rataj, op. cit., p. 416.

They had all been active in the Legions and the P.O.W., and they all shared an absolute faith in the political wisdom of the Marshal. To them he was still the commander of legionary days, to whom unquestioning allegiance was owed, and whose decisions were not to be questioned. Of his immediate entourage, Piłsudski could speak as an equal only with Sławek, one of his oldest political collaborators who had been a leading member of the Military Organization of the P.P.S. between 1905 and 1908. The rest were his 'boys' (*chłopcy*), and he was to them more like a stern and omniscient father than a political leader. They were all strongly élitist in their views, believing that Polish society had been corrupted by the period of enslavement by the partitioning powers and that only they had raised the banner of independence in 1914. The bitter experience of their isolation and political weakness both before and during the war deeply coloured their political outlook. Not all of them, moreover, were capable of carrying out the tasks with which they were entrusted.

However, for the moment, as is abundantly clear from the Cabinet minutes, their influence on the conduct of domestic policy remained small and most government business went through the Cabinet. The Marshal did sometimes overrule Bartel, and force him to change his policy—in the autumn of 1926, when the Sejm voted a compromise budget in accordance with Bartel's wishes, Piłsudski insisted that the Prime Minister reject it;[1] similarly, he forced Bartel to accept, against his original intention, the renomination of two Ministers, Młodzianowski and Sujkowski, against whom the Sejm had passed a vote of no confidence in September 1926[2]—but for the most part Piłsudski gave Bartel considerable leeway. He was even prepared to allow him a certain latitude in the selection of the Cabinet: it was not until May 1930 that he insisted upon the resignation of the Minister of Industry and Commerce, Eugeniusz Kwiatkowski, of whom he had strongly disapproved.[3]

In fact Piłsudski showed little interest in the down-to-earth problems of government. Of the 92 Cabinet meetings which took place between the May coup and the elections of March 1928, he attended only 34, and of these he remained at one for only one

---

[1] Rataj, op. cit., pp. 399–402.
[2] Ibid., pp. 403–4.   [3] Rothschild, op. cit., p. 218.

item.[1] Moreover, we have the testimony of Wacław Grzybowski, head of the Prime Minister's Office at this time, that Bartel remained as fully in command in the period in which he was Vice Premier as he had been when he held the premiership.[2] Indeed, Piłsudski, as Prime Minister between October 1926 and March 1928, attended only 19 out of 59 Cabinet meetings.[3]

Piłsudski was well aware of the differences between his political technique and that of Bartel. He was prepared to wait and see whether Bartel could govern together with parliament. 'I am showing my intention of still maintaining what is called parliamentarianism', he told Baranowski at the end of August 1926:

It is the basis of democracy, for which there is always place in Poland, even directly in governing. I have given proof of this in forcibly keeping Bartel, whose colour and character you know, and who would like soon to resign because of his kidney complaint, which causes him continual pain. But I am determined on a final showdown, and of a brutal type, if they [the Deputies] want to return to their former habits.[3]

Bartel made his own political position clear in two speeches, one in the Sejm on 19 July and the other in the Senate on 30 July, outlining the policy of his Government.[4] He went out of his way to reassure the Deputies, particularly those of the Centre and Left, about the character of the 'blank cheque' they were signing in adopting the constitutional reforms demanded by the Government. He maintained that his Government was a 'Government of Labour', which needed wide powers in order to deal with the financial crisis and to reform the state administration. The Cabinet was planning no 'doctrinaire experiments in social or economic matters',[5] but did intend its measures to be effective. 'To govern', stated Bartel, 'is to implement'.[6] He felt that the new Government would be able to bring in a far-reaching programme of reforms because it was not paralysed by party divisions: 'In the present Government the ministries do not constitute either "allied sovereign states" or, even more, hostile and enemy states.'[7]

[1] P.P.R.M., meetings of 1926, 1927, and 1928.
[2] Grzybowski, op. cit., pp. 110–11.
[3] Baranowski, op. cit., pp. 205–6.
[4] For the Sejm speech, see *S.S.S.R.*, 19 July 1926, cols. 13–31; for the Senate speech, see *S.S.Se.R.*, 30 July 1926, cols. 38–53.
[5] *S.S.S.R.*, 19 July 1926, col. 22.
[6] *S.S.Se.R.*, 30 July 1926, col. 39.
[7] *S.S.S.R.*, 19 July 1926, col. 18.

The Cabinet saw as its principal task the improvement of the economic situation. Its policy did not differ radically from the earlier plans: the budget was to be balanced by cutting government expenditure, and the zloty stabilized; public investment would be used to revive the economy, and the importance of the agricultural sector was stressed. In addition, Bartel proposed a number of other fairly radical reforms. The state administration was to be reorganized to make it more efficient and to render it readily accessible to all members of the population. The legal system was to be modernized, abolishing the differences in law between the various partitions, and a friendlier policy towards the national minorities would be adopted. The Prime Minister affirmed that 'The Government will not allow the just rights of citizens who are not Poles to be endangered. It holds, moreover, that hostility towards any group of citizens because of its language or belief is contrary to the spirit of Poland.'[1] In addition, the Land Reform Law was to be implemented, and servitudes were to be abolished; unemployment would be combated by extending public works; an attempt would be made to limit excessive centralization, and the provinces would not be neglected.

The two speeches were well received, particularly by the politicians of the Left and Centre,[2] perhaps because Bartel's concept of the limited role of Parliament did not emerge from them as clearly as it might have done. He did allow parliament certain functions, such as passing bills on local government and electoral reform. He was even prepared to allow parliament to pass votes of no-confidence in ministers or in policies of the Government. However, he demanded a strict separation between the executive and the legislature: the former was responsible for governing, and should not be impeded in this by the latter. He recognized that political parties had a part to play in increasing political consciousness in the country, and even in exercising some control over the activity of the Government, but felt that they should play no part in the running of the country. 'The Polish reality for which we are working', he stated in the Sejm, 'can in no measure be grasped in a party fashion.'[3] He believed, moreover, that parties had a harmful effect on the functioning of the Government, since they isolated it from expert opinion, on which he set great store. Indeed,

[1] S.S.S.R., 19 July 1926, col. 23.   [2] See, e.g., Rataj, op. cit., p. 380.
[3] S.S.S.R., 19 July 1926, col. 22.

Bartel created a number of new institutions in order to take advantage of the advice of experts. The first of these, created by decree on 12 September 1926, was the Legal Council, which was responsible to the Minister of Justice. Its function was to give expert legal advice on proposed legislation. Three bodies were established in the Prime Minister's Office. The Economic Commission was composed of representatives of industrial, trading, and banking organizations: its chairman was Andrzej Wierzbicki, President of Lewiatan. The Agricultural Commission represented large and small agricultural producers; it was headed by Jan Stecki, a prominent landowner. The Labour Commission was to represent the interests of working people, and sat under the chairmanship of the socialist Bronisław Ziemięcki. Bartel made a point of referring all proposed legislation to one or all of these councils. In this way he felt he upheld the principles of democracy, while at the same time avoiding the harmful effects of excessive dependence on the political parties. He also made considerable use of two bodies composed exclusively of full-time research workers which he had set up under the Ministry of Trade and Industry: the Institute for Investigating Economic Conditions and Prices, and the Commission of Inquiry into the Condition and Costs of Production and Exchange.[1]

The limited role which Bartel assigned to parliament is reflected in his attitude towards the right to question ministers which deputies and senators enjoyed. Before 1926 this privilege had been much abused; many members of parliament had advanced the private interests of their constituents by threatening ministers and civil servants with embarrassing questions in parliament. It was, nevertheless, a valuable and effective means of parliamentary control over the actions of the Government. Bartel considerably narrowed its scope. At the Cabinet meeting of 16 December 1926, he laid down the policy which the new Government was to follow: inquiries by clubs of deputies to governmental authorities, even when in the form of parliamentary questions, did not have to be answered, because these clubs had no legal status; inquiries by deputies or senators about the private affairs of particular individuals, when not in the form of parliamentary questions, did not have to be answered; inquiries by individual deputies or senators

---

[1] For an interesting account of the way in which Bartel conducted his Government, see Grzybowski, op. cit.

on matters of public interest, or of concern to their constituencies, should be answered, although there was no constitutional obligation to do so.[1]

Bartel greatly strengthened the position of the Prime Minister in relation to the other members of the Cabinet. Each minister, on accepting Cabinet office, had to give Bartel an undated letter of resignation. Ironically, Piłsudski himself did so. The functioning of the Cabinet was modified so that the Prime Minister alone was responsible for the agenda of Cabinet meetings; only matters of which he approved could be discussed.[2] The only person, apart from the Prime Minister, who could affect the agenda of the Cabinet was the President. Bartel agreed with Piłsudski that the rights of the President were too restricted. On 9 June 1926 the Cabinet resolved that the President could hold up the discussion of any point on the agenda until the Minister concerned had explained the situation to him. He could also demand that this matter be the subject of an *ad hoc* Cabinet meeting called in his presence.[3] However, in practice Mościcki rarely exercised these rights. From his election at the beginning of June 1926, until March 1928, he attended only three Cabinet meetings.[4]

Parliamentary questions concerning the different departments were dealt with by the Prime Minister. The exposition of the Government's programme was reserved for the Prime Minister. In exceptional cases a Minister might make a policy speech, but it had first to be cleared with the Prime Minister.[5] Bartel's authority seems to have been recognized by the Cabinet. In the nineteen months between the coup and the elections of March 1928 the records show only one occasion on which he was overruled by a majority of his ministers: this was when he opposed the dissolution of the Warsaw City Council at the Cabinet meeting of 16 May 1927.[6]

Bartel also increased the effectiveness of the premiership by reorganizing the Prime Minister's Office by decree on 25 August 1926.[7] The Office was now divided into three sections, the Prime

---

[1] P.P.R.M., 16 December 1926, item 2.
[2] For these changes, see Grzybowski, op. cit., p. 106.
[3] P.P.R.M., 9 June 1926, item 2.
[4] Ibid., meetings of 1926, 1927, and 1928.
[5] Grzybowski, op. cit., p. 106.
[6] P.P.R.M., 16 May 1927, item 34.
[7] For the decree, see Grzybowski, op. cit., p. 107.

Minister's Council, the Prime Minister's Office, and the Prime Minister's Legal Office. The head of the Council, although not responsible for the work of the other two departments, was to link and co-ordinate their activities, the Legal Office was to communicate the position of the Prime Minister to Ministries when they were drafting legislation, while the Prime Minister's Office dealt with the day-to-day business of the Premier. All three divisions were staffed with highly able people who did much to facilitate the work of government.

Bartel placed great stress on the improvement of the quality and efficiency of the administration. On 16 June the Cabinet resolved to create a Commission for the Reorganization of the Administration, composed of the Ministers of the Treasury, of Justice, Trade and Industry, Railways, and Public Works.[1] By the time it was dissolved on 26 November 1926, it had held nine meetings. Its principles for reorganizing the running of ministries had been embodied in a decree on 6 September 1926, and it had also proposed a new statute improving the functioning of the Ministry of Finance.[2]

The Cabinet also reorganized the central administration of the Ministry of Internal Affairs, and made some improvements in local government. For the moment the centralized structure of local administration remained unchanged, but the requirement that the officials of a sub-prefecture should meet regularly, under the chairmanship of the sub-prefect, and submit reports of their meetings to the Ministry of the Interior, was much more effectively implemented. Similarly, the obligation of senior provincial officials to meet periodically, with the Governor in the Chair, was more scrupulously fulfilled.[3]

On 7 March 1927 the Government set up a state Local Government Council, composed largely of representatives of local elected bodies. It was to give its opinion on the projected laws, proclamations and policy statements placed before the Cabinet by the Minister of the Interior. It was also, on its own initiative, to suggest

[1] P.P.R.M., 16 June 1926, item 3.
[2] Ibid., 26 November 1926, item 5, Appendix 4.
[3] This is clear from the reports of these meetings sent to the Ministry of the Interior. See A.A.N., Ministerstwo Spraw Wewnętrznych, Departament Organizacyjno-Prawny: 'Protokóły zebrań periodycznych kierowników władz i urzędów II instancji'; 'Protokóły zebrań periodycznych kierowników władz i urzędów I instancji'.

to the Cabinet reforms of local government and methods of implementing existing laws.[1] In addition, early in 1928 the Government issued a number of decrees designed to diminish the differences in the administrative systems of the former partitions. A start was also made on the unification of the legal system.[2]

Not all the modifications introduced by the new Government proved successful. The abolition of the Ministry of Public Works, for example, an attempt to cut down government expenditure, proved ill-advised, and the Ministry was re-established on 16 December 1926.[3] However, for the most part these reforms did give the new regime more secure control over the civil service than that achieved by any of the governments before the coup, and ensured that its policies were more effectively carried out.

At the same time, the Government steadily decreased the power of elected local bodies, assigning wide-ranging functions to the local administration instead. Increasingly, officials came to be envisaged as a local élite. At a meeting in the Wilejka district (Wilno province), the Sub-Prefect defined the function of a civil servant, apart from his administrative work, as a double one: that of an educator and an advisor.[4] In return, the state demanded far-reaching loyalty from the civil service. The minutes of a meeting of officials of the district of Słupce (Lodz province) on 21 December 1927 make this clear:

Dealing with the attitude of officials to the Government, the Sub-prefect reminded those present of the principle and necessity of absolute loyalty on which the whole governmental apparatus was based . . . All present strongly supported this view of the Sub-prefect's, and assured him that no other view prevailed among them than that of citizen-officials, performing without question all that the Government intended.[5]

One of the less successful of the Government's programmes was the campaign against corruption. Early in 1927 a Special Com-

[1] 'Statut Państwowej Rady Samorządowej', appended to P.P.R.M., meeting of 7 March 1927.
[2] See, e.g., 'Rozporządzenie Prezydenta Rzeczypospolitej z dnia 19 stycznia 1928 r. o organizacji i zakresie działania władz administracji ogólnej', Dz.U.R.P. (1928), no. 11, pp. 154–68; 'Rozporządzenie Ministra Spraw Wewnętrznych z dnia 28 marca 1928 r. w sprawie wojewódzkich i powiatowych organów kolegjalnych administracji ogólnej', Dz.U.R.P. (1928), no. 46, pp. 1013–15.
[3] P.P.R.M., 16 December 1926.
[4] P.Z.P.K. I, Województwo Wileńskie, Powiat Wilejski, 21 December 1929.
[5] P.Z.P.K. I, Województwo Łódzkie, Powiat Słupeckie, meeting of 21 December 1927.

mission to Combat Financial Abuses was created. It was headed by Mieczysław Dębski, a Piłsudski-ite who before 1926 had held an important position in the Main Auditing Office, and it was directly responsible to the Prime Minister's Office. However, the Commission clashed more and more with Bartel, and the amassing of evidence proved rather difficult.[1] Only one successful prosecution was made, against General Żymierski, who in September 1927 was sentenced to five years' imprisonment for abuses in connection with army orders for gas masks from the firm 'Protekta'.[2] Karol Popiel, the N.P.R. deputy, was violently attacked in the government press for his involvement in this affair; he resigned his parliamentary seat, challenging the Government to prosecute him, but the state felt its case too weak to proceed. Similarly, although a parliamentary court held that some of Wojciech Korfanty's dealings 'were not in accord with the provisions of the law and good business principles',[3] no charges were brought against him. The Commission was eventually dissolved in the autumn of 1928.

THE ARMY

One of the first acts of the Government after receiving from parliament its power of issuing decrees was finally to settle the question of the Army. Piłsudski had been very worried by the divisive effects on the Army of the three-day civil war, and indeed, after the coup he tried to keep the Army as remote from political conflict as possible. In the Order of the Day of 22 May he appealed for reconciliation:[4]

Our blood has sunk into one common earth, an earth equally dear to, equally loved by both sides. May this warm blood, this soldiers' blood, the most precious in Poland, be, under our feet, the new seed of brotherhood, may it announce a common truth for brothers.

In a letter to Bartel on 8 June 1926 Piłsudski laid down the conditions under which he would accept the post of Minister of War.

[1] Dębski has described the work of the Commission in his memoirs. See M. Dębski, 'Komisja Nadzwyczajna do Walki z Nadużyciami', N.D.P., 1st ser., viii. 129–44. For the decree setting up the Commission, see Dz.U.R.P. (1927), no. 41, pp. 502–4.

[2] Robotnik, 7 September 1927.

[3] Z. Landau and B. Skrzeszewska, Wojciech Korfanty przed Sądem Marszałkowskim (Katowice, 1964), pp. 167–8.

[4] Piłsudski, P.Z., ix. 10.

He demanded that the Proclamation on 7 January 1921 be re-established as the basis for the constitutional position of the Army, and required an assurance from Bartel that the Army would be 'led by one individual'.[1] He felt that the legal status of the Army should be strictly defined, and the President's position as the highest military authority recognized. In addition, he acknowledged, at least in theory, the Minister of War's responsibility to the Prime Minister by offering to give Bartel a signed, undated letter of resignation on assuming office. He also agreed to uphold his constitutional obligations to the Sejm. Finally, he declared that the Army 'would only not find itself in a false position'[2] if it had as its internal chief and spokesman an officer who, with his staff, would be entrusted with the preparation of plans for a potential future conflict. As Minister of War, Piłsudski stated, he would represent the views of this officer on questions of defence and would be his constitutional shield. On 12 June Piłsudski was appointed by the Cabinet head of the Inner War Council established by the 1921 decree; he thus acquired the post of the 'representative officer' as well as that of Minister of War.

There were certain constitutional objections to this solution, but the matter was finally settled by two decrees decided on at a Cabinet meeting on 5 August 1926.[3] The first stated that in terms of Article 46 of the constitution and the new law empowering the President to issue decrees, those aspects of Army administration not reserved by law for the legislature would be dealt with by decree.[4] The second, on Army organization, merely embodied and made more explicit the provisions of the 1921 decree. The President, it stated, exercised his power as the highest military authority through the Minister of War, on whose advice he nominated officers from the rank of divisional commander upwards. On the basis of a Cabinet resolution taken on the advice of the Minister of War, the President nominated the General Inspector of the Army, the Deputy Minister of War, and the Chief of the General Staff. The Minister of War commanded the Army, and was responsible constitutionally and before Parliament for

[1] Piłsudski, *P.Z.* ix. 36–7.
[2] Ibid., p. 38.
[3] P.P.R.M., 5 August 1926.
[4] 'Rozporządzenie Prezydenta Rzeczypospolitej z dnia 6 sierpnia 1926 r. o wydawaniu dekretów w zakresie Najwyższego Zwierzchnictwa sił zbrojnych Państwa', *Dz.U.R.P.* (1926), no. 79, p. 881.

his actions.[1] The General Inspector of the Army was designated in advance Commander-in-Chief in wartime. He was entrusted with control over all questions which related to the preparation of the Army and the defence of the country in case of war. The General Staff and its Chief and the Army Inspectors were subordinate to him.[2] The decree also affirmed that the Minister of War and the General Inspector would be members of the Council for the Defence of the State,[3] a body created by decree on 25 October 1926.[4] Its functions were to discuss general problems of national defence and work out guidelines for the mobilization and organization of the resources of the state. It was headed by the President of the Republic, and the Prime Minister, the Ministers of War, Foreign Affairs, the Treasury, and the Interior, and the General Inspector of the Army sat on it.

Finally, on 8 August, at the same Cabinet meeting at which the first decree was adopted, the decision was taken, perhaps against Bartel's wishes, certainly against the advice of the Minister of Finance, to raise the salaries of army officers.[5] Though difficult to justify in terms of the economic situation, it certainly improved the material position of the officer corps, and particularly of the more junior officers, many of whom had been in considerable financial difficulties before 1926. It thus did much to overcome the bitterness of the divisions created by the coup.

The principles of Army organization for which Piłsudski had fought for so long were now finally established. They were, however, open to a number of serious objections, and their application had a generally harmful effect on the efficiency of the Army as a fighting force. On the one hand, the Army was granted a far-reaching independence from civilian control and a situation was created which could easily lead to conflict between the military and the politicians. For the time being the fact that Piłsudski was both Minister of War and General Inspector of the Army (he was appointed to this post by presidential decree on 27 August) made

[1] 'Dekret Prezydenta Rzeczpospolitej z dnia 6 sierpnia 1926 r. o sprawowaniu dowództwa nad siłami zbrojnymi w czasie pokoju i o ustanowieniu Generalnego Inspektora sił zbrojnych', *Dz.U.R.P.*, no. 79, p. 882, Articles 1, 2.

[2] Ibid., Articles 3, 4.

[3] Ibid., Article 6.

[4] 'Rozporządzenie z dnia 25 października 1926 r. o utworzeniu Komitetu Obrony Państwa', *Dz.U.R.P.* (1926), no. 108, pp. 1203–4.

[5] P.P.R.M., meeting of 8 August 1926, item 2.

such a clash impossible, though at the cost of destroying completely parliamentary control of the armed forces.

Within the Army too, the scheme had a number of drawbacks. In the first place, it gave to the General Inspector an almost dictatorial power, and considerably lessened the importance of the General Staff. Moreover Piłsudski was not the man to exercise to good account the far-reaching powers he had acquired. A brilliant military amateur, he lacked the staff training and technical expertise which would have enabled him to absorb and apply the rapid advances in military thought which occurred in the 1920s and early 1930s. His extreme remoteness, and the absence in his immediate entourage of anyone with whom he could converse as an equal, exaggerated still further his belief in his own omnicompetence in military matters. In addition the problem created by the Marshal's insistence on running the Army single-handed was intensified by the fact that he would not agree to see anyone on business whom he had not himself summoned nor would he allow matters to be discussed which he did not raise himself.[1] Bearing in mind his somewhat sporadic activity, this meant that many important matters tended to be neglected or bypassed. In his memoirs, Marian Romeyko, who served in the General Staff in this period gives an example of what this meant in practice. In 1927–8, after much preliminary research and the holding of a number of conferences, guidelines for the development of the Polish Navy were worked out by the General Staff and were agreed on by both the Chief of the General Staff, General Piskor and the Head of the Navy, Commander Świrski. Then arose the question of how Piłsudski's approval was to be obtained. It could not be arranged by Commander Świrski, since Piłsudski would not receive him, while General Piskor maintained that he could not raise the matter on his own initiative. To resolve the impasse Piskor proposed the following strategy to Major Skulski, who had drawn up the proposals:

You take the whole scheme and go at once to the President who is at present at his residence at Wisła. I will give you a letter to him. You explain the matter, and ask him in my name, when he returns to Warsaw to invite the Marshal to tea, discuss the development of the navy with him, convince him and get his approval for the proposal.[2]

[1] On this, see M. Romeyko, *Przed i po maju* (Warsaw, 1967), ii. 56–7.
[2] Ibid., p. 57.

Piłsudski's military thinking became increasingly out-of-date. He continued to believe, at least implicitly, that any future war would be a repeat performance of 1920, and this led him to exaggerate the importance of infantry and cavalry at the expense of artillery, communications, and the Air Force. It was because of his belief that flanking cavalry manœuvres could still win decisive victories that he rejected in 1929 General Konarzewski's plan for the gradual motorization of the cavalry. The General had shown that the cost of maintaining a motorized brigade would not be significantly larger than that of maintaining a brigade of cavalry.[1]

The Marshal's growing ill health, particularly after 1928, also meant that his activity in the Army became more and more haphazard, often taking the form of badly thought-out *pronunciamentos* on subjects of which he had little knowledge. His intervention generally had a deleterious effect. An example of the harm Piłsudski's sudden and in many cases ignorant *démarches* could cause can be seen in the case of the Air Force. Between 1926 and 1929 a considerable effort was made to bring the Air Force up to date, and investigations were undertaken concerning the possibilities of resisting a bombing attack and co-operating with the Army during battle. In August 1929, Piłsudski laid down his 'guidelines' for the Air Force. They rested on the entirely outdated view that the Air Force was to be used solely for reconaissance, ruling out its role of instructing the Army in defence against air raids and omitting entirely anti-aircraft defence. Characteristically, Piłsudski issued this order without consulting his Chief of Staff or the Army Inspectors.[2] Under normal circumstances, it would have sufficed for a senior general to go and see the Marshal and arrange for the withdrawal of the order. But these were not normal times.

This was not the only example of Piłsudski's headstrong ways. His unwillingness to accept the fact that conventional artillery could not deal with air attacks delayed until after his death the development of anti-aircraft defence, while his views on communications were merely the commonplaces of World War I. These views of his were the main reason for the rejection of

---

[1] S. Kopański, 'Odpowiedź na list generała Głuchowskiego w sprawie "utechnicznienia" wojska', *Bellona*, no. i (1955), p. 80.

[2] Romeyko, *Przed i po maju*, ii. 116–17.

General Fabrycy's ten-year plan of March 1930, which called for the building up of the armed forces and the provision of up-to-date weapons,[1] and of General Piskor's proposals for modernizing artillery, communications, and sappers, for creating motorized units, and establishing a bombing Air Force.[2] Piłsudski was also largely responsible for the virtually unchallenged acceptance in the Army of the slogan 'Eyes East' (*Oczy na wschód*). This followed naturally from his belief that Poland could only be seriously threatened by Russia, since the alliance with France and the terms of the Treaty of Versailles ensured that Germany would be power-less to act against Poland. As a concept, it affected all Polish military strategy and remained orthodox not only in the 1920s, when it had some objective justification, but also in the 1930s, when the rearmament of Germany and the dynamic force of Nazism had clearly demonstrated its falsity. Moreover the clear distinction Piłsudski insisted on drawing between the peacetime and wartime operations of the Army largely accounts for the fact that during the whole of his rule, no proper system of national defence was adopted and consequently no effective plans for a future war were drawn up.

An important reason for the decline in the strategic and tech-nical effectiveness of the Army after 1926 lay in the downgrading of the General Staff. Before the coup, although in theory the Chief of the General Staff was directly subordinate to the Minister of War, in practice the General Staff controlled Army affairs. This situation changed radically after the coup. Piłsudski, mostly as a result of his own military experiences, had an exaggerated con-tempt for the 'know-alls' of the General Staff, and affirmed repeatedly that he could not endure their 'omnipotence'. In the Army reorganization of August 1926, he considerably diminished the functions of the General Staff. Field officers were effectively subordinate to the Ministry of War, control over promotions was taken from the General Staff and given to the Personnel Bureau of the Ministry, and the organization of the Army in peacetime, which had been the responsibility of the 1st Department of the General Staff, was transferred to the Second Deputy Minister. Moreover, the morale and quality of the General Staff was seriously undermined because of Piłsudski's view that promotion should go

---

[1] E. Kozłowski, *Wojsko Polskie, 1936–1939* (Warsaw, 1964), p. 15.
[2] S. Kopański, 'Odpowiedź na list generała Głuchowskiego . . .', p. 80.

to field officers rather than staff officers. It became increasingly difficult to persuade young officers to take positions in the General Staff or to attend technical courses at the Higher Military School. Already by 1929 there were only about thirty candidates for the sixty free places at the school.[1]

These developments had a deplorable effect on the technical efficiency of the Army and on its grasp of modern strategic considerations. The worst consequences of this system were not felt immediately since Piłsudski appointed as Chief of Staff General Tadeusz Piskor, a competent legionary officer whom he respected and who understood the importance of the General Staff. But even under Piskor, the impossibility of approaching the Marshal directly and the lack of initiatives from above meant that the work of the General Staff tended to stagnate. The appointment of a rather junior officer, Colonel Janusz Gąsiorowski, who had never held a command, to replace Piskor in December 1931 marked a further decline in the General Staff's importance and under him it became little more than a glorified secretariat.

For promotion, too, a Piłsudski-ite past, particularly one involving service in the legions, became increasingly important. Although the purge of the Marshal's opponents did not go as far as some of his more jealous supporters would have liked, a fair number of anti-Piłsudski-ite officers did lose their positions. Between 30 April and 30 June 1927, for instance, 581 officers were retired, including 30 generals and 331 senior officers.[2] Nevertheless, some of Piłsudski's principal adversaries during the coup still remained in the Army. Colonel Anders, Rozwadowski's Chief of Staff, was soon afterwards given the command of an independent cavalry brigade and was eventually, after a long wait, made a general in 1930. Colonel Paszkiewicz, the Commander of the Cadet School and the Officers' Infantry School, was also not long afterwards given a general's rank and even Major Marian Porwit, who had given the order to the Cadets to resist Piłsudski at the Poniatowski Bridge, retained his position as Director of the Officers' Infantry School, although his further advancement was in fact checked.

But from the late 1920s an increasing number of officers who for either political or personal reasons had clashed with Piłsudski's

---

[1] Romeyko, *Przed i po maju*, ii. 385. On the question of the General Staff as a whole, ibid., pp. 78–117.
[2] Kozłowski, p. 304.

close advisers, found their promotions blocked or were forced to retire from the Army, particularly after the relatively scrupulous Colonel Aleksander Prystor was replaced in April 1929 as head of the Personnel Department at the Ministry of War by the fanatical and vengeful legionary, General Michał Karaszewicz-Tokarzewski. He in turn was replaced in the early 1930s by Colonel Ignacy Misiąg, an unimaginative and not very intelligent field officer who proved both incompetent and rather time-serving in the post.

This control over appointments had the desired effect of ensuring Piłsudski-ite dominance in the Army. But it certainly also meant that ability was by no means the primary criterion used in assessing promotions, and the Army suffered accordingly. As early as 1928, of the ten Army Inspectors (who were to be divisional commanders in wartime), eight had actively supported the May coup and six were former legionaries.[1] The transformation was even more thorough at a lower level. Whereas in 1926, only 10 per cent of army officers had been former legionaries, by 1939 they formed 70 per cent of the commanders of infantry divisions and 54 per cent of the commanders of cavalry and motorized armoured brigades.[2]

The Piłsudski-ite officers in many cases lacked formal military training, and had won their spurs in the Polish-Soviet War. In this war, recounts General Jerzy Kirchmayer,

The legionary Captain became a General, the legionary soldier, a Captain . . . Thus our officer corps, or to speak more strictly, that part of it which determined military matters, had every reason never to forget the 1920 War, to return to their experiences on every occasion. This was to return to their own ordeals, to joyful, victorious memories. In this fertile soil, the experiences of that war assumed vast proportions in their eyes.[3]

Their virtual obsession with what they regarded as the strategic lessons of that war, and in particular, with the vital role cavalry would play in future hostilities, further increased resistance in the Army to modernization and to the introduction of technical weapons.

[1] Rothschild, op. cit., pp. 190–1.
[2] A. Grudziński, 'Cyfry mówią', *Wiadomości*, xiv (no. 675), p. 6; S. Kopański, *Moja służba w wojsku polskim 1917–1939* (London, 1965), pp. 302–3.
[3] J. Kirchmayer, *1939–1944; Kilka zagadnień polskich* (Warsaw, 1947), p. 47.

ECONOMIC POLICY

A substantial improvement in economic conditions took place during the first three years of the new regime. As we have seen, this economic revival had already begun before the coup. The number of those employed in factories with more than twenty workers had begun to rise in January 1926,[1] and from that month industrial production had also started to increase, though somewhat unevenly.[2] The number of registered unemployed had begun to fall in March, although it remained high,[3] and the budget deficit had begun to decrease from the first of the year as the effects of Zdziechowski's reforms were felt.[4] From February, small increases could also be detected in monetary circulation and in the credit operations of the banks.[5] The *de facto* devaluation of the zloty aided exports, which had grown in value from 68·8 million zloties in January 1926 to 118·6 million by May.[6]

The effect of the May coup in ending the political instability greatly increased business confidence and fostered economic recovery. By 29 May the zloty had fallen to 11 to the dollar. By 26 June it stood at 10 to the dollar, and by 7 July it reached 9·15.[7] The stock market also began to revive, and registered unemployment fell to 185,000 by the end of September.[8] The uplift in world trade which had begun in 1925 helped exports, as did the British coal strike which started in May 1926. This opened up new markets in Scandinavia which were particularly welcome since the Polish-German tariff war had closed the traditional Polish outlets.[9]

Piłsudski himself was not much interested in economic problems or fully aware of their importance. As he told *Kurjer Warszawski* on 29 November 1924, 'I am never ashamed to acknowledge what I do not know. I could not, for instance, take the Cabinet post of Trade and Industry, or Railways. I don't know about these

[1] *R.S.R.P.* (1927), p. 349, Table II.
[2] *Bulletin statistique du Ministère des Finances* (1927), no. 1, p. 20, Table XXII.
[3] *R.S.R.P.* (1927), p. 356, Table V.
[4] Ibid., p. 511, Table IV.
[5] Ibid., p. 269, Table IX; p. 273, Table XIII.
[6] Ibid., p. 231, Table Ib.
[7] *Messager Polonais*, 9 July 1926.
[8] *R.S.R.P.* (1927), p. 356, Table V.
[9] W. Michowicz, 'Wpływ strajku górników angielskich z 1926 r. na przemysł węglowy w Polsce', *Zeszyty Naukowe Uniwersytetu Łódzkiego*, 1st series, pamphlet 7 (1957), pp. 209–46.

matters.'[1] Świtalski, a later Prime Minister and confidant of Piłsudski's, wrote of the Commander's

quite blatant disregard for economic matters—this took the form, with him, of turning the phrase 'economic committee' ['komitet ekonomiczny'] into 'comic committee' ['komitet aj-komiczny']. One could observe in the Commander a concern for the State Treasury and for the scrupulous accounting of funds. At the same time, however, the Commander was very much against the preponderance of economic over political matters.[2]

Indeed, people with real competence in economic matters were rare in Piłsudski-ite circles. Bartel, who placed much stress on the economy, was thus fortunate in finding two very able men, Gabriel Czechowicz and Eugeniusz Kwiatkowski, to work with him. Czechowicz, a senior civil servant, held the Ministry of Finance from the coup until 4 June 1926. He then returned to his former post of Permanent Under-Secretary to the Ministry, where he remained until 2 October 1926 when he again became Minister, holding the office until March 1929. Kwiatkowski, technical director of the State Nitrate Factory at Chorzów, was Minister of Commerce and Industry from 8 June 1926 until May 1930. Together with Bartel they were responsible for the formulation and implementation of the new Government's economic policy.

Although Czechowicz had, under a pseudonym, strongly criticized the deflationary aspects of Zdziechowski's measures,[3] and although grouped around the radical Piłsudski-ite journals Głos Prawdy and Droga there were many who advocated radical land reform and wide nationalization, the economic policies of the new Government proved to be almost entirely a continuation of those of its predecessors.[4] Already on 8 June Bartel had assured Wierzbicki that 'neither in social nor in economic policies will the Marshal make any experiments. The bases of the financial policies

[1] Quoted in M. Porczak, Rewolucja majowa i jej skutki (Cracow, 1927), pp. 13–14. Rothschild claims (p. 418) that Porczak was a pseudonym for Ignacy Daszyński. There is no evidence whatever for this assertion. In fact, Proczak was a well-known member of the P.P.S. and a publicist in his own right.

[2] A.A.N., Zespoły Szczątkowe, Akta Sprawy Świtalskiego, sygn. II/88, 'Dn. 15 listopada 1935 r. Rozmowa z Prezydentem'. Hereafter cited as A.S.S.

[3] He published in April 1926 under the name G. Leliwa a pamphlet, Problem skarbowy w świetle prawdy (Warsaw, 1926).

[4] For an account of radical Piłsudski-ite views on economic policy, see: S. Starzyński, Program rządu pracy w Polsce (Warsaw, 1926), and Rola państwa w życiu gospodarczym (Warsaw, 1929), and ed. Starzyński, Na froncie gospodarczym. W dziesiątą rocznicę odzyskania niepodległości (Warsaw, n.d.).

of the previous governments will be maintained.'[1] The continuity in economic policy is clear in the statement which Kwiatkowski presented to the Cabinet on 17 June, and which was afterwards communicated to the press.[2] As his main objectives, he stressed the irreproachably orthodox principles of balancing the budget and stabilizing the zloty. He also emphasized the importance of exports, particularly coal. The only innovations in his programme were a greater stress on agriculture, and the promise that the development of Gdynia, the new Polish port on the Baltic, would be accelerated.

In fact, within the framework of the economics of the time, this was the only possible programme: it did aid recovery, although Keynesian reflation might have worked faster. One source of inflation was eliminated as the connection between the salaries of government officials and the cost of living index was ended. Railway deficits were cut when the railway administration was set up as an independent entity. Moreover, the practice of planning monthly budgets which the new Government introduced meant that government income and expenditure did not get too radically out of balance. Whereas in the financial year 1925–6 government income had been 1,570 million zloties and expenditure 1,806 million, in 1926–7 income was 2,133 million and expenditure 1,982 million.[3] The revalorization of some taxes and the increased yield of others as a result of the economic revival also contributed to this improvement.

The Government underlined the importance of foreign capital in economic development.[4] The new stability, the hope that an agreement could be reached with Germany, and the Government's obvious financial orthodoxy all increased the interest of foreign investors. Only two weeks after the coup, the Lodz textile industry received a substantial British credit, while the projected Harriman

---

[1] A. Wierzbicki, 'Uwagi o przewrocie majowym', *N.D.P.*, 1st series, ix (1965), 224.

[2] P.P.R.M., 17 June 1926, Appendix I: 'Program gospodarczy Ministra Przemysłu i Handlu E. Kwiatkowskiego.'

[3] Zweig, op. cit., p. 49; *Materiały odnoszące się do działalności rządu w czasie od 15 maja 1926 do 31 grudnia 1927* (Warsaw, 1928), p. 215. For the economic policy of the new Government see: Landau and Tomaszewski, op. cit.; Landau, *Plan stabilizacyjny*; Michowicz, op. cit.; Zweig, op. cit.; Madajczyk, op. cit.; Landau, 'Misja Kemmerera', *P.H.* xlviii (1957), no. 2, pp. 270–84.

[4] See, e.g., Kwiatkowski's speech in the Sejm on 13 November 1926: *S.S.S.R.*, 13 November 1926, col. 15.

investment in Silesian Zinc, which had been under discussion since the previous November, was agreed on by the end of June.[1] Other large inflows of foreign capital in 1926 came from the creation in July of a Franco-Polish consortium to develop the port of Gdynia and from the large timber concession granted to British interests in October.[2]

However, investment in Poland was small, compared with the massive investment which was taking place at the time in Germany. Most of it, moreover, was short-term. In 1927, capital movement into Poland amounted to 1,536 million zloties: 922 million was short-term and 614 million long-term, but of this only 68 million was invested in Polish industry. The corresponding figures for 1928 were 1,897 million zloties over all, 1,570 million short-term, 327 million long-term with 101 million in industrial investment.[3]

The culmination of the Government's stabilization plan and of its attempts to attract foreign capital was the arrangement of a loan with a group of American and European bankers, represented by the Bankers' Trust Company, the Chase National Bank of New York, and Lazard Brothers and Company. This loan, concluded on somewhat unfavourable terms in October 1927, amounted to $62 million and £2 million sterling, and was intended to underpin the stabilization of the zloty achieved by that date. It was closely linked with a grant of $20 million to the Bank of Poland by the leading central banks in an effort to integrate the Polish credit system with that of the rest of the world. The plan proved successful in establishing the zloty at its new rate of 8·91 to the dollar, but the massive inflow of foreign capital which had been hoped for did not follow.[4] Nevertheless, several loans were obtained in 1928 by local government authorities, among them the province of Silesia and the municipalities of Warsaw, Poznań, and Gdynia.[5]

These developments further stimulated the industrial revival. The reserves of the Bank of Poland rose from 203 million zloties at the end of December 1925 to 1414·6 million in December 1927.[6] The index of industrial production rose from 79·6 in 1926

[1] Landau, *Plan stabilizacyjny*, pp. 48–59.
[2] Ibid., pp. 45–8.
[3] *M.R.S.* (1931), p. 88, Table XXVII.
[4] For the plan see: Landau, *Plan stabilizacyjny*, pp. 121–278; Zweig, op. cit., pp. 50–2.
[5] Landau, *Plan stabilizacyjny*, pp. 258–9; Zweig, op. cit., p. 53.
[6] *R.S.R.P.* (1927), p. 262, Table I; (1928), p. 244, Table I.

to 116·4 in 1928.[1] Exports increased as the new coal markets in Scandinavia were maintained, and so did imports, as much outdated industrial equipment was replaced. In 1927 the trade balance was passive. It became active in 1928, but only because of the inflow of short-term capital.[2] Domestic trade also expanded rapidly.[3]

The position of the industrial working class improved. The number of unemployed fell from 243,000 in June 1926 to 80,000 in September 1928.[4] Money wages rose, and since food prices fell slightly, real wages rose as well, passing the level of early 1925 by the end of 1927. The Government also widened the already extensive system of welfare legislation. In July 1927 the nature and aims of factory inspection were codified, and in November unemployment insurance for salaried workers was modified and compulsory disablement, old age, and widows' and orphans' insurance was extended to all workers. In March 1928 the contractual position of workers was improved. However, these social reforms were coupled with an attack on the P.P.S. control of the social service organizations.[5]

Agriculture also benefited from the economic upturn. It is true that agricultural prices fell slightly from the high level of the beginning of 1925, when they had been inflated by a poor harvest, but they fell more slowly than industrial prices, and for once the price scissors worked in favour of the peasant.[6] Peasant income rose, though this was partly due to the increased opportunities for side employment outside agriculture created by the industrial revival. The return per hectare for a peasant holding of 5–10 hectares rose from 348 zloties in 1926–7 to 586 zloties in 1928–9.[7]

Although Piłsudski had ruled out a radical land reform, the favourable economic conditions induced large landowners to sell

---

[1] Taking the 1925–9 index of industrial production as 100; I. Svennilson, op. cit., pp. 304–5, Table A66.

[2] *M.R.S.* (1931), p. 88, Table XXVII.

[3] Zweig, op. cit., p. 52.

[4] Ed. M. Drozdowski, 'Bezrobocie w Polsce, 1925–1936', *N.D.P.*, 1st ser. (1961), p. 232.

[5] For these developments, see *10 lat polityki społecznej Państwa Polskiego* (Warsaw, 1928); *Polityka społeczna państwa polskiego, 1918–1935* (Warsaw, 1935).

[6] See Landau and Tomaszewski, op. cit., p. 135.

[7] M. Dziewicka, 'Zagadnienie degradacji rolnictwa w Polsce kapitalistycznej', *Ekonomista* (1955), p. 82, Table III.

land voluntarily within the framework of the Land Reform Law. Between 1926 and 1928, the annual provision of 200,000 hectares to be subdivided was exceeded.[1] Parcellation was most rapid in western Poland and in the Eastern Kresy, but it was also fairly important in the former Congress Kingdom. In addition, the Government placed stress on improving other aspects of the agricultural system. The liquidation of servitudes was speeded up as well as the consolidation of holdings and the subdivision of common lands.[2]

Finally, the improvement of economic conditions in Western Europe meant that emigration, a traditional rural safety valve, was again possible on a large scale. Between 1926 and 1928, 552,000 people emigrated, and 197,000 were seasonal migrants.[3]

Large landholders also profited from the improved conditions. The high prices paid for land meant that there was money available for the purchase of agricultural machinery and the intensification of production. The number of tractors imported, for example, rose sixfold between 1926 and 1928.[4]

The economic revival provided a secure base for the activities of the Government. It is true that progress was patchy, and that the economy was excessively dependent upon short-term foreign credits and vulnerable to fluctuations of the world economy, but for the moment, the Government could claim to have dealt successfully with a problem which had been too much for all the pre-coup Cabinets.

THE GOVERNMENT AND THE CHURCH

The Government also succeeded in achieving improved relations with the Church, in spite of the strong anti-clericalism of many of the more radical Piłsudski-ites, and the Church's close links with the Endecja, Piłsudski's bitterest opponents. As late as 22 February 1927 *Głos Prawdy* carried an article describing its inquiry into the state of Catholic belief in the country under the heading 'The Roman Catholic Republic of Poland', with the subheading 'The people have had enough of fattening the bellies of priests.'[5]

The Piłsudski-ite had strongly attacked the terms of the

---

[1] *M.R.S.* (1931), p. 16, Table III.
[2] See Madajczyk, op. cit., pp. 232–60. [3] Ibid., p. 250.
[4] Ibid., p. 253. [5] *Głos Prawdy*, 22 February 1927.

Concordat. On 12 February 1925 *Kurjer Poranny* had called for a postponement of the signing of the agreement; it was held that its conclusion at this time might harm relations with France, since a conflict had broken out between the French Government and the Papacy.[1] On 21 March 1925 *Głos Prawdy* had censured the Polish negotiators as excessively yielding.[2] Moreover, many higher Church dignitaries and parish priests had been enthusiastic supporters of the Endecja, and had violently opposed the coup. Among the unequivocal opponents of Piłsudski in the Polish hierarchy one could include Archbishops Teodorowicz and Sapieha and Bishops Łosiński and Łukomski. After the coup, many priests refused to allow members of the Piłsudski-ite Riflemen's Association to enter churches in uniform, and refused to celebrate mass in honour of the Marshal's name-day.[3]

Nevertheless, the Pope, Pius XI, who had served in Poland as Apostolic Visitor (1918–19) and Papal Nuncio (1919–21), was determined not to precipitate a conflict, and sent a papal blessing to the new Government by means of Archbishop Kakowski, who happened to be in Rome at the time. Kakowski conveyed the Pope's message to Bartel on 28 May 1926.[4] Pius entrusted the carrying out of his conciliatory policy to August Hlond, whom he appointed to the vacant primatial see of Gniezno on 24 June 1926. Hlond, previously Bishop of Katowice, had been for many years a papal administrator in Vienna, and was not closely associated with any political party in Poland. He soon became the most powerful ecclesiastical personage in the country. On 20 June 1927 he was created Cardinal. The Papal Nuncio in Poland at the time of the coup was rather lukewarm about this policy of *rapprochement*, but his successor, Francesco Marmaggi, who arrived in March 1928, supported it strongly.

The new Government, for its part, was determined to be on good terms with the Church, and Piłsudski saw in the achievement of satisfactory relations with Rome an important means of achieving the national consolidation he sought. His policy in this sphere was a further clear indication that he had no intention of

[1] *Kurjer Poranny*, 12 February 1925.

[2] *Głos Prawdy*, 21 March 1925.

[3] See J. Jurkiewicz, *Watykan a Polska w okresie międzywojennym, 1918–39* (Warsaw, 1958), pp. 79–80; Pobóg-Malinowski, op. cit. ii. 499–500.

[4] *Czas*, 30 May 1926. Kakowski explained on the following day that the blessing was granted to all Poland.

adopting a radical political stance. President Mościcki personally attended a Catholic conference held in Warsaw on 27–30 August 1926, a gesture warmly welcomed by Archbishop Kakowski in his address:

By his presence at the Catholic conference, the President has publicly affirmed that the highest representative of the state and lay authority in Poland links himself in thought and spirit with the Catholic population, the overwhelming majority of the nation, and has affirmed that the well-being of that population is his concern.[1]

He further stated that Catholics would support the Government if it respected their rights and religious convictions. However, in spite of a government decree on 25 November 1926 increasing the power of chaplains in the Army, an element of strain persisted. The conference of bishops which met in Warsaw on 30 November to 1 December 1926 expressed concern at attacks on the Church in the 'anti-Catholic press'. 'All these newspapers', it alleged, 'are considered to have the support of official circles.' It complained of the slow implementation of the Concordat, and of proposals for a marriage law repugnant to Catholics.[2] Hlond himself was worried by the anti-government tone of this communiqué, and addressed a letter to Piłsudski in which he claimed that the Church did want 'to co-operate harmoniously with the Government' but demanded in return that the Government 'extend its sincere protection to the Church . . . and avoid anything which could worry Catholics or cause them to become hostile to the Government.'[3]

The central problem was, in fact, the implementation of the Concordat. As we have seen, the Piłsudski-ites believed that the state had made excessive concessions. From 24 November representatives of the Government were negotiating with the Papal Commission over disputed points.[4] On 8 and 13 January, the Ministers involved held two interim meetings to decide on policy, for which the Ministry of Religious Cults and Education prepared

[1] Quoted in Jurkiewicz, op. cit., pp. 84–5.
[2] The Bishops' Declaration is reprinted in *Gazeta Warszawska Poranna*, 2 December 1926.
[3] Quoted in Jurkiewicz, op. cit., pp. 85–6.
[4] The minutes of these meetings are to be found in A.A.N., Prezydium Rady Ministrów grup 97.2, 'Sprawa konkordatu między Polską a Rzymem'.

three undated memoranda.[1] The first of these stressed the far-reaching concessions which the Government felt had been made.[2] The state had only a power of veto in the nomination of bishops, and had no control over the appointment of suffragan bishops, titular bishops, rectors, professors in seminaries, or abbots; the lower clergy took no oath of loyalty to the state; the state had no control over the language used or the subject-matter taught in seminaries; the clause giving the Government the right to demand the removal of a priest could not actually be implemented; and new benefices and monastic orders could be created without government consent.

The second memorandum specified in some detail the points over which the Government questioned the Church's interpretation of the Concordat.[3] These included the power of parish councils (Article 24), and the clauses relating to the property rights of the Church. The exemption from land reform of Church holdings previously seized by the partitioning powers and now in government hands was a case in point (400,000 hectares were involved), as was the claim for the return of all Church buildings in state hands. The Government opposed Rome's demands for the return of some formerly Catholic churches which had been Greek Orthodox since the nineteenth century, as well as the Church's policy of extending the Greek Catholic rite. The level of priests' salaries was also disputed. Finally, the Government accused the Church of not abiding by the Concordat's provision for consultation with the Government over the creation of new monasteries, and claimed that the article stipulating that parish priests must be approved by the Government was not being enforced.

On most of these issues the Government in the end proved willing to make concessions to the Church. In a decree on 9 December 1926, and in a novella to the law on teachers of 15 July 1927, the Government fully recognized the dominant position of the Church in religious education.[4] Catholic schoolchildren

---

[1] Ibid.

[2] Ibid., 'Notatki na sprawę konkordatu'.

[3] Ibid., Memoriał M.W.R. i O.P., 'Sprawa konkordatu między Polską a Rzymem 1927 r.'.

[4] 'Rozporządzenie Ministra Wyznań Religijnych i Oświecenia Publicznego z 9 grudnia 1926 r. o nauce szkolne katolickiej', Dz.U.R.P. (1927), no. 1, pp. 8–9.

were even required to go to confession three times a year. In addition the Minister of Justice established clerical immunity in a decree of 23 February 1927,[1] and some concessions were made concerning the Church's property in the decree of 7 February 1928.[2]

The implementation of the Concordat led to the establishment of satisfactory relations with the Church. Government officials began to take part in religious ceremonies, and in June 1927 the Pope revived the right of the Polish king (in the person of the President) to confer the cardinal's biretta upon those members of the hierarchy resident in Poland who were elevated to the College of Cardinals. In July the President and Piłsudski, as Prime Minister, took part in a ceremonial adorning of the miraculous icon of the Virgin at Wilno. In the speech he made on this occasion Piłsudski stated, 'I wish to say not only that Poland has a devoted friend in the Pope, but that this devotion has been made manifest.'[3]

The Church's policy of cultivating good relations with the Government was further shown in the formation in February 1927 of the Catholic League, which afterwards became a part of Catholic Action.[4] The Government was at first unsympathetic to this lay organization, but soon realized that its 'apolitical' character was merely a device to cut some of the ties between the Church and the Endecja. Many of its most prominent supporters were conservatives, whom the Government was then wooing politically. One of them, the well-known Cracow politician, Professor Władysław Jaworski, made this anti-National Democratic tendency clear: 'The Apostolic work [of the organization]', he wrote in *Czas* on 23 February 1927,

will show that it is not a question of acting against this or that party, but against the tendency which, under the mask of religion, spreads principles which are in complete contradiction to religion, and *which in taking as their motto the love of one's fatherland, spread hate between citizens.*[5]

Nevertheless for most of the parish priests and many of the

---

[1] *Dziennik Urzędowy Ministerstwa Sprawiedliwości* (1927), no. 5.

[2] 'Rozporządzenie Prezydenta Rzeczpospolitej z dnia 7 lutego 1928 o wpisywaniu do ksiąg hipotecznych praw własności polskich osób prawnych kościelnych i zakonnych', *Dz.U.R.P.* (1928), no. 16, pp. 218–19.

[3] Piłsudski, *P.Z.* ix. 77.

[4] See Micewski, op. cit., chap. iii.

[5] (Italics in original.) This was a clear reference to the Endecja.

hierarchy, closely linked emotionally and politically with the Endecja, the *modus vivendi* achieved with the Government was essentially a necessity imposed by the political situation, and not a matter of conviction.

THE NATIONAL MINORITIES

The Government also tried to implement a new policy towards the minorities. Already on 24 May 1926 Kazimierz Młodzianowski, the Minister of the Interior, announced that 'The Government intends to follow a sincere and open policy in that which concerns the affairs and interests of the National Minorities.'[1] Bartel, too, in his exposition of Government policy, as we have seen, made a point of stressing the liberal intentions of the Cabinet in this sphere.

On 16 June 1926 the Cabinet set up a Committee of Experts on the Eastern Provinces and National Minorities. It was headed by Leon Wasilewski, well-known for his liberal views on questions of nationality.[2] The question of government policy was fully discussed at the Cabinet meeting of 18 August.[3] Here Młodzianowski argued that the governments before the coup had pursued no clear policy. One had to recognize that 'the attitude of the masses [of the national minorities] towards the state is unwilling and distrustful'.[4] The administration had proved inadequate, and political matters had been stressed at the expense of economic problems. Far-reaching promises had been made, but not fulfilled, which had caused great resentment. The goal of national assimilation should be renounced, and instead conditions should be created for assimilation to the state structure.

Młodzianowski's suggested outline of policy was adopted by the Cabinet.[5] Prefaced by an extensive and highly competent survey of the problems, it laid down a number of principles to be followed, some general and some applying to particular minorities. The Government was to look to the real interests of the 'broad mass' of the minorities, satisfying both their economic and cultural needs, which an improvement in local administration

[1] *Kurjer Poranny*, 25 May 1926.
[2] P.P.R.M., 16 June 1926, item 4.
[3] Ibid., 18 August 1926.   [4] Ibid., Młodzianowski's speech.
[5] Ibid., 'Konkretnie ujęte zasady planu działania Rządu i jego organów w stosunku do mniejszości narodowej'.

and a revival of local self-government would reveal more clearly. Representatives of the minorities were to sit on expert bodies created by the Government, and an amnesty for political crimes committed before 1923 was called for.

In relation to the Germans, the Government would uphold its treaty obligations. The question of citizenship should be settled, and the impartiality of officials should be ensured. However, the land reform should be accelerated in western Poland. In the eastern provinces, the Government should implement the land reform. The School Law should be amended to make it more acceptable to the minorities, and members of the minorities should be admitted to the civil service. A statute regulating the status of the Orthodox Church should be enacted. The law conferring autonomy on East Galicia should, however, be modified. As regards the Jews, the Government opposed economic anti-Semitism and would ensure adequate credits for Jewish trade. The law on compulsory Sunday rest would be modified, and all still-existing laws which discriminated against Jews would be abrogated. Zionism would be favoured, and the Religious Commune reorganized. Yiddish-language state primary schools were to be created, and government aid would be furnished to Jewish private schools. Finally, pressure should be exerted on the universities to do away with the *numerus clausus*.

Although Młodzianowski was replaced on 2 October 1926 by the unimaginative and far less competent Felicjan Sławoj-Składkowski, some attempt was made to implement this far-reaching policy. The importance of dealing fairly with the minorities was communicated to the local administration. On 21 December 1927 the Sub-Prefect of the district of Słupce in the Lodz province explained the need for the new policy to his officials:

Aware of the palpable and unhappy results of the activity of previous Governments in this sphere until May 1926, society ought patiently and in good faith to await, at least for a couple of years, the results of the present system.[1]

[1] P.Z.P.K. I, Powiat Słupski, województwo Łódzkie, 21 December 1927. Many similar statements by local officials could be cited. See, e.g., the directive of the Governor of the Stanisławów province on political problems, dated 26 November 1929, in P.Z.P.K. I, file 82; the report of the meeting of the local government officials of the Nadwórna district, Stanisławów province, on 30 June 1930, loc. cit.; that of the meeting of officials of the Hrubieszów district, Lublin province, on 13 June 1929, P.Z.P.K. I, file 74.

Nevertheless the Government was not everywhere successful in gaining the support of the civil service for its reforms. In western Poland, in particular in Pomerania, one finds frequent references in the reports of the meetings of local officials to the need for concerted Polish action against the minorities.[1]

In eastern Poland, the Government placed great stress on land reform and on the improvement of the economic situation through the consolidation of holdings and the abolition of servitudes. Subdivision was rapid in the White Russian areas and Volynia, where 70–80 per cent of the land divided went to White Russian and Ukrainian peasants.[2] The economic upturn of the early years of the new regime also encouraged development. Some rather half-hearted attempts were made to improve the school system; however, in practice the liberal programme outlined by Mło-dzianowski proved difficult to carry out in the face of administrative inertia and the opposition of Polish chauvinists. The Government again failed to overcome the obstacles placed by nationalists, both Polish and Ukrainian, in the way of founding a Ukrainian university in Lwów.

Political development also hindered an extensive change in policy. The Communist-dominated White Russian Hromada grew rapidly in size and popularity. From 569 members in July 1926 it had amassed perhaps 100,000 supporters by the time the Government banned it in January 1927.[3] After this, the popularity of Communism declined somewhat, and the Zmahannie, the successor organization to the Hromada, never gained wide support. The underground Communist Party of western White Russia was increasingly paralysed by the internal conflict raging in the Polish Communist Party between the Rightist leadership of Warski and the Left, led by Leszczyński, and split in September 1927. The Communist-controlled White Russian School Organization also split in 1927, and several of its leaders made approaches to the Government. Nevertheless the regime failed to gain any real support in this region, and was at best grudgingly accepted.

[1] See, e.g., P.Z.P.K. I, file 79: report of the meeting of the officials of the Grudziądz district, Pomerania, on 24 March 1928, or of the officials of the Tuchola district on 17 December 1927.

[2] Madajczyk, op. cit., p. 245.

[3] For the Hromada see: Bergman, op. cit.; Reguła, op. cit., pp. 143–218; G. Jackson, *Comintern and Peasant in East Europe, 1919–30* (New York, 1966), pp. 194–214.

The situation was slightly better in Volynia and East Galicia. The new Governor of Volynia, Henryk Józewski, appointed in 1927, did much to win the trust of the local population. In East Galicia the Government seems to have reached some agreement with the main nationalist party, the U.N.D.O. In return for the removal of some officials accused of chauvinism and some modification of the school system, the party was to declare itself loyal to the Polish state. Some parcellation in the area did take place through the U.N.D.O.-controlled Land Bank.[1]

The revolutionary groups here too were greatly weakened by the struggle taking place within the Polish Communist Party and by the disputes over 'national deviationism' (Shumski-ism). Both the Communist Party of the Western Ukraine and its legal front, Sel-Rob, split in 1927.

The Government had its greatest success with the Jews. On 14 October 1927 it issued a decree extending and reorganizing the Jewish communal organizations, thus winning much support among the Orthodox.[2] It also took steps to aid Jewish trade, which benefited as well from the economic revival. On 20 January 1927 the new Minister of Religious Cults and Education, Gustaw Dobrucki, declared himself against the *numerus clausus*,[3] and on 18 July 1927 he reissued a circular of 1925 forbidding its application in institutions of higher learning.[4] However, as so often, good intentions were not enough. The Government could do little against economic anti-Semitism, and by 1928 had not yet abolished all the Tsarist restrictive laws still in operation in Russian Poland. It did not provide funds for Jewish private schools, and in practice the *numerus clausus* was still applied. 'Our attitude to the Government', the Jewish leader Maksimilian Hartglas had stated in the Sejm in January 1927, 'no matter what Government, can be summarized in one phrase . . . "by their deeds shall ye know them". We can wait for these deeds and we can be very patient. But even

[1] This whole matter remains somewhat obscure. *Nasz Przegląd*, the main Jewish daily newspaper, printed a number of articles in December 1926 reporting meetings between the Government and various Ukrainian and White Russian politicians, including members of U.N.D.O. The compromise was also alluded to during the Brześć trial: see *Proces brzeski*, p. 140.

[2] 'Rozporządzenie Prezydenta Rzeczypospolitej z dnia 14 października 1927 r. o uporządkowaniu stanu prawnego w organizacji gmin wyznaniowych żydowskich', *Dz.U.R.P.*, no. 52, pp. 1129–34.

[3] *Robotnik*, 21 January 1927.

[4] *Nasz Przegląd*, 10 August 1927.

our patience has limits.'[1] By October 1927 the Grünbaum group was again dominant in the Jewish Parliamentary Club, and its members sent out a letter to the Government asking when its promises would be fulfilled.[2]

In Poznania and Pomerania the Government established satisfactory relations with the Germans. The question of citizenship had finally been settled by the Vienna Agreement of 30 August 1924, the Government stopped expropriating the property of citizens of the Reich, and although the land reform affected German landholding, the high prices paid somewhat mitigated this grievance.

However, in Upper Silesia the situation was exceedingly unsatisfactory. The new provincial governor, Michał Grażyński, a native of Gdów near Cracow, was an ardent Piłsudski-ite and a former member of the P.O.W. who had taken a prominent part in the Silesian risings. He saw his task as a twofold one, to reinforce the links between Upper Silesia and the rest of Poland, and to increase the strength of the pro-Government political organizations. His activities brought him into conflict with Korfanty, the principal Polish politician in the area, who resisted his plans to diminish Silesian autonomy and to bring in officials from other parts of Poland, notably Galicia. His attempts to outbid Korfanty by exploiting Polish nationalism also brought him into conflict with the German minority.[3] The difficulties came to a head over the issue of the desire of many Poles in the area to send their children to German schools, which were widely believed to offer a superior education. Contrary to the provisions of the Upper Silesia Convention, Grażyński instructed school inspectors to determine whether a child was German or Polish. When the International Court declared this illegal in April 1928, he retaliated by closing a number of German schools, claiming that their number was unjustified by the proportion of Germans in the local population. Conflict also arose over Grażyński's attempts to arrest Otto Ulitz, Secretary-General of the German League, whom he accused of spying. The Silesian Assembly, controlled by Korfanty, refused to waive Ulitz's parliamentary immunity, so that it was only by

---

[1] *S.S.S.R.*, 26 January 1927, col. 47.

[2] The letter was reprinted in *Nasz Przegląd*, 23 November 1927.

[3] For the situation in Upper Silesia see: H. Rechowicz, *Sejm Śląski, 1922–39* (Katowice, 1965), pp. 105–95; J. Krasuski, *Stosunki polsko-niemieckie, 1926–1932* (Poznań, 1964), pp. 312–45.

dissolving the Assembly in February 1929 that Grażyński was able to arrest him. He was eventually acquitted of the charges brought against him.

FOREIGN POLICY

The first years of the new Government saw an improvement in the international position of Poland, largely the result of the relaxation of tension in Europe in the period after Locarno.[1] The credit for this improvement accrued, for the most part, to the new regime. Piłsudski himself took charge of the direction of foreign policy, and the new Foreign Minister, August Zaleski, who had been Ambassador in Rome, was directly responsible to him. The only aspects of foreign policy discussed in the Cabinet were economic questions connected with the trade negotiations with Germany.

Although Piłsudski had strongly criticized the foreign policy of the Governments before the coup, he introduced no changes. Shortly after the coup he told Beck:

Everything seems to indicate that for five years at least there will not occur in Europe upheavals in which our country could find itself involved. We have a little time for our military and internal work. It can hardly be foreseen that we will have to take any important initiatives.[2]

In spite of Piłsudski's great resentment of Locarno, the Treaty of Alliance with France was retained, and relations remained good, though not as close as they had been. The French desire for a *rapprochement* with Germany and the consequent belief in France of the need to revise Germany's eastern frontier somewhat undermined Polish faith in the usefulness of the alliance; so did the French attempts to limit the scope of the agreement in order to avoid involvement in a Polish-German conflict.[3]

The coup was welcomed in Germany, where Piłsudski was believed to be willing to reach a settlement with the Reich. The Marshal did make an effort to improve relations; however, a certain disappointment was inevitable, since Stresemann was

[1] For the international situation see: J. Korbel, op. cit.; Z. Gąsiorowski, 'Stresemann and Poland after Locarno', loc. cit.; Krasuski, *Stosunki polsko-niemieckie, 1926–32*.

[2] J. Beck, *Dernier rapport. politique polonaise, 1926–39* (Neuchâtel, 1951), p. 3.

[3] See Korbel, op. cit., pp. 242–4.

principally interested in regaining the 1914 frontiers, while Piłsudski merely wished to establish a *modus vivendi* by settling a number of disputed issues. That he ever intended making territorial changes is to be doubted.[1] After an initial improvement, relations with Germany deteriorated somewhat in mid-1927 as a result of the Polish desire to extend the Locarno system of guarantees to Germany's eastern frontier, and because of the worsening of the position of the German minority in Upper Silesia. Nevertheless after Piłsudski's meeting with Stresemann at Geneva, in December 1927, a real relaxation of tension took place. In November 1927, an agreement on the position of Polish emigrants in Germany had been signed, as well as one on the right of settlement of Germans in Poland. In the next year, agreement was reached on a number of matters including inheritance rights, customs formalities, frontier regulations, passports, and the export of timber. The vexed question of the compensation due to Germany for the taking over of the munitions factory at Chorzów was settled in November 1928, and in October 1929 an agreement on the liquidation of German property in Poland was signed. Finally, after protracted negotiations, a trade agreement (though not a treaty) was concluded in March 1930, but it was never actually ratified since the impact of the Great Depression led to a more intransigent posture in German foreign policy.

Relations between Russia and Poland after the coup were marked by some initial tension.[2] The assassination in June 1927 of the Soviet Ambassador in Warsaw by a Russian *émigré*, and the threat of war between Poland and Lithuania, which diminished only after Piłsudski's dramatic intervention in Geneva in December 1927,[3] aggravated Soviet fears that Poland would be used as the springboard for an imperialist attack on Russia. From early 1928, however, relations improved somewhat. The Soviet Union resented the loosening of her ties with Germany now that the Reich, once more accepted as a Great Power, had less need of her.

[1] The raising of the frontier question during Herman Diamand's mission to Stresemann in July 1926, and in Prince Michał Radziwiłł's conversations with Stresemann in March 1928, may well have been private initiatives.

[2] For a discussion of the view, held at the time by the Soviet Foreign Office and echoed in recent years by many historians in Poland, that the coup was fomented by the British Foreign Office in order to bring to power in Poland a government which would be more sympathetic to British schemes for armed intervention against the Soviet Union, see Appendix A, pp. 514–17.

[3] See Korbel, *Poland between East and West*, p. 236.

Stresemann's policy was concentrated on good relations with the West, and from 1928 he placed less stress on links with Russia, particularly as he came to resent Communist subversion in Germany. As a result Russia, about to embark upon massive industrialization, sought to safeguard her western frontier by improving relations with Poland. In 1928 an exchange of political prisoners took place, and the two nations signed a railway convention and an agreement on the return of Polish art treasures in Russia. Finally, rather piqued by the lack of interest among the Western Powers in her schemes for outlawing war, Poland together with Rumania, Latvia, and Estonia signed the Litvinov Protocol with Russia in February 1929, implementing in Eastern Europe the principles of the Kellog–Briand Pact.

From about 1927, relations between Poland and Great Britain grew closer, the realization, in a sense, of Skrzyński's foreign policy. Poland came more and more to appear a responsible member of the European Concert, and she shared with Britain a hostility towards the Soviet Union. In October 1929, as a result of this new closeness, the legations in London and Warsaw were elevated to embassies.[1]

THE GOVERNMENT AND PARLIAMENT

Piłsudski had come to power with no clear political principles, apart from a dislike of political parties and of the way in which the parliamentary system had functioned before the coup. Yet in spite of the fact that he was much more interested in administration than in politics, and though many of his actions had no careful planning behind them, he did try in the period after the coup to lay the basis for a broad political organization which would support his rather vague goals. In June 1926 he spoke with Baranowski 'of the necessity to create a single front, with the broadest party span, something he had not yet been able to achieve'.[2] Sławek, Piłsudski's closest associate and confidant, addressing a group of conservative politicians at Dzików in September 1927 told them that they must 'harmonize the stand-

---

[1] On Anglo-Polish relations, see the memoirs of Skirmunt, who was Polish ambassador in London throughout this period: K. Skirmunt, 'Moje wspomnienia' (unpublished. In the Jagiellonian Library, Cracow).

[2] Baranowski, op. cit., p. 198.

points of the Right and Left. For it would not be a healthy situation if the Right alone were to dominate the political life of the state in spite of the existence of substantial segments of left-wing opinion, or *vice versa*.[1] Piłsudski thus sought to widen the basis of his political support and to undercut the National Democrats by trying to win over the political organizations of the large landowners. He had co-operated with the Galician conservatives since before World War I, and had maintained these contacts after Independence. He had also approached some of the other conservative groups both before and after the coup, and his policy towards the Church was to some extent another attempt to win their support. Sławek again gives a key to Piłsudski's thinking:

He [Sławek] regarded as an evil the lack of representation of the conservative element in the life of the state, for the National Democratic Right was anarchistic, and while the Left which had been pro-Independence (Lewica niepodległościowa) was well disposed towards the state, it had introduced into political life an excessive demand for reform. There was thus a need for an element representing moderation and a statist point of view.[2]

In mid-1926 there were three main groupings among the conservatives.[3] The most pro-Government point of view was represented by the Wilno group, the Conservative Organization, led by Eustachy Sapieha and Stanisław Mackiewicz, and linked with the Wilno newspaper *Słowo*. The circle around Prince Lubomirski in Warsaw was similar in outlook. The former Stańczycy in Cracow and the ideologically related Warsaw branch of the Party of the National Right, led by Prince Janusz Radziwiłł, were also pro-Government, but wanted some firm commitments from the régime before they would declare their support. This group also had some links with industry. Radziwiłł himself was as much an industrialist as a landowner, and Maurycy Poznański, the leader of the Lodz branch of the Party of the National Right, was a prominent Jewish mill-owner. The third group, the Christian

---

[1] ed. K. Kersten, 'Protokół konferencji grup konserwatywnych z udziałem przedstawicieli Marszałka Piłsudskiego w Dzikowie w dniach 14–16 września 1927 r.', *N.D.P.* (1st series) ii (1959), pp. 209–10.

[2] Ibid., p. 209.

[3] For the Conservatives see: Micewski, op. cit., chap. iii, pp. 79–141; Mackiewicz, op. cit., pp. 183–9; A. Czubiński, *Centrolew* (Poznań, 1963), pp. 32–7.

National Party, was divided. While Jan Stecki wanted to support the Government, Stroński and Dubanowicz held out for the traditional party alliance with the National Democrats.

Piłsudski, as we have seen, had thought of proposing an eminent conservative for the presidency, and had spoken of Janusz Radziwiłł, who already before 1926 had been urging his political associates to come to terms with Piłsudski, as a possible Foreign Minister. The landowners were not slow to respond to these approaches. On 27 May 1926, at a meeting at Prince Lubomirski's house, a committee was set up under Janusz Radziwiłł to sound Piłsudski's intentions.[1] When the Marshal reformed the Cabinet after the fall of the Bartel Government at the end of September 1926, he included two important landowners from eastern Poland, Aleksander Meysztowicz as Minister of Justice and Karol Niezabytowski as Minister of Agriculture. These links were sealed by Piłsudski's presence at a banquet at Nieśwież, the Radziwiłł family estate in eastern Poland, on 25 October 1926. He was there ostensibly to confer a posthumous decoration on Stanisław Radziwiłł, his aide-de-camp during the 1920 war, but the large number of prominent landowners attending made it clear that a wider significance was intended.

By late 1926 a certain reshaping of conservative political organizations had occurred. In December, the Sapieha and Lubomirski groups united to form the Polish Conservative Organization of State Work.[2] In the same month, the Warsaw and Lodz branches of the Party of the National Right united with the Stańczycy, and in February 1927 a Lwów branch was formed. Both these new groups declared themselves for the Government.

The Government also succeeded in winning the support of the representatives of industry. Andrzej Wierzbicki, President of Lewiatan and a National Democratic Deputy, has described how Bartel arranged a meeting with him and Ministers Zaleski, Makowski, Jurkiewicz, and Klarner on 8 June 1926. There Bartel promised that there would be no radical innovations in economic policy, and stated that while he could not offer Wierzbicki a place in the Cabinet, he would set great store by his advice. In reply, Wierzbicki stressed the willingness of the economic organizations

---

[1] W. Glinka (ed.), 'W rocznicę przewrotu majowego. Dokumenty', *Polityka*, i, no. 11, 6–7.
[2] Polska Organizacja Zachowawczej Pracy Państwowej.

of the country to co-operate with the Government.[1] The creation
of the Economic Council, on which many industrialists sat, and
the generally conservative character of the Government's economic
policies, increased the closeness of this co-operation. On 12 May
1927, the first anniversary of the coup, *Kurjer Polski*, which
represented heavy industry, stated:

If at the outset the supporters of the May Coup encountered unrestrained and violent condemnation, there has followed swiftly—in spite
of the frightful pain and suffering which has claimed so many victims—
a calming of public opinion and even a justification of the Coup, because
of the weight and seriousness of the actions which the so-called May
Coup has undertaken.[2]

The Government also tried, with some success, to avoid
excessively antagonizing the Left. Piłsudski-ites were important
in the Socialist Party, the Liberation, and the Peasant Party, and
the Government hoped, through these supporters, to prevent the
left-wing parties moving to a position of radical opposition.
When the Cabinet was reconstituted in October 1926 the Socialist
Jędrzej Moraczewski became Minister of Public Works, and in
January Bogusław Miedziński of the Liberation became Minister
of Posts. It proved impossible, however, to prevent a split in the
National Workers' Party; the Piłsudski-ites left in June 1926, and
in August, led by Ludwik Waszkiewicz in Łodz and Adam
Ciszak in Poznań, they formed the N.P.R.—Left Wing, which
supported the Government.[3] The small Party of Labour, somewhat weakened by the resignation first of Thugutt and later of
Ludwik Chomiński and Eugeniusz Śmiarowski, still remained
pro-Government. A similar grouping was the League for the
Reform of the Republic,[4] which had followed a radical Activist
line during the war. It had become defunct after Independence,
but was revived in May 1926 by Zdzisław Lechnicki by the
amalgamation of the Association of Settlers, the Riflemen's
Association and the Association of Silesian Rebels. Through its
bi-weekly, *Przełom*, it attempted to win support for the Government and to bring the Cabinet over to its radical statist position.

[1] A. Wierzbicki, 'Uwagi o przewrocie majowym', *N.D.P.* 1st series (1965),
pp. 224–5.
[2] *Kurjer Polski*, 12 May 1927.
[3] *Nowa Sprawa Robotnicza*, 29 August 1926.
[4] Związek Naprawy Rzeczypospolitej.

Its most important member was Michał Grażyński, the Governor of Silesia.[1]

Finally, apart from many who now adhered to the Sanacja for opportunistic reasons (the so-called 4th Brigade), the Government had a fair amount of support among the left-wing intelligentsia, of which some of the views were very like the radical, non-racialist aspirations of Italian Fascism. Representative of this group was the legionary poet, Wacław Sieroszewski, who gave a lecture in Warsaw on 24 October 1926 comparing Piłsudski and Mussolini.[2] There was also a group which included Tadeusz Hołówko, Adam Uziembło and Adam Skwarczyński, associated with the journal *Droga*, which hoped that Piłsudski would adopt a radical economic policy and deal fairly with the minorities. Wojciech Stpiczyński, the gifted though erratic editor of *Głos Prawdy*, which had become a daily since the coup, assumed a radical statist position and hoped to win the support of youth for the Sanacja.

Piłsudski was unwilling to order the dissolution of Parliament until he felt sufficiently well-established in the country and had a sufficiently strong political basis to risk elections. Nevertheless he used the threat of dissolution to prevent the parties of the Centre and Right, which would certainly have suffered heavily in elections, from attempting seriously to disrupt the work of the Government. He wished to take advantage of the far-reaching decree powers which the Government had been granted during the existing parliament, and he was not above violating the spirit, if not the letter, of the constitution by 'interpretations', usually suggested by Stanisław Car, a Piłsudski-ite lawyer. For example, when the Sejm passed a vote of no confidence in two Cabinet ministers, Piłsudski had Bartel resign and reassume office, reconstituting the Cabinet exactly as it had been before, on the grounds that although the Constitution made provision for votes of no confidence, it did not forbid the re-nomination of ministers against whom such votes were directed. A desire to humiliate the Sejm and to compromise it in the eyes of the people may also have played a part in his calculations.[3]

[1] On the Z.N.R., see the memoirs of the first editor of *Przełom*, Tadeusz Katelbach: *Spowiedź pokolenia* (Lippstadt, 1948), pp. 135–50.

[2] *Gazeta Warszawska Poranna*, 25 October 1926.

[3] Piłsudski's intentions remain a matter for speculation. He confided in no one consistently, kept no diary and often surprised even his closest associates by his actions.

When the new parliamentary session opened on 20 September 1926, conflict soon arose between the Government and the Sejm. The parties of the Right were incensed by the purges taking place in the administration and by the unresolved fate of the three generals still in custody. They were determined to show Piłsudski that they were a force to be reckoned with. The Christian Democrats were particularly aggressive, since they feared that moderation might mean a loss of support in favour of the Endecja.[1]

On 23 September, the Budgetary Committee of the Sejm accepted the proposal of Zdziechowski, a National Democrat, that the Government's budget for the last quarter of 1926 be cut by 34 million zloties. Though Bartel inclined towards a compromise solution, Piłsudski insisted that if parliament accepted this proposal, the Government should take it as a vote of no confidence. As a result the Sejm, anxious to avoid a direct clash, rejected the Committee's findings, but instead passed a vote of no confidence in two Government ministers, Młodzianowski and Sujkowski.[2] Bartel again advocated compromise, but as we have seen, Piłsudski insisted upon the renomination of the whole Cabinet, thus significantly widening the scope of the dispute. In retaliation, the Senate cut the 34 million zloties from the budget, and the new Senate proposal was accepted by the Sejm on 30 September. The Government interpreted this as a vote of no confidence. Bartel resigned, and a dissolution was universally expected. Instead, Piłsudski himself formed a Government on 1 October. On 2 October parliament was prorogued until the commencing of the normal budgetary session at the beginning of November.

In the meantime, the political atmosphere deteriorated still further when a number of Piłsudski-ite zealots broke in upon and assaulted Zdziechowski, who had played an important part in precipitating the crisis. This incident apparently took place without Piłsudski's approval, and aroused his anger, but no serious attempt was made to uncover those responsible.[3]

When parliament was reconvened, an almost farcical dispute arose over Piłsudski's demand that, as a sign of respect, deputies should stand while the President's declaration of the opening of

[1] Rataj, op. cit., p. 396.   [2] Ibid., pp. 396–407.
[3] Miedziński told Rataj that Piłsudski 'became mad with anger' when he heard of the attack; Rataj, op. cit., pp. 418–19. The tone of some of the articles in the Piłsudski-ite press was not reassuring, however. See, e.g., *Głos Prawdy*, 1, 2 October 1926, 8 October 1926.

parliament was read. After nearly two weeks, the question was finally resolved by having the President read the message in person in a hall in the Governmental Palace from which all the chairs had been removed.

More serious was the strong opposition aroused in all parties by a decree issued on 4 November which drastically limited the freedom of the press.[1] When the Sejm finally met on 13 November, a motion was presented calling for the abrogation of this decree. It was approved by the Juridical Committee on 15 November. Because of some uncertainty over the method of abrogating decrees, it was then sent to the Constitutional Committee. The Government let it be known that it would not yield, and a clash seemed certain. In the end, however, Piłsudski decided to draw back, and allowed the Sejm to abrogate the decree on 10 December. The situation eased, and parliament approved the Government's provisional budget. As a sign of the relaxation of tension, Piłsudski himself appeared before the Budgetary Committee of the Sejm on 16 December and made a conciliatory speech.[2]

By the end of 1926, the political situation had become somewhat clearer. On the Right, the Christian National Party was seriously split by Piłsudski's approaches to the large landowners. The coup had led to a growth of Right-radicalism and antiparliamentarianism among the National Democrats, and such support as the party still enjoyed among large landowners was threatened by Piłsudski's wooing of the conservatives. To many the coup seemed to illustrate the final bankruptcy of liberal constitutionalism in Poland. At a meeting of the Executive Council of the Popular National Union on 27 November 1926, Dmowski, who had not been active in politics for several years, tried to convince the leaders of the party to transform it into a new 'national

---

[1] 'Rozporządzenie Prezydenta Rzeczypospolitej z dnia 4 listopada 1926 r. o karach za rozpowszechnianie nieprawdziwych wiadomości oraz o karach za zniewagę władz i ich przedstawicieli', *Dz.U.R.P.* (1926), no. 110, pp. 1123–5. For the general question of the Government's treatment of the press and the nature of press censorship in this period, see M. Pietrzak, *Reglamentacja wolności prasy w Polsce (1918–1939)* (Warsaw, 1963).

[2] According to Rataj, op. cit., p. 448, 'The fact that the Government accepted the withdrawal of the press decree without protest, where previously it was ready for extreme measures if this were done, the fact that Piłsudski took part in a normal and polite way in the sessions of the Budget Committee—these facts were universally regarded as the results of a definite change in the course of the Government, in the direction of co-operation with the Sejm.'

movement', based to some extent on the model of similar groups elsewhere in Europe.[1] Although the party leadership did not oppose Dmowski's initiative, the view prevailed that the party in its present form still answered the needs of the political situation.[2] Nevertheless Dmowski decided to launch his Camp for a Great Poland[3] on 4 December in Poznań. It was to be 'the organization of the conscious forces of the nation',[4] hierarchically organized. It did not intend to engage in day-to-day political activity, but hoped through education to unite all 'national elements' in a disciplined and organized body which would eventually take power. For the moment, outside student circles, its support was small.

The Centre parties too were much affected by the new situation. In spite of its apparent unity in parliament, the Christian Democratic Party was deeply divided. Only Korfanty's group in Upper Silesia was determined to pursue intransigent opposition. By the end of 1927, its policy had diverged so far from that of the central office that Korfanty's provincial committee was suspended. The Warsaw section of the party was for moderate opposition, while the group in Lwów led by Professor Stefan Bryl inclined towards co-operation with the Government.[5] In the National Workers' Party the coup led to a split, as we have seen; however, the majority of its members remained faithful to the leadership of Adam Chądzyński and moved into increasing opposition. The Piast decided not to assume a definite position for the time being, hoping that the activities of the Government and new elections would clarify the political scene. At the fifth party congress, held in Cracow on 28 November 1926, a resolution was passed approving the actions of the Parliamentary Club of the party 'in particular, the policy of the defence of parliamentarianism and of parliamentary governments in Poland, based on a stable majority'.

---

[1] The literature on the National Democrats between the wars is extremely scanty, and is one of the main gaps in the historiography of pre-war Poland. See: Micewski, op. cit., chap. ii; A. Garlicki, 'Obóz Wielkiej Polski', *Mówią Wieki* (November 1958), p. 38; Dmowski, *Pisma*, vols. ix, x; A. Wapiński, 'Niektóre problemy ewolucji ideowo-politycznej Endecji w latach 1918–1939' *K.H.* lxxiii (1966), no. 4, 861–77.

[2] The communiqué issued by the party is reprinted in *Gazeta Warszawska Poranna*, 28 November 1926.

[3] Obóz Wielkiej Polski (O.W.P.).

[4] Dmowski, 'Obóz Wielkiej Polski. Deklaracja Ideowa', *Pisma*, ix, p. 95.

[5] Micewski, op. cit., chap. iii; Czubiński, *Centrolew*, pp. 40–1.

At the same time, 'the principle of an objective attitude towards all governments up to the present, including this one' was approved.[1]

On the Left, considerable sympathy for Piłsudski survived, though opposition was growing. This process was to be seen most clearly in the P.P.S. There were many in the party, apart from the dedicated Piłsudski-ites, who hoped that Comrade Ziuk would modify his policy and move towards the Left. The party was thus unwilling to do anything which would excessively antagonize the Government. At the same time, the leadership hesitated to make too many concessions for fear of losing support to the Communists and to the P.P.S.—Left, a group which had split off from the Socialists in June 1926 and soon became a Communist-front organization.[2] During the September budget crisis, the party had voted for the Government until the provocative renomination of the Bartel Cabinet. Disquiet was further aroused by Piłsudski's approaches to the large landowners, although there were many in the party who justified this course as a means of 'encircling' the National Democrats.[3] When Moraczewski joined the Government, the Central Executive Committee of the P.P.S. ruled simply that he had acted on his own initiative, rejecting attempts to expel him from the party. What finally brought the P.P.S. into formal opposition was the press decree. On 11 November the Central Executive Committee resolved to adopt a policy of opposition because of the anti-democratic actions of the Government and its reactionary social and economic policy.[4] However, when the Government softened its course, the party retreated. On 20 December the Executive Council passed a resolution that

the opposition of the Socialist Party does not aim at overthrowing Marshal Piłsudski, the Prime Minister, but at bringing about the reorganization of his Cabinet by the exclusion of monarchist and reactionary elements and at obtaining a modification of internal policy, particularly in relation to the National Minorities.[5]

[1] *Czas*, 1 December 1926. For internal developments in the Piast see: Lato, op. cit., pp. 87–152, and Witos, op. cit. iii. 136–51.
[2] On the P.P.S.—Lewica, see L. Hass, 'P.P.S. Lewica, 1926–31', *N.D.P.*, 1st series, iv (1961), 59–99, and *P.P.S. Lewica, 1926–31. Materiały źródłowe* (Warsaw, 1963). The group's name was a conscious echo of that adopted by the more socially radical part of the P.P.S. which split off from the party in 1906. See above, Chapter II, pp. 62, 68–9.
[3] Rataj comments bitterly on this, op. cit., p. 420.
[4] *Robotnik*, 12 November 1926.   [5] Ibid., 21 December 1926.

The move towards opposition was much slower in the radical peasant parties. On 8 December 1926 the Executive Committee of the Liberation passed a number of resolutions criticizing aspects of the Government's activity, but it concluded merely that the party would oppose 'those acts of the Government which it considered harmful'.[1] Pro-Piłsudski sentiment was strongest in the Peasant Party. On 19 December, Jan Dąbski, writing in the party weekly *Gazeta Chłopska*, stressed that the danger of a coup against democracy came from the Right, not the Sanacja, and criticized the Government only for not doing enough to crush reaction.[2] At the end of December 1926 the Warsaw committee resolved that the party 'has looked, and still looks, with great friendliness upon Marshal Piłsudski's Government', but that this attitude was becoming more difficult to maintain because of the neglect of peasant interests and the approaches to the magnates.[3]

The uneasy truce between the Government and the Sejm which had been achieved in December continued when parliament was reconvened on 25 January 1927. The discussion of the budget for 1927-8 proceeded without difficulty, and when the question of the parliamentary immunity of the Hromada deputies arrested in January was raised, only the P.P.S., the Communists, and the Slavic minorities voted against its being waived. On 15 February the second reading of the budget was approved despite the opposition of the National Democrats, the Christian National Party, the P.P.S., and all the minorities except the Jews. According to Rataj, the National Democrats would have voted for the budget if the Government had not already possessed a majority.[4] When, after the final voting of the budget on 22 March, the Liberation proposed votes of no confidence in Meysztowicz and Niezabytowski, the Right refused to support them, and the motions were thus defeated. On 23 March, *Gazeta Warszawska Poranna*, the National Democratic daily, commented: 'The Popular National Union is a party too mature to sacrifice the fundamental interests of the state to its emotions.'[5]

The situation worsened when the Government suddenly and unexpectedly adjourned parliament on 25 March. Piłsudski told

[1] *Wyzwolenie*, 19 December 1926.
[2] *Gazeta Chłopska*, 19 December 1926.
[3] Ibid., 2 January 1927.
[4] Rataj, op. cit., p. 462.
[5] *Gazeta Warszawska Poranna*, 23 March 1927.

Rataj that this step had been taken because the Government wanted to separate the vote on the budget from other parliamentary business,[1] but it was more likely intended to prevent the passing of a bill on the right of assembly, of which the Government disapproved. The way in which the adjournment was effected was typical of the secrecy with which the Government surrounded much of its activity, and was greatly resented by all the political parties. It pushed the P.P.S. further into opposition. When, on the anniversary of the coup, Daszyński published a pamphlet assessing developments since the previous May, Niedziałkowski commented in *Robotnik* 'his book is the last word of warning to those who today control the state. The last word.'[2] At the end of May, the Executive Council of the party resolved that 'Opposition is the principle of action of all organs of the party and their members.'[3]

The Liberation also moved more clearly into opposition. At its congress in Warsaw on 11 June 1927, it criticized the Government for not dissolving parliament, for attacking parliamentarianism, for not helping the peasants and for co-operating with the clergy and the large landowners. Although it recognized the beneficial effects of the coup, the congress called on the Executive Council of its Parliamentary Club 'to intensify its critical attitude towards the Government'.[4] Of the non-revolutionary parties of the Left, only the Peasant Party remained favourable to the Government. The Piast also hardened its opposition. After bitter discussions, the Parliamentary Club of the party rejected on 10 May by a decisive majority a resolution advocating co-operation with the Government. At the same time an alliance with the Right, advocated by Kiernik and Osiecki, was also rejected.[5] In order to recapture the influence which it had lost since the coup, the party undertook an extensive campaign during the spring and summer in which the Government was strongly criticized, although Piłsudski himself was not directly attacked. The sixth congress of the party, held in Poznań on 8–10 July 1927, reaffirmed this anti-Government position and stressed the importance of defending

[1] Rataj, op. cit., p. 471.
[2] *Robotnik*, 8 May 1927. The pamphlet in question was *W pierwszą rocznicę przewrotu majowego* (Warsaw, 1927).
[3] Quoted in Próchnik, op. cit., p. 259.
[4] *Wyzwolenie*, 19 June 1927.
[5] Lato, op. cit., p. 142.

Democracy, although it also upheld the need for the modification of the 1921 Constitution.[1]

When Parliament reconvened on 20 June, the National Democrats and the P.P.S. co-operated in putting forward a bill which would restore to the Sejm its right of dissolution. This would make it possible to force the holding of elections and thus put an end to the existing situation which was widely felt to be compromising parliament, in that a majority of deputies were powerless against the Government. The bill was passed by 189 votes to 10.[2] The Right also proposed changes in the electoral system which would reduce the number of members and modify the proportional system. Finally, two new and only slightly less harsh decrees on the freedom of the press which the Government had issued in May came before the Juridical Committee on 6 July, where they were violently attacked.[3]

All this was too much for the Government. On 13 July the session was prorogued. The deputies of the P.P.S., Liberation, the Piast, Christian Democracy, the Christian National Party, and the Popular National Union agreed to demand the convening of an extraordinary session of parliament.[4] However, the necessary resolution was only adopted on 2 August, when it was submitted to the President.[5] The fate of General Zagórski, who disappeared on 6 August in rather mysterious circumstances after his alleged release from gaol, contributed to the excitement. He had almost certainly been murdered, perhaps accidentally and probably without direct authorization from Piłsudski.[6] However, the Government adopted delaying tactics in calling this session. It should

---

[1] *Piast*, 17 July 1927.

[2] *S.S.S.R.*, 20 June 1927, cols. 61–2.

[3] 'Rozporządzenie Prezydenta Rzeczypospolitej Polskiej z dnia 10 maja 1927 r. o prawie prasowem', *Dz.U.R.P.* (1927), no. 45, pp. 549–59; 'Rozporządzenie Prezydenta Rzeczypospolitej z dnia 10 maja 1927 r. zmieniające niektóre postanowienia ustaw karnych o rozpowszechnianiu nieprawdziwych wiadomości i o zniewagach', *Dz.U.R.P.* (1927), no. 45, pp. 559–60.

[4] *Gazeta Warszawska Poranna*, 15 July 1927.

[5] Ibid., 3 August 1927.

[6] A large literature has grown up around this subject. See: Lieberman, op. cit., p. 304–12; L. Hass, 'Tajemnicze zniknięcie', *Mówią Wieki*, ii (1959), no. 12, pp. 14–17; and 'Jeszcze raz o generale Zagórskim', *Tygodnik Powszechny*, xiv (1960), no. 8, p. 7; M. Kukiel, 'Jeszcze o majowej wojnie domowej i generale Zagórskim', *Wiadomości*, xiv (12 July 1959), no. 693, p. 6; Pomorski, 'Jak zginął gen. Zagórski', *Nadodrze* (1959), no. 7, p. 6; J. Rawicz, *Gen. Zagórski zginął* (Warsaw, 1963).

have been convened early in September, but was not called until the 22nd, nearly ten days after it should have opened, according to the constitution. Already before it met, a group of deputies, which did not include the socialists, had agreed on a proposed law restoring to the Sejm the right of dissolution by a simple majority. This was considered by *Glos Prawdy* 'a provocation'.[1]

When parliament finally met, it debated the rejection of the press decrees which the Juridical Committee had proposed. Lieberman, for the P.P.S., delivered a fiery speech:

> For former generations and for us, a Polish constitution was to be a charter of rights and privileges, revered by all—for the present Government it is a political toy, a toy for keeping the Right and the Left at bay, nothing but a toy. . . . We will abrogate the decrees of the President as the product of dictatorial ideas and as constituting a danger to the fundamental rights of the whole population. We will abrogate them, and we will abrogate them as many times as they are renewed.[2]

The press decrees were abrogated with only two dissenting votes (both cast by members of the Club of Labour). The Popular National Union then proposed a number of motions, the most important of which demanded the withdrawal of the special powers granted to the Government after the coup and the limiting of the Presidential right to issue decrees to cases of urgent need. The Government's response was again to prorogue parliament. It continued to apply the press decrees, claiming that for them to be revoked a law was necessary, not simply a resolution. The question went to the Supreme Court where in February 1928 it was first decided in the Government's favour, and although the Government later allowed the decrees to be repealed, this concession had by then, as Próchnik remarks, 'only a moral significance'.[3]

The Government reconvened parliament on 21 October, as it was legally obliged to do in order to present the budget. A dispute arose among the parties as to whether parliament should agree to consider the budget or not, but this remained academic since parliament was adjourned immediately after it had been declared

[1] *Glos Prawdy*, 17 September 1927.
[2] *S.S.S.R.*, 22 September 1927, col. 21.
[3] Próchnik, op. cit., p. 262. See below, p. 301.

in session. It remained adjourned until its five-year mandate elapsed on 28 November 1927. The Government had been unable to co-operate with the existing parliament; the elections, which were to be held on 4 and 11 March, would, it hoped, allow it to co-operate with a new one.

VI

THE GROWING CONFLICT WITH PARLIAMENT

The 'Sanacja' camp was, to speak brutally, the camp of those people who placed their money on Piłsudski. There were among them ideologues—some who believed that Piłsudski would create a monarchy in Poland, others that he would introduce a socialist system. There were careerists and speculators who bet on Piłsudski as they would on a racehorse. But the basis, the foundation of this camp was that it had no common ideology, that it was a union of people who expected something from Piłsudski.

Stanisław Mackiewicz, 1941

Any strong man would go through this Poland like a knife through butter. But he would then fall into a void.

Stanisław Thugutt, Autumn 1925

THE ELECTIONS

THE elections of March 1928 initiated a new phase in the conflict between the Government and parliament. The Government saw these elections as a plebiscite on the May coup and on its achievements in the two years following, and was determined that the new parliament should contain a majority with which it could cooperate. It was the Government's aim to contest the elections by appealing to the widest possible support, both on the Right and on the Left. In a confidential speech on 15 September 1927 at the Dzików conference of conservative groups, Sławek made clear the Government's position: 'The elections should be conducted with the slogan "On the one side the pre-May parties, on the other everything which opposes them".' In this way, he added, 'it may be possible to find a common expression for the pro-Government Right and Left'.[1] Yet, although the Government did continue its approaches to both Right and Left, it hesitated for the moment to organize an all-embracing bloc.

Much effort was devoted to cementing the alliance with the

[1] Kersten, op. cit., p. 211.

conservative Right. Sławek, together with Remigiusz Grocholski, Piłsudski's Adjutant, represented the Government at the Dzików conference, held on the estate of Zdzisław Tarnowski, near Tarnów, on 14–16 September 1927.[1] All the main conservative groups were represented, and among the 36 people who attended were most of the prominent large landowners in Poland. In his two speeches, Sławek went out of his way to win their support. He stressed that although the coming elections would be fought under the existing electoral system, the Government regarded constitutional reform, the strengthening of the executive, and the modification of proportional representation, as a pressing need. He even hinted that the Government was not opposed to the restoration of the monarchy, the cherished goal of some of the conservatives. 'The Marshal', he stated, 'understanding that he cannot be replaced, holds that in the future only a symbol will be able to replace him.'[2] In a discussion which took place in Sławek's absence, a difference of opinion emerged between the Party of the National Right and the Conservative Association, which were both very eager to co-operate with the Government, and the Christian National Party which, though also sympathetic towards the Government, was unwilling to break completely its previously strong ties with the National Democrats. An attempt was made to set up a united conservative group, and even Eustachy Sapieha, one of the most pro-Piłsudski-ite of those present, stressed that a general electoral bloc with the Sanacja was not possible, although local arrangements could be reached.

The Dzików meeting was followed by a number of smaller gatherings in Galicia and in Western Poland, where further attempts were made to win over the large landowners. On 24 October the three main conservative groups agreed to set up a Conservative Committee to co-ordinate their activity. A joint programme was issued which called for an increase in the powers of the President, the equalizing of the rights of the Sejm and Senate, a qualified franchise, and fair treatment for the minorities.[3]

The Sanacja retained the support of the large industrialists. On 19 December, 168 important entrepreneurs and landowners issued a long statement implicitly supporting the Government for having established increased political stability. They stressed that a

---

[1] For the minutes of this conference see Kersten, op. cit., pp. 204–15.
[2] Ibid., p. 211.   [3] *Czas*, 31 October 1927.

constitutional system should be maintained, but that the powers of
the executive should be extended, and those of parliament limited.[1]

In addition, the Government tried to maintain and extend the
support it enjoyed on the Centre and Left. Here the only political
groupings openly sympathetic to the regime remained the Party of
Labour, the League for the Reform of the Republic, and the
National Workers' Party—Left Wing. However, there was still
much sympathy and good will, some of it dictated by opportunism,
in most of the Centre and Left parties. The Christian Democrats
remained seriously divided, and the group led by Stefan Bryl in
Lwów tended generally to support the Government.[2] The Piast
too remained internally at odds on the question of its attitude to
the Sanacja. We have seen how, early in 1927, the party had moved
to a position of much stronger opposition to the Government.
This aroused considerable unease among the pro-Piłsudski-ite and
opportunistic members of the party, particularly after Government
circles spread the suggestion that if only the most compromised
members of the Piast, such as Witos, Kiernik, and Osiecki, were
removed from positions of power, the Government would co-
operate with the party. Several unsuccessful attempts were made
to induce Witos to resign as President of the party, and to let Rataj
take his place. The discontent in the party came to a head in
September and October 1927, when Jakub Bojko, one of its oldest
and most respected members, after failing to exclude Witos from
the leadership, issued a manifesto strongly attacking him and
announcing his own intention of co-operating with Piłsudski. He
resigned from the party, taking several others with him. Bojko
founded a weekly, *Chłop Polski*, and a pro-Government peasant
organization, the Association of Polish Peasants.[3]

In spite of the bitter disputes which had characterized relations
between the Cabinet and parliament and the resentment this had
provoked on the Left, the Government still remained hopeful that
it could gain the support of the left-wing parties. Pro-Government sympathies were strongest in the Peasant Party. Świtalski, at
this time Director of the Political Department of the Ministry of
Internal Affairs, who was in charge of the attempt to form a left-

[1] *Dzień Polski*, 22 December 1927.
[2] Czubiński, op. cit., pp. 40–1.
[3] See: Lato, op. cit., pp. 140–52; Witos, op. cit. iii. 143–68; Bojko's manifesto
and Witos's reply are printed in Lato, pp. 237–44.

wing pro-Government bloc, managed to induce the party on
4 November 1927 to propose a common electoral front which
would include the League for the Reform of the Republic, the
Bojko group, the Party of Labour, the Liberation, and the P.P.S.
The bloc failed to materialize, however, because of opposition to
the Government's close links with the landowners, and because the
Liberation and the P.P.S. were unwilling to take part.[1] The refusal
openly to commit the Peasant Party to the Government led to
discontent among the most ardent pro-Piłsudski-ites, whose disruptive activity reached such proportions that their leaders, Jan
Stapiński, for many years the head of the Agricultural Workers'
Union, Hipolit Śliwiński, and Stanisław Wójtowicz were expelled
from the party on 23 December 1927. In January 1928 they formed
a new pro-Government peasant organization, the Peasant Alliance.[2]

Świtalski also made approaches to the Liberation to enter a pro-
Government bloc, threatening the party with dire consequences if
it did not. According to Aleksander Bogusławski, one of its leaders,

When the representatives of the Liberation replied negatively,
Świtalski began to threaten the complete destruction of the party. He
said that they [the Sanacja] possessed large sums of money, nearly 28
million zloties, and they controlled the administrative apparatus, thus
they could easily destroy the Liberation.[3]

It is not clear whether Świtalski made similar approaches to the
P.P.S., but the fact that the overwhelming majority of the Piłsudski-ites, with the exception of Tadeusz Hołówko and Moraczewski,
remained in the party, suggests some contact may have existed.
In January 1928, however, the party split in Upper Silesia, where
a large part of the leadership, headed by Józef Biniszkiewicz, went
over to the Sanacja.[4]

In the first month after the proclamation of new elections the
Government did not proceed in organizing its disparate supporters.
But from December 'non-party' committees to support the Marshal
were being formed, particularly in Galicia and the Eastern Kresy.
With the co-operation of the local authorities, the network of com-
mittees grew rapidly, and by January it was possible to unite them

[1] A.S.S., quoted in Stęborowski, op. cit., p. 76.
[2] Związek Chłopski. For the split see: Lato, op. cit., pp. 155–7; A. Więzikowa,
Stronnictwo Chłopskie (Warsaw, 1963), pp. 102–5.
[3] W. Bogusławski, 'Pamiętnik', Archiwum Zakładu Historii Ruchu Ludowego,
quoted in Lato, op. cit., p. 158.
[4] Rechowicz, op. cit., pp. 125–8.

and to create a 'Non-party Bloc for the Support of the Government'.[1] The membership of the B.B.W.R. was extremely varied. In fact, agreement on the distribution of seats on the general and constituency lists was reached only after much conflict. The general list (i.e. the list of seats divided in proportion to the number of seats won in the country as a whole) was only published on 24 January, the last day possible.[2] The core of the bloc was made up of former legionaries and members of the P.O.W. Walery Sławek was its Chairman and played a large part in its organization. Other legionaries who stood on the bloc's lists included Bogusław Miedziński, Adam Koc, Janusz Jędrzejewicz, Marian Kościałkowski, and Bronisław Pieracki. Ministers were also important in the bloc's membership. Bartel, Czechowicz, and Kwiatkowski stood for the Sejm, while Niezabytowski and Zaleski stood for the Senate.[3] Sławek succeeded in inducing both the Party of the National Right and the Conservative Association to join the bloc along with the Left, in spite of their earlier unwillingness to do so. The Christian National Party split over the question of the bloc. The majority of its members, led by Stroński and Adam Żoltowski, decided to support the National Democrats. The rest seceded and, under the name of the Christian Agricultural Party, joined the bloc.[4] Many prominent landowners and their supporters figured in the B.B.W.R. lists, such as Janusz Radziwiłł and Eustachy Sapieha for the Sejm, and Zdzisław Tarnowski and Franciszek Drucki-Lubecki for the Senate. The bloc also obtained the implicit support of Lewiatan, the Polish Industrialists' Association, and its director, Jan Hołyński, stood on the state list for the Sejm.

In addition, the B.B.W.R. included the pro-Government Left-Wing organizations, the Party of Labour, the League for the Reform of the Republic, and the National Workers' Party—Left Wing. In East Galicia the Christian Democrats joined in too. A considerable attempt was made to obtain peasant support through the secessionists from the various peasant parties. Of those who had left the Piast, Bojko himself, Władysław Wójtowicz, and Władysław Kosyderski stood for the Sejm, while Ignacy Miciński

[1] Bezpartyjny Blok Współpracy z Rządem, known as the B.B.W.R.

[2] *Głos Prawdy*, 25 January 1928.

[3] Most of this information about Government Deputies and Senators is from T. i K. Rzepeccy, *Sejm i Senat, 1928–33* (Poznań, 1928), and T. Łoza, *Czy wiesz kto to jest* (Warsaw, 1938).

[4] *Głos Prawdy*, 19 January 1928.

stood for the Senate. Józef Sanojca and Marian Cieplak, formerly of the Peasant Party, also stood for the Sejm. The small conservative Catholic Peasant Party in Galicia entered the bloc as well.

The B.B.W.R. also included a number of pro-Government figures from the national minorities. Elias Kirszbraun, one of the leaders of the orthodox Agudas Israel, and Wacław Wiślicki, director of the [Jewish] Merchant's Association, stood for the Sejm; Lazar Dal, a Jewish leader in Volynia, stood for the Senate. Several pro-Government White Russians and Ukrainians appeared on the B.B.W.R. lists in Volynia and in the Nowogródek and Wilno provinces.

However, the B.B.W.R. did not comprise all the pro-Government groups contesting the election. In Poznania and Pomerania it proved impossible for the conservative and radical supporters of the Government to reach agreement. The conservatives put up their own list, under the name of the Catholic Union of the Western Territories,[1] which included landowners' groups and some secessions from the Piast. It was to include the Christian Democrats, but they withdrew on orders from the Warsaw headquarters of the party. Nevertheless, the Christian Democratic trade unions continued to support the list.[2] The Radicals—the League for the Reform of the Republic and the N.P.R.—Left—also submitted an independent list of candidates as the National-State Bloc of Labour.[3] In Silesia the pro-Government forces assumed the name of the National-Christian Alliance of Labour[4] because of the importance of political Catholicism in the area, and no B.B.W.R. list was nominated. In Galicia the Peasant League of Jan Stapiński, although it supported the Government, also ran independently.

The aims of the bloc were very vague. Its adherents limited themselves to expressions of support for Piłsudski, to calls for a reform of the constitution which would further increase the power of the executive, and to a rather ill-defined étatism, claiming that the different social groups should subordinate their individual interests to the higher interest of the state. The improvement in conditions after 1926 was constantly alluded to. On 19 January

[1] Katolicka Unia Ziem Zachodnich.
[2] Czubiński, op. cit., pp. 71–2.
[3] Narodowo-Państwowy Blok Pracy.
[4] Narodowo-Chrześcijańskie Zjednoczenie Pracy. See Czubiński, op. cit., p. 73.

1928 the B.B.W.R. published a statement of purpose. After a bitter critique of the way in which the parliamentary system had functioned before 1926, it launched an attack against those politicians, blindly attached to parties, who had 'learned nothing', who wished to return to 'the system of a year and a half ago, a system which they embellish with the name of "parliamentarianism" or "legality".' The results of the activity of the Piłsudski Government, the manifesto continued,

are enough to convince us that Poland has found the right path to consolidate the power of the state and achieve prosperity for its citizens. We do not want to leave this path to become bemired in the old ruts and swamps. The present reorganization must not be a passing phase in the history of reborn Poland, it must be the beginning of a long period of happiness and prosperity, resulting from the harmonious development of all the strength and resources of the state and of the whole population.[1]

The list of undertakings which B.B.W.R. candidates had to sign was also vague. A deputy was to support and respect the power of the President and to work for an increase in the power of the executive. He was to ensure that 'the needs of the State' were not subordinated to those of any group or social class, to treat other B.B.W.R. deputies with respect, and if, after the election, more than one parliamentary group should be organized from among those elected on List 1, he must take no action to join a new group without first consulting Piłsudski.[2]

The main attack of the B.B.W.R. was directed against the National Democrats, both because they were regarded as the most irreconcilable opponents of Piłsudski, and as a means of gaining left-wing support. In turn, the National Democrats strongly criticized the Government because it did not possess a 'National and Catholic' character, and for its disregard of the constitution, though they also called for its modification and for the establishment of an equilibrium between the executive and legislative powers. This was to be maintained by a Constitutional Tribunal which would pronounce on the legality of the actions of both executive and legislature.[3] The party also attacked the Government

---

[1] The declaration was reprinted in *Głos Prawdy*, 20 January 1928.

[2] *Gazeta Warszawska*, 23 February 1928. (The name *Gazeta Warszawska* was reassumed by the paper in January 1928.)

[3] The 'Programme theses' of the Z.L.N. had been adopted by the Supreme Council of the party on 16 October 1927. They are reprinted in *Gazeta Warszawska Poranna*, 17 October 1927.

for what it held to be excessive liberalism towards the national minorities, in particular the Jews and Ukrainians.[1] In addition, its press warned the conservatives that the Piłsudski-ites had not abandoned their radical principles and were merely making use of conservative support to establish what *Kurjer Poznański* called 'Moraczewski-ism',[2] or socialism under a different name.

The National Democrats attempted, moreover, to revive and extend the Christian Alliance for National Unity. The party leadership reached agreement with Dmowski and the O.W.P., hard-pressed by a government order of October 1927 which banned it in the Lwów, Tarnopol, and Stanisławów provinces.[3] The O.W.P. pledged itself to support National Democratic candidates and to make no nominations on its own. The Endecja was also helped by a pastoral letter issued by the Polish bishops on 5 December 1927 which called for united action by Catholics in the coming elections. 'We have no need', it continued, 'to insist on this self-evident truth: that division in circumstances such as those in which we find ourselves weakens the Catholic and national camp.'[4] It is not clear whether the bishops intended the declaration to have an anti-Government character, but its use of traditional National Democratic catch phrases made it seem so to the Endecja.[5] On 11 December the Executive Council of the party resolved to place itself 'on the ground indicated by the bishops' pastoral letter', and declared itself 'favourable to an electoral campaign pursued by a united national camp'.[6] On 13 December 118 leading right-wing politicians and intellectuals signed a public manifesto calling for the creation of a Catholic electoral bloc.[7]

The letter upset the Government, and still more the pro-Government conservatives. The Conservative Committee, the co-ordinating body of the three main conservative groups, sought

[1] For examples of attacks on the Government's policy on national minorities, see *Kurjer Poznański*, 21 November 1927; *Gazeta Warszawska Poranna*, 28 October 1927, 29 October 1927, 5 November 1927, 29 February 1928.

[2] For warnings to the Conservatives, see, e.g., *Gazeta Warszawska Poranna*, 21 October 1927, 27 October 1927, 28 October 1927. 'Moraczewskiism' was an allusion to Jędrzej Moraczewski, a pro-Piłsudski-ite member of the P.P.S. who became a Cabinet Minister in October 1926.

[3] *Gazeta Warszawska Poranna*, 21 October 1927, 25 October 1927.

[4] The letter was printed in *Gazeta Warszawska Poranna*, 7 November 1927.

[5] Pro-Government radicals attributed the letter to the Armenian Archbishop Teodorowicz of Lwów, a strong supporter of the National Democrats.

[6] *Gazeta Warszawska Poranna*, 12 December 1927.

[7] The text was reprinted in *Gazeta Warszawska Poranna*, 13 December 1927.

an audience with Cardinal Kakowski. After it took place a statement was issued to the press affirming that the letter had no anti-
Government intention.[1] When Hlond, who had sent a telegram
from Rome forbidding priests to take part in the election, returned
to Poland with Bishop Przeździecki of Podlasie in mid-January,
rumours circulated that they had brought with them a letter from
the Pope expressing his support for Piłsudski.[2] On 8 February
Janusz Radziwiłł claimed that when he sought Bishop Szelążek's
advice about standing on the B.B.W.R. list he was told 'Not only
do I authorize you to stand on List 1, I urge you to do so.'[3]

Nevertheless, the National Democrats continued to exploit the
bishops' letter. On 12 December they began negotiations with the
Piast, the N.P.R.—Right Wing and the Christian Democrats,
and on 23 December they announced that their electoral list would
be headed 'The Catholic–National Electoral Committee'. However,
on 9 January, when submitting the names of their candidates, they
were forced to admit that apart from a section of the Christian
National Party, they had been unable to enlist the support of any
other political groups.[4]

The Piast, greatly disheartened by Bojko's secession, determined
upon an alliance with the Christian Democrats, and rejected
Witos's call to stand on the National Democratic list. The tone of
the Piast–Christian Democratic programme was markedly clerical,
though not strongly anti-Government: 'We will support the
Government when its acts are just and conform to our views, but
we will oppose, in a legal way, projects contrary to our principles.'[5]
This alliance did not extend to Silesia, where the Christian Democrats were at odds with the Warsaw head office over the parliamentary court's verdict against Korfanty, and decided to nominate an
independent list.

The N.P.R.—Right Wing stood alone, but its strength was confined mainly to Western Poland. Its once-strong Lodz organization
had almost completely gone over to the Piłsudski-ites.

[1] *Czas*, 19 December 1927.
[2] *Głos Prawdy*, 14 January 1928; *Czas*, 10 February 1928.
[3] *Czas*, 10 February 1928.
[4] The communiqué announcing this failure was reprinted in *Gazeta
Warszawska*, 9 January 1928.
[5] *Rzeczpospolita*, 25 January 1928. (This was the main organ of the Christian
Democrats.) For the Piast in this period, see Witos, op. cit. iii. 167–9, and
Lato, op. cit., pp. 159–61.

The parties of the non-revolutionary Left, the P.P.S., the Liberation, and the Peasant Party, avoided directly attacking Piłsudski in their electoral campaigns. They even claimed to be truer exponents of his programme than the B.B.W.R., a claim made more plausible by the fact that Piłsudski's name did not figure on the B.B.W.R. list. A rapid move towards outright opposition to Piłsudski would have cost these parties a great deal of their support.

The Peasant Party remained the most strongly pro-Government, in spite of the bitterness engendered at the time of Stapiński's expulsion.[1] As late as 8 January Andrzej Waleron, one of the party leaders, affirmed: 'The Peasant Party has supported and will support the Government of Marshal Piłsudski, who is an irreproachable man and has performed great services for the Nation and State.'[2] However, the pressure of the Government's electoral campaign provoked a more critical response. On 12 February, for example, the Executive Committee of the party issued a declaration stating that behind the screen of Piłsudski's name, the B.B.W.R. hid landlords, capitalists, and officials in their service, and appealed to peasants to vote against the bloc.[3] In its programme, the party called for the expropriation without compensation of all land in excess of 60 hectares in large estates. It demanded the maintenance of the republican system of government, and declared 'unremitting war against all monarchist or Fascist coups against the constitution'.[4]

The campaigns of the P.P.S. and the Liberation had many similarities. Both called for radical social reforms and for the maintenance of democracy. Both demanded the abolition of the Senate and the granting of territorial autonomy to the Slav minorities.[5] At the same time, they avoided directly attacking Piłsudski, arguing that they, and not the conservative landlords and industrialists, were his true allies, and stressing the danger from the National Democratic Right. According to the Sub-Prefect of Łuków, in the province of Lublin, 'It is characteristic that opposition parties like the P.P.S. and the Liberation, which often quite

---

[1] See above, p. 237.

[2] C.A.M.S.W., Urząd Wojewódzki Kraków, vol. 25-b, p. 23 (speech to the provincial assembly of delegates of the Peasant Party, Cracow, 8 January 1928), quoted in Lato, op. cit., p. 162.

[3] *Gazeta Chłopska*, 12 February 1928.

[4] The programme was reprinted in *Gazeta Chłopska*, 5 February 1928.

[5] The P.P.S. programme was reprinted in *Robotnik*, 1 January 1928, that of the Liberation in *Wyzwolenie*, the party weekly, on 22 January 1928.

passionately attack the Government, not only do not criticize the activity of Marshal Józef Piłsudski, but claim him as their man.'[1] An attempt was made to effect an electoral alliance between the two parties, but this was sabotaged by Świtalski. He told the P.P.S. leaders that the Government's attitude towards their party would be much more hostile if it formed this bloc than if it fought the elections alone.[2] In discussion with the Liberation leaders, he argued that such an alliance would be directed against Piłsudski, that it would strengthen conservative influence among the peasantry, and that the P.P.S. was trying to replace the Liberation in the countryside.[3] Nevertheless, relations between the two groups remained close. In the course of an interview with *Robotnik* on 1 January 1928, for example, Jan Woźnicki, President of the Liberation, stated that in the coming Sejm, the P.P.S. and the Liberation would be the principal forces struggling to maintain democracy.[4]

The main Communist Party list was that of the Worker–Peasant Alliance,[5] but a number of other lists were submitted in case this one should be declared invalid. In addition, a number of Communist-front organizations put up candidates.[6] The debate over the 'May error' had led to the dominance in the party of the minority Leftist group, led by Leszczyński, at the fourth congress of the party in September 1927, a victory achieved partly as a result of Stalin's intervention on their behalf. Warski was excluded from the Central Committee, and a Leftist line, afterwards confirmed at the sixth conference of Comintern (July–September 1928), was adopted. This condemned Social Democracy as the main enemy and rejected out of hand any co-operation with other left-wing parties.[7]

The principal minority list was again that of the Bloc of National Minorities. It now extended to the U.N.D.O. in East Galicia, but did not include the Agudas Israel in former Russian Poland, which had joined the Galician Zionists in rejecting Grünbaum's call for

---

[1] A.A.N., Zespół Ministerstwa Spraw Wewnętrznych, Wydział Organizacyjno-Prawny, Materiały na zjazdy wojewodów i starostów, folio 1.

[2] A.S.S. Quoted in Lato, p. 159.   [3] Ibid., pp. 158–9.

[4] *Robotnik*, 1 January 1928.

[5] Jedność Robotniczo-Chłopska.

[6] These included the Left Peasant Union-Self-Help (Zjednoczenie Lewicy Chłopskiej-Samopomoc) which had replaced the banned Independent Peasant Party, the Ukrainian Worker–Peasant Alliance (Sel-Rob), and the White Russian Demand (Zmahannie) which had replaced the Hromada.

[7] For the Communist Party in this period see: Dziewanowski, op. cit., pp. 120–8; Reguła, op. cit.

an alliance between the Jews and the other national minorities. A number of radical minority organizations also put up lists. The German Socialists reached an agreement with the P.P.S. and stood on its list. The Jewish Bund and Poalej Sion again stood independently, as did the Ukrainian Sel-Rob Left, which had broken with the Sel-Rob over nationality policy in the Soviet Ukraine, and the Ukrainian Electoral Bloc of Worker and Peasant Parties.

The Government actively intervened in the elections. As a first step, it clashed with the Supreme Court which was empowered to nominate three people from among whom the Electoral Commissioner, responsible for the organization of the election, was to be chosen by the President. The Government demanded that the court include as one of its nominees Stanisław Car, the legal expert who had suggested most of the devices for bending the constitution which the Sanacja had employed. When the court twice refused to comply, the Government, acting alone, named him Commissioner.

The administrative apparatus was extensively used to support the Government's campaign. Sławoj-Składkowski, the Minister of the Interior, was quite open about this, stating in the course of the Sejm's debate on his ministry's budget on 5 June 1928:

I consciously took part in the elections for those parties which said they would support Marshal Piłsudski, and I say it openly. . . . When I took this decision to participate in the elections, I called the provincial governors to me and orally advised them to support the B.B.W.R. The governors implemented this through the sub-prefects.[1]

The documents bear this out. On 13 January, the Governor of the Lodz province urged his subordinates to support the B.B.W.R., calling on the head of his political department, Jan Dychdalewicz, to explain the situation. This he did with great directness: 'Today, therefore, since the Government places such stress on the results of the elections, it is the duty of the administration in the first place to support its wants to the fullest extent of its power.'[2] Many examples of the involvement of local officials in the campaign on behalf of the Sanacja could be cited. On 13 January the Sub-Prefect of the Konin district in the province of Lodz instructed his officials to support the Government:

This support could take the form, during the electoral period, of

---

[1] S.S.S.R., 5 June 1928, col. 116.
[2] P.Z.P.K. II, Lodz province, 13 January 1928, folio 60.

settling favourably all those matters which could harmfully affect the attitude of the people to the Government or diminish their support, as, for instance, holding up for the time being distraints for taxes in arrears, allowing relief in their payment, postponing the date of their payment, allowing payment in instalments, through the swift giving of advice and the favourable settlement of matters where there is no legal objection.

He especially appealed to the School Inspector to support the B.B.W.R. campaign through the teachers subordinate to him.[1]

Moreover, the police allowed election meetings of the Sanacja's opponents to be broken up by pro-Government militants, and a number of radical politicians were taken into custody or compelled to report to the police thrice daily during the electoral period.[2] Action was also taken against the anti-Government press by means of the press decree. Right-wing newspapers were particularly affected. *Gazeta Warszawska*, for example, was confiscated on 1, 10, 13, 14, 24, 27, 29 February and 3 March, *Kurjer Poznański* on 18, 22, 23, 29 February and 1 March. Electoral pamphlets were subject to censorship too, and a fair number of those of the Right, as well as a few of those of the P.P.S., were seized.[3]

The B.B.W.R. enjoyed impressive financial reserves, which enabled it to undertake a campaign of almost American dimensions and also to buy off opponents. These funds came not only from the bloc's numerous supporters among the landowners and industrialists, but also from the Treasury as well. 'On the orders of Marshal Piłsudski', wrote Sławoj-Składkowski long afterwards, 'Minister Czechowicz gave me 8 million zloties for the elections, which I accounted for to a Citizens' Commission headed by Zawadzki and Sieroszewski.'[4]

In addition, through its control of the Electoral Commission, the Government was able to invalidate lists when they were sub-

[1] P.Z.P.K. I, Konin sub-prefecture, Lodz province, 13 January 1928, folio 76. There were many such cases. See, e.g., P.Z.P.K. I, folio 76, meeting on 28 December 1927 of the officials of the Łask district, Lodz province; folio 80, meeting on 27 January 1928, of the officials of the Kościan district in Poznania; folio 83, meeting on 3 February 1928 of officials of the Rohatyń district in the Stanisławów province.

[2] See the open letter of one of those affected, A. Kordowski, to the Minister of Justice. *Robotnik*, 12 March 1928.

[3] *B.P.P.P.* 183, pp. 10–12. Complaints about the Government's behaviour in the elections appeared frequently in the Opposition press. See, e.g., *Robotnik*, 12 February 1928, 15 February 1928, 29 February 1928, 3 March 1928.

[4] Letter to W. Pobóg-Malinowski, 9 October 1951, quoted in Pobóg-Malinowski, *Najnowsza historia*, ii. 515.

mitted, a power it used principally against the Communists. In the same way it was able to assess the validity of votes cast in the election, when 320,000 ballots were declared cancelled (i.e. 3·6 per cent)[1] as against 50,000 in 1922. A certain amount of falsification also took place during the counting of votes.

After the elections the Sejm created a Special Commission to Investigate Electoral Abuses.[2] Although a number of constituencies called for a judicial investigation, no action was taken until after Car's resignation from the Commission in December 1929. (He had become Minister of Justice in December 1928.) Between December and April 1930, the Supreme Court declared invalid the results in six constituencies, mostly in Eastern Poland, and in the new elections here the B.B.W.R. lost nearly twenty seats.[3] When the Government's mild course was abandoned in April 1930 no further legal investigation was permitted. It should be stressed, however, that in spite of the irregularities already described, the actual voting took place without administrative interference.

The elections were a qualified success for the B.B.W.R. Whereas Sławek had stated at Dzików that he expected the Government to win 160 seats, the bloc together with the pro-Government N.P.R.—Left and Peasant League won 130 seats (out of 444) in the Sejm, and 25·2 per cent of the vote. The results for the Senate were even better. Pro-Government organizations won 31·7 per cent of the votes and 46 seats (out of 111). The B.B.W.R. did particularly well in the Eastern Kresy, partly as a result of administrative pressure, where it took 37·3 per cent of the Sejm vote and 35 of its seats. In Galicia as a whole it received 24·6 per cent of the vote, with a slightly higher proportion in East Galicia, where it won, together with the Peasant League, 27·8 per cent. In Central Poland (roughly the former Congress Kingdom) it gained 18·9 per cent. It did particularly well in Warsaw, where it won 35·9 per cent of the vote and 6 of the 14 seats.[4]

In western Poland, its results were uneven. In Silesia the National Christian Alliance of Labour did well, winning 30·6 per cent of the votes and 7 of the 17 seats. However, in Poznania and Pomerania the existence of two separate lists hampered the

---

[1] Based on Rzepeccy, op. cit., p. 229.
[2] For this, see below, p. 260.
[3] See below, Chapter VII, p. 307.
[4] The election results are derived from calculations based on the figures given in Rzepeccy, op. cit., *passim*.

TABLE VII. *Results of the Elections to the Sejm, 1928**

Parties	No. of votes (in 1,000s)	Percentage
Pro-Government lists	2,874	25·7
B.B.W.R. (including Silesia)	2,399	21·5
Catholic Union	193	1·7
Bloc of Labour	147	1·3
Peasant League	135	1·2
Right	980	8·8
Monarchists	54	0·5
Catholic National list	926	8·3
Centre	1,141	10·2
Christian Democrats and Piast	771	6·9
Silesian Christian Democrats	142	1·3
N.P.R.	228	2·0
Non-Revolutionary Left	3,000	26·8
Peasant Party	619	5·5
Liberation	834	7·5
Radical Peasant Party (Fr. Okoń)	44	0·4
P.P.S.	1,481	13·2
Independent Socialist Party of Labour	22	0·2
Communist and Pro-Communist	768	6·9
Communist lists	278	2·5
Peasant Self-Help	27	0·2
White Russian pro-Communist lists	140	1·2
Sel-Rob	180	1·7
Sel-Rob Left	143	1·3
National Minorities Nationalist lists	2,042	18·1
Bloc of National Minorities	1,439	12·8
Ukrainian Party of Labour	45	0·4
Ukrainian National Alliance	9	0·1
Ruthenian (Russian)	133	1·2
Galician Zionists	241	2·1
Orthodox Jews	175	1·5
National Minorities: Socialist and Radical lists	380	3·5
Bloc of Ukrainian Socialist and Peasant Parties	269	2·5
Bund	80	0·7
Poalej Sion	31	0·3

* Based on Rzepeccy, op. cit., p. 229.

Government's campaign in this still somewhat hostile area. In Pomerania the Catholic Union of the Western Territories (List 30)

TABLE VIII. *Composition of the Sejm, 1928**

Parties	Deputies No. (of 444)	Percentage
Pro-Government	130	29·3
B.B.W.R.	122	27·6
National Workers' Party—Left	5	1·1
Peasant League	3	0·6
Right	37	8·4
Popular National Union	37	8·4
Centre	54	12·1
Silesian Christian Democrats	3	0·6
Christian Democrats	16	3·6
National Workers' Party	14	3·1
Piast	21	4·8
Non-Communist Left	129	29·2
Peasant Party	26	5·9
Liberation	40	9·1
P.P.S.	63	14·2
Communist and Pro-Communist	19	4·1
Communists	7	1·5
Peasant Self-Help	1	0·2
Sel-Rob	4	0·9
Sel-Rob Left	2	0·4
White Russian Worker–Peasant Club	5	1·1
National Minorities: Nationalist parties	65	14·7
Ukrainian/White Russian Club	30	6·8
Ukrainian Party of Labour	1	0·2
Non-Party White Russians	1	0·2
Russians	1	0·2
Germans	19	4·4
Jews	13	2·9
National Minorities: Socialist and Radical parties	10	2·2
Radical Ukrainians	8	1·8
German Socialists	2	0·4

* Based on Próchnik, op. cit., p. 282, Table XVIII.

won 7·7 per cent of the votes and the State Bloc of Labour (List 21) 0·8 per cent. Neither won any seats. In Poznania List 30 won 6·6 per cent of the vote but no seats, List 21 16 per cent and 4 seats.

The parties of the Left also made a good showing. The P.P.S. won 13 per cent of the votes (as against 10·3 per cent in 1922) and 63 seats (41 in the previous Sejm). For the first time it won 2 seats in Poznania and 1 in Pomerania. But in the industrial areas of Warsaw, Lodz, and the Dąbrowa basin it found its influence challenged by the Communists. The Liberation won 7·3 per cent of the votes and 40 seats, somewhat less than in 1922, largely because of the various splits it had suffered. The Peasant Party, founded late in 1925, won 5·9 per cent of the votes and 26 seats.

The results of the Communists showed a marked increase in support. Altogether, Communist and pro-Communist lists polled 6·6 per cent of the vote, compared with 1·5 per cent in 1922, thus electing 7 openly Communist and 12 fellow-travelling deputies. The number of Communist votes was very likely larger than the official figure, for the majority of the votes disqualified were almost certainly Communist. These disqualifications were most numerous in White Russian areas, where Communist sympathy was strong. In Warsaw the Communists received 14·0 per cent of the vote, as against 9·0 per cent for the P.P.S., in Lodz 18·7 per cent (the P.P.S. 28·1 per cent), and in the Dąbrowa basin 47·3 per cent (the P.P.S. 20·1 per cent).

The parties of the Right and Centre were badly hit by the elections. The Piast won only 21 seats as against 70 in the previous parliament, the Christian Democrats 19 as against 44. Because of the common Christian Democratic–Piast bloc, it is not possible to compare the percentage of the vote each party obtained in the two elections. The N.P.R. maintained its influence in western Poland, where it won 9 of its 14 seats, but lost its strength in Lodz, where it received only 692 votes. Hardest hit were the National Democrats, who won 8·4 per cent of the vote and 37 seats. In the previous parliament they had had 98 deputies. Even in Poznania and Pomerania the Endecja vote declined. Whereas in 1922 the parties of the Christian Alliance of National Unity won 48·9 per cent of the vote in Poznania and 55·7 per cent in Pomerania, the Catholic National List won 17·2 per cent in Poznania and 24·3 per cent in Pomerania.

The Bloc of National Minorities (List 18) won 12·6 per cent of the vote, as against 16 per cent in 1928, largely because many Jews in former Russian Poland voted for the Orthodox list or for the B.B.W.R., and many White Russians and Ukrainians voted for radical and pro-Communist parties. In East Galicia the U.N.D.O., which stood on List 18, showed itself the strongest of the Ukrainian parties, winning 27·3 per cent of the vote and 20 of the 55 seats.

TABLE IX. *Composition of the Senate, 1928**

Parties	Senators No. (of 111)	Percentage
Pro-Government		
B.B.W.R.	46	41·5
Right		
Popular National Union	9	8·0
Centre	12	10·8
Christian Democrats	6	5·4
National Workers' Party	3	2·7
Piast	3	2·7
Left	20	18·0
Peasant Party	3	2·7
Liberation	7	6·3
P.P.S.	10	9·0
Pro-Communist		
Sel-Rob	1	0·9
National Minorities	23	20·8
Ukrainian/White Russian Club	12	10·9
Germans	5	4·5
Jews	6	5·4

* Based on Próchnik, op. cit., p. 287, Table XXI.

The Bloc of Ukrainian Socialist and Peasant Parties won 9·2 per cent (6 seats) and the Galician Zionists 8·5 per cent (5 seats). As we have seen, pro-Communist parties did relatively well in both the White Russian and Ukrainian areas. The Sel-Rob won 1·6 per cent of the vote (4 seats), the Sel-Rob Left 1·2 per cent (2 seats), and the various White Russian lists 1·2 per cent (5 seats).

THE NEW PARLIAMENT

Although the Government had failed to obtain an absolute majority in either House, it regarded the results as highly satisfactory. The election was seen primarily as a crushing defeat for the National Democrats, Piłsudski's bitterest and most irreconcilable opponents. As Wacław Makowski, who had been Minister of Justice immediately after the coup, wrote in *Kurjer Poranny* on 11 March:

> The recent elections . . . have ruined certain political parties, until now very strong, and have given birth to a great Bloc, which does not correspond to previous divisions. The defeated parties are those whose public role should now end; they grew up in the period of our enslavement, and adapted their beliefs to those conditions of existence. What characterized them was the lack of a 'feeling for the state', the exploitation of religious and national slogans . . . the absence of an understanding of the need for national consolidation or any aspiration for national independence. . . . The political catchwords which the absence of independence has allowed to exist until now must finally disappear. . . .

The Government believed, in spite of the clashes in the previous parliament and in the course of the electoral campaign, that it could reach a *modus vivendi* with the parties of the Left. Above all, it did not regard the P.P.S., in which there was still a sizeable group of Piłsudski-ites, as hostile. During the election the Sub-Prefect of Lodz, presumably under Sławoj-Składkowski's instructions, had explained the Government's position to his officials:

> The P.P.S. had its own role, that of combating Communism in the ranks of the workers. . . . The union of the P.P.S. and the local B.B.W.R. committee was not desirable, for it would give the Communists the opportunity to claim that the P.P.S.—a workers' party—had betrayed the interests of the workers.[1]

Of the parties of the Centre only the N.P.R. was intransigently hostile to the Government. The Christian Democrats were severely split, and in both the Warsaw and Galician sections of the party there were important groups who wished to reach some compromise with the Cabinet. The Piast had avoided assuming a posture of rigid opposition. Its position was made clear by Jan

---

[1] P.Z.P.K. I, meeting of officials of the Lodz sub-prefecture, Lodz province, 19 January 1928.

Dębski, president of the Parliamentary Club of the party. Speaking in the Sejm on 31 March, he said

> We will undertake our work in this Sejm in such a way as to preserve and improve, and not destroy, the parliamentary system in Poland. I affirm that the responsibility for this Sejm and its fate will fall on the Government parties and those of the Left. We, as a minority, reserve for ourselves the right of parliamentary opposition, but we inform you in advance that this opposition will not be destructive to Parliament, but will be in accordance with the interests of the state.[1]

Among the National Minorities, the Jewish and German Clubs could generally be counted on to support the Government, while the U.N.D.O. adopted a waiting attitude. Only from the National Democrats, the N.P.R., the Silesian Christian Democrats, and the Communists could the Government expect unremitting hostility, but in all, these groups commanded only 73 votes of the total of 444.

Piłsudski declared himself in favour of co-operation with the new Sejm; however, as so often, what he meant by 'co-operation' had little connection with the basic principles of parliamentarianism. At a private meeting of leading B.B.W.R. members of parliament he outlined his position. After stressing that the most important task of the new parliament would be revision of the constitution,[2] he continued:

> Poland must have a parliamentary constitution—it cannot be an exception in the world, like Italy or Russia. . . . At the same time, the Sejm as an institution has lost its way. It is not the function of the Sejm to exhaust the Government. Moreover, if the Sejm does not wish to co-operate with the Government, it will be driven out.[3]

His public statements were more conciliatory. In the communiqué issued to the press after this meeting it was stated:

> Marshal Piłsudski . . . after having declared that he has always been a supporter of a constitutional regime, with parliament as an indispensable institution alongside the President and the Government, has made it clear that, for the third time, he is trying to make possible collaboration between the Government and the Sejm. Now that the number of those elected on the Government Bloc is considerable, one can hope

[1] *S.S.S.R.*, 31 March 1928, col. 28.
[2] For the second Sejm to amend the constitution a three-fifths majority was required in place of the usual two-thirds.
[3] Piłsudski, 'Przemówienie do grupy posłów i senatorów z B.B.W.R. (13.III.28)', *P.Z.* ix. 106.

that this collaboration will at last be achieved; he believes, moreover, that the Sejm can facilitate this by changing its method of working. . . .[1]

As a pledge of the Sejm's willingness to co-operate, Piłsudski demanded that it accept his nominee for the post of Marshal, proposing Bartel when Miedziński, whom he had asked first, refused. He thus passed over Rataj, who had been Marshal of the previous Sejm, and wished to retain the office. If Piłsudski had sought their support, the parties of the Left, which owed their electoral success at least in part to their connection with him, and which believed that in the new parliament the Government would be forced to co-operate with them, would certainly have complied.[2] But Piłsudski announced Bartel's candidacy two weeks before parliament was to meet: he wanted his candidate to be accepted without any discussion as a sign that the new parliament was willing to come to terms with him. This was too much for the Left. It revived all the resentment provoked by the Government's treatment of parliament in the previous year, and by the abuses of the electoral campaign. At an angry meeting of the P.P.S. Parliamentary Club on 23 March, the anti-Piłsudski-ite Marek was elected President by 47 votes to 16 for the Piłsudski-ite Jaworowski. It was also decided to nominate Daszyński for Marshal.[3] Daszyński agreed to stand in spite of warnings from Sławek, Miedziński, and Bartel that this would greatly antagonize Piłsudski, and his candidacy was supported by the Liberation and the Peasant Party.

Piłsudski decided to open parliament in person on 27 March and to read the Presidential Address himself, intending in this way to underline the importance he attached to the establishment of co-operation between the executive and the legislature. The session went off badly. When Piłsudski started to read his address shouts of 'Down with the Fascist Government of Piłsudski!' arose from the Communist benches. Piłsudski had expected something of this sort, and had told Sławoj-Składkowski to prepare the police for such an eventuality.[4] When the outburst persisted, police were

[1] *Głos Prawdy*, 15 March 1928.
[2] See, e.g., Pragier, op. cit., p. 349.
[3] *Robotnik*, 24 March 1928.
[4] This account of the events is taken from *S.S.S.R.*, 27 March 1928, col. 1–6, and from the contemporary press. Lieberman's allegation that the cries came from the Ukrainian nationalists seems rather unlikely (Lieberman, op. cit., pp. 324–7). For Piłsudski's consultations with Sławoj-Składkowski, see Sławoj-Składkowski, *Strzępy meldunków*, pp. 23–8.

brought in and seven deputies, mostly Communists, expelled. By this violation of parliamentary immunity Piłsudski may have intended to intimidate the supporters of Daszyński, but in fact it did much to strengthen the determination of the Left, and to some extent the Centre, to stand up to the Government. Daszyński was elected Marshal on the second ballot by 206 votes to 141 for Bartel, 37 for the National Democrat, Zwierzyński, and 13 for the Communist, Sypuła. The members of the Piast, most of the Christian Democrats, and some of the radical Ukrainians voted for Daszyński on the second ballot.[1] After the vote was taken, the B.B.W.R. deputies stormed out of the Chamber.

In the Senate the Government's influence was greater, and here its candidate for Marshal, Julian Szymański, was elected with the help of Christian Democratic and Jewish votes.

The Government and the pro-Government press showed extreme irritation at the election of Daszyński. 'The election of Mr. Daszyński', wrote *Epoka* on 28 March, 'cannot but be interpreted as a provocation against the Government.'[2] The fury of *Głos Prawdy* expressed itself in a rather uncharacteristic anti-Semitism:

The Left has, in the last months, claimed to be the champion of parliamentarianism. We radicals . . . declare that this was and is a lie. . . . Yesterday, when the Communists, people in the pay of a foreign country, provoked incidents against the creator of Polish independence, they were applauded by our Left, appallingly corrupted, rotten with the spirit of communizing Jewry. . . .[3]

Action against parliament was widely expected. Yet, when the session commenced, the atmosphere became somewhat calmer, Daszyński paid a courtesy call on Piłsudski and, in return, received a visit from him in the Sejm. The B.B.W.R. Club resolved on 29 March to end its boycott of parliamentary proceedings. On that day the Government placed before the Sejm the budget provisions for the first quarter of the financial year 1928–9, the preliminary proposals for the budget for the entire year, and a proposed law granting special credits for investment. Bartel asked that the first and third of these matters be settled rapidly.[4] Although Marek, for

[1] *S.S.S.R.*, 27 March 1928, cols. 24–5.
[2] *Epoka* was the name adopted by *Nowy Kurjer Polski* in September 1926.
[3] *Głos Prawdy*, 28 March 1928.
[4] *S.S.S.R.*, 29 March 1928, col. 4.

the socialists, opened an attack on the Government for its failure to use the powers it had been granted to introduce radical reforms, for its disregard of the constitution, and for its abuses in the election, the course of the debate was fairly smooth. The budget provisions for the first quarter were sent without difficulty to the Budgetary Committee on the 29th, where the Government text was accepted on the same day. They were returned to the Sejm on the 30th and were accepted without a division, the B.B.W.R., Christian Democrats, Piast, Peasant Party, and Jews supporting the Government. At the same time, however, a proposal to establish a Special Committee to Investigate Electoral Abuses was sent to the Administrative Committee of the Sejm.[1] On the 31st, a motion proposed by the Ukrainian Khrutsky that the preliminary budget for 1928–9 be rejected, was defeated by 275 votes to 39. Only the Communists and the members of the Ukrainian/White Russian Club voted in its favour. The provisional budget was then sent to the Budgetary Committee. On the same day, the investment credits were also voted, and parliament was adjourned until 4 April.[2]

During parliament's adjournment the leadership of both the Liberation and the P.P.S. met to formulate policy. On 15 April the P.P.S. Executive Council resolved that 'fundamental opposition' remain the party's course. It declared itself against any proposed constitutional changes, whether introduced by the Endecja or the B.B.W.R., which were intended to weaken parliamentary democracy. A number of radical social reforms were demanded, and the Communists were condemned as destroyers of working-class unity. Finally, the Council called upon the party's Central Committee to strengthen P.P.S. links with 'Peasant Democracy'. Nevertheless, the resolutions were sufficiently vague still to allow the Piłsudski-ites to remain within the party.[3] The Executive of the Liberation met on 29 April, and resolved that the party would defend the constitution against any attempts to modify its democratic character. The Government, it further stated, had not satisfied the economic needs of small agricultural producers; this, along with the Sanacja's interference in the electoral campaign, 'force the party into an increasingly critical attitude towards the

[1] S.S.S.R., 29 March 1928; 30 March 1928.
[2] Ibid., 31 March 1928.
[3] The resolutions were published in Robotnik, 17 April 1928.

Government and push it by the logic of events in the direction of opposition'.[1]

When the new session opened, relations between the Government and the Sejm remained uneasy. Conflict first developed over the method of abrogating the press decree: whether a simple resolution by the Sejm was sufficient or whether a law passed by both Houses was required. The courts had been forced to uphold convictions under the press decree of May 1927 because the Government had not published the Sejm's resolution of abrogation in the *Digest of Laws*. On 24 April, the socialists proposed an amendment to the law of 27 December 1927 which prescribed the manner in which laws were to be published in the *Digest*. Article I of their proposal stipulated that the Government be obliged to publish the Sejm's resolutions annulling Presidential decrees.[2]

The proposal came before the Sejm Legal Committee on 27 April, and on 8 May Lieberman argued for the new law before a joint meeting of the Constitutional and Legal Committees. In spite of the Government's vigorous opposition, the Constitutional Committee approved his interpretation of the constitution by 19 votes to 12. The draft then came again before the Legal Committee, where debate raged bitterly. The Committee's chairman, Jan Piłsudski, the Marshal's brother, resigned in protest against the activities of the Opposition.[3] The pro-Government press was also harshly critical. 'The resolution', wrote *Czas* on 12 May,

will make almost impossible collaboration between the Government and the Sejm. It must be interpreted as a sign that the majority of the Sejm does not want, and is incapable of, such collaboration and that it considers its principal task that of protesting against dictatorship.[4]

Opposition also arose over a number of new taxes proposed by the Government, which included a tax on buildings in rural municipalities, and an increase in the Land Tax. Czechowicz, the Minister of Finance, attempted to justify them to the Sejm on 22 May as necessary to maintain a balanced budget and to make

[1] For the resolutions, see *Wyzwolenie*, 6 May 1928.
[2] *S.S.S.R.*, 24 April 1928, col. 36. For the text of the law, see *Druki Sejmowe*, 2nd series, no. 51.
[3] The minutes of the debates in the Sejm committees were not published. Their course can easily be followed from the summaries provided in *Druki Sejmowe* and the reports in the contemporary newspapers. Particular use has been made of *Gazeta Warszawska*, *Czas*, and *Robotnik*.
[4] *Czas*, 12 May 1928.

possible the increase in the salaries of officials which had been promised during the election. The proposals were attacked by the Left, and particularly by the radical peasant parties, as a concession to the large landowners by the imposition of further burdens on the peasantry. The Buildings Tax was defeated on its first reading by 189 votes to 149, the Land Tax increase by 190 to 146. The majority included all the Left groups as well as the Ukrainians and White Russians. The Jewish Club, which had always argued that the urban population was excessively taxed to spare the countryside, voted for the law. As a result of these two votes, Czechowicz withdrew a proposed Estate Tax which probably would have been passed.[1]

However, none of the parliamentary groups was prepared to push its opposition to extremes. This became evident in the budget debate which took place on 29, 30, and 31 May.[2] For the Government, Bartel made a moderate speech, and Sławek stressed that the aim of the B.B.W.R. was to harmonize different social interests for the common good. He called for more extensive constitutional reform in order to render impossible 'a return to the methods employed before 1926'. The Government's aim, he continued, was not Fascist,

to liquidate the Sejm or to limit the franchise. No, gentlemen, our aim is that parliament, as a necessary institution, shall learn to deal with state matters in other ways than such as we have seen recently in the speeches of many Deputies in the Committees and in the general debate. It is a question of healing parliament, which is undergoing a serious crisis not only in Poland. There are other examples. Primo de Rivera and Mussolini are more or less models for the radical destruction of parliament. You see and know well that that is not the aim of the Government or the B.B.W.R.[3]

For the socialists, Niedziałkowski declared that the Government was powerless to deal with the pressing social and economic problems because of its heterogeneous class character. The régime stood before a crossroads, and would have to choose between democracy and some form of Fascism. The system could not be

[1] For the course of this debate see: *S.S.S.R.*, 22 May 1928, cols. 16–50; 23 May 1928, cols. 7–44, 49.

[2] *S.S.S.R.*, 29 May 1928, cols. 5–50; 30 May 1928, cols. 3–85; 31 May 1928, cols. 3–49.

[3] Ibid., 30 May 1928, cols. 45–6.

maintained as it was; it was the aim of the P.P.S. 'to see that its liquidation was followed by democracy and not by one or other form of Fascism'.[1] The P.P.S. was thus in 'fundamental opposition' to the Government. It would, however, abstain on the budget since it did not wish to accelerate the crisis.

Niedziałkowski's speech reflected the views of those in the P.P.S. who believed that the B.B.W.R. was bound to split because of its lack of internal cohesion.[2] This point of view was given strength by the resistance which the radicals in the B.B.W.R. had shown to the attempt to give the Bloc a more definite programme. Indeed, the radical groups within the Sanacja had displayed an increasing solidarity. In June the League for the Reform of the Republic and the Party of Labour united, forming the Union of Labour of Town and Country, a grouping with fifteen deputies and three senators.[3] Moreover, there were persistent rumours that Piłsudski was in ill-health, which led to the belief that he might soon die or become incapacitated, thus precipitating a split in the government ranks.[4] At the same time, there were other points of view within the P.P.S. Apart from the out-and-out Piłsudski-ites, there were those who, like Daszyński, hoped that the Government would be forced to reach an agreement with the Left in order to achieve a parliamentary majority. On the Left, there were those like Pragier, Zaremba, and Ciołkosz, members of a secret organization within the party, who believed that a conflict with Piłsudski was inevitable. In such a clash the P.P.S. had a chance of success only if it enjoyed the support of all the peasant parties. For this reason they were prepared to postpone the conflict until the Piast was more willing to co-operate.[5] Thus, for the moment, the majority of the party was united behind the Niedziałkowski line.

In their speeches in the budget debate, both the Liberation and Peasant Party deputies used stronger expressions of opposition

---

[1] Ibid., 29 May 1928, col. 35.

[2] See Niedziałkowski's articles in *Robotnik*, 20 May 1928; 1 June 1928; 7 June 1928.

[3] T. Selimowski, *Polskie legalne stronnictwa polityczne. Zarys popularny* (Warsaw, 1930), p. 31.

[4] Piłsudski's ill-health was frequently alluded to in the press. See, e.g., *Kurjer Poznański*, 11 May 1928 or the London *Times*, 9 May 1928. These rumours were always vehemently denied by the Piłsudski-ite press, although their truth is affirmed both by Piłsudski's own statements and by those of Sławoj-Składkowski in *Nie ostatnie słowo oskarżonego*, p. 131.

[5] See Pragier, op. cit., pp. 353–4.

than they had done previously. However, both parties announced that they would vote for the budget if the Government maintained the credit of 100 million zloties for small agricultural producers which they had proposed. The Piast, Christian Democrats, and N.P.R. all stated that they would vote for the budget, since to do otherwise would precipitate a dangerous situation. On the other hand, the National Democratic spokesman, Roman Rybarski, criticized the Government for not providing sufficient information to make a proper discussion of the budget possible. Of the national minorities, the Jews were divided, while all the other groups declared that they would vote against the budget.

When put to the vote on 15 June, the budget was passed by 218 votes to 54, with 172 abstentions.[1] The B.B.W.R., Piast, Christian Democrats, Peasant Party, and Liberation voted for the motion, the P.P.S., the National Democrats, and the Galician Zionists abstained, and most of the other national minority groups and the Communists voted against it. The budget of the Ministry of the Interior, which was held to be principally responsible for the Government's electoral abuses, was reduced. On the same day the Sejm Administrative Committee finally voted to set up the Committee of Inquiry into the Elections. The budget then went to the Senate, where it was passed on 22 June, although the additional credits proposed by the radical peasant parties were rejected. The session was then immediately declared closed by the Government.

During the recess, Piłsudski resigned the premiership, handing it over to Bartel, and retained only the post of Minister of War. He took this step largely on grounds of ill-health, as he admitted at the Cabinet meeting on 25 June where he announced his resignation, much to the surprise of his ministers.[2] But he was also not unaware that the achievement of satisfactory relations with parliament needed the lighter touch of someone like Bartel. Still, as an indication that a hard course towards parliament could also be adopted, Świtalski, one of the inner group of military advisers around Piłsudski, entered the Cabinet as Minister of Education.

Nevertheless, Piłsudski could not resist giving vent to his irritation with the new parliament. In an interview published in *Głos*

---

[1] *S.S.S.R.*, 15 June 1928, cols. 42–3.
[2] For a description of this meeting, see Sławoj-Składkowski, *Strzępy meldunków*, pp. 28–32.

Prawdy on 1 July[1] he attacked the constitution for excessively limiting the powers of the President, and for imposing too heavy a load on the Prime Minister who, because of the attention he was forced to devote to matters of detail which ought to be delegated, was practically powerless. The most difficult of the Prime Minister's tasks was co-operating with parliament. 'If I had not overcome my inclinations', he confessed, 'I would have done nothing but beat and kick the gentlemen-deputies without ceasing.'[2] He criticized the very nature of parliamentarianism: 'The type of work itself, consisting of the labour of talking, is one of the most miserable ideas ever invented',[2] alleging that the quality of speaking in parliament was so low that even the flies died of boredom. In his opinion the first Sejm (1918–22) had been a 'Harlots' Sejm', and it was only after much thought that he had decided against expelling it. The second Sejm he labelled the 'Sejm of Corruption'. When it seemed to him that the new Sejm had begun to adopt the methods of the first two, he decided he had to 'choose again— either to avoid any co-operation with the Sejm and be at the disposal of the President to impose a new constitution, or to resign'.[3] He had decided to resign, but in any serious crisis he would still be at the disposal of the President.

The interview provoked strong reactions in the country. The government newspapers took the opportunity to demand the reform of the constitution, while supporters of the Right, not without an element of *Schadenfreude*, argued that a Government with as much power as the Sanacja should have been able to overcome the constitutional obstacles, and interpreted the interview as a confession of failure after two years of office.[4] On the Left, opposition was vocal, resulting in the confiscation of a number of issues of left-wing dailies and weeklies. The Executive Committees of the P.P.S., the Liberation, and the Peasant Party, all condemned Piłsudski's attacks on parliament. Daszyński, as Marshal of the Sejm, took pains to rebut the former Prime Minister's accusations in a statement on 3 July, making at the same time a transparent appeal to the Sanacja: 'If one created a stable majority in this parliament, Polish parliamentarianism could

---

[1] Piłsudski, 'Wywiad z redaktorem *Głosu Prawdy* (1.VII.28)', *P.Z.* ix. 109–19.
[2] Ibid., p. 116. [3] Ibid., p. 119.
[4] For the pro-Government view, see *Polska Zbrojna* (the Army organ) 22 July 1928. For that of the Right, see *Gazeta Warszawska*, 11 July 1928; *Rzeczpospolita*, 3 July 1928.

develop slowly but regularly as a powerful factor in the public life of the country . . .'[1]

During the summer, the demand by the Government's supporters for further constitutional changes became more insistent. At the Congress of Legionaries held at Wilno on 12 August, where Piłsudski, contrary to all expectations, made an entirely non-political speech,[2] a resolution was adopted calling for constitutional reforms which would 'consolidate for ever the memorable achievement of Marshal Piłsudski'.[3] Various proposals were discussed by the B.B.W.R., and many rumours circulated as to their character. According to *Robotnik*, what they all had in common were provisions for increasing the powers of the President and the Senate and for diminishing those of the Sejm.[4] Some B.B.W.R. supporters demanded more extreme changes; in the Wilno *Słowo* of 28 August, Mackiewicz called on Piłsudski to establish a hereditary monarchy and found a dynasty.

The most moderate statement of the Government's case was made by Bartel in an interview with *Kurjer Wileński* on 4 October. He argued that there was an inherent contradiction in the principle of parliamentarianism. Since it demanded that the Government be formed with the support of a majority in parliament, the Sejm was, in some sense, responsible for the Cabinet. Yet it was also a function of the Sejm to criticize and control the Government. Bartel felt that this dilemma could only be overcome if the Government were appointed by the President, and were responsible to him. Parliament's function of control could be maintained and should be exercised in an annual no-confidence debate as well as in the budget debate.[5]

---

[1] *Robotnik*, 4 July 1928.
[2] Piłsudski, 'Przemówienie na zjeździe legionistów w Wilnie, 12.VIII.1928', *P.Z.* ix. 119–28.
[3] *Polska Zbrojna*, 13 August 1928.
[4] *Robotnik*, 14 September 1928.
[5] *Kurjer Wileński*, 4 October 1928. The text of the interview was later published as a pamphlet: K. Bartel, *Niedomagania parlamentaryzmu* (Warsaw, 1928). The constitutional question during this period has given rise to an enormous literature. The widely differing views prevalent within the Sanacja are easily traced in the minutes of the conference of leading members of the B.B.W.R. held on 30–1 August 1928 with Makowski in the Chair. See A. Piasecki (ed.), *Sprawozdanie z ankiety przygotowawczej do reformy Konstytucji* (Warsaw, 1928). The entire September issue of *Droga* was devoted to this question. Other interesting products of the debate were: W. Z. Jaworski, 'Ze studiów nad Konstytucją', *Przegląd Współczesny*, no. 77 (1928), pp. 353–73;

THE GROWTH OF OPPOSITION ON THE LEFT

Bartel's speech was interpreted by the Right as evidence of a new conciliatory disposition on the part of the Government. However, on the Centre and Left this public debate on the constitution contributed to an intensified opposition. Early in September representatives of the Christian Democrats and the Piast met; they declared themselves against any increase in the power of the President and for the maintenance of parliamentary democracy.[1] Thugutt, who had rejoined the Liberation during the electoral campaign, attacked the Government for planning to limit democracy,[2] while Diamand of the P.P.S. criticized Bartel's proposals in *Naprzód*: there were only two types of government, he argued, 'people's governments' and 'authoritarian governments'. 'According to Mr. Bartel', he continued, 'there can also be "authoritarian-popular" governments or "dictatorial-democratic" governments. This is not the case, and never will be.'[3]

At the same time, the problem of the national minorities was again becoming acute. It was given token expression during the preparations for the commemoration of the tenth anniversary of Polish Independence. All the representatives of the national minorities, with the exception of the Jews, announced that they would not participate in the celebrations. Discontent was strongest among the Ukrainians. Dmitri Levitsky, head of the U.N.D.O., gave an interview to *Moment* on 13 September in which he stated 'We Ukrainians are not loyal as regards the Polish state, and we do not want to be.' When asked if this meant that the Ukrainians wished to secede, he replied, 'Certainly, and without any doubt.'[4]

The increased hostility of the P.P.S. to the Government was apparent when the party Executive Committee met on 31 September. After two days of discussion, a series of resolutions was adopted which stressed the need to maintain intransigent opposition to 'the present system of government', an 'autocracy' supported by capitalists and large landowners. The Government was accused of

---

J. Growski, *Aforyzmy polityczne nieobowiązujące* (Warsaw, 1929); A. Piasecki, *O kryteriach oceny projektów konstytucji* (Warsaw, 1929).

[1] *Gazeta Warszawska*, 7 September 1928.
[2] *Wyzwolenie*, 19 August 1928.
[3] *Naprzód*, 11 October 1928.
[4] *Moment*, 13 September 1928, reprinted in *Gazeta Warszawska*, 14 September, 1928.

undermining the basis of democracy and of incapacity for dealing with the economic crisis.[1] The Committee rejected the counter-resolutions of Jaworowski, the head of the Warsaw organization of the party and an ardent Piłsudski-ite, which had stressed the importance of parliamentary government, but had called on the party to find a basis for compromise with the Sanacja.[2] The passing of the original resolutions thus represented a victory for those in the party who believed that a clash with Piłsudski was inevitable, and a defeat for the Piłsudski-ites and for those like Daszyński who still hoped to achieve a compromise with the Government. A confrontation between the Central Committee of the P.P.S. and Jaworowski's Warsaw branch, which had vigorously opposed the party's moving into opposition and had fought to prevent Moraczewski's expulsion, seemed inevitable. Many party members resented the tight control exercised by Jaworowski in Warsaw and deplored his questionable methods, in particular the use of his socialist militia to provoke conflicts with political opponents, usually the Communists, and his alleged misappropriation of funds. Already a number of clashes between his organization and the Central Committee had been resolved only with difficulty.[3]

On 10 October the first issue appeared of a new socialist daily, *Przedświt*, edited by Bolesław Czarkowski, to which Moraczewski was a leading contributor. Although it claimed that it had been founded not to split the P.P.S. but to 'deepen the ideology of the party',[4] it made very clear its pro-Government sympathies. The party suspected that Jaworowski was involved in its publication. On 11 October the Central Committee ordered him to dissolve the Trade Union Council he had set up in Warsaw to strengthen his hold there, and to deny any connection with the new daily. When he refused, the Central Committee pronounced the Warsaw party organization dissolved on 17 October.[5] The next day those expelled formed a new group called the P.P.S—Former Revolutionary Fraction,[6] after the organization which Piłsudski had led when he

[1] *Robotnik*, 2 October 1928.
[2] 'Poufny Komunikat Informacyjny m. st. Warszawy', Archiwum Zakładu Historii Partii, quoted in A. Tymieniecka, 'Rozłam w P.P.S. w 1928 roku', *Kwartalnik Historyczny*, lxxii (1965), no. 4, pp. 811–35.
[3] For these developments, see Tymieniecka, op. cit.
[4] *Przedświt*, 10 October 1928.
[5] Tymieniecka, op. cit., pp. 828–30.
[6] P.P.S.—Dawna Frakcja Rewolucyjna, nicknamed P.P.S.—Frak or B.B.S. Both terms were derogatory: the first referred to the alleged desire of the leaders

had resisted before 1914 those in the P.P.S. who wished to place more emphasis on social and less on national issues. The new party criticized the P.P.S. for its unremitting hostility to the Government, which, it claimed, had deprived the working class of any influence in public affairs, and stated that it would adopt an 'objective' attitude, although it would not join any bloc.[1]

The P.P.S.—Frak united with the rebel Silesian party organization, but outside Warsaw the split was relatively unimportant. The new group set up a committee in Lodz and gained control of a number of trade unions. Ten P.P.S. deputies decided to join, and *Przedświt* became the official party organ, though Moraczewski refused to become a member. Not all the Piłsudski-ites left the P.P.S., for some still hoped to heal the split, of whom the most important was Ziemięcki. At its first conference, held at Katowice on 1 November, the new party maintained that the Bartel–Piłsudski Government was a coalition, and demanded only the removal of it of Ministers 'representing reactionary spheres'.[2]

The P.P.S. devoted a great deal of effort to limiting the extent of the split. A provisional party organization, headed by Barlicki, was set up in Warsaw. At the twenty-first party conference, held in Sosnowiec on 1–4 November, a resolution was adopted condemning the secessionists. Nevertheless, some attempts at reconciliation were still made, notably by Daszyński. Towards the Government, the party's attitude was understandably hostile. The feeling of weakness engendered by the split also led to the passing of resolutions which emphasized the importance of co-operation with the radical peasant parties. The left-wing Independent Socialist Party now rejoined the P.P.S.[3]

Parliament was reconvened on 31 October, and devoted its opening sessions to the first reading of the budget for 1929–30.[4] For the Government, Czechowicz explained that expenses had increased somewhat (to 2,802 million zloties) and announced that

of the party for office and preferment (*frak* means 'tail coat', i.e. formal dress); the second suggested the party's close links with the B.B.W.R.

[1] For the party's programmatic declaration of 18 October 1928, see *Przedświt*, 19 October 1928.

[2] Tymieniecka, op. cit., p. 834.

[3] For the police report on the proceedings of this conference, see 'XXI Kongres P.P.S. (1–4.XI.1928)', ed. A. Tymieniecka, *N.D.P.* (1st series), vi (1963), 289–96.

[4] *S.S.S.R.*, 31 October 1928, cols. 6–13; 6 November 1928, cols. 5–43; 13 November 1928, cols. 4–52; 14 November 1928, cols. 4–51.

the Government intended to introduce several new taxes and to modify others in order to prevent a deficit. The debate brought no political surprises. For the socialists, Marek kept to the new hard line, criticizing the Government for looking to the interests of the rich only. When he referred to Piłsudski's July interview as 'the swan-song of the previous Government',[1] however, he came into sudden and violent conflict with Sławek, who denounced this as 'arrant villainy'.[2] Sławek's reaction seems rather excessive, even for so ardent a Piłsudski-ite, and it may well be that some of the colonels, as the ex-legionaries and P.O.W. members around Piłsudski were commonly known, hoped to accelerate the clash with parliament by provoking the deputies in this way. Bartel certainly thought so, for he afterwards firmly refused to have any official dealings with Sławek.[3] In the debate Rybarski, for the National Democrats, deplored the way in which the Government had ignored the budgets in previous years by demanding supplementary credits. On 14 November the Sejm voted to send the Government's proposals to the Budgetary Committee.

The interchange between Marek and Sławek had important political consequences. On 10 November the P.P.S. Parliamentary Club voted to exclude Sławek from among those of its opponents it considered 'worthy of esteem'.[4] Sławek reacted by challenging Niedziałkowski, who had been in the Chair, to a duel, a challenge the latter refused. At the opening of the session the moderate elements in the P.P.S. had been strong. Daszyński, as Marshal, had called together the heads of the Sejm clubs before parliament reconvened to see whether a majority could be formed.[5] He had also made a conciliatory speech during the Sejm's celebration of the tenth anniversary of Independence.[6] However, the obvious unwillingness of the colonels to compromise, and the harsh language of Piłsudski himself, who, on the anniversary of independence, had referred to the Deputies, somewhat portentously, as 'men without a past or a future',[7] strengthened the intransigent group in the party. Relations with the left-wing peasant parties became closer.

---

[1] *S.S.S.R.*, 6 November 1928, col. 13.
[2] 'Bezczelne łajdactwo', *S.S.S.R.*, 6 November 1928, col. 43.
[3] Lato, op. cit., p. 178.
[4] *Robotnik*, 11 November 1928.
[5] Stęborowski, op. cit., pp. 145–8.
[6] *S.S.S.R.*, 10 October 1928, cols. 2–6.
[7] Piłsudski, 'Z przemyśleń Naczelnika Państwa', *P.Z.* ix. 130.

On 14 November the P.P.S., the Liberation and the Peasant Party set up a Consultative Committee of left-wing Parties for the Defence of the Republic and Democracy[1] to facilitate co-operation in upholding the constitution. On all other matters they retained their individual freedom of action.

The question of the way in which the Government had exceeded the credits granted it by parliament arose again during the committee stage of the budget. The National Club had proposed a resolution calling on the Government to present without delay a bill to legalize the supplementary credits obtained during the financial year 1927–8.[2] When the proposal was debated in the Budget Committee on 21 November, Wróblewski, the head of the Main Auditing Office, stated that once that body had become aware of the exceeding of credits, it had called upon the Minister of Finance to regularize the position, but had not felt it necessary to inform the Sejm or the President. Nevertheless, because the parties of the Centre and Left were not yet ready for an open clash with the Government, they accepted Bartel's assurance on 28 November that the Government would soon present the supplementary credits to the Sejm for ratification.[3]

More conflict arose over the budget of the Ministry of the Interior when Sławoj-Składkowski revealed in committee that his Ministry's Secret Service fund, which had been cut to one-quarter in the previous budget, had been restored to its full extent by the Cabinet. This blatant disregard of constitutional procedure infuriated the entire opposition, and on 29 November the Budget Committee voted to cancel all credits for the Secret Service in the coming year.[4]

Relations between the Government and parliament also deteriorated as a result of a dispute over the position of the courts. On 7 February 1928 the Government had issued a decree, to come into force on 1 January 1929, making the organization of the courts

---

[1] Komisja Porozumiewawcza Stronnictw Lewicowych dla Obrony Republiki i Demokracji. See *Robotnik*, 15 November 1928.

[2] In terms of Article 6 of the Treasury Law of 2 March 1927, 'The contracting of credits not included in the budget can take place only on the resolution of the Minister of the Treasury, enacted as a law, on condition that at the same time new financial sources are created to pay for the credits. Ministers are individually responsible for the strict observance of this clause.' *Dz.U.R.P.* (1927), no. 30, p. 313.

[3] *Gazeta Warszawska*, 29 November 1928.

[4] Ibid., 30 November 1928.

uniform in the different partitions.[1] The opposition feared that one of its clauses, suspending for two years the immovability of judges, could be used to undermine the independence of the judiciary. On 18 December, after an angry debate in the Sejm during which B.B.W.R. deputies had attempted a filibuster, a bill was passed by 162 votes to 108 delaying the publication of the decree until 1 January 1930.[2] The Government had no intention of accepting this rebuff, and decided to promulgate the decree in spite of the Sejm's bill. While insisting that action by both Houses was necessary to alter a decree, it held up Senate proceedings by introducing irrelevant matters so that the question could not be brought to a vote in the Upper House. Such unsavoury procedure proved so embarrassing to Meysztowicz, the conservative Minister of Justice, that he resigned on 22 December, to be replaced by his undersecretary, Stanisław Car, the already well-known Piłsudski-ite constitutional lawyer. On 31 December the decree was promulgated in the *Digest of Laws*, and on 12 January 1929 the Senate finally rejected the Sejm's motion.

Car immediately proceeded to settle scores with a number of prominent opponents of the Sanacja on the bench, retiring, among others, Zygmunt Seyda, the National Democratic President of the Supreme Court.[3] On 28 January, the National Club brought a motion of no confidence against Car, which was defeated by the narrow margin of 96 votes (the B.B.W.R., P.P.S.—Frak, N.P.R.—Left) to 84 (National Club, Christian Democrats, Peasant Party, N.P.R.—Right, Communists).[4] The P.P.S., Liberation, and Piast abstained. Afterwards Niedziałkowski justified the socialist abstention, arguing that the conflict was only one episode in the battle between the Government and Democracy; that the democratic camp was far more likely to win on a more popular issue; and that the P.P.S. had no intention of helping the National Democrats. A striking feature of the division was the large number of government abstentions. The left-wing press attributed these to the desire of the 'colonels' group' to provoke a crisis by allowing the motion to be carried. In fact, most of the former legionaries did

---

[1] 'Rozporządzenie Prezydenta Rzeczpospolitej z 6 lutego 1928 r. o ustroju sądów powszechnych', *Dz.U.R.P.* (1928), No. 12, pp. 171–94.

[2] *S.S.S.R.*, 14 December 1928, cols. 24–48; 18 December 1928, cols. 15–74, 78–80.

[3] *Gazeta Warszawska*, 19 January 1929.

[4] *S.S.S.R.*, 28 January 1929, cols. 7–37, 39–42.

vote, and government abstentions were more frequent among the conservatives, irritated by the attacks on the independence of the judiciary and by the events which had led to Meysztowicz's resignation. The crisis over the courts did highlight some of the internal tensions in the B.B.W.R.: both *Epoka* and *Głos Prawdy* carried articles attacking Meysztowicz.[1]

The political tension was heightened by the Government's desire for constitutional reform. On 31 October the B.B.W.R. Parliamentary Club had called upon the Sejm Constitutional Committee to lay down the form in which constitutional amendments should be proposed, and this was finally done on 6 December. But as *Czas* put it on 12 December, it was clear that while the Government counted on parliament to modify the constitution, the majority of the deputies were against the changes demanded by the Government: 'Thus the question remains, what will the Government do if reform through the Sejm proves impossible? This question dominates the situation.'[2]

During the debate on the second reading of the budget on 30 and 31 January, the Opposition parties, both Left and Right, continued their policy of avoiding a direct confrontation with the Government.[3] They did this in spite of the resentment aroused by Piłsudski's refusal to take part personally in, or to send a deputy to, the committee stage of the discussions on the budget of the Ministry of War; he claimed that he feared incidents which might compromise relations between the deputies and the Army.[4] During the general debate Rybarski, for the National Club,[5] once again demanded the legalization of the excess credits obtained by the Government. This time he was supported both by Woźnicki of the Liberation and by Dąbski of the Peasant Party. The budget was finally adopted on 11 February without a division. The B.B.W.R., P.P.S.—Frak, Christian Democrats, N.P.R., and Liberation voted for the budget, the P.P.S., the National Club, and the Piast abstained. The budget of the Ministry of the Interior was reduced,

---

[1] For the view of the Left, see *Robotnik*, 29 January 1929. For attacks on Meysztowicz, see *Głos Prawdy*, 1 January 1929 (the weekly supplement), and *Epoka*, 23 December 1928. The article in *Głos Prawdy* was confiscated by the censor.

[2] *Czas*, 12 December 1928.

[3] *S.S.S.R.*, 30 January 1929, cols. 7–55; 31 January 1929, cols. 3–100.

[4] *Robotnik*, 16 January 1929.

[5] This was the name under which the National Democrats were now known.

as had been suggested in committee, by the deletion of the Secret Service fund, and that of the Ministry of War was also cut, largely in response to Piłsudski's behaviour towards the Budgetary Committee.[1] A notable feature of the meeting was the attempt by the 'colonels' group' in the B.B.W.R. to persuade the opposition to reject the budget, hoping thus to precipitate the conflict between the Government and parliament.[2]

After the vote, Niedziałkowski again felt obliged to explain why his party had abstained. The time was not yet ripe, he claimed, for a clash with the Government, since public opinion had first to be convinced of the true nature of the Sanacja:

In our opinion, the vital problem which has faced the country since the Coup is the problem of the constitution, and it is against this background and over this question that the country's choice between the so-called Sanacja camp and that of democracy must take place, a choice of the utmost importance for Poland and for her future.[3]

The constitutional issue did, in fact, soon become the issue of the day. On 22 January the Sejm accepted the findings of its Constitutional Committee, and resolved that constitutional revision be undertaken by means of resolutions presented to Parliament. On 6 February the B.B.W.R. presented to the Sejm its proposal, prepared by Sławek and Professor Makowski. According to its provisions the President of the Republic was to be elected by all those with the right to vote in Sejm elections. Two candidates were to be presented, one nominated by the Sejm and Senate and one by the Government. The President would enjoy very wide powers: he was to ratify all international conventions, except those imposing financial burdens on private citizens; he was to decide disputed elections, and had a suspensive veto; he could issue decrees when parliament was adjourned or dissolved; he would be Supreme Commander of the Army and could suspend court proceedings before a decision was given; he could not be held responsible for his constitutional acts, though he could be tried for treason, violating the constitution, or for common crimes, if three-fifths of the National Assembly voted to impeach him. The voting age for the Sejm would be raised to twenty-four, and Article 12 of the 1921 Constitution, forbidding military personnel to vote,

---

[1] *S.S.S.R.*, 11 February 1929, cols. 14–21.
[2] Próchnik, op. cit., pp. 306–7.
[3] *S.S.S.R.*, 11 February 1929, col. 15.

would be abrogated. Parliamentary immunity would be curtailed, and deputies could be deprived of their seats by the Tribunal of State at the request of the Minister of Justice. No-confidence motions could only be presented if they had 111 signatures, and required 223 votes to be passed. The number of Senators was to be increased to 150. Of these, 100 were to be elected, and 50 nominated by the President. The Sejm could only reject Senate proposals by a three-fifths majority (the 1921 constitution demanded eleven-twentieths). The Sejm and Senate would have only one ordinary session a year, though extraordinary sessions could be summoned by the President acting on his own initiative, or at the request of 222 deputies. These sessions could only discuss what was specified in the presidential message invoking them.[1]

Not surprisingly, this proposal provoked violent reactions. On 8 February *Robotnik* published an article headed 'The Proposal of the Government Bloc means in practice the liquidation of Parliamentary Democracy.'[2] On 12 February it denounced the project as 'a provocation of the working masses' and as an attempt to introduce 'absolutism'.[3] On 17 February *Gazeta Warszawska* warned that if the proposal were adopted, it would not lead to 'harmony between the higher organs [of the state] but would place them in a state of continuous conflict'.[4] The proposal came before the Sejm on 22 February, and, after an acrimonious four-day debate, was sent to the Constitutional Committee on 4 March.[5] The debate made it abundantly clear that the B.B.W.R. did not command a majority for its proposed changes. Moreover, on the last day of the debate the P.P.S., Liberation, and Peasant Party, in order to underline their opposition to the Government's plan, presented their own proposal for constitutional reform. They demanded the suppression of the Senate and the election of the President by a National Assembly elected by universal suffrage. The independence of the judiciary was to be safeguarded, and the rights of the Sejm in controlling the budget extended. Church and State were to be separated. The territorially compact national

---

[1] 'Wniosek posła Walerego Sławka i kolegów z klubu B.B.W.R. w sprawie zmiany niektórych postanowień ustawy konstytucyjnej w trybie przewidzianym dla jej rewizji', *Druki Sejmowe*, 2nd series, no. 444.

[2] *Robotnik*, 8 February 1929.   [3] Ibid., 12 February 1929.

[4] *Gazeta Warszawska*, 17 February 1929.

[5] *S.S.S.R.*, 22 February 1929, cols. 5–32; 27 February 1929, cols. 4–37; 1 March 1929, cols. 76–100; 4 March 1929, cols. 10–72.

minorities were to be granted autonomy, the branches of production 'ripe for this' were to be nationalized, and land ownership was to be limited to 60 hectares.[1]

THE CZECHOWICZ AFFAIR

However, the collision between Government and parliament did not come over the constitutional issue, but over the old question of the exceeding of credits. On 11 February Woźnicki of the Liberation presented to the Sejm a resolution demanding that Czechowicz, the Minister of Finance, be impeached because he had not submitted the Government's supplementary credits to parliament for ratification.[2] Exceeding the provisions of the budget in this way was a fairly common phenomenon, and although in this case the sums involved were large (about 560 million zloties—£12,700,000 at the contemporary exchange rate), there had been no apparent obstacle to the Government's legalizing its financial actions by obtaining the Sejm's approval. That Czechowicz had wanted to follow the correct procedure is obvious from the letter he wrote to Bartel on 16 November offering his resignation if no action were taken on this question.[3] Bartel too, to judge from his statement to the Budgetary Committee on 28 November, had wanted to settle the matter legally.[4] But both ran into the inflexible opposition of Piłsudski. His attitude may have been dictated by a desire to force a clash with parliament. It seems far more likely, however, to have been the result of his desire to conceal the fact that he had obtained from the Treasury an extraordinary credit of 8 million zloties (£180,000) for the B.B.W.R. election campaign.[5] He must have realized the ridiculous and compromising effect such a revelation would have after his innumerable attacks on corruption in the state, and assertions of his own financial rectitude.

The presentation of the resolution accusing Czechowicz marked

---

[1] 'Wniosek Związku Parlamentarnego Polskich Socjalistów, Klubu Parlamentarnego P.S.L. "Wyzwolenie", Klubu Parlamentarnego Stronnictwa Chłopskiego w sprawie zmiany niektórych postanowień ustawy konstytucyjnej, w trybie przewidzianym dla jej rewizji', *Druki Sejmowe*, 2nd series, no. 555.

[2] Stęborowski, op. cit., p. 203.

[3] The letter is reproduced in Lieberman, op. cit., p. 342.

[4] See above, p. 267.

[5] This was afterwards revealed by the disarmingly frank Sławoj-Składkowski: see above, p. 246.

the adoption by the Liberation of a more strongly anti-Government line. The P.P.S. too had moved to a more uncompromising position; at the meeting of the Executive Council of the party on 24–5 February 1929 the more radical view of Lieberman, Zaremba, and Arciszewski prevailed over that of Niedziałkowski, who still wanted to postpone the confrontation with the Government. The main responsibility for the adoption by the P.P.S. of a hard line over the Czechowicz affair lay almost certainly with the veteran Galician socialist Herman Lieberman. He had been extremely suspicious of Piłsudski's goals and methods in Galicia before 1914, but had been fairly closely associated with the legionaries during the war, and had even defended a number of them before the court martial at Marmaros-Sziget, when they were accused of complicity in General Haller's desertion in March 1918. But after 1918, his old suspicion of the Piłsudski-ites revived, and as the P.P.S. constitutional expert he clashed bitterly with them in the various controversies on the reorganization of the Army, in which he opposed their attempts to establish what he regarded as an excessive independence for the military in relation to parliament. An impressive orator, he had distinguished himself in the Austrian *Reichsrat* before 1914 in exposing the abuses of General Galgoczy, the commander of the Przemyśl fortress. He was to prove a formidable opponent in parliament.

The P.P.S. now established a committee to activate the local party organizations, to prepare for a general strike should the Government try to impose a new constitution by decree, and to co-ordinate the tactics of the left-wing parties in the Sejm. A resolution was passed calling on all 'truly democratic elements' in Poland to unite with the P.P.S. in order to prevent a government coup directed against democracy.[1]

The motion against Czechowicz was formally put before the Sejm on 19 February.[2] In the debate, Bartel angrily attacked its presentation at this time. He announced that he would submit a law concerning the credits only after the accounts for the financial year 1927–8 had been closed, and had been confirmed by the Main Auditing Office. This would have made virtually impossible any investigation of the credits obtained. Thus on 26 February the

---

[1] *Robotnik*, 26 February 1929. For other details of the meeting, see 'Poufny Komunikat Informacyjny', quoted in Stęborowski, op. cit., pp. 210–11.

[2] *S.S.S.R.*, 19 February 1929, col. 71.

resolution was passed by 220 votes to 132, with only the B.B.W.R. and its allies dissenting. On the 27th, a special Sejm committee, headed by Lieberman, was set up to deal with the matter of impeaching Czechowicz.[1]

Piłsudski's reply to the motion took the form of a speech on 28 February to the Senate Budgetary Committee which he agreed to address because it was more sympathetic to the Government than was that of the Sejm.[2] He called upon the Senate to re-grant the credits deleted by the Sejm, explaining that he had not appeared before the Sejm Committee because its method of dealing with budgetary problems, by which a Minister could not himself present his budget, seemed to him irrational, and because he feared that his honour would be impugned. He then proceeded to attack parliament viciously, claiming, among other things, that before 1926 the military budget had frequently been used to keep prostitutes for the deputies. This speech aroused intense resentment among members of parliament. Stanisław Szeptycki, a former Minister of War, attacked Piłsudski in an open letter for failing to make his allegations more precise, and emphatically denied his accusations.[3]

On 8 March Czechowicz resigned his Ministry, much against Piłsudski's will,[4] and appeared before the Sejm Committee. Bartel also submitted his resignation, but it was accepted only on 13 April. Before the Committee, Czechowicz criticized the Sejm for taking action against him only because it did not dare to take action against Piłsudski. He claimed that he could not present the supplementary credits for ratification before the time specified by Bartel.[5] On 12 March, Wróblewski gave evidence, stating that the Main Auditing Office had been aware of the supplementary credits since November 1927. He had attempted to get the Minister to issue the necessary bill for ratification, but had elicited only delaying tactics. He was only informed in December 1928 that the Government had decided to link the question of the supplementary credits with that of the closing of accounts. He regarded all the supplementary credits, altogether 562 million zloties, as illegal.[6] On 14 March the

---

[1] *S.S.S.R.*, 26 February 1929, cols. 4–41.
[2] Piłsudski, 'Przemówienie na komisji budżetowej Senatu (28.II.29)', *P.Z.* x. 132–43.
[3] *Robotnik*, 3 March 1929.
[4] See Piłsudski, 'Dno oka', *P.Z.* ix. 150–1.
[5] *Gazeta Warszawska*, 13 March 1929.
[6] Ibid., 15 March 1929.

Committee voted 18 to 9 to impeach Czechowicz for illegally surpassing the provisions of the budget. It assigned the prosecution to Lieberman, Jan Pieracki of the National Club, and Henryk Wyrzykowski of the Liberation.[1]

On 20 March Lieberman justified the Committee's findings to the Sejm. The government deputies responded by calling into question the honesty and patriotism of the prosecutors. The Committee's recommendation was adopted by 240 votes to 126. On 13 March the Senate passed the budget and on the 25th, immediately after the Sejm had voted on the Senate changes and again deleted the Secret Service fund of the Ministry of the Interior, the session was closed.

It had gone very badly. There was considerable discontent in the conservative ranks of the B.B.W.R., uneasy about Meyszto-wicz's resignation and about the Government's apparent un-willingness to make any concessions over the Czechowicz affair. The P.P.S.—Frak was also showing signs of dissatisfaction over the constitutional proposals and over the conservative character of the Government's economic policies.[2] The economic situation was giving some cause for alarm. The Government's questionable behaviour in the Czechowicz affair brought about a waning in foreign confidence, and the value of Polish government bonds on the world market fell. Dewey, the controller appointed to the Bank of Poland under the terms of the Stabilization Loan, had warned the Government of the danger of forcing the budget through without parliamentary consent.[3]

Piłsudski's reaction to this situation was to place more weight upon the advice of the 'colonels' group', his small clique of military advisers, mostly P.O.W. veterans. As the crisis had worsened, this inner group had tended more and more to take over from the Cabinet the formulation and discussion of policy. Whereas between May and December 1926 there had been 44 Cabinet meetings, and in 1927 38, in 1928 there were 26, in 1929 17, and in 1930 20. Of those in 1929 Piłsudski attended only 4, and of those in 1930 5.[4] He had by now clearly decided on a course of conflict with par-liament, convinced that in the long run he was bound to win. The

[1] *Robotnik*, 15 March 1929.
[2] 'Poufny Komunikat Informacyjny', quoted in Stęborowski, op. cit., p. 239.
[3] *Kurjer Warszawski*, 7 May 1929. Dewey, of course, aware of Polish sensi-tivity about foreign interference, denied that he had intervened with the Cabinet.
[4] P.P.R.M., *passim*.

new, unyielding course was revealed in an article he published in *Głos Prawdy* on 7 April.[1] Its tone was savagely hostile to parliament. In relation to the Czechowicz affair, he declared that he alone bore responsibility for the supplementary credits: 'I have always exerted my utmost efforts to compel Mr. Czechowicz to keep all credits for investment from coming before the Sejm.'[2] He had opposed Czechowicz's desire to appear before the Sejm in order to defend his honour there for 'Where', he asked, 'can one find honour among such apes?'[3] He again resorted to extremely crude language:

If, as I should like in this situation, I am called upon to be Prime Minister, I declare publicly that they will not dare to convene the Tribunal of State [to try Czechowicz] even once, since I will have nothing to do with such as cover themselves with their own excrement (*równi z fajdanami*).[4]

On 11 April, two days before his resignation, Bartel wrote an article in *Kurjer Wileński*.[5] It seemed the final adieu to the moderate course. Although he once more declared himself a convinced parliamentarian, he criticized the 'deformations' which parliamentary government had suffered in Poland. Attempting to justify his political position, he implicitly admitted its ineffectiveness:

My way of interpreting the collaboration of Government and parliament has not found a strong enough echo in parliamentary circles. My approach of patience aimed to free Polish parliamentarianism of its embryonic and deformed features. If certain highly influential people outside parliament have felt that this approach was bound to fail, and that it is necessary to have recourse to somewhat different methods, I, for my part, should not have the flexibility necessary to adopt another course . . .

These 'highly influential people' did now in fact openly take power. The new Government was not headed by Piłsudski, who felt that his health would not allow him to undertake such a burden, but by his close collaborator Świtalski. Świtalski was a political operator of some ability and along with Sławek and Beck he was one of the men Piłsudski most trusted. A lifelong follower of the

---

[1] Piłsudski, 'Dno oka', *P.Z.* ix. 143–54.   [2] Ibid., p. 146.
[3] Ibid., p. 150.   [4] Ibid., p. 153.
[5] *Kurjer Wileński*, 11 April 1929. It was later published as a pamphlet: K. Bartel, *Kilka uwag o praktyce parlamentarnej w Polsce* (Warsaw, 1929).

Marshal, he had been important before World War I in the League for Active Struggle, and as a staff officer in the legions he had been Piłsudski's political specialist. On the Marshal's return from Magdeburg, he was his political secretary and closely associated with him during his 'exile' at Sulejówek. After the coup, he was for a time deputy head of the President's Civil Chancellery and then Director of the Political Department at the Ministry of the Interior, in which capacity he played an important part in organizing the election of March 1928. From June 1928, he was a member of the Government as Minister of Education.

The new Cabinet also included a number of other important members of the 'colonels' group'. Colonel Ignacy Matuszewski became Minister of Finance, Colonel Aleksander Prystor Minister of Labour, and Colonel Ignacy Boerner Minister of Posts, while Car continued to hold the Justice portfolio. Of the fourteen members of the Cabinet, six were military. 'That mysterious power', wrote *Robotnik* on 16 April,

which kept to the corridors, has to some extent officially taken over the Government and assumed all responsibility. Messrs. Świtalski, Matuszewski, Moraczewski, Prystor, and Pieracki[1] . . . represent the group of people who will sail the ship of state in the name of Marshal Piłsudski. . . . Democratic Poland with the P.P.S. at its head, looks to the future with complete calm. After the events of May 1926, it has for a long time foreseen the coming of the 'period of colonels'. Its response will be an increased consolidation of the democratic forces of the country.

In order to strengthen the links between the three non-revolutionary parties of the Left, a permanent Consultative Committee was set up. On it sat Niedziałkowski, Barlicki, and Lieberman for the P.P.S., Woźnicki, Bagiński, and Thugutt for the Liberation, and Dąbski, Roja, and Waleron for the Peasant Party.[2] A collision seemed inevitable.

---

[1] Colonel Bronisław Pieracki, deputy head of the General Staff, had been appointed Under-Secretary to the Ministry of the Interior.

[2] Lato, op. cit., p. 181.

VII

THE CLASH

Until now the situation has been such that economic conditions have served the policies of the Government well.
A Government is in a happy position when it finds
strong support in the favourable development of economic
conditions.

Adam Krzyżanowski, October 1929

The new Cabinet must be considered from the point of
view . . . of its relations with the Sejm. What it represents
is the victory of the 'hard line' with respect to parliament.
This is how public opinion sees it. This is how the Opposition sees it. For a long time we have been aware that there
existed two points of view in government circles, the optimistic point of view represented by Mr. Bartel, and the
pessimistic view represented by what has been popularly
called the 'colonels' group'. The last session of parliament
has weakened the former, and Marshal Piłsudski's article
has swung the balance. The possibility of co-operation
between government circles and parliament has fallen
practically to zero.

Ilustrowany Kurjer Codzienny, 15 April 1929

ALTHOUGH an outright clash between Piłsudski and parliament
appeared imminent, it was to take another seventeen months before
the issue was finally resolved. This was largely the result of the
unwillingness of either side to push the situation to extremes.
The parties of the Left continued to hope that pressure through
parliament would force Piłsudski to compromise with them. The
Marshal, for his part, as in the period between 1923 and 1926, was
unwilling to risk an open confrontation and repeatedly hesitated
on the brink. Nevertheless the prominence assumed by the
Czechowicz affair and the failure of Piłsudski and his entourage
to understand what co-operation with parliament entailed made a
compromise unlikely. The conflict became increasingly intense, the
more so as the impact of the Great Depression in Poland considerably undermined the popularity the Sanacja had enjoyed in its first
three years in office. Yet although the fear of losing power increased

the regime's willingness to resort to more and more dubious means to maintain its hold, the Opposition, perhaps mistakenly, never seriously considered extra-parliamentary action. The conflict grew increasingly bitter and its drastic outcome decisively affected the character of the Piłsudski regime throughout the 1930s.

THE IMPACT OF THE GREAT DEPRESSION

The onset of the political crisis coincided with a serious worsening of the economic situation. Poland had benefited from the general economic revival between 1925 and 1929, and many sectors of the economy had experienced a modest boom. But although the country had become even more closely linked to the international economy, it had not been able to attract much foreign capital which it needed, because of the scarcity of domestic resources, to modernize and develop its industry. Moreover, of the foreign loans obtained, most were short-term, and increased Poland's vulnerability to international economic fluctuations. Foreign trade, another important source of development capital, remained small in scale. In 1929 the total value of Polish exports reached 2,813 million zloties, hardly a very sizeable figure.[1] To make matters worse, these exports had been concentrated, for the most part, in primary products which were affected by the unfavourable terms of trade of raw materials relative to manufacturers. The Polish balance of payments had been negative in both 1928 and 1929. Thus the country was relatively defenceless against the effects of the downturn in international trade and investment which became obvious with the collapse of the Wall Street stock market in late October 1929, although it had in fact begun somewhat earlier.

In Poland the first signs of the coming crisis were felt early in 1929, and were accentuated by the extremely severe winter of that year. Already in February unemployment had risen to 182,000,[2] while in March the prices of shares fell to their lowest level since February 1927.[3] Agricultural prices too, affected by the general world decline, began to fall early in the year. In industry, textiles and the processing of hides and skins were first hit, and output

[1] *M.R.S.* (1931), p. 59, Table I.
[2] *Bezrobocie w Polsce*, ed. Drozdowski, p. 232. For the impact of the Great Depression in Poland see: L. Grosfeld, *Polska w latach kryzysu gospodarczego, 1929–33* (Warsaw, 1952); Landau and Tomaszewski, op. cit., pp. 141–202; Zweig, op. cit., pp. 53–66.   [3] *Messager Polonais*, 23 April 1929.

began to slacken from about April. Small artisan production was also among the first sectors to feel the Depression, particularly in eastern Poland. The crisis then spread to mining and metallurgy, and soon affected all industrial production. From mid-1930 it began to affect banking as well.

The effects of the Depression in Poland were extremely severe. According to estimates made by the University of Birmingham, the Polish national income fell by 25 per cent between 1929 and 1933 (in Great Britain the corresponding figure was 4 per cent.)[1] Worst hit was agriculture, since agricultural prices fell much more rapidly than those of industrial goods. If we take 100 as the index in 1928 both for articles sold by agricultural producers and for those bought by them, in 1929 the former had fallen to 76, while the latter was 101. In 1931 the respective indices were 55 and 91.[2] The result of this price scissors was a drastic decline in peasant income. The net return for 1 hectare of land on estates of 2–50 hectares fell from 214 zloties in 1927–8 to 25 zloties in 1930–1. In 1931–2, the worst year of the crisis, it was only 8 zloties.[3] The peasants were also badly affected, as the Depression continued, by the burden of debt they had acquired in the good years between 1926 and 1929 in order to extend and modernize their plots. Taxes too were increasingly difficult to pay. As a proportion of peasant expenditure, they rose from 12·9 per cent in 1928–9 to 25·7 per cent in 1932–3.[4]

The impoverishment of the peasants meant that it became increasingly difficult for them to buy land made available under the Land Reform scheme. In 1929 164,000 hectares were subdivided, in 1930 130,800, and in 1931 only 105,300.[5] It also made virtually impossible the purchase of agricultural machinery or fertilizers, and thus increased the relative backwardness of Polish agriculture.

Industry was more gradually affected by the Depression. In 1929 the index of industrial production fell to 116·1 from 116·4 in 1928.[6]

[1] *The National Income of Poland*, Birmingham Information Service on Slavonic Countries, Monograph no. 4 (Birmingham, 1937), pp. 5–7.
[2] *M.R.S.* (1935), p. 130, Table I.
[3] Ibid. (1939), p. 74, Table VIII.
[4] *Badania nad opłacalnością gospodarstw włościańskich w roku gospodarczym 1932–33* (Warsaw, 1933), quoted in Landau and Tomaszewski, op. cit., p. 149.
[5] *M.R.S.* (1938), p. 65, Table III.
[6] Index for 1925–9 = 100. Svennilson, op. cit., p. 305, Table A66.

In 1930 it fell to 102·4, and then declined rapidly, reaching 71·2 in 1932. This scale of decline was one of the largest in Europe, and was exceeded only in Germany, Austria, and Czechoslovakia, the countries most drastically affected by the crisis.

The position of those industrial workers who remained employed did not deteriorate radically, at any rate in the initial stages of the Depression. The real value of wages in large and medium industry even rose somewhat as a result of the fall in the price of food. Taking 100 to represent the purchasing power of the average pay packet in 1928, the index rose in 1929 to 109. However it fell to 97 in 1930, to 85 in 1931, and reached 68 in 1932. The 1928 level was again surpassed only in 1937.[1] In addition, unemployment affected a very high percentage of working-class families; in most, probably one member at least lost his job. The number of unemployed had risen by December 1929 to 185,000, and by December of the following year to 299,000, accounting for perhaps 11·5 per cent of the labour force. By March 1931, according to the official figures, it reached 372,000.[2] Unofficial estimates were even higher. According to the Institute of Social Affairs, the number of unemployed in 1931 averaged 520,000, or 25·4 per cent of the labour force.[3] The number of people on short-time also rose, from 21,000 in January 1929 to 142,000 in May 1931.[4]

Members of the intelligentsia were affected as well. Their salaries remained constant, for the most part, but the number of unemployed 'intellectual workers' (a census term) rose from 70,000 in 1929 to 160,000 in 1932–3.[5]

The reaction of almost every government faced with the depression, from the Labour Government in Britain to that of Primo de Rivera in Spain, was to resort to orthodox deflationary economic policies. These policies were more rigidly and inflexibly pursued in Poland than anywhere else in Europe. The departure from the Cabinet first of Czechowicz, who resigned in April 1929 to appear before the Sejm Committee, and later of Kwiatkowski, whom Piłsudski forced to resign in May 1930, and Bartel, who did not hold office after March 1930, robbed the Government of its few truly able economists. Neither Colonel Matuszewski, who became

---

[1] *M.R.S.* (1938), p. 259, Table XXXVIII.
[2] *Bezrobocie w Polsce*, ed. Drozdowski, p. 232.
[3] Instytut Spraw Społecznych, *Młodzież sięga po pracę* (Warsaw, 1938), p. 87.
[4] Próchnik, op. cit., p. 354.
[5] *Młodzież sięga po pracę*, p. 89.

Minister of Finance in April 1929, nor Colonel Prystor, who took the portfolio of Trade and Industry in August 1930, displayed any real competence.

After the first signs of the Depression were seen, the Government responded in April 1929 by raising the bank rate and cutting state expenditure.[1] However it was slow to recognize the seriousness of the situation, and treated the warnings of the Opposition as merely alarmist attempts to discredit the Government. When the Cabinet met to discuss the budget on 8 May 1929, Matuszewski argued, with Piłsudski's support, that the budget could easily be balanced provided the various ministries agreed to economies.[2] It was not until 3 April 1930 that the crisis was seriously discussed by the Cabinet.[3] On this occasion a difference of opinion was evident. Matuszewski advanced the orthodox position, that the Government's primary object must be the maintaining of a balanced budget. Kwiatkowski, on the other hand, stressed the need for a more reflationary policy which would set up public works and provide special credits for those industries in greatest difficulty, such as mining, textiles, timber, and hides and skins. With Kwiatkowski's departure from the Cabinet, the orthodox policy of deflation and budgetary economies was single-mindedly pursued.

The Government saw the stabilization of the zloty as its principal economic achievement since the coup, and the maintenance of a convertible exchange rate soon became the determining factor in its financial policy. This 'struggle to maintain the zloty' was seen as a means for rallying internal support, but it was also undertaken because it would protect the savings in state credit institutions of officials and members of the intelligentsia, groups which had lost heavily in earlier inflations, and because it was believed it would induce foreign capital to move to Poland. In fact, foreign capital avoided Poland, since it was almost universally held that devaluation, or at least exchange control, would eventually have to be applied. Moreover, the doctrinaire desire to maintain the existing exchange rate meant that Polish prices were considerably higher than those of countries which had allowed their currencies

[1] *Czas*, 20 April 1929. The bank rate thus stood at 9 per cent, an indication of how scarce capital was in Poland.

[2] P.P.R.M., 8 May 1929. See also Sławoj-Składkowski, *Strzępy meldunków*, pp. 127–8.

[3] P.P.R.M., 3 April 1930.

to depreciate; as a consequence, it was more difficult for Polish exports to find markets.

In order to halt the decline in agricultural prices, the Government made an attempt to sponsor international co-operation and control. However the International Agricultural Conference held in Warsaw in September 1930 proved a failure. Attempts to deal with the crisis were also hampered by the impact of the Depression in Germany. Because of the situation there, the Reichstag refused to ratify the Trade Treaty with Poland, concluded after arduous and protracted negotiation in April 1930.

When the Government did finally take more vigorous action, its principal objectives were to reduce prices and wages. There was some economic justification for this policy, but it was seriously undermined by the failure to diminish significantly the power of the cartels, which had multiplied greatly during the Depression. In addition, although it was true that real wages had increased in the early stages of the crisis, the Government's attempts to force reductions were bound to cause considerable resentment, particularly since they coincided with an attack on the power of the socialist and Catholic trade unions. It was not until late in 1932 that the Government decided to relieve the heavy burden of indebtedness in the economy by rescaling debts, but even this was no longer of much help to the peasants. In fact, the result of the Government's policies, particularly the desire to maintain the convertibility of the zloty at the existing exchange rate, meant that the Depression continued in Poland until late 1935, when recovery was well under way elsewhere.

The deteriorating economic situation contributed greatly to the general radicalization of politics, both on the Right and on the Left. The hostility of the peasant parties to the Government was especially intensified. Thus the crisis made much more difficult the achievement of any compromise between the Government and the Opposition.

THE TRIAL OF CZECHOWICZ

The clash universally expected after the appointment of the new Cabinet did not take place immediately. In his first statement to the press on 18 April 1929, Świtalski attempted to calm public opinion, advising the assembled journalists not to expect any basic change in government policy, and to judge the new Cabinet by its actions.[1] The tone of the pro-Government press was mild. 'The guidelines of policy', wrote *Polska Zbrojna*, the Army organ, on 17 April, 'have not been modified at all, and it is of little importance that this policy will be implemented by different people.'

In the directing circle of the B.B.W.R., however, a much more aggressive mood prevailed. According to a confidential circular to party officials, the bloc's principal objectives during the parliamentary recess were to be the destruction of the still important influence of the political parties and the consolidation of popular support for the Government's proposed constitutional reforms.[2] In a speech to party functionaries on 16 June, Sławek explained that the Government would prefer to amend the constitution by legal means, but this could only be achieved if strong pressure were brought to bear on the deputies. 'It is sometimes better', he added, 'to break the bones of one Deputy than to be forced to resort to machine guns.'[3]

The Opposition parties were also in a belligerent mood. This was most conspicuous on the Right. The National Party, which had incorporated the Popular National Union and the O.W.P., had adopted a programme in October 1928 which was marked by its strongly anti-Government character as well as by its nationalism and anti-Semitism.[4] The party affirmed its belief in constitutional democracy, although the still largely autonomous O.W.P. was now openly Fascist. At a meeting of the party's Political Committee on 28 January 1929 the Government was again attacked for its autocratic constitutional proposals, its disregard of legality, its supposed hostility to Catholicism, and its alleged softness towards the national minorities. It was also decided to train people in conspiratorial techniques, though conspiratorial action was regarded as premature.[5]

In April and May the party made some attempts to arrange a

[1] *Głos Prawdy*, 19 April 1929.

[2] *Gazeta Warszawska* claimed to have obtained a copy of this circular, and reprinted it on 9 May 1929. The document seems to be genuine.

[3] The speech was later reprinted in *Przełom* (20 July 1929). Its contents became public soon after it was delivered, and naturally infuriated the Opposition. See *Robotnik*, 19 June 1929.

[4] For this programme, see *Gazeta Warszawska*, 16 October 1928.

[5] For these developments see: R. Wapiński, 'Niektóre problemy ewolucji ideowo-politycznej Endecji w latach 1919–39', *K.H.* lxxiii (1966), no. 4, 866–8; Stęborowski, op. cit., pp. 266–7.

combined anti-Government strategy with other Right-Wing and Centre groups. A number of meetings took place with the Christian Democracy, which had also adopted a much more hostile position; representatives of the Piast and the N.P.R. were also sometimes present. As a result, a 'Consultative Committee for the Defence of National Interests' was set up.[1] An unsuccessful attempt was even made in May to co-ordinate the activities of the National Party and the P.P.S.[2]

Radical voices were often heard in the peasant movement as well. In June the Piast executive, meeting in Tarnów, called for an intensification of opposition to the Government,[3] while at the congress of the Peasant Party (7 July), the Sanacja was attacked for behaving 'like a Government of occupation in a conquered country'.[4] The party's representatives in parliament were called upon to bring a motion of no confidence against Świtalski. The congress of the Liberation, meeting in Warsaw on 13–14 June, also advocated 'bitter struggle against the present methods of ruling Poland', but its tone was really rather muted, and the most radical party members, such as Thugutt and Bagiński, were not elected to the executive.[5]

Tentative steps were taken to bring about the union of the three peasant parties, but the old question of the Church proved a stumbling block, as did the fear of the Peasant Party and the Liberation that a united party would be dominated by the Piast. The Piast, on the other hand, criticized the Liberation for its links with the P.P.S. At any rate, a consultative committee of the peasant parties was set up to co-ordinate action in parliament and in the country at large in support of a joint programme for the defence of democracy and the protection of peasant interests.[6]

It was in the P.P.S. that there were most reservations about outright and intransigent opposition. At a meeting on 6 June Daszyński had tried in vain to persuade the Central Committee of the party

---

[1] Komisja Porozumiewawcza dla Obrony Interesów Narodowych.

[2] Stęborowski, op. cit., pp. 266–86.

[3] Czubiński, op. cit., pp. 138–9. The issue of *Gazeta Chłopska* which carried the resolutions (14 July 1929) was confiscated.

[4] Lato, op. cit., p. 190. The issue of *Wyzwolenie* (23 June 1929) which reprinted the resolutions was confiscated.

[5] Ibid., pp. 184–5. The failure of Thugutt and Bagiński to be re-elected may, however, have been connected with attempts to unify the peasant parties, since they were both disliked by the other groups, particularly the Piast.

[6] Ibid., pp. 187–91.

to abandon its policy of strong hostility on the grounds that a clash between the Government and the Left was bound to have disastrous consequences.[1] On 24 June he paid a confidential visit to Piłsudski during which he warned the Marshal of the country's serious economic situation. At the same time, he 'adjured him, by all that was holy, and with all the fervour of his oratory, to make possible a reconciliation, and to create a majority in the Sejm which could co-operate with him'.[2] He offered Piłsudski the support of the P.P.S. and the Liberation. The Marshal was obviously impressed by Daszyński's appeal and replied a number of times, in a subdued voice, 'It all depends on what happens in the business of the Tribunal of State.'[3] It was only somewhat later, just before the beginning of the parliamentary session in October, that Daszyński informed Lieberman, the prime mover in the Czechowicz affair, of the course of this conversation. This prompted Lieberman, writing in exile in 1938, to reflect that if he had been aware of Piłsudski's frame of mind, he might perhaps have acted differently:

It is difficult to judge whether the trial by the Tribunal of State could have been avoided by skilful mediation. In any event, everything possible should have been done to achieve a reasonable compromise, involving no discredit to the honour or dignity of either side.[4]

However, Lieberman was not informed at the time, and in any case by the end of June it was probably too late to undo the corrosive effects of the Czechowicz affair on the political situation.

Although the atmosphere was tense when the trial opened on 26 June, Piłsudski did nothing, in spite of his earlier threats, to prevent its taking its course. This may have been due to Daszyński's appeal, but was more likely the result of the Marshal's belief that if he took upon himself all responsibility for the Cabinet's failure to present the supplementary credits, the judges, the majority of whom he considered to be sympathetic towards him, would bring in a verdict favourable to the Government. 'I am anxious for the

[1] Czubiński, op. cit., p. 136.

[2] Lieberman, op. cit., p. 411. Three accounts of this conversation exist. Piłsudski's is to be found in his article 'Gasnącemu światu', *P.Z.* ix. 186–9, to which Daszyński replied in 'Niewczesne żale', *Robotnik*, 24 September 1929. Both of these accounts were written after the political climate had worsened considerably. The most reliable description seems to be that of Lieberman, which is based on the account of the meeting Daszyński gave him shortly before the opening of parliament.

[3] Lieberman, op. cit., p. 412.   [4] Ibid., pp. 412–13.

Tribunal of State and the Sejm to be further compromised', he told his ministers the day before the opening of the trial.[1] He had already written on 1 June to Stanisław Zaleski, the judge presiding over the preliminary investigation, to explain why he would not appear before him as a witness.[2] In his letter he maintained that he alone had been responsible for the contracting of the supplementary credits. He had been unwilling to present them to the previous 'corrupted' Sejm for ratification, and since the new Sejm had followed the worst traditions of its predecessor, he had decided to continue witholding them. He stressed once more that he had himself prevented Bartel and Czechowicz from presenting the credits at issue, and particularly attacked the calling into question of the ill-fated 8 million zloties granted to the Prime Minister, which had been used, as we have seen, for B.B.W.R. campaign expenses.

On the first day of the trial Czechowicz, in his own defence, argued that the Sejm had accused him on purely technical grounds, and that he should not have been brought to trial until the credits had been examined and the report of the Main Auditing Office had been received.[3] Składkowski and Kwiatkowski both testified that Piłsudski had taken upon himself exclusive responsibility for relations with the Sejm, thus implying that Czechowicz had been accused because the court did not have the courage to try the Marshal.[4]

Piłsudski, in giving evidence, emphasized yet again that the responsibility for contracting the supplementary credits and for failing to submit them to parliament was his alone.[5] He attacked the constitution, the Sejm, and the Tribunal of State: 'I declare to you that I am proud of my actions [with respect to parliament] and that far from considering myself at fault, I regard myself worthy of the highest praise for having curbed the Sejm and destroyed its omnipotence.'[6] The accusation should have been directed against him, he challenged. The trial of Czechowicz was 'a ritual murder committed against a man held responsible for deeds not

---

[1] Sławoj-Składkowski, *Strzępy meldunków*, p. 141.
[2] The letter is printed in *P.Z.* ix. 158–62.
[3] The stenogram of the trial is reprinted in Landau and Skrzeszewska, op. cit., pp. 95–289. For Czechowicz's evidence, see pp. 96–106.
[4] For Sławoj-Składkowski's evidence, ibid., pp. 107–9; for Kwiatkowski's, pp. 109–16.
[5] For his evidence, ibid., pp. 116–22.   [6] Ibid., p. 119.

his own'.[1] He more or less openly admitted that he had taken the 8 million zloties for the elections, and, in concluding, deplored 'the ridiculous situation for which you are responsible, in that a government, led by the greatest man in Poland, whose hands do not stink like yours (pointing at the prosecutors), can be impeached in the first case to come before a Tribunal of State'.[2]

The next day, Lieberman argued that the 8 million zloties illegally obtained for electoral expenses was 'the central point of the trial'.[3] Czechowicz's constitutional responsibilities could not be overlooked simply because he acted upon Piłsudski's arbitrary instructions.[4] Paschalski, for the defence, held that the interest of the state was more important than a strict, legal interpretation of the situation. Czechowicz, he argued, could not be held responsible for Piłsudski's general policies.[5] On 28 June the two other prosecutors spoke, and Lieberman replied to Paschalski.[6]

The unanimous verdict of the thirteen judges was pronounced on the 29th, after ten hours of deliberation.[7] They upheld the principle that, in accordance with the constitution, budgetary control was a fundamental and basic right of the legislature, and that the Government was obliged by law to abide by the budget. Only the Sejm was entitled to approve the credits and expenses contracted by the Government, and it could act to enforce its rights, if the Government did not submit its accounts, without waiting for a proposed bill or for recommendations from the Main Auditing Office. However, the Sejm's resolution of 20 March to impeach Czechowicz did not contain a judgement on the merit of the credits contracted by him. Now, in the documents at the disposal of the Tribunal of State, material providing the basis for such a judgement could be found. It was therefore the decision of the Tribunal of State to 'postpone its proceedings in this case until the Sejm should pass a resolution giving a meritorious assessment, on a formal basis, of the credits questioned by it'.[8]

This verdict was basically unfavourable to the Government, since it was to be expected that when the Sejm met, it would decide against Czechowicz on at least some of the credits contracted.

---

[1] Landau and Skrzeszewska, op. cit., p. 119.   [2] Ibid., p. 121.
[3] Ibid., p. 179.   [4] For his whole speech, ibid., pp. 166–86.
[5] Ibid., pp. 186–219.
[6] For Pieracki's address, ibid., pp. 220–36; for Wyrzykowski's, pp. 236–47; for Lieberman's reply, pp. 247–56.
[7] For the verdict, ibid., pp. 289–91.   [8] Ibid., p. 290.

Lieberman was probably right in attributing the verdict to the defection of General Żeligowski, believed to be one of the Government's supporters on the Tribunal, who had been so disgusted by the actions of the Sanacja since the coup that he had gone over to the Opposition.[1] Nevertheless, the judgement was not a direct condemnation because the pro-Government minority on the Tribunal argued strongly for unanimity; thus its views had to be reflected in the verdict. The pro-Government press tried to claim that the Tribunal had exonerated Czechowicz,[2] but in fact Government circles were extremely dissatisfied with the decision since it was obvious that a serious conflict would develop as soon as parliament met.

THE FALL OF THE ŚWITALSKI CABINET

During the recess, relations between the Government and the P.P.S. deteriorated considerably as a result of the attack by the new Minister of Labour, Colonel Prystor, on the socialists' control of the local sick funds, through which the state medical scheme was administered.[3] These had long been the almost exclusive preserve of the P.P.S., and Prystor's replacement of the elected socialist controlling boards in a number of towns by appointed commissioners aroused great resentment. P.P.S. supporters were also removed from their posts in other government welfare organizations. This attack constituted a serious threat to the financial position of the P.P.S., since many socialist party officials earned their living in the state social services.

The exasperated mood of many P.P.S. members was articulated in a letter addressed by the ninety-four-year-old socialist Bolesław Limanowski to the President. The issue of *Robotnik* in which the letter was published (6 August) was confiscated, but it was distributed as an internal party circular.[4] In it Limanowski attacked

---

[1] He had recorded in his diary his distaste for the methods used in the 1928 elections. See A.A.N., 'Akta gen. Żeligowskiego', file 48, quoted in Stęborowski, op. cit., p. 81. See also Lieberman, op. cit., pp. 408–9.

[2] See, e.g., *Głos Prawdy*, 1 July 1929; 2 July 1929.

[3] See: Z. Zaremba, *Narodziny polskiego faszyzmu* (Warsaw, n.d.), pp. 17–18; Stęborowski, op. cit., pp. 254–6. The P.P.S. issued a leaflet on the subject; see A.Z.H.P., sygn. 114/VI–1926–30, 'Polska Partia Socjalistyczna w obronie samorządu'.

[4] A.Z.H.P., sygn. 114/VI–1926–30, okólnik no. 12 ('W sprawie konfiskaty listu tow. Senatora Bolesława Limanowskiego'), 17 August 1929.

the Government for undermining parliamentarianism, for mis-appropriating funds and for its 'daily breaking of the law'.[1] In closing, he reproached the President for his subservience to the Government, and called on him to uphold the law against the violators of the constitution. His letter thus reflected the conviction of certain Opposition politicians that Mościcki did not approve of the new hard line, and could be persuaded to put pressure on the Government to adopt a more moderate course.

On 3 September, Rybarski of the National Club wrote to the presidents of the Parliamentary Clubs of the Centre and Left, asking them to sign a petition to the President demanding the convocation of an extraordinary session of parliament in order to discuss 'a number of important matters', such as the Czechowicz case, the economic situation, and foreign policy.[2] In an attempt to forestall this move Świtalski went to see Daszyński on 4 September and proposed

a conference of the representatives of parliamentary groups of both Houses to discuss budgetary affairs, in order to give the debate on the budget a rational and effective character. Previous practice had shown that the functioning of parliament had not always possessed such a character.[3]

Piłsudski, he claimed, had expressed his desire to attend.

Piłsudski-ite historians have claimed that this approach was a genuine attempt to reach an accommodation with the Sejm, and had been planned long before.[4] It is true that on 1 July, Piłsudski had told Sławek, Prystor, and Świtalski that he favoured the calling of a meeting of the leaders of the parties to discuss budgetary questions. His aim, he stated, was that the budget be speedily passed, so that 'we can demand that the Sejm occupy itself with the constitution'.[5] He also explained in some detail his strategy in relation to the problem of constitutional reform.

Sławek is to approach the heads of the parties, proposing an agreement on the question of the constitution. When these discussions fail to have any result, the B.B.W.R. is to declare in the Sejm, in the most extreme (*jaskrawy*) fashion, that it will no longer allow the settlement of the

[1] A.Z.H.P., sygn. 114/VI–1926–30, okólnik no. 12 ('W sprawie konfiskaty listu tow. Senatora Bolesława Limanowskiego'), 17 August 1929.
[2] *Gazeta Warszawska*, 4 November 1929.
[3] *Głos Prawdy*, 5 November 1929.   [4] See, e.g., the note in *P.Z.* ix. 185.
[5] A.S.S., 'Konferencja z Komendantem, min. Prystorem, płk. Sławkiem, dn. 1.VII.29'.

constitutional question to be obstructed. This is the moment when one could dissolve the Sejm.[1]

The Opposition parties, particularly those of the Right, felt that the approach was not made in good faith, and saw it also as a sign of weakness on the part of the regime.

Thus, on 11 September, Rybarski, on behalf of his Club, refused to take part in the proposed conference on the grounds that the attitude towards parliament of the Government, and 'in particular the Minister of War', made such a meeting impossible.[2]

The parties of the Left and Centre were undecided. There were some, particularly in the P.P.S., who wished to accept the Prime Minister's invitation. However, after long discussion on 14 September, the six groups of the Centre and Left (the P.P.S., the three peasant parties, the Christian Democrats, and the N.P.R.) issued a joint declaration in effect rejecting the Government's offer. It called upon the Marshal of the Sejm to speed up the calling of parliament, and insisted that during the recess only the Presidium of the Sejm, headed by its Marshal, was empowered to discuss budgetary matters with the Government.[3] This was the first time all these groups had issued a joint statement, and it constituted a basis for the formation of a *Centrolew* alliance. In addition, the Parliamentary Club of the P.P.S., anticipating the refusal to take part in the conference, resolved on 13 September that its objective was the overthrow of the 'post-May system'. The first step towards this goal was to be the passing of a vote of no-confidence in Świtalski.[4]

In spite of this rebuff, the Government made its other planned approach to the Opposition on 20 September, when Sławek proposed a conference of parliamentary groups to discuss constitutional changes.[5] However this was almost universally seen in Opposition circles as a tactical move to prevent the convening of parliament, and it was obvious that the invitation of the B.B.W.R. president would elicit an unfavourable response.

Although Piłsudski was greatly irritated by the failure of these two moves, the tone of the article he wrote on the subject on

[1] Ibid.   [2] *Gazeta Warszawska*, 12 November 1929.
[3] *Robotnik*, 15 November 1929.
[4] *Robotnik*, 14 November 1929. It also resolved not to take part in the conference, but this resolution was not published until the 15th in order, *Robotnik* claimed, not to prejudice the discussions with the other Centre and Left groups.
[5] *Gazeta Warszawska*, 21 September 1929.

22 September was rather milder than some of his other pronounce-ments.[1] He claimed that the proposed budgetary meeting was the logical result of Daszyński's June approach, which he now publicly revealed in a deliberately arrogant way, hoping to embarrass Daszyński within his own party, and to divide the Opposition. Such a conference would, he alleged, have introduced a new and improved method of dealing with the budget, would have created more flexibility, for the requirement that the Government must strictly observe the terms of the budget was 'the most ridiculous barrier to all progress'.[2] He attacked parliament yet again, asserting that the Deputies were the representatives of a 'dying world' and suffered from 'parliamentary diarrhoea' ('fajdanitis poslinis').

The article did not have the hoped-for divisive effects on the P.P.S. Daszyński countered that after all the insults Piłsudski had heaped on the deputies, he should not have been surprised by their refusal to attend a meeting he was to address.[3] Although Barlicki attacked Daszyński for having paid a private call upon Piłsudski, it was generally agreed at the meeting of the party's Central Com-mittee on 25 September that Daszyński had acted in good faith. Piłsudski's revelations merely strengthened the position of the intransigent group, led by Barlicki and Arciszewski, within the P.P.S.[4]

However, Piłsudski did succeed in dividing the Opposition generally, for the fragile unity of the six-party Bloc could not with-stand the strain of his exposures. The Liberation attacked Daszyń-ski for making unjustified statements on its behalf, and both the Piast and the Christian Democracy became much cooler towards the P.P.S. When the parties rejected Sławek's offer, only the Piast and the Christian Democrats issued a joint communique; the others made separate announcements. The National Party also attempted to exploit the incident. It renewed its approaches to the Centre parties, arguing that the Left could never be trusted to conduct a policy truly hostile to the Sanacja because of its previous links with Piłsudski.[5]

The Government was uncertain as to how best to deal with the political situation. One symptom of the conflict within its ranks

[1] 'Gasnącemu światu', *P.Z.* ix. 185–92.
[2] Ibid., p. 188.
[3] *Robotnik*, 24 September 1929.
[4] Stęborowski, op. cit., p. 341.
[5] See, e.g., Stroński's article in *Gazeta Warszawska*, 27 September 1929.

was Bartel's unexplained resignation of his parliamentary seat in
October.[1] In the same month Eustachy Sapieha, one of the leading
conservatives in the B.B.W.R., also resigned his seat.[2] The
divisions were clearly discernible at the meeting of B.B.W.R.
deputies and senators held on 17 October, which was attended by
all members of the Cabinet.[3] The case for a policy of conciliation
was put by Professor Adam Krzyżanowski, deputy for Cracow and
Dean of the Law Faculty at the Jagiellonian University. He insisted
that any improvement in the economic situation, whose seriousness he stressed, required an improvement in relations with parliament. In his opinion, the authority of the Government had declined
radically; the Opposition press was now even attacking Piłsudski.
These moderate views were seconded by Senator Boguszewski.
A middle position was advocated by Radziwiłł, leader of the
B.B.W.R. conservatives, who criticized the Government for failing
in the past to inform the Bloc of its intentions. He hoped that an
outright clash could be avoided, but if it must occur, he believed
that the Government was bound to win. However, the mood of
the majority at the meeting was very bellicose. Deputy Sanojca, a
defector from the Liberation, held that the Sejm should be attacked
'as such'. If all the Deputies in Poland were arrested, he claimed,
nobody would care. The most reliable indication of Piłsudski's
own frame of mind was provided by his close associate, Miedziński.
Political excitement, he asserted, was confined to the intelligentsia.
The Opposition had become hysterical, and had no real support.
The situation did not require haste; Piłsudski would be able to
choose the right amount to act. Piłsudski had indeed expressed
similar views at the meeting with Prystor, Sławek, and Świtalski
on 1 July 1929.[4] Finally, Świtalski himself, concluding the meeting,
emphasized the importance of the issue of constitutional reform
as a means for uniting society behind the Government.

Of the Opposition groups, the Right was determined to use the

[1] *Naprzód*, 27 September 1929.

[2] *Gazeta Chłopska*, 17 October 1929.

[3] A.A.N., P.R.M. sygn. 22, file 127, 'Stenogram konferencji premiera
Świtalskiego z posłami i senatorami B.B., 17.X.29'.

[4] A.S.S., 'Konferencja z Komendantem, min. Prystorem, płk. Sławkiem,
dn. 1.VII.29'. In opposition to his lieutenants, who believed that the position
of the Government was deteriorating and that the clash with parliament should
not be postponed, he affirmed that he did not take 'such a pessimistic view'.
The Left, in particular, he claimed did not possess 'very much impetus', as
could be seen from Daszyński's approach to him.

new session of parliament to attack the Government over the Czechowicz affair. However, on the Centre and Left opinion was divided. Among the Christian Democrats the question of maintaining a political alliance with the Left was provoking dissension. The policy of Chaciński's Warsaw Central Office, that the party should co-operate with the P.P.S. just as Christian Democrats in Belgium and Germany co-operated with socialists, aroused opposition, particularly in the Cracow District Committee. There it was held that attempts should be made to strengthen links with the N.P.R. and the Piast, and to establish contact with the National Party. The Christian Democrats were also internally at odds over the correct strategy to adopt *vis-à-vis* the Świtalski Cabinet. Many held that the forced resignation of this Government 'would not change the situation at all, or would in fact make it worse'.[1]

As for the Piast, Witos was unhappy about too close co-operation with the Left, and entered upon a series of negotiations with the representatives of the Christian Democrats and the National Party with a view to presenting a common front in the budgetary session.[2] In the Liberation, the attempts of pro-Piłsudski-ite elements to moderate the party's hostile stand were defeated, and a radical position was upheld.[3] Radical views also prevailed in the Peasant Party. On 1 October its Parliamentary Club resolved that 'the time is absolutely ripe for the immediate resignation of the whole of the present Cabinet and the liquidation of the entire Sanacja régime....'[4]

The P.P.S. too was in a hostile mood. On 1 October, Niedział-kowski wrote in *Robotnik* that all links between the party and Piłsudski were severed. The Piłsudski of 1905, 1914, 1918 and 1920 'belongs to history'. On 13 October, the Executive Committee of the party again resolved that its aim was the liquidation of the 'post-May system'. It declared itself willing to co-operate with any group 'which sincerely upholds the principle of Democracy'. The parliamentary activity of the party was to be combined with organized mass action: 'If any attempt at a coup is made, it will meet

---

[1] 'Komunikat Informacyjny', no. 110. Quoted in Lato, op. cit., p. 198. For the situation in the Christian Democracy, see Lato, loc. cit.; Stęborowski, op. cit., pp. 349–52.

[2] Lato, op. cit., pp. 197–8.

[3] Ibid., p. 198.

[4] *Gazeta Chłopska*, 10 October 1929. The issue of *Gazeta Chłopska* (6 October 1929) in which the resolutions appeared was confiscated, but Dąbski, who edited the paper managed to get them through the censorship by printing them in an article headed 'What does the semi-official *Epoka* say?'.

with *the most decided resistance from the masses.*[1] However the party's attempts to foster co-operation with the socialist groups among the minorities caused a cooling of its relations with the N.P.R. and the Christian Democrats.

The political differences which separated the Centre and the Left are nicely charted in the replies of the party leaders to a questionnaire issued on the eve of the new parliamentary session by *Tydzień*, a new democratic weekly founded by Thugutt.[2] Asked whether the conflict had reached a decisive stage, and how it could be resolved, only the leaders of the three Left parties proposed that a motion of no confidence be brought against Świtalski. Nevertheless, on 30 October, the Parliamentary Clubs of the Christian Democrats and the Piast both resolved to support such a motion.[3]

As the new session approached, it became evident that the Government had determined on a hard line. The political situation became extremely tense. 'The atmosphere', wrote *Czas* on 28 October, 'is heavy, saturated with electricity, and it recalls the situation just before the Coup.'[4] On the morning of the opening of parliament (31 October) the new pro-Government daily, *Gazeta Polska*, asserted: 'The country has had enough of exhibitions of unrestrained demagogy which hide behind the authority of the so-called legislative power.'[5]

Before the session was to commence, a large number of officers were given verbal orders to assemble near the Sejm. The operation was entrusted to the joint command of Colonel Beck, Colonel Kostek-Biernacki, known for his brutality and his absolute devotion to Piłsudski, and Colonel Dojan-Surówka. One group (approximately 150) remained near the Ujazdowski Hospital as a reserve. The other (100–20), went to the Sejm armed with swords and revolvers at about 4 p.m. Since they did not possess entrance tickets, they were asked to wait; nevertheless they forced their way into the entrance hall. It had been announced that Świtalski was ill, and that Piłsudski would open the new session in person. However, when he arrived, accompanied by Beck and Sławoj-Składkowski, Daszyński refused to open parliament, declaring that 'In the presence of bayonets, revolvers and swords I will not open the

---

[1] Ibid., 15 October 1929.
[2] *Tydzień*, 26 October 1929.
[3] *Gazeta Warszawska*, 31 October 1929.
[4] *Czas*, 28 October 1929.
[5] *Gazeta Polska*, 31 October 1929.

session.'[1] At about 5.30, after a violent interchange, Piłsudski left; at 8.00 the officers finally began to disperse. The session remained unopened.

Exactly what Piłsudski had in mind on this occasion is not clear. It is true that officers had sometimes been present in parliament on important occasions, but never in such numbers. The precedent established at the previous opening, when parliamentary immunity had been violated to expel the Communists, was not encouraging. It may be that Piłsudski intended only to intimidate the deputies but, at the same time, many rumours had circulated about the possibility of violent action. The choice of the relentless and un-scrupulous Kostek-Biernacki is perhaps significant, as is Pragier's claim that the hospitals near the Sejm were told to prepare for an emergency that evening.[2] Lieberman certainly believed that the officers would have attempted to provoke the deputies if the session had been opened.[3] On the other hand, it may be that Piłsudski, as on several previous occasions, shrank at the last from an act so blatantly illegal.

Piłsudski ordered the whole of his conversation with Daszyński, including his own final insults, to be published in order further to inflame the political situation.[4] And indeed, tension did mount. On the evening of the ill-fated opening, the P.P.S. affirmed its 'complete solidarity' with Daszyński's stand, and on 4 November the leaders of all parliamentary groups except the B.B.W.R. and its allies informed the Sejm Marshal that he had their 'complete approval' for all his actions.[5] When Mościcki asked Daszyński to come and explain the situation to him, Daszyński first required an assurance that Piłsudski would not be present. At the meeting, Mościcki attempted to persuade Daszyński to seek a reconciliation with Piłsudski, but Daszyński refused to meet the Marshal outside parliament.[6]

On 5 November parliament was finally convened, and imme-diately prorogued for a month. At the same time, the Govern-

[1] Daszyński's conversation with the Marshal is recorded by Piłsudski, *P.Z.* ix. 192–4. This account of the opening of Parliament is based on the report of the Sejm committee set up to investigate the incident (*Druki Sejmowe*, 2nd series, no. 859), and on Lieberman, op. cit., pp. 413–26.

[2] Pragier, op. cit., p. 364.

[3] Lieberman, op. cit., pp. 424–5.

[4] Sławoj-Składkowski, *Strzępy meldunków*, p. 157.

[5] *Robotnik*, 1 November 1929; 5 November 1929.

[6] Ibid., 5 November 1929.

ment, in its campaign against the Opposition, organized the public collection of 1 million zloties for use against 'espionage'. This was intended to demonstrate society's revulsion at the financial cuts imposed on the Ministry of the Interior.[1]

During the recess, the Government pursued the policy, previously outlined by Świtalski, of attempting to rally popular support by stressing the need for constitutional reform. On 19 November, Świtalski addressed a crowd of more than 2,000 in the concert hall of the Warsaw Philharmonic. His speech was also broadcast by Radio Poland. In a fairly moderate manner, he emphasized the importance of the proposed reforms; Poland, he declared, could not afford the luxury of a weak government. He attempted to defend the regime against charges of autocracy and disregard for public opinion. The reforms would, he hoped, be adopted without difficulty, but 'if we encounter difficulties in our path towards constitutional reform, difficulties resulting from ill-will and systematic destructiveness, it will not be our fault if the conflict assumes a serious character.'[2] Similar speeches were made by a number of other Cabinet ministers.

In addition, attempts were made to divide the Opposition. The Left, claimed Gazeta Polska on 8 November, was doing the Endecja's work, in its intransigent hostility to the Government. The P.P.S. was accused of unpatriotically involving foreigners in Polish affairs because of the support it had received from other European socialist parties. Late in November, a few of the remaining pro-Piłsudski-ites in the P.P.S., of whom the most notable was Emil Bobrowski in Cracow, left the party.[3]

However, although both the Christian Democrats and the N.P.R. stressed that they did not envisage a lasting character for the Centrolew, the unity of the alliance, at least on the question of parliamentary tactics, was firm. On 1 December several joint public meetings were held at which it was affirmed that at the new session of parliament a vote of no confidence in the Prime Minister would be passed.[4] The P.P.S. again maintained that its objective was the 'total liquidation of the post-May system'. The party even formed a clandestine journal, Biuletyn Informacyjny, to circumvent the

[1] Gazeta Polska, 12 November 1929.
[2] Ibid., 20 November 1929.
[3] Ibid., 26 November 1929.
[4] Robotnik, 3 December 1929.

censorship.[1] Yet among the socialists there were doubts about the final goal. In an interview printed in *Naprzód* on 23 November, Diamand, for example, had transparently appealed to the Government to form a coalition with the Left.[2]

Parliament was opened on 5 December. In the intervening period, the Main Auditing Office announced that it could not close the Government's accounts for the financial year 1927-8 because 579 million zloties of supplementary credits had not received legislative approval.[3] After Daszyński, opening the session, had implicitly criticized the Army for its role in the events of 31 October, and after the verdict in the Czechowicz case had been read,[4] Matuszewski, the acting Minister of Finance, opened the debate on the budget proposals for 1930-1. His speech was quiet in tone, and he limited himself to a detailed, factual account of the financial situation, marred somewhat by its over-optimism.[5]

For the socialists, Niedziałkowski stated that the P.P.S. intended to fight, within the bounds of legality, for democracy and socialism, and would resist any attempt at a coup. The present regime was dangerously exasperating political antagonisms, and had provided no solutions for the country's pressing problems; it should be liquidated as a matter of urgency. Thus, as a first step, the parties of the Centrolew had tabled a motion of no-confidence in Świtalski. The Sejm, he was sure, would support any Cabinet determined to dismantle the existing system of government.[6] His views were seconded by Róg of the Liberation.[7] Rybarski's speech, for the National Party, occasioned violent outbursts. When he attacked the Government for taking action against right-wing university students, one of the B.B.W.R. deputies shouted 'Remember the assassination of President Narutowicz, and the action of the youth you led then!' Rybarski replied 'Narutowicz was assassinated by a man who has paid for it with his life, while the murder of Zagórski was committed by men who have succeeded in concealing themselves.'[8] (This accusation aroused tumultuous opposition from the B.B.W.R. ranks.) Finally, Rybarski stated that his party would

[1] Czubiński, op. cit., pp. 152-4.
[2] *Naprzód*, 23 November 1929.
[3] *Robotnik*, 7 November 1929.
[4] *S.S.S.R.*, 5 December 1929, cols. 2-12.
[5] Ibid., cols. 12-32.
[6] Ibid., cols. 32-40.   [7] Ibid., cols. 40-6.
[8] Ibid., col. 54; for the whole speech, cols. 46-58.

support the no-confidence motion, in spite of the 'profound differences' which separated the National Party from some of the other groups supporting it. The remaining Centre and Left groups and the national minorities also attacked the Government.[1]

The no confidence motion came up for debate on 6 December. Its course was stormy.[2] Świtalski accused the Opposition of 'digging the grave of parliamentarianism',[3] which had no rationale in its present form because of the absolute dominance of the parties. The Opposition, he charged, was divided internally and could not form a Government. It was irresponsibly exploiting the economic situation to discredit the Government. Next, Kwiatkowski stated bluntly: 'You gentlemen can vote on your resolution as you wish, as your conscience dictates. We will remain in spite of your paper resolutions.' When there were shouts of protest at the unconstitutional nature of this statement, he insisted that he had actually said 'We, as an attitude to state problems, as a programme and an organization, will remain in spite of your paper resolutions.'[4] The Government's case was also put by Car and Sławoj-Składkowski, while Żuławski (P.P.S.), Putek (Liberation), Rybarski and Stroński (National Party), and Madejczyk (Piast) were the main Opposition speakers. The motion was carried on the same day, by 243 votes to 119, with 7 abstentions. Only the B.B.W.R. and its allies voted against.

Piłsudski hesitated for a time to decide how to deal with the situation. He had already made up his mind that it was not possible to co-operate with the existing Sejm, but was not convinced that this was the correct time to dissolve it and call new elections, since the economic situation had deteriorated and the budget had not yet been voted.[5] Some of his entourage were rather more aggressive. On 14 December, Świtalski, in a speech broadcast from the Warsaw Philharmonic, argued that the actions of the Sejm, led in the previous session by a group of 'hysterical professional politicians' had confirmed the urgent need for constitutional reform. It would be easy, he claimed, to reach an understanding with the country over the heads of the deputies.[6]

[1] Ibid., cols. 58–115.
[2] See ibid., 6 December 1929, cols. 6–112.   [3] Ibid., col. 32.
[4] The Sejm minutes record the latter version on both occasions. S.S.S.R., 6 December 1929, col. 67; this is denied by Próchnik, op. cit., p. 337.
[5] Pobóg-Malinowski, Najnowsza historia, ii. 524.
[6] Gazeta Polska, 15 December 1929.

BARTEL AGAIN BECOMES PRIME MINISTER

This intemperate speech may well have strengthened the belief Piłsudski already held that Świtalski was an unsuitable Prime Minister,[1] and probably increased his determination to change course, at least for a time. Among the Opposition, too, there were many who wanted to avoid an outright clash. On 9 December Daszyński told Mościcki that the majority which had defeated the Cabinet had no intention of forming a Government, and called on the President to exercise a moderating influence in the crisis.[2] On the 17th, Mościcki summoned a number of Opposition leaders to a meeting attended by Świtalski, Sławek, and Car. It was his aim, he stated, to diminish the tensions between the Sejm and the Government. This could be achieved if agreement were reached on constitutional reform.[3] The reply of the Centrolew leaders was moderate. They affirmed that the Sejm was prepared to revise the constitution; although the political atmosphere created by the present system of government made it difficult, reform could be achieved if there were a 'modification of the present régime'.[3] The National Party and the Jewish Club made similar declarations.

As a result, on 21 December, Piłsudski persuaded an unwilling Bartel, in considerable distress because of his kidney complaint, and uneasy about the political and economic situation, to form a Government. He gave him wide-ranging freedom of action, and assured him that he could resign after the adoption of the budget.[4] Bartel himself was quite sincere about his desire to reach an accommodation with parliament. As he told the *Ilustrowany Kurjer Codzienny*, he favoured the 'therapeutic' rather than the 'surgical' method in politics.[5] After some initial difficulty, largely because of opposition from the 'colonels' group', he succeeded in forming a Government on 29 December. He excluded from his Cabinet the most unpopular members of the Świtalski Government: Sławoj-Składkowski, Car, the Minister of Justice, Niezabytowski, the Conservative Minister of Agriculture,[6] Moraczewski, who was held responsible for engineering the split in the P.P.S., and Śwital-

[1] Pobóg-Malinowski, op. cit., p. 524.
[2] *Polonia*, 10 December 1929.
[3] *Robotnik*, 19 December 1929.
[4] Pobóg-Malinowski, *Najnowsza historia*, ii. 525.
[5] *Ilustrowany Kurjer Codzienny*, 25 December 1929.
[6] His successor, Sławomir Czerwiński, was however replaced in January by Leon Janta-Połczyński, another Conservative.

ski himself. Bartel would have liked to dismiss Prystor as well, but Piłsudski refused to permit it.[1] The incoming ministers were much more acceptable to the Sejm, particularly the new Ministers of the Interior, Józewski, who had been Governor of Volynia, and the new, liberal Minister of Justice, Feliks Dutkiewicz. Still, many of the old guard remained in the Cabinet. 'The changes', wrote *Czas* on 1 January, 'must be interpreted as evidence of a willingness to conciliate the Sejm, especially the socialists and the radical peasant groups . . .'.

Although the Budget Committee had been sitting since 28 December, the first full session of parliament took place only on 10 January 1930, when Bartel outlined his Government's policy.[2] The Cabinet changes, he stated, did not mean the abandonment of those 'principles and postulates' which had been 'the basis of the so-called post-May régime'.[3] Nevertheless, he claimed, he came with good will. He knew the views of the deputies just as they knew his. 'Can one not find in both', he asked, 'as much in common as is necessary for the state?'[4] He stressed the importance of constitutional reform and, in particular, the strengthening of the executive so that the 'personal responsibility of the men whom the will of the country places over the state'[5] could be increased. Under his Government, he promised, the civil service and local administration would be impartial, and not favour any one party. He appealed to the deputies to co-operate with the Government in order to overcome the economic crisis. Parliament, he affirmed, 'has a serious job to perform', and 'criticism marked by understanding of the general interest' would be listened to by the Cabinet.[6]

As a further sign of its desire for conciliation, the Government now placed no obstacle in the way of a resolution in the Sejm establishing the proper method of publishing Sejm resolutions. This finally made possible the abrogation of the press decrees of May 1927.[7]

In reply to Bartel's speech, Róg, for the Centrolew, argued that

---

[1] Pobóg-Malinowski, *Najnowsza historia*, ii. 525.
[2] For his speech, which lasted three hours, see *S.S.S.R.*, 10 January 1930, cols. 20–52.
[3] Ibid., col. 21. [4] Ibid., col. 22.
[5] Ibid., col. 24. [6] Ibid., col. 52.
[7] The resolution was adopted the same day. *S.S.S.R.*, 10 January 1930, col. 81.

the aim of the grouping in passing a vote of no confidence in
Świtalski had been a change in the system of governing. The
Centrolew, he continued, had agreed in December that this change
would have to satisfy six demands, stipulating:

1. The full application of the constitution and the statute conferring autonomy on Silesia.
2. The establishment of the principle that constitutional revision
   would only be undertaken legally.
3. The establishment of the independence of the judiciary, Army
   and civil service.
4. The maintenance of the principle of popular participation in
   local government.
5. The ending of administrative arbitrariness in press confiscations and political repression, and the investigation of the
   financial abuses of the Government.
6. The ending of any Treasury subsidies to a political party.

The new Government, he claimed, would be judged by whether it
implemented these principles or not.[1]

For the National Party, Winiarski stated that his Club would
support any actions beneficial to the country. He did not believe,
however, that Bartel's Government 'had the power to effect a basic
improvement'.[2] The leaders of the minorities were also somewhat
sceptical of the Government's ability drastically to modify the
situation.[3]

Work on the budget proceeded fairly smoothly, although once
again the Secret Service fund of the Ministry of the Interior was
cut, this time by 50 per cent. The budget debate took place
between 3 and 12 February.[4] Its course was relatively calm, and
the budget was adopted without a division on both the second and
third readings. The National Party abstained. For the Centrolew,
Niedziałkowski explained that the constituent parties would vote
for the budget since it was granted 'to the state, and not to a system
of government'.[5] However, this was not to be construed as a vote
of confidence; they would not cease their struggle for the establish-

---

[1] S.S.S.R., 15 January 1930, cols. 35–6.
[2] Ibid., col. 42. For the whole speech, cols. 36–43.
[3] Ibid., cols. 43–57.
[4] For the debate see: ibid., 3 February 1930, cols. 3–97; 10 February 1930,
cols. 87–94; 12 February 1930, cols. 3–19.
[5] Ibid., 12 February 1930, col. 12.

ment of democracy. The decision to vote for the budget was strongly criticized by the Left Wing of the P.P.S., led by Barlicki, Pużak, and Zaremba, who had already opposed the softening of opposition following the formation of the Bartel Government. They had also been very uneasy about the association of the party with 'clericalist' and 'right-wing' groups, such as the Piast and the Christian Democrats.[1]

The course of the session in general was not particularly easy, partly because the more zealous supporters of a hard line within the B.B.W.R. were anxious to see Bartel fail. Violent opposition was aroused in the B.B.W.R. by the bill to safeguard the freedom of elections passed on 29 January, following the Supreme Court's invalidation of election results in several constituencies and the submission of the report of the Sejm committee set up to investigate electoral abuses.[2] Conflict also arose in the committee, established largely on Sławek's insistence in an attempt to discredit Daszyński, which was investigating the events in the Sejm on 31 October. It had elicited a number of quite compromising statements from Army officers, and on 13 February the B.B.W.R. members sitting on it refused to participate any longer in its proceedings, claiming that it was not impartial.[3]

Constitutional reform, too, created problems. On 11 January the Constitutional Committee began discussing the two proposals submitted to it (one from the Government, the other from the P.P.S., Liberation, and Peasant Party). On 21 January the Centre parties submitted a draft of their own, which increased the power of the President, but did not curtail the rights of the legislature as drastically as the B.B.W.R. plan. By the beginning of March, no real consensus had been achieved on the type of constitutional changes needed. On 6 and 13 March, the Committee rejected proposals calling for an increase in the powers of the executive. This, according to Mackiewicz, 'emphatically ended any possibility of compromise between the Sejm and the Government of Marshal Piłsudski on the constitution'.[4]

The Czechowicz affair remained a potential threat, for now that

[1] Czubiński, op. cit., pp. 165–6.
[2] For the debate on the bill, see S.S.S.R., 29 January 1930, cols. 13–32. For the Report, Druki Sejmowe, 2nd series, Druk no. 570.
[3] Gazeta Polska, 14 February 1930.
[4] S. Mackiewicz, 'Czterdzieści jeden posiedzeń Komisji Konstytucyjnej', Przegląd Współczesny (1931), no. 108, p. 79.

the budget had been passed, the Opposition could, in the Budget Committee, assess the merits of the credits involved in the case. In fact, the Committee met for this purpose several times in March.[1] In addition, Lieberman had gone to see Bartel and Jó-zewski in order to hear their evidence concerning the matter.[2] But what actually precipitated the fall of Bartel was the proposal on 8 March by the P.P.S. of a motion of no confidence in Prystor, the Minister of Labour. This was intended principally to conciliate the party's Left Wing, and to demonstrate the party's disapproval of Prystor's actions in dealing with the sick funds. No serious challenge to the Government was envisaged. At the same time, the National Club submitted a motion of no confidence in Czerwiński, the Minister of Education and Religious Cults.

Piłsudski had come to the end of his patience. He decided that the time was ripe to act, since public opinion now saw 'on the one hand the conciliatory Government, on the other, the bitter, uncompromising Opposition'.[3] He therefore ordered Bartel to deliver a speech on 12 March, during the budget debate in the Senate, strongly attacking parliament and the dominance of the parties.[4] When the motions of no confidence came up on 14 March, Bartel declared that he regarded them as a test of confidence in his Government.[5] The motion against Prystor was passed without division. Apart from the B.B.W.R., which opposed it as a matter of course, it was supported by all groups except the Peasant Party, the Jews, and the Germans, who abstained. Bartel submitted his resignation on 15 March.

THE FINAL CLASH WITH PARLIAMENT

Piłsudski's plan, now that the budget had to all intents and purposes been passed, was to prolong the search for a new Cabinet until the statutory five months laid down in the constitution for the duration of the budgetary session had elasped. In this way he hoped to prevent the Sejm from adopting the Budget Committee's report concerning the merits of the additional credits for the year 1927–8. This was a damning document which claimed that in

---

[1] *Druki Sejmowe*, 2nd series, no. 861.
[2] Lieberman, op. cit., pp. 426–9.
[3] Pobóg-Malinowski, *Najnowsza historia*, ii. 525.
[4] For the speech, *S.S.Se.R.*, 12 March 1930, cols. 37–46.
[5] *S.S.S.R.*, 14 March 1930, cols. 7–8.

many cases extra credits had been obtained by the Government 'without real thought or plan', and stated that 8 million zloties of these additional funds had been used for the B.B.W.R. electoral campaign. It included a draft resolution to be submitted to parliament, which read:

The Sejm affirms that the Government, in the financial year 1927–8, committed infringements of the budget without legal ratification, unjustified either by the legal obligations of the state or by the requirements of the rise in expenses on payments and estimates of credit included in the budget, to the sum of 230,000,000 zloties.[1]

Piłsudski also intended to compromise the deputies by showing that they were incapable of forming a Government. He thus refused the President's request that he form a Cabinet himself, justifying his decision in *Gazeta Polska*: 'My fundamental disgust for the way in which all parliaments, and, in particular, our Sejm, function is well known. . . . Of all the innovations since Independence, the Deputy is perhaps the basest.'[2] He entrusted the task of forming a Government to the well-meaning but politically inexperienced Marshal of the Senate, Juliusz Szymański, who took his mission so seriously that he had to be enlightened by Sławek as to its true character.[3] On 26 March Szymański announced Piłsudski's four conditions for effective co-operation with the Sejm, with which he identified himself: the deputies and the parties were not to meddle in matters of the personnel or functioning of the Government; the deputies were not to interfere with the implementation of the budget once it had been voted; Article 6 of the Treasury Law (requiring legislative approval for supplementary credits) should be revoked; and the Sejm should sit only six months a year.[4] These were terms of capitulation, and were thus, of course, completely unacceptable to the Opposition. The formation of a Government was next entrusted to Jan Piłsudski, the Marshal's brother, who in his turn began to 'consult' the deputies.

Daszyński was infuriated by this procedure, and decided, contrary to parliamentary practice and in spite of the strong opposition of the B.B.W.R., to call parliament into session before a Government had been formed. He wished, above all, to present

---

[1] For the report, see *Druki Sejmowe*, 2nd series, no. 861.
[2] Piłsudski, *P.Z.* ix. 209, 211.
[3] Pobóg-Malinowski, *Najnowsza historia*, ii. 526.
[4] See Piłsudski, *P.Z.* ix. 214–15.

to parliament the report of the Committee of Inquiry into the events of 31 October and that of the Budget Committee on the supplementary credits.[1] When the session opened on 29 March the atmosphere was tense, and action against the Sejm seemed certain. However, the meeting passed off quietly because Daszyński backed down at the last moment and did not present the Budget Committee's report on the Czechowicz affair.[2] Once it had voted on the Senate's amendments to the budget, the Sejm was immediately adjourned by the new Government, set up that very day and headed by Walery Sławek, Piłsudski's closest collaborator. The composition of the Cabinet was the same as that of its predecessor, except that Car again took the Justice portfolio. Sławek's appointment was universally regarded as signifying the absolute victory of the advocates of a hard line in relation to parliament.

In response, on 5 April the parties of the Centrolew issued an 'Appeal to the Nation'. Poland, they claimed, was living under a disguised dictatorship, incapable of dealing with the economic crisis. The Sejm, in passing votes of no confidence, first in Świtalski and then in Prystor, had demanded a modification of the system. The Government had refused to comply. The President should now dissolve parliament and let the nation choose between the Sejm and Marshal Piłsudski.[3]

The three peasant parties also began to co-operate more closely. Although relations between the Peasant Party and the other two groups had cooled somewhat because of the former's abstention in the no-confidence motion again Prystor, the leaders of the three parties met for an all-day conference on the political and economic situation on 15 April. There it was unanimously resolved that the economic policies of the Government had proved ruinous for the small agricultural producer, and that the Government's hostility to democracy had robbed the peasantry of any influence on the running of the state. The resolution continued:

Under the circumstances, the Parliamentary Clubs [of the three groups] have decided to harmonize their activity, both in parliament and in the country, in order to create a common peasant front for the threatened economic interests and political rights of rural people.[4]

In May, the three parties agreed on a common electoral list for

[1] See Lieberman, op. cit., pp. 431–2. [2] Ibid., pp. 432–6.
[3] *Robotnik*, 6 April 1930. [4] *Wyzwolenie*, 20 April 1930.

local government elections. This increased closeness was greeted with some reserve by the other parties of the Centrolew. The Christian Democrats criticized the Piast for becoming too closely associated with the anti-clerical Liberation and Peasant Party, whereas the P.P.S. remained sceptical towards the premise that all peasants, large and small, had common political and economic interests.[1]

Piłsudski had decided to hold new elections. On 26 May he summoned Sławoj-Składkowski and told him:

The Sejm is going to be dissolved, and you must manage (*zrobić*) the new elections together with Sławek and Świtalski. They have told me that you are indispensable to them for these elections, and you will therefore return to the Ministry of the Interior.[2]

When asked if he could prepare for the elections in six weeks, Sławoj-Składkowski, who became Minister of the Interior again on 3 June, said he needed three months. This was understandable, since the Government's prospects in a free election did not appear very good. In May and June elections were held in three constituencies in which the original results had been disallowed by the Supreme Court. In the new results, the B.B.W.R. lost 7 seats, the P.P.S. 2, the Liberation 1, the Christian Democrats 1, and the Sel-Rob 1. The Peasant Party gained 6, the Minority bloc 3, the National Party 2, and the Ukrainian Socialist Radicals 1.[3] As a consequence of these changes, the Government bloc lost as well 2 more seats elected on the state list. The elections for the Silesian Sejm on 11 May also showed a lessening of support for the Government. Whereas in the 1928 General Election the Government had won 30·6 per cent of the votes, it now won 17·1 per cent. The Christian Democrats won 22·7 per cent, the N.P.R. 6·9 per cent (standing together in 1928 they had won 25·2 per cent), the German nationalists 30 per cent (31·1 per cent), the P.P.S. 8·8 per cent (13·7 per cent), and the Communists 4·6 per cent (3·7 per cent). The P.P.S.—Frak won only 0·8 per cent of the vote.[4] In the plebiscite held among the oil workers in East Galicia to determine how the workers' building fund should be divided, the P.P.S.—

---

[1] Lato, op. cit., pp. 212–14; Czubiński, op. cit., pp. 199–200.
[2] Sławoj-Składkowski, *Strzępy meldunków*, p. 193.
[3] *Gazeta Warszawska*, 11 June 1930.
[4] Rechowicz, op. cit., p. 298, Table VI.

Frak won only 20·9 per cent of the votes, as against 79·1 per cent for the P.P.S.[1]

In the meantime, the Centrolew demanded the calling of an extraordinary session of parliament, presenting a petition with the necessary number of signatures to the President on 9 May. However, in order to forestall discussion of the supplementary credits, the Sejm was once again adjourned as soon as it met on 23 May. Bending the constitution still further, Car refused to summon the Senate along with the Sejm. In response, the parties of the Centrolew issued a joint declaration stating that the adjournment of the Sejm made it impossible to deal with the economic crisis. They also for the first time attacked the President, 'who has allowed himself to be used in the political trick of the camp represented by Mr. Sławek's Cabinet'. The struggle for the removal of dictatorship and the full implementation of the constitution, concluded the statement, would be pursued 'until the final victory of organized democracy'.[2]

Two days before the month's adjournment of parliament was to elapse, the extraordinary session was declared closed on 21 June. On the 25th the National Party held a large protest meeting at which Rybarski spoke,[3] and the Centrolew, which had anticipated the Government's action, had already on 15 June called a mass congress for the 29th to defend 'freedom and law'. It was to be held in Cracow, an old P.P.S. stronghold surrounded by a countryside controlled by the Piast. As the economic situation had deteriorated, clashes had occurred between the police and the unemployed in a number of towns. Although there is some evidence that the reaction of the mass of the population to the depression was one of apathy and inertia, the period saw a strong radicalization of the political parties.

The P.P.S. was in a particularly militant mood, partly because many of its meetings had been broken up, and many of its members attacked, by militants from the P.P.S.—Frak.[4] On 28 May the Party Central Committee stated in a circular to its regional committees: 'We are entering a new period of political struggle which cannot be resolved by the Sejm, but which must be carried through

---

[1] Próchnik, op. cit., p. 356.
[2] The resolution is reprinted in *Wyzwolenie*, 1 June 1930.
[3] *Gazeta Warszawska*, 26 June 1930.
[4] On this, see Próchnik, op. cit., pp. 359–60.

with the greatest effort of the whole population, and, in the first place, of the working class.'[1] The party organized a number of mass meetings to protest against the actions of the Government. The culmination of this campaign, agreed on with the other parties of the Centrolew, was to be the Cracow congress. On 20 June, at a meeting of all Senators and Deputies of the Centrolew, the aims of the bloc were defined in a unanimous declaration.[2] It attacked the Government for its failure to deal with the economic crisis and for its hostility to democracy. The President was again criticized for helping to undermine parliament. Finally, the Centrolew demanded:

1. The withdrawal of the Governments of the dictator, Józef Piłsudski.
2. The formation of a constitutional Government based on the confidence of society, which, together with parliament, could struggle against the economic catastrophe and the misery of the working people of town and country.[2]

The congress took place, as planned, in Cracow on 29 June. In spite of the Government's attempts to diminish attendance by exerting administrative pressure and by sending falsified telegrams to local party organizations announcing that the congress had been called off,[3] it was attended by perhaps 1,500 delegates and 25,000–30,000 supporters.[4] This was not in fact as many as the organizers had hoped for, but it was still a considerable number. The sessions were held in the Old Theatre, and the mood of the delegates was militant.[5] The congress was opened by Róg of the Liberation. For four years, he claimed, the country had been ruled, against its will, by a dictatorship. Moreover, the Government was responsible for the severity of the economic crisis. The six parties of the Centrolew were united in the conviction that the rule of law had to be re-established in Poland. Telegrams of sympathy to the congress from Daszyński, Limanowski, and thirty-eight British Labour M.P.s were then read. Next, representatives of the six parties

[1] Quoted in Czubiński, op. cit., p. 203.
[2] It is reprinted in *Gazeta Warszawska*, 21 June 1930.
[3] These manœuvres were described in *Robotnik* on 1 July 1930; 2 July 1930.
[4] *Robotnik* on 1 July estimated the number as 30,000, Witos in his memoirs as 25,000 (op. cit. iii. 183). The pro-Government *Ilustrowany Kurjer Codzienny* (1 July 1930) claimed that there were altogether 10,000 people present, while *Gazeta Warszawska* (30 June 1930) estimated attendance at 22,000.
[5] For the speeches at the congress see: *Robotnik*, 30 June 1930; 1 July 1930.

made declarations on behalf of their groups. Barlicki spoke for the
P.P.S., Malinowski for the Liberation, Waleron for the Peasant
Party, Witos for the Piast, Kuśnierz for the Christian Democrats,
and Popiel for the N.P.R. The most radical speech was made by
Thugutt, as chairman of the Committee for Freedom of Speech.
The Government, he claimed, was far too preoccupied with
holding power to worry about the economic crisis. Foreign capital
was avoiding Poland because of the unsettled internal situation.
'If the Government and the President of the Republic are not
absolutely certain that they and their partisans are a feeble minority
in Poland,' he challenged, 'let them try to find out through free
elections.'[1]

The congress then, amid loud cheering, adopted a number of
resolutions.[2] For four years, it was stated, Poland had been ruled
by the dictatorship of Piłsudski:

The will of the dictator is exercised through the changing Governments; the President is also subject to the dictator's will. The basis of
society's faith in the law in its own state has been undermined, public
life is continually full of rumours and threats of a new coup; the people
have been deprived of all influence over the internal and foreign policy
of the Republic.

It was then resolved that the struggle for the elimination (usunięcie)
of Piłsudski's dictatorship would be undertaken by all six parties,
and pursued to victory; only a Government with the confidence
of the Sejm and society would be supported by the Centrolew; any
attempt at a coup by the Government would meet with strong
resistance; if such a coup were accomplished, society would be
free from all obligations towards the Government, and debts
incurred abroad by this illegal regime would not be honoured;
any attempt at terror would be countered by physical force; the
President should resign, because he had allowed himself to be used
by the Government in its evasions of the constitution.

Later, a mass meeting was held at the Kleparski Market, attended
by a huge crowd. Jankowski of the N.P.R. attacked the Government for the 'unheard-of obstacles' it had placed in the way of the
congress; Żulawski, for the P.P.S., declared 'We must march together as in 1920. Our only order must be: all to the front, all to

[1] Robotnik, 30 June 1930.
[2] The censorship would not allow the resolutions to be published. They are
reprinted in Lato, op. cit., pp. 259–60.

the war of liberty against dictatorship!'[1] A procession then made its way from the market to the Mickiewicz Memorial in the centre of the town, to an accompaniment of radical slogans, such as 'Down with the puppet President!', 'To the gallows with Piłsudski!'[2] At the Memorial, Mastek of the P.P.S. closed the meeting with the words 'Goodbye, until we meet in Warsaw for the formation of a worker–peasant Government.'[1]

In both the mood of its participants and the tone of its resolutions, the congress was by far the most radical step the Opposition had yet undertaken. According to Witos, the majority of its leaders (whose optimism he did not share) believed that Mościcki would now resign. If he did not, they thought he would dismiss Sławek and create a new compromise Government, or, at the worst, call new elections. They forgot once again, as Witos comments, 'that no speeches could topple Piłsudski's Government'.[3]

The Cabinet's reaction to the congress was one of fury. On 1 July Sławek, who had gone with Sławoj-Składkowski and Tadeusz Schaetzel on the previous day to Piłsudski's summer residence at Druskieniki, threatened to take legal action against its organizers.[4] The Public Prosecutor was ordered to initiate proceedings against thirty of them, in terms of Article 65 of the Austrian penal code, but was forced to abandon the case on 11 July, because there was not sufficient evidence of revolutionary intent.[5]

The anti-Government campaign organized by the Centrolew lost some of its momentum after the congress because the peasants were now fully occupied with the harvest, and because of the traditional suspension of politics during July and August. On 10 July the Centrolew leaders met, and, after long discussion, resolved that the Bloc would submit a petition to the President calling for the convocation of an extraordinary session of the Sejm and Senate. However, they did not specify a date.[6]

---

[1] *Robotnik*, 1 July 1930.

[2] Witos felt this shouting may have been begun by *agents provocateurs*. See Witos, op. cit. iii. 183.

[3] Ibid. 185.

[4] *Ilustrowany Kurjer Codzienny*, 3 July 1930.

[5] *Gazeta Warszawska*, 11 July 1930. Austrian criminal law remained in force in Galicia until 1932; Article 65 reads: 'He is guilty of an offence against public order who publicly or before several people by printed text, written work, or drawing provokes contempt for or hatred of the person of the Emperor, the integrity of the state, the form of government, or the state administration.'

[6] *Robotnik*, 12 July 1930.

The pro-Government parties greatly intensified their activity during this period, and held many meetings. The development of the crisis led to an increase in Right-radicalism in the Sanacja and already in March an openly pro-Fascist weekly, *Nowa Kadrowa*, had been launched, probably by police headquarters. The leading article in the first issue claimed that just as the First Cadre had marched under Piłsudski's command to fight for independence, so the New Cadre would fight under his orders to create a 'Great Power Poland' (*Polska Mocarstwowa*). It affirmed:

> The time has come to launch the slogan, for all citizens of good will to unite and to swell the serried and disciplined ranks of the 'New Cadre' which marches today—not like the First Cadre to fight for lost independence, but to win its own society, to conquer the Bastille of opportunism, party egoism, demagogy, ill will, contradiction, passivity, defeatism, and cowardice.[1]

According to the right-wing press, this journal was closely linked to a secret military society, the Union of the White Eagle,[2] created by Rydz-Śmigły in order to ensure that the Sanacja would retain power if Piłsudski should die. Rumours also circulated of the existence of another secret society with similar aims, the Union of Military Action.[3] These developments aroused increasing dissatisfaction among the more liberal members of the B.B.W.R. During the second half of May, Czechowicz resigned his parliamentary seat and on the 22nd told reporters that the Government was responsible for the delay in settling the matter of the supplementary credits.[4] On 9 July, three B.B.W.R. deputies, led by Marjan Cieplak, announced that they were leaving the bloc since it had become 'more and more indifferent to the peasant masses'. Shortly afterwards, they rejoined the Peasant Party.[5] At the end of July, the Union of Legionaries split, and an Organizational Committee of Democratic Legionaries and P.O.W. members was set up under Arciszewski, Bagiński, Andrzej Strug, and Thugutt. On 10 August, it held a congress in Warsaw attended by sixty delegates

---

[1] *Nowa Kadrowa*, 16 March 1930.

[2] Związek Orła Białego.

[3] Związek Żołnierskiego Czynu. For some of these speculations, see *ABC*, 11, 12, and 16 July 1930; *Polonia*, 13 and 17 July 1930.

[4] *Robotnik*, 23 May 1930.

[5] Ibid., 11 July 1930. In fact, these resignations were probably part of a government plan to infiltrate the Peasant Party, with the object of dislodging it from the Centrolew.

representing thirty local committees. The organization was renamed the Union of Democratic Legionaries.[1]

The Opposition was much encouraged by what it took to be the dissolution of the B.B.W.R., and also by the deterioration of Piłsudski's health, which seemed to indicate that he would soon be forced to withdraw from active politics. On 14 July the Marshal had delegated full control of the War Ministry to his deputy, General Konarzewski. 'We should not be surprised', commented *Robotnik*, 'if Marshal Piłsudski's holiday lasts several months, even more, we should not be at all astonished, and would even regard it as entirely to be expected, if the Marshal retired completely from public life because of his health.'[2] In spite of widely current rumours that he would make an important speech there, Piłsudski did not address the congress of legionaries held in Radom on 10 August, although he did attend, and had resumed the duties of Minister of War on 8 August. Speeches were delivered by Rydz-Śmigły, Sławek, and General Górecki; nevertheless the congress, as a demonstration of support for the Government and a rival to the Cracow congress, proved a disappointment.[3]

The Government also had problems to contend with in Silesia, where the dispute between Governor Grażyński and Korfanty had reached new heights of acrimony. As we have seen, the Government had suffered a defeat in the Silesian elections of May 1930. When the new Sejm met, conflict arose over its attempts to exercise its right of control over the provincial budget. On 1 July the Sejm was adjourned, over the strenuous objections of Korfanty and the P.P.S. Demonstrations were organized all over Silesia to protest against Grażyński's actions.[4]

On 21 August the Centrolew leaders met to discuss the political situation in the country as a whole, and decided to present a petition early in September calling for the convocation of parliament. The next day, after further debate, it was resolved to organize simultaneous protest meetings in twenty-one towns on 14 September. 'The moment has come', wrote *Robotnik*,

to deepen and widen the action we have embarked upon. This time it will be not only in one town, but in twenty-one places over the whole

[1] *Robotnik*, 29 and 30 July 1930, 11 August 1930.
[2] Ibid., 19 July 1930.
[3] For the course of the congress, see *Gazeta Polska*, 11 August 1930.
[4] Rechowicz, op. cit., pp. 173–88.

of the Republic that the worker and peasant masses will assemble on the same day to affirm by the force of their numbers and their unbroken will, their desire to overthrow the hated dictatorship.[1]

However, the Opposition had underestimated Piłsudski. Already on 11 August he had instructed Sławoj-Składkowski to assemble evidence which would make it possible to prefer charges against the leaders of the Centrolew.[2] On the 22nd he informed Car, Beck, and Sławoj-Składkowski that he intended to dissolve parliament and arrest a number of the deputies.[3] The next day Sławek resigned, and Piłsudski became Prime Minister. In his new Cabinet Colonel Beck, the Deputy Prime Minister and Minister without Portfolio, played a key role. Because Car refused to take responsibility for the arrest of the deputies, the Justice portfolio was conferred upon Czesław Michałowski.[4]

Immediately upon taking office, Piłsudski gave an interview to *Gazeta Polska* in which he again attacked the 1921 constitution and the general behaviour of the deputies.[5] His words seemed to invite his supporters to take the law into their own hands against members of parliament, and, indeed, on 29 August Jan Dąbski, the President of the Peasant Party, was severely beaten by 'unknown' Army officers. The following day, parliament was dissolved, and new elections were proclaimed, for the Sejm on 16 November, and for the Senate on 23 November. On 1 September, after reading the list of deputies presented to him by Sławoj-Składkowski, Piłsudski marked 'with a green pencil' those who were to be arrested.[6] He had ruled out, however, the imposition by force of a new constitution or of modification in the electoral system.

The final stage of the clash between the Government and the Opposition coincided with a serious deterioration of the situation in East Galicia. At a congress of Ukrainian Nationalists held in Vienna from 27 January to 3 February 1929, the Ukrainian Military Organization led by Evgeni Konovalets, had combined with a number of smaller Ukrainian groupings. The new body

[1] *Robotnik*, 24 August 1930.
[2] Sławoj-Składkowski, *Strzępy meldunków*, p. 205.
[3] Ibid., pp. 205–6.
[4] Pobóg-Malinowski, *Najnowsza historia*, ii. 528–9.
[5] Piłsudski, *P.Z.* ix. 217–24.
[6] Sławoj-Składkowski, *Strzępy meldunków*, p. 223.

took the name of the Organization of Ukrainian Nationalists (O.U.N.).[1] It assumed a strongly oligarchical character, and, with some help from Germany, began a campaign of sabotage. This was aimed, primarily, at discrediting the more moderate Ukrainian organizations, especially the Right Wing of the U.N.D.O., which had had some contact with the Polish Government, by provoking the authorities to make reprisals.[2] On 28 June 1930, one member of the organization was sentenced to death for sabotage and seven were given prison sentences of between two and four years' hard labour. Nine were acquitted.[3] In retaliation, the group intensified its campaign of sabotage. On 30 July a postal van was attacked near the station at Bóbrka Chlebowiec, and one official was killed; on the night of 6/7 August a large number of fires were started which destroyed the harvest on many Polish estates; on 16 August the telegraph lines between Lwów and Sambor, Przemyśl, and Stanisławów were cut and on 21 August an unsuccessful attempt was made to derail the Stanisławów–Kołomyja express. The sabotage continued throughout August and September. On 10 September, official sources estimated that property worth 6,743,000 zloties had been destroyed, including 62 houses, 67 barns, 112 mills, and 78 other buildings.[4]

Piłsudski reacted by holding villages near places where sabotage had occurred collectively responsible.[5] Cavalry were billeted in them, and fines levied. No one was killed, but those who resisted the troops or were suspected of sabotage were beaten. By the end of November this policy had succeeded in quelling the disturbances, but it left behind a legacy of bitterness. Moreover, nearly thirty Ukrainian deputies and perhaps a hundred other Ukrainian politicians had been arrested. At the same time, however, the Government tried to make approaches to the Ukrainian moderates. Dmitri Levitsky came to Warsaw early in October to discuss the situation with officials in the Ministry of the Interior, but no

---

[1] Organizatsiya Ukrainskikh Natsionalistuv.

[2] For the situation in East Galicia see: Pobóg-Malinowski, *Najnowsza historia*, ii. 537–41; W. Tarnopolsky, 'The Polish-Ukrainian Conflict in East Galicia and its Repercussions in the League of Nations' (Columbia University Master's thesis), Columbia University, 1955; B. Martynets, *Ukrainskie pidpilia vid UVO do OUN* (n.p., 1949).

[3] *Gazeta Warszawska*, 29 June 1930.

[4] Ibid., 10 September 1930.

[5] He gave his instructions to Sławoj-Składkowski on 1 September. Sławoj-Składkowski, *Strzępy meldunków*, p. 223.

agreement was reached.[1] Archbishop Szeptycki also visited Warsaw twice in this period. The Government prevailed upon him to issue a pastoral letter from the Uniate bishops condemning the sabotage. However, when it appeared it also condemned the policy of holding villages collectively responsible, to the Government's intense annoyance.[2]

The outbreak of violence in East Galicia helped the Government considerably in its campaign for re-election. Calls for national consolidation became more readily acceptable and it was much easier to accuse the Centrolew of disloyalty, of being in league with forces aiming to destroy the Polish state. Yet the truth of the matter was that the Christian Democracy, the N.P.R., and to a lesser extent the Piast, were held by even the more moderate Ukrainians in the U.N.D.O. to represent Polish chauvinism. Relations between the U.N.D.O. and the Centrolew were therefore marked by considerable mutual suspicion.

The proclamation of elections led the Centrolew to form a new electoral bloc, the League for the Defence of Law and the People's Freedom, on 9 September. The Christian Democrats did not join, partly because to have done so would have hampered their negotiations with Korfanty's Silesian group over reunification, and partly because it was believed that participation in the bloc would be an electoral liability in western Poland, one of the areas of Christian Democratic strength. The party therefore issued a communiqué stating that though it would continue to co-operate with the other parties of the Centrolew in their struggle against the Government, it could not join the bloc because of its failure to affirm that it would maintain the Concordat.[3]

The programme of the new bloc was issued on 10 September.[4] It attacked the Government for failing to deal with the economic crisis and for destroying respect for the law by its attack on the constitution. Piłsudski had undermined the legend of the legions by his alliance with the conservatives, his Government had no policy in relation to the national minorities, and had taken public funds for its electoral expenses. The aim of the bloc was thus 'the complete and final liquidation of the dictatorship of Józef Pił-

[1] Czubiński, op. cit., pp. 217–18.
[2] The censorship would not allow the whole message to be published. Parts were reprinted in *Czas*, 21 October 1930.
[3] *Rzeczpospolita*, 10 September 1930.
[4] It is reprinted in *Robotnik*, 11 September 1930.

sudski'.[1] The parties of the alliance affirmed their preparedness to take power, and outlined a fairly detailed economic programme.

On the night of 9/10 September, Piłsudski had eleven of the Centrolew's leaders arrested. They were not, on the whole, its most important figures,[2] but were individuals either known for their radicalism or against whom Piłsudski had a personal grudge. Included among them were Barlicki, Lieberman, Pragier, Ciołkosz, and Mastek of the P.P.S., Bagiński of the Liberation, Witos and Kiernik of the Piast, and Karol Popiel of the N.P.R. Dąbski of the National Party, and Józef Baćmaga, a B.B.W.R. deputy accused of embezzlement, were also arrested, as well as four Ukrainian nationalists. On the following night more arrests were made. In an interview on the 13th Piłsudski made light of the political character of the arrests, claiming that they were as much the result of peculation, and again charged the deputies with abusing their parliamentary immunity.[3]

The Centrolew was greatly taken aback by the arrests, so much so that its protests were somewhat halfhearted. Nevertheless meetings were held, as planned, all over the country on the 14th, and in some places reached large proportions, notably in Lublin. In Warsaw during the procession after the meeting someone threw a bomb, as a result of which 300 persons were taken into custody.[4] Large numbers of arrests continued to be made during September and October, further contributing to the disarray of the Opposition. On 25 September the Silesian Sejm was dissolved and Korfanty arrested. By the middle of October, several thousand people were in custody, including sixty-four former deputies, many of whom were confined in the military fortress in Brześć and were not allowed any contact with the outside world.[5] On the night of 12/13 October the police arrested eight members of the P.P.S. militia and charged them with planning an attempt on the life of Piłsudski.[6] Their leader, Piotr Jagodziński, who had been involved in an assassination attempt against the Russian Governor-General

---

[1] Ibid.

[2] Neither Niedziałkowski, the principal instigator of the Centrolew, nor Thugutt, the founder and editor of the Centrolew's weekly, *Tydzień*, were arrested.

[3] Piłsudski, *P.Z.* ix. 230–5.

[4] *Gazeta Warszawska*, 16 September 1930.

[5] Ibid., 20 October 1930.

[6] *Kurjer Poranny*, 14 October 1930; *Robotnik*, 14 October 1930.

in 1906, claimed that the plot was only a subterfuge to uncover police spies.

The Centrolew retained to the last its belief that the electoral confrontation would prove decisive, and refused to resort to illegal measures in its struggle against the Government. When a partial strike broke out in Warsaw on 16 September in protest against the arrests, it was disavowed by the P.P.S. and condemned as a possible provocation.[1] The Executive Council of the party, meeting on the 28th, resolved that only legal means of protest should be employed.[2] As late as 1 October *Robotnik* wrote:

> We should not worry ourselves with the question: What will happen after the elections: Today we have *in the ballot a powerful weapon to struggle with the system*. They have tried and will try to tear these ballots from our hands in a number of ways. But those hands number millions, and if the millions fulfil their obligation—the victory of the working masses is certain.[3]

This 'electoral illusion' was the result partly of the shock induced by the scale of government repression, partly of an awareness that strike action had little hope of success in conditions of mass unemployment. Its principle cause, however, was a pathetic though perhaps commendable faith that once the Centrolew could demonstrate that it had the support of the country the Government would voluntarily abdicate.

The strength of the Centrolew alliance was put to a harsh test as the Government's repression was intensified, and differences of personality and programme became more conspicuous. The greatest reserve was shown by the Peasant Party. It had not taken part in the protest meetings of 14 September, and in early October a group of pro-Government members, led by Tadeusz Rożański and Antoni Hańko tried to take over the party and force it to leave the bloc. A fairly important part in this crisis was played by Piotr Targoński and Piotr Kosiba, the 'defectors' from the B.B.W.R. who had joined the Peasant Party in July. Although the attempt was defeated, and its protagonists were expelled, the internal dissension hampered the party's campaign.[4] The Government also organized a small split in the Piast, and tried to do the same in the

---

[1] Czubiński, op. cit., pp. 226–7.
[2] *Robotnik*, 29 and 30 September 1930.
[3] Ibid., 1 October 1930 (italics in original).
[4] *Gazeta Polska*, 7 October 1930, *Robotnik*, 8 and 11 October 1930.

Liberation.[1] The P.P.S., too, lost a few more members to the Sanacja. In addition, in parts of Poznania the Piast refused to stand on the Centrolew list.

The B.B.W.R. issued no electoral programme, but in its campaign laid most stress on the need for constitutional reform. It continued as before, to be a loose alliance of former legionaries, conservatives, pro-Piłsudski-ite radicals and pro-Government representatives of the national minorities. However, the worsening of climate led to a consolidation of the power of the 'colonels' group' within the bloc, with a corresponding diminution in importance of its other components. Jan Stecki, the first of the conservatives to figure on the B.B.W.R. state list, occupied the tenth place.[2] Unlike 1928, Piłsudski himself occupied first place on the list. He played an active part in the electoral campaign, repeating, in a number of interviews with Miedziński, his by now well-worn criticisms of the deputies and of parliamentary government.[3] As in the previous election, the B.B.W.R. possessed large financial resources, and its campaign was conducted on a massive scale. Politically, it derived considerable support from Germany's increased demands for the revision of Poland's western frontier. It accused the Centrolew of seeking support abroad, and the P.P.S. of excessive sympathy for the German Social Democrats. The Opposition bloc's victory, it was claimed would benefit only the Reich. The Centrolew was also accused of encouraging the unrest in East Galicia. In addition, the B.B.W.R. made serious attempts to win over Catholic support. On 14 October, Janta-Połczyński, the conservative Minister of Agriculture, met the Pope in Rome, and conveyed His Holiness's blessing to Piłsudski as well as to the President and 'the whole Polish nation'.[4] Apart from its attempts to split the rival bloc, the main burden of the Government's attack on the Centrolew stressed its disparate character and its political irresponsibility in fomenting a political crisis at the height of the Depression.

The National Party entered the elections on its own, with a strongly anti-Government programme. Although the Centrolew's approaches to the party had proved unsuccessful, the two groups

---

[1] *Kurjer Poranny*, 9 October 1930.

[2] If we exclude the Minister of Agriculture, Leon Janta-Połczyński, who occupied fourth place. *Gazeta Polska*, 8 October 1930.

[3] Altogether, between 26 August and the elections, he gave seven interviews. For these, see Piłsudski, *P.Z.* ix. 217–57.

[4] *Czas*, 16 October 1930.

agreed not to attack each other. This truce was exploited by the Government, which attacked the left-wing parties for making common cause with their worst enemies. It also made relations between the Centrolew and the national minorities, already uneasy about the chauvinism of such groups as the N.P.R. and the Piast, rather cool.[1]

The Communist Party took an active part in the electoral campaign, centring its attack on the 'social Fascists' and 'populist-Fascists' of the Centrolew whom it accused of deluding the masses, since only revolution could resolve the struggle against the Sanacja.[2] The Government succeeded in preventing the formation of a minorities bloc, but a Ukrainian-White Russian electoral bloc and a German electoral bloc were set up. It proved impossible to unite the different Jewish groups, however, and the Galician Zionists, the Grünbaum Zionists, and the Orthodox all presented separate lists. The Bund put up a common list with the largely Jewish Left-Wing Independent Socialist Party of Labour.

The Government again intervened actively in the elections. On 10 September, Piłsudski told Sławoj-Składkowski to make sure that the attitude of officials to the election was 'as it ought to be'.[3] And indeed, on 29 October we find the Sub-Prefect of the Chodzież district in Poznania instructing a meeting of civil servants:

State officials should support the B.B.W.R. list, the more because the head of the Government has taken the first place on it. It is not enough to be loyal, it is not enough only to give one's vote. The moral obligation of officials is to support the state-consolidating action of the head of the Government most vigorously.[4]

Administrative obstacles were placed in the way of the Opposition parties. They had difficulty in obtaining permission to call meetings or hire halls, and the police refused to stop pro-Government hooligans from breaking up their rallies.[5]

---

[1] There were also other reasons for this coolness. When the Centrolew approached the U.N.D.O., Levitsky refused to stand on a common list claiming that the bloc was a 'living corpse', Czubiński, op. cit., p. 223.

[2] See 'W sprawie akcji wyborczej do Sejmu i Senatu', *K.P.P. Uchwały i rezolucje*, iii. 156–8.

[3] Sławoj-Składkowski, *Strzępy meldunków*, p. 229.

[4] P.Z.P.K. II, 'Powiat Chodzież (Województwo Poznańskie) meeting of 29.X.30'.

[5] See *Robotnik*, 16, 19, and 22 October 1930, to cite only a few instances.

The Government also made use of its control of the electoral machinery. Altogether, the electoral commissioners invalidated 214 lists before the voting commenced. Of these, 14 were submitted by the Centrolew, most of them in areas in which its influence was strongest. The constituencies in which it was forbidden to stand included nos. 6 (Grodno), 15 (Konin), 26 (Lublin), 42 (the area around Cracow) and 47 (Rzeszów).[1] The number of votes invalidated was also considerably higher than in 1928, accounting for 4 per cent of those cast. Most of the invalidations took place in central and southern Poland, and affected the Centrolew particularly.[2] In many places the Government called upon the people to cast their votes openly, as a sign of loyalty.[3] In addition, a certain amount of direct falsification took place, especially in the Kresy.

The elections proved a triumph for the Government, not only because of its repressive measures and its attempts to influence the voting, but also because the feeling developed that it was bound to win, legally or illegally, and that it would therefore be best to give this victory a legal stamp. Moreover the Opposition had underestimated Piłsudski's personal popularity and had failed to realize that the appeal of their sophisticated demands for the maintenance of parliamentary control over the budget was relatively limited.

The B.B.W.R. and the P.P.S.—Frak won 47·4 per cent of the votes for the Sejm and 247 of the 444 seats.[4] This was not, however, the two-thirds majority needed for constitutional revision. The Bloc did even better in the Senate elections, winning 54·7 per cent of the votes and 75 (of 111) seats. In the elections for the Upper Silesian Sejm, the Sanacja also improved on its previous performance, emerging as the largest group, with 19 of the 48 seats (35·7 per cent of the votes), compared with 17 seats (37·2 per cent of the votes) for the Christian Democrats and 7 (13·4 per cent) for the Germans.[5]

In the Sejm elections, the B.B.W.R. did particularly well in the Eastern Kresy, where, with some administrative pressure, it won

[1] Based on *Statystyka Polski*, series C, iv, 'Statystyka wyborów do Sejmu Senatu'. The figures given in Czubiński, op. cit., p. 232, are incorrect.

[2] 'Statystyka wyborów do Sejmu i Senatu', p. xxi, Table VIII.

[3] *Kurjer Warszawski*, 17 November 1930; *Czas*, 18 November 1930.

[4] The electoral results given here are based on the figures in 'Statystyka wyborów do Sejmu i Senatu'. For the results in the Silesian elections see: Rechowicz, op. cit., p. 320, Table X; p. 303, Table X.

[5] The drastic fall in the size of the German vote was brought about by the invalidation of the German list in one of the three Silesian constituencies.

81·1 per cent of the vote. In Galicia, where most Centrolew invalidations took place, it won 53·4 per cent, and in East Galicia
51·2 per cent. In central Poland it received 39·0 per cent and in
Warsaw 40·4 per cent. It remained weakest in western Poland, in
spite of the fact that in this election it had succeeded in uniting its
supporters here and had presented one joint list. It received 31·9
per cent of the vote in Silesia, 24·1 per cent in Poznania, and
21·2 per cent in Pomerania.

The results were a disappointment for the Centrolew, which
won only 17·7 per cent of the votes (if we include the P.P.S. list in
Upper Silesia, where no Centrolew list was presented) and 82
seats. At the beginning of the campaign, its leaders had expected
to win 150–80 seats. The urban parties, particularly the P.P.S.,
did very badly. In Warsaw, the Opposition bloc won only 7·1 per
cent of the vote, in Lodz 9·5 per cent, and in the Dąbrowa basin
13·5 per cent. Altogether the bloc won only 9·5 per cent of the
urban vote. It did much better in the countryside, where it won
20·7 per cent.

The Centrolew's results were best in western Poland, where
administrative pressure was weakest. It won 29·9 per cent of the
vote in Poznania and 32·7 per cent in Pomerania. In Upper Silesia
the P.P.S. won 8·6 per cent of the vote and the Christian Democrats 34·0 per cent. In central Poland the Centrolew won 22·9 per
cent, in Galicia 12·9 per cent, and in the Kresy only 3·2 per cent.

The National Party regained some of the ground it had lost in
1928, winning 12·7 per cent of the vote and 62 seats. Nevertheless,
this was somewhat less than the expected total of 80. In Poznania
the party won 32·0 per cent of the vote, in Pomerania 37·9 per cent,
and in Warsaw 17·9 per cent. In central Poland it won 16·7 per
cent, in Galicia 4·0 per cent, and in the Kresy only 2·6 per cent.

The Communist vote dropped sharply from its 1928 level to
2·5 per cent, and the party won only 5 seats. This was partly the
result of administrative pressure, especially in the Kresy, but more
the effect of the bitter disputes within the party and the small
appeal of its intransigent Leftist slogans. In Warsaw the party won
8·8 per cent of the vote, in Lodz 19·6 per cent, in the Dąbrowa
basin 13·5 per cent, and in Silesia 4·1 per cent.

The minorities too did rather badly. The Ukrainian-White
Russian bloc won 6·4 per cent of the vote and 21 seats. In East
Galicia it won 31·0 per cent of the vote, but in the Kresy only

4·6 per cent. The German bloc won 2·7 per cent of the vote and 5 seats. In Poznania it won 12·0 per cent, in Pomerania 7·8 per cent, and in Upper Silesia 34·0 per cent. The division among the Jews, and the fact that many Jews voted for the Sanacja, reduced the Jewish Club in the Sejm to 7.

At last Piłsudski had a parliament with which he should find it easy to co-operate. In an interview with Miedziński on 26 November, the Marshal stated that the President, the Sejm, and the Government ought now to be able to reach some accommodation. The most important task before the new parliament, he claimed, was the revision of the constitution.[1] On 29 November, as a sign that the crisis was over, Piłsudski resigned, and Sławek again became Prime Minister. Piłsudski's victory, though gained at some cost, was a very conclusive one, and as long as he lived, the Opposition was unable to offer any sort of challenge to the Sanacja. Świtalski, describing the Marshal's remarks at a meeting with himself, Mościcki, Sławek, and Beck after the elections, recounts:

The Commander, on the first occasion he met us after the elections, stopped us, with a school-masterish gesture, from giving way to joy at the victory, and told us that we ought immediately to proceed to our next stage of work, the nature of which was already clear. In general terms, he merely stated that we had five years of the most perfect quiet and that we must know how to make use of it.[2]

The next years would show whether the Sanacja could take full advantage of this opportunity.

[1] Piłsudski, *P.Z.* ix. 257–63.
[2] A.S.S., 'Konferencja u Pana Prezydenta w składzie: Prezydent, Komendant, Sławek i Beck w dniu 18 listopada 1930 r.'.

TABLE IX. *Results of Elections to the Sejm, 1930*

Parties	No. of votes (in 1,000s)	Percentage
Pro-Government	5,367	47·4
B.B.W.R.	5,293	46·7
P.P.S.—Frak	74	0·7
Right	1,445	12·7
National list	1,443	12·7
Monarchists	2	—
Centre and Left	2,519	22·1
Centrolew	1,966	17·3
Christian Democrats	430	3·8
Socialist bloc (i.e. P.P.S. in Silesia)	52	0·4
Left Socialist bloc (Bund and Independent Socialist Party of Labour)	71	0·6
Communist and pro-Communist	283	2·5
Communist lists	236	2·1
Peasant Self-Help	23	0·2
Sel-Rob	24	0·2
Minorities	1,648	14·5
Ukrainian and White Russian electoral bloc	726	6·4
Ruthenian Peasant Organization	11	0·1
German electoral bloc	310	2·7
Grünbaum Zionists	247	2·2
Galician Zionists	185	1·6
Orthodox	150	1·3
Poalei Sion	19	0·2

* Based on *Statystyka Polski*, series C, no. 4, 'Statystyka wyborów do Sejmu i Senatu z dnia 16 i 23 listopada 1930 roku'.

TABLE X. *Composition of the New Sejm, 1930**

Parties	Deputies	
	No.	Percentage
	444	100
Pro-Government		
B.B.W.R.	247	55·6
Right		
National Party	62	14·0
Centre	40	9·0
Christian Democrats	15	3·4
N.P.R.	10	2·2
Piast	15	3·4
Left	57	12·9
Peasant Party	18	4·0
Liberation	15	3·4
P.P.S.	24	5·5
Communist and pro-Communist	5	1·1
Peasant Self-Help	1	0·2
Communists	4	0·9
Minorities	33	7·4
Ukrainian-White Russian Club	18	4·0
Radical Ukrainians	3	0·6
Germans	5	1·2
Jews	6	1·4
Orthodox Jews	1	0·2

* Based on Próchnik, op. cit., p. 395.

TABLE XI. *Composition of the New Senate, 1930**

Parties	Senators	
	No.	Percentage
	111	100
Pro-Government		
B.B.W.R.	75	67·6
Right		
National Party	12	10·8
Centre	8	7·2
Christian Democrats	3	2·7
N.P.R.	3	2·7
Piast	2	1·8
Left	9	8·1
Liberation	4	3·6
P.P.S.	5	4·5
Minorities	7	6·3
Ukrainians and White Russians	4	3·6
Germans	3	2·7

* Based on Próchnik, op. cit., p. 398.

VIII

AFTER BRZEŚĆ

During the last years of the Marshal's life, there emerged
the three C's—the clan, the clique and the claque. The
Army was transformed into a clan devoted to Piłsudski;
the clique—in the form of Piłsudski's entourage—ruled in
the name of the Leader, implementing his obscure directives, which in many cases they did not understand; finally,
the claque, a by-product of Piłsudski's entourage in
the form of militants, served to deal with difficult and
indeed shady matters to the accompaniment of deafening
propaganda.

Marian Romeyko, *Przed i po Maju*

THE period between 1931 and the death of the Marshal in May
1935 lacks the drama of the clash between the Government and
parliament. The Sanacja was now securely in control of the
situation while the Opposition was divided and demoralized. Yet
the surface calm of political life was deceptive, and these years
saw a number of important departures in Polish politics. The progressive disunity and intellectual bankruptcy of the B.B.W.R.
became increasingly evident, while Piłsudski himself, old, tired,
and sick, was unable to provide any sort of direction for his
followers. The divisions within the Sanacja, which were to emerge
openly after the Marshal's death, became more and more obvious.
The Centrolew also began to break up, as the peasant parties
united, the socialists moved towards a Popular Front and the
Christian Democrats asserted their independence. The Right
revived, particularly among university students among whom
near-Fascist ideas became widespread, as the economic crisis wore
on and the Government seemed to lack the will to deal with it
effectively. In relation to the national minorities, changes were
also seen, particularly in East Galicia where the Government had
some success in reaching some sort of *modus vivendi* with the
Ukrainians. Perhaps the most important new departure was in
foreign policy, where with the conclusion of non-aggression pacts
with the Soviet Union in July 1932 and Nazi Germany in January

1934, the Government seemed to have gained a new flexibility and freedom in which to manœuvre. Finally, the period saw, just before Piłsudski's death, the adoption of a new constitution which wrote into law the Marshal's cherished political ideal of making the President the fulcrum of Polish political life and subordinating to him both parliament and the Cabinet.

THE SANACJA AFTER BRZEŚĆ

In the new parliament, the Sanacja possessed a secure majority, though not, indeed, one sufficiently large to vote in a new constitution. Yet the leading members of the Government remained extremely suspicious of any sort of co-operation with even this ostensibly friendly parliament. This suspicion was evident in Piłsudski's provocative choice of Świtalski (the man who had headed the first 'Colonel's Cabinet') for the post of Marshal of the Sejm. Świtalski was chosen, on Piłsudski's own admission, because he could best 'keep order'[1] and his speech on 9 January on accepting office did little to allay Opposition fears.[2] He would not, he stated, allow 'parliamentary debates to be swamped by a flood of words whose sole aim was to effect a demonstration', and stated further that he would not make use of the speakers' prerogative to demand parliamentary immunity for members of the Sejm charged with criminal offences. He made it clear that he saw his role as that of facilitating the conduct of government business and that he would always fix the agenda of full sessions in advance in consultation with the head of the Government.

One of his first achievements was the adoption of a new set of standing orders by the Sejm which considerably cut down the rights of the Opposition.[3] The most important clauses of these new orders, accepted by the Lower House on 16 January, were those which gave to the Marshal the right to suppress from the minutes of parliamentary proceedings speeches which 'infringed the oath taken by the speaker at the commencement of the session, in accordance with Article 89 of the constitution' ('the first duty of a citizen is to be loyal to the Polish Republic'), and increased

[1] A.S.S., Konferencja u Pana Prezydenta w składzie: Prezydent, Komendant, Sławek i Beck w dniu 18 listopada 1930 r.
[2] For this speech, see S.S.S.R., 9 December 1930, cols. 10–12.
[3] For these see Sejm Rzeczypospolitej Polskiej, Okres III, Druk Nr.I.

the number of signatures required for a parliamentary question from fifteen to thirty and for an emergency motion from forty-five to seventy-five.

In private, the leading members of the Government were even more open in their contempt for parliament. At his first meeting with his subordinates after the elections, Piłsudski told them that their tactics in the Sejm should be 'to outvote the Opposition mercilessly from the start'. Any attempt to discuss the arrest of the Opposition leaders was to be treated so as to show 'that we have no intention of concerning ourselves with these matters, and thus interrupting our work'.[1]

Świtalski's own attitude towards parliament was made clear at a meeting with Piłsudski, Prystor, and Sławek on 31 August 1931.[2] Here Świtalski, answering Piłsudski's objections that B.B.W.R. tactics were still too much conditioned by the habit of regarding the Sejm as a hostile body, argued that

since the danger exists that in a future Sejm we may not have a clear majority, is it not more sensible to deprive the present Sejm of its function of always expressing an opinion on every matter, and would it not be better . . . to introduce a system of diminishing the role of parliament to an essential minimum?

At the same meeting, Sławek, with Piłsudski's approval, also suggested that 'in the present session we should pursue the tactic of ignoring the Opposition, of refusing to debate with them at length, thus demoralizing them by showing that their arguments have no significance and that everything is done without any regard for their views.'

Świtalski accepted this, although he believed that the Government stood to gain from confrontations with the weakened Opposition, because he did not wish to oppose Sławek, whose aversion to controversy was well known and because 'the Government team is too weak at present, in the absence of Matuszewski [who was ill], to engage in . . . polemics.'

The Government was able to make use of its parliamentary majority to bring an end to the Czechowicz affair. Already on 10 October 1930, Stanisław Wróblewski resigned as President of

[1] A.S.S., Konferencja u Pana Prezydenta w składzie: Prezydent, Komendant, Sławek i Beck w dniu 18 listopada 1930 r.

[2] A.S.S., Konferencja w Belwederze u Komendanta w składzie: Prystor, Sławek i ja, dn. 31 sierpnia 1931 r.

the Main Auditing Office and was replaced on the 20th by General Jakub Krzemieński, an ardent legionary and Piłsudski-ite who had been President of the Supreme Military Court since the coup. On 21 January, the Budget Committee of the Sejm voted to legalize the supplementary credits of the 1927–8 budget, and on the 27th, its recommendations were accepted by the Sejm.[1]

As one would expect, parliament's role remained small, and it met for the most part only to adopt the budget and to pass laws submitted to it by the Cabinet. Moreover, on 15 March 1932 the Sejm passed a law which gave the President the right to issue decrees during the period between the end of one parliamentary session and the commencement of the next the following autumn.[2] These decrees could deal with economic and financial matters, the unification of the legal system, the administration of justice, and, until the end of 1934, with the reorganization of public administration. The Government took considerable advantage of this power. Between 18 March and 3 November 1932, for example, 106 decrees were issued.[3] The power to issue decrees was renewed by the Sejm on 14 March 1934 and again on 22 March 1935.[4]

The Government made use of its control of parliament and its right to issue decrees to entrench its position still further. On 7 November 1931, the Sejm passed a law providing for the military conscription of railway workers should they strike during a war or a time of 'insecurity threatening the State'.[5] On 11 March 1932, a law was passed requiring administrative approval for all meetings held out of doors.[6] Meetings held indoors had only to be announced in advance, but could be forbidden by administrative order. Since September 1931, summary courts had been in existence to deal with some political offences (mainly Ukrainian sabotage), and they were done away with only on 6 March 1934.[7] The immovability of judges was suspended by decree on 23 August 1932[8] and a decree of 27 October 1932 limited the right to form associations.[9]

In addition, the Government, which had long been irritated

[1] *S.S.S.R.*, 26, 27 January 1931, cols. 142–57.
[2] *Dz.U.R.P.* (1932), no. 22, pp. 319–20.
[3] *Gazeta Polska*, 9 November 1932.
[4] *Dz.U.R.P.* (1934), no. 28, p. 462; (1935), no. 28, p. 479.
[5] Ibid. (1931), no. 109, pp. 1765–6.
[6] Ibid. (1932), no. 48, pp. 815–18.
[7] Ibid. (1932), no. 20, p. 319.
[8] Ibid. (1932), no. 73, pp. 1445–51.
[9] Ibid. (1932), no. 94, pp. 1947–53.

by the anti-Sanacja posture of a number of prominent academics, took the opportunity presented by the anti-Semitic excesses of right-wing university students to introduce legislation on 1 March 1932 curtailing the autonomy of the universities.[1] This legislation gave to the Minister of Education the power to close for a period faculties or universities in which student unrest had got out of hand, and also gave him the right to remove from chairs professors he believed were not fit for their posts. This latter power was used to deprive fifty-one professors of their positions, the most prominent being Professor Stanisław Kot, the eminent Professor of the History of Civilization at the University of Cracow and an outspoken critic of the Government.[2]

Debate on these matters, as indeed on all the legislation introduced by the Government, was reduced to a minimum. In October 1931, the rules of Sejm procedure were further modified to allow the Government to limit the delays previously provided for between the presentation of legislation and its discussion, and between the second and third reading of a bill.[3] In addition, the provision giving a majority the right to limit the length of any speech to an hour was changed, so that speeches could be limited to fifteen minutes and in no case could exceed an hour.

This contempt for parliamentary debate alarmed even some members of the B.B.W.R. Kurjer Poranny, a pro-Government radical paper, quotes one of these as follows:

I have often the impression that our parliament has become a machine which receives on a conveyer belt projects emanating from the Government, noiselessly transforms them and pours them into the *Digest of Laws*. This is not a parliament in the accepted sense of the word, it is an automaton. The Deputies talk, but they might just as well go home, since the same result would be achieved: every draft law suggested by the Cabinet is voted as it is, without changing a comma, by the Sejm and then the Senate.[4]

Censorship of the press too was maintained and even, in the tense period after the elections, somewhat extended. During January 1931, for instance, *Robotnik* was confiscated ten times and *Gazeta Warszawska* seven.[5] The scope of censorship was further

[1] Ibid. (1932), no. 38, pp. 639–45.
[2] *Gazeta Warszawska*, 27 September 1933.
[3] See *Kurjer Warszawski*, 14 October 1931.
[4] *Kurjer Poranny*, 17 October 1931.
[5] B.P.P.P., no. 211, p. 10.

extended by a Sejm decision in February 1931 that censored articles could no longer be incorprated in parliamentary questions.[1]

One of the most obvious reasons for this increased authoritarianism was the growing prominence in this period in all spheres of government of military men, particularly veterans from the P.O.W., generally in positions for which neither their military nor their civilian experience gave them any special qualification. The development of this process is difficult to date exactly, but a qualitative change seems to be evident in the years 1929–30, coinciding with the clash with parliament and the increasing ill health of Piłsudski. In the early years of his administration Piłsudski had tried to recruit eminent civilian specialists. But now, with the increasing political bitterness, it became more and more difficult to find non-party civilian supporters of the Sanacja. As the Marshal's health declined former P.O.W. officers in the inner circle of Piłsudski-ites came to take more initiative, and they largely favoured dependence on military men, particularly those whom they knew and trusted from legionary days.

This military take-over assumed vast proportions in the period after 1930, affecting not only the Cabinet and the ministries, principally Foreign Affairs and the Interior, but also local government and the nationalized industries.[2] In Sławek's Cabinet, for instance, nine ministers were military men and only six were civilians; in those of his successors, Aleksander Prystor (27 May 1931 to 9 May 1933) and Janusz Jędrzejewicz (10 May 1933 to 13 May 1934), the proportion was in each case eight to four.

The penetration of the Foreign Ministry also began around 1929–30, when Beck, having resigned as Private Secretary (*szef gabinetu*) of the Minister of War, became Under-Secretary at the Foreign Office. He appointed, as head of the Press and Propaganda Department, Captain Tomir Drymmer, who had already left the Army for the Foreign Office in 1929. Drymmer was followed into the Ministry by a number of officers formerly in Intelligence, including Colonel Tadeusz Schaetzel, Major Tadeusz Kobylański, and Major Aleksander Lubieński. In the field, a number of Consulates-General and Consulates were entrusted to officers, frequently with the justification that this would aid Intelligence

[1] *S.S.S.R.*, 5 February 1931, cols. 3–8.

[2] For this development, see particularly M. Romeyko, *Przed i po Maju* (Warsaw, 1967), ii. 298–308; P. Stawecki, *Następcy Komendanta* (Warsaw, 1969).

work; however there were few officers among those of ambassadorial rank. One of the curious results of this development was the exclusion from the Foreign Office of Roman Knoll, who, as we have seen, played a moderately important part in facilitating Piłsudski's return to power. He apparently referred to the influx of military men as 'an attack of bandits on a lunatic asylum',[1] for which remark he was removed from the civil service.

Military penetration went furthest in the Ministry of the Interior. By the early 1930s, the majority of provincial governors and a sizeable proportion of sub-prefects were officers, and most of the provincial departments dealing with the nationalities and with security were in the hands of soldiers. By 1935 at least twelve of the seventeen provincial governors were military men.

The state sector of the economy was also flooded by soldiers. General Roman Górecki became Director of the Bank of National Economy, Lieutenant-Colonel Stamirowski took over the Agricultural Bank, while Colonel Adam Koc became Director of the Bank of Poland. One of the reasons for this development was the far-reaching nationalization of war industries which took place in the early 1930s, largely under the aegis of Sławoj-Składkowski, Chief of Army Administration between 1931 and 1936. There was some justification for taking over these industries, vital to national security, since they had to a considerable extent passed into foreign hands. But in this case, the industries concerned were not so much nationalized as militarized. Their administration was handed over to officers, generally closely connected with Składkowski, and generally without any real technical competence. Little control was exercised over their activity and these positions thus became for the most part extremely lucrative sinecures, while the efficiency of military industries correspondingly suffered.

Indeed, the whole phenomenon of what has been called the 'Exodus from the Army' had largely deleterious effects both in adversely affecting the state administration and in undermining the morale of the civil service, since the normal course of promotion tended to be bypassed. It was certainly one of the most significant reasons for the increasing inadequacy and incompetence of the Piłsudski régime in the 1930s. Moreover, though many of the officers in the administration were honest, there was a sizeable minority who were not unwilling to make the most of the perks

[1] Ibid. ii. 303.

of their new posts. Piłsudski's claim to have ended the 'reign of corruption of the sejmocracy' began to look increasingly ill-founded.[1]

The Marshal himself, old, sick, and disillusioned by his need to have recourse to force a second time in the constitutional conflict, contrary to his frequently expressed belief that 'force does not educate, it destroys',[2] withdrew more and more from political life. The country was not treated to any more of his redoubtable political interviews after 1931. His health deteriorated still further in this period and his severe bronchitis necessitated long absences from Poland in Madeira, Rumania, and Egypt. In addition he was suffering from arteriosclerosis and, unknown to his entourage, from cancer of the liver.[3] He had also become convinced that, as he told Sławek, Prystor, Beck, and Świtalski on 29 April 1931, 'he cast too big a shadow on Polish life. Everything hinged on him and he was the deciding element, which was not a healthy situation.'[2]

As a result, though all really important questions were ultimately referred to him, he tended to exercise even less control over the functioning of the Government than he had previously. Moreover, since there was no one among his associates who could easily take the lead, his withdrawal did not stimulate, as he seems to have hoped, any greater political capacity on the part of his 'boys', but, on the contrary meant that more and more the Government lacked direction and failed to take any decisive initiative.

His entourage were determined to carry out the directions of the Commander. But these were often very difficult to ascertain. Piłsudski did not generally discuss problems, but called his inner circle together and made *ex-cathedra* pronouncements. As Sławoj-Składkowski wrote of one of his 'reportings' to the Commander,

Naturally, as always I had no idea what the Marshal would discuss with me—or, rather, say to me.

For, although the Commander liked to call my 'reportings' 'conversations', these were entirely one-sided, since usually the Marshal talked and I noted his words.[4]

[1] See for instance L. Berbecki, *Pamiętniki Generała Broni* (Katowice, 1959), pp. 187–90; Romeyko, *Przed i po Maju*, ii. 425–6.

[2] A.S.S., Narada w Belwederze dnia 29 kwietnie 1931 r.

[3] On Piłsudski's health, see Sławoj-Składkowski, *Strzępy meldunków*, pp. 369–70, 477, 547.

[4] Ibid., p. 507.

It is true that not all Piłsudski's followers were quite as slavish as Sławoj-Składkowski. But even the others frequently had difficulty in ascertaining his intentions, and found themselves labouring at cross-purposes with the Marshal. Świtalski, for instance, records his great surprise when the Marshal told him early in 1931 that he was opposed to the Sejm's ratifying the Trade Treaty with Germany and that he favoured only the acceptance of the Hague Liquidation Agreements. Świtalski, in the meantime, had been devoting an inordinate amount of effort to convincing the unwilling B.B.W.R. deputies of the need to ratify the Treaty.[1] Until a week before Mościcki's term of office expired in May 1933 even Sławek, Prystor, Car, and Świtalski did not know whether Piłsudski wanted to have him re-elected; as it turned out, he did.[2] Sławek submitted his proposal for a Senate made up of an élite of those granted the Cross of Honour for service to the state quite unaware that Piłsudski was not willing to accept it.[3]

Moreover, Piłsudski's actions were increasingly marked by an arbitrariness and often dictated by whim as much as by any distinctly thought-out policy. A good example of this was his decision to force Prystor, with whom he had become offended, to resign as Prime Minister in May 1933. He claimed that Prystor 'relies on his "own men" whom he treats as his confidants and rewards with money or positions'.[4]

Yet Świtalski states that neither he, Beck, Sławek, nor Prystor himself felt that there was any basis for the Marshal's allegations. Indeed, Świtalski attributed the incident to Piłsudski's isolation and lack of contact with those outside his immediate entourage:

My impression is that the Commander is a solitary individual. He cuts himself off from people and is thus the prisoner of the opinions, and even the chance intrigues, of those with whom he speaks and who give him a distorted picture of the internal political situation.[4]

Piłsudski's main interests remained foreign policy and the Army. In both these fields, he tended increasingly to lose his

[1] A.S.S., Rozmowa z Komendantem dn. 30.III.31. godz. 5.30 pp.
[2] A.S.S., Konferencja u Prystora dnia 26.IV.33 o godz. 1.15 w składzie Sławek, Car i ja.
[3] A.S.S., 31 stycznia 1934 r. godz 17.30. Konferencja u Komendanta w składzie: Sławek i ja.
[4] A.S.S., Rozmowa z Komendantem dnia 2.V.33r. w Belwederze o godz. 4 pop. Obecni: Sławek i ja.

touch and could not adjust to the rapidly changing situation of the early 1930s. For the most part, he left the implementation of foreign policy to Józef Beck who became Foreign Minister in November 1932. But he was more than anyone else responsible for the underestimation of the dynamic and aggressive character of Nazism which marked Polish foreign policy throughout the 1930s.[1]

In relation to the Army, too, the early 1930s saw the heightening of those defects which had characterized his administration in the 1920s, the downgrading of the General Staff, a lack of receptivity to new technical changes, favouritism on behalf of former legionaries in promotion, and his own inaccessibility. Between 1930 and 1935, the failure to modernize the Army and adopt new types of weapons became even more exaggerated.[2] The acceptance of modern armoured artillery was extremely slow, while the creation of divisions which could be rapidly transported by lorry hardly took place in the period. Supply and transport columns still went on horseback, long marches were still standard for the infantry. The Air Force too remained backward. No anti-aircraft weapons were provided and it was held that all that was really required to fight off an air attack was a new type of gunsight for machine guns.

Communications too remained extremely primitive, dependent on telephone and telegraph rather than on radio as late as 1935.[3] There was an almost total unwillingness to accept how easily cable, which remained the basis of communications in the Polish Army until the Marshal's death, could be disrupted by aerial bombardment or sabotage. Far too little was done to train officers and men in communications and, indeed, Piłsudski's belief that he had successfully resolved the problem by having a serving officer as Minister of Posts and Telegraphs was unfortunately typical of his running of the Army.

Modernization of the sappers was also neglected, and the number of sapper battalions was cut in the early 1930s from thirty to eight, mainly because of Piłsudski's failure to recognize the need for technical training and his rather confused views that since any future war would be a 'war of movement' on the 1920 pattern,

---

[1] On this, see below, pp. 379–86.
[2] Romeyko throughout the second volume of his memoirs draws a grim but convincing picture of these developments. Romeyko, *Przed i po Maju*, vol. ii.
[3] On this, see Romeyko, *Przed i po Maju*, ii. 200–11.

trenches would not be needed, and therefore neither would sappers. As a result the shortage of sappers was not adequately made up by the outbreak of war in 1939, and was painfully felt in the September campaign.[1]

The failure to modernize the Army was partly the result of the Depression, partly the result of the fact that the Army was constantly kept very near full mobilization, a costly process which left very little money for new equipment and adequate training. In fact, between 1921 and 1935 the Polish Army could in case of war increase its numbers by only about 20 per cent. But a more fundamental reason for the technical backwardness of the Army was the increasing paralysis resulting from the lack of any clear directives from the Marshal.

The officer corps was also weakened as a result of the advancement of Piłsudski-ites by the Head of the Army Personnel Department, General Michał Karaszewicz-Tokarzewski and his successor, the less partisan but unimaginative Colonel Ignacy Misiąg.[2] Piłsudski seems to have been aware of the poor quality of many of his legionary *protégés*. Following a meeting with the Marshal and Sławek on 31 January 1934, Świtalski records 'Critical remarks, often of an extremely unfriendly type were expressed by the Commander concerning our highest ranking legionary officers.'[3] But even if this was his view, he did little to improve the quality of his more senior officers. To make matters worse, from 1931 to 1936 the Army was seriously harmed by having as its Chief of Administration the incompetent Sławoj-Składkowski. This post was a vaguely defined one and 'Sławoj' stretched its functions to include education, general discipline, and even counter-intelligence, adversely affecting all these departments.

The final judgement of Marian Romeyko, one of the most acute observers of the military scene in Poland, on Piłsudski's effect on the Army is indeed a damning one:

Piłsudski not only exercised total power in the military field, but became at the same time the centre of power for the country as a whole. As an old, tired man, sick, nervous and burdened with a whole range of complexes, he was simply unable to penetrate deeply matters which required decision and arbitration as a result of the uncoordinated activity

[1] Ibid., pp. 196–200. [2] Ibid., pp. 78–83.
[3] A.S.S., 31 stycznia 1934 r. godz. 17.30. Konferencja u Komendanta w składzie: Sławek i ja.

of his subordinates. He certainly was not able to follow the rapid development of military thought in Europe, to create his own conception of the war of the future, or, finally, to give detailed directives both military and political which could form the basis of an effective system of national defence. A dictator with a very vigorous mind can impose and realize his ideas without regard to whether they are correct or false. A tired and passive dictator, who devotes himself to a number of problems by fits and starts, from occasion to occasion, who cannot inspire ideals and who does not wish to give up his privileged position, depraves his subordinates, deprives them of initiative, creates a feeling of a lack of responsibility, causes apathy and discouragement, passivity and a lack of belief in oneself. As a result, therefore, he removes from the senior officers and Generals the qualities of higher commanders.[1]

GOVERNMENT AND OPPOSITION

The question of the arrest of many of the leaders of the opposition and their confinement in the military fortress of Brześć dominated political life for several months after the election. Protest was roused in the first place by the treatment which the men had received in gaol. Piłsudski had entrusted the supervision of the prisoners to one of his most ruthless and sadistic subordinates, Colonel Kostek-Biernacki, who had learnt a good deal from his service in the French Foreign Legion before 1914. The Marshal had told him to apply strict military prison regulations to those arrested. They were 'to feel they were in prison', they were not 'to feel in Brześć that they were heroes'.[2]

Kostek-Biernacki implemented fully, and probably considerably surpassed, these instructions.[3] The prisoners were forced to perform humiliating tasks, such as cleaning lavatories, they were beaten, subjected to numerous insults, and given inadequate food. Mock executions were even organized in an attempt to break their spirit. They were, contrary to the provisions of the penal code, allowed no contact with the outside world. Shortly after the election, however, a number were released on bail and ugly intimations of what had taken place in Brześć began to appear in the press. The matter achieved wide publicity in December.

[1] Romeyko, *Przed i po Maju*, ii. 77–8.
[2] Pobóg-Malinowski, *Najnowsza historia*, ii. 717.
[3] For a description of the treatment meted out to the prisoners, see the parliamentary question on this matter submitted on 16 December 1930 by the parties of the Centrolew, *Robotnik*, 18 December 1930.

On the 10th, the parties of the Left submitted a motion to the Sejm demanding the release of those still in custody, while the National Party submitted a motion demanding that the Government take action against the officials, magistrates, and soldiers responsible for the arrest and imprisonment of the parliamentarians in Brześć.[1] Both this motion and the question presented to parliament by the Centrolew contained detailed descriptions of what had taken place in Brześć and both were given extensive coverage in the press.

The revelations caused a revulsion against the Government even among those who had little sympathy with the aims of those arrested, and who had been willing to justify the Government's arrests. Poles had experienced too much at the hands of the partitioning powers not to be sensitive to instances of the arbitrary exercise of power and police brutality. The mood of the intelligentsia was eloquently expressed in an open letter which forty-five professors at the Jagiellonian University addressed to Professor Adam Krzyżanowski, one of their colleagues and a B.B.W.R. deputy. 'Many occurrences in the past few years', they wrote,

are undermining—according to our most earnest belief—the moral basis of social and political life in Poland, and by so doing, threaten the development and even, in the long term, the existence of the Polish State. Among these matters, the most alarming is the question of the prisoners in Brześć. This matter cannot be sanctioned by the silence of the thinking elements of society.[2]

Similar protests were made by academics at Warsaw University, the Warsaw Polytechnic, the Free Polish University, the Universities of Poznań, Lwów, and Wilno, and the Lwów Polytechnic. Students, too, demonstrated in support of their professors. Many prominent writers also protested, among them Andrzej Strug, Maria Dąbrowska, Antoni Słonimski, Julian Tuwim, and Tadeusz Boy-Żeleński. Many legal organizations entered protests. The Circle of Polish Jurists, an organization comprising the leading lawyers in the country, voted on 17 January by 120 to 53 to expel the Minister of Justice, Michałowski, and his predecessor, Car, from membership because of their part in Brześć.[3]

The government ranks were also shaken by the Brześć

[1] *Robotnik*, 18 December 1930.
[2] The letter was reprinted in *Robotnik*, 18 December 1930.
[3] Ibid., 20 January 1931.

revelations. Bartel made a personal protest to Mościcki, three B.B.W.R. deputies, Adam Krzyżanowski, Zdzisław Lechnicki, and Ignacy Nowak, resigned their seats, and Witold Stankiewicz, a former minister, left the B.B.W.R. Tadeusz Hołówko and Zofia Moraczewska were only with difficulty restrained from open protest. Even Mościcki was upset. 'I must confess', he wrote later, 'that I myself was left with a disagreeable impression.'[1] Disapproval seems also to have penetrated the Army, for in the middle of January the acting Minister of War, General Konarzewski, issued a secret order forbidding officers to show open hostility to those who had held office in Brześć.[2]

The inner circles of the Government were divided as to how to react to the situation. Some, including Hołówko, Stamirowski, and perhaps Miedziński, felt that the best tactic would be to admit ɪhat abuses had taken place and put the blame on the officers responsible, thus shielding Piłsudski. A harder line was advocated by Sławek and Świtalski, and was finally adopted on the grounds that any other course would cause division in the Army and that the Commander did not want to repudiate responsibility.[3] Thus the B.B.W.R. voted on 16 December against treating as a matter of urgency the National Party motion on the legality of the Brześć arrests.[4] It only allowed the motion to come up on 26 January and the whole question was then treated with a studied contempt. The debate was only permitted to commence at midnight, and at 4.30 a.m. Sławek read a declaration on behalf of the Government.[5] Its tone was harsh and aggressive. The arrests, he claimed, had become necessary because of threatening anarchy, and those arrested had shown a lack of courage in gaol. In relation to the treatment of prisoners, he claimed, 'I have investigated the matter and have confirmed that there was no sadism and torture, although, as in every prison, obedience had to be obtained by force in the

---

[1] Quoted in Pobóg-Malinowski, *Najnowsza historia*, ii. 719.

[2] Konarzewski admitted the existence of the order, which had been made public by *Gazeta Warszawska*, in the Military Committee of the Sejm on 23 January. *Gazeta Warszawska*, 24 January 1931.

[3] For these discussions, see A.S.S., Konferencja u płk. Sławka w składzie pp. Pieracki, Składkowski, Michałowski, Stamirowski, Jędrzejewicz, Hołówko, Miedziński, Koc i ja, dnia 15 grudnia 1930 r; Dnia 16 grudnia 1930 r, Konferencja w Prezydium Rady Ministrów, w składzie: pp. płk. Sławek, Pieracki, Składkowski, Michałowski, Car, Schaetzel i ja, w dniu 18 grudnia 1930 r.

[4] *S.S.S.R.*, 16 January 1931, cols. 105–7.

[5] Ibid., 26, 27 January 1931, cols. 136–40.

case of resistance.'[1] On the conclusion of his speech, the debate was immediately closed, and the Opposition motion defeated, allowing no further debate on the matter.

No action was taken against those principally responsible for Brześć. Michałowski, who had organized the arrests, remained Minister of Justice. Kostek-Biernacki was even ceremoniously received by Piłsudski and awarded the Cross of Independence 'with swords'.[2] Shortly afterwards he was made Governor of Polesia.

The Government seems to have been in two minds as to what action to take against the arrested politicians, almost all of whom had been released on bail by the end of December. It was only some ten months later that eleven persons were brought to trial in the Warsaw District Court. In the charge, it was alleged that

in the period from 1928 on, after common agreement and conscious of what they were doing, they had together prepared a coup (*zamach*), the aim of which was the removal by force of the members of the Government holding power in Poland and their replacement by other persons, without intending any basic change in the constitution of the State.[3]

Their 'revolutionary' activity was alleged to have consisted of inciting hatred towards the Government among the masses, calling on them to overthrow the regime by force, 'organizing, schooling, and arming revolutionary cadres, and forming a central revolutionary organization under the name of the "Centrolew"'. The indictment further charged that this body had adopted revolutionary resolutions at the Cracow congress and had planned an armed 'March on Warsaw'. This had led to bloody incidents in twenty-two cities on 14 September, but the further development of the revolution had been cut short by the Government.[3] Those accused included six members of the P.P.S., Lieberman, Barlicki, Pragier, Ciołkosz, Dubois, and Mastek, two from the Piast, Witos and Kiernik, two from the Liberation, Bagiński and Putek, and Sawicki of the Peasant Party. The list was significant for its omissions. It included only eleven of the twenty-seven people arrested in September 1930, and did not include Korfanty or Popiel. It did not include the leaders of the parties which had made up the Centrolew, the members of the Centrolew

---

[1] Ibid., col. 139.
[2] *Gazeta Polska*, 15 January 1931, *Robotnik*, 24 January 1931.
[3] *Sprawa brzeska*, p. 27.

Consultative Committee or the most prominent members of the Centrolew Shadow Cabinet. The trial was intended, above all, to offer a justification for the Brześć arrests.

Its course, however, made it clear that although some radical statements had been made, the Centrolew had never intended to go beyond the framework of the constitution in its attempts to dislodge the Government. As Lieberman declared in his statement to the court,

> It is not true that I planned a coup, that I planned a revolution, that I wanted to overthrow the Government of Marshal Piłsudski. The truth is, however, that I wanted to remove this Government and want now to remove it, only, as an old parliamentarian, I want to do this in a democratic, parliamentary manner, and since in a parliamentary struggle the President always has the final word, I wanted to overthrow this Government through the calling of new elections which would convince Marshal Piłsudski that the majority of society supported the Opposition.[1]

The main architect of the Centrolew, Niedziałkowski, when called as a witness, explained the motives behind the resolution at the Cracow congress which urged the President to resign, on which the prosecution laid much stress,

> We modelled ourselves on the analogous resolution of the French *cartel des gauches*, the consequence of which was the resignation of Millerand from the Presidency. That resolution was signed by Herriot and the later President Doumergue, and they were never called to answer for that act.[2]

The court gave its verdict on 13 January 1932, acquitting Sawicki, but finding the rest guilty, not of preparing a coup, but of belonging to a conspiracy whose ultimate aim was a coup. The court held that they had wished to overthrow the Government and had intended to do so using illegal means. These had included 'inciting crowds not to obey the legal orders of the authorities', the resolution of the Cracow congress accusing the President of not adequately fulfilling his office and calling on him to resign, and the organization of demonstrations. One of the three judges submitted a dissenting opinion calling for the acquittal of the accused.[3]

Witos was sentenced to one-and-a-half years' imprisonment,

[1] *Sprawa brzeska*, p. 31.   [2] Ibid., pp. 126–7.
[3] For the verdict, ibid., pp. 233–8.

Bagiński to two years, Barlicki, Lieberman, and Kiernik to two-and-a-half years and the rest to three years. The case came before the Court of Appeal on 7 February 1933. Its verdict increased the sentences of Witos, Bagiński, Lieberman, Barlicki, and Kiernik to three years, and those of the rest to five years. (Sawicki's acquittal had been upheld previously.) This decision was rejected by the Court of Cassation on 9 May 1933, but was upheld by the Court of Appeal on 20 July and confirmed in the Court of Cassation on 5 October. Rather than face imprisonment, Witos, Kiernik, Bagiński, Lieberman, and Pragier went into exile. The others were pardoned and released on 29 September 1934, having spent less than a year in prison.

The decision to go into exile was explained in a 'Farewell Letter', secretly distributed in Poland, in which it was argued that to have accepted the sentences would have meant giving sanction to the 'crime of Brześć'. The length of the sentences and the harsh treatment which would be experienced in gaol were also adduced.[1] Though understandable, the move into exile was probably a tactical mistake, and tension between the *émigré* leaders and their followers in Poland did cause some difficulty on the Left. Nevertheless the issue of the Brześć prisoners hung over the politics of the 1930s. The popularity of Witos, in particular, who was living in Czechoslovakia, rose to almost legendary proportions, and the failure of the Government to issue an amnesty prevented any real *rapprochement* with the parties of the Centre and Left. As Maria Dąbrowska wrote, 'The moral links between the Government and the majority of the population were shattered. From now on, all attempts to restore them, however well-intentioned, proved to be vain.'[2]

The Brześć trial was not the only political trial in this period. Already before the elections of 1930, the socialist Jan Kwapiński had been sentenced to one year's imprisonment for making a radical speech at a meeting, although the verdict was afterwards overturned on appeal. Irena Kosmowska of the Liberation had been sentenced to six months for a similar offence. On 1 December 1930, eight members of the P.P.S. were convicted of being involved in incidents connected with the demonstrations of 14 September in Toruń. Two were condemned to four years' hard labour for

---

[1] For the text of this letter, see Czubiński, *Centrolew*, pp. 264–5.
[2] Quoted in Roos, *A History of Modern Poland*, p. 122.

allegedly shooting at the police, a sentence afterwards reduced
in severity, two received two years and the rest six to nine months.
On 16 February 1931, three of those involved in the alleged plot
on Piłsudski's life received a year's imprisonment; on the 11th,
three members of the P.P.S. were sentenced to four years and
two to two years for their part in the demonstrations of 14 September in Warsaw. In July 1934 the Government set up a concentration camp for political offenders at Bereza Kartuska in eastern
Poland. Most of the prisoners were Right-Wing extremists, Communists, and Ukrainian nationalists. Altogether about 500 people
were held in the camp, which remained in existence until 1939.

In spite of its crushing of the Opposition and the secure control
it enjoyed in parliament, the Government had little to show in the
way of positive achievements in this period. Sławek gave way as
Premier on 27 May to Alexander Prystor who, as Minister of
Labour between April 1929 and the 1930 elections, had been
principally responsible for the attack on the P.P.S. control of the
Sick Funds. He was one of the inner circle of Piłsudski-ites, having
entered the Army after 1926 as a colonel with responsibility for
central staff work, first in the office of the General Inspector and
then in the War Ministry. His Cabinet was intended to deal,
above all, with the difficult economic situation, but its efforts
were hesitant and fumbling.[1] Like all the governments of this
period, it lacked directing force, and the individual ministries
frequently functioned without any real co-ordination of policy.
Prystor resigned, as we have seen, in May 1933, when he found,
to his surprise and dismay, that he had somehow antagonized the
Marshal. He was succeeded by Janusz Jędrzejewicz, who had
been a legionary and one of the leaders of the P.O.W. in 1917 and
1918. He had, however, left the regular Army in 1923 to become
head of the Warsaw Teachers' Training College from 1924 to
1926. After the coup he had been attached to the Cabinet Office
for a while and was elected to the Sejm in 1928, holding the office
of Vice-President of the B.B.W.R. From May 1931 he was
Minister of Education and his appointment may have been
intended to give a more moderate and civilian complexion to the
Cabinet. But he was no more capable of running a government
than his predecessor. After a year in office, he was succeeded on
15 May 1934 by Leon Kozłowski, a professional archaeologist,

[1] This is discussed below, pp. 347–53.

who had been a legionary officer. As Minister of Land Reform (1930–2) he had made a name for himself as one of the more radical of the Government's adherents, and his appointment seems to have resulted from the desire to show that the Sanacja was willing to take radical measures to bring the depression in Poland to an end. But as so often with Piłsudski's subordinates, he too was scarcely equipped for the office he held.

The Government did introduce some important legal reforms, using its decree powers to unite the Criminal Codes of the former partitions on 11 July 1932, and the Codes of Civil Procedure on 1 December 1932.[1] But, at the same time, ostensibly in order to facilitate the introduction of the new codes, it suspended once again from the end of August to the end of October 1931 the immovability of judges. The fears of the Opposition that this power would be used to remove opponents of the Sanacja from the bench proved largely justified. Already by 11 September, according to *Robotnik*, nineteen Vice-Presidents of local courts, nineteen Counsellors of Appeal Courts, and a number of Judges of the First and Second Degree had lost their positions.[2] In addition, though the enactment of a statute creating a uniform system of organization for the Bar all over Poland brought many advantages, it also increased the power of the Government to interfere with members of the legal profession.[3]

A bill reorganizing and unifying the structure of local government was passed on 23 March 1933.[4] Local government reform was a very pressing problem, particularly in Galicia, where a qualified franchise still persisted. A draft proposal had been presented to the Sejm in 1927, but it was never voted on because of the dissolution of parliament. The Sanacja proposal, first presented to parliament in January 1932, did not aim at a complete recasting of the system of local government, but only at creating a uniform pattern, and it applied only to the smaller units, the rural and urban communes and groups of districts. It was, however, open to considerable objection because of the small role it left to elected representatives, and it came under strong criticism from the Opposition, from local government organizations, and

---

[1] *Dz.U.R.P.* (1932), no. 60, pp. 1153–81; no. 112, pp. 2383–454.
[2] *Robotnik*, 11 September 1932.
[3] *Dz.U.R.P.* (1932), no. 86, pp. 1643–52.
[4] Ibid. (1933), no. 35, pp. 693–723.

from official bodies representing local government officers. The Cabinet does seem to have been somewhat affected by these objections, because the bill was brought before parliament only after a long delay and was not passed until March 1933. However, though a number of modifications were made to the original proposals, the essence of the law remained unchanged. The executive organs of local government were strengthened and subjected to closer government scrutiny, while the elected bodies were to be subject to government dissolution. Direct election was retained for the municipal councils of towns, but in those of communes and districts, indirect election was established. The first elections held under the new system in November and December 1933 fully justified fears that this indirect system would lead to large-scale government interference in the voting.[1]

Legislation was also passed on 11 March 1932 to effect a far-reaching reorganization of primary and secondary education.[2] The new law was intended to make access to secondary education easier for students from poorer families and from rural areas. It extended over the whole country the seven-year primary school. (Previously this had been the pattern only in the countryside, while in the towns, those going on to secondary education went to high school after five years.) Secondary education was correspondingly shortened. A certificate of competence was now to be given after four years in a gymnasium. Entrance to university required a further two or three years in a *lycée*. In addition, the number of technical high schools was increased.

On paper, there was much to be said for the new legislation, but it was hurriedly introduced with little prior discussion, and the whole reform thus had a botched-up and provisional character which partly explains its failure to realize the hopes of its initiators. The simultaneous introduction of 'political education' (*wychowanie państwowe*) as a subject for study in the schools was also widely criticized. According to Jędrzejewicz, the Minister of Education, its purpose was to '[educate] our youth in the cult of our state, in a profound respect for its historic tradition, in the sentiment of the bonds which link us with the efforts of previous generations'.[3]

[1] See the discussion in the Administrative Committee of the Sejm, *Kurjer Warszawski*, 18 December 1933.
[2] *Dz.U.R.P.* (1932), no. 38, pp. 639–45.
[3] *Gazeta Polska*, 21 January 1932.

As could perhaps be expected, the new course consisted, for the most part, of a glorification of Piłsudski's role in recent Polish history and a defence of the Sanacja.

The passage of the new Education Act was accompanied by a bill regulating private education which gave the Government the power to refuse to permit the opening of a private school until the founders had taken an oath of loyalty to the State.[1] In addition, schools could be shut down and teachers dismissed for 'disloyalty'. This measure, intended primarily to give the Government more supervision over the schools of the national minorities, made the Church uneasy and provoked an open letter from Cardinals Hlond and Kakowski expressing their dissatisfaction.[2] However, though Sławek did attempt to reassure the hierarchy, the bill was passed unaltered.

THE GOVERNMENT AND THE ECONOMY

Perhaps the greatest failure of the Government in these years was its inability to alleviate the effects of the Great Depression. It may be that no immediate solution was possible, that Poland, a largely agricultural country, poor in capital, overpopulated, and with no outlet for its rapidly rising population, could not, on its own, do much in the short run to restore prosperity and confidence. But none of the ministers in charge of economic affairs exhibited more than a superficial understanding of the problems facing the country, and none was prepared to embark on any sort of radical experiment. The Ministers of Finance, Colonel Matuszewski (14 April 1929 to 26 May 1931), the Marshal's brother, Jan (27 May 1931 to 5 September 1932), and Marian Zawadzki, Professor of Political Economy at Wilno University (5 September 1932 to 12 October 1935), all held fast to the orthodox deflationary policy which had been decided on at the onset of the Depression. The basis of government policy, frequently reiterated, remained the maintenance of a balanced budget, the preservation of the convertibility of the zloty at its existing exchange rate, and adherence to the gold standard.[3] The

---

[1] *Dz.U.R.P.* (1932), no. 33, pp. 545–6.

[2] For this letter see *Gazeta Warszawska*, 19 February 1932.

[3] See for instance, Zawadzki's speech to the B.B.W.R. on 1 June 1932 (*Gazeta Polska*, 2 June 1932); Prystor's speech to the Senate on 15 December

upholding of these canons of financial orthodoxy cost the country dearly, seriously impeding attempts to alleviate the crisis and, in fact, dictating the whole nature of the Government's economic strategy.

The aim was to reduce all prices and costs so that the deflationary effects of the depression were equitably distributed over the whole economy. At the same time, the Government embarked on ruthless economies in order to cut its own expenses so that the budget would balance. Already in June 1930 the estimates for public works were reduced by 160 million zloties, while in April 1931 the pay of all civil servants was cut by 15 per cent, though this was later modified to 5 per cent for army officers.[1] (It was rumoured that it was this favouritism which had provoked Matuszewski's resignation.) The annual increment for civil servants was also done away with. Drastic reorganization took place in the administration. The Ministry of Public Works was abolished, the Ministry of Land Reform merged with that of Agriculture, the Emigration Office was closed, and the activities of the Main Statistical Office were greatly narrowed. In addition, the whole system of welfare benefits was modified in March 1933. Though a pension scheme was now introduced, all other benefits, particularly those for medical treatment, were cut down and workers contributions increased.[2]

These changes did considerably diminish budgetary expenditure, though their wisdom, both from an economic and a social point of view could be questioned. At the same time, however, the decline in economic activity caused Government income to fall, and the budget deficit thus reached 371 million zloties in 1933–4, falling to 236 million zloties in 1934–5.[3] To meet the deficit, the Government issued a semi-voluntary National Loan in September 1933, and also raised direct and indirect taxation, customs, fees, the prices of goods available through government monopolies, and railway fares. This, of course, severely impeded the attempt to achieve a new price level, since it caused a considerable rise in the cost of living and thus increased

1932 (*S.S.Se.R.*, 15 December 1932), or Zawadzki's speech in the budget debate in the Sejm on 3 November 1933 (*S.S.S.R.*, 3 November 1933).

[1] *Gazeta Polska*, 11 April 1931.

[2] On these changes, see *Polityka społeczna Państwa Polskiego, 1918–1935*, p. 273.

[3] *M.R.S.* (1936), p. 265, Table X.

the resistance to the wage and salary cuts which the Government was encouraging industry to make in order to bring down costs.

The Government realized that the main reason for the harshness of the economic crisis in Poland was the severity with which agriculture had been affected. The price scissors continued to work against the peasant. Whereas the price paid for agricultural produce fell from 76 in 1929 to 40 in 1933, 33 in 1934, and 34 in 1935 (1928 = 100) the corresponding figures for the industrial goods bought by farmers were 101, 73, 71, and 67.[1] In other words a peasant, to purchase what he had formerly bought, had to sell double the amount of agricultural produce. When attempts to induce industry to cut prices voluntarily failed, the Government decided to attack the cartels, which already in 1929 had controlled nearly 40 per cent of Polish industrial production and whose sphere of operation had been greatly extended by the crisis. In 1934, for instance, cartel agreements covered firms whose capital made up 65·6 per cent of that of all Polish Joint Stock companies.[2] There was considerable justification for the view that cartel agreements kept prices high. Whereas the index of the prices of raw and semi-manufactured goods fell from 97 in 1929 (1928 = 100) to 64 in 1932, cartelized prices in this field fell from 108 to 104.[1] The Government's new Cartel Law of 28 March 1933 gave the Cabinet far-reaching control over the cartels, and set up a special Cartel Court which had the right, at the request of the Ministry of Industry and Trade, to dissolve cartels or declare their agreements invalid.[3] The Government made some use of these powers, dissolving the cement cartel, the carbide cartel, and a number of others of lesser importance. But in spite of a great deal of sound and fury, the final results were not significant. Whereas uncartelized prices of raw materials and semi-manufactures fell to 57 in 1934 and 55 in 1935, cartelized prices, which still included coal, oil, and sugar, fell to 89 and 83.[1] In fact the Government hesitated to antagonize industry by undertaking an all-out assault on restrictive practices. Moreover, the cartels played an important part in Government economic strategy. Since

[1] Ibid., p. 162, Table I.
[2] Kalecki, 'Udział karteli w działalności przemysłowej na rynku polskim', pp. 4–5.
[3] Dz.U.R.P. (1933), no. 270, pp. 652–6.

it had been decided not to devalue, the payment of Poland's
foreign debts became increasingly burdensome, and to acquire
foreign currency the Government depended more and more on
exporting at prices below the cost of production, while allowing
the industries concerned (primarily coal, oil, and sugar) to recoup
their losses by raising domestic prices. To do this effectively,
maintained prices on the internal market were required, and these
were arranged by the cartels.

The Government attempted further to aid agriculture by
diminishing the burden of debt under which the countryside
laboured. Debts were rescaled by legislation, and the nominal
capital value, the rate of interest, and the period of amortization
were all adjusted in favour of the debtor. But the Government
hesitated to act too radically for fear of hurting the infant capital
market in Poland, and though the burden of debt per hectare was
reduced from 345 zloties in 1931 to 231 zloties in 1935, this aided
primarily the large estates and the more prosperous peasants.[1]
Policies of attempting to raise agricultural prices by bulk buying
and by encouraging export also did little for the smaller peasant,
the man hardest hit by the crisis.

The Government took little positive action to end the industrial
crisis. It did take over a number of large firms which had gone into
liquidation, the most important of these being the Peace Foundry,
a huge Upper Silesian complex, and the great Lodz textile firm
of K. Scheibler and Grohman. A certain amount of public works
was also undertaken in order to reduce unemployment. But
though the number of men employed on these projects grew from
23,000 in 1930 to 98,000 in 1935,[2] their scale was still too small
to alleviate the situation to any significant extent.

None of these measures was more than a palliative, and thus
although there was a slight economic upturn in 1933, the crisis
persisted until early 1936, far longer than in most other countries.
Its effects were most severe in agriculture, where as we have seen
the Government failed materially to reduce the price scissors. The
net income per hectare on farms of 2–50 hectares did rise slightly
from the catastrophic level of 8 zloties in 1931–2, but in the
succeeding years it reached only 26, 35, and 18 zloties.[3] This figure

[1] Landau and Tomaszewski, *Zarys historii gospodarczej Polski*, p. 195.
[2] *M.R.S.* (1936), p. 173, Table I.
[3] Ibid. (1939), p. 74, Table VIII.

moreover does not include farms of 0–2 hectares which made up 34 per cent of all holdings in Poland and which were even more severely hit by the crisis. The rapid rise in population and the virtual impossibility of emigration either to the towns or abroad made the problem of rural over-population even more pressing. It was further aggravated by the severe cutting down of the land reform, which the Government accepted in order to cut expenses. In 1931, only 74,000 hectares (of the 200,000 provided for in law) were subdivided, and in the succeeding years the figure was 84,000, 57,000, and 80,000.[1]

Better than any figures, the remarks of an acute contemporary observer, Jan Michałowski, give an idea of the severity of the catastrophe which had struck the countryside.

Sugar no longer exists in the villages. The majority of children—in the Rzeszów district—have seen it only in the form of sugar-cakes at the Kermis. At present, the grey type of salt is used and sometimes even the red type intended for cattle; in spring, before the harvest, because of the lack of ready cash, even this worst variety is used over and over again, salted water being saved from one meal to cook the next meal's potatoes.

The medium peasant goes about today shod in the same boots, patched and repatched many times, in his one shirt, which is laundered at night. From his others, clothes were long ago made for the children. . . . They have one garment apiece, and feel most painfully their lack of clothes. It is easier in summer, but in winter in the northern part of the district one can meet in huts children who are bundled up to the neck in bags filled with chaff, since without clothing they would freeze in the cold, unheated dwelling.[2]

The impoverishment of the countryside brought about a significant increase in peasant radicalism. 'The peasants', wrote one of those who submitted his autobiography in the competition organized by the Institute of Social Economics, 'only know and say that this is a bad government, that they are disappointed with Independence and they recall Russian times with nostalgia.'[3] One form which the increased radicalism of the countryside took was that of strikes during which peasants refused to sell their produce. Early in 1932 two such strikes took place in Galicia, while in

[1] Ibid. (1938), p. 65.
[2] J. Michałowski, *Wieś nie ma pracy* (Warsaw, 1935), p. 49.
[3] Instytut Gospodarstwa Społecznego, *Pamiętniki chłopów*, 1st series, p. 126.

September of that year the peasants around Warsaw refused for a week to supply the capital with food. Similar demonstrations which on a number of occasions resulted in violence, occurred again in West Galicia in May and June 1933. In October over 130 people received sentences ranging from six months to four years for their part in these disturbances.

Industry remained depressed and failed to show any significant revival until early 1936. The index of industrial production, which had fallen to 54 in 1932 (1929 = 100) rose only to 56 in the following year, to 63 in 1934, and to 66 in 1935.[1] Unemployment too increased greatly. According to the official figures, in December 1930 the number of unemployed was 299·8 thousand. It rose to 312·5 by December 1931, and though it fell to 220·2 in December 1932, by December 1933 it had reached 342·6 and by December 1934 413·7.[2] Moreover, as the officials of the Ministry of the Interior admitted, these statistics did not reflect the real situation and the true figure was in each case as much as 200,000 higher.[3] Thus from 1933 to 1935 the number of unemployed was over 40 per cent of the total labour force, an unprecedently high figure. Moreover even those who had work were affected by wage cuts and the shortening of the working week, so that real wages fell from 108 in 1929 (1928 = 100) to 62 in 1933.[4] The great increase in unemployment led at first to a feeling of helplessness and apathy. But it led also to a growing radicalism. In 1930 and 1931 the number of days lost in strikes fell far below that of 1929. But in 1932 and 1933 it was far in excess, in the latter year by three-and-a-half times.[5]

Small traders and artisans were also extremely hard hit by the crisis as were the intelligentsia, particularly its younger members, who saw no opportunity for themselves in the existing situation. As the Depression wore on, the Government's arguments that the country had merely to wait until the crisis passed became less and less acceptable.

One of the important effects of the crisis was to increase still further the already large role of the state in the Polish economy.

[1] *M.R.S.* (1936), p. 3.

[2] Drozdowski, 'Bezrobocie w Polsce w 1925–1936', p. 232.

[3] On this question, see the confidential report of the Ministry of the Interior published by Drozdowski in 'Bezrobocie w Polsce w 1925–1936'.

[4] *M.R.S.* (1934), p. 136, Table XX.

[5] Ibid. (1936), p. 195, Table XXXIX.

The Depression had dealt some harsh blows to Polish capitalism, never particularly robust. A large number of concerns which had collapsed had, as we have seen, passed into state hands. In 1935 for instance, the total capital of joint-stock companies in Poland was 3,253 million zloties; of this 1,691 million zloties was in the hands of foreign capitalists whose share in the Polish economy also increased in this period. Of the 1,562 million zloties domestically owned, nearly 654 million were in the hands of the state.[1] The extension of étatism was most striking in the financial system. Private banking had been very badly affected by the crisis and the loss of confidence, and its place was more and more taken over by the state. The proportion of deposits held in private banks fell from 38·4 per cent in 1928 to 19·3 per cent in 1935,[2] and in this year 41 per cent of the share capital of private banks was held by the Government.[3] Long-term credit in particular was almost entirely in state hands. The failure of liberal democracy in Poland does seem to have some connection with the failure of Polish capitalism. The inability of the indigenous bourgeoisie to emerge in a form powerful enough to provide for the accumulation of the capital necessary for industrialization is one of the most striking similarities between the situation of Poland in the inter-war period and that of the new states which have emerged in Africa and Asia since World War II.

THE DEVELOPMENT OF THE B.B.W.R.

The B.B.W.R. became increasingly weak and ineffective between 1931 and 1935. The Brześć revelations had caused considerable disquiet, and the resignation of Lechnicki and Nowak meant that the radical 'Union of Town and Country' became for the moment virtually defunct. The B.B.W.R. seemed virtually incapable of combining parliamentary duties with grass-roots activities in the country, and its local organizations tended to become moribund.[4] Świtalski even proposed the establishment of a new

---

[1] R. Gradowski, *Przyczynek do zagadnienia kapitału państwowomonopolistycznego w Polsce, 1918–1939* (Warsaw, 1965), p. 24.
[2] Ibid., p. 40.
[3] Ibid., p. 39.
[4] Świtalski commented on this bitterly. A.S.S., Rozmowa z Panem Prezydentem, dnia 24 marca 1931 r.

pro-Government organization, on the lines of the former 'National League',[1] but this was rejected on the grounds that the B.B.W.R. provided an adequate framework, if only one could breathe life into it ('włożono jednak w nie treści').

The Government's dilemma in attempting to rally popular support was frankly admitted by Sławek in a speech he made to the General Council of the Union of Legionaries on 3 December 1932.[2]

We legionaries and P.O.W. members constitute a minority in the country, and one so restricted that if one considers from the point of view of numbers, we should have no right to govern the State. If we do not have arithmetic on our side, we must ask ourselves how, in accordance with what system, must we govern if we are to fulfil our proper role in the country? As a minority, we could dominate the majority by terror, by a fiercely dictatorial system. . . . But if we reject both dictatorship and terror, we have to find other means. These means are precisely the great principles we represent. We must communicate to society as a whole the views and values which are ours and whose virtues we ourselves know.

There were, he continued, many people in Poland outside the legions who had shown their patriotic devotion and their dedication to the welfare of the country. These people should not be 'pushed to one side. We must, on the contrary, do everything to attach them to our tradition, to our thought, to our respect for the State. This is our method of Government without terror and without dictatorship.'

However, the propagation of the vague cult of Piłsudski which was the only real ideological content of the Sanacja proved increasingly difficult. On 5 August 1934, the twentieth anniversary of the Marshal's crossing of the Austrian frontier, an Institute of Legionary Studies was set up. Its aim, according to its director, Bogusław Miedziński was 'to give a durable expression to the great epoch in which we live, to the great and happy transformation which our country and generation have seen'.[3] But to many, even to those who admired and respected Piłsudski, his adherents, governing in his name, seemed to be 'living on the glory of services

[1] A.S.S., Konferencja w sprawach organizacyjnych u Premiera Sławka w składzie: Skwarczyński, Schaetzel, Jędrzejewicz, Hołówko, Beck, Składkowski, Stamirowski, Siedlecki, dnia 20 marca 1931r. The National League had been an underground organization in the 1880s and 1890s.

[2] *Czas*, 6 December 1932.   [3] *Gazeta Polska*, 6 August 1934.

they rendered in 1905 and 1914',[1] while the continual references
to pre-World War I divisions over orientation had less and less
relevance to the younger generation, brought up under independence, and indifferent to the old and rather tired arguments.

The Government continued its policy of fostering pro-Sanacja
secessions from the Opposition. It had its greatest success in the
trade-union movement. Moraczewski, under the prompting of
Sławek, launched on 25 May 1931 a pro-Government Union of
Trade Unions,[2] to challenge the hold of the Socialist and Christian
Democratic organizations. The Z.Z.Z. called for close collaboration with the state, but demanded some radical changes, including
the forced cartelization and state control of industry, a strongly
progressive income tax, and the implementation of the forty-hour
week.[3] Its semi-official character helped recruitment, particularly
in nationalized industries, and it soon claimed a membership of
150,000. But this still did not rival the combined 250,000 members
of the older bodies.

A National Socialist Party, intended to rally pro-Government
elements in the N.P.R., was formed in April 1932, but had so
little success that it had to be refounded two years later. Neither
the Agricultural Peasant Party, launched in April 1932 and led
by Henryk Dzendzel, a former associate of Witos, nor the Christian
Social Party, created in February 1937 by seceders from the
Christian Democrats, won any significant support. Indeed the
Government's peasant following was racked by dissension between its two youth movements, the 'League of Young Peasants'
and the 'League of Peasant Youth' led by Karol Polakiewicz,
a militant Piłsudski-ite who had left the Peasant Party in 1928.
The feud between these two organizations grew so bitter that
Polakiewicz, though Vice-Marshal of the Sejm and President of
its Administrative Committee, was expelled from the B.B.W.R.
in February 1935.[4]

Within the B.B.W.R., relations between the conservatives and
the radicals became increasingly tense. Although the conservatives had a representative in the Cabinet in Marian Zawadzki, a
professor of Political Economy at Wilno University, who from

[1] As Żuławski, the P.P.S. deputy, put it in the budget debate in the Sejm
on 8 November 1934. *S.S.S.R.*, 8 November 1934.
[2] Zjednoczenie Związków Zawodowych (Z.Z.Z.).
[3] For its programme, see *Kurjer Warszawski*, 27 May 1931.
[4] On the Polakiewicz affair, see Singer, *Od Witosa do Sławka*, pp. 227–31

August 1931 was Under-Secretary in the Ministry of Finance, and Minister from September 1932, they felt increasingly unhappy about the evolution of government policy. They distrusted its progressive étatism in the economic field, and had serious reservations about its growing authoritarianism and police-state methods. At the same time, in the inner circle of Pilsudski-ites there was a strong feeling that the alliance with the conservatives was a liability, particularly as the Depression persisted, and that the close links between the Government and the large landowners and capitalists should be weakened. On 24 March 1931, Świtalski told the President that one of the reasons for B.B.W.R. unpopularity was the fact that its spokesmen in economic matters came almost exclusively from conservative spheres, and that this was an unhealthy phenomenon.[1] Jędrzejewicz, too, confided in Świtalski, shortly after becoming Prime Minister, that he was unhappy about the Government's posture in economic matters, particularly since he felt that Zawadzki was much too sensitive to conservative influence.[2]

The conservative response to this new situation was to intensify their critical attitude towards the Government, while attempting at the same time to unite the different pro-Government conservative organizations. On 2 December 1932, at a political banquet organized by *Czas*, Prince Radziwiłł attributed the growing political malaise to

the disappearance of an independent and responsible public opinion. This situation is aggravated because the Opposition, on the one hand, tendentiously criticizes all the actions of the Government, even its best moves, while on the other, the Governmental groups either do not say anything, or limit themselves to approving the Government's actions.[3]

On 7 December, the three conservative groupings, the Party of the National Right, the Conservative Organization, and the Christian Agricultural Party, met in Warsaw to discuss current politics, and after criticizing some aspects of government policy, set up a committee to study the prospects of union. This led on 27 February to the establishment of a united body, the 'Union of Conservative Political Organizations'.[4]

The divisions in the B.B.W.R. grew much more acrimonious

[1] A.S.S., Rozmowa z Panem Prezydentem, dnia 24 marca 1931 r.
[2] A.S.S., Rozmowa z Jędrzejewiczem, dn. 11 maja 1933 r.
[3] *Czas*, 3 December 1932.   [4] Ibid., 28 February 1933.

with the accession of the Kozłowski Government in May 1934, which attempted to adopt a more radical policy in economic affairs. An open clash came over the role of the conservatives in industries dominated by foreign capital. Already in January 1933, Radziwiłł and other prominent conservatives had been strongly criticized by the Minister of Industry and Trade, Generał Zarzycki, for their connections with the German capitalist Friedrich Flick in Upper Silesia.[1] In 1934, a resounding scandal broke over the administration of the foreign-owned Żyrardów textile mill.[2] This factory, which had been one of the largest in the Congress Kingdom before 1914, was almost entirely destroyed during World War I. It was rebuilt by the Polish government, but had passed in August 1923 to Marcel Boussac, a French textile entrepreneur, who had acquired a large majority of the original shares. Władysław Kucharski, the Minister of Finance responsible for recognizing Boussac's claim for control, had come under considerable fire for his action, but attempts to impeach him had proved unsuccessful. Boussac ran the Żyrardów mills in a way that was widely criticized. He concluded an agreement with a French textile firm owned by himself to supply credit, raw materials, and expertise to Żyrardów and used this to make high profits while running down the mill itself. From 1933 the Polish minority of the shareholders, among whom there were a number of prominent conservatives, attempted to end Boussac's abuses, and in March 1934 the mill was sequestrated pending an investigation. In the hope of avoiding costly legal proceedings, however, an agreement between the minority shareholders and Boussac was reached in July, with the approval of the Polish Minister of Industry and Trade.

The matter now took a more complicated turn because Beck, the Polish Foreign Minister, was attempting at this time to torpedo Barthou's attempts to create an Eastern Bloc to contain Germany,[3] and seems to have felt that the Żyrardów affair could

---

[1] *Gazeta Warszawska*, 26 January 1933.

[2] On the Żyrardów affair, see particularly the report of the Ministry of Foreign Affairs of 1936 reprinted in Z. Landau and J. Tomaszewski, *Kapitały obce w Polsce, 1918–1939. Materiały i dokumenty* (Warsaw, 1964), pp. 117–26, and the article on Aleksander Lednicki, who arranged the compromise between the majority and minority shareholders, in Z. Nagórski, *Ludzie mego czasu*, (Paris, 1964), pp. 139–42, as well as the contemporary press.

[3] See below, pp. 384–6.

be used to work up anti-French sentiment. As a result the pro-Government papers strongly attacked the July agreement claiming that it was a betrayal of Polish national interests, while the Government arrested the two French managers of the plant, as well as Count Henryk Potocki, a pro-Government conservative who had been chairman of the Żyrardów Council of Administration until its sequestration. Another conservative, Senator Artur Dobiecki, resigned his seat following his condemnation by a B.B.W.R. Court of Honour, while Józef Targowski, the President of the B.B.W.R. in the Senate, resigned from the Bloc and demanded to be tried by a Court of Honour.

The whole affair aroused considerable bitterness and was followed by demands in the pro-Government press for a 'movement to the Left', abandoning the conservatives, which would enable the Government to consolidate its position by acquiring worker and peasant support. The conservatives responded by publishing a series of articles in *Czas* on 'The Evolution of the Bloc'.[1] Their main argument was that the real danger to the Government came not from the weakened and divided Left, but from the increasingly strong and self-confident National Democratic Right. Only the conservatives could win these people over to the Government. 'From now on, the evolution of the Government Bloc should be directed to reinforcing its moderate wing. The weakening of this wing will not be a victory for the radical elements of the Bloc, but of their worst enemies, the "National Camp".'[2] The Sanacja did not prove receptive to these arguments. Though attempts to create an 'opening to the Left' were largely unsuccessful, the role of the conservatives within the Bloc continued to decline.

Perhaps the most significant failure of the Bloc was its marked inability to attract significant support among the new generation. Piłsudski and his followers had always held that the vast majority of their contemporaries had been corrupted by the experience of foreign rule and the habits of servitude it had encouraged. It was this which largely explained their élitism, their feeling that they alone had raised the banner of Independence before 1914. But they also believed that the new generation born in freedom would

[1] *Czas*, 10, 12, 13, 14, 15, 20, 21, 22, 26, 27, 30 September 1934; 2, 10 October 1934.
[2] Ibid., 22 September 1934.

recognize the rightness of their views and of their claim to rule the country. This did not happen, for the young were increasingly bored by the old debates about pre-war orientations and saw the Government as tired, repressive, and unimaginative, without any real answers to the pressing problems of the country. Thus the pro-Government youth organizations, in spite of (or perhaps because of) a great deal of fostering and the lavish provision of state finance, never became more than avenues of advance for careerists. Though the pro-Government Riflemen's scouting movement,[1] whose origins went back to before World War I, had in the early 1930s 140,000 members, it was not the largest of the scouting groups in Poland. In an effort to increase its popularity, it was placed, in September 1932, under the control of the Ministry of War and a serving brigadier-general was delegated to serve as 'Commander-in-Chief of the Union of Riflemen'.[2] However, official control proved counter-productive; the Riflemen failed to increase, and provided few recruits for the main pro-Government youth group, the Legion of Youth[3] founded in 1930 at the height of the constitutional conflict. This organization, too, in spite of considerable subsidies, proved relatively unattractive; its attempts to widen its base brought it into conflict with the Bloc conservatives, while the anti-clericalism and social radicalism of some of its members led to its being accused, rather bizarrely, of 'Communism' by the Church hierarchy.[4] From the end of 1934 it underwent a severe internal crisis as its leadership tried to eliminate its most radical members. These efforts proved unsuccessful and in April 1935 its leading patrons in the Government, Sławek, Janusz Jędrzejewicz, and Świtalski, withdrew their support. After this the organization rapidly became defunct.

The Government's failure was most evident at the universities. Here the great majority of the non-Jewish students were extreme nationalists, supporting either the National Democrats or the Fascist groups which emerged in the 1930s. The minority were left-wing, either socialist or populist, so that supporters of the Government were extremely scarce, and were mostly obvious opportunists. There were a number of reasons for the right-wing

---

[1] *Strzelec.*
[2] *Gazeta Polska,* 1 September 1932.
[3] *Legion Młodych.*
[4] A pastoral letter was issued to this effect in February 1934. *Gazeta Warszawska,* 24 February 1934.

extremism prevalent among university students. They tended to come from the intelligentsia, very hard hit by the long-drawn-out Depression. They saw little opportunity for themselves in the existing system, particularly as the economy showed no signs of recovery. Their feeling of insecurity was increased by the competition which the Jewish intelligentsia provided, and this partly explains the prevalence of anti-Semitic views among them, and the frequent demands for a *numerus clausus* (or indeed a *numerus nullus*). In fact, the percentage of Jewish university students declined from about 20·4 per cent in the academic year 1928–9 to 13·2 per cent in 1935–6.[1] Neither figure was particularly high, when one considers that the Jews constituted nearly a third of the urban population, from which the great majority of university students came. Moreover there was a great demand among Jews for university education. In 1928–9, in addition to the 8,700 Jewish university students in Poland, an estimated additional 8,000 young Polish Jews were studying at universities in Western Europe, people who had not been able to find places in their homeland.[2] However, both because of predilection, and to some extent because of discrimination in other fields, Jews tended to be concentrated in certain faculties, notably law and medicine, and the reduction of their numbers here was a continuous demand of the majority of students.

The anti-Sanacja mood at the universities was encouraged by the heavy-handedness of the Government, and especially by the undisguised willingness of the leading Piłsudski-ites to interfere with university autonomy. Already in early 1931 the overwhelming support given by students to their professors who had protested against the incidents in Brześć had shown the extent of their antipathy to the regime. The Government had little idea of what to do when faced with student hostility and it tended to fall back on a maladroit form of 'stick and carrot', offering advancement to those who would support the regime, and taking repressive measures against organizations representing the Opposition students.

It refused, for instance, to give legal recognition to the National Union of Polish University Youth, the principal organization of Polish university students. This body was, indeed, firmly in the

---

[1] S. Segal, *The New Poland and the Jews* (New York, 1938), p. 199.
[2] Ibid., p. 198.

hands of the Right, and its constitution included an 'Aryan' para-graph prohibiting Jews from becoming members. In October 1931 the Minister of Education issued a circular to all rectors of institutions of higher learning, informing them that the National Union was not to be recognized or aided in any way by university authorities and that its forthcoming election of executive officers was not to be allowed.[1] The prohibition was repeated in January 1933, after which the students decided to found a new organiza-tion, the 'General Conference of Students'. But this too was dis-solved by Government order in April 1933. The Government also acted against the student 'brotherhoods' (*Bratnia Pomoc*), organizations for mutual aid which existed at all Polish uni-versities, and forbade the two principal groups of this type, both of which were controlled by the Right, to have branches at more than one university. In addition the Cabinet extended its control over the distribution of bursaries (which were granted to only 2 per cent of all students) so that it could prevent their being granted to students with views clearly hostile to the régime. Some of the Government's actions were small-minded in the extreme. In October 1931, for example, one of the inter-university brother-hoods which had borrowed money from the Bank of National Economy to build co-operative housing for students fell behind in its interest payments. Its buildings were immediately sequestrated by court order.

In this situation, it is perhaps not surprising that the uni-versities were the scene of continuous political upheaval in the early 1930s. In November 1931 student unrest, sparked off by demands for the reduction of the number of Jewish students, led to the closing, for a short period, of the universities of Warsaw and Cracow, and the Warsaw Polytechnic. Student rioting led by the Right took place the following October in Warsaw, Poznań, and Lwów, as a result of the raising of university fees by the Minister of Education. It was followed in November by more incidents of a markedly anti-Semitic character, and these led again to the closing of the University of Warsaw. On the occasion of the passing of the Government's bill limiting the autonomy of the universities in March 1933, the right-wing students organized a strike in all institutions of higher learning. Violent clashes occurred when members of pro-Government organizations refused

[3] *Gazeta Warszawska*, 1 October 1931.

to stay away from lectures. In October 1933 incidents between National Democratic Students and those of the 'Legion of Youth' caused the closing of Warsaw University, this time by the Minister of Education in terms of the powers he now possessed under the act reorganizing higher education. In March 1934 the university was once again closed following anti-Semitic incidents involving the distinguished historian, Professor Marceli Handelsman, who was of Jewish origin.

THE OPPOSITION

The Centrolew did not survive the 1930 elections. In the new parliament, the deputies of the constituent parties were too few to make possible effective co-operation against the Government. Voices critical of the alliance were raised in all the parties, but were strongest in the P.P.S., which, as we have seen, had suffered worst in the elections. Indeed, the period 1931–5 saw a marked decline in the party's power and influence. The circulation of *Robotnik* fell so considerably that the journal underwent a financial crisis in early 1935,[1] the membership of the P.P.S.-dominated trade unions fell by 25 per cent between 1928 and 1934, while that of the party itself also diminished.[2] The party's confidence that the Government could be overthrown by legal and parliamentary means had been shown to be cruelly mistaken, and it proved difficult to find a new course. The belief that the party was too legal-minded and insufficiently radical led to some loss of support to the Communists, particularly among the unemployed. Repression increased, and the Government had some success in persuading or coercing workers to join its own trade-union organization. The persistence of the economic crisis and the growth in unemployment also caused a fall in union membership and this, along with purges of P.P.S. members of the Sick Funds and other welfare organizations, placed the party in serious financial difficulties. At the same time, the National Democrats and their Fascist offshoots undertook a great deal of propagandizing among workers and enjoyed a certain amount of success.

---

[1] Drozdowski and Tymieniecka, 'Mieczysław Niedziałkowski', p. 63.

[2] J. Kowalski, *Trudne lata. Problemy rozwoju polskiego ruchu robotniczego, 1929–1935* (Warsaw, 1966), p. 518.

The dispute in the party over its general political orientation crystallized at its twenty-second congress (23–5 May 1931).[1] Three groups could be distinguished. The first, the so-called 'Old Comrades', the party hierarchy led by Niedziałkowski and Żuławski, had seventy-nine delegates. It supported the Centro-lew and the policy of alliance with other groups in defence of democracy. The Centre, with seventy-one delegates led by Zaremba and Dubois, attacked the alliance with 'bourgeois' parties, and called for joint action with the socialist parties of the national minorities. The Left, led by Drobner, with fifty delegates, wanted a revolutionary policy and proposed talks with the Communists. However, the leadership, in spite of its minority position, secured the adoption of resolutions upholding its past actions and calling on the party to 'co-operate with the democratic peasant movement and to unite all democratic forces in the country'.[2]

During the 1930s the party moved to a more radical position, as the Government became more authoritarian and began to cut down welfare benefits and as the economic crisis showed no sign of coming to an end. International events also played a part, notably the Nazi conquest of power in Germany and the crushing of the Austrian socialists. Liberal democratic forms appeared inadequate to withstand the rising Fascist tide. The Polish regime was held to be 'crypto-Fascist' and many argued that purely legal means would be inadequate to overthrow it. An important straw in the wind was the article 'Mea culpa' published in Robotnik on 1 January 1933 by Norbert Barlicki, one of those convicted in the Brześć trial and a respected, rather Left-of-Centre member of the party. How was it, he asked, that only fourteen years after the most terrible catastrophe the world had seen, the pre-war reactionaries who were responsible for that catastrophe could be in a position again to assume power and abolish the democratic achievements which had followed the war? 'What has happened to that fine revolutionary upsurge of societies and whole nations which—as history shows—stopped the massacres, brought back peace, drove out or annihilated tyrants and founded the freedom of the people on broad democratic foundations?' What had destroyed this upsurge was 'the too early stopping of the revolutionary process',

[1] See 'XII Kongres P.P.S. (23–25.V.1932 r.) w relacji Komunikatu Informacyjnego Komisariatu Rządu w Warszawie', N.D.P., 1st series, 11 (1959), 217–44.
[2] Robotnik, 28 May 1931.

the willingness of the socialists to acquiesce in half measures in the cause of national unity.

The party's Centre and Left were in a considerably stronger position at the twenty-third congress (2–4 February 1934) where they held a clear majority.[1] Though the party hierarchy succeeded in maintaining its position, it was forced to accept a resolution stressing the importance of non-parliamentary forms of struggle and stating that a dictatorship of the proletariat might be necessary as a provisional stage after the overthrow of the bourgeoisie. The Left also demanded, without success, that the P.P.S. deputies withdraw from parliament.

The discontent of the Left again came to a head at the meeting of the Executive Council of the party on 30–1 March 1935.[2] Niedziałkowski's editorial policy in *Robotnik* was strongly attacked as being insufficiently radical. He and Żuławski resigned from the Central Committee and had to be persuaded to withdraw their resignations until the next party congress.

With this increased radicalization, relations with the Communists again became a live issue. The intransigent Leftist line adopted by Comintern in 1928 had been firmly upheld at the fifth congress of the K.P.P., held near Leningrad in August and September 1930.[3] The Leński leadership was maintained and the process of subordinating the party to the directives of Comintern, which now in practice meant Stalin, went even further. The conference rejected any co-operation with the parties of the Centrolew, arguing that their opposition to the Piłsudski régime was an 'internal affair of Fascism'. Since the leadership in the Soviet Union greatly feared foreign intervention in the wake of the famine and virtual civil war which had followed the introduction of collectivization, the K.P.P. adopted as one of its principal tasks the defence of the Soviet state. This was to be achieved by integrating the struggle of workers, peasants, and national minorities. Young party members were to be trained to perform acts of sabotage in the event of a Polish-Soviet conflict and the importance of infiltrating the Polish armed forces was stressed. National

[1] See 'XXIII Kongres P.P.S. (1934 r.) w materiałach i relacjach agenturalnych Komisariatu Rządu na m. st. Warszawę', ed. H. Marek, *Z.P.W.* i (1958), no. 1, 159–202.

[2] J. Żarnowski, *Polska Partia Socjalistyczna w latach 1935–1939* (Warsaw, 1965), p. 22.

[3] On this congress, see K.P.P., *Uchwały i rezolucje*, iii. 109–272.

reunification (i.e. incorporation in the Soviet Union) for western White Russia and the western Ukraine was reaffirmed, while self-determination was demanded for Polish Upper Silesia and (for the first time) for the 'nationally mixed areas of Pomerania'.

This extreme position made impossible any co-operation with the other parties of the Left. Relations deteriorated still further as a result of the party's attitude to the Brześć prisoners, as expressed in a K.P.P.-sponsored article in *Pravda*, 'On the beaten lackeys of Polish Fascism'.[1] Of their trial, the Warsaw correspondent of the Comintern Press Service wrote: 'The Brześć trial is an epilogue of the disputes within the different factions of Polish Fascism. . . . there stands in the dock the morally corrupt so-called "Polish democracy" which is eaten away by inner treachery.'[2]

This extreme Leftist line came under strong attack from some members of the party led by Isaac Deutscher, Paweł Minc, and Abe Flug, who argued that the party could not remain indifferent to the struggle between the political groups in Poland, and that it should defend the remaining vestiges of bourgeois democracy against authoritarianism. However, their calls for a popular front were disregarded, and they were expelled from the K.P.P. at the sixth party congress (November 1932) as 'agents of social-Fascism'.[3] The decisive change in party policy came with Hitler's seizure of power in January 1933, leading as it did to the destruction of the most powerful party in Comintern and to the ending of the political co-operation between Weimar Germany and the Soviet Union. Comintern did not immediately change its policy on Germany, believing that Nazism might prove a transient phenomenon. But after the burning of the Reichstag (March 1933) it encouraged the K.P.P. (and also the Czech Communist Party) to propose to the other socialist groups the 'setting up of a united front of struggle against the capitalist offensive and against Fascism'.[4] The P.P.S. proved somewhat resistant to these approaches, but in August 1934 a provisional agreement was reached with the Bund.[5] Popular Front tendencies were also strong both in the P.P.S. youth movement and in its trade-union organization. Indeed a significant

---

[1] *Pravda*, 29 December 1930.
[2] *International Press Correspondence* (the organ of Comintern), 5 November 1931.
[3] See K.P.P., *Uchwały i rezolucje*, iii. 378.
[4] *International Press Correspondence*, 24 March 1933.
[5] Żarnowski, *Polska Partia Socjalistyczna*, p. 22.

change could be detected in the Party Executive Council's resolution of October 1934, which conceded the importance of uniting the proletariat. However, agreement with the Communists could not be achieved without 'the stopping by the Communists of their attacks in word and in print, and the ending of their splitting tactics in the P.P.S.'[1] These Popular Front tendencies were to develop much more strongly after Piłsudski's death.

The P.P.S. continued to uphold its policy of alliance with the now united Peasant Party, although differences in programme and political tradition hindered co-operation. In the parliament of December 1930, the forty-eight deputies and six senators of the three peasant parties formed a single club, and on 15 March 1931, at a special congress, the three parties were formally united under the name of the Peasant Party.[2] Each of the three constituent groups had an equal number of representatives on the Executive Committee of the new party, while each was assigned the chairmanship of one of the party's three executive organs. The programme adopted was essentially moderate, largely in order to conciliate the Piast;[3] the party claimed to be the 'political organization of the rural population . . . the most numerous stratum (*warstwa*) of the nation' (Article 1). It affirmed its support for a democratic constitution, rejecting dictatorship or extra-parliamentary means of struggle (Articles 2, 3). An ambiguous compromise was reached on the status of the Church. 'The Peasant Party', reads Article 6, 'aims at a regulation of the relationship of religious cults to the state which will ensure the independence of both in fulfilling their functions.' The national minorities were to be guaranteed their rights, although at the same time the party advocated that the towns become 'real centres of Polish culture and Polish economic life' (Articles 9, 10), a reference aimed at the Jews. It also affirmed the necessity of combating the excessive development of intermediary trade. The 'just demands of the mass of the workers' were supported (Article 19), and all land in large estates was to be redistributed, with compensation to the owners (Article 21).

It proved difficult in the initial years of the party to give any

---

[1] Drozdowski, Tymieniecka, 'Mieczysław Niedziałkowski', p. 62.

[2] *Stronnictwo Ludowe.*

[3] For this programme, see *Materiały źródłowe do historii polskiego ruchu ludowego* (Warsaw, 1966), iii. 13–23.

real substance to the new-found unity.[1] The programme, in spite of its moderation, proved too extreme for the more conservative of the Piast's followers in Poznania, who seceded in February 1932. None of the three parties was convinced that the union would last, and all attempted to maintain their links with their former organizations, so as not to lose too much when the expected break came. *Zielony Sztandar*, the organ of the new party, was looked upon, both by the former Liberation and the former Piast leaders as a somewhat unwelcome competitor for their own journals, and they both showed a marked reluctance to furnish lists of their own subscribers so as to enable the new paper to enlarge its circulation. Break-up seemed near on a number of occasions. In May 1932, for instance, a government spy reported:

Predictions of a split, and the conviction that one cannot be avoided, have become notorious among the leading activists of the Peasant Party. Things have gone so far that for a number of days talks have clearly been taking place on the demarcation of respective spheres of influence, so that with the split, there can emerge two, more or less united, Peasant Parties.[2]

But in spite of the initial difficulties, the union proved lasting, and by May 1933 the party could claim, without too much exaggeration, a membership of 120,000.[3] In the new party the former Piast leaders showed most dynamism, and Witos, until his departure to Czechoslovakia, emerged as the dominant personality in the organization. Indeed, the increased strength of the Piast led to secessions by former Peasant Party and Liberation members in 1935.

The party became increasingly radical as the Depression continued and the Government's authoritarianism emerged more clearly. Already in May 1931, Witos supported his local party organization's resolution demanding uncompensated expropriation of the large estates; at the same time he suggested that the Opposition withdraw their deputies from parliament in protest against the Government's blatant disregard of their views,[4] a proposal he repeated on a number of occasions in the following years. The party also led the peasant strikes which took place in 1932

[1] On this, see J. Borkowski, 'Procesy integracyjne w Stronnictwie Ludowym od I do II kongresu, 1931–1933', *R.D.R.L.* vi (1964), 114–61.
[2] Quoted in Borkowski, 'Procesy integracyjne . . .', p. 137.
[3] Ibid., p. 149.
[4] J. Borkowski, 'Odpowiedź polemistom', *Polityka*, 12 February 1965.

and 1933, and a number of its activists were sentenced to imprisonment for their participation.[1] The call for uncompensated land reform, repeated by Witos in an interview with *Naprzód* in December 1932,[2] was adopted by the party at its second congress in May 1933, although its radical character was somewhat modified by the assertion that the estates expropriated should be, in the first instance, those with outstanding taxes or debts to state banks, and those whose owners sent their profits abroad. In addition, stronger methods for dealing with the Sanacja were demanded.[3] *Piast*, for instance, in September 1933, discussing the collapse of the German Social Democrats, commented: 'The assertion that Fascism can be broken only by revolution is undoubtedly correct. . . . all parliamentary discussion and the so-called democratic methods of parliamentarianism have shown themselves anachronisms.'[4] Nevertheless the second congress refused to adopt extra-parliamentary political tactics and demanded only the removal of the dictatorship by new and free elections.[5]

The party continued divided on the question of alliances. A sector of the leadership, notably Rataj and Józef Grudziński, favoured a close alliance with the P.P.S. Witos and his followers, though not opposed to links with the Left, had great reservations. Indeed Witos argued that the P.P.S. saw the Endecja as its main enemy and was tacitly co-operating with the Government, a view his Polish informants confirmed in him during his exile in Czechoslovakia.[6] He wavered in his own characteristic way, between the concept of the peasants standing alone and relying on their own strength, and the resumption of his previous links with the Centre and Right. Indeed, the question of the party's orientation remained unresolved throughout the period. In addition, there were contacts between some of the leadership, certainly Sawicki and perhaps Róg, with the Government, but attempts to induce the party to moderate its opposition proved almost completely unsuccessful.

The Christian Democrats and the National Workers' Party maintained their opposition to the Government in the early 1930s, although they struck off on their own, away from the other parties

---

[1] See above, pp. 351–2.   [2] *Naprzód*, 1 December 1932.
[3] For these resolutions, see *Materiały źródłowe do historii polskiego ruchu ludowego*, iii. 94–7.
[4] *Piast*, 16 September 1933.
[5] *Materiały źródłowe do historii polskiego ruchu ludowego*, iii. 96.
[6] W. Witos, *Moja tułaczka, 1933–1939* (Warsaw, 1967), pp. 330, 400.

of the Centrolew. In October 1930 the Warsaw and Silesia organizations of the Christian Democrats reunited, and in June 1931 Korfanty was elected President of the party. After 1930 the party continued to oppose the Government, resolving in July 1931 that it would fight against 'all manifestations of dictatorship',[1] although it would not use extra-parliamentary means of struggle. It singled out as its main allies the N.P.R. and the National Party. At the same time, most of the pro-Government elements left the Christian Democrats, encouraged to do so by some of the Church hierarchy, embarrassed by the party's anti-Sanacja position. An even larger split took place in February 1934 when a pro-Government Catholic organization, the Christian Social Alliance,[2] was created, led by an important member of the party, Father Szydelski. Another smaller split took place in January 1935. In fact the Christian Democracy never gained the wholehearted support of the Church and it failed in this period significantly to extend its position. Its links with the N.P.R. remained strong, but that party too, was much weakened by pro-Government splits.

The principal political force on the Right thus remained the National Democrats, who had regained some of their lost ground in the elections of November 1930 and who exhibited considerable dynamism in these years.[3] But in spite of the reunification of the O.W.P. and the Popular National Union in October 1928, and the formation of the National Party, the division between the older parliamentary politicians and the young, more and more openly Fascist members of the O.W.P., whose influence grew as the economic crisis persisted and the Government became more authoritarian, continued to plague the Endecja. The party fell more and more under the control of the young Right-radicals, sponsored by Dmowski, whose articles arguing that liberal democracy was merely a shield for 'Jewish-Masonic dominance' and that a 'national revolution' on the Italian pattern was necessary, gained increasing support.[4] Hostility to capitalism as such also

---

[1] Micewski, *Z geografii politycznej II Rzeczypospolitej*, pp. 170–1.

[2] *Zjednoczenie Chrześcijańsko-Społeczne.*

[3] On the Endecja in this period see: R. Wapiński, 'Niektóre problemy ewolucji ideowo-politycznej Endecji w latach 1919–1939', *K.H.* (1966), pp. 861–77; Micewski, *Z geografii politycznej II Rzeczypospolitej*, pp. 261–88; T. Bielecki, *W szkole Dmowskiego* (London, 1968).

[4] Dmowski published the articles he wrote during these years in *Przewrót* (Warsaw, 1934).

became common among nationalist ideologists. According to Adam Doboszyński, whose book *The National Economy* went into several editions, the object of nationalist economic policy should be

the abandonment of machine-made trash and the return to individual craftsmanship . . . And, as a final goal, the creation in society of a healthy class of small artisans, in which fathers will bequeath their workshops to their sons, who will no longer fill the factories or swell the ranks of the unemployed and debased intelligentsia.[1]

The anti-Semitism of the party increased, greatly encouraged by the impunity with which Hitler was able to dispossess and deprive of political rights the wealthiest and most powerful Jewish community in Europe. Demands for the total expulsion of the Jews from Poland, for the severe limitation of their numbers at the universities and for the boycotting of Jewish trade became frequent. As the Left revived in strength, the view grew widespread that the real enemy was not the Sanacja, but the Popular Front, generally called the 'Folks Front' in order to underline its allegedly Jewish character.[2]

The young nationalists undertook large-scale propagandizing among workers and the petit-bourgeois as well as among the intelligentsia. Membership of the O.W.P. rose from 35,000 in January 1930 to 120,000 in May 1932 and its influence was particularly strong at the universities.[3] By early 1933 it could claim nearly a quarter of a million members. The rapid growth of the O.W.P. alarmed the Government and led it to dissolve the organization, first in Pomerania, Poznania, and the Kielce province in September and October 1932, and then in the country as a whole in March 1933. The dissolution of the organization led to a clash between its leaders, who wished to continue their activity underground, and the more conservative, older leadership of the National Party, who opposed conspiracies and wanted the members of the O.W.P. merely to join the youth section of the party. Their advice was followed, but the feeling that the party leaders were 'weak and legalistic' and 'filled with opportunism',

[1] A. Doboszyński, *Gospodarka narodowa* (Warsaw, 1934), p. 122.
[2] 'Folks Front' was the Yiddish translation of Popular Front. It was used rather than the Polish *Front Ludowy*. (The use of the letter 'F' rather than 'V' showed that it was not German.)
[3] Wapiński, 'Niektóre problemy', p. 871.

was increased among the young activists. On the other hand, one group, led by Ryszard Piestrzyński, decided to come to terms with the Sanacja, arguing that the old political differences were irrelevant and that the National Party was dominated by its 'blind and passionate . . . opposition'[1] to everything the Government was doing. The coup of May 1926 had, they felt, elements of a national revolution, and their aim was to push the Government further in a healthy direction.

A second group of the O.W.P. also left the National Party and in April 1934 founded the openly Fascist and violent National Radical Camp,[2] modelled on the Nazis. This group also contained elements who believed that some compromise with the Government should be sought. However, its activities so annoyed the Government that after two months it was dissolved, and most of its members confined in Bereza Kartuska. Nevertheless it remained in existence underground, and after Piłsudski's death a section of its members, led by Bolesław Piasecki, did in fact come to terms with the Government.[3]

Even among the former O.W.P. leadership who remained in the National Party there was considerable dissatisfaction. In April 1934, however, a number of the young extremists, including Tadeusz Bielecki, Jędrzej Giertych, and Jan Matłachowski, were able to force their co-option to the party executive. By February 1935, supported by Dmowski, they had consolidated their power and, as a result, the party as a whole drew increasingly close to Fascism, though it rejected the *Führerprinzip* and the anti-religious character of Nazism. Though a number of people in the party continued to uphold liberal views, its evolution in a generally Fascist and anti-parliamentarian direction was a phenomenon pregnant with danger for the future.

THE NATIONAL MINORITIES

The problem of East Galicia continued to weigh heavily on Polish politics in the early 1930s. The 'pacification', which, Sławoj-Składkowski admitted to the Budget Committee of the Sejm in

---

[1] Ibid., p. 872. [2] Obóz Narodowo-Radykalny.
[3] Piasecki has continued his 'approaches to governments'. During the war he made some approaches to the Wehrmacht and afterwards proposed to the N.K.V.D. to split the Catholic Church in return for his life. His role in the anti-Zionist and anti-Jewish campaign in Poland in 1968 was considerable.

January 1931, had led to the arrest of nearly 1,800 people,[1] left a considerable residue of bitterness. Though many of those arrested were soon released, a significant proportion were brought to trial, some receiving heavy sentences. In addition, a number of people, including the prominent U.N.D.O. politician Dmitri Levitsky, were still kept in preventive custody. The three government-supported Ukrainian Gymnasiums at Tarnopol, Drohobycz, and Rohatyn, which had been centres of nationalist unrest, were not reopened.

The Ukrainians had not been as hard hit as the Centrolew by government repression during the elections. Altogether twenty Ukrainian Nationalist deputies were elected, seventeen from the U.N.D.O. and three from the Ukrainian Socialist Revolutionary Party. In addition, seven pro-Government Ukrainians were elected in Volynia and two in East Galicia. In the new parliament the Ukrainian deputies presented a motion in December 1930 demanding a full inquiry into the pacification so that those responsible could be punished and those injured indemnified.[2] Gaining no satisfaction, they addressed a petition to the League of Nations in January 1931 claiming that the Government had violated the provisions of the Minority Treaty by its actions in East Galicia.[1]

The Government did make some attempt to improve relations with the Ukrainians. In March 1931, for instance, Janusz Jedrzejewicz, at this time president of the B.B.W.R., and the group's vice-president Tadeusz Hołówko, well-known for his sympathy for the minorities, undertook talks with three of the leading Ukrainian politicians, deputed by the U.N.D.O. In return for a declaration of loyalty and the withdrawal of the Ukrainian petition at the League of Nations, Jędrzejewicz and Hołówko offered to intercede with the Polish population of East Galicia to effect 'a radical change in their attitude' to the Ukrainians. The satisfaction by the Government of certain Ukrainian demands was also offered.[3] However, their approach failed and the petition went before the League, which delegated the Japanese representative to draft a report which was issued in January 1932.[4]

[1] *Gazeta Polska*, 10 January 1931.
[2] *Robotnik*, 28 December 1930.
[3] *Gazeta Warszawska*, 11 March 1931.
[4] Ibid., 1 February 1932.

It held that the Polish Government 'had not intended to apply towards the Ukrainian minority a policy of systematic oppression and force'. The sabotage in East Galicia, it argued, had been organized by 'certain Ukrainian nationalist elements'. 'I feel myself obliged to express regret', commented the reporter, 'that an action of this kind should attempt to hide behind the system of minority protection of the League of Nations.' At the same time, the Polish Government was criticized for allowing a state of affairs to develop which 'did not conform entirely to what should be ensured to National Minorities'. It was conceded that a number of officers had been punished for excesses during the pacification, but no indemnity had yet been given to innocent parties affected by their actions.

Further attempts were made by the Government to come to terms with the Ukrainian leadership. They were assisted by a revulsion among some elements of Ukrainian society against the terrorists of the O.U.N., whose financial dependence on the German Foreign Office was becoming increasingly obvious.[1] Late in March 1931, Bishop Khomshyn, the Uniate Bishop of Stanisławów issued a pastoral letter strongly condemning 'all acts of sabotage and all subversive organizations' and calling on Ukrainians to change their attitude to the Polish state and concede to it a loyalty which would ensure it 'strength and security'.[2] 'Let us imagine', he continued, perhaps prophetically,

that one day the Poles, hated by the Ukrainians, depart and leave us to ourselves. Then what would become of us? From the other side of the Zbrucz, in a few hours, there would come hordes of Bolsheviks. They would close our churches, transforming them into houses of debauchery, they would deport part of the clergy and intelligentsia, they would oppress the people, destroying in them what is human and reducing them to a condition worse than they have ever experienced. As to the peasants, who are the basis of our nation, they would be reduced to serfs of the state.

The Government's attempts had most success in Volynia, where under the aegis of Governor Józewski, it succeeded in June 1931 in setting up a pro-Polish Ukrainian Union of Volynia

---

[1] A number of documents describing these contacts was published in the press in September 1931. See *Ilustrowany Kurjer Codzienny*, 10 September 1931.

[2] The letter was reprinted in *Czas*, 24, 25 March 1931.

which enjoyed the support of the Greek Orthodox Metropolitan of Poland. In July Dmitri Levitsky was released from preventive custody,[1] while in January 1932, Różniecki, the Governor of the Lwów province, addressed a conference of the main Ukrainian economic and cultural organizations, and offered them fairly far-reaching reforms.[2]

In spite of these rather sporadic efforts, however, the situation in East Galicia showed no marked improvement. The harshness of Polish repression was not easily forgotten, and the discontent of the Ukrainian peasantry was increased by the severity of the economic crisis. In the summer of 1931, there was a new outbreak of terrorism by the O.U.N. In July, a Post Office vehicle carrying money was attacked near Zbrucz and one of the police escort killed; in August, an armed band stole 30,000 zloties from a post office at Truskawiec. Lesser acts of sabotage also took place. Mills and granaries were burnt down and telephone and telegraph wires cut. At the end of August, members of the O.U.N., true to their policy of preventing any Polish-Ukrainian *rapprochement*, assassinated Tadeusz Hołówko, one of the most ardent exponents of a *détente* in the Government. More armed robberies took place in November and December 1932. However, the O.U.N. sabotage was increasingly resented by the large majority of the Ukrainian population, and from late 1932 the organization devoted more attention to organizing a boycott of the bilingual government schools.

But even though sabotage declined, Polish-Ukrainian relations deteriorated further in this period. Little was done to follow up government approaches, and the new Local Government Law (March 1933), which diminished the rights of self-governing villages and made Polish the official language in all local government bodies, was very much resented. Unease was also aroused by Poland's unilateral abrogation in September 1934 of the National Minorities Treaty, although this action was provoked more by the impending entry of the Soviet Union into the League of Nations than by any internal considerations.

From late 1933, however, the situation began to change. In the U.N.D.O. there was increasing dissatisfaction with a totally negative policy of non-co-operation but also with the violence of

---

[1] *ABC*, 15 July 1931; *Robotnik*, 21 July 1931.
[2] *Gazeta Warszawska*, 5 January 1932.

the O.U.N. and the repression it brought.[1] As a result the party resolved to struggle for territorial autonomy for the West Ukrainian lands within the Polish state and held that the achievement of this demand could form the basis for the normalization of Polish-Ukrainian relations. Strong pressure for the adoption of this moderate policy was exerted by the leaders of the extensive Ukrainian co-operative movement, which stood to suffer most from political intransigence. The increasingly repressive national policy being pursued at this time in the Soviet Ukraine also exerted a moderating influence. In March 1932 the U.N.D.O. attacked Soviet 'terror', while in August 1933 the Greek Catholic Episcopate issued a pastoral letter entitled 'The Ukraine in the Arms of Death'.[2] The O.U.N., too, shared in this mood, and in October 1933 one of its members killed an official in the Soviet Consulate in Lwów in an attempt to assassinate the Consul. The Polish-Russian and Polish-German *rapprochements* of these years also dictated a more moderate policy, diminishing as they did the prospect of help from outside.

On the Polish side, too, there seemed to be a greater willingness to compromise. A government-sponsored 'Polish-Ukrainian Bulletin' (*Biuletyn Polsko-Ukraiński*) was founded in Warsaw in December 1933, and Prime Minister Jędrzejewicz's speech in the Budget Committee of the Sejm in January 1934 also sounded a new note.[3] He affirmed his strong sympathies for the Ukrainian people, among whom he was born and brought up, and stressed that the difficult situation in East Galicia resulted from faults committed 'by both sides', a concession welcomed by Levitsky. Paradoxically, the movement towards reconciliation was accelerated by the assassination in June 1934 of Bronisław Pieracki, the Minister of the Interior, by a member of the O.U.N.[4] This action was condemned by the U.N.D.O. executive, who sent a delegation to the new Minister of the Interior to inform him of their attitude. Archbishop Szeptycki also strongly attacked the assassination. Some political discussions between the U.N.D.O. and the

---

[1] On this development, see S. Vytvytsky and S. Baran, 'Western Ukraine under Poland', in *Ukraine; a Concise Encyclopedia* (Toronto, 1963), pp. 838–46.
[2] Ibid., p. 844–5.   [3] *Gazeta Polska*, 19 January 1934.
[4] The assassination was an attempt to torpedo the development of the *détente* between Poland and Germany, which had led the German army to instruct the O.U.N. to stop sabotage in East Galicia. See Roos, *Polen und Europa*, pp. 152–3.

Government were initiated, and though nothing concrete was achieved, the basis for the limited agreement reached after Piłsudski's death had been laid.

None of the other minorities played as prominent a role as the Ukrainians in the politics of this period. In White Russia, pro-Soviet sympathies continued to be strong and in January 1931, four deputies of the White Russian Workers and Peasants Parliamentary Club were sentenced to eight years' imprisonment for planning revolutionary acts aimed at dislodging from Poland her north-eastern territories and incorporating them in the Soviet Union.[1] But government repression, coupled with increasing disillusionment with the Soviet Union, as White Russian political and cultural organizations were liquidated and collectivization was ruthlessly pursued, led to political quiescence in the area.

The German minority presented rather different problems. The extremely tense state of relations between Poland and the Reich and the strongly pro-revisionist and anti-Polish mood prevalent in Germany brought this group under suspicion, as did their increasing sympathy for National Socialism. In 1931, for instance, a new *Jung-deutsche Partei* was founded in Bielsko-Biała by Richard Wiesner. This party modelled itself on the Nazis and rapidly extended its influence over the whole country.[2] The older *Volksbund* too, became increasingly nationalistic and sympathetic to German revisionism.

In this situation, disputes were bound to arise, and their bitterness was increased by the heavy-handedness of the Polish authorities and their fear of making any significant concessions to the German minority, lest this should pave the way for the revision of the western frontier. The storm centre remained Upper Silesia, where Governor Grażyński continued his efforts to win support for the Sanacja by outbidding Korfanty's Christian Democracy in Polish chauvinism. He provoked great resentment by his repressive actions against the list of the German minority in the national elections (16 and 23 November 1930) and the elections to the Silesian Sejm (23 November), in which, amidst much administrative chicanery, the German list had been disallowed in one of the three Silesian constituencies. The German government

---

[1] *Gazeta Warszawska*, 15 January 1931.
[2] W. Kuhn, 'Das Deutschtum in Polen und sein Schicksal in Kriegs- und nach-Kriegszeit', *O.E.H.P.*, p. 149.

protested to the League of Nations against Grażyński's actions, while the *Volksbund* submitted a petition in January 1931 complaining about the abuses. The Council of the League criticized Grażyński's activities, and recommended that the Polish authorities take action to restore the confidence of the minority. In September, the Council held that the Polish Government's assurances concerning the actions it had taken were satisfactory.[1] This, however, did not satisfy the German minority and bitterness remained. Moreover, although Zaleski, the Polish Foreign Minister, affirmed that his Government would respect the decision of the International Court at the Hague that parents should decide whether to send their children to German- or Polish-medium schools in Upper Silesia, administrative pressure in this sphere continued and was also much resented. The situation remained extremely sensitive throughout 1932 and 1933 and disputes also arose in Poznania and Pomerania about the implementation of the land reform and the distribution of liquor licences, in which the Germans claimed they were being discriminated against.

Tension mounted still further with the Nazi accession to power and the obvious sympathy with which this even was greeted by the majority of Germans in Poland. Otto Ulitz, the leader of the *Volksbund*, for instance, at a public meeting in Katowice in May 1933, affirmed that his organization regarded the appellation 'Nazi', which Poles were using to characterize the *Volksbund*, as a compliment.[2] The Polish-German Non-aggression Pact of January 1934 brought a superficial alleviation, however, and in July of that year both the *Volksbund* and the *Jung-deutsche Partei* proclaimed their loyalty to the Polish state.[3] But no basic reconciliation took place, little was done to end German grievances, and there was no real acceptance by the German minority, or, indeed, by the German government, of the existing western frontier.

The position of the Jews also deteriorated in this period. This was the result not so much of government policy as of the Depression, which hit Jewish traders and artisans particularly hard, and also virtually brought to an end the possibility of emigration.

---

[1] On this see: Krasuski, *Stosunki polsko-niemieckie, 1926–1932*, pp. 296–309; Rechowicz, *Sejm Śląski, 1922–1939*, pp. 240–2.

[2] Ibid., p. 244.

[3] Ibid., p. 248.

The increasing anti-Semitism of the Right also increased Jewish anxieties. The Government remained hostile to any anti-Jewish activity, taking strong action, as we have seen, against students campaigning for the exclusion of Jews from the universities. The National Democratic proposal for the introduction of a *numerus clausus* in institutions of higher education was condemned in the Sejm Education Committee by Stypiński, the Director of Higher Education, and rejected by the majority of the Committee on 4 March 1932.[1] The Government also refused to give way to the frequent demands of the right to end the 'privileged' position of the Jews. Pieracki, the Minister of the Interior, stated in parliament that

the ethnic Polish group enjoys in the State, by the very nature of things, the greatest privilege, that is the privilege of being in a majority. The State is thus *eo ipso* the most important organ of the Polish *raison d'état*. This is why every privilege can derive only from the service rendered to the state by any given individual and not at all from the fact that he belongs to this or that ethnic group.[2]

The demands of the Right for action against the Jews were lent strength by Hitler's conquest of power and the ease with which he was able to take action against German Jewry. The violent outbursts of anti-Semitism in Germany after January 1933 were widely reported in the Polish press and even led to a number of attempts to emulate them. It was this which induced the Government to ban the O.W.P. on 28 March 1933. This did not, however, end the agitation. The Polish abrogation of the Minorities Treaty even encouraged *Gazeta Warszawska* to ask whether Beck had gone far enough. Referring to the issue of the reform of the constitution, it went on:

There exists at present in Poland a current of opinion, growing ever stronger, which demands that by this reform, the Jewish population be deprived of its political rights and that, while retaining a certain liberty in running its own affairs, should not be able to intervene, by its votes and influence in general questions, in Polish questions.

This 'current' was to increase greatly in strength after Pił- sudski's death.

[1] *Gazeta Polska*, 9 March 1932.
[2] Ibid., 8 September 1932.

FOREIGN POLICY

The years after 1930 saw important new departures in foreign policy. The period of relative international calm which, as Piłsudski had told Beck shortly after the coup, would mean that Poland would not need to take any major steps in foreign affairs for 'five years at least', was coming to an end. The negotiations to achieve general disarmament were having little success, the League was declining in prestige, while the threat of political upheaval in Germany, with the prospect of a more aggressive pursuit of revisionist aims, was increasing. To Poland, a particularly dangerous feature of the situation was the evident weakness of France, more and more concerned to take no major initiative without English approval. Moreover, influential circles in France and Britain were prepared to appease Germany by frontier modifications at Poland's expense. At the same time, the pressure on Poland's eastern frontier was considerably lightened by the internal difficulties caused in the Soviet Union by the introduction of collectivization and the first Five-Year Plan, and by the Japanese invasion of Manchuria in September 1931.

Piłsudski too, having settled the internal political conflict, felt that the time was right for the country to pursue a more active foreign policy. As instrument of this 'new course', he chose the somewhat enigmatic figure of Józef Beck, who had been an Intelligence Officer in the P.O.W. and after a career in the Army in independent Poland, had been Piłsudski's *chef de cabinet* in the Ministry of War between the coup and August 1930. He then became a member of the Cabinet as a Secretary of State and had been one of those principally responsible for the implementation of the hard line in the conflict with parliament. In December 1930 he was made Secretary of State in the Foreign Ministry, and in November 1932 took over the office of Foreign Minister from Zaleski, a position he held until the collapse of the Polish state. Beck, ambitious, arrogant, intelligent, but often devious, stamped his mark strongly on Polish policy, particularly after 1935 when he continued rigidly and somewhat unimaginatively to implement the 'guidelines' laid down by the Marshal. These 'guidelines' marked an important break with the policy pursued between 1926 and 1930, which, under the influence of Zaleski, had still emphasized the pre-eminence of the alliance with France and Polish obligations to the League. From 1930 on, the major factor in Polish policy was to be a reliance on the country's own strength, followed by the establishment of good relations with its two neighbours 'built on the basis of strict mutuality'.[1] The country's next concern was to be the achievement of 'close co-operation with the states of the geopolitical region in which Poland lies'. Only after this came 'alliance as a coefficient of security'. Piłsudski had strong reservations about how far France would fulfil her treaty obligations to Poland and the extent to which these obligations had been modified by the Locarno agreements. The victory of the Left in the French elections of 1932 had increased the Marshal's scepticism.

The general direction of the new policy was sketched in more detail at a meeting between Beck and Piłsudski at the end of 1931.[2] Here it was agreed that 'the foundations of European politics were becoming increasingly weak. 'This', commented Beck,

imposed a greater vigilance and obliged Poland to adopt a more indi-vidualistic attitude, since one could rely less and less on collective security; but this could also give us the opportunity to settle a number of 'unsolved problems'. On the Marshal's demand, I classed these in four groups: Danzig, the minorities treaty, Lithuania, and the Cieszyn area.

Piłsudski agreed with this general analysis, and it was decided that strong measures should be taken if Poland's rights were further restricted in Danzig, the minorities treaty should eventually be denounced by a *fait accompli*, while secret negotiations with Lithuania should be begun. As regards Cieszyn, the Marshal held that it could not be acquired until the dissolution of Czecho-slovakia, which he regarded as inevitable, but which Polish policy should not aim at accelerating.

The first major change in policy came in Polish-Soviet rela-tions.[3] These had improved somewhat in 1928 and early 1929 with the signing of the Litvinov Protocol, but had deteriorated sharply in the second half of 1929. By the spring and summer of 1930, tension was so high that Zaleski was forced in an official statement

---

[1] This account follows that of one of Piłsudski's close adherents, J. Łukasiewicz, *Polska jest mocarstwem* (Warsaw, 1939), p. 23.

[2] Beck, *Dernier Rapport*, pp. 8–10.

[3] On this, see B. Budurowycz, *Polish-Soviet Relations, 1932–1939* (New York and London, 1963), pp. 3–50.

to deny rumours of an impending Russo-Polish war.[1] But from early 1931 relations again improved. The Soviet Union began negotiations with France in May, Russian relations with Weimar cooled, and Japanese aggression in Manchuria compelled a redeployment of Soviet forces in the Far East. Negotiations to bring about a non-aggression treaty between Poland and the Soviet Union began in August 1931 and led to the initialling of a pact on 25 January 1932, which was finally ratified by both sides the following July. The two governments promised to 'refrain from taking any aggressive action against, or invading the territory of, the other party either alone or in conjunction with other powers'.[2] In addition each bound itself to remain neutral if the other became a victim of aggression and undertook not to take part in any agreement directed against the other party. These were both significant concessions by the Soviet Union and marked a notable movement away from the Rapallo policy of co-operation with Germany against Poland.

Though each side remained sceptical of the other's intentions, a real improvement in relations took place. A mutual exchange of political prisoners was made, cultural links were increased and in May 1933, Piłsudski granted the Soviet ambassador, Antonov-Ovseyenko, the rare privilege of a personal interview. In July 1933 closer links were established when Poland joined Afghanistan, Estonia, Latvia, Persia, Rumania, and Turkey in signing with the Soviet Union a Convention for the Definition of Aggression. Piłsudski, however, did not modify his belief that the Soviet Union constituted the major threat to Poland's independence.[3]

At the same time, Poland was increasingly preoccupied with her relations with Germany, where the political and economic crisis had brought Hitler to power on 30 January 1933 as head of a coalition government of Nazis and German Nationalists. It has been fairly widely accepted that Piłsudski reacted to the Nazi takeover by proposing to the French in March and again in April a preventative war to effect the displacement of Hitler, or to enforce on him acceptance of the disarmament clauses of the Versailles Treaty. It was the failure of the French to respond to

---

[1] Ibid., p. 8. [2] Ibid., p. 16.
[3] As, for instance, he had told Jerzy Potocki, the new Polish ambassador to Turkey in May 1933. Potocki's account of his conversation with the Marshal is reproduced by W. Jędrzejewicz in his article 'Piłsudski i Kemal', *Wiadomości*, 23 May 1954, p. 2.

these advances which, it has been argued, led the Marshal to seek an accommodation with Hitler. However, there seems to be no foundation for these claims; on the contrary, they are an interesting example of the type of rationalization and self-justification indulged in by the epigones of the Marshal.[1] Piłsudski, as we have seen, had tried from the coup itself, and in accordance with his belief that Russia was the more dangerous enemy, to reach some sort of accommodation with Germany. Though some alleviation of tension had been achieved, these attempts had had no significant results because of the universal demand in Germany for the revision of the Polish western frontier. Relations had indeed deteriorated as the political crisis in Germany gave added strength to the nationalist extremists. Tension had centred, as Beck had correctly pointed out, on Polish rights in Danzig. In June 1932 there was a near-collision when Piłsudski sent the Polish destroyer *Wicher* into Danzig harbour, ostensibly to pay a courtesy call on a visiting British squadron, but in fact to enforce Polish rights there.

At the same time, however, Piłsudski was not particularly alarmed by the German political crisis. Indeed, he welcomed it, believing that a protracted period of civil strife would weaken the Reich at a time when Poland, internally consolidated, was growing stronger. He was not worried by the rise of the Nazis—they were 'nothing but windbags'[2]—and anyway they seemed less

---

[1] The question of Piłsudski's alleged 'preventive war' has given rise to an enormous literature of which only the most important items can be mentioned here: H. Roos, 'Die Präventivkriegspläne Piłsudskis von 1933', *Vierteljahrshefte für Zeitgeschichte*, iii (October 1955), 344–63; B. Celovsky, 'Piłsudskis Präventivkrieg gegen das nationalsozialistische Deutschland. Entstehung, Verbreitung and Widerlegung einer Legende', *Die Welt als Geschichte* (1954), Heft I, pp. 53–70; Z. Gąsiorowski, 'Did Piłsudski attempt to initiate a preventive war in 1933?', *Journal of Modern History*, xxvii (June 1955), 135–51; T. Kuźmiński, *Polska, Francja, Niemcy, 1933–35* (Warsaw, 1963), chap. ii, pp. 40–89. Since most of the evidence held to prove that Piłsudski did intend some sort of military action comes in memoirs written by Piłsudski-ites after World War II (see, for instance, Miedziński's articles 'Popioły są jeszcze gorące', *Wiadomości*, 26 October 1952, 9 November 1952), a source of particular significance is the letter written by Count Szembek to Count Raczyński, the Ambassador of the Polish government-in-exile in London on 31 August 1942 *Diariusz i teki Jana Szembeka*, ed. T. Komarnicki (London, 1965), ii. 4–10). Szembek, who as Under-Secretary of State, and a man close to Beck, should have had some wind of possible plans, denies any knowledge whatsoever of a proposed preventative war in March or April 1933.

[2] As he told Colonel d'Arbonneau the French military attaché. Laroche, *La Pologne de Piłsudski*, p. 113.

dangerous and less hostile to Poland than old-style Prussians like von Schleicher. In fact the general development of the German situation seemed to him to favour his policy of achieving a Polish-German *rapprochement*.[1] Already in November 1932 he had sent Count Szembek, one of Beck's most trusted aides, to Berlin to sound the possibility of achieving a *modus vivendi*.

His policy on Hitler's coming to power was thus to enforce Polish rights by a show of strength in Danzig in March 1933, while at the same time refusing to be provoked, and holding out the prospect of the normalization of relations with the Reich. He does not seem ever to have seriously considered a preventative war. For one thing, he knew that France would not be a party to such a scheme. The French had already in December 1932, under British pressure, accepted in principle the German claim to equality of rights as regards armaments, and had eagerly greeted Mussolini's scheme in March 1933 for a European four-power directorate, which would in practice direct German revisionism towards Poland. He was also well aware that Poland was in no position, either militarily or economically, to go to war. Moreover, he had no wish to force out Hitler, of whom he was not particularly apprehensive and who he did not believe could seriously undermine the disarmament clauses of the Versailles Treaty.

Therefore when the Danzig Senate under German pressure withdrew its abrogation of the agreement of 1923 concerning the harbour police which had provoked the Polish reaction in March, Piłsudski began to make soundings through Wysocki, the Polish minister in Berlin, as to whether an accommodation with Germany could be reached. In September 1933, Beck produced a memorandum outlining his attitude to Hitler, a memorandum with which Piłsudski expressed his agreement and which sets out clearly the underlying motivation of Polish policy.[2] Beck maintained that the Nazi régime, aiming as it did at a revolutionary transformation of Germany, would need a period of calm in foreign affairs. He attached great importance to the fact that neither Hitler nor his closest collaborators were Prussian and that

[1] For a useful account of the evolution of Piłsudski's ideas on Nazism, see the article by Józef Lipski, who, as ambassador in Berlin from July 1933, played a key role in implementing the policy of Polish-German *détente*. J. Lipski, 'Przyczynki do polsko-niemieckiej deklaracji o nieagresji', *Bellona* (January–June 1951), pp. 18–37; (July–September 1951), pp. 3–21.

[2] Beck, *Dernier Rapport*, pp. 28–9.

they thus did not share the anti-Polish sentiments of his predecessors. Hitler himself the Foreign Minister saw as primarily interested in obtaining the national unification of all Germans. From all this, he concluded, 'we find ourselves with a unique opportunity to restore our position in the European equilibrium'.[1]

Hitler, too, was not unwilling to respond to these advances. The underlying motive of his foreign policy was always to acquire *Lebensraum* for German settlement in the east and he thought he might persuade the Poles to co-operate with his plans for a partition of Russia. His anti-Bolshevism also predisposed him to abandon the Rapallo policy, while he was an astute enough tactician to realize the advantages which even a temporary accommodation with Poland would bring in weakening the French alliance system and the stability of the Versailles Treaty arrangements.

The Polish-German contacts continued after the German withdrawal from the League of Nations in October 1933 and led to the German-Polish Declaration of 26 January 1934, affirming that the two governments would 'settle directly all questions whatsoever which concern their mutual relations'.[2] If this proved impossible, other peaceful means would be employed, and the use of force was ruled out. Finally, previous international arrangements, and here the Franco-Polish alliance was principally involved, were held not to conflict with the agreement or to be affected by it.

Following the signing of this declaration, Beck went to Moscow in February in order to reassure the Russians that the new agreement had no anti-Soviet content. The principle of 'balance' was thus adhered to, and in consequence the Poles refused to respond to German proposals for a Polish-German alliance directed against the Soviet Union in terms of which Poland was to make territorial cessions to Germany in the west in return for compensation in the Ukraine.[3] The German-Polish Declaration seemed, in fact, to have brought great benefit to Poland. The pressure for the revision of the frontier eased, and German expansion was directed towards Austria, *Anschluss* seeming to Piłsudski to hold no dangers for

[1] Beck, *Dernier Rapport*, p. 29.
[2] Z. Gąsiorowski, 'The German-Polish Nonaggression Pact of 1934', *J.C.E.A.*, xv (April 1955), no. 1, p. 25.
[3] On these, see Roos, *Polen und Europa*, pp. 208–12.

Poland, and also towards Czechoslovakia, whose collapse had long been predicted by the Marshal. The Danzig question ceased to be a sore point, the agitation of the German and, to a lesser extent, the Ukrainian minorities tapered off, and the long-drawn-out economic conflict with the Reich was brought to an end. Poland was now in a position to denounce the Minorities Treaty unilaterally in September 1934. Beck was further able to pursue a strongly anti-Czech policy, with continual demands for the redress of the grievances of the Polish minority in the trans-Olza region of Austrian Silesia.

These gains were, however, somewhat illusory. Although no secret anti-Soviet agreement existed between Poland and Germany, the suspicion that some bargain of this nature had been entered into caused a deterioration in Polish-Soviet relations which, though remaining correct, became rather cool. Relations with France, too, which was not informed in advance of the Polish-German negotiations, became notably more distant. Moreover, though Piłsudski would probably have refused anyway to participate in Barthou's scheme for an Eastern Pact of Guarantee including the Soviet Union, the Polish veto seemed to many in the Quai d'Orsay to imply that there was more to the Polish-German declaration than appeared on the surface. On 3 February 1935, the French Ambassador in Poland, Jules Laroche, told Szembek that 'the idea of the alliance is profoundly shaken'.[1] As France attempted to compensate for the weakening of her Polish ties by closer links with the Soviet Union, culminating in the Franco-Soviet Treaty of Mutual Assistance of 2 May 1935, so correspondingly the Polish-German *entente* became firmer.

The main beneficiary of these developments was Germany. It may be that Piłsudski was right to be sceptical of the French willingness to honour their treaty obligations in Eastern Europe. It may be, too, that his suspicion of the Soviet Union was justified. But Poland in the long run could only lose by any modification of the Versailles settlement which, far more than her own strength, was the main guarantee of her continued existence within the 1921 frontiers. The foreign policy of the Soviet Union in this period was motivated largely by her internal situation, the Far-Eastern conflict, and the threat which Nazi Germany posed to her. Her move away from the revisionist and towards the *status*

---

[1] *Diariusz i teki Jana Szembeka* i. 227.

quo powers thus seems to have had a real basis. A policy less
determined to assert Polish independence and more bent on
co-operation with France, Czechoslovakia, and Russia to maintain
the frontiers and disarmament provisions of the Versailles settlement would therefore seem, from today's perspective, to have
been more to Poland's advantage. It is true that in 1933 German
rearmament posed no threat to Poland. But when it began to
gather momentum in 1934, Franco-Polish suspicion was too great
to make possible effective co-operation against it. Moreover,
Piłsudski, dying of cancer, was in no position to take bold initiatives, while Beck was prepared to go much further than the
Marshal to maintain good relations with Germany and to attribute
benevolent intentions to Hitler.

THE NEW CONSTITUTION

As Piłsudski's increasing ill health became more and more
apparent to his entourage, the need for enacting a new constitution
which would give lasting form to his ideas on political organization, and which would also ensure the maintenance of power by
the Sanacja after his death, became more urgent. The question of
constitutional revision had lain virtually dormant since the elections of November 1930 had failed to give the B.B.W.R. the two-
thirds majority necessary for modification. On 2 February 1931,
the 1929 constitutional proposals of the Bloc were presented to
the Sejm and discussion of them was resumed in the Constitutional
Committee on 5 March. These discussions dragged on with little
result, and it was only on 26 January 1934 that the conclusions
of the Committee were submitted to the Sejm. Now, however,
desperate to ensure their continuance in power after the Marshal's
death, the leading members of the Sanacja forced the adoption of
a new constitution by a manœuvre that was without doubt illegal.

When the conclusions of the Constitutional Committee were
finally submitted to the Sejm, the Opposition groups, declaring
that they would give the Government no help in modifying the
constitution, boycotted the debate.[1] The 63 'constitutional theses'
submitted by the Committee were, however, arranged in such
a way that if all were accepted individually, they would form

---

[1] For this session, see *S.S.S.R.*, 26 January 1934, cols. 3–56.

a new constitution. The B.B.W.R., at the instigation of Car and over the strong protests of Stroński, the sole remaining representative of the Opposition, thus rapidly voted in the new constitution article by article, obtaining the necessary two-thirds majority before the Opposition Deputies could return. This procedure certainly contravened the provision of the 1921 constitution (Article 125) that two weeks' notice had to be given for the presentation of constitutional amendments.

Piłsudski, who may not have been consulted in advance,[1] seems to have been somewhat unhappy about this procedure. On 31 January, he told Sławek and Świtalski that he was not in principle opposed to what they had done but that 'it was not healthy that a Constitutional Law should be adopted by a trick or a joke.'[2] He insisted that the constitution should be made more legitimate by detailed discussion and modification in the Senate. Thus more than a year went by before the new constitution obtained a two-thirds majority in the Senate on 16 January 1935, and it was only finally approved by the Sejm on 23 March. Since on this occasion it was only a question of voting on the Senate changes, it was held that a majority of eleven-twentieths (Article 35) was sufficient.

The new constitution was intended to give lasting form to the principles of government for which Piłsudski had fought for so long, and which he believed he had implemented since the coup.[3] The key position was held by the President, who was to exercise those functions of supervision and control over the whole governmental apparatus which had in fact been performed by Piłsudski since 1926. 'The President of the Republic,' stated Article 11, 'being the highest authority in the State, co-ordinates the activity of the superior organs of the State.'[4] He was to appoint the Prime Minister, and, on the latter's advice, the other ministers. He was also empowered to appoint, without the counter-signature of the Prime Minister, the President of the Supreme Court, the President of the Main Auditing Office, the General Inspector of the Armed

---

[1] Singer states that Prystor was given the task of obtaining Piłsudski's approval by telephone after the session had started. Singer, *Od Witosa do Sławka*, p. 188.

[2] A.S.S., 31 stycznia 1934 r. godz 17.30. Konferencja u Komendanta w składzie: Sławek i ja.

[3] For the constitution, see *Sejm Rzeczypospolitej Polskiej. Kadencja IV*, Druk no. 2, 'Ustawa Konstytucyjna z dnia 23.IV.1935 r.' (Warsaw, n.d.).

[4] Ibid., p. 4.

Forces, the Supreme Commander, the members of the Tribunal of State, and one-third of the members of the Senate. He could, on his own initiative, dissolve parliament, he was the highest military authority, and represented the state in its dealings with foreign powers. He could not be held personally responsible for his official acts.[1]

The President was to be elected for seven years by universal suffrage from two candidates. Of these one was to be nominated by the retiring President (who in time of war could nominate his own successor), the other by an Electoral Assembly composed of the Marshals of the Sejm and Senate, the Prime Minister, the President of the Supreme Court, the General Inspector of the Armed Forces, and seventy-five electors, two-thirds of whom would be chosen by the Sejm and one-third by the Senate. If the outgoing President did not present a nominee, the candidate of the Electoral Assembly was held to be elected.[2]

The Government, composed of the Prime Minister and his Cabinet, was to 'direct those affairs of the State which do not fall to the competence of the other organs of authority'.[3] Its members were politically responsible to the President, who could demand their resignation at any time. The Sejm could pass a vote of no confidence in the Government or in an individual minister, but such a proposal could not be voted on at the same session at which it was presented, and had subsequently to be approved by the Senate. If it was adopted, the President had to dismiss the Government or the minister concerned, or dissolve parliament.[4]

The functions of legislation were to be exercised by the Sejm and Senate, although the number of matters which could be dealt with by decree was increased. The right of initiating legislation was restricted to the Government and the Sejm. A law rejected by the Senate required a three-fifths majority in the Sejm to be passed. The President possessed a suspensive veto for one month.[5]

The Sejm deputies were to be elected by universal, secret, equal, and direct (though not proportional) suffrage. The Sejm was to sit for five years, but could be dissolved before that date by the President.[6] Every year it was to hold an ordinary session,

---

[1] 'Ustawa Konst. z dnia 23.IV.1935 r.', Articles 12–15, pp. 4–6.
[2] Ibid., Article 16, pp. 6–7.   [3] Ibid., Article 25, pp. 10–11.
[4] Ibid., Articles 25, 26, 28, 29, pp. 11–13.
[5] Ibid., Articles 49–57, pp. 22–5.   [6] Ibid., Article 32, p. 14.

lasting four months, to vote on the budget. If the Sejm did not adopt a budget, the Government's proposal automatically gained the force of law.[1] Half the members of the Sejm could demand an extraordinary session, but this could only discuss the matters listed in the presidential decree convoking it. The scope of parliamentary immunity was greatly narrowed.[2]

The Senate was to be two-thirds elected and one-third nominated by the President. The method of election was to be established subsequently.[3]

The military aspects of the constitution also embodied Piłsudski's long-fought-for principles. The President was empowered to issue decrees dealing with the organization of the Supreme Command, and was given the right to nominate the Supreme Commander, who had full power over the Army and was responsible to the President.[4]

This constitution was the means by which the Marshal 'sought to ensure the permanence of his life's work'.[5] In theory, its attempt to combine popular control with firm government seemed a reasonable answer to the problems of a country like Poland, lacking political experience and facing difficult social and economic problems. But in practice, after Piłsudski's death, his successors were concerned far more to exploit the wide powers which the constitution gave to the Government to maintain themselves in power. They thus exposed the insignificance of the safeguards supposedly enshrined in the new fundamental law.

The enactment of the constitution did not long precede Piłsudski's death. From the end of 1934, his health deteriorated visibly, and on 23 April 1935 Professor Wenkebach, brought to Warsaw from Vienna, diagnosed incurable cancer of the liver and stomach. His condition worsened rapidly and on 12 May, the tenth anniversary of the coup, he died. His body was buried in the crypt of Wawel Cathedral in Cracow where lay the Polish kings, while his heart was buried with the body of his mother in Wilno. The country was torn by a deep feeling of grief and anguish. The régime had become increasingly alienated from public opinion, but Piłsudski himself had been widely respected

[1] Ibid., Articles 58–60, pp. 25–8.
[2] Ibid., Articles 36, 41, pp. 16, 17–18.
[3] Ibid., Article 47, p. 21.
[4] Ibid., Article 63, pp. 28–9.
[5] Roos, *A History of Modern Poland*, p. 141.

as honest, far-seeing, and noble. The shock of his death was the greater, since all rumours of his illness had been fiercely denied by his entourage. It remained to be seen how far he had schooled his 'boys' to take over from him, and how far he had, as he believed, laid the foundations for the secure political evolution of Poland.

IX

POLAND WITHOUT PIŁSUDSKI
POLITICAL DEVELOPMENTS 1935–1939

> Until now there has existed an arbiter, or rather a super-
> arbiter, not foreseen in the constitution, kept in office by a
> legend stronger than all those clauses in the constitution
> which favour the Government. The legend gave him the
> right to superiority. But legends cannot be bequeathed . . .
> When our rulers again began to stir themselves, when
> they shake off the numbness caused by the funeral, the eyes
> of society will turn towards them and will watch attentively
> and critically. The mythical secret power hidden in the
> Belvedere has ceased to exist. The period of economic crisis,
> of unresolved social and national problems, of political
> activity within the framework of the new constitution, of
> the increasingly bitter clash of opinions, is beginning. No
> factor as strong as the legend will be here to settle disputes
> with a word. The time of trial is beginning.
>
> Bernard Singer, *Nasz Przegląd*, 21 May 1936

THE death of Piłsudski proved extremely disruptive to the coher-
ence of the Sanacja. Though the Marshal, in his later years, had
played little actual part in the running of the government, his mere
presence had provided an ultimate authority which could settle all
disputes over the direction of policy and which could unite the
somewhat disparate elements which made up his régime. After his
death, there was no one among his successors who could assume
his authority and exercise his control. As a result, from 1935 the
Government was riven by deep divisions of personality and
policy, and a decisive confrontation was prevented only by the
increasingly threatening nature of the external situation. Indeed
the growing insecurity of Poland's international position came
more and more to dominate politics. In 1932 Poland, with an army
of 266,000 men, had stood in a fairly satisfactory position in relation to Germany, whose military force was limited to 100,000 men
and to the Soviet Union whose 562,000-strong army was to a
considerable extent deployed in the Far East. But by 1936, this

situation had undergone a radical transformation. Germany's re-armament was successfully under way, and as early as autumn 1935, she could put into the field an army of at least 450,000 men. Russia's armed strength, too, grew in this period to something approaching a million men. Although some attempts were made between 1935 and 1939 to modernize the Polish Army,[1] the dis-crepancy in numbers remained shattering and it proved a slow and difficult task to overcome the negative effects of Piłsudski's last years on the organization of the fighting forces.

The increasingly perilous basis of Polish independence thus contributed, as the period advanced, to a heightened nationalism, which manifested itself primarily in a growing anti-Semitism and in the Government's heavy-handedness in dealing with the other national minorities. It led too to a softening of internal political antagonisms, though the Sanacja never succeeded in reaching a compromise with either the Right or the Left Opposition. Poland's weakness in relation to her neighbours was further highlighted by her slow recovery from the economic crisis. Unemployment rose, reaching 466,000 in 1936,[2] and there was a great increase in work-ing-class militancy and in the number of strikes. However, from mid-1936, after Kwiatkowski's break with the extreme *laisser-faire* policies which had been pursued throughout the Depression, the situation improved somewhat. Yet by 1939, though something had been achieved, unemployment remained at an extremely high level, and the desperate condition of the countryside continued largely unrelieved. Finally, as the period wore on, the bankruptcy of Beck's rigid application of the Piłsudski-ite formula that Poland should pursue a policy of 'balance' between her two powerful neighbours became ever more evident. Its abandonment, brought about by the growing aggressiveness of Nazi Germany, came too late to save the country's independence.

THE STRUGGLE OVER THE SUCCESSION

Sławek, in a speech to the Parliamentary Club of the B.B.W.R. on 5 July 1935, told his audience that the Marshal's death meant that new political methods would have to be adopted in Poland. 'Attempts to find another man who, by his greatness, could possess such superior moral authority will not be successful.' Between 1926

---

[1] See below, pp. 483–93.   [2] *M.R.S.* (1937), Table XXV, p. 249.

and 1935, Piłsudski had constituted the ultimate authority for his followers. His role was to be replaced by the new constitution. 'The law, as the highest authority, is to govern us and, within the framework of the law, he whom the law appoints.'[1]

However Sławek's hopes were not fulfilled, and the new constitution proved a disappointment in operation. In the first place, there was no-one among the Piłsudski-ites who could effectively exercise the vast powers it granted to the President. Piłsudski had left no written political testament but he had given a number of verbal instructions to his entourage. On a number of occasions he had specified that Sławek, his closest and perhaps his only confidant, was to succeed Mościcki as soon as the new constitution had been adopted.[2] This was not a happy choice. Sławek, the soul of honour and a man of irreproachable character and decency, 'the epitome of the romantic fighter for independence in its finest form, that deriving from the Eastern Kresy'[3] was politically naïve and quite unable to assume the heavy responsibilities of the Presidency. Used to implementing blindly the instructions of the Commander, he was left devastated by his idol's death and showed himself almost incapable of action in the tense period after May 1935. Prystor, who was deputed by the inner group of 'colonels' to try and galvanize Sławek at this period, had the impression that even now 'Walery at a moment's notice would reach for the telephone to ask the Commander for an appointment.'[4]

Sławek's obvious lack of political awareness required to deal with the pressing difficulties which faced both the country and the Government soon became clear to a number of the leading Piłsudski-ites. Mościcki, who in the period immediately after Piłsudski's death would have resigned the Presidency under the slightest pressure, thus became increasingly unwilling to relinquish his office. As early as 6 August he gave Konrad Wrzos, a pro-Government journalist, an evasive answer when asked if he would resign before the end of his term. 'I will always do what is necessary for the State—I will take steps in future with this criterion solely in mind.'[5]

Mościcki's decision to refuse to give way to Sławek was partly dictated by his own belief that Sławek had neither the ability nor

[1] Quoted in Póbog-Malinowski, *Najnowsza historia*, ii. 773.
[2] Ibid., pp. 769–70.   [3] Ibid., p. 770.   [4] Ibid., p. 774.
[5] *Ilustrowany Kurjer Codzienny*, 7 August 1935.

the force of character to hold the Presidency successfully. Surprisingly, Mościcki, whose tenure of the Presidency during Piłsudski's lifetime had been characterized by his almost mindless compliance with the demands of the Marshal, emerged after 1935 as a politician of some intelligence and subtlety. He was further impelled to continue in office by the prompting of some of his associates, notably Eugeniusz Kwiatkowski and Wojciech Stpiczyński. Kwiatkowski was a close friend of Mościcki's and had been appointed by him as technical director of the great chemical works at Chorzów in 1922. It was under the President's aegis that he had entered Bartel's Cabinet as Minister of Trade and Industry, a position he had held until May 1930 and in which he had shown considerable ability. He had lost his position as a result of a clash with Piłsudski, who distrusted his economic ideas and his links with the Opposition. Kwiatkowski knew that Sławek, true to the directives of the Marshal, would never allow him to hold Cabinet office, and saw in Mościcki's continued hold of the Presidency his only real hope of again entering the Government.

Stpiczyński, an able but emotional and demagogic Piłsudski-ite journalist, who between 1924 and 1929 had edited *Głos Prawdy*, also had personal reasons for opposing Sławek, who together with Koc had been responsible for his losing his post when *Głos Prawdy* was transformed into *Gazeta Polska*. A consumptive, he was also extremely ambitious, and his feeling towards Sławek, whom he regarded as a potentially disastrous President, bordered on hatred. In a long talk with Mościcki at the President's summer residence in Spała he used all the force of his oratory to persuade him not to resign. It was shortly after this conversation that Mościcki sought the advice of a number of leading lawyers, who told him there were no legal reasons why he should give up office.[1]

Faced with this new situation, the inner circle of Piłsudski-ites, the 'colonels' Prystor, Janusz Jędrzejewicz, Beck, and Miedziński, decided that steps should at once be taken to force Mościcki to resign. However Miedziński's suggestion that a number of the leading personalities should approach the President individually and demand his resignation in accordance with Piłsudski's wishes was rejected by Sławek on the grounds that he regarded such pres-

---

[1] Pobóg-Malinowski, *Najnowsza historia*, ii. 776–7. Pobóg-Malinowski's account of events immediately following the Marshal's death, though strongly sympathetic to Sławek and hostile to Kwiatkowski, is, on the whole reliable.

sure on the Head of State as 'impermissible'.[1] Sławek indeed was hardly the man to force Mościcki's resignation. Asked some two years later by Stanisław Mackiewicz, the conservative journalist, why he had not exerted greater pressure to force the President to withdraw, he replied, 'How could I do it! You know that then I would have had to take his place.'[2] Yet this was the man Piłsudski had chosen as his successor.

Piłsudski's instructions were more successfully followed in relation to the distribution of the senior posts in the Army. On the night of the Marshal's death, the President, acting with the approval of the Cabinet, appointed to the Ministry of War General Tadeusz Kasprzycki, who had been Deputy Minister of War since 1934. To the more important post of General Inspector of Armed Forces, who was to be the Commander-in-Chief in wartime and who also enjoyed wide powers in peacetime, he appointed General Edward Rydz-Śmigły whom Piłsudski had long marked for this office.[3] Rydz-Śmigły had been one of Piłsudski's closest military collaborators and had been a leader of the legionary movement in Galicia before World War I. From 1914 to 1917, he was a senior officer in the legions and in 1917 and 1918, after Piłsudski's imprisonment in Magdeburg, Commanding Officer of the P.O.W. In the Popular Government set up under Moraczewski in Lublin in November 1918, he accepted the position of Minister of Defence, an initiative which was later criticized by the Marshal as committing the Piłsudski-ites to support the Moraczewski Government. Between 1919 and 1921 he held various senior posts in the Army including that of Commander of the Third Army in the Polish-Soviet war. From 1921 he was an Army Inspector, and thus one of the generals who were to be divisional commanders in wartime. He was not one of the inner circle of Piłsudski-ites and had taken no part either in the preparation of the coup or in any of the major political decisions between May 1926 and 1935.

In designating Rydz to succeed him, Piłsudski seems to have been moved principally by his desire to keep the Army out of politics. Rydz, though a fairly competent soldier, had little gift for

---

[1] Ibid., p. 777.
[2] Mackiewicz, op. cit., p. 275.
[3] Pobóg-Mallnowski, *Najnowsza historia*, ii. 766–9; Mackiewicz, op. cit., p. 274.

politics and had never been entrusted with political duties by the Marshal. Piłsudski thus passed over the much more able and imaginative General Kazimierz Sosnkowski, who had been his Chief of Staff between 1914 and 1916 and who had been Minister of War between 1920 and 1923 and again in 1924. As we have seen, Sosnkowski was the general commanding the Poznań district in 1926, and although extremely close to the Marshal, had not been informed in advance of his plans for an armed demonstration. Faced with the agonizing dilemma of whether to support Piłsudski or not on 12 May, he seems to have attempted suicide, and though he remained a general, becoming an Army Inspector in 1929, he was never again fully trusted by the Marshal. Piłsudski's decision to pass over Sosnkowski in favour of Rydz-Śmigły may have been dictated by the former's failure to support him unreservedly during the coup. (Piłsudski's memory for slights was elephantine.) But it seems more likely that he was motivated by his desire to keep Rydz out of political life,[1] and his belief that Sosnkowski would have an important role to play in politics. According to Pobóg-Malinowski, he had already once designated Sosnkowski in early 1933 as the head of a Government of National Unity in the case of a war with Germany.[2]

Piłsudski's choice did not go unchallenged on the night of 12 May. A number of the 'colonels', uneasy about Rydz's ability, wanted Sosnkowski to be appointed as General Inspector. However, the opinion of Sławek, who was unwilling to flout the clearly expressed view of the Marshal although he was personally on bad terms with Rydz and should have seen in him a potential rival for power, prevailed and Rydz was appointed.[3] It was a disastrous choice. Rydz would have made an able, if not highly imaginative, divisional commander, but he was neither intellectually nor temperamentally fitted to hold the post of Supreme Commander. Moreover, the powers of the General Inspector were so large and the prestige of the Army so great, that he was bound, in spite of Piłsudski's belief that by his reorganization of the High Command he had taken the Army out of politics, to play a large political role. For this he was quite unsuitable. Contemporary observers are

---

[1] According to Mackiewicz, op. cit., p. 274, there was talk in 1935 of sending Rydz to political 'Siberia' by making him General Inspector.

[2] Pobóg-Malinowski, *Najnowsza historia*, ii. 769.

[3] Mackiewicz, op. cit., p. 274.

unanimous about him. Mackiewicz, writing in exile in London in 1941 after the fall of Poland, commented:

After everything that has happened and which can now no longer be disputed, one must ask in what strange way could this man, without intelligence, without character, small and petty, vacant and empty, impose himself for so long. It must be attributed to favourable internal conditions, a sympathetic appearance, an oratorical gift, the ability to speak in fine flowing phrases, a good seat on a horse, his friendly manner towards people, and his habit of never expressing an opinion on matters which surpassed his intelligence.[1]

Leon Noël, the last French ambassador in Poland before the war described him as follows:

Honest, upright and at the same time not lacking in *finesse*, cultivated, possessing, for example, a deep knowledge of the Napoleonic era, he was far from being without merits, but Pilsudski's favour and events laid upon him responsibilities which he certainly did not seek and for which he was not prepared.[2]

Not only was there no one among the Pilsudski-ites who could take over the role of the Marshal and thus make the new constitution function effectively, but its residual parliamentarianism was soon undermined. The first inroads were made by the new electoral laws for the Sejm and Senate which came into force on 8 July 1935 and which made virtually impossible a free selection of candidates and increased enormously the control the Government could exercise over an election. In the law for the Lower House,[3] proportional representation was abandoned, and the country was divided into 104 two-member constituencies. Candidates had to be nominated by a special assembly in each constituency composed of local officials and representatives of elected local government bodies, economic organizations, such as chambers of commerce, industry and agriculture, organizations of lawyers, doctors, teachers and university professors, and other professional associations. In addition any group of 500 persons was entitled to one representative on the assembly. If only four candidates were presented by the assembly, all could stand in the election. If more than four

---

[1] Ibid., p. 278.
[2] L. Noël, *L'Agression allemande contre la Pologne* (Paris, 1946), p. 26.
[3] *Dz.U.R.P.* (1935), no. 47, pp. 795–810.

were nominated, only those who obtained more than one-quarter of the votes of the assembly in a single ballot (each member having the right to vote for four persons) could stand. As will be obvious, the scope for electoral manipulation by the Government was enormous.

Similar élitist conceptions were embodied in the electoral law for the Senate.[1] The membership of the upper house was reduced to 96. One-third of this was to be appointed by the President. The remaining two-thirds were to be chosen by Provincial Electoral Councils. These in turn, were elected by those who had received certain decorations, those who possessed secondary school diplomas, by elected members on local government bodies, persons holding elective office in local economic organizations, presidents of professional organizations, and persons holding high office in the administration of any of these bodies.

The way in which this decisive break with liberal parliamentarianism was adopted remains somewhat obscure. The laws were first laid before parliament on 7 May before the Marshal's death and it is impossible to know how far they reflected his own views.[2] Their main authors seem to have been Sławek, Bohdan Podoski, a leading member of the B.B.W.R. and one of the main architects of the 1935 constitution, Eugeniusz Kozłowski, Premier from May 1934 to March 1935, and perhaps Stanisław Car, the old expert at twisting and bending laws to suit the purposes of the Sanacja.[3] To Podoski and Kozłowski the constitution was merely a clever trick to maintain the régime in office, in the face of the waning of its support caused by the death of Piłsudski. Sławek however, had more elevated goals. He saw the law as the culminating point of the Marshal's attempts to destroy party dominance of Polish political life. It was intended to make possible 'a closer, more direct link between the Sejm and society', and would thus 'take away from the party chiefs their monopoly in putting up

[1] *Dz.U.R.P.* (1935), no. 47, pp. 810–15.

[2] According to Singer, Kozłowski claimed that Piłsudski had approved the new law, telling him, 'You have found the eye of a needle. Now you must organize elections which can be honest.' (Singer, *Od Witosa do Sławka*, p. 252.) But this is merely contemporary gossip.

[3] Ibid., pp. 239–41, 251–3. Jędruszczak, claims that Car was one of the law's inventors. (T. Jędruszczak, *Piłsudczycy bez Piłsudskiego* (Warsaw, 1963), p. 58). But Świtalski, in his private notes, states that Car was opposed to the law and merely implemented unwillingly Sławek's instructions (A.S.S., Dnia 19 listopada 1935. Rozmowa z Carem).

candidates'.[1] Sławek's political *naïveté* was such that he certainly believed these assertions.

The new law did not go unchallenged. It was of course vigorously attacked by the parties of the Opposition, who claimed that they would boycott any election held under the new system. But it also aroused a fair amount of criticism from members of the B.B.W.R. in the Constitutional Committees of the Sejm and the Senate. In the latter, both Senator Radziwiłł, perhaps the leading conservative, and Senator Ewert claimed that its introduction would be disastrous.[2] Jędrzej Moraczewski, head of the Government-sponsored Union of Trade Unions (Z.Z.Z.) also condemned the law,[3] while Świtalski, writing on 19 November 1935, speculated that his refusal to make public his criticisms of it at its introduction, dictated by an unwillingness to reveal the divisions with the Sanacja, had been a grave error.[4]

The first elections under the new system were held on 8 September. All the Opposition parties with the exception of a group from the Peasant Party, led by Malinowski, Róg, Smoła, and Woźnicki, all former members of the Liberation, observed the boycott. The Government did however manage to reach arrangements with the Ukrainians, Jews, Germans, and some White Russian groups so that they could nominate their own candidates. The boycott proved, if not quite as successful as the Opposition had hoped, a decisive rebuff for the Government, a 'catastrophe', according to Świtalski.[5] 'Society has rejected the electoral law at its fourth reading', commented Singer, pungent as ever.[6] According to the official figures, of the 16,282,347 people entitled to vote, 7,575,681 or 46·5 per cent had done so.[7] This compared with 78·3 per cent in 1928 and 74·8 per cent in 1930. The Government claimed this was a victory, since the proportion of votes cast for the B.B.W.R. had risen from 43·1 per cent in 1928 to 46·5 per cent. But this was merely a forlorn attempt to explain away the widespread rejection of the Sanacja. It is difficult to subject the

[1] Pobóg-Malinowski, *Najnowsza historia*, ii. 777.
[2] Singer, *Od Witosa do Sławka*, pp. 239–41.
[3] J. Żarnowski, 'Lewica sanacyjna w latach 1935–1939', *Przegląd Historyczny* (1958), no. 4, pp. 715–16.
[4] A.S.S., Dnia 19 listopada 1935 r. Rozmowa z samym sobą.
[5] A.S.S., Rozmowa z Prezydentem. Dnia 30-go września 1935 r.
[6] Singer, *Od Witosa do Sławka*, p. 266.
[7] *Gazeta Polska*, 10 September 1935.

election to detailed analysis, since the Government never brought out an official account of the results such as had been published by the G.U.S. after earlier elections. Indeed, *Kurjer Poznański* claimed that this was because the results were much worse than those suggested by the initially published figures.[1] It is certainly true that the figure of 46·5 per cent is misleading. In the first place, the Government could not claim the votes cast for the eleven U.N.D.O. and four Jewish deputies or for the unsuccessful Germans and White Russians. Those who cast blank votes were reckoned with those who voted. Their number was significant in Silesia, where they made up nearly 30 per cent of the voters. In addition there was a fair amount of administrative pressure, particularly in Eastern Poland. Moreover, as *Wieczór Warszawski*, a pro-Government newspaper, pointed out, there was something curious about the figures. According to the official press agency P.A.T., 7,576,000 people had voted. Each elector had two votes; yet if one added up the number of votes cast and divided it by two one obtained the figure of 5,674,000. It is true that some people could have cast one vote only, but the discrepancy, nearly 2 million, is striking.[2] Some indication of the country's mood can be gleaned from the other figures given by the P.A.T.[3] These revealed that the lowest proportion of votes was cast in the capital (23 per cent). Western and Central Poland also showed relatively low participation. In Poznania, 23 per cent voted, in Pomerania 30 per cent, in the Lodz province 27 per cent, in the Kielce province 29 per cent, and in the Warsaw province 36 per cent. Only in the eastern provinces, where administrative pressure was greatest, was the proportion high, as in Polesia (59 per cent) or the Nowogródek province (56 per cent). East Galicia, where the U.N.D.O. was given a virtual monopoly of seats, also showed a high percentage of voting. But even here the proportion was much below 1928 and 1930. In the Tarnopol province, where the percentage of voters was highest, the figure was only 57 per cent.

The disastrous results of the election, 'the plebiscite which the Government had organized against itself',[4] made still deeper the

[1] 1 January 1936.
[2] *Wieczór Warszawski*, 10 September 1935.
[3] *ABC*, 12 September 193~
[4] As Stanisław Kot wrote: o Paderewski on 3 November 1935. Quoted in Jędruszczak, op. cit., p. 29.

political divisions within the Sanacja. Mościcki became more than ever convinced that Sławek's political judgement was faulty and he was determined not to give up office when the political scene was, as he described it, 'threatening'.[1] He also seems to have convinced himself that when Piłsudski decided that Sławek should be President, he did not envisage his own imminent death, and that he had intended to exercise close control over Sławek's actions. Thus, when Sławek tried once again, shortly after the convening of parliament at the beginning of October, to induce the President to resign, Mościcki refused, and in spite of a bitter interchange, would not give way.[2]

The dispute soon widened in scope. Mościcki was convinced, perhaps under Kwiatkowski's influence, that the over-riding reason for the political malaise was the persistence of the economic crisis in Poland. In order to bring it to an end, he was prepared to break with the rigidly *laisser-faire* policies which had been applied since the beginning of the crisis and to embark on a fairly radical interventionist attempt to revive production. The chief implementer of this new policy was to be Kwiatkowski, who was to be given not only the post of Minister of Trade and Industry, but also that of Deputy Prime Minister, with control over all economic matters. Sławek would not accept this. He shared the economic conservatism as well as the lack of comprehension of economic issues which characterized the 'colonels'. He believed, too, that Mościcki's intention to nominate a minister directly conflicted with the constitution, which delegated the appointment of ministers to the Prime Minister.

Mościcki realized fairly early that he could not work with Sławek, and, having seen the ease with which he had renounced his claim to the Presidency, became determined to force him to resign as Prime Minister. Already on 6 September he had asked Świtalski, the man in the 'colonels group' with whom he was on closest terms, whether he would become Prime Minister if Sławek resigned.[1] On 22 September, the President asked Świtalski whether Sławek had said anything to him about his desire to resign. 'I gained the impression', commented Świtalski, 'that the President eagerly awaited news of Sławek's intention of resigning.[1] The offer

---

[1] A.S.S., *Może przesilenie?* 26 września 1935 roku.
[2] Pobóg-Malinowski, *Najnowsza historia*, ii. 776–9.

to Świtalski of the Premiership was renewed on 26 September. Świtalski however gave a definite refusal on 30 September. He, like Sławek, was unhappy about Kwiatkowski's economic radicalism and about the fact that the Minister of Trade and Industry would be appointed by the President and not the Prime Minister.[1] It is not clear from the available material who else Mościcki approached, although he did tell Świtalski that he regarded Prystor as 'insufficiently competent' to handle the existing situation.[1] Indeed he was unable to find a Premier from among the 'colonels', who in spite of the differences between them, all showed their solidarity with Sławek against the President. On 11 October, however, he managed to persuade one of the younger Piłsudski-ites, Marian Zyndram-Kościałkowski, to form a Cabinet.[2] Zyndram-Kościałkowski, well known for his radical sympathies, had been Minister of the Interior from June 1934. Although he was not one of the inner circle of Piłsudski-ites, he had long been linked with the Marshal, but through the Polish Military Organization (P.O.W.) rather than the Legions. In 1911, he had been one of the founders of the League of Active Struggle in St. Petersburg, and from 1914, one of the leaders of the P.O.W. in the Congress Kingdom. In the following years, he became active in peasant politics, and was elected Vice-President of the Liberation. When he left that party, he became a Vice-President of the B.B.W.R. and a leading member of the League for the Reform of the Republic (the Naprawiacze), which had recovered considerably by the mid-thirties from its political setbacks in the period after the Brześć trial. Both as Governor of the Białystok province and as Minister of the Interior he had enjoyed the reputation of a liberal, and his Premiership was welcomed by the Opposition, particularly on the Centre and Left, as marking the return to a more civilian form of government.

His appointment was not acquiesced in without a struggle. When Mościcki's intention of nominating him became known, Rydz went to the President and strongly attempted to dissuade him.[2] On the following day (12 October) Beck, too, put strong pressure on the President to change his mind, threatening to refuse to serve under Kościałkowski. Mościcki however stood firm, Sławek resigned, and Beck, rather than give up his post, did not

---

[1] A.S.S., Może przesilenie? 26 września 1935 roku.
[2] A.S.S., Dalszy ciąg przesilenia dn. 18.X.35 r.

carry out his threat. Since the conflict in the Sanacja was carefully kept within the directing circle, Kościałkowski had relatively little difficulty in forming a government. Kwiatkowski was given the post of Minister of Finance, so that he could initiate a new economic policy, as Mościcki had intended.

Sławek's defeat was followed by the dissolution of the B.B.W.R. on 30 October 1935, a step which further undermined the Piłsudski-ite system. Sławek appears to have taken this action on his own initiative, without really consulting his political associates. He justified it on the grounds that the new electoral law had ended the need for political parties. A member of parliament now 'had no need of an organization of a political type which will unnecessarily come between him and the country'.[1] Certain other considerations also seem to have influenced him. He felt that the B.B.W.R. had become encumbered by opportunists and careerists and that this partly explained its unpopularity in the country. In addition, the divisions within the organization had increased considerably after Piłsudski's death. The conservatives in particular were strongly critical of the Government, and *Czas* became involved in a violent polemic with the official *Gazeta Polska* in May 1935. At one stage this led the Warsaw municipality to close *Czas*'s new offices (the paper had moved to Warsaw in January 1935) on the grounds that they contravened the health regulations. Murmurings were also heard on the Left Wing of the Bloc. The Union of Trade Unions (Z.Z.Z.) had, as we have seen, strongly attacked the new electoral law, while the League for the Reform of the Republic became increasingly active, seeing in the death of Piłsudski the opportunity for obtaining high political office always denied them (with the exception of Governor Grażyński in Silesia) during the Marshal's lifetime. They did not observe Sławek's appeal that little active campaigning should take place during the elections and thus emerged as a significant group in the new parliament.[2] Finally, in dissolving the Bloc Sławek seems to have been motivated by a certain pique. The B.B.W.R. was his own creation and, as he complained bitterly to Świtalski, after the formation of the Kościałkowski Government, 'My authority is being undermined and the B.B. is being criticized, by which an

---

[1] *Gazeta Polska*, 31 October 1935.
[2] The National Christian Union of Labour, the organization of the bloc in Silesia, dominated as it was by the Naprawiacze, was not in fact dissolved.

attack on me is intended.'[1] Thus Sławek once again displayed his deplorable lack of political judgement. The dissolution of the Bloc caused a serious political vacuum, for although Piłsudski had often attacked partisanship and had resented parliamentary attempts to control his actions, he did realize the need for an organization such as the B.B.W.R. to uphold the Government's case in parliament. Sławek does seem to have intended to replace the bloc by a 'Universal Organization of Society'[2] (P.O.S.) through which local government authorities were to select 'the best among them' to sit on councils to select members of parliament, who were to be the highest organ of the P.O.S.[3] This conception was so patently absurd that it was rapidly torpedoed by Sławek's associates.

The appointment of the Kościałkowski Government and the dissolution of the B.B.W.R. marked an important stage in the evolution of the political scene after Piłsudski's death. These two events marked the virtual disappearance as a coherent political entity of the 'colonels' group', that inner circle of Piłsudski-ites who had virtually run the country under the Marshal's orders since 1929. The 'colonels' were still united in their hostility to the new Government, particularly because of the way in which Sławek had been slighted. Their opposition was made painfully obvious to Kościałkowski at the meeting of former Prime Ministers on 9 November when Świtalski told the new Premier that he was allowing himself to be made the tool of the President and Kwiatkowski.[4] It was also due to the opposition of the 'colonels', in particular of Car, who was Marshal of the Sejm, and Prystor, who was Marshal of the Senate, that the Government was granted special powers to issue decrees only until the end of January, and not until June, as it had hoped.[5] Some of the wilder members of the group, like former Premier Kozłowski, even talked of passing a vote of no confidence in the new Government in parliament, where Sławek's influence was strong, but this was ruled out on the grounds that it would make too obvious to the Opposition the divisions within the Sanacja.[6]

[1] A.S.S., Rozmowa ze Sławkiem w końcu października 1935 r.
[2] Powszechna Organizacja Społeczeństwa.
[3] Pobóg-Malinowski, *Najnowsza historia*, ii. 795.
[4] A.S.S., On 9 listopada 1935 r. Tak zwane Zgromadzenie Lokatorów w Prezydium Rady Ministrów.
[5] A.S.S., Dalszy ciąg przesilenia dn 18.X.35 r.
[6] Pobóg-Malinowski, *Najnowsza historia*, ii. 782.

But though they were united in their opposition to Kościał-kowski, the 'colonels' were internally at odds on virtually all other questions. A number had become deeply disillusioned with Sławek and his apparent lack of political understanding. Miedziński, the influential editor of *Gazeta Polska*, attacked Sławek at a meeting of deputies and senators on 25 October, claiming that his arguments against creating political groupings in the new parliament were ridiculous and that this kind of organization was a 'natural phenomenon'.[1] His desire to bring Sosnkowski back into political life and to broaden the base of the Government was also opposed by Sławek.[2] As his relations with Sławek worsened, he looked more and more to Rydz-Śmigły, although it was only from early 1937 that he began to envisage a political role for the General Inspector. Koc and Składkowski too, discontented with Sławek, began to orient themselves more and more towards Rydz. Świtalski also decided fairly early that he could not, as he told the President, 'co-operate politically with Sławek at this time'.[3] Already at the end of September he had decided to take the non-political post of Governor of the Cracow province, so that he could return to political life when Sławek's policies had led to the unfortunate results he feared.[3]

Even those among the colonels who remained loyal to Sławek had great misgivings. Beck, who told Świtalski that he supported Sławek's aim of taking party considerations out of Polish political life,[4] did not press his support for the former Prime Minister so far as to resign when Kościałkowski formed his Government. Both Prystor and Car continued to support Sławek, but were strongly critical of his actions.[5] Sławek by now, though still a major political figure, had already lost a great deal of the credit he had enjoyed in May 1935 as the Marshal's declared political heir.

---

[1] A.S.S., Dnia 25 października 1935 roku. Konferencja u Góreckiego w B.G.K.

[2] Pobóg-Malinowski, *Najnowsza historia*, ii. 783.

[3] A.S.S., Rozmowa z Prezydentem. Dnia 30-go września 1936 r.

[4] A.S.S., Rozmowa z Beckiem. 1.X.35.

[5] For Prystor's attitude; A.S.S., Dnia 28 listopada 1935 r. Zebranie u Kościałkowskiego w składzie: Sławek, Prystor i ja. For Car's — A.S.S., Dnia 19 listopada 1936 r. Rozmowa z Carem.

THE COMPROMISE BETWEEN RYDZ - ŚMIGŁY AND MOŚCICKI
(NOVEMBER 1935 TO JULY 1936)

The formation of the Kościałkowski Government did not resolve
the crisis in the upper ranks of the Sanacja. What Mościcki
referred to as the Piłsudski-ites' 'search for a Pope'[1] continued in an
intensified form in the months after November 1935. As a result
of the growing disillusionment with Sławek, Rydz emerged as the
most obvious candidate for the role. His stock rose fast within
government circles, and the Sanacja press, especially *Gazeta
Polska* and *Kurjer Poranny* (edited by Rydz's ardent supporter
Stpiczyński) began to propagate his cult. Rydz himself, at a
meeting in December to celebrate the anniversary of the Poznań
rising of 1918, stressed the special role the Army played in Polish
political life.[2] The implications were clearly spelled out in *Kurjer
Poranny*. An anonymous article, 'The Polish Soldier in the Movement for Social Reform', described the speech as underlining 'the
quite exceptional position which the National Army and its leader
hold in the life of our Republic'. This 'leader' was the natural
implementer of radical social change: 'No-one else will more carefully or more assiduously take care that the processes necessary for
the crystallization of new form of society will take place within the
framework of the Polish *raison d'État* without external pressure.'[3]
The claim that Rydz was an exponent of a 'Left' orientation within
the Sanacja was also assiduously propagated by Stpiczyński in
parliament.

There was little truth in this claim, for Rydz, a man with few
political ideas, inclined rather to a somewhat simple-minded form
of nationalism. But he had not been one of the inner circle of
Piłsudski-ites and he thus did not share the stigma which they
bore in the eyes of society at large, while his refusal to make clear
pronouncements allowed his reputation to grow by leaps and
bounds. Already on 21 May 1935 Marian Kukiel wrote to Sylwin
Strakacz, Paderewski's secretary, of 'Rydz's undoubtedly good
intentions', while on 27 May, Stanisław Kot wrote to Paderewski
that 'Rydz is gathering around him the so-called decent Piłsudski-
ites.'[4] These views were shared by the Left. Lieberman, writing in

[1] A.S.S. Rozmowa z Prezydentem dn. 1 listopada 1935 r.
[2] Jędruszczak, op. cit., pp. 79–80.   [3] *Kurjer Poranny*, 5 January 1936.
[4] Quoted in J. Żarnowski, *Polska Partia Socjalistyczna w latach 1935–1939*
(Warsaw, 1966), p. 29.

exile in August 1935, surmised that Rydz 'intends to condemn the colonels' régime, his political views do not coincide at all with those of the ruling circles'.[1] Hopes of a 'Leftward' turn by Rydz were cherished by the P.P.S. executive, and even by the Communists. On 12 October 1935 the Secretariat of the K.P.P. issued a statement which underlined the deep differences within the Sanacja and remarked that 'the continued stressing by Rydz of his anti-German sentiments . . . is not purely a tactical move'.[2]

The growing power of Rydz was an obvious threat to Mościcki. Rydz had strongly opposed the formation of the Kościałkowski Government, and Stpiczyński was one of those most eager for a Sejm vote of no confidence in the new Cabinet. As a result the President decided, perhaps at the prompting of Kwiatkowski, that he would have to compromise with Rydz. An agreement between the two men was reached in December 1935.[3] Its terms remain somewhat obscure, but it seems to have provided that the Kościałkowski Cabinet would remain in office until the end of the budgetary session, when a new Government would be formed reflecting the close co-operation of Rydz and Mościcki.

Kościałkowski was not informed that the fate of his Cabinet had been sealed, and he thus embarked with some verve on an attempt to win at least the tacit support of the Centre and Left. In his first address to parliament, he was conciliatory, claiming that he had no intention of preventing 'healthy, objective, ideologically-motivated criticism' of the Government and that he hoped to establish between the Government and the country 'the simple link of confidence which should exist between those who struggle for the same cause'.[4] His Minister of the Interior, Władysław Raczkiewicz, also appealed to the Centre and Left in a long speech in parliament on 24 February in which he claimed that the main enemies of the Republic were the Communists and the Nationalist Right.[5]

The attempted *apertura a sinistra* proved a failure. This was not so much because of the intransigence of the Left—indeed the

---

[1] H. Lieberman, 'La dictature polonaise privée de son chef', *Informations Internationales, publicés pour la presse par le Sécretariat d'Internationale Ouvrière Socialiste*, vol. xii, no. 26, 3 August 1935. Quoted in Żarnowski, *Polska Partia Socjalistyczna*, p. 29.

[2] Quoted in ibid., p. 63.

[3] Pobóg-Malinowski, *Najnowsza historia*, ii. 783–4.

[4] *S.S.S.R.*, 17 February 1936.   [5] Ibid., 24 February 1936.

P.P.S. was at first extremely responsive to Kościałkowski's approaches—as to the half-hearted character of the Government's actions. Though an Amnesty Law applying both to political and ordinary criminals was passed in parliament in January,[1] the Government refused to extend it to the political *émigrés* from the Brześć trial or to those detained in the concentration camp of Bereza Kartuska, which would greatly have eased the political situation. Press censorship remained strongly in force and was even intensified in this period, leading the Union of Journalists to complain to the Prime Minister in April 1936.[2]

The political standing of the Government was finally undermined by a serious outbreak of labour unrest in the spring of 1936. By this time, the seemingly unending economic crisis, and the ever-higher level of unemployment had thoroughly exasperated the working class, which was increasingly prepared to turn to newer and more violent methods of struggle. One of the most popular was the sit-in, or 'Italian' strike, in which workers took over a factory and refused to leave. Following a strike of this type at the end of March at the Semperit factory in Cracow, violence erupted between workers and police and six people were killed and twenty wounded. There followed violent disturbances in Częstochowa and, in the middle of April, in Lwów, in which eight people were killed and sixty wounded.

The Government was not directly responsible for these incidents, which were the result more of the intransigence of the local authorities, especially Świtalski, who as Governor of the Cracow province committed several appalling blunders. The violence did not end the possibility of a reconciliation with the Left, because the P.P.S., aware of the colonels' hostility towards the Government, was unwilling to do anything to hasten its fall. It certainly confirmed the opinion of Rydz and also of the colonels that Kościałkowski was too weak. But in a paradoxical way, the labour unrest slightly delayed his fall. When an article appeared on 17 April in *Gazeta Polska* (whose editor, Miedziński, had been informed by Rydz that the Prime Minister was to be replaced) attacking Kościałkowski's handling of the strikers, he reacted by confiscating the issue.[3] Rydz was furious at Miedziński for having

---

[1] *Dz.U.R.P.* (1936), no. 1, pp. 1–3.
[2] *Warszawski Dziennik Narodowy*, 9 April 1936.
[3] Pobóg-Malinowski, *Najnowsza historia*, ii. 784.

abused his confidence and neither he nor Mościcki was prepared to let Kościałkowski resign in such a way as to make it seem he had done so under pressure from *Gazeta Polska*. As a result, Kościałkowski remained in office until 15 May.

The formation of a new Government was delayed by disputes over who should be Prime Minister. Among those considered was General Sosnkowski, who was proposed to Rydz by Miedziński some weeks before the ill-fated article appeared in *Gazeta Polksa*. This suggestion was rejected by the President, perhaps on Kwiatkowski's advice.[1] Sosnkowski himself seems to have made an approach to Rydz himself on 13 May 1936, but his offer to head a government was refused.[2] It is not clear who else was put forward, but it seems certain that the appointment of the egregious Sławoj-Składkowski was intended only as a provisional measure. It was only with strong misgivings that his candidacy was approved by the President, and then only on condition that Kwiatkowski enter the Cabinet as 'Economic Vice Prime Minister'. Yet as so often happens in politics, this 'provisional' Government proved surprisingly durable, and survived until the fall of the Polish state.

Enough has already been said about Składkowski to show that he was totally unsuited for the office he held. Indeed, the only reason that his tenure of it did not have more disastrous consequences was that all important decisions were taken out of his hands. The composition of the Cabinet was agreed upon in terms of the compromise between Rydz and Mościcki. It was divided into two groups, 'The President's Ministers' and 'Rydz's Ministers'. The first group comprised Kwiatkowski, Juliusz Poniatowski, the Minister of Agriculture, Wojciech Świętosławski, the Minister of Education, Emil Kaliński, the Minister of Posts and Telegraphs, and Kościałkowski, who took the portfolio of Social Welfare. Rydz's group included Składkowski himself, General Kasprzycki, the Minister of War, Colonel Ulrych, the Minister of Transport, and Witold Grabowski, the Public Prosecutor in the Brześć trial, as Minister of Justice. Beck occupied a special position in the Cabinet, and was allowed one minister of his own, Antoni Roman, the Minister of Trade and Industry, who had previously been the Polish Minister in Stockholm. When Składkowski asked

[1] Ibid., pp. 784-5.
[2] Kazimierz Sosnkowski, *Materiały historyczne* (London, 1966), biographical details by J. Matecki, p. xvi.

plaintively 'Can I choose at least one of "my" ministers for "my" Cabinet?'[1] he was allowed to keep the portfolio of Minister of the Interior for himself. It was also partly through his pressure, that Kościałkowski remained in the Cabinet.

The next months saw the emergence of Rydz as the dominant personality in the Government. Already on 9 May, a new decree on Army organization had specified more distinctly the functions of the Minister of War and the General Inspector and had clearly emphasized the primacy of the latter.[2] Składkowski, in his own inimitable way, accurately characterized the new Government a few days after its formation. 'By the order of the President of the Republic and of General Rydz-Śmigły, I have become Prime Minister. . . . Today, comrades, together with General Rydz-Śmigły, I am going out on patrol.'[3] In his first speech to parliament, he underlined the fact that Rydz had inherited the Marshal's mantle. 'We have a leader, whom the Commander has designated as the guardian of the frontiers of the Republic and who at the same time keeps careful watch over the spirit of the nation.'[4] Rydz sedulously cultivated this role. He attended the first meeting of the new Cabinet, an action totally unwarranted by his constitutional position. At the thirteenth congress of legionaries, on 24 May 1936, he launched a widely publicized appeal for national consolidation. Stressing the perilous international situation of the country, he appealed to all men of good will to unite for the defence of Polish independence.[5] The speech, with its patriotic phraseology and absence of legionary élitism, was well received in the country as a whole. The congress of legionaries also marked a further strengthening by Rydz of his position within the Sanacja. The civilian 'Union of Legionaries' was amalgamated with the military 'Legionary Regimental Circles' and on the executive of the united organization there was no representative of the 'colonels' group'. Sławek, who had been President of the Union of Legionaries, was replaced by Koc, now a strong supporter of Rydz.

Rydz also tried to attract support outside the Government.

---

[1] Quoted in Pobóg-Malinowski, *Najnowsza historia*, ii. 785.

[2] *Dz.U.R.P.* (1936), no. 38, pp. 647-9.

[3] *Gazeta Polska*, 19 May 1936.

[4] *S.S.S.R.*, 4 June 1935.

[5] *Gazeta Polska*, 25 May 1936. This speech is discussed in more detail below, see pp. 419-20.

At the prompting of Stpiczyński, the General, who was himself of peasant origins, attended a mass rally of the Peasant Party at Nowosielce on 29 June 1936 in honour of Michał Pyrz, who had organized the village to defend itself against the Tartars in the seventeenth century. But though there were shouts in support of the 'Supreme Commander' from the 120,000 peasants present, the occasion was not a success. A petition was presented to Rydz calling for the re-establishment of parliamentary democracy, for an amnesty for the *émigré* leader of the peasant party, and for an end to the pro-German foreign policy of Beck. The cry 'We want Witos' was repeatedly raised. Rydz, infuriated, left the meeting early.[1]

Rydz's growing influence did not go unchallenged. Mościcki, worried by the General's extension of his power, and also by Składkowski's suggestion that he should let Rydz take the Presidency, called a Cabinet meeting in the middle of June, at which he stressed that the obligation of all its members was to observe the provisions of the new constitution. The Premier and his Cabinet were politically responsible only to the President; they could not be regarded as subordinate to anyone else. This challenge to his authority came as a surprise to Rydz, but it did not achieve its desired effect. Mościcki, now 69 and no longer in good health, had been greatly worn down by the strain of office and by his clashes firstly with Sławek and now with Rydz. In the midst of his pronouncement, he lost the thread of what he was saying, giving the impression of an 'incapable and helpless old man.'[2] His failure to assert himself effectively seems to have led Kwiatkowski to the conclusion that Rydz's growing power could not be effectively challenged, and that a new compromise would have to be reached. He thus persuaded the President that he should show the greatest goodwill towards the General, 'so that he would feel grateful and obliged and, in addition to this, standing in the state hierarchy just next to the President, he would be clearly dependent on him'.[3] Mościcki seems to have adopted this advice, and in early July told Składkowski that all members of the Government should treat the General Inspector 'with the greatest respect,

---

[1] See Mackiewicz, op. cit., p. 299.
[2] Pobóg-Malinowski, *Najnowsza historia*, ii. 787. This account of the meeting follows that of Pobóg-Malinowski, ii. 786–8.
[3] Ibid., p. 788.

since he had the most important responsibility in the country after the President, that of defending the country'.[1] Składkowski implemented this instruction with his usual clumsiness and ineptitude. On 15 July 1936, he issued a circular to all Ministries and provincial authorities. 'In accordance with the will of the President of the Republic', it stated,

General Rydz-Śmigły, designated by Marshal Piłsudski as the first defender of the Fatherland, and as the first collaborator of the President in ruling the country, is to be regarded and respected as the first person in Poland after the President of the Republic. All state functionaries, with the Prime Minister at the head, are obliged to show him respect and obedience.[2]

This almost certainly went far beyond what Mościcki had intended. Although strictly speaking it had no legal force, since the constitution could not be altered by a Ministerial circular, it certainly marked a further break with the principles of the 1935 constitution. Piłsudski's ideal of the parallel obedience of the Prime Minister and the General Inspector to the President was deformed by making the General Inspector second in power to the President, and in fact the possessor of greater authority in relation to the Cabinet than the Prime Minister.

Rydz's position as the 'second man in the State' was further underlined in November, when he was made a Marshal. Presenting him with his baton, Mościcki affirmed,

Today, I entrust to you the baton of Marshal, as a symbol of your great role in the State. The hetman's baton which you are about to receive is not only the attribute of the highest military rank. Contemporary reality demands that this solemn act be understood in a particularly large sense. Together with the President of the Republic, always respecting his constitutional obligations, you are to lead Poland to the highest glory.[3]

THE OPPOSITION

The death of Piłsudski was also followed by important changes in the Opposition. The P.P.S., which had long prophesied the collapse

[1] Pobóg-Malinowski, *Najnowsza historia*, ii. 788.
[2] *Gazeta Polska*, 16 July 1936.   [3] Ibid., 11 November 1936.

of the Sanacja, believed that it could not long be delayed. The main danger thus lay in an agreement between the National Party, which the socialists now regarded as their main enemy, and the right wing of the Government bloc. It was largely in the hope of maintaining their old contacts with government circles dating from legionary days that Arciszewski, Niedziałkowski, and a number of other members of the Central Committee attended the Marshal's funeral, for which they were strongly attacked by younger members of the party.[1] However, hopes for a reorganization of the Government and for some concessions to the Left were dashed by the new electoral law, and the P.P.S. was one of the main advocates of the electoral boycott. Nevertheless the Kościałkowski government was greeted with some sympathy, particularly at the beginning of its period of office. 'Kościałkowski', commented *Robotnik* on 15 October,

represents a type of man different from those who have governed the State in the last few years. His is the generation after Mr. Sławek's, that of the 'Polish Military Organization' rather than the legions. With him will come a more sober political line, one which takes more regard of the social forces in the country—those forces which Mr. Sławek, filled with fanatical hatred saw only as the manifestation of partisan spirit.

The Central Committee of the party was well aware of the conflicts in the ruling circles of the Sanacja and it was largely because of their belief that too radical action would play into the hands of the colonels, who opposed the Kościałkowski Government, that they argued against taking a particularly militant course during the labour unrest of March and April 1936. The formation of the Sławoj-Składkowski Cabinet came as a considerable surprise to the party leadership, and was received with 'much consternation' because of the fear that Government repression would be intensified.[2] The party became convinced that hopes for an 'opening to the Left' by the Government were largely illusory, although attempts were still made to win over some of the left-wing elements in the Sanacja, principally in the Legion of Youth and in the circle of radical journalists at *Kurjer Poranny* led by Wincenty Rzymowski. Indeed in July 1936 the Legion of Youth

---

[1] Żarnowski, *Polska Partia Socjalistyczna*, pp. 25–8.
[2] According to the information of the Government Commissioner in Warsaw. Quoted in ibid., p. 136.

split, and one section openly declared its sympathy for the P.P.S., joining its youth movement in 1937.[1]

Calls for a popular front with the Communists also became stronger in this period, although there were still many among the socialists who continued to regard the Communists with extreme distrust. The K.P.P. was advancing its new united front policy with considerable eagerness. It was given international Communist legitimacy at the Seventh Comintern Congress (July–August 1935) and the changed international situation, with the Soviet Union joining the League of Nations in 1934, concluding alliances with France and Czechoslovakia in May 1935 and becoming a leading exponent of collective security, also gave the policy new impetus. In July 1935 the P.P.S. and the K.P.P. agreed on a 'pact of non-aggression'. This involved a mutual cessation of attacks in the party press and at meetings as well as joint campaigns against Beck's foreign policy and the concentration camp of Bereza Kartuska.[2] It was following this agreement that Niedziałkowski, writing in *Robotnik*, commented, 'The differences dividing the workers' class movement internally have diminished enormously.'[3] The popular front had some enthusiastic supporters on the left wing of the P.P.S. including Barlicki, Dubois, and Próchnik. In October 1936, a popular front newspaper, *Dziennik Popularny*, was founded and socialists collaborated closely with the Communists in the Lodz municipal elections of that year. Relations soon cooled somewhat, both because of the P.P.S.'s opposition to the Communist leaders' desire to use the labour difficulties of early 1936 to provoke an all-out clash with the Sanacja, and because of the beginning of the purges in Russia and the execution of Kamenev and Zinoviev in October 1936. The attempts of the Communists to infiltrate various P.P.S. organizations were also greatly resented. Already in May 1936, the Executive Council of the socialists, while upholding the non-aggression pact, resolved that 'positive collaboration of the P.P.S. and K.P.P. is impossible because of both practical and ideological reasons'.[4] The non-aggression pact was finally renounced at the meeting of the Executive Council in November 1936.[5] At the same time, the

[1] Micewski, *Z geografii politycznej II Rzeczypospolitej*, pp. 277–8.
[2] Żarnowski, *Polska Partia Socjalistyczna*, pp. 43–4.
[3] *Robotnik*, 2 August 1935.   [4] Ibid., 11 May 1936.
[5] M. Drozdowski and A. Tymieniecka, 'Mieczysław Niedziałkowski', *Najnowsze dzieje Polski: materiały i studia z okresu 1914–1939*, ix (1965), 69.

party remained firm in its attempts to achieve co-operation with the Peasant Party and some success was achieved in negotiations with Rataj and Grudziński in early 1936. Co-operation with the socialist parties of the minorities, particularly the Bund, also increased greatly at this time.

The period was indeed one of growing strength for the P.P.S. 'Socialism is undoubtedly on the way up', commented the Christian Democratic *Głos Narodu* in May 1936.[1] 1936 was, as we have seen, a year of great labour unrest, and altogether 3,950,000 working days were lost in strikes, the highest figure in the whole inter-war period.[2] In most of these strikes the P.P.S. played a prominent role, though some were organized by the Communists. On the anniversary of 'Bloody Wednesday' (the day in September 1906 when Tsarist police savagely crushed a P.P.S. demonstration in Warsaw) the party mounted a huge parade in Warsaw, with many thousands of participants, an impressive show of strength. The most striking victory of the socialists in these years was in the Lodz municipal elections where, in collaboration with the Communists, the party won thirty-four of the seventy-two seats. Together with the Bund's total of six seats this was an absolute majority. The groupings supporting the Government did not win a single seat, the National Party won twenty-seven seats, and the other Jewish groups won five seats.[3]

These were also years of growth for the united Peasant Party. The party had been somewhat weakened by the secession of a number of its members who opposed the boycott of the 1935 elections. In August 1936 one faction, led by the former Peasant Party leader Andrzej Waleron and close to the Naprawa group, formed a new pro-Government peasant grouping. But this setback did not prove lasting and indeed it was in the countryside that the boycott of the elections proved most successful. The new programme, adopted at the third party congress on 7-8 December, was far-reaching in its claims and reflected a new self-confidence.[4] The rural population, stated Article 1, 'because of its numbers, its physical and moral vigour resulting from its link with the land, as well as its national and state values, is justified in regarding

[1] *Głos Narodu*, 6 May 1936.
[2] *M.R.S.* (1939), Table XLVII, p. 284.
[3] *Robotnik*, 29 September 1936.
[4] For the programme, see *Materiały źródłowe do historii polskiego ruchu ludowego* (Warsaw, 1966), iii. 13-23.

itself as the natural ruler (*gospodarz*) of Poland'. The party also became more clerical, calling for unconditional observance of the principles of Christian morality in public life (Article 4). Capitalism was condemned as incapable of solving the economic problems of the country, and a planned economy was demanded (Article 5). The insistence upon uncompensated expropriation of the large estates was reiterated, and the 'individual self-sufficient plot' was to be the basis of the agricultural system (Article 6). In addition, the new programme was more anti-Semitic. The presence of the Jews, it claimed, made impossible the development of a native Polish middle class; the Jewish problem should be resolved by encouraging Jewish emigration, although Jews in Poland should not be deprived of their civil rights (Article 7).

The Party became steadily more radical as the crisis in the countryside showed little signs of coming to an end. Though the leadership of the party, especially Rataj and Grudziński, hesitated to seek an outright clash with the Government, which they believed could only result in defeat, calls for more determined action increased, particularly among the youth section of the party, the so-called *Wici*. The summer of 1936 saw several outbreaks of peasant violence. Clashes between striking agricultural labourers and blacklegs in West Galicia in June and July led to a number of deaths. After a meeting at Witos's birthplace, Wierzchosławice, in August, a number of *Wici* members attempted to surround and burn down the police station. One of the demonstrators was killed and a policeman gravely wounded. In August and September, peasant strikes, in which agricultural produce was not delivered to the towns broke out in the Zamość area as well as in Volynia. Calls for a nation-wide peasant strike gained increasing currency.

The National Party too saw in the weakening of the Sanacja which followed Piłsudski's death, the opportunity to make its bid for power. It was now to a great extent under the control of the younger disciples of Dmowski, whose Fascist sympathies became increasingly pronounced. An indication of the tone of party propaganda can be culled from the 'order of the day' issued at a demonstration of the party outside Warsaw to celebrate the anniversary of the 'miracle on the Vistula'.

The danger of the Judaeo-Communist conspiracy dispelled by the Polish victory of 1920 has increased seriously in the last few years and has made the menace of revolution hang over our country and over the other countries of Europe, particularly over those which have not yet succeeded in giving themselves a solid national regime. The victory of anarcho-Communist forces is particularly in the interest of the Jews, who are threatened by the tide of National movements, growing stronger every day.[1]

The party attempted to use the Jewish question to win support and to embarrass the Government, and its anti-Jewish methods became increasingly violent. In the single month of December 1935, according to police records, there were twenty-seven cases of Nationalist vigilantes beating up Jews, one of which was fatal, thirty-four cases of breaking the windows of Jewish houses, and six of the destruction of Jewish property.[2] However, these criminal methods were opposed by some of the more civilized members of the party, whose leadership was increasingly divided on questions of tactics. The great wave of labour unrest of early 1936 even led the executive of the party to instruct the party activists to avoid direct clashes with the police, and to aid them in clashes with the Left.[3] The tendency towards reconciliation with the Government was to become stronger as time went on.

The small Fascist offshoots of the National Party continued to divide after 1935. One section of the O.N.R.–A.B.C. attempted at the end of 1936 to reach some compromise with the executive of the party. Piasecki's O.N.R.–Falanga, on the other hand, became increasingly close to the Sanacja with which it began to co-operate in 1937. Another group of former O.N.R. members, led by Stanisław Strzetelski and Tadeusz Kobylański also approached the Government early in 1937 through Kwiatkowski. A concensus was achieved on a number of disputed points, including the constitution, foreign policy and the Jewish question, but no lasting agreement was reached.[4] Another pro-Government secession from the Nationalists was the group around Jan Rembieliński and Stanisław Miklaszewski who in November 1936 founded a weekly, *Podbipięta*, which advanced views in favour of a corporate state and also supported the Government, arguing that the only matter now dividing Sanacja and Endecja was the Jewish question.

[1] *Warszawski Dziennik Narodowy*, 17 August 1936.
[2] R. Wapiński, 'Niektóre problemy ewolucji ideowo-polityčznej Endecji w latach 1919–1939', p. 874.
[3] Ibid., p. 875.
[4] Pobóg-Malinowski, *Najnowsza historia*, ii. 799–800.

The increasing demogogy of the National Party and its virtual acceptance of a Fascist programme led to much unease in the more responsible part of the Polish Right. One result of this was the agreement reached between the former Premier Paderewski, General Haller, and Witos in February 1936. This 'Morges Front' named after the town in Switzerland where Paderewski was living, aimed at creating a broad coalition of the Centre and Right including the Peasant Party, the National Democrats, the Christian Democrats and the National Workers' Party. It called for the re-establishment of a democratic system in Poland and in foreign policy was strongly Francophile, urging the abandonment of Beck's pro-German line. It was prepared, moreover, to compromise with the 'decent elements' in the Sanacja.[1]

The Front did not attain wide support in Poland itself. The National Democrats, and especially Dmowski himself, were hostile to it, criticizing it for its Francophilia and its liberal character which, it was believed, made it susceptible to 'Masonic and Jewish' influences. In addition, in spite of Witos's sponsorship, the leadership of the Peasant Party in Poland suspected the Front of being too right wing, although it had significant support in a number of local branches. But it did gain a number of notable adherents, among whom were General Sikorski and the eminent National Democratic journalist Stanisław Stroński. It was also strongly supported by both the Christian Democrats and the N.P.R. As a result, these two parties united in October 1937 to form the Party of Labour, headed by Korfanty and Popiel. Sikorski was important in the achievement of this union, and General Haller and Kukiel also joined the party, which upheld a liberal Catholic point of view. It was also joined by a number of people who had no previous connection either with the N.P.R. or with the Christian Democrats, including the former President Wojciechowski and Gabriel Czechowicz.[2] However its strength was not great outside Upper Silesia, for its general anti-Government position meant that it was opposed by many powerful members of the Church hierarchy and by Catholic Action. The emergence of the Morges Front as a potential alternative on the right both to the Sanacja and to the Endecja was significant, and was to prove of great importance after the outbreak of the war.

---

[1] On this, see Micewski, *Z geografii politycznej II Rzeczypospolitej*, pp. 257–9.
[2] *Kurjer Warszawski*, 11 October 1937.

THE CAMP OF NATIONAL UNITY (JULY 1936 TO MARCH 1938)

The Government's obvious weakness and lack of support in the country, shown both in the elections of September 1935 and in the labour troubles of early 1936, alarmed many leading members of the Sanacja. Calls for the setting up of a new political organization to replace the B.B.W.R. became increasingly frequent. At an extraordinary congress of the Federation of Former Polish Combatants, held on 18 April 1936, a resolution was passed in the presence of the Prime Minister and Minister of the Interior affirming that

considering the present situation of our State and of the country, we regard as an imperative necessity the setting up, with the shortest possible delay, of a political camp with a clearly defined programme which will be in conformity with the ideology of Marshal Piłsudski. . . . It is necessary to undertake an ideological offensive, on a broad front which will use all possible means. . . . At all costs, we must throw a bridge between the Federation and the younger generation.[1]

Similar calls were made at this time both by *Gazeta Polska* and by *Czas*.[2]

It is not clear when it was finally decided to launch a new party. Its establishment may have been a part of the December agreement between Rydz and the President, and was certainly given a fillip by the increase in Rydz's power which followed the formation of the Składkowski Government. Ten days afterwards, on 24 May, Rydz in a speech at the Union of Legionaries issued a call for national unity, a unity which, it was implied, would take an institutional form.[3] He stressed Poland's weak position in relation to her two increasingly powerful neighbours and argued that the country could only maintain its independence by the unified exercise of the national will. The only slogan under which this national consolidation could be achieved, he felt, was that of 'national defence', which he defined as the releasing of the moral and creative forces in the nation. The situation was a difficult one and the time for political divisions had passed. 'There is no

---

[1] *Gazeta Polska*, 19 April 1936.
[2] Ibid., 23 April 1936; *Czas*, 22 April 1936.
[3] See above, p. 410.

choice, one must speak plainly; you must either stand here in the ranks with us, like a brother or—you are not our brother!'[1]

The new political organization Rydz proposed was slow in taking form. Its setting up was entrusted to Adam Koc, one of the younger Piłsudski-ites (in 1936 he was 46) who had come out strongly for Rydz and who replaced Sławek as Head of the Union of Legionaries in May 1936. He too was a disastrous choice. Koc had a distinguished past. During the war, he had been one of the leaders of the P.O.W. in the Congress Kingdom, and had been severely wounded in the campaigns of the First Brigade in 1915–16. After 1918, he entered the Army and was one of Piłsudski's main sources of contact with his military supporters after his resignation of his military positions in May 1923. After the coup, Koc was sent as chief of staff to Sikorski in Lwów, in order to place him under close government surveillance. From 1928 he was a Deputy to the Sejm and in 1929 and 1930 was also chief editor of *Gazeta Polska*. In 1930 he joined the Ministry of Finance as Under-Secretary and in 1936 became President of the Bank of Poland. In economic matters he was an ardent supporter of *laisser-faire* liberalism and had in fact resigned from the Bank of Poland in May 1936 rather than implement Kwiatkowski's policy of limiting the freedom of exchange of Polish currency. A man of restricted outlook, his political views were ingenuous, and were largely characterized by a strong conservatism and by his belief that the basis of government support should be widened by coming to terms with the younger nationalists. In addition, his war injuries, which had never healed properly, meant that his health was relatively poor and contributed to his almost pathological inability to take decisive steps. Pobóg-Malinowski's description of him is a damning indictment: 'By 1936', he concludes,

he was only a sybarite, skilled in the culinary arts, fond of comfort, not inclined to great effort, and, in addition, a snob, gathering round him people with famous names or inherited titles. Of the fine radicalism of his youth no trace remained; he was by conviction an extreme conservative, even a reactionary. Having accepted the position of leader of the new camp, he sank into sluggish reflection, equivalent in fact to almost complete inactivity.[2]

[1] *Gazeta Polska*, 25 May 1936.
[2] Pobóg-Malinowski, *Najnowsza historia*, 1st ed., ii. 606. This description was considerably toned down in the second edition.

Koc did virtually nothing in the first few months after Rydz's speech to launch the new organization. In the meantime, Rydz's prestige inside Poland had grown considerably as a result of his official visit to France in the first week of September. Though this did not lead, as some had hoped, to the dismissal of Beck,[1] it did result in the negotiation of a substantial French loan for Poland and it seemed to presage some modification of Beck's pro-German policy. Even *Robotnik* commented that Rydz had 'exercised a *very good* influence' on Polish foreign policy.[2] While in France, addressing Polish emigrants, Rydz repeated his call for the achievement of greater national consolidation.[3]

Koc however took his time. Though innumerable rumours circulated that a new pro-government organization was soon to appear, months went by, consumed by negotiations with various opposition politicians, discussions of a proposed programme, and sheer inactivity. The consensus of opinion held that the new organization would attempt to widen the basis of the Government's support by attempting to compromise with the National Democratic Right. '40 per cent nationalism, 30 per cent social radicalism, 20 per cent agrarianism, 10 per cent anti-Semitism' was how the right-wing *Goniec Warszawski* assessed the new formula early in September.[4] Some indication of Koc's plans was given in a new weekly, *Zaczyn* ('Ferment'), founded under his clandestine patronage in December 1936. In its first issue, it claimed that Koc did not intend 'to follow the B.B.W.R. tradition', and that his goal was the creation of 'a strong and lasting organization'. Its basis was to be the greatness and strength of the State, at the head of which stood the Leader (*wódz*). 'In the Army the idea remained, there was no break, the leader was, the leader is, the leader rules, directs, commands. The leader's words will now be a command for more than the Army.' To aid the leader an organization had to be created, and this was Koc's task.[5]

One of the main reasons for the delay in setting up the new body was the attempt to widen its scope by bringing into it a number of Opposition groups. They were mostly from the extreme Right. Koc made contact with Bolesław Piasecki, the leader of the

[1] See below, pp. 479–80.
[2] *Robotnik*, 13 September 1936.
[3] *Kurjer Poranny*, 9 September 1936.
[4] *Goniec Warszawski*, 4 September 1936.
[5] *Zaczyn*, 3 December 1936.

underground O.N.R.–Falanga, and was taken to a meeting on an estate near Pilica. According to Pobóg-Malinowski, 'Koc returned from this excursion shocked and enchanted: he was impressed by the iron discipline prevailing in this group, by the unconditional obedience for the "Leader"—Piasecki—and by its members' unusual facility in giving prepared and categorical answers to all, even the most complicated, questions.'[1] He therefore determined to delegate the running of his group's youth section, the League of Young Poland, to the Falanga, and in fact entrusted its organization to Piasecki's deputy, Jerzy Rutkowski. Negotiations with another group of O.N.R. members, that led by Kobylański and Strzetelski, were conducted by Miedziński, one of the strongest exponents in the colonels' group of the 'opening to the Right'. But though a substantial consensus was achieved, no formal agreement was reached. Attempts were also made to win over the Peasant Party, and negotiations began with Rataj and Dębski. They demanded, however, the modification of the electoral system, the speeding up of land reform and an amnesty for Witos. Though negotiations were not broken off, no real progress was made.[2]

Koc's obvious intention of coming to terms with the more discreditable (and indeed discredited) sections of the nationalist right caused considerable unease in left-wing legionary and Sanacja circles. A striking reflection of this dissatisfaction was the New Year article in *Kurjer Poranny* by Jan Czarnocki. It attacked both the new electoral law and the dissolution of the B.B.W.R. and called for a broad 'democratic' coalition, including the P.P.S., the Peasant Party, and left-wing legionary circles. It ruled out compromise either with the nationalist Right or with the conservatives.[3] It was as a result of this article that the radical Piłsudski-ites were deprived of control of *Kurjer Poranny*, which was handed over to a pro-Government offshoot of the National Democrats, the League of Young Nationalists.[4] The Naprawa group was also alarmed at the thought of losing its autonomy. Its organization in Silesia, the National Christian Alliance of Labour, had remained in existence after the dissolution of the B.B.W.R. In June the group held a Congress in Warsaw at which it improved

---

[1] Pobóg-Malinowski, *Najnowsza historia*, ii. 798–9.
[2] Ibid., pp. 800–1.   [3] *Kurjer Poranny*, 1 January 1937.
[4] Związek Młodych Narodowców. J. Żarnowski, 'Lewica sanacyjna', p. 723.

its organization and adopted fairly radical resolutions.[1] The conservatives, too, were alarmed by the evolution of the Sanacja. They became polarized in two groups, the liberal-conservatives, linked with *Czas*, and the nationalist-conservatives, linked with the Wilno *Słowo* and its effervescent editor, Cat-Mackiewicz. Both groups opposed the growing tendency towards totalitarianism in the Sanacja and both feared the adoption of more radical measures of land reform. In addition a number of younger conservatives were grouped around the periodical *Bunt Młodych*. They tended to be critical of the Government and were close to the nationalist group of conservatives, though more radical in their social programme.

The establishment of the new pro-Government organization was also delayed by disputes over its programme. What little we know of this comes from Pobóg-Malinowski who, as one of the leading government ideologists, witnessed the process at first hand.[2] According to him, Koc continually put off the issuing of a political and ideological declaration until Miedziński, infuriated by his procrastination, drafted his own declaration which was accepted by Koc's collaborators. Rydz, however, objected to the programme as being too radical and wrote a new, very conservative declaration. With some difficulty Miedziński was able to get Rydz and Koc to agree to tone down its most extreme formulations, particularly in relation to land reform, and this revised version was finally made public by Koc in a radio broadcast on 21 February 1937. It was vague, somewhat conservative and nationalistic, and unspecific on the question of whether a totalitarian system was proposed.[3] Introducing the declaration, Koc claimed that he appealed to all those who sincerely wished to make Poland a great nation.

We stretch out our hand across the hedges and walls, real or non-existent, which have until now divided citizens. Let the politicians guard these walls, let them fortify them with barbed wire for the defence of their ambitions and interests, or those of their party. We want nothing to do with these fossils of the sad past. . . . It is high time to appeal to persevering daily effort, to combine our energy and to exploit it by the most rational and economic means.[3]

The new constitution, which placed a brake on the excesses of

[1] *Kurjer Warszawski*, 15 June 1936.
[2] Pobóg-Malinowski, *Najnowsza historia*, ii. 801.
[3] For the declaration, see *Gazeta Polska*, 22 February 1937.

parliamentarianism, was to remain the basis of political life. The Army held a special place in the state and the concept of national defence was to 'unite all citizens and silence their sterile and demoralizing discords'. The clauses on the Catholic Church were far more openly clerical than pronouncements of the Sanacja had previously been, an attempt to win over the nationalist Right. Those on social matters were vague and tended to be conservative, reflecting the views of Rydz and Koc rather than those of Miedziński. All 'abstract doctrines, corresponding to the interests of a particular group and not of society as a whole' were rejected, and Communism was particularly strongly condemned. Economic and social problems were to be dealt with principally in their relation to the defence and power of the state and violent change was ruled out. Private enterprise was to be respected in industry, but to be placed under state supervision. Class hatred was condemned and the state was to protect the interests of the workers.

The section on land reform was also vague. The difficult situation of the peasant farmer was to be relieved by a number of measures such as increasing the amount of land in peasant hands, consolidation of holdings, land amelioration, the improvement of agricultural technique, the rationalization of the system of distribution and sale, and the improvement of credit facilities. The increase in economic opportunities in the towns would also help absorb the surplus rural population. The question of what sort of land reform was envisaged was left studiously vague.

The policy of the new organization towards the national minorities contained some significant concessions to the point of view of the National Democrats. The desire to 'coexist fraternally' with the national minorities was stressed:

We are conscious of the characteristics which constitute the difference between them and us. We will respect these national characteristics as long as they do not threaten the interest of the State, and are not exploited to erect a Chinese Wall between us and to cultivate hatred. As regards the Jewish group, our attitude is as follows:

We have too high an idea of our civilization and we respect too strongly the order and peace which every state needs to approve brutal anti-semitic acts which harm the dignity and prestige of a great country. At the same time, it is understandable that the country should possess the instinct impelling it to defend its culture, and it is natural that Polish society should seek economic self-sufficiency.

In the period following the issuing of this declaration, attempts were made to set up a new political organization, to which the name the Camp of National Unity (OZON) was given.[1] In its first weeks, its nominal membership grew rapidly, and it attracted a large number of Piłsudski-ite organizations: the National Christian Alliance of Labour, the various pro-Government secessions from the Peasant Party, the pro-Government rump of the N.P.R. in Poznania, the Union of Young Nationalists, which had seceded from the Endecja in 1934 and, with some reservations, the Naprawa group. Various semi-political Piłsudski-ite groups also proclaimed their accession. These included the Federation of Polish Associations of Defenders of the Fatherland, which comprised thirty-four organizations of former combatants, the Riflemen's Union, and the Union of Polish Scouts. Lewiatan, the organization of Polish industrialists, also declared its readiness to support Koc's initiative.[2] In addition, the executive organs of a large number of non-political bodies including the Association of Firemen and the Association of Post Office Workers joined on behalf of their members. It was as a result of accessions of this type that Koc was able to claim that more than 2 million people had applied for membership of OZON within its first weeks.

However, the list of groups which refused to support the Camp was also significant. No major political group outside the Sanacja joined and even within its ranks there was considerable dissatisfaction. It was strongest in Left-legionary circles, and a number of organizations, including Moraczewski's Union of Trade Unions (Z.Z.Z.), the two unions of intellectual workers, and the pro-Sanacja League of Polish Teachers, responded unfavourably. So did the conservatives. The liberal conservatives distrusted the new grouping, regarding its members as largely unprincipled opportunists, and their paper, *Czas*, expressed the fear that OZON would merely duplicate the faults of the B.B.W.R.[3] The nationalist conservatives were more enthusiastic, but demanded more information about the relationship of OZON to the Government.[4]

This was indeed the key question. Though Koc was received by the President and the Prime Minister after the publication of

---

[1] Obóz Zjednoczenia Narodowego.
[2] Quoted in Jędruszczak, op. cit., p. 142.
[3] See for instance, the article in *Czas* on 13 March 1937.
[4] *Słowo*, 12 March 1937.

his declaration, the activities of Poniatowski, the Minister of Land Reform, and of Kwiatkowski himself seemed at odds with the OZON programme. Mościcki appeared to settle this question in his radio address of 19 May. He stressed that the initiative in creating OZON had come from Rydz himself, who had been designated by Piłsudski Leader of the Army and who should be regarded as 'Leader of the Nation'. He expressed his solidarity with Rydz's attempt to achieve 'national consolidation' and expressed his agreement with the programme of the Camp.[1] Yet in spite of his address, the relationship between Government and party still remained unclear. As affairs stood, a number of OZON's adherents, unhappy about the course of Government policy, saw the organization as a means for putting pressure on the Cabinet.

Another unanswered question was how far the creation of the Camp was intended to be the first stage in the introduction of a one-party system. The internal structure of the new grouping was, in this respect, not reassuring. The matter was placed in the hands of Colonel Jan Kowalewski, formerly Military Attaché in Bucharest, who was given the characteristic pseudo-military title of 'Chief of the General Staff', and who proceeded to organize the Camp on hierarchical principles. OZON was divided into a rural and an urban section, and all the leading positions were filled by appoint-ment. Kowalewski denied that the Camp aimed to create a 'mono-party', and affirmed that other parties would not be banned. He did however stress that the goal was a 'guided democracy' and claimed that he favoured a widening of the Camp's support, both on the Right and on the Left.[2]

Koc himself had stronger sympathies for totalitarianism. On 31 May he asserted:

the task of directing this or that aspect of national life cannot be assumed by one political group or faction, but only by the Camp of National Unity, homogeneous and disciplined. Our goal is to create in Poland a new democracy, working for the good of the Nation and of the State, in which the interest of the individual and that of the State will be indissolubly united.[3]

In July, he went further still:

outdated forms and opportunistic habits stand in the way of the crystal-

[1] *Gazeta Polska*, 20 March 1937.
[2] See his interviews with the press on 20 April and 19 August 1937.
[3] *Gazeta Polska*, 1 June 1937.

lization and regrouping of the creative forces of the Nation and State. They have against them, on the other side of the barricade, the 'Folks-front'.[1]

Indeed, all the major initiatives of OZON to widen its political support were made in the direction of the Right. We have already noted how the programme of the Camp in relation to the Jews resembled that of the National Democrats. This similarity was underlined by Kowalewski on 22 April in a statement which made virtually impossible Jewish membership of OZON. While recognizing that there were some Jews who had sincerely adopted Polish nationality, he continued:

Nevertheless, Christian principles, which are the basis of Colonel Koc's declaration, will be the decisive factor in the choice of members. In exceptional cases, Polishness must be established not only by the fact of accepting this nationality, but by the sacrifice of blood voluntarily split, or by other services rendered to the Fatherland, in the course of a whole life, which bear witness to the fact that a person truly belongs to the Polish nation. We have in Poland Jews who have fought for the independence of the country and who, by virtue of this, are organized in the Association of Jews who have fought for Polish Independence.[2] We respect this page of their life, which proves that they are good citizens, just as we respect the attachment, which they do not hide, to their Jewish nationality. It is obvious that they cannot belong to the Camp of National Unity. All the more so, Jews who do not have a past of this type cannot be given privileges by the mere action of professing Polish nationality.[3]

Rydz himself, in an attempt to win over the nationalist students, accepted an invitation to attend a banquet given by the old-established student society Arkonja, which had long been virtually controlled by the Endecja and its offshoots. On this occasion, referred to by Cat-Mackiewicz as an imitation of Piłsudski's visit to Nieśwież,[4] Rydz stressed that he had come 'primarily to attest my faith in the soul of Polish youth'.[5] 'The gulf between the nationalists and the legionaries is gradually being filled', commented the right-wing *Goniec Warszawski*.[5]

Another indication of the growing links with the nationalist

---

[1] Quoted in Singer, *Od Witosa do Sławka*, pp. 342–3.
[2] A reference to the Piłsudski-ite Union of Jews who have taken part in the Struggles for the Independence of Poland.
[3] *Gazeta Polska*, 22 April 1937.   [4] Mackiewicz, op. cit., p. 298.
[5] *Goniec Warszawski*, 20 May 1937.

Right was the creation of the Club of 11 November under the patronage of Grabowski, the Minister of Justice, and Rydz himself.[1] It was attended by members of the O.N.R. and the League of Young Nationalists and published a number of the lectures and discussions which took place there in the form of brochures. Rydz's adjutant Tadeusz Karszo-Siedlewski was present at most of its meetings and Rydz himself was reputed to pay great attention to the proceedings of the Club. The youth movement of OZON, the League of Polish Youth,[2] headed by Jerzy Rutkowski, Piasecki's second-in-command, and expounding corporatist and anti-Semitic ideas, constituted another attempt to reconcile the quarrel between Dmowski and Piłsudski.

The growing *rapprochement* with the nationalist Right was interrupted for a time by the almost ridiculous *brouhaha* which arose in June and July 1937 when Archbishop Sapieha, without consulting the Government, moved Piłsudski's remains from one crypt in Wawel cathedral to another, on the grounds that the peace of the sanctuary was being disturbed by the large influx of visitors, many of whom were 'strangers to Catholicism'.[3] But calls for a union of the Right against the Communist danger continued to grow. The inevitable clash between the openly totalitarian and the more liberal elements within the Sanacja was precipitated by two events. The first was the ten-day peasant strike called by the Peasant Party on 15 August 1937, probably the most serious outbreak of social unrest in Poland in the whole of the inter-war period. The Peasant Party had been growing steadily more radical. At the extraordinary party congress held in Warsaw in January 1937, the party had demanded the 'full democratization of the constitution of Poland' and threatened to resort to an agricultural strike if its demands were not met.[4] Some months later Rataj, always a believer in moderate tactics, gave up his position as party leader, ostensibly on grounds of ill health. He was succeeded by Stanisław Mikołajczyk, a close follower of Witos himself, who agreed with the latter's policy of forcing a confrontation with the Government.[5] The strike, during which peasants were to refuse

---

[1] On this see: Jędruszczak, op. cit., pp. 155–6; Mackiewicz, op. cit., p. 300.

[2] Związek Młodzieży Polskiej.

[3] *Kurjer Warszawski*, 25 June 1937.

[4] *Materiały źródłowe do historii polskiego ruchu ludowego*, iii. 329–30.

[5] W. Matuszewska, *U źródeł strajku chłopskiego w r. 1937* (Warsaw, 1962), pp. 138–9.

to supply the towns, was the logical outcome of this policy. It was intended as a show of strength to force concessions from the Government and its goals were openly political. The manifesto proclaiming the strike called for the 'liquidation of the Sanacja system', an amnesty for the Brześć exiles, the re-establishment of democracy, and a change in foreign policy.[1]

The strike was fairly widely observed, particularly in Galicia. It was for the most part peaceful, but the Government's attempts to break down the baricades which the peasants had erected led to considerable violence. Altogether, according to the official figures, 42 people were killed. More than 1,200 were arrested, of whom about 500 received prison sentences.[2] Witos and Mikołajczyk were less sympathetic than Rataj to the P.P.S., which at its twenty-fourth congress in Radom had specifically rejected a Popular Front with the Communists and had called for the strengthening of links with the Peasant Party. Nevertheless, some attempts were made to initiate common action during the strike, and workers undertook one-day sympathy strikes in a number of towns, including Bochnia, Tarnów, Cracow, and Kielce.[3] After the end of the peasant strike, the links between the two parties were further strengthened.

The Government was severely shaken by this manifestation of peasant radicalism which, even to such a moderate observer as Marian Kukiel, Sikorski's close friend, seemed the precursor of 'civil war'.[4] The divisions within the Sanacja were further intensified by Składkowski's suspension on 30 September of the Executive Committee of the Union of Polish Teachers and his handing over of its affairs to a government commissioner, Paweł Musioł, a leading member of the Falanga. The Union of Polish Teachers was a radical Piłsudski-ite organization which had been fostered by all Ministers of Education since the coup, in preference to its Catholic and nationalist rival organization. From early 1936 it had become more radical and anti-clerical. Already in that year, one issue of its children's paper Płomyk ('The Flame') had been confiscated for praising the Soviet Union. The organization had refused to join OZON and it confirmed this refusal in September

[1] Materiały źródłowe do historii polskiego ruchu ludowego, iii. 343–4.
[2] Pobóg-Malinowski, Najnowsza historia, ii. 835.
[3] Żarnowski, Polska Partia Socjalistyczna, pp. 257–65.
[4] Quoted in Strajk chłopski w 1937 r., dokumenty archiwalne, i (Warsaw, 1960), 212.

1936, while in the following year the number of Left-Wingers on the executive was increased. These seem to have been the main reasons for Składkowski's move, which took place under pressure from Koc, although the Prime Minister claimed he was forced to act because of the support the organization had given to Communism and pacifism, and because of its financial irregularities.[1]

His handling of the problem was maladroit in the extreme, particularly his nomination of a young Fascist as Commissioner, and led to a storm of protest from the left-wing Opposition and from radical Sanacja circles. Following the intervention of a number of important people, including Piłsudski's widow, Składkowski gave way, and in February 1938 the Executive Committee was finally re-elected in its original form without objection from the Government. Koc's initial success in his attack on the Teachers Union seems to have emboldened him to attempt an attack on the left-wing Opposition. At a meeting of the Cabinet on 10 October, in the presence of Rydz-Śmigły, Koc supported Składkowski, who affirmed that recent events had 'to a large extent undermined the Sanacja régime',[2] and argued that there was a high probability that new peasant strikes would occur and that these would stimulate sympathy strikes by the workers. To prevent this, Koc proposed the liquidation of the trade-union movement in its existing form and the setting up of a system of corporations on the Fascist model. To carry through this scheme, he had 'tens of thousands of young men at his disposal'.[2] He was supported in his demands by Rydz, who referred to Koc as 'his man, executing only his commands'.[3] Koc's wild plans for a new coup were strongly opposed by the President and 'his' ministers, Poniatowski and, less strongly, Kwiatkowski. They were also

---

[1] A rather tendentious account of this crisis can be found in Wanda Wasilewska, *Historia jednego strajku* (Warsaw, 1946).

[2] This account of the events at the two meetings is based on the document in the Paderewski Archive entitled 'Wewnętrzne położenie Polski', a document without a date or a signature and the K.P.P. 'List z Domu' of 16 October 1937. Both are quoted in Jędruszczak, op. cit., pp. 191–3.

[3] Ibid., pp. 191–2. On these events see: Jędruszczak, op. cit., pp. 191–3; Żarnowski, *Polska Partia Socjalistyczna*, pp. 272–5; S. Szechter, 'Próby faszystowskiego przewrotu (październik 1937 r.)', *Wieś Współczesna* (1960), no. 10, pp. 129–34; W. Myślek, 'Nieudany pucz Śmigłego', *Polityka*, 3 March 1962; H. Dzendzel, 'Witos, Śmigły-Rydz, ONR', *Polityka*, 24 March 1962.

resisted by Kościałkowski and Beck. As a result, no action was taken.

A similar meeting took place several days later, though probably without the presence of Rydz. Koc and his adherents once again strongly attacked the President and attempted to force him to agree to a modification of the Government and the exclusion from it of his Ministers. The new Prime Minister was to be Grabowski, the Minister of Justice, well known for his Fascist sympathies, who promised that immediately after taking office he would crush 'Judeao-Communism', ban the P.P.S., *Robotnik*, and some other left-wing papers, abolish the Trade Union movement, and pass anti-Semitic legislation. Mościcki, however, was again able to prevent any change in the Government. This apparently induced Koc and Rydz-Śmigły to consider a coup of their own, a Polish 'St. Bartholomew's Night' for 25-6 October. It was to involve the arrest or murder of perhaps 1,500 politicians, including Mościcki, and was to be carried out by Koc, with his Falanga supporters, Paciorkowski, the Deputy Minister of the Interior, and the ruthless Lieutenant-Colonel Zygmunt Wenda, reputed to be one of the murderers of Zagórski, who had replaced Kowalewski as OZON Chief of Staff. At the same time, Koc attempted to put pressure on Car, the Marshal of the Sejm, to transform parliament into a one-party body on the model of Germany and Italy. When Car refused to comply, insisting that he would uphold the constitution, Koc is alleged to have replied: 'We will see which is stronger, the constitution or thirty divisions.'[1]

Car however, was more than a match for the intemperate Koc. On 20 October he called a meeting of the leaders of the regional groupings into which the Sejm, in the absence of party divisions, was organized, at which Rydz and Koc were strongly attacked.[2] Determined opposition to any plans for a coup was also expressed by left-wing Sanacja circles and the strength of this reaction may have induced Koc to hold back his plans for the moment. Already on 14 October, under the auspices of the Naprawa group, an 'Inter-union Consultative Committee of Polish Youth Organizations' was set up. This included the Riflemen's Union, the Piłsudski-ite Union of Young Peasants, the Union of Polish Scouts, and the Organization of Working Youth. A Union of the Patriotic Left

---

[1] Quoted in Mackiewicz, op. cit., p. 304.
[2] Jędruszczak, op. cit., p. 193.

was also established, made up of Moraczewski's Union of Trade Unions, Jaworowski's P.P.S.—Revolutionary Fraction, the unions of the intellectual workers, and the Legion of Youth. At the same time, Democratic Clubs were set up in a number of towns. Among the leading members of the Warsaw Democratic Club were the eminent historian Marceli Handelsman, Regina Fleszarowa, a radical member of the Senate, and Wincenty Rzymowski, the radical journalist who had lost his position when the editorial board of *Kurjer Poranny* had been changed in 1937. The journal *Czarno na Białem*, founded in September 1937 by January Grzędziński, was another important source of opposition to Rydz and a forum where the different factions of the Left could discuss their problems.[1] Koc may also have hesitated to act because of Lieberman's leaking of rumours of a possible coup to the Western press.[2]

Rydz and Koc seem to have seen this as only a temporary set-back to their totalitarian ambitions. At a meeting of the leaders of the Union of Legionaries and the P.O.W. on 30 October, Rydz attacked his critics within the legionary movement. He spoke 'nervously, chaotically, derisively, defiantly, trying to imitate Piłsudski's tone'. He scoffed at those who feared a 'St. Bartholomew's Night'. 'Where are your nerves? You pride yourselves on the fact that the Army and police are on your side. What have you got to fear?'[3] Koc too pushed on with his plans to increase his power in parliament by setting up an OZON club there. It was eventually established after some difficulty on 29 November.[4] In addition, on 9 December *Gazeta Polska* announced that it was becoming the official organ of OZON.

But attempts to introduce a totalitarian system were meeting growing opposition in Government circles. An indication of this was the joint Congress of the Union of Legionaries and the P.O.W. in East Galicia early in November, at which totalitarianism was criticized, and the activities of the OZON youth organization, the Union of Polish Youth, were attacked.[5] General Żeligowski, a man with much prestige in legionary circles, criticized OZON's

---

[1] Jędruszczak, op. cit., p. 193.

[2] Żarnowski, *Polska Partia Socjalistyczna*, pp. 273-4.

[3] A.A.N., Archiwum Paderewskiege. 667. Komunikat Informacyjny no. 14 z 22.XI.1937. Quoted in Jędruszczak, op. cit., pp. 195-6.

[4] *Kurjer Warszawski*, 30 November 1937.

[5] *Ilustrowany Kurjer Codzienny*, 8 November 1937.

totalitarian tendencies in parliament on 2 December. He also attacked the circular proclaiming Rydz to be the second personage in the state as unconstitutional.[1] Żeligowski was supported in parliament by Colonel Tadeusz Schaetzel, an ally of Sławek. He also enjoyed a fair amount of support from pro-Government circles in the country, particularly in Wilno, where the local leader of OZON declared his sympathy with the General. Mościcki too was emboldened to strengthen his position. On 13 November he received a delegation from the P.P.S. which handed him a memorandum and spent two hours with him discussing the political situation. The memorandum attacked Beck's foreign policy, OZON, and anti-Semitism. It called for the introduction of a planned economy to deal with the economic crisis and for a new electoral system and the re-establishment of a full democracy.[2] It is not clear whether the initiative for this meeting came from the President or the P.P.S., and Pobóg-Malinowski's assertion[3] that the delegation had been invited by Kwiatkowski must be treated with some reserve. Certainly strong pressure was put on Mościcki by some Government circles to refuse to see the delegation. The fact that he did receive it undeniably strengthened his hand against Rydz and Koc. The proposal is most likely to have come from the P.P.S. which in this instance acted in consultation with the Peasant Party. The party leadership, under the influence of Arciszewski and Pużak, had come increasingly to believe that the principal danger in Poland was a Fascist coup, and that contact should be increased with the more democratic elements in the Sanacja to prevent this. The party leadership also seems to have believed that it might be possible to detach Rydz from Koc and his entourage. It stressed the party's positive attitude to the Army as a principal means for maintaining independence, and as a result the party participated in a march-past before the Marshal in Warsaw on 11 November.[4]

These hopes, illustrative of the P.P.S.'s unwillingness to risk again, after the débâcle of 1930, an all-out attack on the Government, had a certain basis. From about the end of 1937 Rydz became increasingly unhappy about the direction OZON was

[1] *S.S.S.R.*, 2 December 1937.

[2] The memorandum was printed in *Robotnik* on 14 November 1937.

[3] Pobóg-Malinowski, *Najnowsza historia*, ii. 854.

[4] On these developments, see Żarnowski, *Polska Partia Socjalistyczna*, pp. 283–8.

taking under Koc's leadership. He particularly disliked the Falanga's control of the Camp's youth organization. He tried through Miedziński to induce Koc to change his line, and when these attempts failed, he agreed to comply with Mościcki's demand that Koc be deprived of his position. Koc resigned as head of OZON on 10 January.[1]

He was succeeded by General Stanisław Skwarczyński, the brother of the radical Piłsudski-ite Adam Skwarczyński, who had died in April 1934. General Skwarczyński, a legionary before 1914, had served in the Austrian Army during World War I. In August 1918 he had deserted in order to join the P.O.W. and had supported Piłsudski during the coup. He became a general in 1928, and was a serving military officer until he replaced Koc. His appointment was widely regarded as a shift to the Left by OZON, although the more radical Piłsudski-ites would have preferred Michał Grażynski. Skwarczyński's speech on the first anniversary of Koc's declaration to some extent bore this out. He stressed the need for radical measures to remove the causes of social unrest, for rapid industrialization and for measures to raise the level of peasant agriculture.[2] But he was above all a military man with military interests, and under his direction OZON became more and more a medium for mobilizing civilian support for the Army's efforts to organize the country's defence. Cat-Mackiewicz comments acidly:

Skwarczyński deprived OZON of any political character. OZON became an organization of political opportunism. He called out continually, 'Forward March, Forward March together.' Yet no-one knew where they were marching, to a fire, to a wedding, to a church, or to a play, to the Left or to the Right. They did indeed say that one should march where Rydz commanded, but of them all, Rydz knew least about the direction of the march, having no programme himself.[3]

Skwarczyński did end the monopoly enjoyed by the Falanga in the OZON youth movement. Early in February 1938 he created a new organization, the 'Service of Youth', which was closely supervised by him. Tension between the OZON leadership and Rutkowski and his associates in the League of Polish Youth grew until Rutkowski withdrew from OZON on 20 April taking many of his supporters with him.

---

[1] Pobóg-Malinowski, *Najnowsza historia*, ii. 804.
[2] *Gazeta Polska*, 22 February 1938.   [3] Mackiewicz, op. cit., p. 403.

Though the conflict between the more authoritarian and the more liberal elements in the Government was not yet settled, Mościcki and his followers now consolidated their position. On 14 January, the President received a delegation from the Democratic Club which stressed the need for a modification of the electoral law.[1] Both Mościcki's speech on Piłsudski's name-day[2] and Skwarczyński's on 11 April[3] underlined the need for winning peasant support by radical measures in the countryside. Kwiatkowski's speech in Katowice on 24 April calling for united efforts to deal with the economic crisis in Poland also sounded a new note, and seemed to offer the prospect of a meaningful collaboration between the Government and the Opposition.[4]

DOMESTIC CONFLICT WANES AS THE INTERNATIONAL SITUATION BECOMES MORE THREATENING (MARCH 1938 TO SEPTEMBER 1939)

From the spring of 1938, the atmosphere of politics began to change, and the intensity of the conflicts both within the Government and between it and the Opposition diminished considerably. With the German annexation of Austria in March, questions of foreign policy and national security grew ever more prominent and the bitterness of internal controversies tended to lessen. In the face of external threats, support rallied to the Government, which was basking in the apparent success of Beck's foreign policy. He had forced Lithuania to establish diplomatic relations with Poland in March 1938, and had gained the Trans-Olza part of Austrian Silesia from Czechoslovakia in October. The economic situation also improved, the result both of Kwiatkowski's policies and of the upturn in the world economy, and this too diminished the Government's unpopularity. The final decisions on what concessions should be made to the Opposition were put off, and the uneasy compromise struck in May 1936 was to last until the collapse of the Polish state in September 1939.

However, conflict within the Government ranks was not yet over, and parliament now became the main area. From the start,

[1] *Robotnik*, 16 January 1938.
[2] *Gazeta Polska*, 20 March 1938.
[3] Ibid., 12 April 1938.
[4] *Robotnik*, 25 April 1938. This speech was not commented on by *Gazeta Polska* and only short extracts from it were reprinted in *Kurjer Poranny*.

the parliamentary group of OZON proved difficult to control and was plagued by dissension. On 10 February its chairman, Colonel Bolesław Swidzyński, resigned from the Club, largely on the grounds that it had abandoned the right-wing character of Koc's original declaration.[1] He was supported by Leon Kozłowski, a former Prime Minister, who had also shown increasing right-wing sympathies and was much obsessed by the dangers of Masonic penetration in Poland. A further split took place late in April when the editor of the weekly *Jutro Pracy*, Jerzy Budzyński, was expelled from the Club. He was followed by thirteen other members of parliament and was also supported by Kozłowski.[2] Justifying their action, the group issued a statement claiming that OZON had abandoned 'the national and Christian orientation' of Koc's declaration.

The relative lack of support which the Government enjoyed in parliament was made painfully obvious in June when, following the death of Car, the Marshal of the Sejm, Sławek was elected to fill his place. Sławek's candidacy seems to have been sponsored by Żeligowski, and it was bitterly opposed by a number of the Government's followers, above all Miedziński, who supported Ignacy Nowak, a Silesian member of the Naprawa group. Sławek's victory was a convincing one, for he obtained 144 votes to 30 for Nowak, with 32 blank votes. This constituted a threat both to Mościcki's supporters (the so-called Zamek group)[3] and to those of Rydz, since the President, whose office was to fall vacant in 1940, was chosen primarily by the Sejm and Senate. It was probably Sławek's success which induced Mościcki to dissolve parliament on 13 September and call new elections for 6 and 13 November. According to Pobóg-Malinowski, whose narrative is admittedly marked by a strong hostility to Kwiatkowski, the Minister of Finance had been pressing the President since the end of March to dissolve parliament but was only able to obtain Rydz's assent, without which Mościcki would do nothing, after Sławek's election.[4] The dissolution came as a complete surprise to the entire Opposition and indeed to many of the leading members of the Sanacja, including Sławek and Prystor.

---

[1] *Kurjer Warszawski*, 11 February 1938.
[2] *Czas*, 1 May 1938.
[3] The nickname 'Zamek' came from the President's palace, the Zamek.
[4] Pobóg-Malinowski, *Najnowsza historia*, ii. 853.

The electoral campaign revealed the deep divisions in the Government. Both Mościcki and Kwiatkowski emphasized the need for a new electoral system and promised that the introduction of suitable legislation would be one of the first tasks of the new Assembly. Kwiatkowski in a speech at Katowice on 16 October went out of his way to stress his sympathy for the nationalist, socialist, and populist opposition and to assert his belief that these groups had a role to play in the running of the country. He also acknowledged the importance of parliamentary control of the actions of the Government.[1] The most radical parts of his speech were not even printed in the official *Gazeta Polska*. Składkowski's speech at Turek on 23 October struck a different note. He attacked the Opposition parties for their refusal to participate in the elections and compared the behaviour of the party leaders to that of the *szlachta* just before the partition of Poland.[2]

However, the Opposition boycott was much less successful than that of 1935. Altogether 67·3 per cent of those eligible voted, and according to the official figures only 4·2 per cent of the votes cast were invalid. The percentage of voters was highest in Eastern Poland (Tarnopol province—82·1; Stanisławów province—66·2; Lwów province—64·5; Polesia—72·8; Wilno province—70·8; Nowogródek province—68·5). But it was also high in Silesia (83·2), perhaps because of Kwiatkowski's speech. The most striking differences between the 1935 and 1938 results were in Central Poland. In Warsaw 53·3 per cent voted (29·4 per cent in 1935); Warsaw province 66·2 per cent (37·3 per cent); Kielce province 67·2 per cent (36·6 per cent); Lodz province 60 per cent (36·7 per cent); Lublin province 71·7 per cent (39·9 per cent); Białystok province 76·7 per cent (57·2 per cent). The Government also did well in traditionally National Democratic Western Poland, winning 63·7 per cent of the votes in Poznania and 64·9 per cent in Pomerania. The boycott was most successful in West Galicia, long a stronghold of the Peasant Party, where only 47·1 per cent of the electorate voted.[3]

These results were undoubtedly a triumph for the Government, as was conceded by the Opposition.[4] Attempts have been made to

[1] *Robotnik*, 17 October 1938.
[2] *Gazeta Polska*, 24 October 1938.
[3] Ibid., 8 November 1938.
[4] See, for instance, the articles in *Nasz Przegląd* on 8 November 1938 and *Robotnik* on 20 November 1938.

show that a high percentage of voters cast only one of their two votes and that this should be taken as an indication of sympathy for the Opposition. In the more highly developed part of the country (so-called Poland 'A'), only 47·4 per cent of the voters cast two votes, as they were entitled to.[1] But this figure is far more likely to reflect misunderstandings over the highly complicated electoral system than a desire to express solidarity with the boycott. There were a number of reasons for the Government's success. The Cabinet were determined that there would be no repetition of the fiasco of 1935. Public prosecutors were informed that agitation in favour of an electoral boycott was illegal in terms of Article 156 of the Penal Code, and carried a penalty of imprisonment of up to two years. This threat of possible legal reprisal was carried in the press.[2] Censorship of the press was so intensified that the Warsaw Journalists' Association protested against its severity on 14 October.[3] The Government exercised all possible pressure, and fear of the consequences of not voting was a major factor in the high turn-out at the polls. It was also able to induce Cardinal Hlond to condemn the boycott and assert that it was a 'patriotic obligation' to vote.[4] In addition, the Government benefited from the popularity it enjoyed in the country as a whole, largely as a result of Beck's spurious triumph in acquiring the Trans-Olza part of Austrian Silesia after Munich. In fact, the Opposition was itself rather half-hearted about the boycott. Unsuccessful negotiations were undertaken between the Government and both the P.P.S. and the Peasant Party to enable them to participate in the elections.[5] This halfheartedness was partially the result of the implied threat that if the boycott were too successful, the proposed reform of the electoral system would not take place. One of the Government's electoral slogans was this rhyme:

Voters, don't forget the saw,
No Sejm, no electoral law.[6]

---

[1] This is the main argument of the article by Bolesław Morka, 'Nie zwycięstwo OZN lecz klęska', in *Czarno na Białem* on 8 January 1939. His conclusions are uncritically reproduced by M. Turlejska in *Rok przed klęska* (3rd ed., Warsaw, 1965), pp. 142–3.

[2] *Gazeta Polska*, 18 October 1938.

[3] *Warszawski Dziennik Narodowy*, 1 November 1938.

[4] Pobóg-Malinowski, *Najnowsza historia*, ii. 854.

[5] Żarnowski, *Polska Partia Socjalistyczna*, pp. 322–3.

[6] Zapamięta jcztery słowa, Sejm to ordynacja nowa.

The election accomplished the political extinction of Sławek. Through its control of the electoral assemblies, the Government had exercised strong pressure in the selection of candidates and in the Sejm 161 of the 208 deputies were members of OZON. Moreover Sławek was personally defeated in Warsaw, although his ally, Żeligowski, was successful in Wilno, and he was badly hurt by this rebuff. This, together with his fears for the future of Poland and his belief that he had failed his beloved Marshal, were responsible for his suicide in March 1939. The members of the new parliament were mostly men with no political past. Lewiatan had no representative in the new Sejm, and the number of conservatives was greatly reduced.[1] Cat-Mackiewicz's predictions that the Government's aim in the elections was to 'form a "pseudo-monoparty" parliament composed of officials'[2] was unfortunately realized.

The period after the election saw an intensification of repressive action by the Government. The new press decree, issued on 21 November, ostensibly to unite the laws governing the press in the different parts of the country, further limited the freedom of the press. Penalties for infractions of the law were increased and newspapers could now be forced to publish government communiqués of up to 1,250 lines.[3] Another decree of 22 November to 'protect certain interests of the State' imposed potentially very severe limitations on political freedom. It made illegal and introduced drastic penalties for all 'defeatist' propaganda, strikes in military factories, general or peasant strikes or entering into contact 'with a person who serves a foreign government or an international organization with the intention of harming the Polish State'. Many clauses, such as that just cited, were formulated in such general terms as to make it possible for the Government to make illegal all opposition.[4] At the same time, Masonic organizations were banned, an ominous gesture to win over those who believed that Poland was threatened by a 'Jewish-Masonic plot'. The clauses of this decree were also so vague that they could be employed against any conspiratorial organization.[5]

The growing totalitarian tendencies within the Government

---

[1] *Kurjer Warszawski*, 8 and 9 November 1938.
[2] *Słowo*, 25 October 1938.
[3] *Dz.U.R.P.* (1938), no. 89, pp. 1333–41.
[4] Ibid., no. 91, pp. 1370–2.
[5] Ibid., p. 1372.

even emboldened Zygmunt Wenda, the Chief of Staff of OZON and its *de facto* director, to attempt to overthrow Kwiatkowski and end the power of the Zamek faction. Wenda, a 'Lieutenant-Colonel with the ambitions of a General'[1] and an open supporter of the introduction of a totalitarian system, attacked Kwiatkowski in parliament on 3 December, claiming that his economic policy resulted from an over-optimistic assessment of the situation and was 'not daring enough'.[2] However Wenda overestimated his own strength and obtained little backing even from those who would have liked to support him. Kwiatkowski's position was strengthened, and on 9 December Wenda was forced to admit that he had expressed only 'his personal views'.[3]

Given the delicate balance of forces within the Sanacja, the Government's decision to allow the holding of the long overdue elections for local government bodies assumed a special importance. The elections were to be held over a two-year period: in late 1938 they were to take place in 49 towns in southern and western Poland and in 30,000 village communes in central and eastern Poland; in early 1939, elections were scheduled for 89 towns, mostly in western Poland. In May 1939 the towns in central and eastern Poland were to vote, as well as 10,500 village communes in the central and southern Poland. Elections were also planned for 1,100 rural councils in the west and south.

Partly as a concession to Opposition demands, the Government promised that the elections would be a free and unfettered expression of public opinion. Administrative interference was kept within reasonable limits, particularly in the larger towns, and Składkowski's instructions to local government officials, that 'electors should be free both from improper interference by the authorities, as well as from pressure by unauthorized bodies',[4] was for the most part observed.

The Opposition, eager to show its own strength and conscious of the fact that Primo de Rivera's fall in Spain in 1931 had followed his defeat in local government elections, devoted much attention to the campaign. The results were somewhat inconclusive, but they clearly showed the falsity of the Government's

[1] Pobóg-Malinowski, *Najnowsza historia,* ii. 805.
[2] *S.S.S.R.,* 3 December 1938.
[3] Ibid., 9 December 1938.
[4] *Zielony Sztandar,* 18 December 1938.

claims that it enjoyed a clear majority in the country. By June 1939, the elections in the towns had been completed.

Over the country as a whole, the results seemed to favour the Government. According to *Gazeta Polska*, OZON and its allies won 48·1 per cent of the seats in the 394 towns where elections were held, as against 15·6 per cent for the National Party, 10·8 per cent for the P.P.S., 17·4 per cent for the Jewish groupings and 8·1 per cent for other parties.[1] But this gives a rather misleading picture, for many of the towns involved were little more than villages in which the Government still found it easy to exert pressure. If one looks at the distribution of seats in the 160 larger towns in which the P.P.S. put forward candidates, the picture looks somewhat different. Here OZON, often in alliance with other groups, won around 30 per cent of the seats, the P.P.S. around 25 per cent and the National Party around 17 per cent.

TABLE XII.* *Results of Local Government Elections in the 160 Towns contested by the P.P.S. in 1938 and 1939*

Political grouping	Seats
Total:	3,944
P.P.S.	1,078
National Party	671
OZON	864
OZON in alliance with other groups (principally the National Party and the Christian Democrats)	468
Peasant Party	26
Party of Labour	55
Christian Democracy	16
National Radicals	6
P.P.S.—Former Revolutionary Fraction	2
Non-party	56
Bund	141
Other Jewish lists	503
Ukrainians	30
Germans	26
Czechs	2

* Żarnowski, *Polska Partia Socjalistyczna*, p. 330.

P.P.S. spokesmen claimed, moreover, that to assess the results solely in terms of seats was misleading, since OZON had done

[1] *Gazeta Polska*, 1 July 1939.

particularly well in the smaller towns where administrative pressure was greatest. The results in the forty-eight towns with a population of more than 25,000 were certainly a more convincing indication of socialist strength.[1]

An interesting indication of political attitudes on the eve of the war is revealed in the results of the six largest towns. In Warsaw, a town of officials and civil servants, the Government did well. It was helped too by the prestige of the mayor, Stefan Starzyński, a prominent member of OZON and also of the Naprawa group. The Government bloc won 40 seats, the P.P.S. 27, the Bund 16, the National Party 11, the National Radicals 5, other Jewish groups 4. In Lodz, the P.P.S. scored a notable triumph, for of the 72 seats it won 35, against 11 for OZON, 18 for the National Party, 11 for the Bund, 6 for other Jewish groups, and 5 for the Germans. In Cracow, no single group stands out. OZON in alliance with the Party of Labour won 23 seats of 72; the P.P.S. won 24, the National Party 12, Jewish groups 13. Poznań remained a National Democratic stronghold; of 72 seats, the National Party won 52, OZON 19, the P.P.S. 1. In Eastern Poland, victory was shared by the Government and the nationalists. In Wilno, OZON won 19 seats, the socialists 9, the nationalists 26; in Lwów, OZON was 23, the P.P.S. won 9, the nationalists won 22, the Jewish groups 16.

[1] Votes in towns with more than 25,000 inhabitants. (Based on Żarnowski *Polska Partia Socjalistyczna*, p. 331.)

Party	Percentage
P.P.S.	26·8
OZON	29·0
National Party	18·8
Bund	9·5
Party of Labour	1·6
National Radicals	1·2
Others	13·1
	100

The P.P.S. won an absolute majority in Sosnowiec, Radom, Borysław, Dąbrowa Górnicza, Ostrowiec, and Kalisz and won a majority together with the Bund or the Poalei Sion in Lodz, Piotrków, Włocławek, Grodno, Tarnów, Siedlce, Płock, Nowy Sącz, and Zamość. OZON won an absolute majority only in Brześć and Kolomyja, and a majority in alliance with so-called non-party groups in Równe, Tarnopol, Stryj, and Włodzimierz Wołyński, all smaller towns in Eastern Poland subject to strong administrative pressure.

As will be evident from these figures, one of the most striking features of the elections was the emergence of the Bund as the dominant political force in the Jewish community. Another interesting feature was the way OZON was able to make alliances with the National Party, particularly in the smaller towns. It is much more difficult to subject the electoral results in the rural communes to analysis, because elections in these small places tended to be decided on questions of personality, and national questions were not particularly important. But here too, the Government was unable to dominate the new elected councils and the Peasant Party proved to be a force in the countryside.[1]

The results of the local government elections were variously interpreted. *Gazeta Polska* hesitated for some days after the December elections to print anything, while *Kurjer Poranny* claimed that the results 'had a purely local significance'.[2] To the Opposition press, the elections were proof that the Government did not possess sufficient following in the country to introduce a single party system. 'They show', wrote the popular Catholic paper *Mały Dziennik*, 'that none of the major political groupings has enough credit or prestige to have the right to claim a monopoly of power without, in so doing, weakening the State. . . .'[3]

The relative success of the Opposition in the elections led its spokesmen once again to press the Government to say when it would proceed to reform the electoral law as it had promised. On 18 January Senator Dębski, who had been nominated by Mościcki to represent the Opposition, demanded to know when the Government would take action. He received an ambiguous answer from Sławoj-Składkowski. 'As regards the attitude of the Government,' affirmed the Prime Minister, 'I can assure you that it is cognizant of this question, and that it considers it highly important for the future of the Polish State.'[4]

The Government appeared in no hurry to undertake a reform which could well undermine its power, and its spokesmen attempted continually to postpone the settlement of the question for as long as possible. When electoral reform was demanded by two independent deputies, Juliusz Dudziński and Franciszek Stoch, in

---

[1] Turlejska, *Rok przed klęska*, p. 147.
[2] *Kurjer Poranny*, 20 December 1938.
[3] 20 December 1938.
[4] *S.S.Se.R.*, 18 January 1939.

mid-February, General Skwarczyński replied that OZON was aware of the importance of the problem and would only pass legislation which had been 'deliberately thought out'. He claimed no time limit had been set in the President's message as to when the new electoral law should be introduced.[1]

All the while, the international situation was becoming more threatening. German power in Eastern Europe had been enormously increased by the Munich agreement and the destruction of the military potential of Czechoslovakia. Hitler did not yet contemplate renouncing the Declaration of Non-Aggression with Poland, still unclear whether to move East or West and hoping to reduce Poland to a sort of satellite against either eventuality. He saw that the increased strength of the Reich would allow him to place his relationship with the Poles on a new and more advantageous footing.

On 24 October 1938, Ribbentrop for the first time, in conversation with Lipski, the Polish Ambassador in Berlin, demanded the 'return of Danzig' and the construction of an extra-territorial *Autobahn* across Pomerania to link East and West Prussia. These demands were repeated to Beck on 4 January 1939 on his return through Germany from France. Beck, in his memoirs, noted the new tone employed by Hitler in these conversations.[2] In the discussions Ribbentrop was particularly unyielding. The serious nature of the German claims became even clearer on Ribbentrop's visit to Warsaw on 24 January 1939. On this occasion the demands for Danzig and an *Autobahn* were repeated, and in addition strong pressure was exerted on Poland to join the Anti-Comintern Pact. German demands took on an even more threatening form after the final dissolution of Czechoslovakia on 14 March, with the incorporation of Bohemia and Moravia into the Reich and the setting up of an independent Slovakia, dependent on Germany. On 21 March, the claims for Danzig and the *Autobahn* were reaffirmed, while Nazi-sponsored anti-Polish demonstrations were organized in the Free City.

At the same time, the annexation of Bohemia and Moravia caused a revulsion in British public opinion which led to a modification of British policy. This culminated in the offer of a

[1] *S.S.S.R.*, 16 February 1939.
[2] J. Beck, *Dernier Rapport: politique polonaise, 1926–1939* (Neuchatel, 1951), pp. 180–1.

guarantee to the Poles, which Beck was able to modify into an agreement involving mutual obligations in case of attack. Thus on 6 April an Anglo-Polish communiqué was issued announcing that a formal agreement would shortly be signed, providing for mutual aid in the case of a direct or indirect threat to the independence of the United Kingdom or Poland. On 28 April the German Government renounced the German-Polish Non-Aggression Declaration of 1934.

These developments naturally dominated Polish political life and internal conflict diminished considerably in intensity. Indeed, the Government's new foreign policy enjoyed widespread support among the Opposition. Poland's increasingly insecure position gave greater strength to Government calls for national consolidation. Already in January, the Executive Committee of the Peasant Party resolved that 'the slogan of the unification of society around the defence of the State finds a vigorous response in the Peasant Party'.[1]

The National Party, perhaps weakened by the death of Dmowski in January 1939, also moderated its opposition. From February, one of its leaders, Stanisław Kozicki, sought contact with the Government and had a number of talks with General Skwarczyński.[2] Rydz-Śmigły, as the embodiment of the Army, also became much more popular; this led Miedziński, who was again emerging as a political force, to propose around the end of February that the Marshal take over the Presidency from Mościcki, whose health seemed to be failing. The scheme came to nothing, however, when the President's health took an unexpected turn for the better.[3]

The Government decided to take advantage of the patriotic éclat aroused by the German threats to launch an internal loan to raise money for military aviation and anti-aircraft artillery at the end of March. The committee which organized support for the loan included prominent representatives from the main Opposition parties: the Peasant Party, the National Party, the P.P.S., the Party of Labour, and even the National Radicals lent their support. The loan was an enormous success, and by the end of June General Berbecki, its Commissioner-General, was able to

[1] *Materiały źródłowe do historii polskiego ruchu ludowego*, iii. 407.
[2] Pobóg-Malinowski, *Najnowsza historia*, ii. 855–6.
[3] Ibid., p. 855.

announce that it had raised 404 million zloties against the 180 million the Government had hoped for, and that 3·1 million people had subscribed.[1]

At the same time, the question of the political *émigrés* was now finally settled. After prior discussion with Polish diplomatic officials, Witos, Bagiński, Kiernik, and Korfanty, who had been living in Czechoslovakia, returned to Poland. After several days' nominal imprisonment, they were all set at liberty. Of those who had stood trial at Brześć, only Hermann Lieberman remained abroad.

But though it was prepared to make conciliatory gestures towards the Opposition, the Government was not prepared to share its power and create a Government of national unity. On 1 April the P.P.S. submitted a memorandum to the President calling on the Government to reform the electoral system so that in 1940 the President could be chosen by a parliament elected on a democratic franchise. The Government's reaction was to prevent the publication of the memorandum in the press.[2] Indeed, in response to further calls for the reform of the electoral system, *Kurjer Poranny*, fully supported by *Gazeta Polska*, held on 25 April that discussions 'on this or that internal programme can only undermine the development of the national morale and weaken the consolidation of national energy'.[3]

At the end of May the pro-Government press went so far as to launch an extremely bitter compaign aimed at discrediting Witos, who, it was alleged, had been contacted by the Gestapo in Bohemia after its incorporation into the Reich.

> In the name of the German government, the Gestapo promised him that he could return without fear to Poland and would take power there as head of a broadly-based Popular Government. The Gestapo asked in return only that he concede autonomy to the Germans in Poland and the other national minorities.[4]

The only truth in these highly compromising allegations was that after the annexation of Bohemia the German authorities had attempted unsuccessfully to make contact with Witos. Certain written propositions relating to the minorities and economic questions had been passed on to him by a third party. These had

---

[1] *Gazeta Polska*, 27 June 1939.
[2] Żarnowski, *Polska Partia Socjalistyczna*, pp. 341–2.
[3] *Kurjer Poranny*, 25 April 1939. [4] Ibid., 31 May 1939.

been rejected, and the Polish diplomatic representative in Prague was informed by Witos of the whole course of events.

The revelation of the truth did not deter *Kurjer Poranny*, and the campaign against Witos was pursued unabated throughout June. As *Robotnik* pointed out, these were strange methods by which to achieve national consolidation.[1] It was clear that the Government was not interested in co-operation with the Opposition except on its own terms. In June the principal members of the Sanacja, together with Rydz-Śmigły, finally decided not to widen the basis of their support and create an all-party coalition.[2] As a result, Poland entered the war with the regime jealously guarding its political monopoly, a fact which was to have great significance after the rapid defeat of the Polish armies.

[1] *Robotnik*, 4 June 1939.
[2] Pobóg-Malinowski, *Najnowsza historia*, ii. 856–7.

X

ECONOMICS, THE NATIONAL MINORITIES, AND FOREIGN POLICY 1935–1939

Poland will be a great power or she will not exist.
Józef Piłsudski

THE years between 1935 and 1939 saw important departures in foreign policy, in relations with the national minorities, and in foreign affairs. Kwiatkowski's measures from mid-1936 effected a hopeful revival in industry, although the position of the peasant farmer was not to any marked extent alleviated. As for the national minorities, Polish policy was dictated more and more by fears that any encouragement of national separateness might foster secessionist ambitions and weaken the country's security. As a result, the formulation of policy was increasingly entrusted to the Army, especially in Eastern Poland. Neither was there much success in foreign policy, in spite of Beck's pseudo-triumphs. The Foreign Minister's unimaginative application of Piłsudski's principle of 'balance' between the country's two powerful neighbours placed Poland in an increasingly exposed position in relation to Nazi Germany. Moreover, the failure to effectively reorganize the Polish Army meant that his foreign policy was based to a large extent on bluff; this was to be cruelly exposed in the three-week campaign of September 1939.

THE ECONOMIC SITUATION

The Government did enjoy a certain success in stimulating the growth of the economy, particularly after the abandonment of the orthodox deflationary policy which had been pursued since the onset of the Depression. This policy, which as we have seen, led to the persistence of depressed economic conditions in Poland for much longer than elsewhere in Europe, was undermined in several ways. With the death of Piłsudski the chief brake on the adoption of a more adventurous economic policy was removed. At the same time, attempts to stimulate economic recovery by deficit financing and government programmes of public works could be seen in successful operation in the United States, Germany, and elsewhere. The first two five-year plans in Russia also increased the feeling that the resolution of the economic crisis lay in the abandonment of *laisser-faire* and the adoption of economic planning. The rigidly deflationary policy pursued in Poland was, moreover, not proving successful. In spite of drastic cuts in government expenditure, it proved impossible to balance the budget, and the deficit rose from 115·8 million zloties in 1934–5 to 307·0 million zloties in 1935–6.[1] Unemployment remained extremely high and led in early 1936 to a wave of strikes and industrial violence. In March the Security Department of the Ministry of the Interior warned that if an explosive situation was to be avoided, 'much more decisive steps should be taken to relieve the pressure on the labour market'.[2]

In addition, the assumptions on which the deflation had been pursued now seemed to have less justification. The guarantee extended to foreign investors that they could freely transfer their assets, which forced the maintenance in Poland of extremely high rates of interest, had been decided upon in the belief that it would stimulate new foreign investment in the country. Yet the tense international situation discouraged the inflow of new capital. The increase in international trade which was expected with the waning of the Depression also did not occur. If we take the 1929 index as 100, whereas international industrial production had risen from 74 in 1932 to 127 in 1937, international trade rose only by 74·1 to 96·2.[3] This phenomenon was largely the result of the widespread adoption of high protectionist tariffs. Yet Polish policy presupposed that the recovery of the country's economy would follow a revival of international trade.

A final factor stimulating a shift in policy was the widespread dissatisfaction deflation had aroused in left-wing Sanacja circles. Stpiczyński, writing in *Kurjer Poranny* in the second half of 1935, attacked the alleged dependence of government economic policy on the large landowners and the big industrialists of Lewiatan.[4]

---

[1] *M.R.S.* (1939), Table XII, pp. 376–7.
[2] 'Bezrobocie w Polsce w latach 1925–1936', *Najnowsze dzieje Polski. Materiały i studia z okresu 1914–1939*, ed. M. Drozdowski, iv. 231. The whole report covers pp. 212–38.   [3] *M.R.S.* (1939), pp. 1, 162.
[4] See, e.g., *Kurjer Poranny*, 22 November 1935.

These pressures were, however, relatively slow to take effect. Professor Marian Zawadzki remained the main architect of economic policy in the Sławek Cabinet, which held office until 12 October 1935, and no significant departures were made from the deflationary course he had pursued since his appointment in September 1932. The Government continued the 'draining' of the credit market by issuing internal loans to which civil servants were virtually forced to contribute, which were intended to make up the budget deficit. In July 1935, for instance, a 6 per cent Investment Loan of 50 million zloties was floated. Some attempts were made to relieve the burden of agricultural indebtedness and to increase foreign trade by negotiating commercial agreements. In November and December 1935 agreements were reached with importers of coal in Yugoslavia, Denmark, Norway, and Finland to increase the amount of Polish coal they bought.[1]

Nevertheless, Zawadzki's policies had little success. The fall in Government revenue made it impossible to balance the budget in spite of stringent cuts in expenditure. Industrial production increased somewhat, though in 1935 the index stood at only 85 (1928 = 100).[2] Indeed, 1935 saw both monetary circulation and prices reach their lowest level during the Depression, and there was a further fall in the amount of coal mined and of oil extracted. Unemployment, too, remained extremely high, falling only from 414,000 in December 1934 to 403,000 in December 1935.[3]

Pressure for a modification of economic policy became stronger after the débâcle of the elections of September 1935, which so exposed the weakness of the Sanacja. Mościcki firmly believed that the economic issue was the most pressing of the day, and he was determined to secure the appointment of his friend Eugeniusz Kwiatkowski as Minister of Finance in the Kościałkowski Cabinet set up in October. Kwiatkowski, perhaps the ablest economist among the Piłsudski-ites, had left the Cabinet in May 1930 after a dispute with the Marshal, and had from 1930 to 1935 been the Director of the State Chemical Works at Mościce. Kwiatkowski's economic views were not particularly radical, though he had come to the conclusion, as a result of the Depression, that strong controls over foreign trade were a necessity if any economic recovery was

---

[1] On these policies, see M. Drozdowski, *Polityka gospodarcza rządu polskiego, 1936–39* (Warsaw, 1963), pp. 30–8.

[2] *M.R.S.* (1939), Table II, p. 3.   [3] 'Bezrobocie w Polsce', p. 232.

to be achieved in Poland. On the other hand, he was an extremely able administrator and the policy he at first pursued differed from that of Zawadzki primarily in the efficiency with which it was implemented.[1]

He saw as his prime task the balancing of the budget, which he regarded as the necessary precondition for any economic recovery. He increased government revenue by imposing a special tax on salaries from public funds and by lowering the level at which people were liable to income tax. He also cut expenses by a tighter control of local government spending and by diminishing the pensions to retired persons and invalids. He rejected any further use of the practice of floating loans to meet government deficits, which he regarded as harmful to the private credit market. His measures had the desired effect, and the budget for 1936–7 showed a surplus of 4 million zloties as against the large deficit of the previous year.[2]

Kwiatkowski's policy also differed from that of his predecessor in his more energetic attempt to diminish the hold of cartels on the national economy. By a new decree of 27 November 1935, the Minister was given the right to dissolve cartels, and not merely to suspend their operation as previously.[3] These powers were used to dissolve nearly 100 cartels and led to the lowering of prices of a number of articles in common use. But as before, the cartels proved far too useful to the Government, particularly in its foreign trading, for the campaign against them to be too vigorously pursued.

He also attempted to make the economy less rigid by diminishing the role of government-owned enterprises. In December 1935 his Minister of Trade and Industry, Roman Górecki, called a conference to investigate methods of exercising more effective control over state enterprises. This conference set up an 'Étatist Commission' on which prominent industrialists were represented, and in March 1936 the Cabinet drew up a list of Government concerns which were to be investigated by the Commission to see whether any could be handed back to private enterprise. But given the weakness of private domestic capital in Poland, calls for the diminution of the role of the state in the economy had little effect. Indeed 1936 saw a significant extension of the percentage of Polish

[1] Drozdowski, *Polityka gospodarcza*, pp. 47–65.
[2] *M.R.S.* (1939), pp. 376–7, Table XII.
[3] *Dz.U.R.P.* (1935), no. 86, pp. 1397–8.

industry in state hands, with the taking over by the Government of the 'Community of Interests', the largest Silesian mining and foundry complex, which accounted for 56 per cent of Polish steel and 12 per cent of Polish coal production. When the Żyrardów affair was finally settled in autumn 1936, the majority of shares in the mills were taken over by the Bank of National Economy.[1]

None of these measures constituted a major change of policy, which came only with the financial crisis caused in the first nine months of 1936 by the fall of the Laval Government in January and the coming to power of the Popular Front. Following a run on the franc, France left the gold standard in September and allowed the value of the franc to fall. The crisis of the franc, with which the zloty was closely linked, accelerated the flight from money which had been apparent in Poland since the spring of 1935, when rumours about a future devaluation of the zloty gathered force. Since money could be freely transferred from the country, these rumours led to a rapid outflow of capital. The gold and currency reserves of the Bank of Poland fell rapidly, and 57 million zloties were lost in April 1936 alone.[2] This outflow adversely affected both the country's balance of trade and her balance of payments.

The Government's reaction to the crisis was to abandon the free transfer of currency from Poland and introduce a strict system of exchange control on 26 April 1936.[3] Only the Bank of Poland and certain other specified banks were given the right to deal in foreign currency, and a special Foreign Exchange Commission was established to supervise their activity. Since this did not prove sufficient, the Government decided on 24 July 1936 to suspend cash transfers for the service of foreign loans, a decisive break with previous policy which had always regarded the prompt fulfilment of the country's financial obligations a paramount goal.[4]

In February 1937 terms were agreed with Poland's creditors for rescaling her debts. Strict controls were also introduced on foreign trade. On 7 May 1936, the importing of goods was prohibited without a licence obtained from a newly established Commission for Trade. Exporters were also obliged to notify the Commission of their transactions, and obtain a foreign exchange permit.[5] The

[1] Landau and Tomaszewski, op. cit., pp. 234–5.
[2] Z. Karpiński, *Bank Polski, 1924–1939* (Warsaw, 1957), p. 169.
[3] *Dz.U.R.P.* (1936), no. 32, pp. 559–62.
[4] Ibid., no. 57, pp. 925–8.
[5] Ibid., no. 36, p. 624.

regulations were further tightened on 3 November 1936 by the establishment of a Polish Clearing Institute which was assigned the task of carrying out clearing agreements by which imports from a particular country had to be balanced by exports to it and of arranging the necessary compensatory transactions.[1] There was also in the last two years before the war an intensification of exchange control regulations. By a decree of 7 November 1938 Polish residents had to register their assets abroad, and could be compelled to sell them to the Bank of Poland.[2] In addition, in terms of legislation of November 1938 and January 1939, the export of jewels or precious metals was prohibited, and the amount of foreign currency which could be taken abroad severely restricted.[3]

These measures did stem the outflow of capital and end the atmosphere of panic. A positive balance of trade was maintained in 1936, though relatively small deficits occurred in 1937 and 1938. But the level of Polish trade was much below that of the best years of the 1920s. Exports, for instance, in 1935 were only 44·8 per cent of their 1928 figure in value and in 1938, the best year before the war, had risen only to 57·1 per cent.[4] Part of this loss was caused by the fall in the price of agricultural products, which constituted Poland's main export, but it also reflected the results of the increasingly restrictive character of international trade.

The introduction of exchange control and control over foreign trade precipitated the split between Kwiatkowski and those representatives of the colonels—in particular Koc, Lechnicki, and Matuszewski—who regarded these measures as an unjustified departure from financial orthodoxy. Koc resigned as Director of the Bank of Poland in March 1936. The orthodox deflationary policy was also supported by the conservatives, both in *Czas* and in Mackiewicz's *Słowo*.[5] Its abandonment marked a further diminution of the importance of the conservatives within the Sanacja.

Against Kwiatkowski's policy of rigid exchange control, Koc and Matuszewski advocated a devaluation of the zloty, perhaps followed by adherence to the sterling bloc. There was much to be said for this policy, but Kwiatkowski, who at first regarded the

---

[1] Ibid., no. 84, pp. 1390–1.
[2] Ibid. (1938), no. 88, pp. 1299–1300.
[3] Ibid., no. 85, pp. 1285–9; (1939), no. 7, pp. 61–3.
[4] Based on *M.R.S.* (1939), Table I, p. 162.
[5] See for instance, the article in *Czas* on 10 May 1936.

controls he had introduced as purely temporary expedients, opposed it on the grounds that the rise in the price of imported raw
materials which would have ensued, would have outweighed any
gain, while the burden of Poland's foreign debts would have been
increased. He also felt that national prestige was involved in maintaining the parity of the zloty, and may have had doubts as to the
possibility of a real increase in the volume of world trade, on which
the success of devaluation would have depended.

The introduction of controls over foreign exchange and trade
made possible further departures in economic policy. A dispute
now arose within the Government. The military on the one hand,
led by Rydz-Śmigły and Wenda, wanted to abandon entirely
orthodox budgetary financing and embark on a course of expansion
based on a planned inflation, as was being pursued in Germany.
This course was opposed by Kwiatkowski on the grounds that

we are a young state with a population not skilled in financial matters
and distrustful of them, not used to our own national economy. The
corner-stone of our financial policy must be the sums saved by moderately
rich and indeed poor people. In the case of the disappearance or devaluation of these hard-won savings we would be morally undermined
and destroyed as a functioning society, even without a war with
Germany.[1]

Kwiatkowski's more cautious approach was, for the next part,
adopted. In July 1936, he set out a four-year plan in terms of
which the Government would invest between 1,650 and 1,800
million zloties. The financing for this plan was to be provided by
the mobilization of all the idle resources which had accumulated in
public and private banks and savings institutions since the onset
of the Depression. This was to be underwritten by the issue of
Treasury bills and of promissory notes on state enterprises. In
addition, credits were to be obtained from the Labour Fund, which
was responsible for public works programmes, and the note issue
of the Bank of Poland was somewhat increased.[2]

At the same time, the Ministry of War and the General Staff
also prepared a six-year investment programme to step up the

[1] F. Sławoj-Składkowski, 'Opowieści administracyjne czyli pamiętnik niebohaterski', *Kultura* (1951), no. 9/47, p. 122.
[2] On this see: Drozdowski, *Polityka gospodarcza*, pp. 66–73; Landau and
Tomaszewski, op. cit., pp. 212–27.

production of armaments.[1] This plan reflected the dissatisfaction of the military with what they regarded as the excessively cautious character of Kwiatkowski's scheme, and the lack of co-ordination between the two plans caused a certain amount of difficulty.

The sums initially proposed in Kwiatkowski's plan were not particularly large. In the first year there was to be an investment of around 340 million zloties, not significantly more than government outlays on investment in the early 1930s. What enabled the plan to take larger dimensions was the French loan of £12½ million granted to Poland in autumn 1936. By this time, Kwiatkowski had become dissatisfied by what he regarded as the excessive dissipation of resources. Government investment was thus concentrated in one particular area, the Central Industrial Region, bounded approximately by Kielce, Radom, Lublin, Przemyśl, and Tarnów. This area, unlike Poland's older industrial complexes, was remote from the frontier, a region in which there was little industry and in which agricultural under-employment was particularly acute. Government investment was now stepped up and private investment given new tax incentives by legislation in April 1938. By March 1939, the objectives of the first four-year plan had been achieved and 2,400 million zloties had been invested by the Government, as against the 1,800 million originally proposed.[2]

Kwiatkowski now favoured a rather more radical approach. He proposed a fifteen-year plan to modernize the country, the first three years of which were to be mainly devoted to increasing Poland's military potential and during which the spending of 2,000 million zloties was envisaged. The financing of the new plan was less concerned with preventing inflation than Kwiatkowski's earlier policies had been. Between early 1938 and July 1939, monetary circulation rose from 1,659 million zloties to 2,383 million zloties.[3] The new statute of the Bank of Poland adopted in March 1939 also provided for the first time for the bank to emit a fiduciary issue of up to 800 million zloties and to provide large credits to the Treasury.[4] The evolution of this plan was, of course, cut short by the war. The industrial situation certainly improved after 1936. The index of industrial production rose from

[1] On this, see also below, pp. 487–9.
[2] Landau and Tomaszewski, op. cit., pp. 211–12.
[3] Wiadomości Statystyczne, 18 July 1939.
[4] Dz.U.R.P. (1939), no. 23, pp. 413–20.

94·3 in that year (1928 = 100) to 110·7 in 1937 and 119·3 in 1938. By June 1939 it had reached 129·8.[1] The rise in the output of producer goods was even more striking. The index rose from 103·1 in 1936 to 156·8 in June 1939.[1] The number of those employed also rose, but tended to lag behind production. In 1939, the number of industrial workers was only slightly higher than in 1928. As a result, though the real wages of those employed rose between 1936 and 1939, the number of unemployed remained extremely high, fluctuating only slightly from 466,000 in 1936 to 456,000 in 1938.[2] The increase in production was partly caused by the general upturn in world economic conditions. But as we have seen, Polish foreign trade was still in 1938 far below the level of 1928, and the main credit for the advances made in the years before the war must go to Kwiatkowski.[3]

The Government was much less successful in dealing with the agricultural problem. From the appointment of Juliusz Poniatowski as Minister of Agriculture in June 1934, it had pursued a rather more radical policy. The pace of land reform had been speeded up from the low level to which it had fallen during the Depression, and the amount of land subdivided rose from 79·8 thousand hectares in 1935 to 119·2 thousand hectares in 1938.[4] But even this last figure was significantly below the annual quota of 200,000 hectares provided for in the Land Reform Law. The Government also significantly stepped up other measures designed to improve the structure of agriculture. The consolidation of holdings and the abolition of common lands and servitudes were all greatly accelerated in this period. In addition, the attempt to diminish the

[1] Drozdowski, *Polityka gospodarcza*, p. 96.

[2] *M.R.S.* (1939), Table XXV, p. 268.

[3] The extent to which the economic improvement of these years was the result of Kwiatkowski's own policies or of the general upturn in world trade has occasioned some controversy. See M. Drozdowski, 'Polityka gospodarcza Eugeniusza Kwiatkowskiego w latach 1938–1939' (Komunikat naukowy). VIII Powszechny Zjazd Historyków Polskich w Krakowie 14–17:X.1958. VI— Historia gospodarcza Polski, Polskie Towarzystwo Historyczne (Warsaw, 1960); Z. Landau, 'Głos w dyskusji nad komunikatem M. Drozdowskiego: Polityka gospodarcza Eugeniusza Kwiatkowskiego w latach 1938–1939', VIII Powszechny Zjazd Historyków Polskich w Krakowie; Z. Landau, 'Polityka t. zw. nakręcania koniunktury w Polsce w okresie 1936–1939', *N.D.P.*, 1st series (1959), no. 2, pp. 75–92; M. Drozdowski, 'W sprawie polityki gospodarczej rządu polskiego w latach 1936–1939', *N.D.P.*, 1st series (1960), no. 3, pp. 263–8; Z. Landau, 'Jeszcze raz w sprawie polityki gospodarczej rządu polskiego w latach 1936–1939', *N.D.P.*, 1st series (1960), no. 4, pp. 239–46.

[4] *M.R.S.* (1939), Table III, p. 70.

indebtedness of farmers, embarked upon in 1932, was continued. The rate of interest on their debts was lowered and the period over which they had to be paid was extended. Debt conversion reached its highest level between 1934 and 1936, but the Government hesitated to take really radical action for fear of harming the weak capital market in Poland. The results of this policy were thus rather insignificant; the indebtedness of small and medium plots diminished only from 366 zloties per hectare in 1933–4 to 296 zloties per hectare in 1937–8.[1] In 1935 the Government embarked on a policy of buying up grain in periods in which the price was low, in order to stabilize prices; however, its resources were far too small to have any marked effect. In April 1937 it also introduced legislation prohibiting the subdivision of plots acquired under the land reform.[2] Although some advocated the enactment of a law based on the Nazi model which would prohibit the subdivision of any holding below a stated size, it was never introduced, largely as a result of the fear that it would provoke great popular unrest.

All these measures were little more than palliatives. Between 1935 and 1937 agricultural prices rose, mainly as a result of the situation on the world market, and the position of farmers improved. But in 1938, prices began to fall again and this drop had not been halted by the outbreak of the war. Indeed, the rise in the standard of living of the urban classes in Poland was achieved to a considerable extent as a result of the decline of that of the peasantry. Table XIII shows the course of the price scissors in the last years before the war.

TABLE XIII.* *Index of Retail Prices 1935–8*
(1928 = 100)

	Industrial articles bought by farmers	Articles sold directly by farmers
1935	66·3	35·8
1936	64·6	38·7
1937	66·2	49·2
1938	65·2	43·8

* *Koniunktura Gospodarcza*, z spec., p. 22, Table 6. Quoted in Drozdowski, *Polityka gospodarcza*, p. 196.

[1] *M.R.S.* (1939), p. 74, Table VIII.
[2] *Dz.U.R.P.* (1937), no. 36, pp. 739–40.

At the same time, the rise in the rural population was more than outweighing the effect of the land reform. According to the Institute of Social Studies, the annual increase of the economically active population in agriculture was approximately 230,000. Of these about 30,000 moved to the towns and another 50,000 acquired land, either from the subdivision of holdings or from the extension of cultivable land. This meant that the annual increase in the surplus population in agriculture was something like 100,000. By the outbreak of the war, the number of people who, with their dependants, could have left the countryside without any harmful effect on production was probably over 8 million.[1] This pressure on the land forced the increased subdivision of holdings and the emergence of more and more economically unviable plots. Moreover, the size of the surplus agricultural population was now so great that even a radical land reform could not on its own relieve pressure on the land. By 1939, only 14 per cent of the total arable land was still in farms of more than 50 hectares, leaving perhaps a further 3 million hectares still to be subdivided.[2] Bearing in mind the fact that the 2,654,000 hectares which had already been distributed under the land reform had scarcely alleviated the situation, the agricultural problem was clearly further from solution in 1939 than it had been in 1918.

THE NATIONAL MINORITIES

The problem of the national minorities remained one of the most acute the state had to face. The Government did succeed in improving somewhat relations with the Ukrainians in East Galicia. From late 1934 the Cabinet had been negotiating with the more moderate elements in the U.N.D.O. led by Vladimir Tselevitch and Vasyl Mudry. These negotiations were successfully concluded on the eve of the elections of September 1935. In return for being allowed to propose its own candidates in East Galicia (which virtually ensured their election) the U.N.D.O., while not renouncing its demands for self-determination, undertook to respect Polish 'state needs' and to vote for the budget.[3] In the election thirteen U.N.D.O. deputies and four senators were returned. In addition, one deputy and one senator from the Ukrainian Catholic National

---

[1] Drozdowski, *Polityka gospodarcza*, p. 200.
[2] Zweig, *Poland between Two Wars*, p. 134.
[3] Pobóg-Malinowski, *Najnowsza historia*, ii. 821.

Party were elected in East Galicia. The other Ukrainian parties here boycotted the election. In Volynia five deputies and one senator were elected and formed the pro-Government Parliamentary Regional Group of Volynia.

After the election, the Government made a number of further concessions. Vasyl Mudry, who succeeded the more intransigent Dmitri Levitsky as President of the U.N.D.O. Central Committee in October 1935, was elected a Vice-Marshal of the Sejm. The great majority of the Ukrainians confined in Bereza Kartuska were released, and the Government accepted the amendments proposed by U.N.D.O. to the amnesty law of January 1936. Credits were now granted to Ukrainian economic institutions in East Galicia and the Cabinet halted the practice of annually holding plebiscites in Ukrainian areas, in terms of the Grabski Education Act of 1924, to determine whether Polish, Ukrainian, or both should be the medium of instruction in the schools. These plebiscites had been open to strong official pressure and had caused much bitterness among the Ukrainians.

The *rapprochement* with the Government, usually referred to as the policy of 'normalization', was not universally accepted in Ukrainian political circles. One faction of the U.N.D.O. leadership, grouped around the editors of *Dilo* (Kedryn-Rudnitsky, Kuzmovich, Nymchuk, and Levitsky) soon moved into opposition to the policy, which had never been accepted by the two socialist groupings, the Ukrainian Social-Democratic Party and the Ukrainian Social-Radical Party. Neither was the compromise accepted by the pro-Facist Front of National Union, which had split off from U.N.D.O. in 1933, or the influential Union of Ukrainian Women which declared its hostility in 1936. In 1937 these different groups established a co-ordinating committee of a rather loose character to organize their opposition to the dominant faction of the U.N.D.O.[1]

The success of 'normalization' did not prove lasting. As so often before, it proved easy to make liberal declarations in Warsaw, but far more difficult to have them carried out by local officials. Moreover, as Poland's external situation became more threatening, policy towards the Ukrainians was more and more dominated by the military, above all by the forces stationed in the areas concerned, for whom the maintenance of 'security' was the

---

[1] On these developments, see Vytvytsky and Baran, 'Western Ukraine under Poland', pp. 843–8.

pre-eminent consideration. Conflict had arisen already in 1935 and 1936 because of the U.N.D.O.'s desire to extend its influence over Volynia and the other formerly Russian Ukrainian areas. The atmosphere deteriorated considerably in 1938 as a result of the Army's attempts to foster the separate identity of the three mountain groups or tribes living in the Carpathians in the southern part of East Galicia, the Lemki, the Bojki, and the Huculi.[1] Their links with Poland were fostered, the desire of some of the Lemki to leave the Uniate Church and become orthodox was encouraged, teaching in the Lemki dialect, for which a new alphabet was developed, was begun, and Ukrainian teachers removed from Lemki schools. This policy was moderately successful, but it was bitterly resented by the Ukrainians and attacked as the 'artificial creation of national groups' and a new form of the Austrian tactic of 'divide and rule'.

Even more resented was the attempt, also fostered by the military, to claim as Polish the large numbers of mostly Ukrainianized petty gentry in East Galicia.[2] With the encouragement of the local officials, many of these 'barefoot gentry', differentiated from the mass of the peasantry only by the possession of their jealously guarded titles of nobility, abandoned Ukrainian co-operatives and social organizations, and proclaimed their Polish identity. By early 1939, they had created some 800 local branches with a membership of about 530,000. Their behaviour was strongly attacked by Ukrainian nationalists and led to a number of outbreaks of communal violence. The most serious of these, that in the Tarnopol province, was brutally crushed by the sadistic General Gustaw Paszkiewicz, who similarly distinguished himself after World War II in crushing the remnants of the Polish underground for the Communists.

What finally destroyed 'normalization' was the increased dynamism of German foreign policy, which led the majority of Ukrainians to look to Hitler for the realization of their national objectives. Already, on 23 February 1938, Vasyl Mudry had announced that the U.N.D.O. would abstain on the voting of the budget because of its dissatisfaction with the policies of the Ministries of Agriculture, Education, and Justice.[3] On 7 May the Central Committee of the U.N.D.O. issued a declaration stating that the policy of 'normalization' had not achieved the desired results, and that

[1] Pobóg-Malinowski, *Najnowsza historia*, ii. 823.
[2] Ibid., pp. 823–4.   [3] *S.S.S.R.*, 23 February 1938.

relations between Poles and Ukrainians would only be placed on a satisfactory basis once the Ukrainians in Poland had been granted territorial autonomy.[1] At the beginning of 1939, the leadership of the U.N.D.O. finally decided to join the Ukrainian Consultative Committee, formed to oppose the policy of 'normalization'.[2] The political ferment among the Ukrainians was enormously increased following the establishment, after the Munich agreement, of an autonomous régime in Subcarpathian Ruthenia under Father Voloshyn. This area was seen by many of the Ukrainians in Poland as the 'Ukrainian Piedmont' and many members of the Sich, a leading Ukrainian youth organization, flocked to the capital of Khust to help the new regime.

Ukrainian disillusionment was great when this 'Piedmont' was soon abandoned by Hitler and made over to the Hungarians, who proceeded to crush all manifestations of Ukrainian nationalism. This disillusionment with the Führer, 'the liberator of oppressed peoples', as he was described on a bouquet given him by a group of East Galician nationalists on his entry to Vienna in March 1938,[3] caused a return to a pro-Polish orientation by the U.N.D.O. Its leadership supported the Internal Loan for Anti-Aircraft Defence in April 1939. On 27 April, Mudry proclaimed on behalf of his organization that its first objective must be to preserve 'the Ukrainian national substance in Poland', and that its members would fulfil their obligations to the state.[4] But the bitterness which had been created by the twenty years of Polish rule in East Galicia was to emerge with renewed force after the Polish defeat.

Government policy was no more successful in Volynia. This too was largely the result of maladroit intervention by the local military. Until the spring of 1938, Governor Józewski was able to pursue a policy which had some success in winning the allegiance of the local population. However, he was the object of bitter attacks from the local Poles and also from the Army, especially the Intelligence Section of the General Staff, which increasingly controlled nationality policy in this period. His control over his local officials diminished continuously until he was virtually forced to resign early in 1938.[5]

[1] *Gazeta Polska*, 12 May 1938.
[2] Vytvytsky and Baran, 'Western Ukraine under Poland', p. 848.
[3] R. Buell, *Poland; Key to Europe* (New York, 1939), p. 274.
[4] *Robotnik*, 27 April 1939.
[5] Pobóg-Malinowski, *Najnowsza historia*, ii. 825–7.

There were now continual efforts to forcibly assimilate the local population. The most unfortunate of these was the attempt, largely pursued under the initiative of the local military commanders to convert the Orthodox population in Volynia and the Chełm region to Catholicism. In the nineteenth century the Uniate Church had been strong in these areas, and had thus been subject to unremitting pressure from the Russian Government in favour of Orthodoxy. Many Catholic and Uniate churches had indeed been forcibly converted to Orthodox use. A commission set up before 1926 had found that of 389 local Orthodox churches and chapels, 51 would fulfil the needs of the Orthodox population and suggested that the rest should be returned to the Catholics. However justified such a policy may have seemed in view of the Russian Government's actions in the nineteenth century, it was politically exceedingly misguided, and after the coup the Government hesitated to embark on it. What was worrying the military authorities now was the phenomenon of local Uniates turning to Orthodoxy from 1936 onwards, which was believed to be the result of Ukrainian nationalist agitation. In response, the local authorities began to take over Orthodox churches. Nearly 150 were given to the Catholics and Uniates, while something like 120 were destroyed.[1] It was claimed that the overwhelming majority of those destroyed were disused chapels, but as could have been expected, strong local resentment was provoked. Pobóg-Malinowski claims that the Government in Warsaw opposed this policy, but could not control the local army commanders.[2] Whether this is true or not, the policy was certainly halted by early 1939. But by then much of the goodwill created by Józewski had been destroyed.

The White Russians were also subjected to increased pressures for Polonization in this period. A number of White Russian cultural institutions were closed down, including the White Russian Teachers Association, the School Society, and the Institute of Economy and Culture.[3] In January 1938 the National White Russian Committee, one of the principal White Russian political organizations, was dissolved on the grounds that it had maintained links with subversive organizations in Poland and abroad.[4] Politically the area remained relatively quiescent and there was no

---

[1] Pobóg-Malinowski, *Najnowsza historia*, ii. 827–9.   [2] Ibid., p. 829.
[3] A. Horak, *Poland and her National Minorities* (New York, 1961), p. 175.
[4] *Kurjer Poranny*, 18 January 1936.

resurgence of terrorism on the pattern of the late 1920s. The Government also attempted to foster economic development in the area, particularly by giving tax exemption to private investment there, but the provinces with White Russian majorities remained in 1939 the most backward economically in Poland.

The central feature of the history of the German minority between 1935 and 1939 was its almost complete conversion to National Socialism. This development did not, as in Czechoslovakia, take the form of the emergence of a single party which eventually succeeded in winning the allegiance of the majority of Germans. The role of the Sudeten German Party was indeed aspired to by the Jung-deutsche Partei, established in former Austrian Silesia in 1931 by Richard Wiesner, which was openly sympathetic to Hitler. However, Wiesner's attempt to unite German political life under his control met with strong resistance from the older German nationalist organizations such as the Deutscher Volksbund and Deutscher Volksblock in Upper Silesia, the Deutsche Vereinigung für Posen und Pomerellen in Western Poland, and the Deutscher Volksverband in Central and Eastern Poland.[1] These organizations established in 1934 a rather loose alliance, the Rat der Deutschen in Polen, to co-ordinate their activities, though it did not prove particularly effective. But in spite of these older groupings' opposition to Wiesner, they too, after 1933, became more and more sympathetic to National Socialism. From the 1920s they had maintained fairly close links with both the German Foreign Ministry and the Volksbund für das Deutschtum im Ausland, and this proved more than enough to offset the support the Jung-deutsche Partei enjoyed from the foreign organization of the National Socialist Party, particularly from the Landesgruppe Polens der N.S.D.A.P. and from Forster, the Nazi leader in Danzig. Nevertheless, in January 1937 the Volksdeutsche Mittelstelle, the S.S. agency for minority affairs, attempted to unite German organizations in Poland in a Bund der Deutschtum in Polen.[2] This attempt failed, both because of the opposition of the German Foreign Ministry, which felt that it would cause a deterioration in the position of the Germans in Poland, and because

---

[1] W. Kühn, 'Das Deutschtum in Polen und sein Schicksal in Kriegs- und Nach-Kriegszeit', *O.E.H.P.*, p. 149.

[2] M. Cygański, *Mniejszość niemiecka w Polsce centralnej w latach 1919-1939* (Lodz, 1962), pp. 98-9.

of the intransigence of the leadership of the Jung-deutsche Partei, which demanded control of the new organization. But the two factions co-operated increasingly closely, as in the Lodz municipal election of autumn 1938. They thus effectively destroyed the power of the German socialist and Catholic parties, which declined into insignificance in this period. They were also able to obtain official Polish recognition of the principle that the Germans in Poland were a *Volksgruppe*, that they were no longer Polish citizens of German nationality, but a part of the German nation, with which they were united by a common *Weltanschauung* and an allegiance to the state of that nation, the Greater German Reich. Links between both groups and Germany itself increased enormously.

The Government's policy following the Polish-German Non-Aggression Pact was to reduce as far as possible the sources of friction with the German minority. After the end of the fifteen-year period in which Upper Silesia was subject to the Geneva Convention, various Polish-German agreements were made to deal with the problems created by its termination, and on 5 November 1937 an agreement was reached between Warsaw and Berlin on the general question of their respective national minorities. In terms of this accord, both sides renounced policies of forcible national assimilation and promised to recognize the right of members of the minority to use their mother tongue, to organize cultural and economic institutions, and to establish schools. No obstacles were to be placed in the way of 'the choice or the exercise of an economic activity'. These rights did not diminish the minorities' obligation of 'absolute loyalty to the state in which they live'.[1]

In accordance with this policy, the Polish Government did virtually nothing to halt the spreading of Nazi views among the German minority. It tried, too, to alleviate some of the more pressing complaints of the Germans. In the 1935 elections, it sponsored the candidacy of Richard Wiesner of the Jung-deutsche Partei and Edward Hasbach, a representative of the older national-ist groups, to the Senate. In 1938 Hasbach was again chosen as Senator, along with another representative of the Young Germans, Max Warnbeck.

Nonetheless tension remained, particularly in Western Poland and Silesia, where local officials were keen to continue the work of undoing the effects of German rule, and where the loyalty of

---

[1] *Gazeta Polska*, 6 November 1937.

the local German population was often suspect. In June 1936, for instance, 86 Germans were convicted in Katowice of having formed an underground organization, the National-Sozialistische Deutsche Arbeiter Bewegung, whose aim was to detach Upper Silesia from Poland by an armed uprising.[1] Bitterness was increased by the Government's attempt to support the pro-Polish minority within the Augsburg Evangelical Church, the largest Protestant Church in Poland, against the majority of the Church's synod,[2] by the implementation of the land reform in Western Poland and in Upper Silesia after the expiration of the Geneva Convention, and by the withdrawal of teaching certificates from a number of extreme German nationalists. While Polish opinion was greatly aroused by the increased pressure exercised by the German government on the Polish minority in Germany, the sympathy of the Germans in Poland for the Reich, and their growing hostility to the Polish State, were nourished by the triumphs of German foreign policy in 1938.

The situation deteriorated rapidly after Polish-German relations took a sharp turn for the worse in March 1939. The Polish Government feared the German minority as a potential fifth column, and indeed the September campaign revealed how many of them had undertaken diversionary and espionage work for the Reich. From May to August, a large number of German activists were arrested, and German schools, co-operatives, newspapers, and organizations were shut down. Many Germans fled to the Reich. By the end of August, the German Government claimed it had given shelter to 70,000 'victims of Polish terror', and these people constituted a useful weapon for Goebbels's propaganda machine. The September campaign witnessed a further sad story of intolerance on both sides.

The position of the Jews deteriorated radically in the last years before the war. Anti-Semitism began to play an ever-increasing role in the political stance of the Government, both as a means of winning over the younger nationalists and to divert attention from other social problems. The closer ties with Germany which followed the Non-Aggression Declaration, along with the greater flow of propaganda from the Reich and the ease with which the Nuremberg laws were passed in autumn 1935, greatly encouraged anti-Jewish feeling in Poland. As *Czas* commented as early as 2 January 1936, 'Anti-Semitic agitation is spreading like an avalanche.'

[1] *Robotnik*, 21 June 1936.
[2] Kühn, 'Das Deutschtum in Polen', p. 132.

H h

The campaign to persuade peasants to boycott Jewish shops and stalls in small market towns took more violent forms, and led to incidents such as those in Przytyk and Mińsk Mazowiecki in June 1936 and in Czyżewo in December 1936 and January 1937 which can only be described as pogroms. Moreover, though the Government condemned anti-Jewish violence, its attempts to suppress it were somewhat half-hearted. It did not apparently see anything objectionable in the boycott as such. It was after the incidents of June 1936 that Sławoj-Skladkowski told the Sejm 'My Government considers that nobody in Poland should be injured. An honest host does not allow anybody to be harmed in his house. An economic struggle? That's different (*Owszem*).'[1]

As we have seen, when OZON was formed its programme on the Jewish question approached that of the National Democrats. While condemning violence, it argued that 'cultural self-defence' and the 'movement of the Polish people towards economic independence' should be supported.[2] According to Koc's Chief of Staff, Colonel Kowalewski, Jews, even those who had fought in the Polish struggle for independence, could not be members of OZON any more than 'Poles can belong to a Zionist organization'.[3] The party became still more explicit in the last year before the war; in December 1938, General Skwarczyński and 116 of his parliamentary colleagues addressed a question to the Prime Minister on the Jewish problem, in which they stressed that they regarded as a necessity 'the radical reduction of the number of Jews in Poland by means of a massive emigration'.[4]

The development of these attitudes on the part of the Government members of parliament led too, to a bill being passed in April 1936, prohibiting Jewish ritual slaughter.[5] It is true that arrangements were made to provide Jews with kosher meat, but this did not undo the bill's harmful effects, for since the great majority of butchering in Poland had been done by Jews, a large number of Jewish butchers lost their jobs.

The situation of Jews at the universities also deteriorated. Their numbers diminished, and those who were admitted were subject to continual harassment. In the academic year 1935–6 both Warsaw

---

[1] *S.S.S.R.*, 4 June 1936, col. 7.
[2] *Kurjer Poranny*, 22 February 1937.
[3] Ibid., 21 April 1937.
[4] *Gazeta Polska*, 22 December 1938.
[5] *Dz.U.R.P.* (1936), no. 29, pp. 528–9.

and Poznań Universities were closed for short periods as a result of anti-Semitic disturbances among the students. This violence, which generally took the form of a demand for separate 'ghetto benches' for Jewish students (as a first stage in their total exclusion from the universities), assumed even larger proportions in the academic year 1936–7, during which there were severe student troubles at a vast number of institutions of higher learning, including Lwów's University and Polytechnic, Warsaw's University, School of Commerce and Polytechnic, and the Universities of Wilno, Cracow, and Poznań. Though the Minister of Education, Wojciech Świętosławski, had stated in parliament in January 1937 that he regarded as 'impossible' the establishment of ghetto benches,[1] he changed his mind following a request by the rectors of universities and other institutions of higher learning in October 1937, for fear of further disturbances.[2] Many professors, particularly in Warsaw, Wilno, and Poznań, opposed this decision, but the institution of ghetto benches soon became common practice in most Polish Universities and Polytechnics. Many Jewish students stood through lectures rather than submit to the indignity of accepting their 'racial' place.

Resistance to Jews in the professions also grew in this period. In February 1937 the Union of Agents to the Military Administration voted to request its administrative council to end all commercial dealings with Jewish firms,[3] while in March the Warsaw section of the Confederation of Polish Electrical Engineers voted 107 to 23 to admit only 'Aryans' to its membership.[4] A similar decision was taken in May 1937, though by the narrow margin of 140 to 130, by the annual conference of the Association of Doctors,[5] while in the same month, the League of Polish lawyers at its conference, voted in favour of preventing the further entry of Jews to the profession.[6]

The Government increasingly came to see the only solution for the Jewish problem in large-scale emigration. On Beck's instructions, the Polish delegate to the Economic Commission of the League of Nations raised the question of Jewish emigration on 5 October 1936, claiming that the Jewish problem in Poland

[1] *S.S.S.R.*, 23 January 1937.   [2] *Gazeta Polska*, 8 October 1937.
[3] *Warszawski Dziennik Narodowy*, 2 March 1937.
[4] Ibid., 3 March 1937.   [5] *Gazeta Polska*, 11 May 1937.
[6] Żarnowski, *Struktura społeczna inteligencji*, pp. 223–4.

required 'rapid measures of relief'.[1] The Government strongly supported Jewish aspirations in Palestine, and entered into close contact with international Zionist organizations, the World Zionist Organization of Chaim Weizmann, the Jewish Agency, and the Revisionists, led by Vladimir Jabotinsky. It was realized, however, that even if unimpeded Jewish emigration to Palestine was permitted by the British mandatory authorities (from August 1937 Jewish emigration was restricted to 1,000 persons a month), that country could never support more than a fraction of the Jews in Eastern Europe. Thus on 6 October 1936 Tytus Komarnicki, the Polish delegate at the Political Commission of the League of Nations, again raised the question of Jewish emigration. After stressing the importance of Jewish rights in Palestine, he claimed that because of the size of the Jewish population, not only in Poland but in Eastern Europe generally, other outlets for emigration had to be found. Some success was achieved with President Roosevelt's help, in inducing a number of Latin American states to increase their quota of Jewish immigrants. In May 1937 a group of Polish experts even went to Paris to discuss with the French the possibility of Jewish settlement in Madagascar, and in the following year a non-Zionist Jewish Committee for Colonization, headed by the Jewish Senator Moses Schorr, was set up under ministerial patronage to foster emigration to countries other than Palestine.[2] These efforts had little success. With the flood of refugees pouring out of Germany, Austria, and Czechoslovakia, to say nothing of the other states of Eastern Europe, country after country was closing its doors to the Jews. In 1937 barely 9,000 Jews were able to emigrate from Poland. It was all very well to say, as the pro-Government Senator Petrażycki did in parliament on 12 February 1937, that by refusing to emigrate the Jews were 'bringing water to the mill of anti-Semitism'.[3] But where could they go?

For the nationalist opposition, the Government's policy was far too moderate. It was not enough, insisted the main National Democratic paper *Warszawski Dziennik Narodowy* on 20 November 1938, 'to show the Jews the door; one should push them through by means of a "surgical operation" [*sic*] which would deprive them legally of the means to live in Poland'.[4]

[1] Pobóg-Malinowski, *Najnowsza historia*, ii. 813–14.
[2] *Gazeta Polska*, 10 December 1938.   [3] *S.S.S.R.*, 12 February 1937.
[4] *Warszawski Dziennik Narodowy*, 20 November 1938.

This approach commended itself to some members of OZON. In January 1939 two deputies, Benedykt Kienc and Franciszek Stoch, presented to the Sejm a proposal for a law 'to partially regulate the position of persons of Jewish nationality *vis-à-vis* the Polish state'.[1] This would have deprived the overwhelming majority of Jews of their civil and political rights, of the right to vote, to be an official, to exercise one of the free professions, to possess immovable property, to take part in court cases. Jewish emigration would thus be accelerated, and was to be financed by the creation of an 'Emigration Fund' supported by forced contributions from Jewish organizations and wealthy Jews. It is difficult to decide what would have happened to this proposal had Polish-German relations not taken a rapid turn for the worse.

The effect of the growing anti-Semitism, coupled with the actions of the Government, was the progressive economic ruin of the Jewish community. In some fields, as in the sponsoring of peasant co-operatives to bypass Jewish middle men, this was not the principal intention of the Government. But in many areas the Government pursued policies which could only have the effect of destroying the economic basis of the Jews in Poland without any evident gain to society as a whole. The Government's virtual exclusion of Jews from the country's timber trade, in which they had hitherto played a prominent part, and their replacement by state officials, led to a radical decline in efficiency,[2] while the refusal to add a moratorium on the debts of traders when one was imposed on those of peasants in 1933 ruined a large number of Jewish shopkeepers.[3] The tax burden on the occupations in which Jews predominated was also extremely heavy. According to Segal, the Jews, 10 per cent of the population, paid between 35 and 40 per cent of all taxes.[4] Moreover, though the Government complained of the excessive number of Jews in commerce, it allowed restrictions on the entry of Jews both to trade schools, where new skills could be acquired, and to universities. It also began to refuse to recognize professional qualifications acquired abroad by those who had been refused entry to Polish universities. By this 'cold pogrom' the Government believed it would force the Jews to emigrate. But as we have seen, emigration on a large scale was impossible.

[1] *Kurjer Warszawski*, 19 January 1939.
[2] S. Segal, *The New Poland and the Jews* (New York, 1938), pp. 132–4.
[3] Ibid., pp. 145–6.　　　　　　　　　　　　　　　[4] Ibid., p. 141.

All that was achieved was the extensive pauperization of a large section of the state's inhabitants. By the outbreak of the war, perhaps 1 million of the 3 million Jews in Poland were almost entirely dependent on relief, largely from private Jewish organizations financed from the United States.

The character of the situation can be judged from the fact that in 1938, 50 per cent of the Jews in Poland could not afford to pay a 5 zloty ($12\frac{1}{2}$p.) communal tax; 50 per cent of the rest could not afford 10 zloties.[1] A prominent Jewish leader in Lwów reported with awful foresight: 'A year or two ago, 40 per cent of our people applied for aid to the community, this year it is 50 per cent., the next year or the year after that it will be 60 per cent. We are waiting for death.'[2]

FOREIGN POLICY

Throughout the period between 1935 and 1939, Polish foreign policy remained exclusively under the control of Colonel Józef Beck, the man Piłsudski had long designated as his successor in this field. Beck ostensibly held to the Marshal's principle that Poland should strive to keep a balance in her relations with her two powerful neighbours. In fact, however, the basis of his policy was changed, and its key became the maintenance of the good relations with Germany which had been achieved by the Non-Aggression Declaration of 26 January 1934. Beck welcomed the increasing freedom of manœuvre which the *rapprochement* gave to Poland, and he was prepared to make significant concessions in order to maintain it. This attitude is reflected in his policy on Danzig: he co-operated with the Reich in diminishing the rights of the League of Nations' Commissioner and acquiesced in the rapid Nazification of the Free City.[3] At the same time, he was quite unwilling to enter any sort of alliance with Germany, and turned a deaf ear to further suggestions of a common Polish-German campaign against the Soviet Union. In his first meeting with Hitler after the Marshal's death, he did not respond to the Führer's suggestions that German-

---

[1] O. Janowsky, *People at Bay: the Jewish Problem in East Central Europe* (London, 1938), pp. 92–3.

[2] Ibid., p. 97.

[3] On this, see B. Dopierała, *Gdańska polityka Józefa Becka* (Poznań, 1967).

Polish relations should be strengthened 'in the face of the eventual common danger'.[1]

Beck believed that Nazi dynamism posed no threat to Poland because of the fundamental antagonism between the Reich and Russia. As Lipski, the Polish Ambassador in Berlin, told Szembek, the Permanent Under-Secretary in the Polish Foreign Ministry, on 27 May 1935, 'Opposition to Russia, as well as the *rapprochement* with Poland, have become axioms of German policy.'[2] Beck believed that German expansion would first take a south-easterly direction, towards Austria and Czechoslovakia (whose disappearance, he told Szembek on 12 June 1935, was bound to occur 'sooner or later'),[3] and would then be directed against the Soviet Union. He saw no real danger to Poland in this development, and indeed believed that in its initial stages it would increase his freedom of manœuvre.

He also continued to uphold the Franco-Polish alliance as a counterweight to the new ties with Berlin, though he had little faith either in the willingness or in the ability of the French to honour their commitments in Eastern Europe. As he told his subordinates on 2 July,

Either the 'Popular Front', subordinated to Moscow, will come to power, and then, if the Franco-Soviet *rapprochement* develops still further, it will be necessary to strengthen our relations with Germany; or the parties of the Right will come to power, and, following our example, will seek to accommodate themselves with Berlin.[4]

At the same time, he cultivated Polish relations with Britain, which he came to regard as more important than France, in order to provide a further safeguard should German ambitions turn towards Poland.

Beck attempted to maintain correct relations with the Soviet Union in accordance with the Non-Aggression Treaty of November 1932. At the same time, however, he regarded the Soviet Union as Poland's principal enemy, and was hostile to its attempts to build up a system of collective security, which he regarded as a pretext for increasing Soviet influence in Europe. It was for this reason that he opposed the Franco-Soviet and Czechoslovak-Soviet

---

[1] *Diariusz i teki Jana Szembeka*, ed. T. Komarnicki, i (London, 1964), 331. This edition of Szembek's diary is cited hereafter as Szembek, *Diariusz*.
[2] Ibid. i. 306.
[3] Ibid., p. 316.
[4] Ibid., p. 328.

Alliances, which made these countries tools 'in the hands of Comintern'.[1] It also explains the Polish diplomatic activity which was instrumental in achieving the fall in August 1936 of the Rumanian Foreign Minister Titulescu, who was believed to favour closer ties with the Soviet Union.[2] Thus it is not surprising that along with increasingly close links with Berlin, there went a deterioration of Polish-Soviet relations.

In addition to the general aim of safeguarding Poland's security, Beck's policy also had some subordinate goals. He wanted, in the first place, to achieve 'Great Power status', by which he meant that Poland should participate in any future schemes for the establishment of a European Directorate, on the lines of Mussolini's 'Four-Power Pact' of March 1933. He also hoped to sponsor the emergence of a 'Third Europe', composed of the states from the Baltic to the Black Sea, which would be independent of both the London–Paris and the Rome–Berlin Axes. Poland's primary interest in this regard was the Baltic, referred to by *Polska Zbrojna* on 9 September 1937 as Poland's 'natural sphere of influence'.[3] But Beck also hoped, as a result of the disappearance of Czechoslovakia, to achieve a common Polish-Hungarian frontier. Close relations could then be built up between Poland, Hungary, Italy, Yugoslavia, and Rumania. This new combination would provide a barrier to German eastward expansion.

The evolution of Beck's policy between 1935 and the outbreak of the war must be seen largely in terms of the development of Polish-German relations. Between the Marshal's death in May 1935 and March 1936, these relations followed the pattern they had taken since the signing of the Non-Aggression Pact. To a Germany almost entirely isolated, a friendly Poland was of great importance. The German authorities therefore placed much stress on keeping on good terms with the Poles. Hitler assured Beck, for instance, on 3 July that 'it would be madness to attempt to seize territories from Poland or—and this he underlined with force—to push her back from the Baltic'.[4] The close links Hitler had established with Beck were of considerable help to him. They made it much easier for him to reject the various proposals for a system of collective

[1] Szembek, *Diariusz*, ii. 197.
[2] See S. Mikulicz, 'Wpływ dyplomacji sanacyjnej na obalenie Titulescu', *Sprawy Międzynarodowe*, xii (1959), nos. 7/8, pp. 104–23.
[3] *Polska Zbrojna*, 9 September 1937.
[4] Szembek, *Diariusz*, i. 330.

security advanced at this time, and enabled him to initiate the first and most dangerous phase of German rearmament without having to worry about a hostile Polish reaction. As a result German strength increased dramatically by early 1936, with the introduction of compulsory military service, the creation of an army of thirty-six infantry divisions and the building up of the Air Force and Navy.

This period came to an end with the German remilitarization of the Rhineland, which drastically undermined the strategic basis of France's alliances in Eastern Europe. The characteristics of Beck's policy emerged clearly during this crisis, when he sought, through an elaborate double game, to improve his relations with France, and thus to diminish the significance of the Franco-Soviet alliance and, at the same time, to maintain his good relations with Germany. He had decided already in February 1936 that France would not use force to undo the remilitarization of the Rhineland, which he did not regard as a *casus foederis* in terms of the Franco-Polish alliance. Thus, when the German troops marched in, he informed the French on 7 March that he would aid them in whatever way was needed, fully aware that he would not need to make good this offer. At the same time, he let the Germans know that he had nothing against their action. The nature of this intricate manoeuvre soon became evident to the French, and thus, far from improving relations with France, Beck's action heightened the already great suspicions of him in the Quai d'Orsay.[1]

From March 1936 to October–November 1937, the *rapprochement* with Poland was no longer as important for Germany. This was a period in which Europe increasingly seemed divided into a Fascist and an anti-Fascist camp, and political conflicts became extremely bitter, with the victory of the Popular Front in France in May 1936 and the outbreak of the Spanish Civil War in June. Germany was now able to establish close ties with Italy, embittered towards Britain and France because of the sanctions imposed over Abyssinia, and with Japan. Hitler seems to have realized that Poland would only really be valuable to him either as an ally in a war with the Soviet Union or as a friendly neutral in a war with the West. Before Poland would accept either of these roles it was clear she would have to be forced into the position of little more than a

[1] On this question, see M. Wojciechowski, *Stosunki polsko-niemieckie, 1933–1938* (Poznań, 1965), pp. 257–91.

German satellite. There are indeed examples of increased German pressure on Poland during this period, although they still did not take a very drastic form. The Germans suggested the cession of an extra-territorial *Autobahn* across the Corridor,[1] the situation in Danzig, Piłsudski's 'barometer for Polish-German relations', again became tense and there were a number of attempts to isolate Poland from the Western Powers, as in the negotiations for a Four-Power Pact which followed the remilitarization of the Rhineland.

In spite of these rather worrying developments, there was no significant change in Polish policy. Largely under pressure from Rydz, who in May 1935 had already resumed staff contacts with the French Army broken off under Piłsudski, Beck was forced to make a rather unwilling attempt to improve his relations with France. But though an agreement was reached at Rambouillet in September 1936 on a French credit for the development of the armaments industry in Poland, the French were unable to obtain any real modification of Polish policy, particularly in relation to Czechoslovakia. Moreover, Beck went out of his way to inform Berlin that these talks had in no way affected the Polish-German *rapprochement*.

At the same time, Beck was unwilling to make his relations with Germany any closer, and made it clear on several occasions that Poland would not join the Anti-Comintern Pact concluded between Germany and Japan in November 1936, to which Italy adhered a year later.[2] The Poles also remained quite deaf to the various German hints of territorial advantages in the Ukraine which would accrue from a common anti-Russian campaign. At the same time Polish-Soviet relations deteriorated still further, with the outbreak in July 1937 of the Sino-Japanese war and with the increasingly close ties between Poland and Japan. However, Beck, wary of a possible involvement in the Anti-Comintern Pact, warned his ambassador in Japan not to enter into any formal undertakings.[3]

By October and November 1937, the situation had changed.

[1] As in the conversations between Rydz and Goering on 16 February 1937. Letter from Moltke to Weizsäcker, 23 February 1937, Politisches Archiv des Auswärtigen Amts. Bonn. Quoted in Wojciechowski, *Stosunki polsko-niemieckie*, p. 320.

[2] As in the Beck-inspired article of Miedziński in *Gazeta Polska* on 24 December 1936.

[3] Letter of the Polish ambassador in Tokyo, Tadeusz Romer to B. Budurowycz, 31 July 1938. Quoted in B. Budurowycz, *Polish-Soviet Relations, 1932–1939* (New York, 1963), p. 101.

Hitler was by now clearly determined on expansion, on the absorption of Austria, and the destruction of Czechoslovakia. At the same time, from October 1937, the British government was set on a policy of attempting to satisfy what it regarded as the more moderate of Hitler's aims by negotiation, while the French, increasingly conscious of their own weakness, felt they had no alternative but to support the new British policy. Hitler, however, had decided to obtain his objectives not through British mediation, but by his own strength. As a result he again had considerable need of the goodwill of the Poles, and took steps to calm the situation in Danzig, telling Lipski on 5 November that he had no intention of altering the statute of the Free City.[1]

Beck responded eagerly to the German approaches. His assessment of Polish interests did, indeed, run parallel to the new German line, particularly in relation to Czechoslovakia. He was, moreover, convinced that the Western powers would not go to war to prevent Hitler's getting his way on either Austria or Czechoslovakia, and thus came to the conclusion that to oppose him on these matters would merely jeopardize the Polish-German understanding to no purpose. Beck did nothing to hinder the growing German pressure on Austria in late 1937, and in fact did what he could to frustrate the Austrians' attempt to get Czechoslovak and Hungarian support against the Reich, largely because of his hostility to the Czechs. The Poles accepted the *Anschluss* without protest, referring to it as an 'internal matter for Austria'.[2] Indeed, Beck made use of the fortuitous coincidence of a frontier incident on the Lithuanian border in the same week to issue an ultimatum to Kaunas, forcing the Lithuanian government to initiate diplomatic relations with Poland. He thus closed a long-standing gap in Poland's Baltic links, though at the cost of creating the impression (false in this case) of acting in collusion with Germany.

In relation to Czechoslovakia Beck went further. He had long felt that the destruction of Czechoslovakia was in the Polish interest. Not only would credit accrue to the Government if it could settle the frontier dispute arising from the fact that the Trans-Olza area of Austrian Silesia, with a large Polish population, had gone to the

[1] Report of Lipski, *Official Documents concerning Polish-German and Polish-Soviet Relations 1933–1939* (London and Melbourne, 1939; hereafter cited as *Polish White Book*), Document 34, pp. 41–2.
[2] Telegram of Moltke of 13 March 1938, *Documents on German Foreign Policy*, series D, no. V (cited hereafter as D.G.F.P.), Document no. 32, p. 41.

Czechs in 1919, but the collapse of Czechoslovakia would enormously weaken Soviet influence in Europe. Through the emergence of an independent or semi-independent Slovakia and the incorporation of Subcarpathian Ruthenia in Hungary, a common Polish-Hungarian frontier would be created and the basis laid for his cherished schemes for a 'Third Europe'.[1]

He thus co-ordinated his campaign of pressure on Prague on behalf of the Polish minority in Czechoslovakia with Hitler's activities for the Sudeten Germans, at the same time consulting the Hungarians, who were making similar demands. He refused to consider a *rapprochement* with Czechoslovakia, as was urged on him by the French, and also spurned the approaches made to him by the Czechs. In addition, he put strong pressure on the Rumanians to refuse French demand to permit the free passage of Soviet troops. This whole policy was based on the assumption that France would not go to war over Czechoslovakia. Characteristically, however, Beck decided that should a European war break out on this issue, Poland could not fight on the same side as Germany, and would 'within twenty-four hours' be compelled to transform her foreign policy so as to fulfil her obligations to France.[2]

The Munich agreement constituted a major defeat for Beck. Not only had the conference been a reincarnation of the European 'directorate' of 1933, and Poland not consulted in its decisions, but Polish claims to the Trans-Olza area were postponed for future settlement. Beck's reaction was to issue an ultimatum on 30 September, demanding that the Czechs cede the area. Though this ultimatum was issued without prior consultation with the Germans, it was accorded their 'complete understanding',[3] and was accepted by the Czechs on the following day.

But this hollow triumph could not disguise the true nature of the situation Poland now faced. Czechoslovakia did not in fact disintegrate, and the whole country fell under German influence, encircling Poland on the south and undermining her strategic position. Subcarpathian Ruthenia, far from being ceded to Hun-

---

[1] On these developments, see particularly S. Stanisławska, *Wielka i mała polityka Józefa Becka* (Warsaw, 1962); idem, *Polska a Monachium* (Warsaw, 1967); H. Roos, *Polen und Europa. Studien zur polnischen Aussenpolitik, 1931–1939* (Tübingen, 1957), pp. 273–357. Beck's policy has given rise to an enormous literature, some of which is listed in the Bibliography.

[2] Beck, *Dernier Rapport*, p. 163.

[3] D.G.F.P., series D, No. V, Document 55, p. 80.

gary, became a Ukrainian 'Piedmont', and under the control of its Prime Minister, Voloshyn, who was close to the Ukrainian Military Organization, exercised a strong and disruptive influence on the Ukrainians in Poland. German influence also grew appreciably, following Munich, in Lithuania, Hungary, and, to a lesser extent, Rumania. Moreover, both Britain and France seemed prepared to give Hitler a 'free hand' in Eastern Europe.

Under these new conditions Hitler thought the time was again ripe to put pressure on Poland over Danzig, in order to force her into an alliance which would, in fact, make the country a German dependency, and would thus free him to move either east or west. Towards the end of October, in order to appease the Poles, he damped down his Ukrainian propaganda, and on 24 October got Ribbentrop to propose to Lipski an 'over-all solution' of Polish-German relations. This was to involve the return of Danzig to the Reich, with safeguards for Polish rights, and an extra-territorial *Autobahn* across the corridor. In return, the Polish-German frontier was to be recognized. Poland was, finally, to join the Anti-Comintern Pact.[1]

Beck knew that although he had regarded Danzig as 'a lost post' since 1938,[2] neither the Polish Government nor Polish public opinion would countenance its cession. He realized too that the acceptance of the German terms would mean the end of Polish independence. His reaction was to act on the assumption that the Germans were trying to get their way by bluff, while at the same time trying to increase his freedom of manœuvre. But he must have realized that the whole basis of his foreign policy was falling apart. As Szembek remarked on 10 December to Grzybowski, the Polish Ambassador in Moscow,

> It is extremely difficult to maintain the balance between Russia and Germany. Our relations with the latter are entirely founded on the view of leading personalities in the Reich that in a future Russo-German conflict, Poland will be the natural ally of Germany. In these conditions, the policy of good neighbourliness which has its origin in the agreement of 1934 could easily disappear as a pure fiction.[3]

[1] D.G.F.P., series D, No. V, Document 81, pp. 104-7; *Polish White Book*, Document 44, pp. 47-8.
[2] He had expressed this view to the head of his office, Michał Łubieński in 1938. M. Łubieński, 'Ostatnie negocjacje w sprawie Gdańska', *Dziennik Polski*, 3 December 1953.
[3] J. Szembek, *Journal, 1933–1939* (Paris, 1952), pp. 386-7.

On 5–6 January Beck, in consultation with Rydz and Mościcki, decided that to accept the German offer would make Poland a 'vassal state'.[1] Yet Beck still hoped that a compromise could be reached, and was even prepared to offer a German-Polish condominium in Danzig.[2] However, by Ribbentrop's visit to Poland on 25 January he had finally decided not to make any real concessions. With the German destruction of Czechoslovakia in March, and the absorption of Bohemia and Moravia into the Reich, the situation developed rapidly. On the one hand, the Germans were now putting their demands to Poland in a much more pressing form. At the same time, the shock caused by Hitler's action against Czechoslovakia caused an enormous change in public opinion in Britain and in the Conservative Party itself. This brought about a modification of British policy, which led to the British guarantee to Poland of 30 March. This was transformed by the agreement of 6 April into a virtual alliance.

Beck apparently continued to believe that Germany was only trying to obtain concessions by bluff and was thus unlikely to go to war, and that she would be unable to reach an agreement with the Soviet Union. He may also have over-estimated the ability of the Polish Army to resist the *Reichswehr*. Thus, though he attempted to improve relations with the Soviet Union, and a Trade Agreement between the two countries was signed on 19 February, he refused to consider closer ties with the Russians on the grounds that this would endanger Polish independence and unnecessarily provoke Germany. He categorically refused to accede to demands that Russian troops be allowed to cross Polish soil, the point which, above all, led to the breakdown of the Anglo-Russian talks of mid-1939.[3] The rest of the story, the conclusion of the Soviet-German Non-Aggression Treaty, with its secret protocol providing for the partition of Poland and the division of Eastern Europe into German and Russian spheres of influence is, of course, well known.

It may be that the Anglo-Russian talks never had any chance of success, and that the Russians were attempting, from Munich on, to reach an agreement with the Germans. What seems more likely is that the Russians were weighing up the offers of both sides for an alliance, and that a greater willingness on the part of the Poles

[1] Beck, *Dernier Rapport*, p. 184.
[2] Łubieński, 'Ostatnie negocjacje w sprawie Gdańska'.
[3] On this, see particularly Budurowycz, *Polish-Soviet Relations*, pp. 126–69.

to compromise could have led to successful negotiations which, at the cost of a diminution of Polish freedom or manœuvre, might have given her more chance to resist the Germans or even have deterred Hitler from war. But until the Russian documents are made available, we can only speculate.

Beck's foreign policy aroused a certain amount of dissent within the Government, and on several occasions he even seemed close to being overthrown. The first of these was during the conflict with Danzig which broke out in June 1935 as a result of the devaluation of the *Gulden* and the introduction by the Senate of the Free City, without prior consultation with the Poles, of exchange control against Poland. Beck's policy during this crisis, of making a number of concessions in order to maintain the Polish-German *rapprochement*, aroused strong opposition from several members of the Cabinet, notably Colonel Floyar-Rajchman, the Minister of Trade and Industry, and Zawadzki, the Minister of Finance. The fact that Beck had the support of the Prime Minister was not of great assistance, since Sławek's political influence was clearly on the wane, a process which culminated in his resignation in October 1935. Beck's position appeared extremely shaky, so that Lipski told Szembek on 7 August that 'the conflict with Danzig has created an immensely difficult situation and threatens to cause the resignation of Beck, and indeed of the whole Cabinet'.[1] However, Beck was able to win over Rydz-Śmigły, whose political influence was steadily increasing and whose anti-German standpoint was above question. He was thus able to end the conflict with Danzig by a compromise agreement reached at Sopot on 21 September. Yet even after this, attacks on his policy continued, and on 12 October a meeting he held with the President to discuss his line of action had a 'dramatic course'.[2] Rumours even circulated that when the Kościałkowski Cabinet was formed, Sosnkowski was considered for the post of Foreign Minister in place of Beck.[3]

Kościałkowski himself told Szembek on 15 March 1936 that while 'he regarded it as necessary to maintain in its general outline the policy of *détente* with Germany' he did not regard as desirable 'a moral demobilization or an attitude filled with quietism towards the Reich'.[4]

Beck's policy again came under attack in 1936 from those in the

[1] Szembek, *Diariusz*, i. 346.   [2] Ibid., p. 381.
[3] Ibid., p. 403.   [4] Ibid. ii. 129.

Government, above all Kwiatkowski, Koc, and Rydz-Śmigły, who were unhappy about the deterioration in Franco-Polish relations caused by the *rapprochement* with Germany. The visit of Rydz-Śmigły to France in September–October 1936, which constituted a major attempt to improve relations with the French, was planned without prior consultation with Beck.[1] It also gave Léon Noël, the French Ambassador in Poland, and a strong opponent of the Polish Foreign Minister, an opportunity to attempt Beck's overthrow.[2] Noël persuaded Delbos, the French Foreign Minister, to make the granting of any credits to the Poles for rearmament conditional on the improvement of Polish-Czech relations and the replacement of Beck. However, Beck himself got wind of the scheme and was able again to win over Rydz, so that the visit passed off with no real danger to him or any modification of Polish policy.

After this, Beck faced no serious challenge from within the Government, although a further attempt was made by Noël in the spring of 1937 to secure his overthrow,[3] and he was again criticized by a number of ministers, including Kwiatkowski, for his actions in 1938.[4] There was also a fair amount of opposition from the Army, and above all from Sosnkowski, to his policy towards Czechoslovakia.[5] His continued tenure of the post of Foreign Minister, in spite of his relative isolation within the Sanacja (he refused, for instance, to join OZON), was above all a tribute to the posthumous influence of Piłsudski over his followers. Beck was the Marshal's designated successor in foreign affairs, and thus Piłsudski-ites like Rydz-Śmigły were prepared to waive their own better judgement rather than challenge his political line. Moreover, Beck was one of the ablest of the Piłsudski-ite politicians and was easily able to hold his own in the political skirmishing after 1935, while his position was further strengthened by a number of successes and pseudo-successes in foreign policy. Again, to have forced his resignation would have caused a sharp deterioration of relations with the Reich, since he was closely identified with the improvement in Polish-German relations, and would have meant conceding the validity of the Opposition's objections to his policy, thus further weakening the position of the régime.

---

[1] On this, see Beck, *Dernier Rapport*, p. 124.

[2] L. Noël, *L'Aggression allemande contre la Pologne*, pp. 139–47.

[3] Roos, *Polen und Europa*, p. 246.   [4] Ibid., p. 357.

[5] Szembek, *Journal*, p. 275; Report of Moltke, 2 September 1938, D.G.F.P., series D, No. V, Document 53, p. 77.

Beck's policy of *rapprochement* with Germany was treated with great suspicion by Polish public opinion. Such backing as it had came largely from various conservative factions including Mackiewicz, *Czas*, and the Young Conservatives linked with the weekly *Polityka*. Even here there were some critical voices, though these objected above all to Beck's failure to take his policy to what was held to be its logical conclusion, an alliance with Germany against the Soviet Union. Beck was well aware of the limitations his internal isolation imposed on him. When he spent an evening with a group of Young Conservatives on 6 November 1937 he admitted that 'the direction of foreign policy is, to a considerable degree, tied to the internal situation of the country and even depends on it' and, after listening to his hosts' 'pessimistic assessment' of the situation, exhorted them to propagate their views 'by word and pen'.[1]

His conduct of foreign affairs was especially strongly criticized in the first years after the Marshal's death, when the general view was neatly expressed by Bolesław Koskowski, who in *Kurjer Warszawski* on 28 January 1936 argued that 'all the costs of the agreement of 1934 have been met by Poland alone'.[2] Germany had achieved, as a result of it a much larger freedom of manœuvre, while the resolution of the basic points at issue between Poland and Germany had merely been postponed. As Świtalski told the President on 15 November 1935, 'the attack of Polish opinion on the foreign policy of Beck is at present so strong that if the Commander were still alive, he would certainly attribute this to the work of foreign agents'.[3]

Beck's line on Danzig aroused particular opposition, so much so that the Minister of the Interior felt compelled to forbid a meeting called to discuss the question in December 1936 by the former Foreign Minister Zaleski, the former Polish Commissioner in Danzig, Henryk Strasburger, and Bolesław Koskowski.[4]

It is true that the Government was able to win a good deal of popularity in 1938 by its assertion of Poland's 'Great Power status' in relation to Lithuania and Czechoslovakia, and that Beck succeeded in exploiting the widely held anti-Czech feelings of the

---

[1] Szembek, *Diariusz*, iii. 168–9.
[2] *Kurjer Warszawski*, 28 January 1936.
[3] A.S.S., Dn. 15 listopada 1935 r. Rozmowa z Prezydentem.
[4] *Robotnik*, 17 December 1936.

Poles and their sympathy for the Polish minority in Czecho-slovakia. But there were also considerable misgivings. The danger-ous implications of Beck's policy towards the Czechs were most clearly realized by the older 'professors' group' in the Endecja, of whom Stroński was the most eloquent, and by the Morges Front. *Kurjer Warszawski*, close to both Sikorski and Stroński, was con-sistent in its opposition to Beck's policy of favouring the break-up of Czechoslovakia. Similar views were expressed by both the Peasant Party and the socialists. According to *Robotnik* on 10 June 1938, there were two aspects to the Czechoslovak problem: that of the Polish minority in Czechoslovakia, on which all were agreed, and that, infinitely more serious, of the 'Hitlerite thrust', which the Government was reproached for completely ignoring.

The acquisition of the Trans-Olza district was greeted with almost unanimous approval by the Poles. But it soon became evident at what cost this 'triumph' had been achieved. As a result of the *Anschluss* and the partition of Czechoslovakia, wrote *Robotnik* on 31 December 1938, Poland was 'face-to-face with the German colossus'.[1] The awareness that Polish opinion would not accept a situation in which Poland was a German dependency was an important factor in inducing Beck, and the Government as a whole, to reject the German proposals advanced from October 1938 on. Beck's refusal to give way was enthusiastically supported, and there was little criticism of his refusal to make any significant concessions to the Russians. As Sikorski wrote to Paderewski on 11 June 1939, 'In Poland, our position has triumphed all along the line. But the people who have advanced it still remain in the shadows.'[2]

Attempts have been made to defend Beck's policy on the grounds that the unwillingness of Britain and France seriously to resist Hitler left him with no alternative but to seek the sort of accommodation he favoured with Germany.[3] The failure of his policy is admitted, but it is argued that no alternative would have proved more successful. These conclusions are not convincing. Beck consistently failed to grasp the aggressive and dynamic character of Nazism, a failing he shared with many Western states-men. But in his case, this was rather more serious because of the

---

[1] *Robotnik*, 31 December 1938.
[2] Quoted in Żarnowski, *Polska Partia Socjalistyczna*, p. 340.
[3] See, for instance, A. Cienciała, *Poland and the Western Powers, 1938–1939* (London, 1968).

many unsolved issues between Germany and Poland. His refusal to consider any form of collective security between 1933 and 1936 was a major factor in enabling Hitler successfully to rearm and to attack the Versailles system. Beck's belief that Poland's security rested not on this system but on the country's own strength seems in retrospect to have been both short-sighted and ill-judged. His whole policy towards Czechoslovakia, too, rested on misconceptions which were fairly obvious at the time, that an independent Slovakia would gravitate towards Hungary and Poland, rather than Germany, and that the Hungarians were a military force to be reckoned with. In addition, though his mistrust of the Soviet Union can be understood, its results were largely harmful, since it was a major factor in his decision to loosen his ties with France and his hostility to systems of collective security. Moreover, with the rise of Nazism and the outbreak of the Sino-Japanese conflict, the Soviet Union had become increasingly willing to underwrite many aspects of the *status quo* in Eastern Europe. Beck's preoccupation with questions of prestige, both national and personal, and his vindictiveness, which can be seen in his strong resentment of the position accorded Beneš at the League of Nations, also proved rather sterile guides in the formulation of policy. Whether a different policy would have worked better remains a matter of conjecture and depends to some extent on how one assesses Russian intentions, a particularly difficult problem given the lack of documentation. But one cannot help feeling that a more resolute attempt to defend the Versailles system would have increased the commitment of the French to the *status quo* in Eastern Europe and might well have proved more effective in deterring Hitler.

THE ARMY 1935–1939

Beck's ambitious foreign policy rested almost entirely on bluff, for although serious attempts were made between 1935 and 1939 to repair the ravages which Piłsudski's administration had inflicted on the Army, by the outbreak of the war the Polish Army was still an inadequate fighting force. At the Marshal's death its level of effectiveness was, indeed, woefully low. On paper it appeared formidable, with a peace-time strength of thirty infantry divisions (which could be increased by a general mobilization to thirty-nine), eleven cavalry brigades, ten armoured battalions and ten Air Force regiments, and had nearly 325,000 men under arms.[1] But although the annual expenditure on the Army had remained between 750 and 850 million zloties in the years between 1926 and 1935 (nearly a third of all budget expenditure) very little had been done to modernize and bring up to date its equipment, which was for the most part outdated and highly inadequate.

This was most clearly the plight of the infantry, which, as in other European armies, formed the basis of the Polish forces. But whereas there was elsewhere a general tendency for the proportion of infantry in the army to decline, this was slow to take effect in Poland. According to a study undertaken by the Polish General Staff at the end of 1935 and the beginning of 1936, the proportion of infantry in the Polish Army was 57·2 per cent, compared with 50·5 per cent in France, 43·5 per cent in Germany, and 43·3 per cent in the Soviet Union.[2] Moreover, a Polish infantry division was very backward in its equipment, which, as General Sosnkowski admitted in April 1937, barely surpassed the level of 1914.[3] Compared with a German or Russian division it was weak in artillery, in the means for undertaking reconaissance and communications, in machine-guns, and in its sapper and chemical sub-departments. It was entirely without organic heavy artillery, anti-tank artillery, and tanks, and was still very slow in movement, being largely dependent on horse-drawn carts.[4]

The same backwardness characterized the cavalry, which was still seen as a fighting arm of vital significance, and which constituted 10·5 per cent of the Army, as against 6·4 per cent in France (much of this motorized), 6·2 per cent in the Soviet Union, and 2·6 per cent in Germany.[5] Yet compared with these countries, in spite of the significance assigned to it, the Polish cavalry brigade possessed the lowest number of officers and men, had the smallest

[1] J. Zając, 'Nasze przygotowanie do wojny', *Kultura* (Paris), no. 1–2 (1961), pp. 161–2; E. Kozłowski, 'Stany liczebne polskich sił zbrojnych w latach 1936–1939', *Biuletyn Informacyjny Wojskowego Instytutu Historycznego* (1961), no. 17, pp. 49–64.

[2] C.A.W., Akta Szefa S.G. Zestawienie porównawcze wojska polskiego na stopie pokojowej i wojennej z wojskiem niemieckim i francuskim. Quoted in E. Kozłowski, *Wojsko Polskie, 1936–1939* (Warsaw, 1964), p. 15. (Hereafter cited as Zestawienie porównawcze.)

[3] E. Kozłowski (ed.), 'Protokóły Komitetu Wyższej Szkoły Wojennej', *Biuletyn Wojskowej Akademii Politycznej* (1959), no. 3, p. 55.

[4] C.A.W., Akta Szefa S.G. Studium organizacji i wyposażenia dywizji piechoty, Oddział I S.G. Quoted in Kozłowski, op. cit., p. 83.

[5] Zestawienie porównawcze, Kozłowski, op. cit., p. 15.

amount of motorized equipment, and was much worse provided with machine-guns and armoured weapons.[1]

When it came to technical weapons, the situation was even worse. Polish artillery had barely advanced since 1914 and its effectiveness was hampered by its extreme lack of manœuvrability, dependent as it was on horse-drawn transport. Moreover, with only twelve artillery batteries to a division, the army was not capable of matching the firepower of either the Germans or the Russians.[1] The introduction of tanks had also been slow, in accordance with the French strategic principles which had survived Piłsudski's dismissal of the French Military Mission in 1928. The view prevailed that armoured weapons were not capable of autonomous action and should only play a supporting role in infantry operations.[2] The overwhelming majority of Polish tanks in 1935 were, therefore, of a light reconnaissance character and there were no large armoured or motorized units, which were increasingly becoming a feature of modern armies. The general level of motorization was also deplorably low.[3] As we have already seen, Piłsudski himself had been responsible for the reduction of sapper units in the Army, so that by May 1929 of the original ten sapper regiments only eight battalions remained. The equipment they possessed was largely outdated and primitive. They had no light bridge-building equipment or mechanized means for building roads, bridges, or field fortifications. Their level of motorization lagged far behind that of their counterparts in Germany or Russia.[3] Communications had also failed to develop. Communication by wire was adequate, but because of Piłsudski's insistence that the state telephone and telegraph system should form the basis for military communications during wartime, the adoption of radio as a means of communication was in 1935 still in its infancy.[4]

The Polish Air Force was in a particularly bad state. In accordance with French strategic doctrine, the view prevailed that the Air Force could only play a subordinate role, and should be used for distant reconnaissance or for supporting large units of infantry or cavalry. No attempts were made to develop an independent fighting or bombing force. As regards equipment, the attempt of

[1] Ibid., Kozłowski, op. cit., p. 16.
[2] On this, L. Stankiewicz, 'Rozwój broni pancernej', *Bellona* (London) (1941), no. 3, pp. 12–21.
[3] Zestawienie porównawcze, Kozłowski, op. cit., pp. 16–17.
[4] Ibid., Kozłowski, op. cit., pp. 17–18.

General Rayski, who took control of the Air Force after the May coup, to end Poland's dependence on French equipment by building up a native Polish aircraft industry had largely disastrous results. Whereas in the late 1920s, the Polish Air Force, with nearly 800 planes, had been the second largest in Europe, by 1936 its number of effective aircraft had fallen to 417—this after an annual expenditure of nearly 60 million zloties and in a period of enormously rapid expansion in the air power of both Germany and Russia.[1]

Moreover the strategy and thinking of the Army was dominated by Piłsudski-ite concepts, most of which were, by 1935, almost entirely anachronistic and incapable of application.[2] Military planning was dominated by the belief that Poland should be prepared above all for a war against the Soviet Union. Planning for a war against Germany occupied a relatively minor place, since it was believed that the restrictions imposed by the Treaty of Versailles would mean that it would be many years before the German Army could re-emerge as a formidable fighting force. Moreover it was believed that in a future war with Germany the major burden of the fighting would fall on France, and that the Polish front would be of secondary importance.

Linked with the belief that any future war would have to be fought in the east, was Piłsudski's view that this war would be a 'war of motion'. This was obviously true in the sense that trench warfare on the model of 1914 was a phenomenon of the past. But to Piłsudski and his disciples in the armed forces, the concept was tied to a belief that any future conflict would follow the pattern of the Polish-Soviet war of 1920, in which they had obtained their battle experience. As then, cavalry would play a major role, and battles would be won by rapid counterthrusts on the wings and at the rear of the enemy. This whole concept was, of course, almost

---

[1] Zestawienie porównawcze, Kozłowski, op. cit., p. 18. M. Romeyko, 'Rayskie' czasy lotnictwa polskiego (London, 1949); M. Romeyko, Przed i po maju, ii. 118–85; T. Królikiewicz, 'Lotnictwo polskie w okresie międzywojennym', Wojskowy Przegląd Historyczny, no. 3 (1957), pp. 95–144.

[2] On this see: S. Lityński, 'Udział Wyższej Szkoły Wojennej przed r. 1939 w kształtowaniu polskiej doktryny wojennej', Bellona (1955), no. 1, pp. 30–8; G. Łowczowski, 'Polska doktryna wojenna, 1919–1939', ibid. (1960), no. 1, pp. 3–24; W. Wisłocki, 'Polemika w sprawie doktryny', ibid. (1960), no. 4, pp. 303–5; T. Machalski, 'Polska doktryna wojenna, 1919–1939', ibid. (1960), no. 4, pp. 248–99; J. Kirchmayer, 1939 i 1944. Kilka zagadnień polskich (Warsaw, 1957).

entirely anachronistic, given the rapid development of artillery and tank warfare. What is more, the Polish Army's dependence on horse-drawn transport meant that it lacked the mobility for the rapid and bold manœuvres required by Piłsudski-ite strategy.

A fundamental feature of Piłsudski's military thinking was the belief that in a future war a decisive role would be played by the superior quality of the Polish officer corps. Yet this superiority was, to say the least, dubious. We have already seen how Piłsudski's dislike of theoretical problems had led, after 1926, to a downgrading of the position of the General Staff and how his followers in leading positions in the Army had acquired from him a strong distrust of technical training. As late as 1939, only 4·84 per cent of the officer corps had acquired diplomas in military academies.[1] A large majority of the officers were brave and competent soldiers, but Piłsudski's concept of the 'specific example' which held that war was essentially a series of unpredictable conflicts and could therefore not be planned in advance, led to a neglect of staff work and planning, particularly at higher levels of command.[2] This development was intensified by the distinction between the peacetime and wartime organization of the Army introduced by the Marshal after the coup. This meant that the peacetime commanders of the ten divisional corps into which the Army was divided were replaced, at the outbreak of war, by the Army Inspectors, who had not recently been in command of armies or operational groups, and who lacked effective staffs when they took command.

The death of Piłsudski made possible a new approach to Army problems. Already in early 1936 the General Staff, which under the able direction of General Stachiewicz had again begun to play a leading role in Army affairs, made a comparative study of the Polish, French, German, and Russian armies, which revealed the extreme weakness of Poland in relation to her neighbours.[3] At the same time, intelligence reports on Germany were confirming the alarming rate of German rearmament.[4] In these circumstances,

---

[1] Kozłowski, op. cit., p. 77.

[2] Note the comments on this of the Chief of the General Staff, General Stachiewicz, on 30 April 1936. E. Kozłowski (ed.), 'Protokóły Komitetu Wyższej Szkoły Wojennej', p. 41.

[3] See pp. 484–5.

[4] This was most clearly revealed by the study 'Niemcy', W. Steblik, 'Studium Niemcy z maja 1936 r.', *Wojskowy Przeglad Historyczny* (1960), no. 3, pp. 334–59.

the modernization of the Army and the development of its military effectiveness was a matter of urgency, and in the spring of 1936 the General Staff undertook the necessary preparations.[1] The plan was developed under the personal supervision of General Stachiewicz, and it was originally scheduled for completion in October 1936 so that it could be submitted to the General Inspector of the Army in November. However, it proved impossible to keep to this deadline, and different parts of the plan were submitted to the General Inspector's Committee on Rearmament and Equipment between August 1936 and December 1937, a procedure not particularly conducive to efficiency.

The plan did not aim at a fundamental reorganization of the Army; its creators were far too close to Piłsudski to make a frontal attack on his achievements. It aimed rather at rationalizing the organization of the different parts of the Army and especially at modernizing its equipment, providing it with those weapons which had been neglected before 1935. The plan also envisaged the rapid building up of Polish military industry by extensive state intervention, and a six-year programme for this purpose was adopted on 28 July 1936 by the General Staff.[2] At the same time a new body, the Committee for the Defence of the Republic, was set up by decree on 9 May 1936.[3] Its secretariat rapidly assumed large powers over the country's economy, particularly in the creation and development of industry, the use of raw materials, and the placing of civilian firms under military control. In terms of a Prime Ministerial directive of 13 July and a circular of 22 July 1936, ministers had to obtain the agreement of the Secretariat in all matters concerned directly or indirectly with the country's defence.[4]

It was estimated in 1937 that the implementation of the plan for the Army, which was to take six years, would need an additional 790–800 million zloties above what was assigned to the Army in the budget. Expenditure on this scale was far beyond what the rather slender financial resources of the country could support,

[1] On the plan, see Kozłowski, op. cit., pp. 22–44; *Polskie Siły Zbrojne w drugiej wojny światowej*, vol. i, part 1 (London, 1951), pp. 168–9.

[2] C.A.W., Akta SeKOR, vol. 54. 'Program rozbudowy przemysłu wojennego' pismo Szefa S.G. do gen. dyw. K. Sosnkowskiego (L. dz. 127) SeKOR (tj.) z 28.VII. 36. Quoted in Kozłowski, op. cit., p. 31.

[3] Dekret Prezydenta RP z 9.V.1936 o sprawowaniu zwierzchnictwa nad siłami zbrojnynii i organizacji naczelnych władz wojskowych w czasie pokoju. *Dz.U.R.P.* (1936), no. 38, pp. 647–9.

[4] Kozłowski, op. cit., p. 23.

and it soon became clear that it would be optimistic to think in terms of an expenditure of more than 500-50 million zloties annually. In fact in the budget years of 1936-7 and 1937-8 only 50 per cent of this sum was spent. By 1938 the worsening international climate led to a further intensification of investment and a new plan seems to have been adopted in that year which increased the amount to be spent by 303 million zloties, mostly to be expended on the Air Force and on anti-aircraft defence. However, it was recognized that expenditure could not be carried on at this level for any length of time, and the term for the implementation of the whole plan was thus extended from six to ten years.

In spite of fairly heavy investment and a good deal of effort, the plan did not succeed in materially improving the strength of the Polish armed forces. Though there was some improvement in the firepower of the Polish infantry, a Polish division still remained far behind a German division. This was most evident in relation to artillery, where the Germans had a 2 : 1 predominance, mortars (2·7 : 1), and machine-guns and pistols (10 : 1).[1] Moreover, very little progress was made in motorization, and the Polish infantry remained dependent on horse-drawn transport with all its disadvantages.

Cavalry retained its position as one of the principle branches of the Army, and General Wiatr's assertions after the war that it was being run down in the last years before 1939 have no documentary basis.[2] An effort was made to build up its firepower, particularly with anti-tank and anti-aircraft artillery, but by 1939 the firepower of the Polish cavalry was still significantly below that of Russia and Germany. Moreover, little attempt was made to create cavalry units larger than a brigade, although only large units could have had any hope of fulfilling the tasks assigned to the cavalry in Polish military thinking.

Little progress, too, was made in bridging the gap between Polish artillery and that of her neighbours. In 1939, the Army still lacked very heavy long-range weapons and many of its lighter guns were quite outdated. There had been very little advance in motorization and ammunition columns were still horsedrawn. According to General Miller, who was in charge of artillery questions on the

---

[1] Ibid., p. 90.
[2] J. Wiatr, 'Przyczynki do historii materiałowego przygotowania obrony Polski w latach 1921-1939', *Bellona* (London) (1959), no. 3, 246.

staff of the General Inspector, the artillery firepower of a Polish infantry division in June 1939 was only one-third that of a German division.[1]

In relation to armoured weapons, the Army still held to the principle that tanks were to be used only to support the infantry and cavalry, and for reconnaissance purposes. The new models of light and pursuit tanks provided for in the plan had only begun to be introduced in 1939, and most equipment was old and out-of-date. The German predominance in this field was quite startling. In August 1939, for instance, the Poles possessed 313 light and medium tanks, against Germany's 3,200. In addition they possessed only 574 reconnaissance tanks and 100 armoured cars. This was not a striking rise since 1935.[2] Only one large armoured military unit had become fully operational on the outbreak of war, though a second was planned to be ready for action by mid-October 1939. In practice, this second unit was able to play virtually no role in the September campaign. All in all, by September 1939 the Poles possessed only one armoured military brigade, three battalions of light tanks, eleven armoured divisions (reconnaissance), eighteen companies of reconnaissance tanks and ten armoured trains.[3]

Some progress was made in increasing the number of trained sappers, but their equipment and level of motorization still remained very inadequate. Communications at a lower level also developed fairly satisfactorily after 1935, with radio now widely introduced. But the principle adopted in the Army, contrary to all accepted rules, that a subordinate was to maintain communications with his superior officer, proved extremely misguided. Moreover, the radio stations provided for divisions and armies proved to have a range of 15–20 km. as against the 30–50 km. required.[4] The combination of these two factors proved disastrous during the September campaign, during which the system of command from a division upwards rapidly broke down.

Modernization was least successful in the Air Force. This was largely the result of the extreme incompetence of the Air Force commander, General Rayski. His scope for action was considerably increased after the death of the Marshal, with the creation of a

---

[1] C.A.W., Akta Dep. Art. M.S. Wojsk, t. 89. Uwagi generała do prac artyleryjskich przy G.I.S.Z. st. Miller (L. dz. 5190/tj) z 13.X.1938 o wyszkoleniu oddziałów i kadry oficerskiej artylerii. Kozłowski, op. cit., p. 150.

[2] Ibid., p. 164.

[3] Ibid., pp. 186–7.   [4] Ibid., pp. 209–11.

Higher Aviation School and an Air Force Staff attached to the General Staff. But he remained totally absorbed in his main preoccupation of developing prototypes for Polish military aircraft, and made no attempt to rethink the role the Air Force could play in a future war. Rayski's plan for the modernization of the Air Force envisaged the increase of its front-line aircraft from 464 in April 1937 to 886 by April 1942. This would make possible the creation of eight squadrons of pursuit planes (reconnaissance), thirty-two of line planes (reconnaissance), ten of accompanying planes, eighteen of pursuit planes, and thirty of bombers. This plan was considerably cut down by the General Staff, and the target of 688 front-line planes for 1942 was finally accepted on 13 October 1936.[1]

By early 1939, however, it had become apparent that Rayski was not capable of implementing even this scheme and that he had been culpably optimistic about the ability of the Polish aircraft industry to fulfil the tasks he had assigned to it. He was finally replaced by General Kalkus, who was to command the Air Force in peacetime, and General Zając, who was to take over on the outbreak of war. But this was too late to remedy the previous errors and neglect. In September 1939 the state of the Air Force was indeed worse than it had been in 1935. The front-line fighting force comprised four bomber squadrons, thirteen of line aircraft, fifteen of fighter aircraft, and eleven of accompanying aircraft, altogether 388 planes,[2] and this after an expenditure of 567 million zloties between 1932 and 1939. However, some progress had been achieved in the development of anti-aircraft defence, particularly after the creation of the Inspectorate of Anti-Aircraft Defence, headed by the capable General Zając, on 4 July 1936.

The reasons for the failure of the Army plan are fairly obvious. It was extremely difficult, in the short time available, to overcome Poland's military backwardness, and though the outlays made between 1935 and 1939 were large by Polish standards, they were not sufficient to effect a qualitative change. Poland just did not have the economic and financial resources to undertake a radical

---

[1] C.A.W., Akta SeKOR, vol. 3. Notatka gen. Malinowskiego zał. nr. 1, 'Rozbudowa jednostek bojowych wg. projektu Szefa Departamentu Aero' Kozłowski, op. cit., p. 232.

[2] *Boje polskie, 1939–1941* (London, 1941), pp. 36–8. A higher estimate of approximately 550 front-line planes was made by T. Cyprian in *Komisja stwierdziła . . . Londyn, 1942* (Warsaw, 1960), pp. 319–24, 331–4.

re-equipment of her Army in a short period. Furthermore, the outlays which were made were not used in the most efficient way. The attempt to modernize all sectors of the Army caused excessive dispersal of resources, while the decision to create new units as new equipment became available, rather than modify older units, involved a wasteful maintenance of men under arms. The practice of maintaining a peacetime Army of thirty infantry divisions (nearly 75 per cent of the mobilized strength of the Army) diverged from the general European pattern of keeping only half of the mobilized army in being. It was extremely costly and consumed resources which could have been much better employed on modernization and re-equipment. The large role assigned to the cavalry, an extremely costly branch of the Army, also absorbed funds which could have been better used elsewhere. Finally, the policy of the state-owned armaments industry of continuing to export weapons between 1936 and 1938, including planes and anti-tank and anti-aircraft guns, was shortsighted in the extreme.

But the basic reasons for the lack of any really effective changes lay in the failure to make a fundamental reassessment of army organization, strategy, and tactics. The Piłsudski-ite officers who were so important in the Army between 1935 and 1939, though they recognized the ill-effects of the Marshal's last years on military affairs, could not bring themselves to break decisively with his thinking. Moreover after his death French strategic concepts again became popular, and these tended to underestimate the importance of the Air Force and of armoured weapons. The basic strategy and tactics of the Army underwent no significant changes between 1935 and 1939 and were thus hopelessly out of date, particularly in relation to Germany.

Moreover, Rydz-Śmigły, who as General Inspector was the most powerful man in the Army, was singularly ill-fitted for the tasks which fell to him. He had no higher military training and, even more than some of the other Piłsudski-ite officers, was still deeply influenced by his experience in 1920. More than anyone else he was responsible for the High Command's unwillingness to organize war games and operational training at the highest level, a mistake which was to have serious consequences during the September campaign. Though some attempts were made to organize exercises and war games on an operational level from 1938 on, it proved too late to remedy the obvious weaknesses.

Furthermore, though the General Staff played a larger role after 1935, it proved to be rather difficult to overcome the Piłsudski-ite hostility to staff work on the part of many senior officers. As a result the General Staff was still rather short-handed and was unable to perform all the tasks assigned to it. It is true that it was able to prepare a new mobilization plan in April 1938 which could be adapted to suit a war in the east or in the west, but other aspects of staff work were rather neglected. This was particularly true of the third section of the General Staff, that concerned with operational planning, which was seriously undermanned. This section had drawn up an operational plan 'East' by March 1939, but because of its lack of staff, only introductory work on plan 'West' had been begun before the outbreak of the war.

THE COLLAPSE OF THE POLISH STATE

Polish public opinion greeted the onset of the war with great equanimity. Government propaganda asserting the 'Great Power status' of the country and the 'triumphs' of 1938 had created an exaggerated idea of its strength, and it was generally believed that, in alliance with Britain and France, Poland would be more than a match for the German forces. According to Lieutenant-Colonel Roman Umiastowski, of the propaganda department of the Supreme Command, speaking on the radio on 4 September,

Our Supreme Commander held command on the front in 1920, when he was 33 ... The military experience of the commanders in the German army is limited ... Our army is prepared for war like no other. It is true that it has less equipment than the enemy, but it has instead soldiers and commanders of a type not possessed by the enemy—above all, young commanders.[1]

These views were widely shared. According to Studnicki, 'many sensible people', including men like Maciej Rataj, 'were enthusiastic for war'.[2]

The prevalent optimism had no basis in the real situation. As a result of pressure from Britain and France, who were still hoping to reach a negotiated settlement with Hitler, general mobilization

---

[1] Quoted in M. Turlejska, *Prawdy i fikcje; wrzesień 1939–grudzień 1941* (Warsaw, 1966), p. 65.

[2] Pobóg-Malinowski, *Najnowsza historia*, iii. 33.

had been delayed by one day, and had only started on 31 August. Thus, though large sections of the Army had already been organized in earlier 'quiet' mobilizations, it had not reached its full strength when the German attack began on 1 September. On that date the Poles had under arms twenty-seven infantry divisions, three reserve infantry divisions, eight cavalry brigades, three mountain brigades, one armoured motorized brigade, and a number of special units and voluntary militia battalions. The force numbered 840,000 men, 70 per cent of the total provided for in the mobilization plan.[1] It is true that mobilization continued after the onset of hostilities, but it was considerably impeded by the German Air Force's disruption of communications. Against the Poles, the Germans had mobilized thirty-seven divisions and improvised infantry groups amounting to another nine divisions, one mountain division, and fourteen mechanized or partially mechanized divisions. Their mobilization had gone much further than that of the Poles and 88 per cent of their total planned force of approximately 1·6 million men was under arms when hostilities began.[2] The German mechanized divisions, which comprised six armoured divisions, four light divisions (motorized infantry with two armoured units), and four motorized divisions were to prove particularly effective against the Polish Army in which, as we have seen, the process of modernization had made little progress. The gap in equipment between the two armies was striking. The Germans possessed 2,700 tanks against the Poles' 313 light and medium tanks and 574 reconnaissance tanks. They had 6,000 guns and mortars to the Poles' 4,800, 4,500 anti-tank guns to the Poles' 1,250, and they were able to employ about 1,900 aircraft against the Poles' miserable force of 388 front-line planes.[3]

Although the Poles pinned great hopes on effective intervention by the British and French, they knew this could not take place immediately.[4] Their aim was thus to contain the German attack

[1] T. Rawski, Z. Stąpor, and J. Zamojski (edd.), *Wojna wyzwoleńcza narodu polskiego w latach 1939–1945* (2nd ed., Warsaw, 1966), pp. 132–7; H. Piątkowski, *Kampania Wrześniowa w Polsce 1939 r.* (London, 1946), p. 40.

[2] *Wojna wyzwoleńcza*, pp. 128–32, 137.

[3] Ibid., p. 103; Kozłowski, op. cit., p. 164.

[4] 'Protokóły polsko-brytyjskich rozmów sztabowych odbytych w Warszawie w maju 1939 r. Przyczynki i materiały do historii kampanii wrześniowej 1939 r.' *Bellona* (London) (1957), no. 3/4, pp. 25–57; 'Protokóły polsko-francuskich rozmów sztabowych odbytych w Paryżu w maju 1939 r. Przyczynki i materiały do historii kampanii wrześniowej 1939 r.', ibid. (London) (1958), no. 2, 165–79.

and to prevent their own forces from being destroyed, so that they could undertake a counter-offensive when the British and French moved into action against the Germans. They were not, however, in a strong position to carry out this plan.[1] Poland, with its extensive frontier with Germany, which had been increased from 1,250 to 1,750 miles by the annexation of Moravia and the establishment of a German protectorate over independent Slovakia, and with its flat and relatively open terrain, was desperately vulnerable to the highly mobile German Army. Moreover the line chosen for defence by the Poles was not the most suitable. It ran along virtually the whole of the country's western, north-western, and south-western frontiers. It was originally intended to abandon Danzig and the Corridor, but with the fear that Hitler might limit himself merely to seizing the Free City, the Poles felt compelled to prepare themselves to respond to an action of this type. The forces in the Corridor were thus increased by two infantry divisions which, in the event, were rapidly cut off by the German attack.[2] It would have been strategically more sensible to base the line of defence further back from the frontier, on the Narew, Vistula, and San rivers, but this was rejected on the grounds that it would have meant abandoning most of the country's industrial areas, and also as a result of over-confidence and an unwillingness easily to cede Polish soil. Furthermore, though the initial stages of the plan for a war with Germany had been worked out, the further evolution of the campaign, and in particular the direction of a possible retreat, had not been decided in detail before the outbreak of war.[3] The Army was further handicapped in conducting a defensive operation of the type envisaged by the fact that there was no command on the army group level, and that the line of command thus went straight from the Supreme Commander to the individual army commanders.

In these conditions the outcome of the campaign was a foregone conclusion. More important than the German numerical predominance were the fourteen mechanized and partially mechanized German divisions. With their rapid and deep thrusting power they penetrated the thin and widely stretched Polish defensive

[1] The literature on the September campaign is enormous. For some of the more important items, see the section of the Bibliography dealing with this subject, p. 559.

[2] Piątkowski, op. cit., pp. 33–5.

[3] *Polskie Siły Zbrojne*, vol. i, part 1, p. 278.

line, and since their greater speed of manœuvre impeded Polish withdrawals from the line along the border, they were able to prevent the Polish Army from fighting a series of delaying operations. The overwhelming German predominance in the air proved another vital factor. The Polish Air Force was able, by dispersing its aircraft, to avoid destruction by the *Luftwaffe*, but it was too small to counteract German operations in the air, which were able to put the Polish railway system out of action and also to destroy large sections of the communications network. This, coupled with German broadcasts intended to mislead the Polish forces, meant that the military system of communications virtually ceased to function after the first few days of the war.

The German plan of attack envisaged two thrusts, one in the north and a rather stronger one in the south, which were to break through the Polish positions and to meet in two places, east and west of Warsaw, thus cutting off the Polish forces west of the Vistula and encircling the Polish capital. The plan succeeded extremely well, in spite of the vigorous resistance put up by the Poles. By 3 September, the German army group 'North', commanded by General von Bock, had cut off the Polish forces in the Corridor and as one part reached the Vistula near Warsaw another advanced beyond Warsaw from the north. The army group 'South', commanded by General von Rundstedt, with its great armoured strength, had broken through the Polish forces and had forced the Poles to fall back from Cracow. By 6 September General von Reichenau, Commander of the tenth Army of the army group 'South', which possessed the most armoured weapons, had advanced beyond Lodz and was moving past Kielce towards Warsaw. The Polish lines of defence had been effectively breached and the Polish Army had ceased to operate in a unified way, the individual units offering resistance where they could to the nearest German column.

Rydz's aim was now to withdraw what he could of the Polish forces across the Vistula, San, and Narew and to form a new line of defence. This proved impossible in the face of the rapid German onslaught and the breakdown of communications, which deteriorated still further when Rydz withdrew with most of his staff from Warsaw to Brześć on the night of 6–7 September. On 8 September one of Reichenau's armoured corps was able to break through to Warsaw after the encirclement of the Polish 'Prussian' reserve army.

The following day German troops besieged Warsaw from the east while further units in the north were also converging on the eastern side of the Polish capital. After some debate, the Germans now decided that the bulk of the Polish forces had not been able successfully to retreat to the east. They thus modified their plan, and by placing most of their troops along the Bzura river, west of Warsaw, were able to cut off the Polish Poznanian and Pomeranian armies under General Kutrzeba, which found themselves forced on 9–10 September to break through the German lines. This 'battle on the Bzura', which lasted nearly eight days, at first went well for the Poles.[1] In the end, however, German armoured reinforcements proved decisive. Only a small section of the Polish troops were able to break free of the German encirclement, while the overwhelming majority were killed or taken prisoner.

On 10 September, after receiving information that the Germans had crossed the Vistula and the Bug, Rydz-Śmigły decided on a further retreat, this time to East Galicia, where it was believed the Polish forces could be supplied from Rumania. This new line of defence also had little chance of success. Already by the 9th, the number of men under arms had fallen to 400,000. The encirclement of the Pomeranian and Poznanian armies in the battle on the Bzura limited still further the number of troops at the disposal of the Supreme Commander. General Sosnkowski, who was placed in command of the South-East Army Group (rather belatedly, army group commands were established after the first week of the campaign) did, however, have some success in holding up the German advance. But he was outflanked by the deep German penetration both to the north and to the south of him. By 12 September the Germans had reached Lwów and on the 15th, the fortress of Brześć was surrounded and compelled to surrender after two days. By now the collapse of Poland was only a matter of time. It is true that the Germans were running into a certain amount of trouble because of a shortage of fuel and the breakdown of some of their armoured vehicles. But the Polish Army was by this stage so disorganized that it was in no position to take advantage of the German difficulties. Indeed from about the 14th, Rydz-Śmigły ceased to exercise any real control over the Army and local commanders were forced to act almost entirely on their own

[1] T. Kutrzeba, 'Bitwa nad Bzurą, 9–22 września, 1939 r.', *Wojskowy Przegląd Historyczny* (1956), no. 1, pp. 237–305; (1957), no. 1, pp. 267–308.

initiative.[1] The intervention of the Soviet Union on 17 September thus did not effect the outcome of the campaign, though it did shorten its duration. The advance of the Red Army took place through territories in which there were few Polish forces and thus met relatively little resistance. On the same day as the Soviet invasion, the Polish government, together with the Supreme Commander, left Poland for Rumania and the campaign was virtually over. Warsaw, however, only surrendered on 27 September, while some other units continued to fight until 5 October.

The line of demarcation between the German and Russian zones of occupation differed somewhat from that laid down in the secret protocol to the Non-Aggression Pact, by which the boundary was to be drawn approximately on the Narew, Vistula, and San rivers.[2] Stalin renounced some parts of central Poland inhabited overwhelmingly by Poles, and in return Lithuania was assigned to his sphere of influence.[3] His main preoccupation seems to have been to ensure the credibility of his claim that he had acted on behalf of the White Russian and Ukrainian 'blood-brothers' of the Soviet Union. Nevertheless, the areas incorporated in the Soviet Union had a population of 4–5 million Poles out of perhaps 13 million, and included a number of areas in which Poles constituted the majority.[4] The question of whether a rump Polish state was to be established after the campaign had been left open in the protocol, but both Stalin and Hitler seem to have been opposed to such a step at this time;[5] thus Poland, the 'ugly offspring of the Versailles treaty',[6] in Molotov's phrase, disappeared from the map. The 'reorganization' of Polish territory would, claimed the Friendship and Frontier Treaty concluded between Germany and the Soviet Union on 28 September, provide 'a firm foundation for a progressive further development of the friendly relations between their peoples'.[7] In addition, both sides in a secret protocol pledged themselves not to allow 'Polish agitation which affects the territories

---

[1] *Wojna wyzwoleńcza*, p. 166.
[2] D.G.F.P., series D, No. VII, Document 284, pp. 295–6.
[3] D.G.F.P., series D, No. VIII, Document 152, pp. 159–61.
[4] Notably the towns of Wilno and Białystok and the areas around them.
[5] L. Herzog, 'Czy Hitler chciał utworzyć buforowe państewko polskie?' *Wojskowy Przegląd Historyczny* (1962), no. 4, pp. 295–316; M. Broszat, *National-sozialistische Polenpolitik, 1939–1945* (paperback ed., Frankfurt am Main, 1965), pp. 15–19.
[6] Ed. J. Degras, *Soviet Documents on Foreign Policy* (London, 1953), iii. 388.
[7] D.G.F.P., series D, No. VIII, Document 157, p. 165.

of the other party', and to 'suppress in their territories all beginnings of such agitation and inform each other concerning suitable measures for this purpose.'[1]

The Poles had received little help from the West. In terms of the Franco-Polish staff talks of May 1939, the French had agreed to undertake a limited offensive three days after the beginning of their general mobilization, and an offensive 'with our main forces, when the principal German effort is directed against Poland' fifteen days after mobilization. Both the British and the French had agreed to bomb German military installations.[2] As regards aerial bombardment, virtually nothing was done, apart from a British attack on the German naval base at Heligoland. British planes did, however, drop anti-Nazi leaflets over German cities! The reasons for this failure have been variously explained. The fear of alienating neutral (particularly American) opinion, of exposing Britain and France to German bombardment, and of placing the Royal Air Force in unnecessary danger, all seem to have played a role. The land operations of the French were scarcely more impressive. The Germans had only forty-four infantry divisions on their western frontier against France's ninety-two tactical units, which included seventy-two infantry divisions. On the night of 6–7 September, a small attack was mounted, which continued on the 8th and resulted in the capture of a small area in front of the Siegfried Line. The offensive was then stopped, and on 12 September General Gamelin, the French Commander-in-Chief, gave the order to abandon offence for defence.[3] The reasons for the French failure to act lie both in the strategic situation and in the defects of interwar French military thinking. The military situation was, in fact, by no means as favourable as the discrepancy between the armed forces of the two sides suggested. The French north-western frontier was approximately 500 miles long. But unless they violated the neutrality of Belgium and Luxemburg, the French had to advance along a narrow 90-mile-wide strip, heavily mined and defended by the best German forces. The French Army was, moreover, not suited to an action of this type. Its mobilization was slow, so that its main offensive could not be undertaken before 17 September.

---

[1] D.G.F.P., series D, No. VIII, Document 160, p. 166.

[2] 'Protokóly polsko-francuskich rozmów sztabowych', pp. 167, 171, 176–7; 'Protokóly polsko-angielskich rozmów sztabowych', pp. 28–9.

[3] A. Goutard, *The Battle of France, 1940* (translated by A. R. P. Burgess, London, 1958), p. 69.

By this date, the defeat of Poland had virtually been accomplished, and any relieving action would have been in vain. Moreover French tactical principles which stipulated that any attack had to be preceeded by a prolonged artillery barrage, as during World War I, hindered the adoption of a strategy of rapid movement, particularly since the French heavy artillery had to be taken out of storage, and could not be employed until the last stage of mobilization. Under these conditions, there was little effective help which the French could give to the Poles, something for which both were to pay dearly.

The Polish Government was severely compromised, both by the rapidity of the Polish defeat and by its own conduct during the campaign. Even after the outbreak of war, the Cabinet had refused to consider a coalition, or even the widening of its ranks.[1] Zygmunt Zaremba, a prominent member of the P.P.S., relates the response of Colonel Wenda, one of the leaders of OZON, to a delegation of the P.P.S., the Peasant Party, and the Democratic Party, which on 4 September proposed the establishment of a Government of National Unity: 'We have begun the struggle and we have no intention of sharing the victory with anyone.'[2]

Statements of this type were to prove an enormous liability in the shock and humiliation of defeat. The Government was criticized for its failure to prepare adequately for the war, and also, rather more unjustly, for failing to remain in the front line and for being too concerned for the safety of its members. Already on 4 September the Government had started to evacuate much of its personnel from Warsaw, and on the night of 6–7 September Rydz-Śmigły himself left the capital. The evacuation had not been adequately planned, and this contributed to the growing air of panic.[3] The call on 6–7 September for all men capable of bearing arms to leave Warsaw for the east, where they could be organized into military units, was particularly maladroit and, though later countermanded, added greatly to the confusion resulting from the move. By 9 September, the Cabinet had come to the conclusion that the campaign had been lost, and the question of whether it should not leave the country in order to maintain the continuity

---

[1] F. Sławoj-Składkowski, 'Prace i czynności rządu polskiego we wrześniu 1939', *Kultura* (Paris) (1948), no. 5, pp. 86–7.

[2] Z. Zaremba, *Wojna i konspiracja* (London, 1957), p. 23.

[3] Pobóg-Malinowski, *Najnowsza historia*, iii. 51–4.

of the Polish Government and defend the Polish cause became insistent.[1] On that date, Szembek had spoken to Noël, the French Ambassador, in order to ascertain the French attitude should the Polish Government leave Poland.[2] Two days later, Beck also discussed with Noël the prospect of the Government's withdrawing to France.[3] From the 14th, the Cabinet established itself in the extreme south-east of Poland, in the region of Kosowo and Kuty, and from here it endeavoured to obtain *droit de passage* for itself through Rumania, and *droit de résidence* in France. The response of the Rumanians, under strong pressure from the Germans and, to a lesser extent, the Russians, and unwilling to compromise their neutrality, was not encouraging.[4] The French were rather more sympathetic but, as Noël pointed out on the 17th, although his Government understood the Polish predicament, difficulties of communication had prevented the establishment of the exact terms of an agreement on *droit de résidence*.[5]

With the Soviet invasion, the withdrawal of the Government became a matter of urgency, if its members were to escape capture. Thus on the evening of the 17th Mościcki, together with the Cabinet, crossed the bridge at Czeremosz into Rumania. It has been claimed that the Rumanians had already agreed to give the Government *droit de passage*,[6] but there is no documentary evidence and it seems somewhat doubtful, in view of the assurances which the Rumanians were giving to the Germans at this time. Some surprise was occasioned by the fact that Rydz-Śmigły also crossed into Rumania, particularly since the Cabinet had decided on the afternoon of the 17th that he should remain in Poland. His decision seems to have been motivated by the promptings of Sławoj-Składkowski, fearing that he would be isolated in the Cabinet in exile, by Rydz-Śmigły's belief that his absence would expose the Government to more pressure from the Allies, and by his ambitions for the Presidency, which in terms of the constitution was to fall vacant in 1940. His action was a psychological

[1] Ibid., p. 56.
[2] W. Pobóg-Malinowski, 'Na rozdrożu rumuńskim', *Kultura* (Paris) (1948), no. 7, p. 128.   [3] Ibid., p. 129.
[4] See, for instance, the conversation between the Rumanian Foreign Minister, Grigore Gafencu, and the German representative in Bucharest, Wilhelm Fabricius, on 11 September: D.G.F.P., series D, No. VIII, Document 50, pp. 47-8.
[5] Pobóg-Malinowski, *Najnowsza historia*, iii. 58.
[6] W. Pobóg-Malinowski, 'Na rozdrożu rumuńskim', pp. 129-30.

blunder of the first order, and undermined still further the authority of the Sanacja, both in Poland itself and among the *émigrés*.[1]

The appearance of this large group of Polish officials caused considerable embarrassment to the Rumanians and, under pressure from the Reich, they demanded that the members of the Government and the Supreme Commander renounce their functions as a condition for their being granted transit.[2] When the Poles refused to comply, they were interned in a number of places in the country. They had, moreover, obligingly furnished the Rumanians with several pretexts for their action since Mościcki, in sending a message to Paris and London from Czernowitz on 18 September, had, in fact, violated Rumanian neutrality, and since the Hague agreement on *droit de passage* specifically excluded military personnel.

The internment seems, above all, to have been the result of Rumanian fears of Germany. There is virtually no evidence to substantiate the argument that some of the Polish diplomatic staff in Bucharest, in particular the Ambassador Roger Raczyński, his First Secretary, Alfred Poniński, and the Military Attaché, Lieutenant-Colonel Zakrzewski, connived at the internment in co-operation with Noël, in order to secure the overthrow of the Government.[3] The Polish Ambassadors in Britain and France intervened strenuously on behalf of the interned politicians, but to no avail.[4] As a result from 17 September Poland was in the view of Edward Raczyński, the Ambassador in Britain, 'for practical purposes without a government . . . Consequently, the idea gained ground that both the President and the Government would have to be replaced by new men.'[4]

The nature of the situation was also rapidly grasped by Mościcki in Rumania, and thus in order to keep power in the hands of the

[1] On this, see Pobóg-Malinowski, *Najnowsza historia*, iii. 60–5.
[2] F. Sławoj-Składkowski, 'Prezydent Mościcki', *Kultura* (Paris) (1956), no. 10, pp. 117–19.
[3] For this view, see Pobóg-Malinowski, *Najnowsza historia*, iii. 68–74. More adequate accounts are found in S. Zabiełło, 'Sprawa polska na arenie między-narodowej', in W. Góry and J. Gołębiowski (edd.), *Z najnowszych dziejów Polski, 1939–1947* (Warsaw, 1961), p. 55; S. Zabiełło, 'Na emigracji 1939/1940', *Sprawy Międzynarodowe*, 9 (1956), 43–6; idem, *O rząd i granice* (Warsaw, 2nd ed., 1965), pp. 13–16. Poniński gave his own version of what took place in 'Wrzesień 1939 r. w Rumunii', *Zeszyty Historyczne*, no. vi (Paris, 1964), pp. 146–202.
[4] E. Raczyński, *In Allied London* (London, 1962), pp. 39–40.

Piłsudski-ites, he gave Roger Raczyński on 20 September a sealed envelope to be sent to Łukasiewicz, the Ambassador to Paris, nominating Colonel Bolesław Wieniawa-Długoszowski as his successor.[1] He also sent the head of his civil chancellory, Stanisław Łepkowski, to Paris to ensure that the succession went smoothly.[2] Unfortunately the choice of Wieniawa-Długoszowski was a disastrous one. He was generally regarded in Poland as a charming but feckless and irresponsible cavalry officer, well known in Warsaw café society.[3] He was also a dedicated Piłsudski-ite and a strong supporter of Beck, and in this capacity had been given the post of Ambassador to Italy in April 1938. His appointment was not only bound to arouse strong opposition in Polish circles and among many of the Piłsudski-ites, but he was also, because of his close links with Beck and his alleged support for Italian territorial claims against France, *persona non grata* to the French. The Poles in Paris thus felt compelled to abandon his candidacy because of the opposition of the Quai d'Orsay.[4] On 27 September Łukasiewicz told his associates in the Paris Embassy that he and Edward Raczyński had been entrusted with the choice of a new President. Three candidates were considered, Paderewski, at this time living in Switzerland, Zaleski, Foreign Minister between May 1926 and November 1932 and known for his strong opposition to Beck, and Władysław Raczkiewicz. Paderewski was generally held to be too sick to hold the office, and the choice thus fell on Raczkiewicz, who was regarded as a compromise candidate acceptable to both Piłsudski-ites and non-Piłsudski-ites.[5] He had been one of the main organizers of the Polish military forces in Russia in 1917 and 1918 and had held office as Minister of the Interior, both before and after the May coup (in 1921, 1925-6, and 1935-6). He had also been Governor of the Nowogródek province (1921-4), the Wilno province (1926-30), and Pomerania (1936-9), and between 1930 and 1935 he had been Marshal of the Senate. As President of the World Union of Poles Abroad, he was fairly well known to Poles outside Poland, particularly in the U.S.A. His candidature, which was accepted on

[1] R. Raczyński, 'Zapiski', *Kultura* (Paris) (1948), nos. 9-10, p. 122.

[2] A. Poniński, 'Wrzesień 1939 w Rumunii', pp. 188-9, 191.

[3] See, for instance, M. Romeyko, *Wspomnienia o Wieniawie i o rzymskich czasach* (London, 1969), pp. 9-19.

[4] E. Raczyński, *In Allied London*, pp. 40-2.

[5] Ibid., p. 42. Łukasiewicz's unpublished memoirs (which I have not seen) are in the Józef Piłsudski Institute in New York.

30 September, signified an extension of the Government beyond the confines of the inner circle of the Piłsudski-ites.

This transformation was to go much further. Already on 28 September Łukasiewicz was forced by pressure both from the Poles in exile and the French to appoint Sikorski Commander of the Polish forces being organized in France.[1] On the 30th, Raczkiewicz attempted to form a Government. His first intention was to entrust the Premiership to Zaleski, but this fell through because of Sikorski's objections. He then called on Stanisław Stroński, a moderate National Democrat, well known for his opposition to Beck. Stroński declined in favour of Sikorski, who was soon able to form a Government.[2] This was his attempt to create a broadly based Cabinet of national unity, but its core was made up of men close to Sikorski himself and linked with the Morges Front. They included Stroński, who held the post of Deputy Prime Minister and Minister of Information, General Marian Kukiel, Sikorski's deputy as Minister of War, and General J. Haller, Minister without Portfolio. It also comprised a number of more respectable Piłsudski-ites, such as Zaleski (Foreign Affairs) and Sosnkowski, who joined the Cabinet in November following his arrival in Paris. Adam Koc, who had been a firm advocate of a change in the Government,[3] in spite of his rather dubious past, was Minister of Finance, a post he held only until December. Marian Seyda represented the National Democrats, Jan Stańczyk the P.P.S., and Alexander Ładoś the Peasant Party.

The final stage in the changeover came when Rydz-Śmigły, under pressure from Raczkiewicz, resigned as Supreme Commander on 27 October, and was replaced by Sikorski on 9 November.[4] On 2 November the Sejm and Senate were dissolved, and a new National Council of twenty-two members was established, representing all the main political parties as well as the main Jewish groupings. It met for the first time in January 1940 and elected Paderewski President, and Bielecki, Lieberman, and Mikołajczyk Vice-Presidents. A beginning was also made in establishing contact with the underground forces in Poland itself.

[1] J. Łukasiewicz, 'Memoirs'. Quoted in Pobóg-Malinowski, *Najnowsza historia*, iii. 80–1.

[2] S. Stroński, 'Jak to było 30 września 1939', *Dziennik Polski*, 13 July 1951.

[3] Pobóg-Malinowski, *Najnowsza historia*, iii. 81.

[4] Idem, 'Ostatnie decyzje marszałka Śmigłego', *Kultura* (Paris) (1951), no. 12/50, pp. 109–10.

The new Government stressed its break with the autocratic features of the pre-1939 regime. The President agreed that, though the constitution could not be radically modified, he would not make use of the vast powers of his office, and that decrees would not be issued by the President, but jointly by the Prime Minister and the Minister concerned.[1] A significant indication of the new atmosphere was the issuing of a decree on 10 November granting an amnesty and a 'full rehabilitation' to the Brześć prisoners.[2] On 30 November, in a radio address, Raczkiewicz affirmed that after victory, the Government would respect the rule of law and the freedom of the individual and would introduce basic social reforms. Elections would be free, and equality for all citizens of Poland 'without destinction of religion or nationality' would be established.[3] The change in the character of the Government was strongly stressed by Sikorski himself. The new Poland, he claimed, would be a land of political freedom and social justice. He strongly criticized the policy followed after the May coup of making appointments solely on grounds of political loyalty, which had weakened the state economically and militarily. In his New Year address in 1940 he called for a break with the tradition of governments 'not subject to control and acting outside and even against the public opinion of the Nation'.[4]

On this new Government fell the heavy task of continuing the war with Germany and defending the Polish cause. Its establishment did not end the political conflicts among the *émigrés* which became particularly bitter after the death of Sikorski in August 1943. Moreover, as it turned out, it was unable to reach an accord with the Russians. As a result, with the victory of the Soviet Union in Eastern Europe, the Poles were not given a second chance to see if they could make democracy work.

---

[1] Turlejska, *Prawdy i fikcje*, pp. 165–6.
[2] Pobóg-Malinowski, *Najnowsza historia*, iii. 90.
[3] Quoted in Turlejska, *Prawdy i fikcje*, p. 167.
[4] Ibid., p. 168.

CONCLUSION

There was no post-May system. There was only at first
Piłsudski, minor noble of genius from the Eastern Kresy,
with the intuition of a statesman and the temperament of
a revolutionary, lordly and coarse, at the same time near
triviality—Piłsudski, for whom, Poland was a great estate,
a Żułów or a Piekiliszki, in which he walked around, brow-
beating bailiffs and managers. With his renaissance *lar-
gesse*, the broadness of his conceptions, and the smallness
of his vindictiveness, he surrounded his person with legend
and dominated a whole period of Polish history. . . . And
then there was Piłsudski old and sick, and then the struggle
among his successors.

Kajetan Morawski, *Tamten brzeg*

IT is in many ways a disheartening experience to recount the
history of the reborn Polish state. Independence, achieved after
so much suffering, and greeted with such high hopes presented the
Poles with daunting and, in the end, insuperable problems. This
is not to deny that a great deal was accomplished; the differences
which had arisen between the various partitions as a result of 130
years of foreign rule were rapidly diminished, and Polish national
consciousness was extended much more widely, particularly
among the peasantry. The creation of an economic unit out of the
disparate areas which made up the country was well under way by
1939, and there was substantial economic progress, particularly
after 1936. The Poles gained valuable experience in running their
own state and in building up a civil service. In the arts too,
independence acted as a new stimulus to creativity.

But against these achievements must be set the shortcomings of
the new state. Of these the most obvious was the failure to maintain
independence. It is, of course, abundantly clear that this failure
was precipitated by the aggressive designs of Nazi Germany. No
Polish government in 1939 could have long resisted the massive
force of Hitler's military machine. The Western policy of appeasement and the Soviet Union's willingness to come to terms with
Hitler also contributed to the Polish collapse. But the Polish
Government cannot be absolved of responsibility for the September catastrophe. Beck's foreign policy from 1934 made Poland

seem almost an ally of Nazi Germany, and paved the way for Hitler's destruction of the Versailles settlement in Eastern Europe. Although it is impossible to know whether an alternative course could have succeeded, it seems likely that a policy more determined to uphold the *status quo* in Eastern Europe and less concerned to assert Poland's 'Great Power status' would have been more effective in protecting the country's interests.

The Polish Army was not well prepared for war with Germany. While it is true that none of Hitler's opponents in the first three years of the war made a particularly impressive showing, and while the Poles resisted with their traditional gallantry and heroism, this cannot disguise the fact that Poland was defeated within barely three weeks, and that defeat was a foregone conclusion before the intervention of the Soviet Union. Piłsudski-ite views on military affairs, above all the inability to appreciate the significance of mechanization and armoured weapons and the continued belief in the efficacy of cavalry against tanks, meant that the Poles had virtually no hope of resisting the Germans effectively. A more carefully thought-out strategy and a more rational plan for military expenditure would certainly have brought better results, and might have allowed the Poles to contain the Germans long enough to make possible some sort of Allied counter-attack in the West (though, of course, French strategic concepts made this rather unlikely).

The new state never overcame its economic problems. It proved extremely difficult to undo the economic effects of partition, and the level of production in the 1920s never surpassed that of 1913. Furthermore the harsh impact of the Great Depression was intensified by a rigid adherence to deflationary policies until early 1936. There was fairly rapid industrial progress from 1936 until the war, but it failed significantly to reduce the very high level of unemployment. Agriculture, too, remained depressed throughout the 1930s. This was for the most part the result of the international economic situation, and of the catastrophic fall in agricultural prices which had begun in the 1920s. The rapid rise in population also intensified the agricultural crisis. Indeed, pressure on the land could only have been alleviated by a radical programme of planned industrialization, a programme which was only embarked on in 1936.

Finally, independent Poland was highly unsuccessful in its treatment of its national minorities, and by 1939 all were seriously alienated from the state. This was partially the result of the political inflexibility of the Ukrainians in East Galicia and of the close links which bound the Germans to the Reich. But it was above all the result of the failure of the Poles to adapt themselves to conditions of independence in a state with large national minorities. Too many Poles still held to the political maxims of the years before 1914, when Polish national survival had been the pre-eminent consideration in political life. The low quality of the lesser bureaucracy also impeded satisfactorary relations with the minorities. It proved relatively easy to make liberal declarations in Warsaw, but far more difficult to have them applied in the provinces. It has been argued that the frontiers of 1921 were, in the long run, untenable, that they made impossible a reasonable relationship with either Germany or the Soviet Union. Germany, it is claimed, would never accept the loss of part of Upper Silesia and the creation of the Corridor, while the Soviet Union was bound to attempt the overthrow of the Treaty of Riga, in order to incorporate the Western Ukraine and Western White Russia. This seems an exaggeration. Frontiers have a habit of becoming fixed, merely because they are established. But at the same time, the failure of the Poles to reconcile their Ukrainian, White Russian, and German minorities to existence within the framework of the Polish state did much to undermine the viability of the 1921 borders. Moreover the concessions made to anti-Semitic agitation from 1935 onwards, were clearly a mistake. They weakened the state economically, had a largely negative effect on the internal political situation, where they strengthened the extreme Right, and contributed to the disillusionment with independent Eastern Europe in the West which was an important factor in fostering the adoption of policies of appeasement.

Almost all these failings can be traced to the political inadequacies of the new state. Neither the democratic constitution of 1921 nor Piłsudski's semi-autocratic regime was able to answer Poland's pressing problems. It is easy to see why the democratic constitution worked so badly and, looking back, its failure seems almost inevitable. But in the optimistic years after World War I, the Wilsonian heresy, the view that liberal parliamentary democracy was the only defensible political system, held virtually universal sway. The situation in Poland was not analogous to that of the states in Asia and Africa which have obtained their independence since World War II. Poland was a part of Europe, a poor and backward part, it is true, but it had shared in many of the developments of European civilization since the Middle Ages. But, in the precedence which the national problem assumed in its politics, in the pressing nature of its social and political problems, and in the prestige and importance which the Army enjoyed in its political life, it does suggest some similarities in political development to countries in Asia, Africa, and Latin America. The course of the constitutional experience in Poland is thus not without wider relevance.

The malfunctioning of the 1921 constitution was evident almost from its adoption. The differences between the former partitions, combined with a high degree of proportional representation, led to the fragmentation of political parties. The lack of political experience and the weakness of the Cabinet in relation to the Sejm made for governmental instability. The temptation to indulge in demagogy, and the political patterns developed under foreign rule, obscured for many the necessity to accord fair treatment to Poland's own national minorities, who made up a third of her population and who were bound, in a democratic system with universal suffrage, to be a force in politics. Moreover, the Polish parties in the *Reichsrat*, the *Reichstag*, and the *Duma* had been small groups, concerned almost exclusively with Polish problems and with attempts to gain redress for political grievances. This was a training singularly unsuited to assuming the responsibilities of a national parliament, with real control over the course of policy in the new country, confronted from its inception with daunting problems. War destruction had been devastating, and the difficulties involved in integrating areas which had long been intimately linked economically with Russia, Germany, and Austria-Hungary were enormous. Then, the perilous international position of Poland, exposed to demands for the revision of her frontiers from both Germany and Russia, and determined to defend her newly regained independence, lent substance to proposals for a stronger executive on the grounds that only a firm and stable government could guarantee the country's existence. This feeling was reinforced by a widespread belief that Poland owed her decline and partition to the weakness of her monarchy. Finally, the scale of corruption in public life, partly the result of political inexperience, partly inherited from Russia and Austria, resulted in a disillusionment with parliamentary government, and did much to discredit the 1921 Constitution.

However, the constitution's greatest failing was its specific aim of excluding Piłsudski from political life. All historical speculation is idle, but it seems likely that had a Presidency with rather more power been established, Piłsudski might have been integrated into the political system. His principal interest was not politics, but the Army and foreign policy, and, as we have seen, it was only with extreme reluctance that he was able to bring himself to make the coup. But the bitterness of the conflict between Piłsudski and the National Democrats before and during World War I, largely anachronistic once independence had been achieved, made any solution of this type impossible. The National Democrats, adopting the extreme and rather bloodless rationalism of Dmowski, never really understood the emotional appeal which Piłsudski communicated to large numbers of his countrymen. They had campaigned so long against what they regarded as the suicidal and criminal tradition of 'gentry revolutionaries' that they failed to realize that the Marshal's gestures, such as his formation of the legions, or his refusal to take the oath of allegiance to the German Emperor, futile though they seemed in practical terms, struck a sympathetic chord, and gave him an authority not easily overthrown. The 1920 war, rash folly though it seemed to the National Democrats, appeared to many others a glorious and noble attempt to safeguard Poland's national existence. It is true that the attempt to dislodge the Ukraine and White Russia from the Soviet Union had failed, but, as they saw it, the war had culminated in a great victory over Poland's hereditary enemy, soothing balm for more than a century of national humiliation. There was no other individual in Poland who could command Piłsudski's charismatic power.

It would have been more difficult to predict the failure of the semi-parliamentary form of government adopted by the Marshal after the May coup. Attempts have been made to claim for Piłsudski some conscious attempts to develop a political system. However his actions show that although he did have some long-term aims, he generally worked from day to day in politics, and his acts are marked by an absence of any real ideological foundation. It was this which led him to eschew any attempt to set up a totalitarian or Fascist system, and induced him to attempt to work within the

1921 constitution, making only moderate changes in it after the coup.

His alternative to undiluted parliamentary democracy failed partly because of its anachronistic character. The methods of parliamentary control which Giolitti had employed in Italy before 1914, or which Taaffe had used in Austria, could no longer easily be applied after the revolutionary upheavals of World War I. Moreover, Piłsudski and his associates had little idea of what it meant to co-operate with even a weak and subservient parliament. Their political training had been concentrated in conspiratorial techniques, and they had little understanding of the nature of parliamentary debate, or of the function of parliamentary criticism of the Government. In addition, the contempt which Piłsudski came to hold for all politicians made difficult the achievement of smooth relations with the Sejm. The parties of the Centre and Left were only too willing, after the coup, to accept a strong Government, headed by the Marshal. All that would have been required to gain their support were a few sympathetic words from Piłsudski, but these were never forthcoming. Piłsudski also never fully comprehended that the parliamentarians were bound to resent his illegalities. The 1928 election is an interesting case in point, for it is clear that neither Piłsudski nor Sławoj-Składkowski saw anything fundamentally wrong in the misappropriation of state funds to help pay for the B.B.W.R. campaign. Yet it was over this issue that the decisive clash between the Government and parliament arose. It must also be remembered that in the years after 1926 Piłsudski's health deteriorated seriously. This certainly impaired the quality of his leadership, and may have been one of the reasons for the crudity of the language with which he attacked the deputies.

Another source of difficulty was Piłsudski's extreme isolation. There was no one among his lieutenants, not even Sławek, with whom he felt he could talk on any sort of equal footing. His understanding of the political situation was therefore dependent upon the often distorted information which he gleaned from his few close associates, not all of whom were distinguished by their intelligence or discernment. To them he remained, not a political leader, but the Commander of legionary days, to whom unquestioning obedience was owed. Within the Government, the interchange of opinion and the discussion of alternative political possibilities atrophied almost completely. It is for this reason that although

Piłsudski played little formal role in the Government during the last three or four years of his life, his mere existence was crucial to the stability of his 'system', which evinced so little substance or cohesion after his death. Once the Marshal was no longer there to pronounce on any important proposal, the Sanacja's ideological content was seen to be almost nil. What Piłsudski had provided was an almost mystical, cohesive presence which proved irreplaceable. His chosen successor, Sławek, meant well, but was totally incapable of performing such a role, and Rydz-Śmigły's attempt to replace him can hardly be regarded as successful.

Finally, the severe impact of the Great Depression in Poland increased the intransigence of both the Government and the Opposition and made more difficult the achievement of any kind of compromise.

The failure to avert a clash between Government and parliament made the Sanacja increasingly authoritarian after 1930. Though Piłsudski was personally still widely respected, the government was never able to regain the trust of large sections of the population. Indeed between 1930 and 1939 the government achieved little more than the democratic cabinets of the despised 'sejmocracy'. It is undeniable that the constitution had functioned badly before 1926, and that the activity of the parties was open to strong criticism. There was much to be said for some sort of 'guided democracy' in Poland, providing a strong Government, which yet allowed a relatively free press and parliamentary criticism. Neither can the achievements of Piłsudski's regime be denied. The political stability which followed the coup certainly aided economic recovery; improvement took place in Poland's international position and, to some extent, in her treatment of her minorities. But after 1930, the Government became increasingly isolated from society. It is true that Poland never became a totalitarian state. Parties survived, the press was fairly free, criticism was allowed. Yet, after the death of Piłsudski exposed its lack of programme, the Sanacja was divided between those who favoured a return to a constitutional system and those who favoured open authoritarianism. This conflict had not been resolved by the outbreak of the war, and it would be rash to predict what its final outcome might have been had the September catastrophe not happened. Rydz, the man most likely to emerge in a dominant position, was certainly not at all equipped for such a role. Indeed, the evolution of politics between 1935 and

1939 showed how little substance there was in Piłsudski's boast that he had laid a firm foundation for the political future of the country. The growth of right-wing extremism, both within the Government and among the nationalist Right, was certainly a worrying development for the future political evolution of the country.

At the same time, however, a striking feature of the 1930s was the increased maturity and responsibility of the democratic parties of the Centre and Left. Their victory, a brief and perhaps inconclusive one, came after the Polish defeat which cruelly exposed the emptiness of the Piłsudski-ites' insistence that they had created a 'Great Power Poland'. The Government formed in France by General Sikorski comprised representatives of the Morges Front, the P.P.S., the Peasant Party, and the liberal elements of the National Party. Its politics were unquestionably democratic in the Western sense, and it may well have been able to function effectively in the post-war situation in Poland. After all, several countries in which constitutional government broke down in the inter-war period, such as Italy and Austria, have worked democratic systems successfully since 1945. Poland's geographic situation made this impossible. The Government-in-exile was unable to convince the Soviet Union that it could be trusted, and failed to reach agreement with the Russians on the frontiers of post-war Poland. Since 1945, the existence of Poland within the borders established at Yalta has been effectively guaranteed by the alliance with the Soviet Union. At the same time, the security which has been achieved has involved the loss of a good deal of freedom of manoeuvre, both in internal and external affairs. Whether internal freedom and true national independence are possible for Poland and for the other states of Eastern Europe remains an open question.

APPENDIX A

WAS THE BRITISH FOREIGN OFFICE
RESPONSIBLE FOR THE PIŁSUDSKI COUP?

THE Polish Right, which was addicted to conspiracy theories of politics, held the view that the Piłsudski coup was the work of the British Foreign Office.[1] This was also the contemporary Soviet opinion, as described by Karol Poznański, a member of the Polish Foreign Office who was in Moscow during the May coup to see to the implementation of a Consular Convention he had signed. The Polish Embassy in Moscow sent him to Narkomindiel to reassure Soviet officials that the coup would not affect Polish-Soviet relations. There one Stein, head of the department dealing with Poland and the Baltic States, told him that

> In spite of the failure of Denikin, Wrangel, and other 'White' generals, England has not renounced the idea of overthrowing the government in Russia through external military intervention. England is aware that, in the present political configuration, only Poland can be a jumping-off point for military intervention. England could not reach agreement with any of the successive Polish governments because no Polish government wanted to take part in the realization of an interventionist scheme. The new Witos Government would certainly not have agreed to take part in such a venture. England has thus sought an arrangement with Piłsudski, and he has approved their plans for intervention. . . .[2]

This interpretation has been adopted by many Polish historians in recent years, sometimes with the modification that Locarno was an attempt to bring Germany and Poland closer together in order to facilitate intervention in Russia.[3] Support is drawn from visits made by Sir William Max-Müller, the British Ambassador, and by the British Military Attaché to Sulejówek. But these may have been no more than courtesy visits to one of the undoubtedly important figures in Poland. One of the first duties carried out by the new French Ambassador to

---

[1] See, for example, *Kurjer Poznański*, 17 May 1926.

[2] K. Poznański, 'Wypadki majowe widziane od strony Moskwy', *Wiadomości*, vol. xii, no. 586 (23 June 1957), p. 3.

[3] For some proponents of this view see: K. Lapter, 'Międzynarodowe tło przewrotu majowego', *Sprawy Międzynarodowe*, vol. ix (1956), no. 5, pp. 43–60; no. 6, pp. 54–71; S. Arski, *My Pierwsza Brygada* (Warsaw, 1963), pp. 435–43; Ajnenkiel, *Od 'rządów ludowych'*, p. 293; S. Stęborowski, *Geneza Centrolewu* (Warsaw, 1963), p. 22.

Poland, Jules Laroche (appointed in April 1926), was to pay a visit to the 'Recluse of Sulejówek'.[1]

The only documentary evidence adduced is a cable which Kajetan Morawski, writing thirty years after the events he describes, claims to have seen after the coup. A British diplomat in the Middle East is supposed to have shown it to a Polish official there nearly two weeks before the coup occurred. The telegram stated that the Witos Government then being formed would be overthrown by violence, and that this turn of events served British interests.[2] The reliability of this evidence is very doubtful. It is strange that the telegram should have been shown to a Polish official, and its contents argue a rather exceptional, perhaps incredible, foresight on the part of the British Foreign Office. It certainly cannot be taken as proof of British complicity in the coup.

In fact, the theory rests on a number of misconceptions. In the first place, the aims of the Locarno Treaty were not anti-Soviet. Its intention was to reconcile France and Germany, while at the same time reaffirming the British guarantee of France's eastern frontier. It was essentially a political gesture intended to reassure France while Germany was again being eased into the European state system.[3]

Austen Chamberlain, the British Foreign Secretary, described the Soviet misinterpretation in a cable to Sir Ralph Hodgson, the British Ambassador in Moscow, on 26 April 1926:

> 2. It is useless to argue with Soviet authorities upon supposed anti-Soviet object of Locarno treaties. They have been told in every capital of Europe that these treaties had no such object and that His Majesty's Government have never sought to form any kind of anti-Soviet bloc. They are really suffering from swollen head. They are of less consequence to us than they suppose, and they grossly flatter themselves when they suppose that British policy is dictated by them.[4]

The Foreign Office knew, moreover, that Stresemann had no intention of breaking Weimar Germany's strong ties with the Soviet Union. Thus it did not oppose the concluding of the German-Soviet neutrality pact of April 1926. On 6 April 1926 Sir William Tyrell minuted a dispatch concerning this pact from Viscount D'Abernon, British Ambassador in Berlin:

> Whatever the motives may be, it would be a mistake on our part not to accept this as a *fait accompli* and make the best of it, as Mr. Gregory

---

[1] J. Laroche, *La Pologne de Pilsudski* (Paris, 1953), pp. 25–9.

[2] Morawski, op. cit., p. 2.

[3] See: A. J. P. Taylor, *The Origins of the Second World War* (London, 1961), pp. 40–60; F. Northedge, *Britain, The Troubled Giant* (London, 1966).

[4] *Documents on British Foreign Policy, 1919–39*, ed. W. Medlicott, D. Dakin, and M. Lambert (London, 1966), series IA, i. 671.

suggests, by intensifying our present policy of encouraging Germany to look West and not East.[1]

Austen Chamberlain minuted his agreement.

Although British relations with the Soviet Union were strained, the Foreign Office hoped that Russia could eventually be reintegrated into the Concert of Europe. It did not believe that the Soviet government was weak or that it could be overthrown by military intervention. On 6 May Sir Ralph Hodgson wrote to Austen Chamberlain:

2. . . . It is a truism that the process of pacification in Europe cannot be regarded as complete as long as Soviet Russia remains outside the scope of those agreements by which it is sought to attain that consummation. . . .

7. It stands to reason that all this would be of no account if the Soviet government is tottering towards its fall. It is not—on the contrary, it is, in spite of many troubles, gaining ground, winning through to solidity.[2]

To this last statement Austen Chamberlain minuted, 'I have throughout held this opinion.'[3]

In relation to Poland, British policy was principally concerned with achieving a German-Polish *rapprochement* and, if possible, some frontier modifications. It was for this reason that the Foreign Office liked Skrzyński as Foreign Minister, since he had signed the Locarno agreements and had secured their ratification by the Polish parliament. When Konstanty Skirmunt, Polish Ambassador in London, told Donald Gregory, head of the Northern Department of the Foreign Office, that Polish foreign policy would not be modified by the coup, Gregory replied, 'The best guarantee of this policy would be the return of Skrzyński to the Foreign Ministry.'[4] Piłsudski's opposition to Locarno was well known, and it is *a priori* unlikely that the British should have engineered his return.

The absence of British involvement in the coup emerges clearly in Donald Gregory's memorandum on the Polish situation, dated 17 May, to which Austen Chamberlain minuted his general agreement. Its tone is one of relief, relief that Piłsudski did not appear to intend to overthrow the constitution, relief (unjustified) that Skrzyński would return to the Foreign Ministry, relief that Britain would not be faced with the dilemma of whether to recognize a revolutionary government or not:

There seems, in other words, no reason to take tragically what has happened, but to regard it not so much as a national crime but as a

---

[1] *Documents on British Foreign Policy, 1919–39*, ed. W. Medlicott, D. Dakin, and M. Lambert (London, 1966), series IA, pp. 567–8.

[2] Ibid., pp. 724, 726.   [3] Ibid., p. 726.

[4] 'Raport polityczny nr 16/26 w związku z kryzysem państwowym w Polsce 20.V.1926 r.', published by Z. Landau in *K.H.*, vol. lxvi (1959), no. 1, p. 155.

national disaster, such as an earthquake or some uncontrollable upheaval. . . . German and Russian propaganda, particularly the former,
will utilise this incident to demonstrate once again the historical instability of Poland and to spread the usual gloomy rumours about a future
partition. Our way of countering that is by an indulgent attitude in regard
to the political lapse of last week and continued benevolence towards the
Polish state. The worst that we could do would be to return to the school-
mastering attitude, to put it at its mildest, that characterised our relations
with Poland from 1919 to 1923. As this synchronised with almost the
whole of the last Piłsudski regime, it is astonishing that he should preserve
any regard for us at all.[1]

Hardly the words of a man whose department had just successfully
engineered a coup.

[1] 'Memorandum by Mr. Gregory respecting the Polish situation', 17 May
1926, *Documents on British Foreign Policy*, pp. 757–8.

APPENDIX B

POLISH PRIME MINISTERS
NOVEMBER 1918 to MAY 1926

Jędrzej Moraczewski (P.P.S.)	18 Nov. 1918–16 Jan. 1919
Ignacy Paderewski (non-party)	16 Jan. 1919–9 Dec. 1919
Leopold Skulski (non-party)	13 Dec. 1919–9 June 1920
Władysław Grabski (non-party)	23 June 1920–24 July 1920
Wincenty Witos (Piast)	24 July 1920–13 Sept. 1921
Antoni Ponikowski (non-party)	19 Sept. 1921–5 Mar. 1922
	10 Mar. 1922–6 June 1922
Artur Śliwiński (non-party)	28 June 1922–7 July 1922
Julian Nowak (non-party)	31 July 1922–14 Dec. 1922
Władysław Sikorski (non-party)	16 Dec. 1922–26 May 1923
Wincenty Witos (Piast)	28 May 1923–14 Dec. 1923
Władysław Grabski (non-party)	19 Dec. 1923–14 Nov. 1925
Aleksander Skrzyński (non-party)	20 Nov. 1925–5 May 1926
Wincenty Witos (Piast)	10–15 May 1926

POLISH PRIME MINISTERS:
MAY 1926–SEPTEMBER 1939

Kazimierz Bartel	15 May 1926–4 June 1926
	8 June–24 Sept. 1926
	27–30 Sept. 1926
Józef Piłsudski	2 Oct. 1926–27 June 1928
Kazimierz Bartel	27 June 1928–13 Apr. 1929
Kazimierz Świtalski	14 Apr. 1929–7 Dec. 1929
Kazimierz Bartel	29 Dec. 1929–15 Mar. 1930
Walery Sławek	29 Mar. 1930–23 Aug. 1930
Józef Piłsudski	25 Aug. 1930–4 Dec. 1930
Walery Sławek	4 Dec. 1930–26 May 1931
Aleksander Prystor	27 May 1931–9 May 1933
Janusz Jędrzejewicz	10 May 1933–13 May 1934
Leon Kozłowski	15 May 1934–28 Mar. 1935
Walery Sławek	28 Mar.–12 Oct. 1935
Marian Zyndram-Kościałkowski	13 Oct. 1935–15 May 1936
Felicjan Sławoj-Składkowski	15 May 1936–30 Sept. 1939

APPENDIX C

SOME ECONOMIC STATISTICS

1. *The Effect of the War on Polish Industry*

THE following tables give some idea of the effect of wartime destruction and requisitions on the Polish economy.

TABLE I. *The Textile Industry in Poland in 1920**

Machinery in operation	Percentage of no. in use in 1914
Fine-spinning cotton spindles	44·1
Mechanical cotton spindles	34·2
Long wool spindles	19·9
Short wool spindles	36·3
Textile machine factories	11·2

* H. Gliwic, 'Przemysł i handel Polski', *Polska w czasie wielkiej wojny*, iii. 178.

TABLE II. *Industrial Production in Poland**

	1913 tons	1920 tons
Coal	8,974,201	6,411,668
Oil	1,113,668	765,025
Paraffin wax	1,353	368
Crude iron	330,318	119,474
Processed iron†	418,416	42,610
Rolling mills†	467,100	48,970

* *R.S.R.P.* i (1920–2), 134–5.
† Only the Congress Kingdom.

The oil industry was seriously affected by the fighting in Galicia. By 1919 its output had fallen to 1·12 per cent of total world production, from 4 per cent in 1909. Sugar refining had dropped to one-third of the pre-war level by 1918, to one-sixth by 1919.

Agricultural output too was greatly diminished as a result of the war. In 1919, 4·5 million hectares of land lay fallow, mostly the property of soldiers, and the number of cattle had fallen to 62·5 per cent of the pre-war figure, the number of pigs to 53 per cent, and of sheep to 40 per cent.[1] Table III illustrates the decline in harvests.

TABLE III. *Harvests**

	1908–13 (annual average) quintals	1918 quintals
Wheat	16,782,700	5,356,800
Rye	57,111,600	28,753,100
Barley	14,889,900	6,998,700
Oats	28,143,400	12,309,600
Potatoes	247,899,200	140,704,800

* W. Grabski, J. Stojanowski, and J. Waręzak, 'Rolnictwo Polski, 1914–20', *Polska w czasie wielkiej wojny*, iii. 478.

2. The Comparative Yield of Large and Small Farms

TABLE IV. *The Yield of Polish Agriculture in 1938**

	I. Estates quintals per hectare	II. Lesser ownership quintals per hectare	Percentage I:II
Wheat	15·3	11·8	129·7
Rye	14·9	12·0	124·2
Barley	15·7	10·9	144·0
Oats	14·0	11·3	123·9
Potatoes	125·3	113·0	110·9
Sugar-beets	220·1	196·0	112·3

* Mieszczankowski, op. cit., p. 322. Though this table relates to 1938, the situation in the earlier years did not differ materially.

3. The Agricultural Census of 1921

Though largely accurate, the 1921 census took place under difficult conditions and its findings thus require a certain amount of modification. It did not include Upper Silesia; many soldiers had not yet returned when the census was taken; the state apparatus was still inadequate; and many peasants falsified the size of their holdings, both because of lack of trust in the officials, and in the hope that if they understated

[1] W. Grabski, J. Stojanowski, and J. Waręzak, 'Rolnictwo Polski, 1914–20', *Polska w czasie wielkiej wojny*, iii. 473.

their holdings they might obtain more in land reform. In Tables V and VI the census figures are given alongside the corrections suggested by Mieszczankowski.[1]

TABLE V. *Number of Holdings in 1921*

Hectares	No. of holdings (1000s)		Percentage		Difference (percentage)
	Census	Correction	Census	Correction	
0–2	1,108·8	1,013·4	33·9	29·0	−4·9
2–5	1,001·8	1,138·5	30·7	32·6	−1·9
5–10	733·3	861·1	22·5	24·7	−2·2
10–20	311·5	360·0	9·6	10·3	−0·7
20–50	76·4	87·6	2·4	2·5	−0·1
Over 50	30·1	30·1	0·9	0·9	—
Total	3,261·9	3,490·67	100·0	100·0	—

TABLE VI. *Distribution of Land*

Holdings hectares	Area (1000 hectares)		Percentage of total		Difference (percentage)
	Census	Correction	Census	Correction	
0–2	1,075·6	1,060·7	3·5	2·8	−0·7
2–5	3,432·6	4,248·3	11·3	11·2	−0·1
5–10	5,156·8	6,562·6	17·0	17·3	−0·3
10–20	4,190·2	5,201·7	13·8	13·7	−0·1
20–50	2,141·4	2,611·1	7·1	6·9	−0·2
Large estates and public land	14,344·1	18,241·6	47·3	48·1	−0·8
Total	30,340·7	37,926·0	100·0	100·0	—

[1] For the census figures: *R.S.R.P.* iv (1925–6), 106, Table I. For the corrections: Mieszczankowski, op. cit., pp. 339–40.

4. *Polish Agricultural Exports*

TABLE VII. *Exports* (in millions of zloties)*

	1928	1929	1930
All exports†	2,508	2,813	2,433

Wood products‡			
Timber	317	254	211
Round timber	226	169	91
Wood manufactures	45	57	44
	588	480	346

Farm produce§	1928–9		1929–30	
Plant produce	277		326	
Animal produce	583		602	
(*a*) Live animals		219		203
(*b*) Animals products		364		399
Agricultural-industrial produce	180		253	
	1,040		1,181	

* The figures are not strictly comparable, because most agricultural exports (though not timber) are given in accordance with the economic year, i.e. 1 August to 31 July.
† *M.R.S.* (1931), p. 59, Table II.
‡ Ibid., p. 62, Table IV.
§ Ibid., p. 62, Table V.

5. Artisans in Poland

Table VIII will give some indication of the wide range of artisan crafts in Poland.

TABLE VIII. *Varieties of Artisan Industry**

	No. of workshops	No. of workers
Tinsmiths	3,770	11,200
Engravers	1,430	4,680
Coppersmiths	40	130
Smiths	40,050	109,000
Brass-smiths	360	80
Locksmiths	4,800	15,960
Watch-makers	2,990	8,600
Coopers	3,410	3,840
Carpenters	4,790	10,870
Basket-makers	640	3,800
Wheelwrights	8,930	19,740
Cabinet-makers	24,280	64,560
Dyers	890	3,340
Soap-makers	300	1,060
Launderers	180	750
Tanners	1,330	9,320
Gaiter-makers	6,970	18,300
Glove-makers	40	200
Harness-makers	4,240	12,080
Shoemakers	81,680	205,060
Linen-makers	590	2,260
Hat-makers	4,760	12,900
Furriers	490	1,150
Tailors	40,770	106,500
Ropemakers	1,210	3,200
Wigmakers	4,160	11,270
Haberdashers	520	1,330
Knitters	120	680
Upholsterers	49	1,380
Weavers	1,270	5,700
Printers	1,110	5,320
Bookbinders	890	2,950
Comb-makers	630	1,830
Masons	2,790	10,510
Bricklayers	4,440	30,510
Glaziers	1,190	2,960
Potters	1,390	5,100
Painters	1,230	3,020
Bakers	60,330	185,400

* H. Mianowski, 'O rzemiośle', *Dziesięciolecie Polski Odrodzonej*, p. 1086.

BIBLIOGRAPHY

This bibliography does not pretend to completeness, as will be obvious from the sections dealing with social and economic matters, national minorities, and foreign policy, which were peripheral to my main interest, though important. As for general political works, I have included here only those books and articles which I felt to be of value.

I. ARCHIVAL MATERIAL

ARCHIWUM AKT NOWYCH (WARSAW)

i. *Zespół Prezydium Rady Ministrów*

1. Protokóły Posiedzeń Rady Ministrów, 1926–1931, vols. 32–57.
2. General (Rektyfikaty)

Rekt. No. 22, Biuro prezydialne Prezydium Rady Ministrów.
Folder 35: Depesze i pisma skierowane do Marszałka J. Piłsudskiego (1926–30).
36: Depesze i listy do premiera K. Bartla (1927, 1929, 1930).
38: Depesze i listy gratulacyjne do premiera K. Świtalskiego oraz rezolucje (1929).
41: Pisma skierowane do premiera W. Sławka (1930–1).
55: Referat dotyczący analizy sytuacji polityki rolniczej, budżetowej, podatkowej, zagranicznej, społecznej i kolejowej 1930 r.
71: Materiały dotyczące zamachu majowego.
77: Wycinki z gazet, wyciągi z prasy, komunikaty informacyjne oraz odezwa P.P.S.—Lewicy do kolejarzy. Statut klubu 'Proemteusz'.
127: Stenogram konferencji premiera Świtalskiego z posłami i senatorami B.B. 17.X.29.
Rekt. No. 24, Exposé premierów.
Folder 6: Exposé premiera Dr. Kazimierza Bartla 1926 r.
7: Przemówienie płk. Sławka na plenarnem posiedzeniu B.B.W.R. 14.XII.28.
8: Przemówienia posłów.
Rekt. No. 64, Sprawy językowe.
Folder 4: Korespondencja w sprawie używania języka żydowskiego na zebraniach publicznych, 1918–23.

3. Grouped items (Grupowe)

2–7 (17): Gabinet P.R.M. prof. dr. K. Bartla, 15.V.26–30.IX.26.
2–7 (19): Gabinet P.R.M. Bartla, 27.VI.28–13.IV.29.
2–21 (1): Korespondencja prywatna premierów Walerego Sławka i Leona Kozłowskiego.
3–3: Korespondencja w sprawie ordynacji wyborczej do Sejmu i Senatu, 1932, 1935, 1938.

3–23: Odpowiedzi na interpelacje poselskie i senackie — tryb postępowania.

3–36: Stosunek rządu do Sejmu i Senatu, debata generalna w Sejmie (1923, 1925, 1926, 1928, 1930, 1939).

5–2 (1): Sprawy zmiany konstytucji R.P. 1930–5.

64–5: Materiały Instytutu Badania Spraw Narodowościowych w sprawie potrzeb gospodarczych ludności żydowskiej w Polsce (1931–1934);

64–8: Materiały Instytutu Badania Spraw Narodowościowych w sprawach konfliktów polsko-ukraińskich (1932–3).

97–2: Sprawa konkordatu między Polską a Rzymem 1927 r.

97–7: Wykształcenie religijne w szkołach, 1926 r.

97–8: Okólnik arcybiskupa Hlonda.

ii. *Zespół Ministerstwa Spraw Wewnętrznych. Departament Organizacyjny*

a. Wydział organizacyjno-prawny.

Files 55–69: Protokóły zebrań periodycznych kierowników władz i urzędów IIej instancji.

71–87: Protokóły zebrań periodycznych kierowników władz i urzędów Iej instancji.

104, 107, 108, 110: Sprawozdania wojewodów.

111: Protokóły posiedzeń Rad Wojewódzkich w województwie Wileńskim i Wołyńskim.

112–29: Protokóły zjazdów starostów.

b. Wydział społeczno-polityczny.

File 860: Biuletyn wyborczy P.A.T.

861: Plakat przedwyborczy.

864: Wybory w Warszawie, 1930 r.

866: Materiały S.N.

871: Odezwa Wyzwolenia, 1927 r.

872: Odezwa Stronnictwa Chłopskiego, 1926 r.

876: Działalności P.P.S., 1930–9.

877: Blok Jedności Robotniczej w Górnym Śląsku, 1927–33.

878: Centrolew.

884: Pamflet przeciw Piłsudskiemu.

885: Odezwa organizacji oficerów do armii, 1929 r.

892, 893, 899: Towarzystwo Uniwersytetu Robotniczego.

919–20: Prasa zagraniczna o Polsce.

c. Wydział narodowościowy.

File 947: Sprawozdanie o działalności Instytutu Badania Spraw Narodowościowych.

956–60: Przegląd prasy narodowościowej.

961: Sprawozdania o mniejszościach, 1926–7 r.

962: Sprawozdania o mniejszościach, 1928 r.

973: Niemieckie ugrupowania polityczne, 1927 r.

1036: Ruchy polityczne ukraińskie w 1927 r.

1038: Wiadomości Ukraińskie.

1046: Wykład o wykształceniu Ukraińców, 1926.
1047: Interpelacje Ukraińców.
1050: Okólnik Klubu Ukraińskiego w Sejmie, 1929.
1062: Żydowskie ugrupowania polityczne, 1927.
1063: Okólnik M.S.W. o Sjonizmie, 1926.
1077: Kościół Unicki w Wołyniu, 1927.

iii. *Zespoły szczątkowe*
sygn. II/88. Kazimierz Świtalski.

ARCHIWUM ZAKŁADU HISTORII PARTII (WARSAW)
Archiwum P.P.S. (1919–39)
ysgn. 114/IV. P.P.S. — Centralny Komitet Wykonawczy. Okólniki, instrukcje, komunikaty, pisma, zaświadczenia.
sygn. 114/IV. P.P.S. — Centralny Komitet Wykonawczy. Biuletyn Informacyjny, 1926–27 r.
sygn. 114/VI. P.P.S. — Centralny Komitet Wykonawczy. Odezwy.
sygn. 114/XXIII. Wybory do Sejmu. Okręgowe Komitety Wyborcze, 1928 r.

JAGELLONIAN LIBRARY (MANUSCRIPT SECTION)
30/62; 31/62. Papiery Stanisława Kozickiego (contains letters of Dmowski).

ARCHIVE OF THE JÓZEF PIŁSUDSKI HISTORICAL INSTITUTE (LONDON)
i: *Relacje*[1]
1957, Relacja Pani Marszałkowej.
1957, Relacja generała Krok-Paszkowskiego.
20 January 1957, Relacja pułkownika Alf-Tarczyńskiego.
n.d., List pułkownika A. Mniszka.
19 August 1957, Relacja majora W. Podhorskiego.
13 June 1957, Relacja podpułkownika W. Mączewskiego.
15 June 1957, Relacja majora W. Żebrowskiego.
1958, Relacja rotmistrza F. Poraj-Wilczyńskiego.
March 1958, Relacja generała F. Narbut-Łuczyńskiego.
October 1957, Wspomnienia generała F. Głuchowskiego.
n.d., Relacja generała L. Kmicic-Skrzyńskiego.
n.d., Druga relacja generała Kmicic-Skrzyńskiego.
n.d., Relacja Wacława Jędrzejewicza.
1 November 1957, Relacja pułkownika T. Schaetzla.
6 June 1957, Dyskusja nad relacjami.
17 August 1957, Relacja generała Sawickiego.
4 May 1957, Relacja pułkownika Ulrycha.
n.d., Relacja generała Skwarczyńskiego.
1957, K. Sawicki, 36pp. w przełomie majowym.

[1] All items are cited in the order in which they are filed.

6 July 1957, Protokół z dyskusji nad relacjami o przewrocie majowym generała Skwarczyńskiego i generała Sawickiego.

ii. *Organizacja naczelnych władz wojskowych*

1. Notatka związana głównie ze sprawa organizacji naczelnych władz wojskowych.
2. A. Piłsudska, Relacja stosunku Marszałka Piłsudskiego do najwyższych władz wojskowych.
3. Materiały do sprawy organizacji najwyższych władz wojskowych.
4. J. Piłsudski, Wypowiedzi w sprawie organizacji naczelnych władz wojskowych (zebrane przez wydział studiów Instytutu Józefa Piłsudskiego) oraz krótka relacja Al. Piłsudskiej, 1952.
5. Instytut J. Piłsudskiego, Materiały do zagadnienia organizacji naczelnych władz sił zbrojnych, n.d.
6. L. Zakrocki, Rozwój organizacji naczelnych władz wojskowych na tle ustawodawczym.

II. NEWSPAPERS

Poland in the period under discussion possessed a very lively and extensive press. Use has been made of the following periodicals (except where otherwise stated, they were published in Warsaw):

DAILIES

ABC National Democrat, close to O.W.P.

Czas (Cracow, later Warsaw). Conservative.

Dzień Polski. Conservative.

Gazeta Polska. Sanacja. Formed in October 1929 by the merger of *Epoka* and *Głos Prawdy.*

Gazeta Poranna. National Democrat. United in October 1925 with *Gazeta Warszawska.*

Gazeta Warszawska. National Democrat.

Głos Prawdy. Radical Piłsudski-ite; a weekly until May 1926.

Ilustrowany Kurjer Codzienny (Cracow). Popular; before the coup close to the Piast, afterwards pro-Sanacja.

Kurjer Polski. Non-party Right Wing; represented business interests.

Kurjer Poranny. Radical pro-Piłsudski-ite.

Kurjer Poznański (Poznań). National Democrat.

Kurjer Warszawski. Non-party Right Wing.

Kurjer Wileński (Wilno). Radical pro-Piłsudski-ite.

Le Messager Polonais. Founded January 1925; semi-official.

Naprzód (Cracow). Socialist.

Nasz Przegląd. Jewish, general Zionist.

Nowy Kurjer Polski. Radical pro-Piłsudski-ite; founded January 1926; renamed *Epoka* in September 1926.

Polonia (Katowice). Christian Democrat.

Polska Zbrojna. The Army organ; after the coup, Piłsudski-ite.

Robotnik. Socialist.
Rzeczpospolita. Christian Democrat.
Słowo (Wilno). Conservative.

WEEKLIES

Gazeta Chłopska. Peasant Party.
Głos Prawdy. Radical Piłsudski-ite; became a daily after the coup.
Nowa Kadrowa. Pro-Government, near Fascist; founded March 1930, became defunct after two issues in 1931.
Nowa Sprawa Robotnicza. N.P.R.—Left (i.e. pro-Sanacja); appeared between 29 May and 29 August 1926.
Piast. Piast.
Tydzień. Centrolew; founded October 1929.
Wyzwolenie. Liberation.

BI-WEEKLIES

Przełom. Radical Piłsudski-ite; founded May 1926.

MONTHLIES

Droga. Radical Piłsudski-ite.
Przegląd Współczesny. Independent.

OCCASIONAL

Nakazy Chwili. Pro-Sanacja; nine issues appeared after the coup.
Nowy Przegląd. Communist; a reprint of this journal for the period 1922–9 has been published by Książka i Wiedza, Warsaw, 1957–66.
Zaczyn. Linked with Adam Koc.

Use has also been made of the semi-confidential press digest published by the French Foreign Office, *Bulletin Périodique de la Presse Polonaise.*

III. GOVERNMENT PUBLICATIONS

Druki sejmowe, 1926–31.
Komisja Ankietowa. *Sprawozdanie Komisji Ankietowej. Badania warunków produkcji oraz wymiany.* 15 vols. Warsaw, 1928.
Kwartalnik Statystyczny, 1924–30.
Mały Rocznik Statystyczny, 1931–9.
Materiały odnoszące się do działalności rządu w czasie od 15 maja 1926 do 31 grudnia 1927. Warsaw, 1928.
Materiały odnoszące się do działalności rządu za 1928 rok. Warsaw 1929.
Materiały Komisji dla Usprawnienia Administracji Publicznej przy Prezesie Rady Ministrów. Warsaw, 1929.
Rocznik Ministerstwa Skarbu, 1927–30.
Rocznik Statystyki Rzeczypospolitej Polskiej, 1920–30.
Sprawozdanie stenograficzne Sejmu Rzeczypospolitej, 1922–39.
Sprawozdanie stenograficzne Senatu Rzeczypospolitej, 1922–39.

Statystyka Polski, 1922–35.
Statystyka Pracy, 1922–31.

IV. PUBLISHED DOCUMENTS

Codzienne zapiski oficera Wydziału Społeczno-Politycznego Komisariatu Rządu na m. st. Warszawę (1 lipiec–31 grudzień 1935). *Najnowsze dzieje Polski: studia i materiały z okresu 1914–1939*, viii (1964), 89–121.
Documents on British Foreign Policy, 1919–1939, ed. W. Medlicott, D. Dakin, and M. Lambert, Series IA. I. London, 1966.
Dokumenty chwili. i: *12 do 16 maja 1926r. w Warszawie*. Warsaw, 1926.
Dokumenty chwili. ii: *Od Belwederu do Zamku*. Warsaw, 1926.
Galicyjska działalność wojskowa Piłsudskiego, 1906–1914. Dokumenty, ed. S. Arski and J. Chudek. Warsaw, 1967.
'Jak doszło do wojny domowej' i 'Przewrót majowy', ed. M. Pietrzak, *Kwartalnik Historyczny*, lxvi (1959), no. 1, 127–54.
Kapitały obce w Polsce, 1918–1939. Materiały i dokumenty, ed. Z. Landau and J. Tomaszewski. Warsaw, 1964.
Komunistczna Frakcja poselska w sejmie, 1921–1935. Warsaw, 1958.
K.P.P. Uchwały i rezolucje. 3 vols. Warsaw, 1955.
'XXI Kongres P.P.S. (1–4.XI.1928)', ed. J. Żarnowski, *Najnowsze dzieje Polski: materiały i studia z okresu 1914–1939*, vi (1963), 289–96.
'XXII Kongres P.P.S. (23–24.V.1931 r.) w relacji Komunikatu Informacyjnego Komisariatu Rządu w Warszawie', ed. J. Żarnowski, *Najnowsze dzieje Polski: materiały i studia z okresu 1914–1939*, ii (1959), 217–46.
'XXIII Kongres P.P.S. (1934 r.) w materiałach i relacjach agenturalnych Komisariatu Rządu na m. st. Warszawę', ed. H. Marek, *Z Pola Walki*, i (1958), no. 1, 159–202.
'XXIV Kongres P.P.S.', ibid. v (1962), no. 4, 183–208.
Konstytucja 17 marca 1921 r. Warsaw, 1921.
Materiały do badań nad gospodarką Polski, Part i, 1918–39. Warsaw, 1956.
Materiały do historii Klubów Demokratycznych i Stronnictwa Demokratycznego w latach 1937–1939. 2 vols. Warsaw, 1964.
Materiały źródłowe do historii K.P.P. w Zagłębiu Dąbrowskim w latach 1920–1939, ed. M. Antonow and R. Rechowicz. Katowice, 1961.
Materiały źródłowe do historii polskiego ruchu ludowego, i: 1864–1918; ii: 1918–31; iii: 1931–9. Warsaw, 1966.
'Narada krakowska z lutego 1918 r.', ed. J. Holzer, *Przegląd Historyczny*, xlix (1958), no. 3, 538–67.
Official Documents concerning Polish-German and Polish-Soviet Relations, 1933–1939 (The Polish White Book). London and Melbourne, 1940.
'Ostatnia wola Piłsudskiego', *Kultura* (Paris), no. 31 (1951), 5–6.
Położenie klasy robotniczej w Polsce, 1929–1939. Studia i materiały. Warsaw, 1965.
Posłowie rewolucyjne w Sejmie, lata 1920–1935. Wybór przemówień, interpelacji i wniosków, ed. T. Daniszewski, G. Iwański, and M. Minkowski. Warsaw, 1960.

M m

P.P.S.—Lewica 1906–1918. Materiały i dokumenty, ed. F. Tych, vol. i, Warsaw, 1961; vol. ii, Warsaw, 1962.

P.P.S.—Lewica 1926–31. Materiały źródłowe, ed. L. Hass. Warsaw, 1960.

Proces brzeski. Toledo, Ohio, n.d.

Proces Eligjusza Niewiadomskiego. Warsaw, 1923.

Proces 11 więźniów brzeskich przed Sądem Okręgowym w Warszawie. Cieszyn, 1931.

'Protokóły Komitetu Wyższej Szkoły Wojennej' ed. E. Kozłowski, *Biuletyn Wojskowej Akademii Politycznej* (1959), no. 3 (Supplement).

'Protokół konferencji grup konserwatywnych z udziałem Marszałka Piłsudskiego' w Dzikowie w dniach 14–16 września 1927 r.', ed. K. Kersten, *Najnowsze dzieje Polski: materiały i studia z okresu 1914– 1939*, ii (1959), 199–215.

'Protokóły polsko-brytyjskich rozmów sztabowych odbytych w Warszawie w maju 1939 r.' *Bellona* (1957), no. 3/4, 26–57.

'Protokóły polsko-francuskich rozmów sztabowych odbytych w Paryżu w maju 1939 r.', ibid. (1958), no. 2, 165–79.

'Protokóły rozmów polskiej misji wojskowej w Londynie we wrześniu 1939 r.' ed. P. Stawecki, *Wojskowy Przegląd Historyczny* (1961), no. 2, 218–30.

'Protokół tajnego posiedzenia Rady Ministrów RP z dnia 28.II.30', *Kultura* (Paris), no. 5/67 (1953), 83–7.

'Przewrót majowy w raportach poselstwa R.P. w Londynie', ed. Z. Landau *Kwartalnik Historyczny*, lxvi (1959), no. 1, 154–8.

Republika Tarnobrzeska w świetle faktów i dokumentów, ed. Z. Trawińska and A. Ciulik. Rzeszów, 1958.

'Rozmowy między kierownictwem K.P.P. a kierownictwem P.P.S. w sprawie zawarcia porozumień o wspólnej akcji w jednolitym froncie w lecie 1935 r.', ed. J. Żarnowski, *Najnowsze dzieje Polski: materiały i studia z okresu 1914–1939*, ii (1959), 247–53.

S.D.K.P. i L. Materiały i dokumenty. 2 vols. Warsaw, 1962.

Sprawa brzeska. London, 1941.

Sprawa Gabriela Czechowicza przed Trybunałem Stanu, ed. Z. Landau and S. Skrzeszewska. Warsaw, 1961.

Sprawozdanie z ankiety przygotowawczej do reformy Konstytucji, odbytej w dniach 30, 31 lipca i 1 sierpnia 1928 r., ed. A. Piasecki. Warsaw, 1928.

'Stosunki polsko-niemieckie przed II wojną światową. Dokumenty z Archiwum Generalnego Inspektora Sił Zbrojnych', ed. E. Kozłowski, *Najnowsze dzieje Polski: studia i materiały z okresu 1914–1939*, iii (1960), 195–261.

Strajk chłopski w 1937 r. Dokumenty archiwalne. 2 vols. Warsaw, 1960.

Strajki rolne w Wielkopolsce, 1919–1922. Materiały archiwalne. Warsaw, 1959.

Ustawa Konstytucyjna z dnia 23.IV.1935 r., Sejm Rzeczypospolitej Polskiej, Kadencja iv, Druk no. 2. Warsaw, n.d.

Wojciech Korfanty przed Sądem Marszałkowskim, ed. B. Skrzeszewska and Z. Landau. Katowice, 1964.

Współpraca rządu ze sferami gospodarczymi państwa. Warsaw, 1927.

V. MEMOIRS

Baranowski, W. *Rozmowy z Piłsudskim, 1916 r.–1931 r.* Warsaw, 1938.
Beck, J. *Dernier Rapport: politique polonaise, 1926–1939.* Neuchâtel, 1951.
Berbecki, L. *Pamiętniki Generała broni Leona Berbeckiego.* Katowice, 1959.
Bojko, J. *Ze wspomnień.* Ed. with an introduction by K. Dunin-Wąsowicz. Warsaw, 1959.
Chrząszczewski, A. 'Kartki z mego pamiętnika', *Tygodnik Zachodni* ii (1957), no. 19, 1–2; no. 20, 1–2; no. 21, 2, 7,; no. 22, 2; no. 23, 2.
Ciołkosz, A. *Trzy wspomnienia.* London, 1945.
Cretzianu, A. 'Rumunia a wrzesień 1939 r'. *Kultura* (Paris), no. 3/77 (1954), 106–15.
Daszyński, I. *Pamiętniki.* 2 vols. Warsaw, 1957.
Dębski, M. 'Komisja Nadzwyczajna do walki z nadużyciami', *Najnowsze dzieje Polski: materiały i studia z okresu 1914–1939*, viii (1964), 129–44.
Diamand, H. *Pamiętnik zebrany z wyjątków listów do żony.* Cracow, 1932.
Dzendzel, H. 'W dniach zamachu majowego', *Tygodnik Demokratyczny*, no. 415 (1961), 5; no. 416 (1961), 6.
Fiderkiewicz, A. '*Dobre czasy*', *Wspomnienia z lat 1922–1927.* Warsaw, 1958.
—— *Burzliwe lata. Wspomnienia z lat 1928–1939.* Warsaw, 1963.
Fołta, W. *Wspomnienia z walk młodzieży chłopskiej.* Warsaw, 1956.
Głąbiński, S. *Wspomnienia polityczne.* Pelplin, 1939. This deals with the period until 1926. For his treatment of events between 1926 and 1939, see the unpublished manuscript 26/59 in the Jagellonian Library, Cracow.
Glinka, W. 'W rocznicę przewrotu majowego', *Polityka*, i, no. xi (8–14 May 1957), 6–7.
Grabski, W. *Dwa lata pracy u podstaw państwowości naszej (1924–1925).* Warsaw, 1927.
Grzędziński, J. *Maj 1926.* Paris, 1965.
Grzybowski, W. 'Premier Kazimierz Bartel', *Kultura*, no. 13 (1948), 99–114.
—— 'Spotkania i rozmowy z Józefem Piłsudskim', *Niepodległość*, i (1948), 89–100.
Haller, J. *Pamiętniki.* London, 1964.
Haller, S. *Wypadki warszawskie od 12 do 15 maja 1926 r.* Cracow, 1926.
Hełczyński, B. 'Prezydent Ignacy Mościcki widziany oczami szefa jego kancelarii cywilnej', *Niepodległość*, N.S. vi (1958), 228–33.
Hupka, J. *Z czasów wielkiej wojny.* Niwiska, 1936.
Jędrzejewicz, J. 'Reforma szkolnictwa', *Niepodległość*, v (1953), 29–59.
Katelbach, T. *Spowiedź pokolenia.* Lippstadt, 1948.
Kopański, S. *Moja służba w wojsku polskim, 1917–1939.* London, 1965.
Korzycki, A. *Fragmenty wspomnień, 1924–1933.* Warsaw, 1962.

Kowalewski, J. 'Gdy ministrowie byli wywrotowcami', *Kultura* (Paris) 1949, no. 8/25, 114–23; no. 9/25, 125–37.

Kozicki, S. 'Półstulecie życia politycznego. Pamiętnik St. Kozickiego.' (Unpublished manuscript 80/56 deposited in the Jagellonian Library, Cracow.)

Krzemieński, J. 'Rozmowa Komendanta ze mną (Wspomnienia Szefa Sądownictwa Wojskowego z lat 1919–1923)', *Niepodległość*, N.S. v (1955), 212–16.

Laroche, J. *La Pologne de Pilsudski: souvenirs d'une ambassade, 1926–1935.* Paris, 1953.

Lieberman, H. 'Pamiętniki.' (Unpublished; typescript in the possession of Mr. A. Ciołkosz, London.) Excerpts have been published in *Kultura* (Warsaw), 27 February, 12 and 19 March 1967.

Lipski, J. *Diplomat in Berlin, 1933–1939. Papers and Memoirs of Józef Lipski, Ambassador of Poland.* Ed. W. Jędrzejewicz, Cambridge, 1968.

Łubieński, M. 'Ostatnie negocjacje w sprawie Gdańska', *Dziennik Polski*, 3 December 1953.

Mercik, W. 'Wspomnienia z wypadków majowych', *Zeszyty Historyczne*, iii (1963), 103–11.

Mitkiewicz, L. 'Czy był możliwy front anti-niemiecki'. *Kultura* (Paris), no. 12 (1959), 99–121.

Mościcki, I. 'Wspomnienia', *Niepodległość*, N.S. vi (1958), 188–204.

Noël, L. *L'Agression allemande contre la Pologne.* Paris, 1946.

Piątkowski, H. 'Wspomnienia z "wypadków majowych" 1926 roku', *Bellona*, iii, iv (1961), 182–213.

Piłsudska, A. *Memoirs.* London, 1940.

—— *Wspomnienia.* London, 1960.

Popiel, K. *Od Brześcia do "Polonii".* London, 1967.

Poznański, K. 'Wypadki majowe widziane od strony Moskwy', *Wiadomości*, xii, no. 586 (23 June 1957), 3.

Pragier, A. *Czas przeszły dokonany.* London, 1966.

Pruszyński, K. *Wybór pism publicystycznych.* vol. i, Cracow, 1966.

Raczyński, E. *In Allied London: the Wartime Diaries of the Polish Ambassador Count Edward Raczyński.* London, 1962.

Raczyński, R. 'Zapiski', *Kultura* (Paris), no. 9 (1948), 116–29.

Rataj, M. *Pamiętniki.* Warsaw, 1965.

Romer, J. *Pamiętniki.* Lwów, 1938.

Romeyko, M. 'Pierwsze dni niepodległości i zamach stanu', *Kultura* (Paris), no. 12/158 (1960), 81–100.

—— *Przed i po maju 1926 r.* 2 vols. Warsaw, 1967.

—— *Wspomnienia o Wieniawie i o rzymskich czasach.* London, 1969.

Rómmel, J. *Za honor i Ojczyznę.* Warsaw, 1958.

Rowecki, S. *Wspomnienia i notatki, czerwiec–wrzesień 1939 r.* Warsaw, 1957.

Rybak, J. *Pamiętniki generała Rybaka.* Warsaw, 1954.

Rydz-Śmigły, E. 'Relacja', *Na Straży* (Jerusalem), no. 32 (1947), 7–8.

Rzepecki, J. *Wspomnienia i przyczynki historyczne.* Warsaw, 1956.

Sikorski, W. 'Kartki z dziennika', *Żołnierz Polski*, xiii (July 1957), 4–6; xiv (July 1957), 14–15.

Skirmunt, J. 'Moje wspomnienia.' (Unpublished manuscript 36/60 in the Jagiellonian Library, Cracow.)

Skotnicki, J. *Przy sztalugach i przy biurku.* Warsaw, 1957.

Sławoj-Składkowski, F. *Kwiatuszki administracyjne i inne.* London, 1959.

—— *Nie ostatnie słowo oskarżonego.* London, 1964.

—— 'Opowieści administracyjne czyli Pamiętnik Niebohaterski', *Kultura* (Paris), no. 7/45–8/46 (1951), 172–95; No. 9/47 (1951), 114–34.

—— 'Prace i czynności Rządu Polskiego we wrześniu 1939 r.', ibid., no. 5 (1948), 75–127; no. 6 (1948), 107–27.

—— 'Prezydent Mościcki', ibid., no. 10 (1956), 98–122.

—— *Strzępy meldunków.* Warsaw, 1938.

Śliwiński, A. 'Marszałek Piłsudski o sobie', *Niepodległość*, vol. xvii (1938), 23–33, 342–53.

Słonimski, A. *Kroniki tygodniowe, 1927–1939 (wybór).* Warsaw, 1956.

Sosnkowski, K. *Materiały historyczne.* London, 1966.

Stapiński, J. *Pamiętnik.* Ed. with an introduction by K. Dunin-Wąsowicz. Warsaw, 1959.

Szembek, J. *Diariusz i teki Jana Szembeka.* Ed. T. Komarnicki. i, London, 1964; ii, London, 1966; iii, London, 1969.

—— *Journal, 1933–1939.* Paris, 1952.

Szymański, A. *Zły sąsiad. Niemcy, 1932–1939, w oświetleniu polskiego attaché wojskowego w Berlinie.* London, 1962.

Świerzewski, S. 'Oczami świadka "operacji wojskowej" Piłsudskiego', *Prawo i Życie*, v (1958), 6.

Thugutt, S. *Wybór pism i autobiografia.* Warsaw, 1939.

Wachowicz, H. 'Relacja o XXIV Kongresie PPS', *Z Pola Walki* (1962), no. 4, 208–12.

Walewski, J. 'Omyłka Wincentego Witosa', *Kultura* (Paris), no. 3/197 (1964), 115–20.

Wańkowicz, M. 'Ostatnia rozmowa z Beckiem i Rydzem-Śmygłym', *Więź* (1959), no. 7–8, 232–42.

Wierzbicki, A. *Wspomnienia i dokumenty.* Warsaw, 1957.

—— 'Uwagi o przewrocie majowym', *Najnowsze dzieje Polski: materiały i studia z okresu 1914–1939*, ix (1965), 205–25.

—— 'Fragmenty wspomnień' (1928–30), *Najnowsze dzieje Polski: materiały i studia z okresu 1914–1939*, x (1966), 222–34.

Witos, W. 'Listy W. Witosa do H. Libermana z lat 1937–1939', *Najnowsze dzieje Polski: materiały i studia z okresu 1914–1939*, vi (1963), 161–89.

—— *Moja tułaczka, 1933–1939.* Warsaw, 1967.

—— *Moje wspomnienia.* 3 vols. Paris, 1964–5.

Wrzeciona, E. 'Bereza Kartuska z innej strony', *Kultura* (Paris) no. 4/30, 1950, 115–26.

Zdziechowski, J. 'Wspomnienia o Stanisławie Wojciechowskim', *Dziennik Polski* (23 April 1953), p. 2.

Zdziechowski, M. 'Ze wspomnień o Józefie Piłsudskim', *Myśl Polska*, iii, no. 1 (1–15 January 1938), 2–3.

Zyndram-Kościałkowski, W. 'Moje wspomnienia o Kazimierzu Bartlu', *Wiadomości*, xiv, no. 684 (10 May 1959), 2.

VI. SECONDARY WORKS

a. GENERAL POLITICAL

Ajnenkiel, A. 'Kilka uwag w sprawie badań nad dwudziestoleciem między-wojennym', *Kwartalnik Historyczny*, lxiii (1956), no. 6, 173–7.

—— 'Materiały do dziejów politycznych Polski w latach 1924–1927', *Historia i nauka o konstytucji*, v (1957), no. 6, 432–47.

—— 'Z dziejów tymczasowego rządu ludowego w Lublinie', *Kwartalnik Historyczny*, lxv (1958), no. 4, 1057–90.

—— *Od 'rządów ludowych' do przewrotu majowego: zarys dziejów politycz-nych Polski, 1918–1926*. Warsaw, 1964.

Anusz, A. *O Wincentym Witosie*. Warsaw, 1925.

—— *Rola Józefa Piłsudskiego w życiu narodu i państwa*. Warsaw, 1927.

Arski, S. *My Pierwsza Brygada*. Warsaw, 1962.

B. H. 'Ukraińskie wspomnienia z Berezy', *Kultura* (Paris), no. 12/98 (1955), 78–85.

Babiński, J. *Geografia polityczna w Polsce w końcu roku 1936*. Warsaw, 1936.

Badeni, S. 'O generale Rozwadowskim', *Wiadomości*, xvi, no. 789 (14 May 1961), 1.

Bandos, A. *Walki chłopskie 1937 roku, szkic popularny*. Warsaw, 1963.

Bardziński, A. *Moje chłopskie rozważania*. 2nd ed. Częstochowa, 1931.

Barlicki, N. *Aleksander Dębski. Życie i działalność, 1857–1935*. Warsaw, 1937.

—— *Wybór przemówień i artykułów z lat 1918–1939*. Ed. J. Tomicki. Warsaw, 1964.

Bartel, K. *Dwie polskie rzeczywistości. Rozmowa z prezesem Rady Ministrów prof. dr. K. Bartlem ogłoszona w 'Kurierze Wileńskim'*. Warsaw, 1928.

—— *Mowy parlamentarne*. Warsaw, 1928.

—— *Wykresy charakteryzujące rozwój życia gospodarczego Polski w latach 1924–1927 włącznie*. Warsaw, 1928.

—— *Niedomagania parlamentaryzmu*. Warsaw, 1929.

—— *Kilka uwag o praktyce parlamentarnej w Polsce*. Warsaw, 1929.

Bartel, P. *Le Maréchal Piłsudski*. Paris, 1935.

Barthélemy, J. *La Crise de la démocratie contemporaine*. Paris, 1931.

Bartoszewicz, J. *Podręczny słownik polityczny. Do użytku posłów, urzędni-ków państwowych, członków ciał samorządowych i wyborców*. Warsaw, 1922.

Bazylowski, S. 'Sprawa Dojlid jako przyczynek do przeprowadzenia re-formy rolnej na początku II Rzeczypospolitej', *Najnowsze dzieje Polski: materiały i studia z okresu 1914–1939*, viii (1964), 19–50.

Bełcikowska, A. *Stronnictwa i związki polityczne w Polsce*. Warsaw, 1925.

—— *Walki majowe w Warszawie 11 maj — 16 maj 1926*. Warsaw, 1926.

Bełcikowski, J. *Charakterystyki i programy stronnictw politycznych na terenie Rzeczypospolitej*. Warsaw, 1928.

Benedykt, S. 'O przełomie majowym', *Wiadomości*, xiv, no. 667 (11 January 1959), 1.

Bitner, W. 'O prawdziwe oblicze "Partii Katolickiej" w dwudziestoleciu', *Więź*, lxii (1963), no. 6, 110–12.

Blit, L. *The Eastern Pretender*. London, 1965.

Bobrzyński, J. *Odrodzenie państwa przez obiektywizm gospodarczy*. Warsaw, 1927.

—— *Na drodze walki*. Warsaw, 1928.

—— *Problem konsolidacji ugrupowań zachowawczych w Polsce*. Warsaw, 1929.

—— *Sprzeczności idei demokratycznej*. Warsaw, 1929.

Bobrzyński, M. *O zespoleniu dzielnic Rzeczypospolitej*. Cracow, 1919.

—— *Wskrzeszenie Państwa Polskiego*. Cracow, vol. i, 1920, vol. ii, 1926.

—— *Dzieje Polski w zarysie*. 4th ed. 2 vols. Warsaw, 1927.

—— *Z moich pamiętników*. Ed. A. Galos. Wrocław–Cracow, 1957.

Bogusławski, A. 'Ruch ludowy w czasie wojny, 1914–1918, w Królestwie Polskim w świetle wspomnień', *Roczniki Dziejów Ruchu Ludowego*, i (1959), 260–87; ii (1960), 279–316.

Borkowski, J. 'Procesy integracyjne w Stronnictwie Ludowym od I do II Kongresu 1931–33', ibid. vi (1964), 114–61.

—— 'Odśrodkowe i dośrodkowe tendencje w Stronnictwie Ludowym, 1933–1935', ibid. (1965), 104–69.

—— 'Odpowiedź polemistom', *Polityka*, 12 February 1966.

Bratkovski, J. *Poland on the Road to Revolutionary Crisis*. London, 1933.

Brock, P. 'The Early Years of the Polish Peasant Party, 1895–1907', *Journal of Central European Affairs*, xiv (1954), no. 3, 219–35.

Bromke, A. *Poland's Politics: Idealism v. Realism*. Cambridge (Mass.), 1967.

Brus, W. *Polska 1918–1926*. Warsaw, 1946.

Buell, R. L. *Poland: Key to Europe*. New York, 1939.

Buszko, J. *Sejmowa reforma wyborcza w Galicji, 1905–1914*. Warsaw, 1956.

Car, S. *Konstytucja 17 marca a polska rzeczywistość*. Warsaw, 1931.

—— *Na drodze ku nowej konstytucji*. Warsaw, 1934.

Chrząszczewski, A. *Od sejmowładztwa do dyktatury*. Warsaw, 1930.

—— 'Uwagi w sprawie "Granatów nad Belwederem" ', *Za i Przeciw*, iv (1960), no. 30, 14.

Ciołkosz, A. 'Tomasz Arciszewski', *Kultura* (Paris), no. 1/99 (1956), 99–105.

Czerpak, S. 'Ruch chłopski w pow. tarnobrzeskim w latach 1918–1921', *Roczniki Dziejów Ruchu Ludowego*, iii (1961), 72–113.

Czubiński, A. 'Przewrót majowy 1926 roku', *Zeszyty Naukowe Uniwersytetu im. Adama Mickiewicza*, xiii (1958), 77–151.

—— 'Wielkopolska i Pomorze wobec zamachu stanu w maju 1926 r.' *Studia i materiały do dziejów Wielkopolski i Pomorza*, vi, no. 1 (1960), 153–207.

—— *Centrolew*. Poznań, 1963.

Daniszewski, T. 'Droga walki K.P.P.', *Nowe Drogi*, xii (November–December 1948), 119–50.

—— *Historia ruchu robotniczego w Polsce*. 5 vols. Warsaw, 1949.

Daniszewski, T. 'K.P.P. a sojusz robotniczo-chłopski', *Kwartalnik Historyczny*, lxi (1954), no. 1, 3–43.

Daszyński, I. *Wielki człowiek w Polsce: szkic psychologiczno-polityczny.* Warsaw, 1925.

—— *Sejm. Rząd. Król. Dyktator. Uwagi na czasie.* Warsaw, 1926.

—— *W pierwszą rocznicę przewrotu majowego.* Warsaw, 1927.

Dąb, J. *Dola chłopów robotników w Polsce.* Warsaw, 1930.

Dąbrowski, S. 'Zamach majowy i kryzys państwa', *Tygodnik Warszawski*, ii (1946), no. 23, 2–3.

Dąbski, J. *Ideologia chłopska.* Warsaw, 1929.

Deptula, W. *Akcja katolicja a chrześcijański ruch robotniczy w Polsce.* Lublin, 1934.

Deutscher, I. *The Tragedy of Polish Communism Between the Wars.* London, n.d.

Dębski, J. 'Maciej Rataj, 1884–1940', *Roczniki Dziejów Ruchu Ludowego*, ii (1960), 418–20.

Dmowski, R. *Pisma.* 9 vols., numbered ii–x. Częstochowa, 1937–9. (Vol. i, a proposed biography of Dmowski, was never published.)

Doboszyński, A. *Gospodarka narodowa.* 2nd ed. Warsaw, 1936.

Dreszer, Z. 'Czy zamach majowy był dziełem tajnej organizacji?' *Polityka*, ix, no. 23 (25 September, 1938), 4–5.

Drobner, B. *Moje cztery procesy.* Warsaw, 1962.

Drozdowski, M. 'Na marginesie zbioru dokumentów archiwalnych "strajk chłopski w 1937 roku"', *Roczniki Dziejów Ruchu Ludowego* (1960), no. 2, pp. 204–18.

—— 'Śmierć Walerego Sławka', *Odnowa* (1959), no. 25 (47).

Drozdowski, M., and Tymieniecka, A. 'Mieczysław Niedziałkowski', *Najnowsze dzieje Polski: materiały i studia z okresu 1914–1939*, ix (1965), 39–85.

Drzymała, F. *Przyczynki do historii i działalności senatu w Polsce, 1922–1926 r.* Warsaw, 1946.

Dubanowicz, E. *Rewizja Konstytucji.* Poznań, 1926.

—— *Z zagadnień konstytucyjnych. Ograniczenia w sposobie wykonywania przez parlament prawa odpowiedzialności ministrów.* Lwów–Warszawa, 1928.

Dunin-Borkowski, P. 'Idea państwowa w Poznańskiem', *Droga*, x (1928), 837–45.

Dunin-Wąsowicz, K. *Dzieje Stronnictwa Ludowego w Galicji.* Warsaw, 1956.

—— *Czasopiśmiennictwo ludowe w Galicji.* Wrocław, 1962.

Dymek, B. 'Z polityki polskiego Stronnictwa Ludowego "Piast" — Pakt Lanckoroński 17.V.1923', *Zeszyty Historyczne Uniwersytetu Warszawskiego*, ii (1961), 143–60.

Dymek, B., and Hass, L. (edd.) *Zjednoczenie Lewicy Chłopskiej 'Samopomoc', 1928–31.* Warsaw, 1964.

—— *Dwadzieścia lat Rzeczypospolitej Polskiej, 1918–1938.* Lwów, n.d.

Dzendzel, H. 'Witos, Śmigły-Rydz, ONR', *Polityka* (24 March 1962).

Dzieduszycki, T. *O zawodowy ustrój państwa.* Warsaw, 1928.

Dzieduszycki, *Dyktatura czy amerykanizacja*. Warsaw, 1928.
—— *Polityka konserwatywna*. Warsaw, 1928.
—— *Dziesięciolecie Polski odrodzonej, 1918–1928*. Cracow–Warsaw, 1928.
Dziewanowski, M. K. 'Piłsudski's Federal Policy, 1919–1921', *Journal of Central European Affairs*, x (1950), no. 2, 113–28; no. 3, 271–87.
—— *The Communist Party of Poland*. Cambridge, Mass., 1959.
Estreicher, S. 'Walka z partyjnictwem', *Przegląd Współczesny* (1929), no. 132, 3–19.
Feldman, W. *Geschichte der politischen Ideen in Polen*. Munich, 1917.
Fiala, V. *La Pologne d'aujourd'hui*. Paris, 1936.
Fiedler, F. 'Komunistyczna Partia Polski', *Nowe Drogi*, xii (November–December 1948), 96–118.
Filipajtis, E. *Lewica akademicka w Wilnie*. Białystok, 1965.
Frankel, H. *Poland: The struggle for Power 1772–1939*. London, 1946.
Gałaj, D. *Powstanie Związku Młodzieży Wiejskiej R.P. 'Wici'*. Warsaw, 1959.
Garlicki, A. 'Obóz Wielkiej Polski', *Mówią Wieki*, ii, no. 6 (June 1959), 32.
—— 'Założenie tygodnika "Piast" w 1913 r.' *Rocznik Historii Czasopiśmiennictwa Polskiego XIX i XX w.*, ii (1962), 169–84.
—— *Geneza Legionów*. Warsaw, 1964.
—— *Powstanie Polskiego Stronnictwa Ludowego — Piast. 1913–1914*. Warsaw, 1966.
Garlicki, A., Kasprzakowa, J., Tymieniecka, A., and Żarnowska, A., 'Stan badań nad dziejami P.P.S. (1892–1939)', *Z Pola Walki*, v (1962), no. 4, 128–60.
Gąsiorowska-Grabowska, N. *Z dziejów przemysłu w Królestwie Polskim, 1815–1918*. Warsaw, 1965.
Giza, S. 'Wincenty Baranowski, 1877–1957', *Roczniki Dziejów Ruchu Ludowego*, iii (1961), 329–55.
—— 'Jan Dąbski, 1880–1931', ibid. iv (1962), 303–34.
Gliwic, H. *Nieco optymizmu. Zbiór artykułów i mów*. Warsaw, 1930.
Gójski, J. *Strajki i bunty chłopskie w Polsce*. Warsaw, 1949.
Górnicki, W. *Trzy skandale*. Warsaw, 1956.
—— 'Ostatni rokosz w Warszawie', *Świat*, vi (1956), no. 20, 8–9; no. 21, 8–9; no. 22, 20–21.
Grabski, S. *Rzym czy Moskwa*. Poznań, 1927.
—— *Państwo narodowe*. Lwów, 1929.
Grabski, W. *Kryzys rolniczy w Polsce*. Poznań, 1929.
Grabski, W. J. 'Ostatnie rozmowy Piłsudskiego z Wojciechowskim', *Kierunki*, v, no. 19 (15 May 1960), 3, 11.
Grobicki, J. 'Dwa niedoszłe zamachy', *Zeszyty Historyczne*, iii (1963), 93–102.
Groth, A. J. 'Proportional Representation in Prewar Poland', *Slavic Review*, xxiii (1964), no. 1, 103–14.
—— 'Parliament and the Electoral System in Poland, 1918–1935.' Columbia University Ph.D. thesis. 1960.

Growski, J. *Aforyzmy polityczne niebowiązujące*. Warsaw, 1929.

Grudziński, 'A. Cyfry mówią', *Wiadomości*, xiv, no. 675 (8 March 1959), 6.

Grzybowski, K. 'Wybory 1930 r.', *Przegląd Współczesny* (1930), no. 104, 465–75.

—— *Polityka Watykanu, 1917–1929*. Warsaw, 1958.

—— 'Parlamentaryzm polski w dwudziestoleciu (1918–1939)', *VIII Powszechny Zjazd Historyków Polskich: Historia najnowsza Polski*, pp. 229–64.

Grzymała Grabowiecki, J. *Tablica synchronistyczna rozwoju Polski współczesnej, 1918–1933*. Warsaw, n.d.

Gurnicz, A. *Program gospodarczy ruchu chłopskiego w okresie drugiej niepodległości Polski*. Lublin, 1959.

Gwiżdż, A. 'Prawo interpelacji posła na Sejm P.R.L.', *Państwo i Prawo* (1956), no. 10, 757–75.

—— *Burżuazyjno-obszarnicza konstytucja z 1921 r. w praktyce*. Warsaw 1956.

—— 'Frakcja komunistyczna w burżuazyjnych sejmach polskich, 1921–1935', *Z Pola Walki*, i (1958), no. 4, 64–100.

Hass, L. 'Tajemnicze zniknięcie', *Mówią Wieki*, ii (1959), no. 12, 14–17.

—— 'Jeszcze raz o generale Zagórskim', *Tygodnik Powszechny*, xiv (1960), 7.

—— 'P.P.S. Lewica, 1926–1931', *Najnowsze dzieje Polski: materiały i studia z okresu 1914–1939*, iv (1961), 59–99.

—— 'Kształtowanie się lewicowego nurtu w Polskiej Partii Socjalistycznej na tle sytuacji wewnątrzpartyjnej (listopad 1923 — maj 1926)', *Kwartalnik Historyczny*, lxviii (1961), no. 1, 69–102.

Hofmokl-Ostrowski, Z. *Sprawa ministra Czechowicza*. Warsaw, 1929.

—— *Brześć*. Warsaw, 1932.

Hołówko, T. *Dlaczego trzeba zmienić konstytucję*. Warsaw, 1931.

—— *Ostatni rok*. Warsaw, 1932.

—— *O zmianę konstytucji. Uwagi z powodu rządowego projektu wzmocnienia władzy wykonawczej*. Warsaw, 1932.

Holzer, J. 'Nurt opozycyjny w P.P.S. frakcji rewolucyjnej i P.P.S. opozycja. (1909–14)', *Przegląd Historyczny*, lxvi (1959), no. 3, 545–68.

—— 'Polityka kierownictwa P.P.S.D. w przeddzień powstania niepodległego państwa polskiego (luty — październik 1918 r.)', *Z Pola Walki*, iii (1960), no. 1, 35–57.

—— *Polska Partia Socjalistyczna w latach 1917–1919*. Warsaw, 1962.

Honowski, F. *Prawno-polityczne dążenia wsi polskiej ne tle literatury ludowej. Rok 1918–1939*. Warsaw, 1939.

Horak, A. 'Edward Rydz', *Kraj pamięta, mówi, oskarża i żąda*. (London, n.d.)

—— *Edward Śmigły-Rydz, Generalny Inspektor Sił Zbrojnych i Naczelny Wódz przed i podczas kampanii wrześniowej*. Lodz, 1945.

Ignar, S. *Agraryzm*. Warsaw, 1953.

Jabłoński, H. *U źródeł teraźniejszości*. Warsaw, 1937.

—— 'Konstytucje polskie', *Państwo i Prawo* (1952), no. 3, 367–405.

—— *Polityka Polskiej Partii Socjalistycznej w czasie wojny 1914–1918.* Warsaw, 1958.

—— *Narodziny drugiej Rzeczypospolitej* (1918–19). Warsaw, 1962.

—— 'Z dziejów obozu legiono-peowiackiego', *Dzieje Najnowsze* (1948), no. 1–2, 40–60.

Jabłoński, T. *Zarys historii P.P.S.* Warsaw, 1946.

Jachieć, F. '10 pułk piechoty w wypadkach majowych 1926 r.', *Wojskowy Przegląd Historyczny*, vi (1960), no. 2, 337–45.

Jackson, G. D., Jr. *Comintern and Peasant in East Europe, 1919–1930.* New York, 1966.

Jankowski, K. 'Droga zdrady narodowej. W 25tą rocznicę przewrotu Piłsudskiego', *Nowe Drogi*, ii (March–April 1951), no. 26, 69–88.

Janowska, H. (ed.) *Przewrót majowy: pierwsze lata rządów sanacji (1926–1928).* Warsaw, 1960.

Jarecka, S. 'Stosunek Niezależnej Partii Chłopskiej do przewrotu majowego i Piłsudskiego w świetle materiałów policyjnych', *Wieś Współczesna*, i (April–May 1957), nos. 2–3, 151–7.

—— *Niezależna Partia Chłopska (1924–1927).* Warsaw, 1961.

—— 'Sylwester Wojewódzki', *Roczniki Dziejów Ruchu Ludowego*, iv (1962), 335–50.

Jaworski, W. L. *Projekt konstytucji.* Cracow, 1928.

—— 'Ze studiów nad konstytucją', *Przegląd Współczesny* (1928), no. 77, 353–73.

Jędruszczak, T. *Piłsudczycy bez Piłsudskiego.* Warsaw, 1963.

Jędrychowski, S. 'Konstytucje Polski przedwrześniowej', *Nowe Drogi*, v (September–October 1951), no. 29, 33–53.

Johnpoll, B. K. *The Politics of Futility. The General Jewish Workers' Bund in Poland, 1917–1943.* Ithaca, N.Y., 1967.

Jurkiewicz, J. 'Konkordat z r. 1925 na tle polityki kurii rzymskiej w okresie międzywojennym', *Kwartalnik Historyczny*, lx (1953), no. 4, 57–85.

—— *Nuncjatura Achillesa Ratti w Polsce.* Warsaw, 1955.

—— *Watykan a Polska w okresie międzywojennym, 1918–1939.* Warsaw, 1958.

Juryś, R. 'Proces brzeski', *Prawo i Życie* (1957), no. 22, 4–5.

—— 'Brześć. O aresztowaniu posłów Centrolewu', *Chłopska Droga* (1960), no. 82, 5.

Kaeckenbeeck, G. *The International Experiment of Upper Silesia.* London, 1942.

Kalicka, F. *Powstanie krakowskie 1923 r.* Warsaw, 1953.

—— *Z zagadnień jednolitego frontu K.P.P. i P.P.S. w latach 1933–1934.* Warsaw, 1967.

Karbowski, W. 'Wypadki majowe w 1926r.' *Wojskowy Przegląd Historyczny*, iv (1959), no. 2, 328–78.

Karpatowicz, L. '18 Brumaire'a Józefa Piłsudskiego?', *Więź*, iv (May 1961), no. 5, 85–112.

Kasprzakowa, J. 'Z dziejów P.P.S.-Lewica w latach 1911–14', *Z Pola Walki*, ii (1959), no. 1, pp. 5–30.

Katelbach, S. 'Loże', *Zeszyty Historyczne*, iii (1963), 199–208.

Kauzik, S. (under pseudonym S. Dołęga-Modrzewski), 'Ś.p. Stanisław Wojciechowski', *Orzeł Biały* (23 May 1953), p. 3.

Kieszczyński, L. *Strajk powszechny w Łodzi 1933 r.* Lodz, 1955.

Koc, A. *Deklaracja ideowa*. Warsaw, 1937.

Kociowa, R. *Irena Kosmowska*. Warsaw, 1960.

Koitz, H. *Männer um Pilsudski*. Breslau, 1934.

Komarnicki, T. 'Początki odrodzonego państwa polskiego po I wojnie światowej', *Bellona* (July–December 1958), nos. 3–4, 255–66.

Komarnicki, W. *O zmianie konstytucji polskiej*. Wilno, 1927.

—— *O praworządność i zdrowy ustrój państwowy. Aktualne zagadnienia konstytucyjne z okresu maj 1926 — marzec 1928.* Wilno, 1928.

—— *O konstytucję narodową*. Warsaw, 1930.

Konopczyński, W. *Sejm 1922–27 bez obsłonek*. Cracow, 1928.

Kora, S. *Wincenty Witos a państwo polskie*. Lwów, 1936.

Kormanowa, Z. *Materiały do bibliografii polskiego ruchu robotniczego, 1918–1939.* Warsaw, 1960.

Kościałkowski, S. 'Marian Zdziechowski', *Kultura* (Paris) no. 1/195–2/196 (1964), 166–84.

Koszutska, M. (also known under pseudonym Kostrzewa, W.) *Pisma i przemówienia*, vol. iii: *1926–1929*. Warsaw, 1962.

Kowal, J. *'Wici', powstanie i działalność społeczno-wychowawcza. 1928–1939.* Warsaw, 1964.

—— *Z dziejów Z.M.W. RP 'Wici'*. Warsaw, 1952.

Kowalczyk, J. *Antysemityzm wczoraj i dziś*. Moscow, 1931.

—— *Co dała chłopom Polska faszystowska?* Moscow–Leningrad, 1934.

—— *Oblicze socjalfaszyzmu polskiego. P.P.S. na procesie brzeskim.* Moscow, 1932.

Kowalczyk, S. 'Przegląd stanu badań nad historią ruchu ludowego w latach 1918–1939', *Roczniki Dziejów Ruchu Ludowego*, i (1959), 167–195.

Kowalczyk, S., Kowal, J., Stankiewicz, W., and Stański, M. *Zarys historii polskiego ruchu ludowego.* i: *1864–1918*. Warsaw, 1963.

Kowalski, J. *Zarys historii polskiego ruchu robotniczego w latach 1918–1939* i: *1918–1926*. Warsaw, 1959.

—— 'Rozwój sytuacji wewnętrznej w K.P.P. po przewrocie majowym 1926 r.' *Z Pola Walki*, vi (1963), no. 4, 123–79.

—— *Trudne lata. Problemy rozwoju polskiego ruchu robotniczego, 1929–1935.* Warsaw, 1966.

Kozicki, S. *Historia Ligi Narodowej*. London, 1964.

Krzyżanowski, A. *Pauperyzacja Polski współczesnej*. Warsaw, 1925.

—— *Dwa programy finansowe (jesień 1925 — wiosna 1927)*. Cracow, 1927.

—— *Dlaczego kandyduję z listy Nr I Bezpartyjnego Bloku Współpracy z Rządem*. Warsaw, 1928.

—— *Rządy marszałka Piłsudskiego*. 2nd ed. Cracow, 1928.

—— 'Dziesięć lat niepodległości', *Przegląd Współczesny* (1928), no. 78, 3–28; no. 79, 224–45.

—— 'Ewolucja parlamentaryzmu i gospodarki światowej', *Przegląd Współczesny* (1934), no. 151, 279–95.

Kukiel, M. 'Jeszcze o majowej wojnie domowej i generale Zagórskim', *Wiadomości*, xiv, no. 693 (12 July 1959), 6.

—— 'Jeszcze o przełomie majowym', ibid. xiii, no. 678–9 (29 March–5 April 1959), 16.

—— *Księga jubileuszowa P.P.S.*, *1892–1932*. Warsaw, 1933.

Kukułka, J. 'Podstawowe założenia ideowo-programowe Zjednoczenia Lewicy Chłopskiej "Samopomoc" ', *Roczniki Dziejów Ruchu Ludowego*, iii (1961), 269–91.

Kuszyk, W. *Wrzenie rewolucyjne na wsi polskiej w latach 1917–1919.* Warsaw, 1957.

Kułakowski, M. *Roman Dmowski w świetle listów i wspomnień*, vol. i, London, 1968.

Kutrzeba, S. *Polska odrodzona, 1914–1928.* 4th ed. Warsaw, 1935.

Kuźmińska, J. 'Związek Ludowo-Narodowy nową formą organizacyjną Obozu Narodowo-Demokratycznego. Struktura i organizacja w latach 1922–1926', *Zeszyty Naukowe Uniwersytetu Warszawskiego*, ii (1961), 98–142.

Kuźmiński, T. *Wieś w walce o Polskę ludową, 1918–1920.* Warsaw, 1960.

Kwiatkowski, E. *Kryzys współczesny i zagadnienie odbudowy życia gospodarczego.* Warsaw, 1935.

—— *Przez zjednoczenie ku potężnej Polsce.* Warsaw, 1938.

Laeuen, H. *Polnische Tragödie.* 2nd ed. Stuttgart, 1956.

Landau, R. *Pilsudski, Hero of Poland.* London, 1930.

Lasocki, Z. *Z lat niedoli Wincentego Witosa.* Cracow, 1947.

Lato, S. 'Udział Stronnictw Ludowych w powstaniu i akcji Centrolewu', *Roczniki Dziejów Ruchu Ludowego*, vi (1964), 162–92.

—— *Ruch ludowy i Centrolew.* Warsaw, 1965.

Leczyk, M. *Komitet Narodowy Polski a Ententa i Stany Zjednoczone, 1917–1919.* Warsaw, 1966.

Lednicki, W. 'Z dziejów pewnego protestu', *Wiadomości*, x (25 December 1955), no. 507–8, 10.

Leinwand, A. *Polska Partia Socjalistyczna wobec wojny polsko-radzieckiej 1919–20.* Warsaw, 1964.

Leński-Leszczyński, J. *O front ludowy w Polsce, 1934–1937. Publicystyka.* Warsaw, 1956.

Lepecki, M. B. 'Zamach na ministra Pierackiego i gorzkie tego następstwa', *Wiadomości*, xi, no. 550 (14 October 1956), 1.

Lewandowski, J. *Imperializm słabości.* Warsaw, 1967.

Lipiński, W. 'Wywiad u marszałka Piłsudskiego w Sulejówku z dn. 10. II.1924 r.' *Niepodległość*, 1st series, vii (1933), no. 15, 63–80.

Lisiewicz, M. 'Związek wojskowy "Honor i Ojczyzna" ', *Bellona*, xxxvi (1954), no. 3, 47–53.

Litwin, A. *Dzieje jednego strajku. Łódź 1936.* Warsaw, 1957.

—— *Samorząd w Polsce burżuazyjno-obszarniczej w latach 1918–39.* Warsaw, 1954.

Lubodziecki, S. 'Sprawa Michała Żymierskiego', *Kultura* (Paris) no. 1/39 (1951), 112–19.

Łoś, S. 'Reforma konstytucji', *Przegląd Współczesny* (1931), no. 108, 81–98.

Łoza, T. *Czy wiesz kto to jest?* Warsaw, 1938.

Łukawski, Z. *Koło Polskie w Rosyjskiej Dumie Państwowej w latach 1906–1909.* Wrocław–Warsaw–Cracow, 1967.

Macartney, C., and Palmer, A. *Independent Eastern Europe. A History.* London, 1962.

Machray, R. *The Poland of Pilsudski.* London, 1936.

Mackiewicz, S. 'Czterdzieści jeden posiedzeń Komisji Konstytucyjnej', *Przegląd Współczesny* (1931), no. 108, 67–80.

—— *Historia Polski od 11 listopada 1918 do 17 września 1939.* London, 1941.

—— *Klucz do Pilsudskiego,* London, 1943.

Madajczyk, C. *Burżuazyjno-obszarnicza reforma rolna w Polsce.* Warsaw, 1956.

Makowski, W. *Uwagi o projekcie reformy konstytucji.* Warsaw, 1930.

Malicki, J. K. *Marszałek Pilsudski a Sejm.* Warsaw, 1936.

Mały słownik historii Polski. 3rd ed. Warsaw, 1964.

Markert, W. (ed.) *Osteuropa-Handbuch: Polen.* Cologne, 1959

Matsko, A. N. *Borba trudiashchikh Pol'shi i zapadnoi Bielarusii protiv fashizma, 1933–1939 gg.* Minsk, 1963.

Matuszewska, W. *U źródeł strajku chłopskiego w r. 1937.* Warsaw, 1962.

Matuszewski, I. *Wybór pism.* London–New York, 1952.

Matuszewski, J. *Próby syntez.* Warsaw, 1936.

Micewski, A. *W cieniu marszałka Pilsudskiego.* Warsaw, 1968.

—— *Z geografii politycznej II Rzeczypospolitej.* Warsaw, 1964.

Miedziński, B. 'Fantastyczne "tło" ', *Kultura* (Paris), no. 12/110 (1956), 106–11.

Mieszkowski, J. 'Zamach majowy "Towarzysza Ziuka" ', *Prawo i Życie,* no. 2 (1958), 4–5.

Migdał, S. *Pilsudczyzna w latach pierwszej wojny światowej.* Katowice, 1961.

Mioduchowska, M. 'Klub poselski Niezależnej Partii Chłopskiej w obronie mas chłopskich', *Roczniki Dziejów Ruchu Ludowego,* i (1959), 120–34.

Monasterska, T. 'Narodowy Związek Robotniczy w latach 1905–14', *Z Pola Walki,* vii (1964), no. 1, 3–31.

Moraczewski, J. *Rozważania nad położeniem politycznym i gospodarczym Polski.* Warsaw, 1938.

Morawski, K. *Tamten brzeg.* Paris, 1962.

—— *Wspólna droga.* Paris, 1962.

—— 'Przewrót majowy', *Wiadomości,* xii, no. 566 (3 February 1957), 1–2.

Mysłek, W. *Kościół Katolicki w Polsce w latach 1918–39.* Warsaw, 1966.

—— 'Nieudany pucz Śmigłego', *Polityka,* 3 March 1962.

Nagórski, Z., Sr. *Ludzie mego czasu.* Paris, 1964.

Negrzyński, J. 'Gospodarka Narodowa', *Kultura* (Paris), no. 9/107 (1956), 76–104.

Nettl, J. P. *Rosa Luxemburg.* 2 vols. London, 1966.

Niedziałkowski, M. *Demokracja parlamentarna w Polsce.* Warsaw, 1930.

Orzechowski, M. *Narodowa Demokracja na Górnym Śląsku (do 1918 roku).* Wrocław–Warsaw–Cracow, 1965.

Ostrowski, K. 'Paradoksy Romana Knolla', *Wiadomości,* xii, no. 571 (10 March 1957), 6.

Peretiatkowicz, A. *Współczesne konstytucje.* Warsaw, 1928.

Piasecka, J., and Auerbach, J. 'Stan organizacyjny KPP w latach 1929–1933'. *Z Pola Walki* (1965), no. 1, 43–57.

Piasecki, A. *O kryteriach oceny projektów konstytucji.* Warsaw, 1929.

—— 'Reforma konstytucyjna w Polsce', *Przegląd Współczesny* (1934), no. 147–8, 197–220.

Picheta, H. 'Przełom majowy', *Tydzień Polski* (9 May 1959), p. 3.

Pietrzak, M. 'Prasa chłopska w latach 1926–1939 w świetle konfiskat prasowych', *Wieś Współczesna* (1958), no. 6, 102–17; nos. 7–8, 158–74.

—— *Reglamentacja wolności prasy w Polsce (1918–1939).* Warsaw, 1963.

Piłsudski, J. *Pisma zbiorowe.* 10 vols. Warsaw, 1937–8.

Pobóg-Malinowski, W. *Narodowa Demokracja.* Warsaw, 1933.

—— *Józef Piłsudski.* Warsaw, 1937. (Under pseudonym J. Woyszwiłło.)

—— *Najnowsza historia polityczna Polski, 1864–1945.* 1st ed.: vol. i, Paris, 1953; vol. ii, London, 1956; vol. iii, London, 1960. 2nd ed. (revised): vol. i, London, 1963; vol. ii, London, 1967.

—— 'Skoro nie szablą, to piórem', *Kultura* (Paris), no. 5/151 (1960), 99–134.

Pod rządami bezprawia i terroru. Warsaw, 1952.

Podoski, B. 'Organizacja naczelnych władz obrony państwa: szkic historyczny', *Niepodległość,* new series, vii (1962), 181–99.

La Pologne, 1919–39. 3 vols. Neuchâtel, 1946–7.

Polska Akademia Nauk: Instytut Historii. *Historia Polski.* Vol. iv, Part I: 1918–21 (ed. L. Grosfeld and H. Zieliński), chaps. i–xiii. Warsaw, 1966.

'Polska niepodległa i druga wojna światowa, 1918–1945', *Polska i jej dorobek dziejowy,* ed. H. Paszkiewicz. Part VI. London 1959.

Polska w czasie wielkiej wojny. 3 vols. Warsaw, 1936.

Polski słownik biograficzny. 12 vols. (A–Kąs.). Warsaw, 1935–66.

Pomorski, S. 'Jak zginął gen. Zagórski', *Nadodrze* (1959), no. 7, 3.

Popiel, K. 'Wybór Prezydenta I. Mościckiego', *Zeszyty Historyczne,* ix (1966), 46–51.

Porczak, M. *Walka robotników z reakcją w 1923 r.* Cracow, 1926.

—— *Rewolucja majowa i jej skutki.* Cracow, 1927.

—— *Walka a demokrację w Polsce.* Cracow, 1929.

—— *Dyktator J. Piłsudski i piłsudczycy.* Cracow, 1930.

Prawin, J. *Bereziacy.* Warsaw, 1965.

Próchnik, A. *Ignacy Daszyński: życie, praca, walka.* Warsaw, 1946.

—— *Pierwsze piętnastolecie Polski niepodległej.* Warsaw, 1957.

—— 'O polskim ruchu ludowym', *Najnowsze dzieje Polski: materiały i studia z okresu 1914–1939,* iv (1961), 135–55.

Puttkamer, E. von. *Die polnische National-Demokratie.* Cracow, 1943.

Radlak, B. *S.D.K.P. i L. w latach 1914–1917.* Warsaw, 1967.

Rawicz, J. *General Zagórski zaginął. Z tajemnic lat międzywojennych.* Warsaw, 1963.

Rechowicz, H. *Rok 1936 w Zagłębiu Dąbrowskim.* Katowice, 1957.

—— *Sejm śląski, 1922–1939.* Katowice, 1965.

Reddaway, W. F. *Marshal Piłsudski,* London, 1939.

Reddaway, W. F., Penson, J., Halecki, O. and Dyboski, R. *The Cambridge History of Poland.* Vol. ii: 1696–1935. Cambridge, 1950.

Reeberg, S. 'The antecedents of the Polish defeat', *J.C.E.A.* i (1942), no. 4, 373–99.

Reguła, J. A. *Historia Komunistycznej Partii Polski w świetle faktów i dokumentów.* 2nd ed. (revised). Warsaw, 1934.

Rek, T. *Ruch ludowy w Polsce.* 3 vols. Warsaw, 1947.

—— *Chjeno-Piast, 1922–1926, w świetle obrad sejmu i senatu.* Warsaw, 1955.

—— *Pierwsze lata dyktatury Piłsudskiego, 1926–1930.* Warsaw, 1956.

—— 'Jeszcze o sprawie brzeskiej', *Prawo i Życie,* nos. 26–7 (1957), 8.

—— 'Sprawa Bagińskiego i Wieczorkiewicza', *Prawo i Życie,* no. 17 (1958), 4–5.

—— *Ksiądz Eugeniusz Okoń (1881–1949).* Warsaw, 1962.

Roczniki Pracowniczych Związków Zawodowych w Polsce. 3 vols. Warsaw, 1930–2.

Roos, H. *Polen und Europa.* Tübingen, 1957.

—— 'Józef Piłsudski i Charles de Gaulle', *Kultura* (Paris), no. 5/151 (1960), 11–20.

—— *A History of Modern Poland.* London, 1966. (Translated from the German edition, Stuttgart, 1961.)

Rose, W. J. *The Drama of Upper Silesia.* London, 1936.

—— *The Rise of Polish Democracy.* London, 1944.

—— *Poland's Political Parties, 1919–1939.* Surbiton, 1947.

Rosenberg, K. (under pseud. K. Wrzos). *Piłsudski i piłsudczycy.* Warsaw, 1936.

Rothschild, J. 'The Military Background of Piłsudski's Coup d'État', *Slavic Review,* xxi (1962), no. 2, 241–60.

—— *Piłsudski's Coup d'État.* New York, 1966.

Ruch robotniczy i ludowy w latach 1914–1923. Warsaw, 1961.

Rudnicki, S. 'Program społeczny Obozu Narodowo-Radykalnego (ONR). Stosunek do kwestii robotniczej', *Z Pola Walki* (1965), no. 3, 25–46.

Rudziński, E. 'Bojówki ONR na ulicach Warszawy w 1934 r.' *Pokolenie* (1962), no. 4–5, 103–9.

—— 'Kształtowanie systemu prasy kontrolowanej w Polsce w latach 1921–1939', *Dzieje Najnowsze,* i (1969), 89–112.

—— 'Stanisław Dubois a radykalizacja O.M. T.U.R. i kształtowanie lewego skrzydła P.P.S.' *Kwartalnik Historyczny,* lxv (1958), no. 4, 1110–34.

—— *Działalność polityczna O.M. T.U.R. 1931–1936.* Warsaw, 1961.

Ryng, J. *Wybór pism.* Warsaw, 1958.

Ryszka, F. (ed.) *Historia państwa i prawa Polski, 1918–1939.* Part I. Warsaw, 1962.

Rzepecki, J. 'Jeszcze o maju 1926', *Wojskowy Przegląd Historyczny*, v (1960), no. 2, 346–9.

—— 'Rozejście się Sikorskiego z Piłsudskim w świetle korespondencji Izy Moszczeńskiej z sierpnia 1915 r.', *Kwartalnik Historyczny*, lxvii (1960), no. 3, 728–39.

Rzepecki, T. and Rzepecki, W. *Sejm i Senat, 1922–1927.* Poznań, 1923.

—— *Sejm i Senat, 1928–1933.* Poznań, 1928.

Rzymowski, W. *W walce i burzy: Tadeusz Hołówko na tle epoki.* Warsaw, 1933.

Santoro, E. *Through Poland during the Elections of 1930.* Geneva, 1931.

Schaetzel, T. *Pułkownik Walery Sławek.* Jerusalem, 1947.

—— 'Przełom majowy', *Wiadomości*, xiv, no. 684 (10 May 1959), 6.

—— 'Ustalenie faktów', ibid., no. 698 (16 August 1959), 6.

Schmitt, B. *Poland.* Berkeley and Los Angeles (Cal.), 1945.

Selimowski, T. *Polskie legalne stronnictwa polityczne.* Warsaw, 1930.

Seton-Watson, H. *Eastern Europe between the Wars, 1918–1941.* 3rd ed. Hamden, Conn., 1962.

Singer, B. *Od Witosa do Sławka.* Paris, 1962.

Skwarczyński, A. 'O co toczy się walka', *Droga*, no. 6 (1930), 446–52.

—— *Pod znakiem odpowiedzialności i pracy.* Warsaw, 1933.

Skwarczyński, T. 'Generał Sikorski podczas przewrotu majowego', *Polityka*, iii, no. 31 (1 August 1959), 1.

Smogrzewski, K. *La Pologne restaurée.* Paris, 1927.

Sobieski, W. *Dzieje Polski.* 2nd ed., revised by S. Kozicki. Warsaw, 1938.

Sołtys, J. 'Za kulisami przewrotu Piłsudskiego', *Żołnierz Polski*, no. 3 (18–24 January 1952), 12.

Sontag, E. *Adelbert (Wojciech) Korfanty, ein Beitrag zur Geschichte der polnischen Ansprüche auf Ostoberschlesien.* Kitzingen-Main, 1954.

Srokowski, W. 'Obrona Belwederu', *Kultura* (Paris), no. 5/115 (1957), 87–104.

Stahl, Z. *System Dmowskiego wczoraj i dziś.* London, 1953.

Stankiewicz, W. 'Pakt Lanckoroński', *Roczniki Dziejów Ruchu Ludowego*, i (1959), 196–219.

Starzewski, J. (under pseud. 'Jast'). *Podłoże dziejowe i znaczenie warszawskich wypadków majowych w roku 1926.* Cracow, 1926.

—— *Józef Piłsudski.* Warsaw, 1930.

Starzyński, S. 'Walka z parlamentaryzmem', *Przegląd Współczesny* (1923), no. 13, 175–91.

—— *Projekt reformy konstytucji polskiej.* Lwów, 1928.

Stawecki, P. 'Niektóre aspekty udziału wojska w życiu politycznym w Polsce w latach 1926–1939', *Dzieje Najnowsze*, i (1969), 89–112.

—— 'O dominacji wojskowych w państwowym aparacie cywilnym w Polsce w latach 1926–1939', *Wojskowy Przegląd Historyczny*, x (1965), no. 3, 328–46.

Stęborowski, P. *Geneza Centrolewu.* Warsaw, 1963.

Stpiczyński, W. *Polska, która idzie.* Warsaw, 1929.

Strapiński, A. *Wywrotowe partie polityczne.* Warsaw, 1933.

Strobel, G. W. 'Arbeiterschaft und Linksparteien in Polen, 1928–1938', *Jahrbücher für Geschichte Osteuropas*, x (1962), no. 1, 67–102.

Stroński, S. *Pierwsze lat dziesięć.* Lwów–Warsaw, 1928.

Szczechura, T. *Związek Nauczycilstwa Polskiego.* Warsaw, 1937.

Szechter, S. 'Próby faszystowskiego przewrotu' (październik 1937 r.), *Wieś Współczesna* (1960), no. 10, 129–34.

Śliwiński, A. 'Marszałek Piłsudski o sobie', *Niepodległość*, 1st series, xvi, no. 43 (September–October 1937), 367–73.

Świderski, B. 'Brześć', *Kronika* (London), 5 February 1966.

Świtalski, K. *O rewizji Konstytucji.* Warsaw, 1930.

Tims, R. *Germanising Prussian Poland.* New York, 1941.

Tomicki, J. 'Norbert Barlicki', *Z Pola Walki*, iii (1960), no. 1, 135–73.

Tommassini, F. *La risurrezione della Polonia.* Milan, 1925.

—— *Marsz na Warszawę.* Warsaw, 1929.

Turlejska, M. *Rok przed klęską.* 3rd ed. Warsaw, 1965.

—— *Prawdy i fikcje, wrzesień 1939 — grudzień 1941.* Warsaw, 1966.

Tych, F. *P.P.S.—Lewica w latach wojny 1914–1918.* Warsaw, 1960.

Tymieniecka, A. 'Rozłam w P.P.S. w 1928 roku', *Kwartalnik Historyczny*, lxxii (1965), no. 4, 811–36.

Wańkowicz, M. 'Z polemiki Cata-Mackiewicza z "Narodowcem"', *Słowo Powszechne*, 10 March 1960.

Wapiński, R. *Działalność Narodowej Partii Robotniczej na terenie województwa pomorskiego w latach 1920–1930.* Gdańsk, 1962.

—— 'Działalność Narodowej Demokracji na Pomorzu Gdańskim w latach 1920–1926', *Zapiski Historyczne*, xxix (1964), no. 1, 7–37.

—— 'Niektóre problemy ewolucji ideowo-politycznej Endecji w latach 1919–1939', *Kwartalnik Historyczny* lxxiii (1966), no. 4, 861–77.

—— 'Miejsce Narodowej Demokracji w życiu politycznym II Rzeczypospolitej', *Dzieje Najnowsze*, i (1969), 47–62.

Warski, A. *Wybór pism i przemówień.* Warsaw, 1958.

Wasilewska, W. *Historia jednego strajku.* Warsaw, 1949.

Wasilewski, L. *Józef Piłsudski jakim go znałem.* Warsaw, 1936.

Wenda, Z. *O silę własną Polski.* Warsaw, 1938.

Wiatr, J. 'List do Redakcji', *Kultura* (Paris), no. 12/110 (1956), 111–13.

Wierzchowski, M. *Sprawy Polski w III i IV Dumie państwowej.* Warsaw, 1966.

Więzikowa, A. 'Zjednoczenie Stronnictw Ludowych w 1931 roku', *Wieś Współczesna*, vi (1959), no. 6, 91–114.

—— 'O działalności Stronnictwa Chłopskiego w latach 1926–1931', *Roczniki Dziejów Ruchu Ludowego*, ii (1960), 147–80.

—— 'Powstanie i geneza Stronnictwa Chłopskiego, 1923–1926', *Zeszyty Historyczne Uniwersytetu Warszawskiego*, ii (1961), 280–310.

—— *Stronnictwo Chłopskie.* Warsaw, 1963.

Witos, W. *Czasy i ludzie.* Tarnów, 1926.

—— *Wybór pism i mów.* Lwów, 1939.

Wolikowska, I. *Roman Dmowski. Człowiek, Polak, przyjaciel.* Chicago, 1961.

Woszczyński, B. 'Wypadki majowe 1926 roku w liczbach', *Najnowsze Dzieje Polski: materiały i studia z okresu 1914–1939*, x (1966), 235–41.

Wycech, C. 'Polityczna myśl ludowa w świetle programów stronnictw chłopskich', *Roczniki Dziejów Ruchu Ludowego*, i (1959), 6–57.

Wyglenda, J. *Plebiscyt i powstania śląskie*. Opole, 1966.

Zaleski, S. (ed.) *Bilans gospodarczy dziesięciolecia Polski odrodzonej*. 2 vols. Warsaw, 1929.

Zaremba, Z. *Narodziny polskiego faszyzmu*. Warsaw, n.d.

—— *60 lat walki i pracy P.P.S.* London, 1952.

Zbyszewski, W. 'Generał Haller', *Kultura* (Paris), no. 10/156 (1960), 106–11.

—— 'Nieznane "testimonium" o Piłsudskim', *Zeszyty Historyczne*, iv (1963), 45–51.

Ziembiński, J. 'Z zagadnień genezy i podstawowych założeń ideowo-politycznych agraryzmu w Polsce', *Roczniki Dziejów Ruchu Ludowego*, ii (1960), 108–47.

Zuyev, F. G., Manushevits, A. J., and Khrenov, I. A. *Istoria Polshi*. Vol. iii. Moscow, 1958.

Zweig, F. *Poland Between Two Wars*. London, 1944.

Żarnowska, A. *Geneza rozłamu w Polskiej Partii Socjalistycznej 1904–1906*. Warsaw, 1965.

Żarnowski, J. 'Lewica sanacyjna w latach 1935–1939', *Przegląd Historyczny* (1958), no. 4, 714–37.

—— *Polska Partia Socjalistyczna w latach 1935–39*. Warsaw, 1965.

—— *Przed świtem. Opowiadania o buntach chłopskich 1932–1937*. Warsaw, 1953.

—— *W dwudziestolecie wielkiego strajku chłopskiego, 1937–1957*. Warsaw, 1957.

b. SOCIAL AND ECONOMIC

Ajnenkiel, A. *Położenie prawne robotników rolnych w Polsce (1918–1939)*. Warsaw, 1962.

Arnekker, E. *Przejawy kryzysu w rzemiośle i chałupnictwie*. Warsaw, 1934.

Bajer, K. '*Przemysł włókienniczy na ziemiach polskich od początku XIX w do 1939, Zarys ekonomiczny i historyczny*. Lodz, 1958.

Bernadzikiewicz, T. *Przerosty etatyzmu*. Warsaw, 1936.

—— *Udział państwa w spółkach handlowych*. Warsaw, 1938.

Billing, W. 'Spór o inteligencji', *Nowe Drogi*, 5 (119), (May 1959), 21–35.

Brodowska, H. *Ruch chłopski po uwłaszczeniu w Królestwie Polskim*. Warsaw, 1967.

Chałasiński, J. *Droga awansu społecznego robotnika*. Poznań, 1931.

—— *Młode pokolenie chłopów*. 2 vols. Rome, 1946.

—— *Przeszłość i przyszłość inteligencji polskiej*. Warsaw, 1958.

Ciechocińska, M. 'Pożyczki wewnętrzne w latach 1933–1934', *Najnowsze Dzieje Polski: materiały i studia z okresu 1914–1939*, iii (1960), 51–91.

Curzytek, J. *Badanie nad opłacalnością gospodarstw drobnych*. Warsaw, 1936.

Czajkowski, T. and Derengowski, J. *Bezrobocie pracowników umysłowych w Polsce, 1927–1932*. Warsaw, 1933.

Czarnocki, N. 'Grzechy i omyłki inteligencji pracującej', *Droga* (1924), no. 8, 32–7.

Czechowicz, J. (under pseud. G. Leliwa). *Problem skarbowy w świetle prawdy*. Warsaw, 1926.

Drozdowski, M. 'W sprawie badań nad gospodarką Polski przedwrześniowej', *Przegląd Historyczny*, xlviii (1957), no. 1, 117–25.

—— 'W sprawie polityki gospodarczej rządu polskiego w latach 1936–1939', *Najnowsze Dzieje Polski: studia i materiały z okresu 1914–1939*, 111 (1960), 263–8.

—— 'Polityka gospodarcza Eugeniusza Kwiatkowskiego w latach 1938–1939.' (Komunikat naukowy.) VIII Powszechny Zjazd Historyków Polskich w Krakowie 14–17.X.1958. Historia gospodarcza Polski, Polskie Towarzystwo Historyczne. Warsaw, 1960.

—— 'Położenie i struktura klasy robotniczej Polski w latach 1918–1939 w literaturze naukowej dwudziestolecia', *Z Pola Walki*, iv (1961), no. 1, 35–61.

—— *Polityka gospodarcza rządu polskiego, 1936–39*. Warsaw, 1963.

Drozdowski, M. (ed.) 'Bezrobocie w Polsce w latach 1925–1936', *Najnowsze dzieje Polski: materiały i studia z okresu 1924–1939*, iv (1969), 211–38.

10 lat polityki społecznej Państwa Polskiego, 1918–1928. Warsaw, 1928.

Dziewicka, M. 'Zagadnienie degradacji rolnictwa w Polsce kapitalistycznej', *Ekonomista* (1955), no. 1, 76–93.

Grabowski, T. *Rola państwa w gospodarce Polski (1918–1928)*. Warsaw, 1967.

Gradowski, R. 'Rola i miejsce Polski burżuazyjno-obszarniczej w systemie kapitalizmu światowego', *Ekonomista* (1955), no. 3, 100–21.

—— *Niektóre problemy kapitalizmu monopolistycznego*. Warsaw, 1959.

—— *Przyczynek do zagadnienia kapitału państwowo-monopolistycznego w Polsce*. Warsaw, 1965.

Groniowski, K. *Realizacja reformy uwłaszczeniowej 1864 roku*. Warsaw, 1963.

—— *Kwestia agrarna w Królestwie Polskim, 1871–1914*. Warsaw, 1966.

Grosfeld, L. *Państwo przedwrześniowe w służbie monopoli kapitalistycznych*. Warsaw, 1951.

—— *Polska w latach kryzysu gospodarczego 1929–1933*. Warsaw, 1952.

Gross, F. *The Polish Worker*. New York, 1945.

Heidenkorn, B. 'Proletaryzacja inteligencji zawodowej', *Droga* (1930), no. 1, 67–74.

Hertz, A. 'Spór o inteligencję', *Droga* (1929), no. 10, 846–55.

—— 'Inteligencja wobec bolszewizmu', ibid. (1931), no. 3, 193–207.

—— 'Sprawa klerków', ibid. (1933), no. 1, 229–40.

—— 'The Social Background of the Pre-war Polish Political Structure', *J.C.E.A.* ii (1942), no. 2, 145–61.

—— 'The Case of an East European Intelligentsia', ibid. xi (1951), no. 1, 10–26.

Holzer, J. 'Powstanie Lewiatana', *Uniwersytet Warszawski. Zeszyty Historyczne* (1961), no. 2, 79–97.

Ignar, S. *Kwestia rolna w Polsce kapitalistycznej.* Warsaw, 1952.

Instytut Gospodarstwa Społecznego. *Pamiętniki chłopów.* Warsaw, 1935.

—— *Struktura agrarna wsi polskiej.* Warsaw, 1937.

Instytut Spraw Społecznych. *Młodzież sięga no pracę.* Warsaw, 1938.

Jedlicki, J. *Nieudana próba kapitalistycznej industrializacji.* Warsaw, 1964.

Jędruszczak, H. *Płace robotników przemysłowych w Polsce w latach 1924–39.* Warsaw, 1963.

Kagan, G. 'Agrarian Regime of Pre-war Poland', *J.C.E.A.* iii (1943), no. 3, 241–69.

Kalecki, M. 'Udział karteli w działalności przemysłowej na rynku polskim', *Prace Instytutu Badania Konjunktur Gospodarczych i Cen,* iii (1933), no. 2, 3–7.

Kalecki, M. and Landau, L. *Szacunek dochodu społecznego w r. 1929.* Warsaw, 1934.

Karpiński, Z. *Bank Polski, 1924–1939.* Warsaw, 1958.

Klarner, C. *Dochód społeczny wsi i miast w Polsce w okresie przesilenia gospodarczego 1929–1936.* Lwów, 1937.

Kołodziejczyk, R. 'Z zagadnień kształtowania się burżuazji polskiej', *Kwartalnik Historyczny,* lxiii (1956), no. 1, 12–54.

Kosieradzki, W. *Plan C.O.P.* Warsaw, 1937.

Koszutski, S. *Rozwój ekonomiczny Królestwa Polskiego w ostatnim trzydziestoleciu.* Warsaw, 1905.

Kula, W. *Historia gospodarcza Polski w dobie popowstaniowej. 1864–1918.* Warsaw, 1947.

—— (ed.) *Społeczeństwo Królestwa Polskiego.* Vol. i: Warsaw, 1965; vol. ii: Warsaw, 1966.

Kwiatkowski, E. *Postęp gospodarczy Polski.* Warsaw, 1927.

—— *Współczesne zagadnienia ekonomiczne na tle zagadnień politycznych.* Warsaw, 1928.

—— *Dysproporcje. Rzecz o Polsce przeszłej i obecnej.* Cracow, n.d.

Landau, L. *Wybór pism.* Warsaw, 1957.

Landau, L., Pański, S., and Strzelecki, E. *Bezrobocie wśród chłopów.* Warsaw, 1935.

Landau, Z. 'Pożyczka tytoniowa', *Zeszyty Naukowe Szkoły Głównej Planowania i Statystyki* (1956), no. 3, pp. 61–82.

—— 'Misja Kemmerera', *Przegląd Historyczny,* xlviii (1957), no. 2, 270–84.

—— 'Pożyczka dillonowska', *Kwartalnik Historyczny,* lxiv (1957), no. 3, 79–85.

—— 'Polityczne aspekty działalności misji doradców finansowych E. Hiltona Younga w Polsce (1923–24)', *Zeszyty Naukowe Szkoły Głównej Planowania i Statystyki* (1958), no. 9, 71–112.

—— 'Działalność koncernu Kreugera w Polsce', *Przegląd Historyczny,* xlix (1958), no. 1, 90–120.

—— 'Władysław Grabski a pożyczki zagraniczne', *Kwartalnik Historyczny,* lxvi (1959), no. 4, 1185–1205.

—— 'Polityka tzw. nakręcania koniunktury w Polsce w okresie 1936–1939', *Najnowsze Dzieje Polski: studia i materiały z okresu 1914–1939,* ii (1959), 75–92.

Landau, Z. ('Głos w dyskusji nad komunikatem M. Drozdowskiego: Polityka gospodarcza Eugeniusza Kwiatkowskiego w latach 1938–1939'.) VIII Powszechny Zjazd Historyków Polskich w Krakowie 14–17.X. 1958. VI Historia Gospodarcza Polski, Polskie Towarzystwo Historyczne. Warsaw, 1960.

—— 'Jeszcze raz w sprawie polityki gospodarczej rządu polskiego w latach 1936–1939', *Najnowsze Dzieje Polski: materiały i studia z okresu 1914–1939*, iv (1960), 239–46.

—— 'Wpływ zamachu majowego na gospodarkę polską', *Przegląd Historyczny*, liii (1962), no. 3, 502–18.

—— *Plan Stabilizacyjny, 1927–1930*. Warsaw, 1963.

Landau, Z. and Tomaszewski, T. *Zarys historii gospodarczej Polski, 1918–1939*. 2nd ed. Warsaw, 1962.

Lulek, T. (ed.) *Etatyzm w Polsce*. Cracow, 1932.

Luxemburg, R. *Die industrielle Entwicklung Polens*. Leipzig, 1898.

Michałowski, J. *Wieś nie ma pracy*. Warsaw, 1935.

Michowicz, W. 'Wpływ strajku górników angielskich z 1926 r. na przemysł węglowy w Polsce', *Zeszyty Naukowe Uniwersytetu Łódzkiego*, 1st series, Pamphlet 7 (1957), 209–46.

Mieszczankowski, M. 'Podatki rolne w Polsce międzywojennej', *Roczniki Dziejów Ruchu Ludowego*, iii (1961), 114–58.

—— *Struktura agrarna Polski międzywojennej*. Warsaw, 1960.

Moore, F. W. *Economic Demography of Eastern and Southern Europe*. Geneva, 1945.

Niewadzi, C. 'Przemysł drobny i rzemiosła w Polsce burżuazyjno-obszarniczej', *Zeszyty Naukowe Szkoły Głównej Planowania i Statystyki*, ii (1955), 141–93.

Pięć lat na froncie gospodarczym, 1926–1931. 2 vols. Warsaw, 1931.

Polityka społeczna państwa polskiego, 1918–1935. Warsaw, 1935.

Poniatowski, Józef. *Przeludnienie wsi i rolnictwa*. Warsaw, 1935.

Poniatowski, Juliusz. *Cele i założenia reformy rolnej w dwudziestoleciu niepodległym*. London, 1951.

Popiołek, K. 'Rozwój kapitalistycznego przemysłu na Śląsku, 1850–1910', *Konferencja Śląska: Instytut Historyczny P.A.N.* i. 191–265. Wrocław, 1954.

Popkiewicz, J. and Ryszka, F. *Przemysł ciężki Górnego Śląska w gospodarce Polski międzywojennej (1922–1939)*. Opole, 1959.

Popkiewicz, K. and Ryszka, F. 'Górnośląski przemysł w latach 1922–1929', *Kwartalnik Historyczny*, lxiii (1956), nos. 4–5, 417–39.

Radkiewicz, W. 'Kilka uwag w związku z artykułem R. Kołodziejczyka o kształtowaniu się burżuazji polskiej', ibid. lxiii (1956), no. 6, 88–95.

Rakowski, J. *Linia rozwojowe gospodarstwa polskiego*. Warsaw, 1938.

—— 'Ideologia gespodarcza epoki J. Piłsudskiego', *Niepodległość* (1948), i. 117–35.

Rudzki, A. *Zarys polskiej polityki komunikacyjnej*. London, 1945.

Rzepecki, B. *Zatarg gospodarczy polsko-niemiecki*. Warsaw, 1930.

Schön, J. *Die polnische Bankwesen*. Katowice, 1928.

Starzyński, S. *Program rządu pracy w Polsce*. Warsaw, 1926.

—— S. *Rok 1926 w życiu gospodarczym Polski.* Warsaw, 1927.

—— *Rola państwa w życiu gospodarczym.* Warsaw, 1929.

—— (ed.) *Na froncie gospodarczym. W dziesiątą rocznicę odzyskania niepodległości.* Warsaw, n.d.

Stein, K., Ritterman, S., Friediger, B., Zauberman, H., and Lange, O. *Przewroty walutowe i gospodarcze po wielkiej wojnie.* Cracow, 1928.

Svennilson, I. *Growth and Stagnation in the European Economy.* Geneva, 1954.

Szczepański, J. 'Struktura inteligencji w Polsce', *Kultura i Społeczeństwo,* iv (1960), nos. 1–2, 19–48.

—— 'The Polish Intelligentsia: Past and Present', *World Politics* (1962), no. 3, 406–20.

Szturm de Sztrem, E. *Kartele w życiu gospodarczym i społecznym.* Warsaw, 1935.

Taylor, E. *Inflacja Polska.* Poznań, 1926.

—— *Druga inflacja polska. Przyczyny — przebieg — środki zaradcze.* Poznań, 1926.

—— *Finanz und Steuersystem der Republik Polens.* Jena, 1928.

Taylor, J. *The Economic Development of Poland, 1919–1950.* Ithaca, N.Y., 1952.

Tennenbaum, H. *Finansowanie inwestycji.* Warsaw, 1939.

Thomas, W. and Znaniecki, F. *The Polish Peasant in Europe and America.* 5 vols. Boston, 1918.

Tomaszewski, J. 'Polityka stabilizacyjna Władysława Grabskiego, 1923–1925', *Najnowsze Dzieje Polski: materiały i studia z okresu 1914–1939,* i (1958), 77–102.

—— 'Gospodarka drobnotowarowa w Polsce międzywojennej', *Zeszyty Naukowe Szkoły Głównej Planowania i Statystyki,* xv (1959), 27–58.

—— *Stabilizacja waluty w Polsce, 1924–1925.* Warsaw, 1961.

Wellisz, L. *Foreign Capital in Poland.* London, 1938.

Wieś w liczbach w Polsce burżuazyjno-obszarniczej i w Polsce ludowej. 3rd ed. Warsaw, 1954.

Wittlin, J. 'Inwentarz kultury narodowej', *Skamander* (1925), no. 38, 76–93.

Zdziechowski, J. *Mit złotej waluty.* Warsaw, 1938.

—— *Skarb i pieniądz, 1919–1939.* London, 1955.

Zniszczenia wojenne i odbudowa Polski. Warsaw, 1929.

Zweig, F. *The Planning of Free Societies.* London 1943.

Żarnowski, J. 'Struktura i podłoże społeczne obozu rządzącego w Polsce w latach 1926–39', *Najnowsze Dzieje Polski: materiały i studia z okresu 1914–1939,* x (1966), 67–84.

—— *Struktura społeczna inteligencji w Polsce w latach 1918–1939.* Warsaw, 1964.

c. NATIONAL MINORITIES

Aland, A. 'Układ stosunków wyznaniowo-zawodowych wśród ludności 3 województw południowo-wschodnich', *Sprawy Narodowościowe* (1939), nos. 1–2, 14–42.

Alter, W. *Antisemityzm gospodarczych w świetle cyfr.* Warsaw, 1937.

Auerbach, J. 'Ogólnożydowska Partia Pracy', Biuletyn Żydowskiego Instytutu Historycznego, iv–vi (1964), no. 50, 37–58.

—— 'Niektóre zagadnienia działalności KPP w środowisku żydowskim w latach kryzysu (1929–1933)', ibid. vii–ix (1965), no. 55, 31–56.

Bączkowski, W. 'Sprawa ukraińska', Kultura (Paris), nos. 7/57, 8/58 (1952), 64–9.

Bergman, A. 'Białoruska Włościańsko-Robotnicza Hromada (1925–1927)', Z Pola Walki, v (1962), no. 3, 73–99.

Bergman, S., Karwacki, F., and Stankiewicz, W. 'Komunistyczna Partia Zachodniej Białorusi', Nowe Drogi (1959), no. 5, 86–93.

Białoruskie ugrupowania polityczne w Polsce w dniu 1 kwietnia 1927 roku. Warsaw, 1927.

Bierschenek, T. Die deutsche Volksgruppe in Polen 1934–1939. Kitzingen 1954.

Bornstein, J. Rzemiosło żydowskie w Polsce. Warsaw, 1926.

—— 'Struktura zawodowa i społeczna ludności żydowskiej w Polsce', Sprawy Narodowościowe (1939), nos. 1–2, 43–98.

Borski, J. M. Sprawa żydowska a socjalizm. Warsaw, 1937.

Bronsztejn, S. Ludność żydowska w Polsce w okresie międzywojennym. Wrocław–Warsaw–Cracow, 1963.

Budurowycz, B. 'The Ukrainian Problem in International Politics, October 1938 to March 1939', Canadian Slavonic Papers, iii (1958), 59–75.

Chmielewski, S. 'Stan szkolnictwa wśród żydów w Polsce', Sprawy Narodowościowe (1937), nos. 1–2, 32–74.

Cygański, M. Mniejszość niemiecka w Polsce centralnej w latach 1918–1939. Lodz, 1962.

—— 'Wpływ rewizjonistycznej polityki rządów republiki weimarskiej na mniejszość niemiecką w Polsce', Najnowsze Dzieje Polski: materiały i studia z okresu 1914–1939, x (1966), 157–62.

Dmitryshyn, B. Moscow and the Ukraine, 1918–1953. New York, 1956.

Dreszer, Z. Sprawa mniejszości narodowych w Polsce a program państwowy demokracji. Warsaw, 1926.

Dunin-Borkowski, P. 'Punkt wyjścia w sprawie ukraińskiej w Małopolsce wschodniej', Droga (1929), no. 6, 561–72.

Feliński, M. Ukraińcy w Polsce. Warsaw, 1931.

Finfuntzwantsik Yor Zamlbuch. Gevidmet dem 25-yoriken Yubileum fun der Yiddisher Arbeter-bevegung. Warsaw, 1922.

Gerasymenko, M. and Dudykevich, B. Borotba trudyashchykh Zakhidnoi Ukrainy za vozziednania z Radianskoyu Ukrainoyu. Kiev, 1955.

Gliksman, J. L'Aspect économique de la question juive en Pologne. Paris, 1929.

—— Struktura zawodowa i społeczna ludności żydowskiej w Polsce. Warsaw, 1930.

Goguel, R. 'W sprawie kilku nowszych publikacji zachodnio-niemieckich, na temat mniejszości niemieckiej z Polsce', Najnowsze Dzieje Polski: materiały i studia z okresu 1914–1939, x (1966), 147–56.

Gorzuchowski, S. Ludność litewska na kresach Pa stwa Polskiego. Warsaw, 1929.

Grünbaum, I. *Milkhamot ha-Yehudim bePolaniya.* Jerusalem, 1946.

Grünberg, K. *Nazi-Front Schlesien. Niemieckie organizacje polityczne w wojewódzwie śląskim w latach 1933–1939.* Katowice, 1963.

Halpern, L. *Polityka żydowska w Sejmie i Senacie Rzeczypospolitej Polskiej, 1919–1933.* Warsaw, 1933.

Heike, O. *Das Deutschtum in Polen, 1918–39.* Bonn, 1955.

Hertz, A. *Żydzi w kulturze polskiej.* Paris, 1961.

Hertz, J. (ed.) *Doires Bundisten.* New York, 1956.

—— *Der Bund in Bilder, 1897–1957.* New York, 1958.

Heydenkhorn, B. 'Wolne miasto Gdańsk' [describes Ukrainian nationalist activity here], *Kultura* (Paris), no. 6/140 (1959), 131–5.

Horak, S. *Poland and her National Minorities.* New York, 1961.

Hrushevsky, M. *A History of Ukraine.* New Haven (Conn.), 1941.

Ilnytzkyj, R. *Deutschland und die Ukraine, 1934–1945.* Vol. i. Munich, 1955.

Istoria Bielaruskoi S.S.S.R. Minsk, 1961.

J. S. (identity unknown). *W kościele i w cerkwi — praktyczny wykład obrządków rzymskiego i greckiego.* Cracow, 1926.

Janowsky, O. I. *People at Bay: the Jewish Problem in East Central Europe.* London, 1938.

Kazet, P. 'Niemieckie ugrupowania polityczne w Polsce', *Sprawy Narodowościowe* (1927), no. 2, 110–21.

Kierski, K. *Prawa mniejszości narodowych.* Poznań, 1923.

Korus-Kabacińska, J. 'Położenie ludności białoruskiej w Rzeczypospolitej Palskiej w latach 1924–26', *Zeszyty Historyczne Uniwersytetu Warszawskiego,* ii (1961), 166–221.

Kravets, M. *Napisy robitnichego rikhy v zakhidny Ukrainy v 1921–39.* Kiev, 1959.

Krysiński, A. *Liczba i rozmieszczenie Ukraińców w Polsce.* Warsaw, 1929.

—— *Liczba i rozmieszczenie ludności poskiej na kresach wschodnich.* Warsaw, 1930.

Kühn, W. *Die jungen Deutschen Sprachinseln in Galizien.* Münster, 1930.

Lestchinsky, J. *Di ekonomishe lage fun Yidn in Poiln.* Berlin, 1931.

—— *Yidn in der shtotisher bafelkerung fun unaphengign Poiln.* New York, 1943.

—— 'The Jews in the Cities of the Republic of Poland', *Yivo Annual of Jewish Social Science,* i (1946), 156–77.

—— 'The Industrial and Social Structure of the Jewish Population in Interbellum Poland', *Yivo Annual of Jewish Social Science,* ix (1956–7), 243–69.

Lewandowski, J. *Federalizm: Litwa i Białoruś w polityce obozu belwederskiego (XI.1918 — IV.1920).* Warsaw, 1962.

Łoś, S. ' "Galicja Wschodnia" ', *Droga* (1931), no. 7–8, 543–61.

Mahler, R. 'Jews in Public Service and the Liberal Professions in Poland 1918–1939', *Jewish Social Studies,* vi (1944), no. 4, 291–350.

Makar, V. 'Stril v oboroni milioniv', *Almanakh-Kalendar Homonu Ukrainy na 1956 rik,* pp. 145–54. Toronto, 1956.

Makukh, J. *Na narodnii sluzhbi.* Munich, 1958.

554 BIBLIOGRAPHY

Margolin, A. *The Jews of Eastern Europe*. New York, 1926.

Matsko, A. N., and Tsamutin, B. E. (eds.) *Revolyutsonnii put' Kompartii zapadnoi Bielarusii, 1921–1939 gg.* Minsk, 1966.

Miedziński, M. *Uwagi o sprawie żydowskiej*. Warsaw, 1937.

Mirtshuk, J. 'The Ukranian Uniat Church', *Slavonic Review*, x (1931–2), 377–85.

Motzkin, L. *La Campagne antisémite en Pologne*. Paris, 1932.

Nasarski, P. *Deutsche Jugendbewegung und Tugendarbeit in Polen, 1919–1939*. Würzburg, 1957.

Paneyko, B. 'Galicia and the Polish-Ukranian Problem', *Slavonic Review*, ix (1930–1), 567–87.

—— 'Germany, Poland and the Ukraine', *The Nineteenth Century and After*, cxxv (January 1939), 34–43.

Paprocki, S. *Minority Affairs and Poland*. Warsaw, 1935.

Parkes, J. *The Emergence of the Jewish Problem*. Oxford, 1946.

Petrusewicz, K. *Proces białoruskiej włościańsko-robotniczej Hromady. Mowy obrończe*. Wilno, 1928.

Podoski, B. 'Białoruska Włościańsko-Robotnicza Hromada', *Niepodległość*, 2nd series, vi (1958), 205–7.

Poluian, V., and Poluian, J. *Revolyutsonnoe i natsionalno-osvoboditelnoe dvizhenie z Zapadnoi Bielarusi v 1920–1939*. Minsk, 1962.

Prokoptschuk, G. *Der Metropolit. Leben und Wirken des grossen Förderers der Kirchenunion, Graf Andreas Scheptytzkyj*. Munich, 1955.

Reshetar, J. S. 'Ukrainian Nationalism and the Orthodox Church', *American Slavonic and East European Review*, x (1951), 38–49.

Revyuk, E. *Polish Atrocities in Ukraine*. New York, 1931.

Robinson, J., Karbach, O., Laserson, M., Robinson, N., and Nichniak, M. *Were the Minorities Treaties a Failure?* New York, 1943.

Rogala, W. 'Wzrost nastrojów rewizjonistycznych wśród niemieckiej mniejszości narodowej w Polsce', *Przegląd Zachodni*, xv (1959), no. 6, 298–317.

Sabotaż ukraiński i akcja pacyfikacyjna. Warsaw, 1931.

Schiper, I., Tartakower, A., and Hafftka, A. (eds.) *Żydzi w Polsce odrodzonej*. 2 vols. Warsaw, 1933

Segal, S. *The New Poland and the Jews*. New York, 1950.

Shukman, H. 'The Relations between the Jewish Bund and the R.S.D.R.P., 1897–1903.' (Oxford University D.Phil. thesis. 1961.)

Shutovich, J. *Kshendz Adam Stankievich u 25-ya ukhodki svyashchenstva bielaruskai natsjonalnai dzeynashchi (10.I.1915–10.I.1940)*. Wilno, 1940.

Sorochtej, L. 'Sprawa ukraińska w Polsce a rząd Władysława Grabskiego.' (Warsaw University Doctoral thesis. 1962).

Srokowski, S. 'The Ukrainian Problem in Poland: A Polish View', *Slavonic Review*, ix (1930–1), 588–97.

Staniewicz, R. 'Mniejszość niemiecka w Polsce — V kolumna Hitlera?', *Przegląd Zachodni*, xv (1959), no. 2, 395–438.

Stoliński, Z. *Les Allemands en Pologne*. Warsaw, 1927.

—— *Szkolnictwo niemieckie w Polsce*. Warsaw, 1927.

—— 'Niemcy w Sejmie i w Senacie, 1919–1927', *Sprawy Narodowościowe* (1928), no. 1, 21–32.

Symmons-Symonelewicz, K. 'Polish Political Thought and the Problem of the Eastern Borderlands', *The Polish Review*, iv, no. 1/2 (Winter–Spring 1959), 65–81.

Szczyrba, M. 'Komunistyczna Partia Zachodniej Ukrainy', *Nowe Drogi* (1959), no. 1, 79–86.

Tarashevich, I. *Bielarusy w shviatle pravdy.* Wilno, 1935.

Tarnopolsky, W. 'The Polish-Ukrainian Conflict in Eastern Galicia in 1930 and its Repercussions in the League of Nations.' (Columbia University M.A. thesis. 1955.)

Tomaszewski, J. *Z dziejów Polesia, 1921–1939.* Warsaw, 1963.

Tomkiewicz, W. *Ukraina między Wschodem i Zachodem.* Warsaw, 1938.

Ukraińskie i ruskie ugrupowania polityczne w Polsce w dniu 1 kwietnia 1927 r. Warsaw, 1927.

Urbański, Z. *Mniejszości narodowe w Polsce.* Warsaw, 1932.

Vakar, N. *Belorussia. The Making of a Nation.* Cambridge (Mass.), 1956.

Vytvytsky, S. and Baran, S. 'Western Ukraine under Poland', *Encyclopedia of the Ukraine*, pp. 833–50.

Wasilewski, L. *Kresy Wschodnie. Litwa i Białoruś — Podlasie i Chełmszczyzna. Galicja Wschodnia — Ukraina.* Warsaw, 1917.

—— *Sprawy narodowościowe w teorii i w życiu.* Warsaw, 1929.

Wasiutyński, B. *Ludność żydowska w Polsce w wiekach XIX i XX.* Warsaw, 1930.

Wysłouch, S. *Rola komunistycznej partji zachodniej Białorusi w ruchu narodowym Białorusinów w Polsce.* Wilno, 1933.

Zachariasz, S. *Di komunistishe bevegung unter dem yidishen arbetenden befelkerung in Poiln.* Warsaw, 1954.

Ziemiński, J. *Problem emigracji żydowskiej.* Warsaw 1937.

Żółtowski, A. *Border of Europe. A Study of the Polish Eastern Provinces.* London, 1950.

Orhanizatsya Ukrainskykh Natsionalistiv, 1929–1954. N.p., 1955.

d. FOREIGN POLICY

b.e.h. 'Nieznana inicjatywa Piłsudskiego', *Kultura* (Paris), no. 5/103 (1956), 124–7. An account of an article by Professor Smal-Stocki on his attempt to act as a mediator, at Piłsudski's behest, between Poland and Lithuania.

Balcerak, W. 'Polska polityka zagraniczna wobec układów lokarneńskich', *Przegląd Zachodni*, xv (1959), no. 6, 259–97.

Barański, Z. *Niemiecki tranzyt kolejowy przez Polskę w latach 1919–1939.* Poznań, 1957.

Batowski, H. *Kryzys dyplomatyczny w Europie: jesień 1938 — wiosna 1939.* Warsaw, 1962.

Beck, J. *Przemówienia, deklaracje, wywiady (1931–1939).* 2nd ed. Warsaw, 1939.

556 BIBLIOGRAPHY

Bonnet, G. *Fin d'une Europe*. Geneva, 1948.

Breyer, R. *Das Deutsche Reich und Polen, 1932–1937: Aussenpolitik und Volksgruppenfragen*. Würzburg, 1955.

Budurowycz, B. *Polish-Soviet Relations, 1932–1939*. New York, 1963.

Celovsky, B. 'Pilsudskis Präventivkrieg gegen das nationalsozialistische Deutschland (Entstehung, Verbreitung und Widerlegung einer Legende)', *Die Welt als Geschichte* (1954), i, 53–70.

Czarnecki, B. 'Gdy Niemcy chcieli z Polską pokoju', *Sprawy Między-narodowe*, xi (1958), no. 12, 69–82.

Dębicki, R. *The Foreign Policy of Poland, 1919–1939*. New York, 1962.

Dopierała, B. *Gdańska polityka Józefa Becka*. Poznań, 1967.

Flandin, P. E. *Politique française 1919–1940*. Paris, 1947.

François-Poncet, A. *Souvenirs d'une ambassade à Berlin. Septembre 1931 — Octobre 1938*. Paris, 1946.

Gąsiorowski, Z. J. 'Did Piłsudski Attempt to Initiate a Preventive War in 1933?' *Journal of Modern History*, xxvii (June 1955), 135–51.

—— 'The German-Polish Nonaggression Pact of 1934', *J.C.E.A.* xv (1955), no. 1, 3–29.

—— 'Polish-Czechoslovak Relations, 1918–1922', *Slavonic and East European Review*, xxxv (December 1956), 173–93.

—— 'Polish-Czechoslovak Relations, 1922–1926', ibid. xxxv (June 1957), 473–504.

—— 'Stresemann and Poland before Locarno', *J.C.E.A.*, xviii (1958), no. 1, 25–47.

—— 'Stresemann and Poland after Locarno', ibid. xviii (1958), no. 3, 292–317.

Jabłoński, H. 'Z tajnej dyplomacji Władysława Grabskiego w r. 1924', *Kwartalnik Historyczny*, lxiii (1956), no. 4–5, 440–55.

Jaworznicki, B. 'Pakt wschodni', *Sprawy Międzynarodowe*, ii (July–December 1949), no. 3–4, 91–109.

—— 'Polsko-radziecki pakt o nieagresji z r. 1932', ibid. (1952), v, 70–82.

Jędrzejewicz, W. 'Piłsudski i Kemal', *Wiadomości*, ix, no. 425 (23 May 1954), 2.

Jurkiewicz, J. 'Polska wobec planów Paktu Wschodniego w latach 1934–1935', *Sprawy Międzynarodowe* xii (1959), no. 3, 18–51.

—— *Pakt wschodni: z historii stosunków międzynarodowych w latach 1934–1935*. Warsaw, 1963.

—— (ed.) 'Tajne posiedzenie Rady Ligi Narodów w grudniu 1927 r. i spotkanie Piłsudskiego z Stresemannem', *Sprawy Międzynaro dowe* xiii (1960), no. 2, 88–96.

Kahanek, F. *Beneš contra Beck. Reportaže a dokumenty*. Prague, 1938.

Komarnicki, T. *The Rebirth of the Polish Republic*. London, 1957.

Korbel, J. *Poland Between East and West: Soviet and German Diplomacy Toward Poland, 1919–1933*. Princeton (N.J.), 1963.

Kozeński, J. *Czechosłowacja w polskiej polityce zagranicznej w latach 1932–1938*. Poznań, 1964.

Krasuski, J. *Stosunki polsko-niemieckie, 1919–1925*. Poznań, 1962.

—— *Stosunki polsko-niemieckie, 1926–1932.* Poznań, 1964.

Kruszewski, C. 'The German-Polish Tariff War (1925–1934) and its Aftermath', *J.C.E.A.* iii (1943), no. 3, 294–315.

Kuźmiński, T. *Polska, Francja, Niemcy, 1933–1935.* Warsaw, 1963.

Landau, Z., and Tomaszewski, J. 'O polityce zagranicznej Polski w latach 1924–1925', *Kwartalnik Historyczny*, lxviii (1961), no. 3, 725–38.

Lapter, K. 'Międzynarodowe tło przewrotu majowego', *Sprawy Między-narodowe*, ix (1956), no. 5, 43–60; no. 6, 54–71.

—— 'Polityka Józefa Becka', ibid. xi (1958), no. 5, 47–69.

—— *Pakt Piłsudski–Hitler 1934.* Warsaw, 1962.

Lepecki, M. B. 'Marszałek Piłsudski i przewidywana w roku 1933 wojna z Niemcami', *Wiadomości*, iv, no. 129 (26 June 1949), 1.

Lipski, J. 'Przyczynki do polsko-niemieckiej deklaracji o nieagresji', *Bellona*, iii. 18–37, iv. 3–21.

Łukasiewicz, J. 'Okupacja Nadrenii i Rambouillet', *Wiadomości Polskie* (London) 1942, no. 21 (115) 3.

—— 'Sprawa czechosłowacka na tle stosunków polsko-francuskich', *Sprawy Międzynarodowe* (London, 1948) nos. 2–3/6–7, 27–60.

—— *Polska jest mocarstwem.* Warsaw, 1939.

Mackiewicz, S. *Polityka Becka.* London, 1942.

Miedziński, B. 'Popioły są jeszcze gorące', *Wiadomości*, vii, no. 343 (26 October 1952), 1; no. 345 (9 November 1952), 2.

—— 'Prawe oko Nelsona', ibid. (1964), no. 49/975, 2.

Mikulicz, S. 'Wpływ dyplomacji sanacyjnej na obalenie Titulescu', *Sprawy Międzynarodowe* (1959), no. 7–8, 104–123.

Northedge, F. S. *The Troubled Giant, Britain among the Great Powers, 1916–1939.* London, 1966.

Orlicz, J., Zwit, J. 'Wywiad polski w III Rzeszy', *Polityka*, 23 September 1960, 1 October 1960.

Pajewski, S. (ed.) *Problem Polsko-Niemiecki w Traktacie Wersalskim.* Poznań, 1963.

Raczyński, E. *The British-Polish Alliance: its Origin and Meaning.* London, 1948.

Ratyńska, B. 'Geneza wojny celnej polsko-niemieckiej', *Najnowsze Dzieje Polski: materiały i studia z okresu 1914–1939*, vi (1963), 77–103.

Roos, H. 'Die "Präventivkriegspläne" Piłsudskis von 1933' *Vierteljahrs-hefte für Zeitgeschichte*, iii (October 1955), 344–63.

—— *Polen und Europa. Studien zur polnischen Aussenpolitik, 1931–1939.* Tübingen, 1957.

Senn, A. E. 'The Polish-Lithuanian War Scare, 1927', *J.C.E.A.*, xxi (1961), no. 3, 267–84.

Skubiszewski, K. 'Gdańsk w prawie międzynarodowym w latach 1919–1939', *Czasopismo Prawno-Historyczne*, viii (1956), no. 1, 258–72.

Sokolnicki, M. 'Józef Piłsudski a zagadnienie Rosji', *Niepodległość*, i (1950), 51–70.

—— 'Archiwum ministra Szembeka' *Kultura* (Paris), no. 9/59 (1952), 111–22.

—— 'Polityka Piłsudskiego a Turcja', *Niepodleglość*, vi (1958), 5–23.

Sokulski, H. 'Wojna celna Rzeszy przeciw Polsce w latach 1925–1934', *Sprawy Międzynarodowe*, viii (1958), no. 9, 54–65.

Stanisławska, S. 'Stosunek opozycji polskiej do polityki Becka wobec Czechosłowacji wiosną 1938 r.' ibid. xii (1959), no. 11/12, 30–67.

—— *Wielka i mała. Polityka Józefa Becka*. Warsaw, 1962.

—— *Polska a Monachium*. Warsaw, 1967.

Strzetelski, S. *Where the Storm Broke: Poland from Yesterday to Tomorrow*. New York, 1942.

—— *Goering poluje na rysie*. London, 1942.

Trocka, H. *Gdańsk w planach imperializmu niemieckiego przed II wojną światową (1933–1939)*. Maszynopis pracy doktorskiej Warsaw University, 1960.

Umiastowski, R. *Russia and the Polish Republic, 1918–1941*. London, 1945.

Wandycz, P. S. *France and her Eastern Allies, 1919–1925*. Minneapolis (Minn.), 1962.

Wojciechowski, M. *Stosunki polsko-niemieckie, 1933–1938*. Poznań, 1965.

e. MILITARY MATTERS

Cyprian, T. *Komisja stwierdziła . . . Londyn, 1942*. Warsaw, 1961.

Fabrycy, K. 'Komórka specjalna', *Niepodległość*, v (1955), 217–27.

Glabisz, K. 'Laboratorium', ibid. vi (1958), 220–7.

Grudziński, A. 'Cyfry mówią', *Wiadomości*, xiv, no. 675 (8 March 1959), 6.

Kirchmayer, J. 'O sztabach i sztabowcach w przedwrześniowym wojsku', *Wojskowy Przegląd Historyczny* (1960), no. 4, 274–308; no. 2, 175–206.

Kopański, S. *Moja służba w wojsku polskim, 1917–1939*. London, 1965.

Kozłowski, E. 'Stany liczebne polskich sit zbrojnych w latach 1936–1939', *Biuletyn Informacyjny Wojskowego Instytutu Historycznego* (1961), no. 17, 49–64.

—— *Wojsko Polskie, 1936–1939*. Warsaw, 1964.

Królikiewicz, T. 'Lotnictwo polskie w okresie międzywojennym', *Wojskowy Przegląd Historyczny* (1957), no. 3, 95–144.

Lityński, S. 'Udział Wyższej Szkoły Wojennej przed r. 1939 w kształowaniu polskiej doktryny wojennej', *Bellona* (1955), no. 1, 30–8.

Łowczowski, G. 'Polska doktryna wojenna, 1919–1939', ibid. (1960), no. 1, 3–24.

Machalski, T. 'Polska doktryna wojenna, 1919–1939', ibid. no. 4, 248–99.

Pstrzokoński, S. 'Interna', *Wiadomości*, v, no. 218 (4 June 1950), 2.

Rayski, L. *Słowo prawdy o lotnictwie polskim, 1919–1939*. London, 1948.

Romeyko, M. *'Rayskie' czasy lotnictwa polskiego*. London, 1949.

Roos, H. 'Die militär-politische lage und Planung Polens gegenüber Deutschland vor 1939', *Wehrwissenschafftliche Rundschau*, no. 4 (1957).

Stachiewicz, W. 'L'offensive pour la Pologne', *Kultura* (Paris), no. 2–3 (1951), 128–60.

Stawecki, P. 'Przyczynek do historii polskiego przemysłu zbrojeniowego', *Wojskowy Przegląd Historyczny* (1963), no. 2, 284–340.

Steblik, W. 'Studium Niemcy z maja 1936 r.', ibid. (1960), no. 3, 334–59.

Wiatr, J. 'Przyczynki do historii materiałowego przygotowania obrony Polski w latach 1921–1939', *Bellona*, iii (1959), 235–56.

—— 'Możliwości przygotowania do wojny w okresie dwudziestolecia', *Kultura* (Paris), nos. 7/165–8/166 (1961), 166–80.

Wisłocki, W. 'Polemika w sprawie doktryny', *Bellona* (1960), no. 4, 303–5.

Zając, J. 'Nasze przygotowania do wojny', *Kultura* (Paris), nos. 1/159, 2/160 (1961), 161–88.

f. THE FALL OF THE POLISH STATE

i. *The September Campaign*

Dom, S. (Izydor Modelski?) *Uwagi o kampanii wrześniowej 1939 roku.* Edinburgh, 1941.

Jaklicz, J. 'Kampania wrześniowa 1939 w Polsce', in *11.XI.1941*, pp. 17–151. Grenoble, 1941.

Kennedy, R. M. *The German Campaign in Poland (1939)*. Department of the Army. Pamphlet no. 20–255. Washington, 1956.

Kirchmayer, J. *1939 i 1944. Kilka zagadnień polskich.* Warsaw, 1958.

—— *Kampania wrześniowa.* Warsaw, 1946.

Kutrzeba, T. 'Bitwa nad Bzurą 9–22 września 1939 r.' *Wojskowy Przegląd Historyczny* (1956), no. 1, 237–305; (1957), no. 1, 267–308.

Norwid-Neugebauer, M. *Kampania wrześniowa 1939 w Polsce.* London, 1941.

Piątkowski, H. ibid. 1946.

Polskie Siły Zbrojne, Vol. i, Part I, ibid. 1951.

Pragłowski, A. 'Kampania wrześniowa', *Kultura* (Paris), no. 9 (1959), 72–86.

Rawski, T., Stąpor, Z., and Zamojski, J. (eds.) *Wojna wyzwoleńcza narodu polskiego w latach 1939–1945.* 2nd ed. Warsaw, 1966.

S. K., F. H., and W. Ż. 'Lotnictwo Polskie w kampanii wrześniowej 1939 roku', *Bellona* (1942), no. 9, 26–53; no. 11, 9–32.

Szymański, A. 'Fragmenty niemieckich przygotowań wojskowych w ostatnim przedwojennym półroczu 1939', ibid. (1954), no. 3, 4–11.

Tomaszewski, T. *Byłem szefem sztabu obrony Warszawy w 1939 r.* London, 1961.

Vormann, N. *Der Feldzug 1939 in Polen. Die Operationen des Heeres.* Weissenburg, 1958.

ii. *The Change of Government*

Broszat, M. *Nationalsozialistische polenpolitik, 1939–1945.* Paperback ed. Stuttgart, 1965.

Drymmer, W. T. 'Z Kut do Bicaz', *Na Straży* (Jerusalem) (1946), 28–30, pp. 6–8.

Goetel, F. *Czasy wojny.* London, 1955.

560 BIBLIOGRAPHY

Hertzog, L. 'Czy Hitler chciał utworzyć buforowe państewko polskie?' *Wojskowy Przegląd Historyczny* (1962), no. 4, 295–316.

Pobóg-Malinowski, W. 'Na rumuńskim rozdrożu', *Kultura* (Paris), no. 7 (1948), 116–33; no. 8 (1948), 80–110; no. 9/10 (1948), 130–78.

—— 'Ostatnie decyzje marszałka Śmigłego', ibid., no. 50 (1951), 100–10.

Poniński, A. 'Wrzesień 1939 r. w Rumunii', *Zeszyty Historyczne* (Paris), no. vi, 146–202.

Stroński, S. 'Paderewski — śmierć na posterunku', *Dziennik Polski*, 6 July 1951.

—— 'Jak to było 30 września 1939', ibid. 13 July 1951.

Tokarzewski-Karaszewicz, M. 'U podstaw tworzenia Armii Krajowej,' *Zeszyty Historyczne* (Paris), vi. 17–44.

Zabiełło, S. 'Na emigracji, 1939–1940', *Sprawy Międzynarodowe* (1956), no. 9, 41–51.

—— 'Sprawa polska na arenie międzynarodowej', *Z najnowszych dziejów Polski, 1939–1947. Zbiór artykułów pod redakcją Władysława Góry i Janusza Gołębiowskiego*, pp. 53–90. Warsaw, 1961.

—— *O rząd i granice.* 2nd ed. Warsaw, 1965.

INDEX